Introducing
Autodesk® Maya® 2014

Introducing
Autodesk® Maya® 2014

DARIUSH DERAKHSHANI

AUTODESK®
Official Press

SYBEX®
A Wiley Brand

Acquisitions Editor: Mariann Barsolo
Development Editor: Stephanie Barton
Technical Editor: Keith Reicher
Production Editor: Eric Charbonneau
Copy Editor: Kim Wimpsett
Editorial Manager: Pete Gaughan
Production Manager: Tim Tate
Vice President and Executive Group Publisher: Richard Swadley
Vice President and Publisher: Neil Edde
Book Designer: Caryl Gorska
Compositor: Kate Kaminski, Happenstance Type-O-Rama
Proofreader: Sara Eddleman and James Saturnio, Word One New York
Indexer: Ted Laux
Project Coordinator, Cover: Katherine Crocker
Cover Designer: Ryan Sneed
Cover Image: Dariush Derakhshani

Dear Reader,

Thank you for choosing *Introducing Autodesk Maya 2014*. This book is part of a family of premium-quality Sybex books, all of which are written by outstanding authors who combine practical experience with a gift for teaching.

Sybex was founded in 1976. More than 30 years later, we're still committed to producing consistently exceptional books. With each of our titles, we're working hard to set a new standard for the industry. From the paper we print on to the authors we work with, our goal is to bring you the best books available.

I hope you see all that reflected in these pages. I'd be very interested to hear your comments and get your feedback on how we're doing. Feel free to let me know what you think about this or any other Sybex book by sending me an email at nedde@wiley.com. If you think you've found a technical error in this book, please visit http://sybex.custhelp.com. Customer feedback is critical to our efforts at Sybex.

Best regards,

Neil Edde
Vice President and Publisher
Sybex, an Imprint of Wiley

To Max Henry

Acknowledgments

As this book goes into its 10th edition, I am thrilled that the Introducing Maya series is a favorite resource for students and teachers of the Autodesk® Maya® software. Education is the foundation for a happy life, and with that in mind, I'd like to thank the outstanding teachers from whom I have had the privilege to learn. You can remember what you've been taught—or, just as important; you can remember those who have taught you. ■ I also want to thank my students, who have taught me as much as they have learned themselves. Juan Gutierrez, Victor J. Garza, Robert Jauregui, and Peter Gend deserve special thanks for helping me complete the models and images for this book. Thanks to the student artists who contributed to the color section, and, of course, thanks to my colleagues, and friends at work for showing me everything I've learned and making it interesting to be in the effects business. Special thanks to HP for its support and keeping me on the cutting edge of workstations. ■ Thanks to my editors at Sybex and the folks at Autodesk for their support and help and for making this process fun. Thanks to the book team for bringing it all together: Mariann Barsolo, Stephanie Barton, Eric Charbonneau, and Kim Wimpsett. My appreciation also goes tenfold to technical editor Keith Reicher. ■ Thank you to my mom and brothers for your strength, wisdom, and love throughout. And a special thank-you to my lovely wife, Randi, and our son, Max Henry, for putting up with the long nights at the keyboard; the grumpy, sleep-deprived mornings; and the blinking and buzzing of all my machines in our apartment. Family!

About the Author

Dariush Derakhshani is a VFX and CG supervisor in Los Angeles, California. Dariush has been working in CG for more than 16 years and teaching classes in CG and effects production for close to 15. He is the best-selling author of a handful of books, including the popular Introducing Maya series. He is also co-creator of Learning Autodesk Maya: A Video Introduction, available from Wiley and http://video2brain.com/Lynda.com. You can find out information on this video series and more at www.koosh3d.com.

Dariush started using the Autodesk® AutoCAD® software in his architecture days and then migrated to using 3D programs when his firm's principal architects needed to show their clients design work on the computer. Starting with Alias PowerAnimator version 6, which he encountered when he enrolled in the University of Southern California Film School's animation program, and working for a short while in Autodesk® 3ds Max® before moving on to Maya® jobs, Dariush has been using Autodesk animation software for the past 17 years.

He received an MFA in film, video, and computer animation in 1997 from USC. Dariush also holds a BA in architecture and theatre from Lehigh University in Pennsylvania and worked at a New Jersey architecture firm before moving to Los Angeles for film school. He has worked on feature films, music videos, and countless commercials as a 3D animator and VFX supervisor, garnering honors from the London International Advertising Awards, the ADDY Awards, the Telly Awards, and a nomination from the Visual Effects Society Awards. He is bald and has flat feet.

CONTENTS AT A GLANCE

Contents

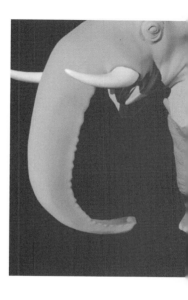

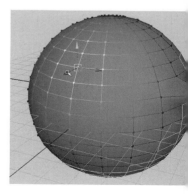

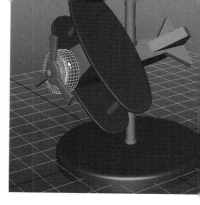

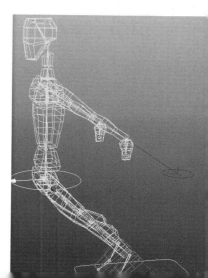

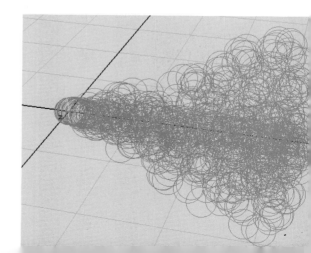

Introduction

Welcome to *Introducing Autodesk Maya 2014* and the world of computer-generated imagery (CGI). Whether you're new to 3D graphics or venturing into Autodesk's powerhouse animation software from another 3D application, you'll find this book a perfect primer. It introduces you to the Autodesk® Maya® software and shows how you can work with Maya to create your art, whether it's animated or static in design.

The first edition of this book was written out of the author's desire for solid, comprehensive, and yet open-ended teaching material about Maya for his classes. This book exposes you to all the facets of Maya by introducing and explaining its tools and functions to help you understand how Maya operates. In addition, you'll find hands-on examples and tutorials that give you firsthand experience with the toolsets. Working through these will help you develop skills as well as knowledge. These tutorials expose you to various ways of accomplishing tasks with this intricate and comprehensive artistic tool.

Finally, this book explains workflow. You'll learn not only how specific tasks are accomplished but why—that is, how they fit into the larger process of producing 3D animation. By doing that, these chapters should give you the confidence to venture deeper into the Maya feature set on your own or by using any of the other Maya learning tools and books as a guide.

It can be frustrating to learn a powerful tool such as Maya, so it's important to remember to pace yourself. The number-one complaint of readers of books like this is a sense that either the pace is too fast or the steps are too complicated or overwhelming. That's a tough nut to crack, to be sure, and no two readers are the same. But this book offers you the chance to run things at your own pace. The exercises and steps may seem challenging at times, but keep in mind that the more you try—even the more you fail at some attempts—the more you'll learn about how to operate Maya. Experience is the key to learning workflows in any software program, and with experience come failure and aggravation. Nevertheless, try and try again, and you'll see that further attempts will be easier and more fruitful.

Above all, this book aims to inspire you to use Maya as a creative tool to achieve and explore your own artistic vision.

What You'll Learn from This Book

Introducing Autodesk Maya 2014 will show you how Maya works and introduce you to every part of the toolset to give you a glimpse of the possibilities available with Maya.

You'll learn the basic concepts underlying animation and 3D and how to work with the Maya interface. You'll then learn the basic methods of modeling—creating objects and characters that appear to exist in three-dimensional space and that can be animated. You'll also explore shading and texturing—the techniques of applying surfaces to the objects you create—and you'll learn how to create lights and shadows in a scene. Animation is an enormously rich topic, but the practice and theory provided here will give you a solid footing. Next, you'll learn how to control the process of rendering, turning your images into files that can be viewed. Perhaps the most dazzling capability of Maya is its dynamics engine, software that allows you to make objects behave as if controlled by the real-world laws of physics.

After you've finished this book and its exercises, you'll have experience in almost everything Maya offers, giving you a solid foundation on which to base the rest of your Maya and CGI experience.

The goal of this book is to get you familiar enough with all the parts of Maya that you can work on your own and start a long, healthy education in a powerful and flexible tool.

You will, however, learn the most from yourself.

Who Should Read This Book

Anyone who is curious about learning Maya or who is migrating from another 3D software package can learn something from this book. Even if you're highly experienced in another 3D package such as the open source Blender or Autodesk® 3ds Max® or Softimage®, you'll find this book helpful in showing you how Maya operates, so you can migrate your existing skill set quickly and efficiently. By being exposed to everything Maya has to offer, you'll better understand how you can use its toolset to create or improve on your art and work.

If you already have cursory or even intermediate experience with Maya, culled from time spent learning at home, you can fill many holes with the information in this book as well as expand your experience. Self-education is a powerful tool, and the more you expose yourself to different sources, opinions, and methods, the better educated you'll be.

In addition, this book is invaluable for teachers in the CG field. This book was written to cater to those who want to pick up the fundamentals of Maya as well as those who want to teach classes based on a solid body of course material. You won't find a better basis for a class when you combine this book with your own curriculum.

How to Use This Book

To begin reading this book, open it to some page, and read.

Introducing Autodesk Maya 2014 approaches the subject in a linear fashion that tracks how most animation productions are undertaken. But the book has numerous cross-references to make sure the chapters make sense no matter in which order you want to tackle them. You can open this book to any chapter and work through the tutorials and examples laid out for the Maya task being covered. Feel free to browse the chapters and jump into anything that strikes your fancy. However, if you're completely new to CG, you may want to take the chapters in order.

Although you can learn a lot just by reading the explanations and studying the illustrations, it's best to read this book while you're using Maya 2014 so that you can try the exercises for yourself as you read them. If you don't already have Maya, you can download an educational license if you are a qualifying student or faculty member at www.students.autodesk.com/ or a 30-day trial version of the software at www.autodesk.com/maya. This book refers to a companion web page (www.sybex.com/go/introducingmaya2014) that contains all the example and support files you'll need for the exercises in the text, which is valuable as an educational aid. You can use the example files to check the progress of your work, or you can use them as a starting point if you want to skip ahead within an exercise. The latter can save the more experienced reader tons of time. You'll also find it valuable to examine these files in depth to see how scenes are set up and how some of the concepts introduced in the book are implemented. Because Maya is a complex, professional software application, the exercises are both realistically ambitious and simple enough for new users to complete. Take them one step at a time and find your own pace, accepting aggravations and failures as part of the process. Take your time; you're not working on deadline—yet.

How This Book Is Organized

Chapter 1, "Introduction to Computer Graphics and 3D," introduces you to common computer graphics terms and concepts to give you a basic overview of how CG happens and how Maya relates to the overall process. This chapter explores the basics of CG creation and its core concepts. In addition, it describes the process of CG production and discusses how to establish a commonly used workflow.

Chapter 2, "Jumping in Headfirst, with Both Feet," creates a simple animation to introduce you to the Maya interface and workflow and give you a taste of how things work right off the bat. By animating the planets in our solar system, you'll learn basic concepts of creating and animating in Maya and how to use its powerful object structure.

Chapter 3, "The Autodesk Maya 2014 Interface," presents the entire Maya interface and shows you how it's used in production. Beginning with a roadmap of the screen, this chapter also explains how Maya defines and organizes objects in a scene while you are set to the task of building a decorative box model.

Chapter 4, "Beginning Polygonal Modeling," is an introduction to modeling concepts and workflows in general. It shows you how to start modeling using polygonal geometry to create various objects, from a basic-looking hand to a catapult, using some of the new tools incorporated into Autodesk Maya 2014.

Chapter 5, "Modeling with NURBS Surfaces and Deformers," takes your lesson in modeling a step further. It shows you how to model with deformers and surfacing techniques, using NURBS to create a patch model detail for a larger locomotive scene. You'll also learn how to convert NURBS surfaces into polygon meshes easily.

Chapter 6, "Practical Experience," rounds out your modeling lessons with a comprehensive exercise showing you how to model a child's table lamp using polygons as well as some NURBS surfacing. The chapter also exposes you the powerful File Referencing workflow available in Maya.

Chapter 7, "Autodesk Maya Shading and Texturing," shows you how to assign textures and shaders to your models. Using a toy wagon model, you'll learn how to texture it to look like a real toy wagon as well as lay out its UVs for proper texture placement. Then, you'll create detailed photorealistic textures based on photos for the decorative box and table lamp models. You'll also learn how to take advantage of Maya 2014's ability to work with layered Photoshop files.

Chapter 8, "Introduction to Animation," covers the basics of how to animate a bouncing ball using keyframes and moves on to creating more complex animation—throwing an axe and firing a catapult. You'll also learn how to import objects into an existing animation and transfer animation from one object to another, a common exercise in professional productions. In addition, you'll learn how to use the Graph Editor to edit and finesse your animation as well as animate objects along paths.

Chapter 9, "More Animation!" expands on Chapter 8 to show you how to use the Maya skeleton and kinematics system to create a simple walk cycle. This chapter also covers how to animate objects by using relationships between them. A thrilling exercise shows you how to rig a locomotive model for automated animation, one of the most productive uses of Maya.

Chapter 10, "Autodesk Maya Lighting," begins by showing you how to light a 3D scene as you learn how to light the table lamp and box that you modeled and textured earlier in the book. It also shows you how to use the tools to create and edit Maya lights for illumination, shadows, and special lighting effects. The mental ray for Maya Physical Sun and Sky feature is explored in this chapter as an introduction to some sophisticated techniques for mental ray lighting.

Chapter 11, "Autodesk Maya Rendering," explains how to create image files from your Maya scene and how to achieve the best look for your animation using proper cameras and rendering settings. You'll work with displacement maps to create details in a model. You'll also learn about the Maya renderer, the Vector renderer, and Final Gather using HDRI and image-based lighting through mental ray for Maya, as well as raytracing, motion blur, and depth of field. You'll have a chance to render the table lamp and decorative box to round out your skills.

Chapter 12, "Autodesk Maya Dynamics and Effects," introduces you to the powerful Maya dynamics animation system as well as nParticle technology. You'll animate pool balls colliding with one another using rigid body dynamics, and you'll fire the catapult. Using nParticle animation, you'll also create steam to add to your locomotive scene. You will then be exposed to nCloth to create a tablecloth and a flag. This chapter also shows you how to use Paint Effects to create animated flowers and grass within minutes, and it introduces you to using toon shading to achieve a cartoon look to your renders.

Hardware and Software Considerations

Because computer hardware is a quickly moving target and Maya now runs on three distinct operating systems (Windows XP/Windows 7, Linux, and Mac OS X), specifying which hardware components will work with Maya is something of a challenge. Fortunately, Autodesk has a "qualified hardware" page on its website that describes the latest hardware to be qualified to work with Maya for each operating system, as well as whether you're running the 32-bit or 64-bit version. Go to the following site for the most up-to-date information on system requirements:

    www.autodesk.com/maya

Although you can find specific hardware recommendations on these web pages, some general statements can be made about what constitutes a good platform on which to run Maya. First, be sure to get a fast processor; Maya eats through CPU cycles like crazy, so a fast processor is important. Second, you need lots of RAM (memory) to run Maya—at least 2 GB, but 8 GB or more is better to have, especially if you're working with large scene files and are on a 64-bit system. Third, if you expect to interact well with your Maya scenes, a powerful video card is a must; although Maya will mosey along with a poor graphics card, screen redraws will be slow with complex scenes, which can quickly become frustrating.

You may want to consider a workstation graphics card for the best compatibility (rather than a consumer-grade gaming video card). Several companies make entry-level through top-performing workstation cards to fit any budget. A large hard disk is also important—most computers these days come with huge drives anyway.

Fortunately, computer hardware is so fast that even laptop computers can now run Maya well. Additionally, even hardware that is not officially supported by Autodesk can often run Maya—just remember that you won't be able to get technical support if your system doesn't meet the company's qualifications.

Free Autodesk Software for Students and Educators

The Autodesk Education Community is an online resource with more than five million members that enables educators and students to download—for free (see website for terms and conditions)—the same software used by professionals worldwide. You can also access additional tools and materials to help you design, visualize, and simulate ideas. Connect with other learners to stay current with the latest industry trends and get the most out of your designs. Get started today at www.autodesk.com/joinedu.

The Next Step

By the time you finish *Introducing Autodesk Maya 2014*, you'll have some solid skills for using Maya. When you're ready to move on to another level, be sure to check out other Maya titles from Sybex at www.sybex.com and additional resources at www.koosh3d.com.

You can contact the author through www.koosh3d.com. You may also go to the book's web page at www.sybex.com/go/introducingmaya2014.

CHAPTER 1

Introduction to Computer Graphics and 3D

This book will introduce you to the workings of 3D animation (called *computer graphics* [CG]) with one of the most popular programs on the market, the Autodesk® Maya® software. It will introduce you to many of the features and capabilities of Maya with the intent of energizing you to study further.

The best way to succeed at anything is to practice. Go through the exercises in this book (more than once if you care to), and also think of exercises and projects that can take you further in your learning process. A book, class, or video can take you only so far; the rest is up to you. Imagination and exploration will serve you well.

This is not to say you can't be a casual visitor to working in CG—far from it. Playing around and seeing what you can create in this medium is just flat-out fun. Don't lose sight of that. If you feel the enjoyment slipping away, step away from the screen for a while. Understanding your own learning pace is important.

Throughout this book, you'll learn how to work with Maya tools and techniques at a pace you set for yourself. This chapter will prepare you for the hands-on study that follows by introducing the most important CG concepts and the roles they will play in your Maya work. When you're learning how to work with Maya, the most important concept is discovering how you work as an artist. If you have a basic understanding of the methodology and terms of computer art and CG, you can skim or even skip this chapter and jump right into working with Maya.

Learning Outcomes: In this chapter, you will be able to

- Distinguish bitmap art from vector art
- Understand the basic workflow for a production
- Choose the correct file format for a project
- Choose the color level and resolution for output
- Arrange objects to follow good design principles
- Recognize key terms and concepts in film and animation

Art?

Art, in many instances, requires transcendence of its medium; it speaks of its own accord. Art goes beyond the mechanics of how you create it (whether by brush or mouse) and takes on its own life. Learning to look beyond what you're working *with* and seeing what you're working *for* is the key in my humble opinion. Try not to view this experience as learning a software package but as learning a way of working to an end.

> Above all, relax and enjoy yourself.

It's hard to relax when you're trying to cram so much information into your brain. But keep in mind that you should try not to make this experience about how a software program works; instead, make it about how you work with the software. Maya is only your tool; you're the boss.

When hiring professional 3D artists, studios demand a strong artistic sense, whether in a traditional portfolio or a CG reel. So, fortify the artist within yourself and practice traditional art such as life drawing, photography, painting, or sculpture as you learn CG.

> Skip to Chapter 2, "Jumping in Headfirst, with Both Feet," if you want to get working right away, though it's best to arm yourself with the fundamentals of CG first!

So, before you start learning a particular CG tool—Maya, in this case—make sure you have a grasp of the fundamental issues underlying CG.

Computer Graphics

CG and CGI are the abbreviations for *computer graphics* and *computer graphics imagery*, respectively, and are often used interchangeably. CG refers to any picture or series of pictures that is generated by an artist on a computer. However, the industry convention is to use the terms *CG* and *CGI* to refer to 3D graphics and not to images created using 2D image or paint programs such as Adobe Photoshop.

Most 2D graphics software is bitmap based, whereas all 3D software is vector based. Bitmap-based software creates an image as a mosaic of pixels, filled in one at a time. Vector-based software creates an image as a series of mathematical instructions from one graphed point to another. This much more powerful method for creating graphics is behind all the impressive CG images you've seen in movies, videogames, and so on. You'll learn more about vectors and bitmaps in the section "Computer Graphics Concepts" later in this chapter.

If you're familiar with 2D graphics software, such as Adobe Illustrator or Adobe Flash, you already know something about vectors. Maya and other 3D-graphics tools add the calculation of depth. Instead of drawing objects on a flat plane, they're defined in three-dimensional space. This makes the artist's job fairly cerebral and very different than it is for 2D art; in 3D art, there is more of a dialogue between the left and right sides of the brain, causing them to smash together at times!

A Preview of the CG Process

The process of creating in CG requires that you either model or arrange prebuilt objects in a scene, give them color and light, and render them through a virtual camera to make an image. It's a lot like directing a live-action production but without any actor tantrums.

> A large community on the Web provides free and for-pay models that you can use in your scenes. Sites such as www.turbosquid.com, www.cgtextures.com, and www.archive3d.net can cut out a lot of the time you might spend creating all the models or textures for a scene.

With CG, you work in 3D space—an open area in which you define your objects, set their colors and textures, and position lights as if you were setting up for a live photo shoot.

After you build your scene in 3D using models, lights, and a camera, the computer *renders* the scene, converting it to a 2D image. Through setup and rendering, CGI is born—and, with a little luck, a CG artist is also born.

Rendering is the process of calculating lights and shadows, placing textures and colors on models, moving animated objects, and so on, to produce a sequence of 2D pictures that effectively "shoot" your virtual scene. Instead of an envelope of 4×6 glossy prints, you get a sequence of 2D computer images (or a QuickTime or Audio Video Interleave [AVI] movie file) that sit on your hard drive or get shared on YouTube or Vimeo, waiting to be seen, and invariably commented on, by your know-it-all friends. And that, in a nutshell, is the CG workflow.

Animation

Animation shows *change over time*. In other words, animation is the simulation of an object changing over a period of time, whether it's that object's position or size or even color or shape.

All animation, from paper flipbooks to film to Maya, is based on the principle of *persistence of vision* that when we see a series of rapidly changing images, we perceive the changing of the image to be in continuous motion. If you have a chance to pause and step through an animated film, frame by frame, on your DVD player or DVR, then you'll see how animation comes together, step-by-step.

To create CG animation yourself, you have to create scene files with objects that exhibit some sort of change, whether through movement, color shift, growth, or other behavior. But just as with flipbooks and film animation, the change you're animating occurs between static images, called *frames* (a term carried over from film). You define the object's animation using a *timeline* measured in these single frames.

You'll learn more in the section "Basic Animation Concepts" later in this chapter. For now, let's move on to the stages of CG production.

The Stages of Production

The CG animation industry inherited a workflow from the film industry that consists of three broad stages: preproduction, production, and postproduction. In film, *preproduction* is the process in which the script and storyboards are written, costumes and sets are designed and built, actors are cast and rehearse, the crew is hired, and the equipment is rented and set up. In the *production* phase, scenes are taped or filmed in the most efficient order. *Postproduction* (often simply called *post*) describes everything that happens afterward: the scenes are edited into a story; a musical score, sound effects, and additional dialogue are added; and visual effects may also be added. (In a film that has special effects or animation, the actual CG creation is usually completed in postproduction. However, it may start in the preproduction phases of the film or project.)

Although the work performed at each stage is radically different, this framework is useful for understanding the process of creating CG as well.

Preproduction

Preproduction for a CG animation means gathering reference materials, motion tests, layout drawings, model sketches, and such together to make the actual CG production as straightforward as possible. Whether you're working on a small job or a complex film, entering into production without a good plan of attack will not only cause trouble but also stunt the growth of your project. Not only that, but having different perspectives on a subject based on research is the key to understanding it.

The Script

To tell a story, CG or not, you should put it in words. A story doesn't need to contain dialogue for it to benefit from a script. Even abstract animations benefit from a detailed explanation of timings and colors laid out in a treatment (because there is likely no dialogue). The script or treatment serves as the initial blueprint for the animation.

The Storyboard

A storyboard is a further definition of the script. Even a rudimentary storyboard with stick figures on napkins is useful to a production. You break the script into sequences, and then you break those sequences into shots. Next, you sketch out each shot in a panel of a storyboard. The panels are laid out in order according to the script to give a visual and linear explanation of the story. Storyboards are useful for planning camera angles (framing a shot), position of characters, lighting, mood, and so on. Figure 1.1 shows a rough storyboard for a character falling asleep while watching TV.

Figure 1.1

A storyboard helps define the action.

The Conceptual Art

Conceptual artworks are the design elements that you may need for the CG production. Typically, characters are drawn into character sheets in three different neutral poses: from the front, from the side, and from an angle called a *3/4 view*. You can also create color art for the various sets, props, and characters to better visualize the colors, textures, and lighting that will be needed. Props and sets are identified from the script and boards and then sketched out into model sheets. The better you visualize the conceptual art, the easier it will be to model, texture, and light everything in CG.

Production

Production begins when you start creating models from the boards, model sheets, and concept art. You model the characters, sets, and props, and then you assign textures (colors and patterns). The animators take these *assets* and animate everything according to the boards and script. Shots are then lit and ready for rendering. To make a long story short, 3D scenes are created, lit, and animated in the production phase.

Postproduction

After all the scenes have been set up with props and characters, and everything is animated, postproduction can begin. Postproduction for a CG project is similar to postproduction for a film. This is where all of a CG film's elements are brought together and assembled into the final form.

Rendering

Rendering is the process by which the computer calculates how everything in the scene should look and then displays it. As you'll learn throughout this book, the decisions you make when creating the objects in a scene can make a big difference in how the rest of the process goes.

Rendering makes significant processing demands on your computer, usually requiring the full attention of your PC. This can take a considerable amount of time when rendering multiple frames. You can render one scene while working on another scene, but asking a computer that is rendering to multitask isn't advisable in most cases.

When everything is rendered properly, the final images are sorted, and the assembly of the CG project begins. Rendering is discussed more fully in Chapter 11, "Autodesk Maya Rendering."

You'll take a quick look at three more postproduction activities: compositing, editing, and adding sound. These are advanced topics, and complete coverage is beyond the scope of *Introducing Autodesk Maya 2014*. However, a multitude of books are available on these topics for further study, and some are listed at the end of this chapter.

Compositing

Quite often, CG is rendered in different layers and segments, which need to be put back together. In a particular scene, for example, multiple characters interact. Each character is rendered separately from the others and from the backgrounds. They're then put together in *compositing*, or the process of bringing together scene elements that were created separately to form the final scene. Maya makes this process easier with render layers, which you'll experience in Chapter 11.

Compositing programs such as Autodesk Composite, The Foundry's NUKE, eyeon Fusion, and Adobe After Effects allow you to compose CG elements together, and give you some additional control over color, timing, and a host of other additions and alterations you can make to the images. Compositing can greatly affect the look of a CG project and can be an integral part of CG creation.

Many new CG artists try to generate their final images in a single rendering of their scene, without needing to do so. Realizing the component nature of CG is important; you can use components to your advantage by rendering items separately and compositing them in the finishing stage. This approach gives you a lot of control in finishing the images to your satisfaction without always having to go back, change the scene, and re-render it.

Editing

The rendered and composited CG footage is collected and edited together to conform to the script and boards. Some scenes are cut or moved around to heighten the story. This process is essentially the same as for film editing, with one big difference: the amount of footage used.

A typical film uses a fraction of all the film or video that is shot. But because creating CG is typically more time-consuming and expensive than shooting live-action, scenes and shots are often tightly arranged in preproduction boards, so not much effort is wasted. The entire production is edited with great care beforehand, and the scenes are built and animated to match the story, almost down to the frame. Consequently, the physical editing process mostly consists of assembling the scenes into the sequence of the story. This is also why a good preproduction process is important. When you plan what you want to get, you're much more likely to get it.

Sound

Sound design is critical to CG because viewers associate visuals with audio. A basic soundtrack can give a significant punch to a simple animation by helping provide realism, mood, narrative, and so on, adding a greater impact to the CG.

Sound effects, such as footsteps, that are inserted to match the action on the screen are known as *Foley sound*. Music is scored and added to match the film. Quite often, the dialogue or musical score inspires a character's actions or body language. Again, this is much the same procedure as in film, with one exception. In the event that a CG project requires dialogue, the dialogue must be recorded and edited before CG production can begin. Dialogue is part of the preproduction phase as well as a component of postproduction. This is because animators need to hear the dialogue being spoken so they can coordinate the lip movements of the characters speaking, a process known as *lip-synch*.

How It All Works Together

The process behind making a *South Park* episode is a perfect workflow example. Although the show appears to be animated using paper cutouts, as was the original Christmas short, the actual production work is done using CG. In preproduction on a typical episode, the writers hammer out the script, and the voice talent records all the voices before the art department creates the visuals for the show. The script is storyboarded, and copies are distributed to all the animators and layout artists.

At the beginning of the production phase, each scene is set up with the proper backgrounds and characters and then handed off for lip-synch, which is the first step in the animation of the scene. The voices are digitized into computer files for lip-synch animators who animate the mouths of the characters. The lip-synched animation is then passed to character animators who use the storyboards and the soundtrack to animate the characters in the CG scene.

The animation is then rendered to start the post, edited together following the boards, and then sent back to the sound department for any sound effects needed to round out the scene. The episode is assembled and then sent off on tape for broadcast.

The CG Production Workflow

Modeling almost always begins the CG process, which then can lead into texturing and then to animation (or animation and then texturing). Lighting should follow, with rendering pulling up the rear as it must. (Of course, the process isn't completely linear; you'll often go back and forth adjusting models, lights, and textures throughout the process.) Chapters 4 through 11 follow this overall sequence, presenting the major Maya operations in the same order you'll use in real-world CG projects.

Modeling

Modeling, the topic of Chapters 4 through 6, is usually the first step in creating CG. It's the topic that garners a lot of coverage in publications and captures the interest of most budding CG artists. Downloading or purchasing models from the Internet can often cut down the amount of time you spend on your project, if you don't prefer modeling or texturing.

There are many modeling techniques, and each could be the subject of its own book. The choice of which technique to use typically depends on the outcome desired as well as the modeler's taste and preferred workflow. The choices are among polygonal modeling (Chapter 4, "Beginning Polygonal Modeling"), NURBS modeling, and subdivision surface (SubD) modeling (Chapter 5, "Modeling with NURBS Surfaces and Deformers"). Knowing how an object is used in a scene gives you its criteria for modeling. You never want to spend more time on a model than is needed. Creating a highly detailed model for a faraway shot will waste your time and expand rendering times needlessly. You can create any required details that are seen from afar by just adding textures to the model. However, if that model is featured prominently in a close-up, it needs as much detail as possible because viewers will see more of it. You'll learn more about this aspect of modeling in Chapter 4.

When you're starting out, it's a good idea to lavish as much attention on detail as you can; this can teach you perhaps 70 percent of what you can learn about modeling, which in turn will benefit your overall speed and technique. As you gain more experience, you'll be able to discern exactly how much detail to add to a scene and not go overboard.

> Because your computer stores everything in the scene as vector math, the term *geometry* refers to all the surfaces and models in a scene.

Texturing

When the models are complete, it's a good idea to begin *texturing* and *shading*, the process of applying colors and material textures to an object to make it renderable. When you create an object in Maya, for example, a simple gray default shader is automatically assigned to it that will let you see the object when you light and render the scene. In Figure 1.2, an elephant model is shown, with textures applied to its lower body.

Figure 1.2

Texturing adds detail to an otherwise flat model.

Because the textures may look different after animating and lighting the scene, it's wise to leave the final adjustments for later. Just as a painter will pencil in a sketch before adding details, you don't need to make all the shading adjustments right away; you can return to any part of your scene in Maya and adjust it to fine-tune the picture.

You'll learn more about texturing and shading in Chapter 7, "Autodesk Maya Shading and Texturing."

Animation

You can make or break your scene with animation. We all have an innate sense of how things are supposed to move on a visceral level, if not an academic one. We understand how physics applies to objects and how people and animals move around. Because of this, we tend to be mostly critical of CG's motion. Put bluntly, you know when something doesn't look right, and so will the people watching your animation.

To animate something properly, you may need to do quite a lot of setup beyond just modeling. Depending on the kind of animating you'll be doing, you may need to set up the models for whatever methods you've decided to animate them. For example, for character animation, you'll need to create and attach an armature, or skeleton, to manipulate the character and to make it move like a puppet.

Taking the models you've spent hours detailing and reworking them to give them life is thrilling and can make any detailed modeling and setup routine well worth the effort.

I cover animation techniques in Maya in Chapter 8, "Introduction to Animation," and Chapter 9, "More Animation!"

Lighting

In my opinion, *CG is fundamentally all about light*. Manipulating how light is created and reflected is what you're doing with CG. Without light, we wouldn't see anything, so it makes sense that simulating light is the most influential step in CG. Lighting greatly affects the believability of your models and textures and creates and heightens mood.

During the lighting step, you set up virtual lights in your scene to illuminate your objects and action. Although you can set up some initial lights during the texturing of the scene, the serious lighting should be the last thing you do, aside from changes and tweaks.

When you gain more experience with lighting, you'll notice that lighting affects every part of your CG creation. Before long, you'll start modeling and texturing differently— that is, working with the final lighting of the scene in mind.

As you'll learn in Chapter 10, "Autodesk Maya Lighting," virtual lights in Maya are similar to lights used in the real world, from a single point of light, such as a bulb, to directed beams, such as spotlights.

Rendering

At this stage, your computer takes your scene and makes all the computations it needs to create raster (bitmapped) images for your movie. Rendering time depends on how much geometry is used in the scene as well as on the number of lights, the size of your textures, and the quality and size of your output: the more efficient your scene, the shorter the rendering times.

How long should a frame take to render? That's a subjective question with no real answer. Your frames will take as long as they need for them to look the way you want. Of course, if you have tight time or budgetary constraints, you need simple scenes to keep the render resources and times to a minimum. That being said, it's important to understand *how* a scene is put together before you learn to put a scene together *efficiently*. While you're learning, use as many lights and as much geometry as you think you need for your scenes. The more experience you gain, the more efficient your eye will become.

Core Concepts

CG animation draws from many disciplines. While learning Maya, you'll work with concepts derived not only from computer graphics but also from design, film and cinematography, and traditional animation. The following sections summarize the most important of those concepts as they apply to Maya.

Computer Graphics Concepts

Knowing a bit about the general terminology and methodology of computer graphics will help you understand how Maya works. Let's begin with the crucial distinction between raster (bitmapped) and vector graphics and how this distinction affects you as a Maya user.

Raster Images

Raster images (a.k.a. bitmapped images) make up the world of computer images today. A raster or bitmap image is a mosaic of pixels, an arrangement of colored pixels onscreen or dots on a print to display an image. Everything you create in Maya will eventually be seen as a raster image, even though you first create it using vectors.

Raster image programs, such as Adobe Photoshop, let you adjust existing settings such as color, size, and position for all or part of an image. These programs affect pixels directly, giving you the tools to change pixels to form images. For instance, you can use a scanned photo of your house in Photoshop to paint the side of the house red to see what it might look like before you run down to the local paint store.

The *resolution* of an image is defined by the number of pixels in the horizontal and vertical directions. Because the pixels are based on a grid of a fixed size, the closer you get to a raster image, the bigger the pixels become, making the image look blocky, or *pixelated*. To make large raster images, you need to begin with a higher resolution. The higher the resolution, the larger the file size will be. Figure 1.3 shows what happens when you blow up a raster image.

Figure 1.3

A raster image at its original size (left) and blown up several times (right)

Vector Images

Vector images are created in a completely different way. They're formed using mathematical algorithms and geometric functions. Instead of defining the color of each and every pixel in a grid of a raster image, a vector image uses coordinates and geometric formulas to plot points that define *areas*, *volumes*, and *shapes*.

Popular vector-based image applications include Adobe Illustrator and Flash, as well as practically all computer-aided design (CAD) programs, such as the Autodesk® AutoCAD® software and SolidWorks. These programs let you define shapes and volumes, and add color and texture to them through their toolsets. This vector information is then converted into raster images (called *rasterization*) through rendering so you can view the final image or animation.

When scaled, vector graphics don't suffer from the same limitations as raster images. As you can see in Figure 1.4, vectors can be scaled with no loss of quality; they will never pixelate.

Figure 1.4

A vector image at its original size (left) and blown up quite a bit (right)

When you work in Maya, vectors are displayed as wireframes. When you finish your scene, Maya renders the image, converting the vector information into a sequence of raster images you can play back.

Image Output

When you're finished with your animation, you'll probably want as many people as possible to see it (and like it!). To make that happen, you have to render it into a file sequence or a movie file. The file can be saved in any number of ways, depending on how you intend it to be viewed.

COLOR DEPTH

An image file stores the color of each pixel as three values representing red, green, and blue. The image type depends on how much storage is allotted to each pixel (the *color depth*). These are the color depths common to image files in CG production:

Grayscale The image is black and white with varying degrees of gray in between, typically 256 shades of gray. Grayscale images are good for rendering out black-and-white subjects as well as being used for some types of texture maps like displacement maps.

8-Bit Image File (a.k.a. 24-Bit Color Display) Referred to as *24-bit color display* or *True Color* in desktop settings for Windows, each color channel is given 8 bits for a range of 256 shades of each red, green, and blue channel, for a total of 16 million colors in the image. This color depth gives good color quality for an image and is widely used in most animation applications. Most of your renders from Maya will probably be as 8-bit image files, because almost all consumer monitors are only capable of 8-bit color reproduction in playback.

16-Bit Image File   Used in television and film work with such file types as TIFF16, a 16-bit image file holds 16 bits of information for each color channel, resulting in an impressive number of color levels and ranges. These files are primarily used in professional productions, although they're being supplanted by the use of 32-bit images.

32-Bit Image File   This is where the big kids play. Used primarily for film work but increasingly in general use, 32-bit image files, such as the OpenEXR format, give you an incredible amount of range in each color channel. This lets you adjust a wide range of tones and hues in your rendered output for the fullest detail.

High Dynamic Range Imagery (HDRI)   HDRI images are 32-bit float images that are created by combining several digital photos into one image file. For example, photos are taken of a subject with different levels of light using various exposures during photography. With a "32-bit float" file format, a lot of information can be stored about the colors in the image—that is, a very high bit depth is achieved. These files are traditionally used as lighting and rendering setups, a workflow you'll explore in Chapter 11.

COLOR CHANNELS

As mentioned, each image file holds the color information in *channels*. All color images have red, green, and blue color channels that, when viewed together, give a color image. Each channel is a measurement of how much red, green, or blue is in areas of the image. A fourth channel, called the *alpha* channel, is used as a transparency channel. This channel, also known as the *matte* channel, defines which portions of the image are transparent or opaque. Not all image files have alpha channels. You can read more about alpha channels in Chapter 7.

FILE FORMATS

In addition to image types, several image file formats are available today. The most common is probably JPEG (Joint Photographic Experts Group), which is widely used on the Internet.

The main difference between file formats is how the image is stored. Some formats compress the file to reduce its size. However, as the degree of compression increases, the color quality of the image decreases.

The popular formats to render into from Maya are TIFF (Tagged Image File Format), Maya IFF (Maya Image File Format), and Targa. These file formats maintain a good 8-bit image file, are either uncompressed or barely compressed (lossless compression), and are frequently used for broadcast or film work. These formats also have an alpha channel, giving you better control when you later composite images. If you're not concerned with an alpha channel and don't plan to composite, rendering to JPEGs works well. To see an animation rendered in a file sequence of TIFFs or JPEGs, for example, you must play them back using a frame player, such as FCheck (which is included with Maya) or IRIDAS

FrameCycler, or compile them into a movie file using a program such as Adobe After Effects.

Ultimately, your final image format depends on the next step in your project. For example, if you plan to composite your CG, you'll need to output a format that can be imported by your compositing or editing program. TIFF files are perhaps the best format to use, because they're widely compatible, have good color accuracy, and have an alpha channel. You might also consider outputting to 16-bit or even 32-bit float images to give you the greatest range of color when you fine-tune the image sequences. For the vast majority of your work as a beginner, you'll be working in 8-bit format.

MOVIE FILES

Animations can also be output to movie files such as AVI or QuickTime. These usually large files, are self-contained, and hold all the images necessary for the animation that they play back as frames. Movie files can also be compressed, but they suffer from quality loss the more they're compressed.

Maya can render directly to an uncompressed AVI movie format, saving you the seeming hassle of having to render out a large sequence of files, although it's best to render a sequence of files that can easily be compiled into a movie file later using a program such as Adobe After Effects, Premiere Pro, or QuickTime Pro. The primary reason is simple: your render may crash, or your machine may freeze. In such an event, you need to start your AVI render from the beginning, whereas with images (such as TIFFs) you can pick up right after the last rendered frame. Rendering frames is just the better way to go.

Color

Color is how we perceive the differences in the wavelengths of light. The wide range of colors that we see (the visible spectrum) results when any of three *primary colors* of light—red, green, and blue—are "mixed" together. You can mix color in two ways: subtractive and additive. These color definitions are most often displayed in *color wheels*, which equally space the primary colors around a ring and place the resultant colors when primaries are mixed in between the appropriate primaries.

Knowing more about color will help you understand how your CG's color scheme will work and help you design your shots with greater authority.

SUBTRACTIVE AND ADDITIVE COLOR

Subtractive color mixing is used when the image will be seen with an external light source. It's based on the way reflected light creates color. Light rays bounce off colored surfaces and are tinted by the different pigments on the surface. These pigments absorb and reflect only certain frequencies of the light hitting them, in essence *subtracting* certain colors from the light before it gets to your eyes. Pile up enough different colors of paint, and you get black; all the colors are absorbed by the pigment, and only black is reflected.

When subtractive color mixing is used in painting, the traditional color wheel's primary colors are red, yellow, and blue. These three pigments can be mixed together to form any other color pigment, and they form the basis for the color wheel most people are exposed to in art education in primary school. In the world of print production, however, a CMYK (Cyan, Magenta, Yellow, and blacK) color wheel is used. Cyan, yellow, and magenta ink colors are the primary colors used to mix all the other ink colors for print work.

Projected light is mixed as *additive color*. Each light's frequency adds on to another's to form color. The additive primary colors are red, green, and blue. These three colors, when mixed in certain ratios, form the entire range of color. When all are equally mixed together, they form a white light.

A computer monitor uses additive color, mixing each color with amounts of red, green, and blue (RGB).

Warm colors are those in the magenta to red to yellow range, and *cool colors* are those in the green to cyan to blue range of the additive color wheel. Warm colors seem to advance from the frame, and cool colors seem to recede into the frame.

HOW A COMPUTER DEFINES COLOR

Computers represent all information, including color, as sets of numeric values made up of binary numbers—0s and 1s (bits). In an 8-bit color file, each pixel is represented by three 8-bit values corresponding to the red, green, and blue channels of the image. An 8-bit binary number ranges from 0 to 255, so for each primary color you have 256 possible levels. With three channels, you have 256×256×256 (16.7 million) possible combinations of each primary color mixed to form the final color.

Color value can also be set on the hue, saturation, and value (HSV) channels. Again, each channel holds a value from 0 to 255 (in an 8-bit image file); these values combine to define the final color. The hue value defines the actual tint (from red to green to violet) of the color. The saturation defines *how much* of that tint is present in the color. The higher the saturation value, the deeper the color will be. Finally, value defines the brightness of the color, from black to white. The higher the value, the brighter the color will be.

All the colors available in Maya, from textures to lights, are defined as either RGB or HSV values for the best flexibility. You can switch from HSV to RGB definition in Maya at any time depending on your preference.

VIEWING COLOR

The broadcast standard for North America is NTSC (National Television System Committee). One joke in the industry is that the acronym means Never The Same Color, referring to the fact that the color you see on one TV screen will be different from what you see on another screen. The same holds true for computer monitors, especially flat-panel displays. All displays are calibrated differently, and what you see on one screen may not be exactly what you see on another screen.

If it's important to have consistent color on different screens, say between your home and school computers, you can use traditional color bars downloaded from the Internet or your own custom-made color chart to adjust the settings of the monitors you work with so they match more closely. If color is absolutely critical when you're working in a group, it's important for everyone to view color output on a single screen.

Resolution, Aspect Ratio, and Frame Rate

Resolution denotes the size of an image by the number of horizontal and vertical pixels, usually expressed as #×# (for example, 640×480). The higher the resolution, the finer the image detail will be.

You'll adjust your final render size to suit the final medium for which you're creating the animation. Table 1.1 lists some standard resolutions.

NAME	SIZE	NOTES
VGA (Video Graphics Array)	640×480	Formerly the standard computing resolution and still a popular television resolution for tape output.
NTSC D1	720×486	The standard resolution for broadcast television in North America.
NTSC DV	720×480	Close to the NTSC D1 resolution, this is the typical resolution of digital video cameras.
PAL (Phase Alternation Line)	720×586	The standard broadcast resolution for most European countries.
HDTV (High-Definition TV)	1280×720	This is the lower of the two HDTV resolutions and is often referred to as 720p.
HDTV (High-Definition TV)	1920×1080	The emerging television standard, sometimes also referred to as 1080i (interlaced frames) or 1080p (progressive frames).
1K Academy (1K refers to 1,000 pixels across the frame)	1024×768	Typically the lowest allowable resolution for film production at Academy ratio (see Table 1.2). Because film is an optical format (whereas TV is a raster format), there is no set defined resolution for film. Suffice it to say, the higher the better.
2K Academy (2K refers to 2,000 pixels across)	2048×1556	Most studios output CG for film at this resolution, which gives the best size-to-performance ratio.
4K Projection (4K is 4,000 pixels across)	4096×2160	High-resolution monitors and televisions for ultra-high-definition video.

Table 1.1

Typical video resolutions

Any discussion of resolution must include the matter of *aspect ratio*. Aspect ratio is the ratio of the screen's *width* to its *height*. Table 1.2 lists aspect ratio standards.

The number of frames played back per second determines the *frame rate* of the animation. This is denoted as *fps*, or frames per second. The following are the three standard frame rates for media:

- NTSC: 30fps
- PAL: 25fps
- Film: 24fps

Table 1.2

Aspect ratio standards

NAME	SIZE	NOTES
Academy Standard	1.33:1 or 4:3	The most common aspect ratio. The width is 1.33 times the length of the height. This is the NTSC television aspect ratio as well as the aspect ratio of 16mm films and some 35mm films, including classics such as *Gone with the Wind*.
Widescreen TV	1.78:1 or 16:9	With HD and widescreen TVs gaining popularity, the 16:9 standard is commonplace now. This aspect is used in HD programming and is also the aspect ratio of many widescreen computer monitors and laptops. This aspect is very close to the way most films are displayed (1.85:1, as shown next).
Widescreen Film (a.k.a. Academy Flat)	1.85:1	The most-often-used 35mm film aspect today. When it's displayed on a television, horizontal black bars appear above and below the picture so the edges aren't cropped off (an effect called *letterboxing*).
Anamorphic Ratio	2.35:1	Using an *anamorphic* lens, the image captured to 35mm film is squeezed. When played back with a projector with an anamorphic lens, the image is projected with a width at 2.35 times its height. On a standard TV, the letterboxing is more severe to avoid cropping the sides.

Knowing your output medium is important when beginning an animation project. Although it isn't crucial, it can affect how you design your framing, create your movements, render your project, and so on. You can change the frame rate and render resolution at any time in Maya, but it's always better to know as best you can what the final resolution and fps will be before you begin.

Playing back a 24fps animation at 30fps will show a slower-moving animation and will necessitate either repeating some frames to fill in the gaps or ending the animation early. Conversely, playing a 30fps animation at 24fps will create a faster-moving animation that will either skip some frames or end later than it should.

3D Coordinate Space, World Axis, and Local Axis

Three-dimensional space is based on the Cartesian coordinate system, a geometric map of sorts developed by the brainy René Descartes. Knowing where you are at all times is essential with a 3D program.

Space is defined in three axes—*X*, *Y*, and *Z*—representing width, height, and depth. The three axes form a numeric grid in which a particular point is defined by *coordinates* set forth as (#,#,#), corresponding to (*X*,*Y*,*Z*), respectively.

At the zero point of these axes is the *origin*. This is at (0,0,0) and is the intersection of all three axes. The 3D space defined by these three axes is called the *World axis*, in which the *XYZ* axes are *fixed references*. The axis in *World Space* is always fixed and is represented in Maya by the XYZ Axis icon in the lower-left corner of the Perspective windows.

Because objects can be oriented in all sorts of directions within the World axis, it's necessary for each object to have its own width, height, and depth axis independent of the World axis. This is called the *Local axis*. The *Local axis* is the *XYZ*-coordinate space that is attached to every object in Maya. When that object rotates or moves, its Local axis rotates and moves with it. This is necessary to make animating an object easier as it moves and orients around in the World axis.

You'll get a hands-on introduction to the Cartesian coordinate space in the tutorial in Chapter 2, where you'll re-create the solar system with the Sun placed at the origin, the planets orbiting the World axis and rotating on their own Local axes, and moons orbiting the planets and also rotating (see Figure 1.5).

Figure 1.5

The Sun at the origin, Earth and other planets orbiting the World axis while rotating on their own axes, and the Moon orbiting Earth

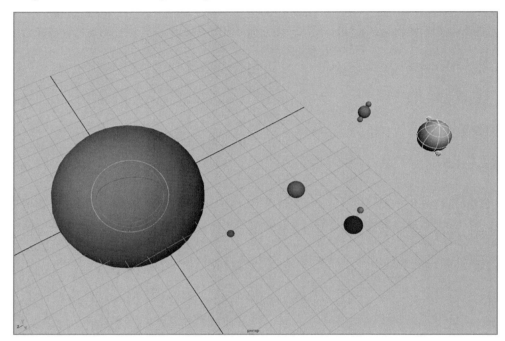

Basic Design Concepts

Composition is all about how you lay out your scene and design your colors. Creating a dynamic frame that not only catches the eye but also informs and intrigues is itself an art form.

Some background in basic design is definitely helpful, and you'll want to look at design books as you further your education in 3D. Understanding the fundamentals of layout and design makes for better-looking scenes and easier setup. The concepts presented here will get you started. Design theory may not seem specifically pertinent to CG right now, but recognizing that there is a logical system behind every pretty picture will help you progress, both as an artist and as an animator.

Form, Space, and Composition

Space is your canvas. Because your canvas ultimately will be a rendered image, your composition needs to fit within your rendered image frame. Whether that frame falls into a tiny web window or a huge IMAX screen, the basics of design always apply: how you arrange your forms and divide your space says a lot.

In the design lexicon, *form* means anything you can see; it has some sort of shape, color, or texture that distinguishes it from its frame. How your scene's objects lie in the frame defines your composition. The space behind and between what is rendered out is the ground, or background plane. Objects become *positive space*, and the background becomes *negative space*. Playing with the position of positive and negative space greatly affects the dynamics of your frame.

Design a static frame in which the objects are all centered and evenly spaced, and your viewers will wonder why they're looking at your composition. Arrange the composition so that your subjects occupy more interesting areas of the frame in which they play with negative space, and the eye is drawn all over the frame, creating a dynamic composition. This principle applies to still images as well as to animation. Figure 1.6 illustrates the difference between a centered, static frame and a frame with a more dynamic negative space.

Figure 1.6

A purely centered frame looks static; the boy seems still with nowhere to go. More interesting framing helps create or heighten a sense of motion, giving space for the boy to run.

In the tutorial in Chapter 10, you'll use light and shadow to turn a still life of fruit into a dynamic and interestingly composed frame.

Balance and Symmetry

Balance in a frame suggests an even amount of positive space from one side of the frame to the other. A frame that is heavier on one side can create a more dynamic composition.

Symmetrical objects in a frame are mirrored from one side to another and create a certain static balance in the frame. An asymmetrical composition, therefore, denotes movement in the composition.

A popular technique used by painters, photographers, and cinematographers is called *framing in thirds*. With this technique, the frame is divided into a grid of thirds vertically and horizontally. Interesting parts of the frame, or focal points of the subjects, are placed at strategic locations in the grid. Placing your subject in the lower third makes it seem small or insignificant, static, or even boring. Placing it in the upper third makes the image more dynamic, magnifying its perceived scale or importance, and even tells a better story.

Contrast

Contrast in design describes how much your foreground subject "pops" from the background. As you can see in Figure 1.7, when you create an area in your frame that contains little variation in color and light, the image seems flat and uneventful. Using dark shadows and light highlights increases the perceived depth in the image, and helps pop out the subject from the background. Animating contrast can help increase or decrease the depth of your frame.

Figure 1.7

With low contrast, the subject seems to disappear into the background. If you add shadows and highlights, the subject pops out.

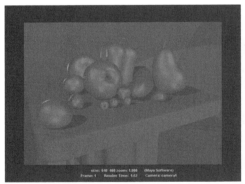 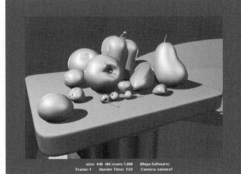

As you'll see in Chapter 10, light plays an important role in creating dynamic contrasts within your frame.

Color

Your use of color also plays a big part in creating impact in your frame. As stated earlier, warm colors tend to advance toward you, and cooler colors seem to recede into the frame. Placing a warm color on a subject on a cool background creates a nice color contrast to help the dynamics of your frame.

Colors opposite each other on the color wheel are *complementary* colors and usually clash when put together. Using complementary colors can create a wide variation of contrast in your scene.

Narrative

A *narrative film* is a film that tells a story of a hero, called a *protagonist*, and that hero's struggle against an *antagonist*. Even in the most abstract concept, there can be a perceived journey: a change that somehow occurs, even if it's a change in the viewer as they view the imagery.

Convincing art creates a sense of change or arc for the audience. This adds an important dimension to your work. When the viewer feels you have something to say, your work becomes that much more touching.

Basic Film Concepts

In addition to the design concepts used in framing a shot, you'll want to understand some fundamental filmmaking concepts.

> There's nothing more important than having a solid, manageable, and achievable plan for your conceptual goal. Put together a good plan, and you'll be set for a good production.

Planning a Production

Most narrative films are broken into acts, which comprise sequences made up of scenes, which in turn are made up of shots. By using a similar layout in the scripting and storyboarding of your own short, you'll find that the entire production process becomes easier and the effect of your film is stronger.

Narrative films are typically divided into three *acts*. The first act establishes the main characters and the conflict or struggle that will define the story. The second act covers most of the action of the story as the hero attempts to overcome this conflict. The third act concludes the film by resolving the action in the story and tying up all the loose ends.

Acts can be deconstructed further into *sequences*, which are groups of sequential scenes that unite around a particular dramatic or narrative point.

A *scene* is a part of a film that takes place in a specific place or time with specific characters to present that part of the story. Films are broken into scenes for organizational purposes by their locations (that is, by where or when they take place).

> Don't confuse the filmmaking concept of a scene with the word *scene* in CG terminology. The latter refers to the elements in the 3D file that make up the CG and may be referred to as a *scene file*.

Scenes are then broken into *shots*, which correspond to a particular camera angle or *framing*. Shots break up the monotony of a scene by giving different views of the scene and its characters. Shots are separated by *cuts* between each shot.

Shots are defined by angle of view, which is the point of view (POV) of the camera. Shots change as soon as the camera's view is changed.

Lighting

Although CG lighting techniques may seem completely different from lighting in real life, the desired results are quite often the same. The more you understand how real lights affect your subjects in photography, the better you'll be at CG lighting.

How you light your scene affects the contrast of the frame as well as the color balance and overall design impact. If the lights in your scene are too flat or too even, they weaken your composition and abate your scene's impact.

You'll learn more about Maya lighting techniques in Chapter 10.

Basic Animation Concepts

As mentioned at the beginning of this chapter, animation is the representation of change over time. This concept is the basis for an amazing art form that has been practiced in one way or another for quite some time. The following sections define the key terms you'll come across numerous times on your journey into animation and CG.

Frames, Keyframes, and In-Betweens

Each drawing of an animation—or, in the case of CG, a single rendered image—is called a *frame*. The term *frame* also refers to a unit of time in animation whose exact chronological length depends on how fast the animation will eventually play back (frame rate). For example, at film rate (24fps), a single frame lasts 1/24 of a second. At NTSC video rate (30fps), that same frame lasts 1/30 of a second.

Keyframes are frames in which the animator creates a pose for a character (or whatever is being animated). In CG terms, a keyframe is a frame in which a pose, a position, or some other such value has been saved in time. Animation is created when an object travels or changes from one keyframe to another. You'll see firsthand how creating poses for animation works in Chapter 9 when you create the poses for a simple walking human figure.

In CG, a keyframe can be set on almost any aspect of an object—its color, position, size, and so on. Maya then interpolates the *in-between* frames between the keyframes set by the animator. In reality, you can set several keyframes on any one frame in CG animation. Figure 1.8 illustrates a keyframe sequence in Maya.

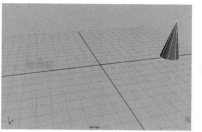

Keyframe at frame 1

Figure 1.8

In the first frame of this sequence, a keyframe is set on the position, rotation, and scale of the cone. On frame 30, the same properties are again keyframed. Maya calculates all the movement in between.

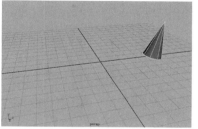

Frame 5

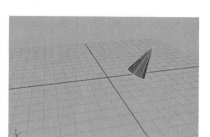

Frame 10

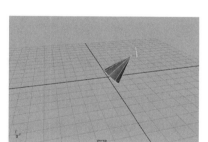

Frame 15

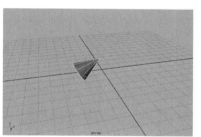

Frame 20

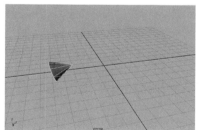

Frame 25

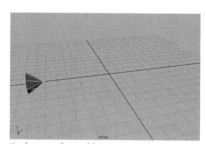

Keyframe at frame 30

Weight

Weight is an implied, if not critical, concept in design and animation. The weight of your subject in the frame is a function of the way it's colored; its contrast, shape, and location in the frame; and the negative space around it. In animation, how you show an object's weight in motion greatly affects its believability. As you'll see in the Axe tutorial in Chapter 8, creating proper motion to reflect the object's weight goes a long way toward producing believable animation.

Weight in animation is a perception of mass. An object's movement, how it reacts in motion, and how it reacts to other objects together convey the feeling of weight. Otherwise, the animation will look bogus—or, as they say, "cartoonish."

Weight can be created with a variety of techniques developed by traditional animators over the years. Each technique distorts the shape of the object or character in some way to make it look as if it's moving. Although it may seem strange to distort an object's dimensions, doing so makes its motion more realistic. Chapter 8 will touch more on creating weight in animation. Here's a quick preview.

SQUASH AND STRETCH

This technique makes a character, for example, respond to gravity, movement, and inertia by squashing it down and stretching it up when it moves. For example, a cartoon character will squeeze down when it's about to jump up, stretch out a bit while it's flying in the air, and squash back down when it lands to make the character look as if it's reacting to gravity.

EASE-IN AND EASE-OUT

Objects never really stop suddenly. Everything comes to rest in its own time, slowing before coming to a complete stop in most cases. This is referred to as *ease-out*.

Just as objects don't stop suddenly, they don't immediately start moving. Most things need to accelerate a bit before reaching full speed. This is referred to as *ease-in*. The bouncing-ball tutorial in Chapter 8 illustrates ease-in and ease-out.

FOLLOW-THROUGH AND ANTICIPATION

Sometimes you have to exaggerate the weight of an object in animation, especially in cartoons. You can exaggerate a character's weight, for instance, by using well-designed follow-through and anticipation.

You should create a bit of movement in your character or object *before* it moves. *Anticipation* is a technique in which a character or object winds up before it moves, like a spring that coils inward before it bounces.

Likewise, objects ending an action typically have a *follow-through*. Think about the movement of gymnasts. When they land, they need to bend a bit at the knees and waist to stabilize their landing. In the same way, a cape on a jumping character will continue to move even after the character lands.

The Axe tutorial in Chapter 8 will give you a chance to implement these two concepts.

SUGGESTED READING

The more you know about all the arts that make up CG, the more confident you'll feel among your peers. For my video tutorials and reference on Maya, you can visit www.video2brain.com/en/courses/learning-autodesk-maya-2013-a-video-introduction. This 2013 versions of the videos will work perfectly with Maya 2014. You can also check out the following excellent resources.

ART AND DESIGN

These books provide valuable insights into the mechanics and art of design. The more you understand design theory, the stronger your art will be.

Bowers, John. *Introduction to Two-Dimensional Design: Understanding Form and Function*. New York: John Wiley & Sons, 2008.

Itten, Johannes. *Design and Form: The Basic Course at the Bauhaus and Later*. New York: John Wiley & Sons, 1976.

Ocvirk, Otto G., et al. *Art Fundamentals: Theory and Practice*. New York: McGraw-Hill, 2012.

Wong, Wucius. *Principles of Form and Design*. New York: John Wiley & Sons, 1993.

CG

CG has an interesting history, and it's evolving at breakneck speed. Acquiring a solid knowledge of this history and evolution is as important as keeping up with current trends.

Kerlow, Isaac. *The Art of 3D Computer Animation and Effects*. New York: John Wiley & Sons, 2009.

Kuperberg, Marcia. *Guide to Computer Animation*. Burlington, MA: Focal Press, 2002.

Masson, Terrence. *CG 101: A Computer Graphics Industry Reference, Second Edition*. Williamstown, MA: Digital Fauxtography, 2007.

Palamar, Todd, and Lee Lanier, and Anthony Honn. *Mastering Autodesk Maya 2013*. New York: John Wiley & Sons, 2012.

PERIODICALS

Computer Graphics World (free subscription for those who qualify): www.cgw.com

Cinefex: www.cinefex.com

3D World: www.3Dworldmag.com

WEBSITES

www.koosh3d.com

www.animationartist.com

www.awn.com

www.creativecrash.com

www.learning-maya.com

FILM

Block, Bruce. *The Visual Story: Seeing the Structure of Film, TV, and New Media*. Burlington, MA: Focal Press, 2001.

MUST-READ

Myers, Dale K. *Computer Animation: Expert Advice on Breaking into the Business*. Milford, MI: Oak Cliff Press, 1999.

Summary

In this chapter, you learned the basic process of working in CG, called a *workflow*, and how it relates to the process of working on a typical live film production. In addition, you were introduced to the core concepts of CG creation and the fundamentals of digital images. Some important ideas in design as well as traditional animation concepts were also covered.

Now that you have a foundation in CG and 3D terminology and core concepts, you're ready to tackle the software. Maya is a capable, intricate program. The more you understand how *you* work artistically, the better use you'll make of this exceptional tool.

There is a lot to think about before putting objects into a scene and rendering them. With practice and some design tinkering, though, all this will become intuitive. As you move forward in your animation education, stay diligent, be patient, and never pass up a chance to learn something new. Above all else, have fun.

CHAPTER 2

Jumping in Headfirst, with Both Feet

In this chapter, you'll start using the Autodesk® Maya® software and get your groove on. This will be a quick primer on the Maya interface so you experience tasks right away. The next chapter will show you more details, and provide additional explanations and a reference of how the entire Maya interface works.

This chapter will take you through the creation of a solar system exercise and the mechanics of animating orbits. With this exercise, you'll dive into creating simple objects, setting keyframes, and stacking your animation to get planets and moons to orbit each other and the sun. This will expose you to object creation, simple modeling, object components, pivot-point placement, grouping and hierarchies, basic keyframing, and timing.

Learning Outcomes: In this chapter, you will be able to

- Gain a working understanding of the user interface and how to navigate in 3D space
- Learn project structure in Maya and how to create projects in Maya
- Create, name, and manipulate simple objects with Move, Rotate, and Scale tools
- Make and apply simple shaders to scene geometry through the Hypershade
- Add keyframes to objects to create animation
- Adjust pivot points
- Create and edit hierarchies by using groups
- Output your animation through playblasting

You Put the *U* in UI

Fire up your computer, and let's get this project going. This section will introduce you to getting around the Maya user interface (UI). It may seem difficult at first, but it will make sense as you move along.

You'll find everything you ever wanted to know about the interface and more in Chapter 3, "The Autodesk Maya 2014 Interface." The overall goal of *this* chapter is to expose you to Maya UI basics as well as important scene creation and editing tools. You can consider the next chapter a debriefing of sorts to fill in UI details that aren't covered in this chapter.

KEYBOARD AND SYMBOL CONVENTIONS USED IN THIS BOOK

The following terms are used throughout this book:

Click and LMB+Click   These refer to a mouse click with the primary (left) mouse button.

RMB+Click   This refers to a mouse click with the right mouse button.

MMB+Click   This refers to a mouse click with the middle mouse button.

Shift+Click   This indicates you should hold down the Shift key as you click with the primary (left) mouse button.

Shift+Select   This indicates you should hold down the Shift key as you select the next object for multiple selections.

Right-Click   This refers to clicking with the right mouse button.

The ☐ Symbol   This, next to a menu command, indicates that you should click the box (☐) next to the menu command to open the options for that command.

A Quick Screen Roadmap

Let's get to the basics of how Maya is laid out (see Figure 2.1). Running across the top of the screen, right under the application's title bar, are the UI elements: the Main Menu bar, the Status line, and the Shelf. On a Macintosh system running OS X, note that the Main Menu bar runs at the very top of the screen, above the application's title bar.

Figure 2.1 shows the major parts of the UI. In the middle of the interface is the *work-space*, which is host to your *panels* (or Scene windows) and their menu options (known as *views* or *viewports* in some other 3D packages). This is where most of your focus will be; this is where you create and manipulate your 3D objects.

Click inside the large Perspective view panel (named *persp*) with the mouse to activate the panel, highlighting its border slightly. Press the spacebar to display a four-panel layout, which gives you top, front, and side views, as well as the Perspective view. Press the spacebar in any of the panels to display a large view of that panel.

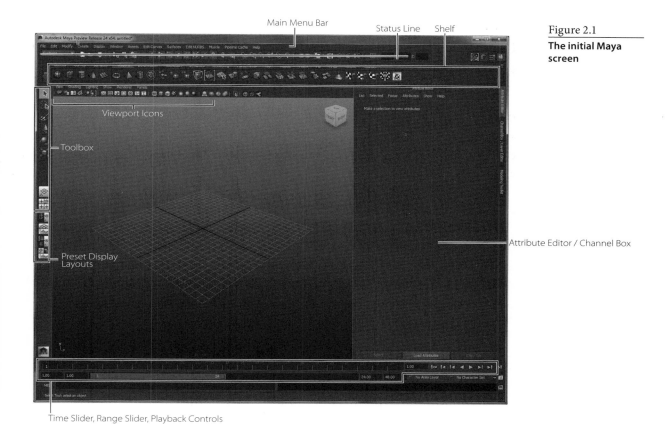

Main Menu Bar — Status Line — Shelf

Viewport Icons

Toolbox

Preset Display
Layouts

Attribute Editor / Channel Box

Time Slider, Range Slider, Playback Controls

Figure 2.1

**The initial Maya
screen**

To the right of the panels is the Attribute Editor/Channel Box/Modeling Toolkit. This is where most of the information (attributes) about a selected object is displayed and edited, as well as where you can access the newly added Modeling Toolkit suite of polygon modeling tools in Maya 2014. Simply click any of the tabs to access these functions. Furthermore, pressing Ctrl+A toggles between the Attribute Editor and the Channel Box. In short, the Attribute Editor gives you access to all of an object's attributes, whereas the Channel Box is a quicker display of the most commonly animated attributes of the selected object. The Attribute Editor is typically wider than the Channel Box, so you'll notice a shift in your view panels when you toggle between them. You can set preferences in Maya to treat the Attribute Editor as its own window to prevent it from displaying on the right side of the UI. You'll learn more about this in the next chapter.

Keys and Syntax in Maya

Maya is case sensitive (i.e. it distinguishes between lowercase and uppercase letters.) The conventions of this book are to always print an uppercase letter to denote which key you must press but to specify "Shift + the letter" when you must press the uppercase of that key. In other words, when I ask you to press the E key, for example, you should simply press the E key on your keyboard, lowercase. When an uppercase letter is called for, the book tells you to press Shift+E, requiring you to enter the uppercase letter E into Maya. Make sure your Caps Lock key is turned off.

SHORTCUTS TO NAVIGATING

Here's a rundown of how to navigate Maya. Keep in mind that the Option key is used on a Macintosh in place of the Alt key on a PC.

Alt+MMB+Click   This tracks around a window. Tracking moves left, right, up, or down in two dimensions; hold down the Alt key, press and hold the MMB, and drag the mouse.

Alt+RMB+Click   This dollies into or out of a view, essentially zooming the view in and out. To dolly, hold down the Alt key, press and hold the RMB, and drag the mouse.

Scroll Wheel   The scroll wheel, in addition to acting as a middle mouse button, can also dolly into or out of a view just like the Alt+RMB+click combination. Scrolling up dollies in, and scrolling down dollies out.

Alt+Click   This rotates or orbits the camera around in a Perspective window. Orbiting lets you get around your object to observe it from different vantage points. To orbit, hold down the Alt key and the LMB. This move is called a *tumble*. You can't tumble your view in an orthographic panel.

Alt+Ctrl+Click and Drag   Dollies your view into the screen area specified in your mouse drag. Hold down the Alt and Ctrl keys while using the LMB to outline a window in the panel to execute this *bounding box dolly*. This action is commonly referred to as a *window zoom* in other applications.

The ViewCube   This part of a panel's interface lets you easily change your current panel view from, for example, perspective to side or top and then back to perspective with just a click. By clicking an area of the ViewCube (shown here), you can switch to other views inside that panel. Clicking one of the conical axis markers gives you an orthogonal view from that direction. Clicking the center square gives you the perspective view. You can toggle the ViewCube in the preferences by choosing Window → Settings/ Preferences → Preferences and clicking the ViewCube category.

Macintosh Keys   The major difference in keys between a PC and a Mac for using Maya is that the Option key on a Mac serves the same function as the Alt key on a PC. Although a few Ctrl key combinations in Windows are accessed via the Command key on a Mac, Mac users can generally use the Mac's Ctrl key for their key combinations just like PC users do.

Mouse Controls

Maya requires the use of a three-button mouse, even on a Macintosh system. The clickable scroll wheel found on most mice can be used as the third button by pressing down to click with the wheel. Scrolling the wheel lets you zoom into or out of a view panel.

In Maya, you press and hold the Alt key on a PC (or the Option key on a Mac) along with the appropriate mouse button to move in the view panel:

- The left mouse button (LMB) acts as the primary selection button and allows you to orbit around objects when used with the Alt key.

- The right mouse button (RMB) activates numerous shortcut menus and lets you zoom when used with the Alt key.

- The middle mouse button (MMB) used with the Alt key lets you move within the Maya interface panels, and the mouse's wheel can be used to zoom in and out as well.

Making Selections

Selecting objects in a view panel is as easy as clicking them. If the object is displayed in Wireframe mode, its wireframe turns green while it's selected. If the object is displayed in a Shaded mode, the object's wireframe will appear around the object. Shaded mode is a way of seeing your objects in the view panel with a basic surface, as opposed to a wireframe that you can see through. You'll see this as you do the following exercise:

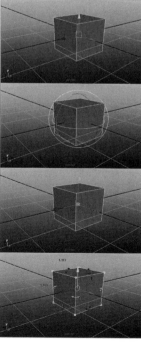

Figure 2.2

The Maya Manipulators

- As you select an object, its attributes appear in the Attribute Editor or Channel Box on the right.

- To select multiple objects, simply hold the Shift key as you click objects to add to your current selection. The previous selection's wireframe turns white, and the new selection is now green. If you press Ctrl+LMB (that is, press the Ctrl key and click) an active object, you'll deselect it. To clear all of your current selections, click anywhere in the empty areas of the view panel.

> Remember: Use Shift+click to select, and Maya adds to the current selection. Use Ctrl+click, and Maya deselects the object you clicked.

Manipulating Objects

When you select an object and enable one of the transformation tools (tools that allow you to move, rotate, or scale an object), you'll see a Manipulator appear at or around the selected object. Figure 2.2 shows the three distinct and most common Manipulators for all objects in Maya (Move, Rotate, and Scale) as well as the Universal Manipulator. You use these Manipulators to adjust attributes of the objects visually and in real time.

To activate a Transform tool, select an object and then click one of the Transform tool icons in the Tool Box, shown in Figure 2.3.

Try This   Let's put some of this into action, shall we?

Press 4 for Wireframe mode; press 5 for Shaded mode.

Choose Create → NURBS Primitives → Sphere. Drag in a view panel anywhere on its grid to create a wireframe sphere, and then size it to your liking. In one of the view panels, press the 5 key on your keyboard, and the display of the sphere will become solid gray, as opposed to open wireframe. This is called *Shaded mode*. Press the 4 key to return to Wireframe mode. You should also see an in-view message at the top of your view stating "shaded display is now on. Press 4 to display objects in wireframe mode."

You can turn off in-view messages by toggling off the In-View Messages check box under Display → Heads Up Display.

With the sphere selected, select the Move tool ( ) from the Tool Box. The first Manipulator shown in Figure 2.2 should appear in the middle of the sphere. The three arrows represent the three axes of possible movement for the object.

Red is for the X-axis, green is for the Y-axis, and blue is for the Z-axis. Cyan is for free movement in both axes of the active panel view.

Clicking any one of the three arrows lets you move the object only on that particular axis. The square in the middle of the Manipulator lets you move the object freely around the plane of the view panel, regardless of the axis. When you select a Manipulator handle for movement, it turns yellow. The Free Movement box in the center then turns back to its regular color, cyan.

Figure 2.3

The Transform tools in the Tool Box

Transform Tools

Next, select the Rotate tool ( ) from the Tool Box, and you'll see the second Manipulator in Figure 2.2. The three colored circles represent the three axes of rotation for the object—red for X, green for Y, and blue for Z. Select a circle to rotate the object on that axis. The yellow circle surrounding the three axis circles lets you freely rotate the object on all three axes. The Free rotation handle also turns cyan when an axis handle is active.

Now, try selecting the Scale tool ( ) to see the third Manipulator in Figure 2.2. By selecting one of the axis handles and dragging the mouse, you can scale the object in a non-uniform manner in that axis. The middle cyan box scales the object uniformly on all three axes.

Now try selecting the Universal Manipulator, which is not shown in the Tool Box but is found by choosing Modify →

Transformation Tools → Universal Manipulator. Its icon (▨) appears under the Tool Box after you select it from the menu. This tool acts in place of all three Manipulators you just tried. Grabbing the familiar arrows translates the sphere. Selecting any of the curved arrows in the middle of the edges of the Manipulator box lets you rotate the sphere in that axis. Finally, selecting and dragging the cyan boxes in the corners of the Manipulator box lets you scale the sphere. If you hold down the Ctrl key as you drag, you can scale the sphere in just one axis.

Go ahead and click around the interface some more. Create more primitive objects, and tool around a bit. Move around the view panels and see how it feels. Give the tires a good kick.

Enough chatting—let's jump into the solar system exercise.

Project Overview: The Solar System

This project focuses on familiarizing you with the fundamentals of navigating Maya, object creation, hierarchy, and pivots, all of which are important concepts for scene manipulation and animation within Maya. In this exercise, you'll create and animate a simple simulation of your working solar system. (You may have done this in school using coat hanger wire and Styrofoam balls.) This time-tested tutorial is great practice for getting used to object creation, hierarchies, scene manipulation, UI navigation, and working with objects and selections. It shows you how to set up hierarchies and gives you experience in working with the proper nodes within a group to create hierarchically layered animation.

The Preproduction Process: Planning

Every smooth operation begins with a good plan. The more research and focused information you gather, the better off you'll be in your work. For this exercise, you need to find out where each of the planets is in relation to the sun and to the other planets and also how many moons it has.

Starting with the sun in the center, the planets in order are Mercury, Venus, Earth, Mars, Jupiter, Saturn, Uranus, Neptune, and Pluto. (Yes, yes, I know Pluto isn't classified as a planet anymore.) All these planets actually orbit the sun in ellipses, but you'll give them circular orbits for this exercise. Most planets have a number of moons that orbit them, and a few including Saturn, have large rings that circle around it.

Earth	1 moon
Mars	2 small moons
Jupiter	16+ moons
Saturn	3 large rings and 18+ moons
Uranus	18 moons
Neptune	8 moons
Pluto	1 moon

Creating and animating all those objects may seem overwhelming, but it's a great way to become comfortable with Maya and animation. Because the goal of the project is achievable without making every moon, you'll cut most of them out of your scene and make a maximum of two moons per planet.

The more you run this exercise, the clearer the scene manipulation and hierarchy structure will become to you. Art is a marriage of inspiration, hard work, and practice.

Creating a Project

Projects are the way Maya manages a scene's assets. A file and folder structure keeps your files organized according to projects. You'll have a project for the solar system exercise.

Start by creating a new project for this assignment. Choose File → Project Window to open the Project Window and then click the New button. (Figure 2.4 shows the Mac OS X version; the Windows version has the same fields.) Files are organized in a particular way in Maya. The top level of this organization is the *Project folder*. Within the Project folder are numerous file folders that hold your files. The two most important types are the Scenes and Images folders. The Scenes folder stores your scene files, which contain all the information for your scene. The Images folder stores images you've rendered from your scene. As with clothing and other items around your house, keeping your files and projects organized is a good practice.

NAMING OBJECTS AND KEEPING THE SCENE ORGANIZED

In Maya and most other CG packages, keeping things organized and as clean as possible is more important than you probably realize. When you pick up a disorganized scene, it is very time-consuming to figure out exactly how everything works together. Many professional studios have strict naming procedures and conventions to minimize the confusion their artists may have when working in a pipeline. Even if you're the only person who will ever see your scene in Maya, it's a good idea to name and organize your objects. Get into the habit of naming your objects and keeping a clean scene. You'll waste a lot of time if you don't, and you'll be bombarded by dirty looks from other artists when they have to handle your cluttered scenes.

The scene files discussed in this chapter are included on the book's web page, www.sybex .com/go/introducingmaya2014. They are in a project layout explained in the following text. Copy the scene files on the web page for this project into your own Project folders after you create the project.

To create a new project, follow these steps:

1. In the Current Project field in the Project Window, enter **Solar_System** as the name for your project. In the Location box, type the location where you want to store your projects.

   The default location for Windows XP, Vista, and Windows 7 is in the current user's My Documents folder: My Documents\maya\projects; for Macs, the default location is Home (`/Users/<yourname>`) in the `Documents/maya/projects/default` folder; and for Windows 8 users it is found under the Documents location under the Start menu. If you prefer, you can put projects in a folder on a secondary or external hard drive to keep them separate from your operating system; this allows for easier backup and is generally a safer environment.

2. If you're using a Windows system, create a folder on your hard drive called **Projects** using Windows Explorer. If you're using a Mac, select a drive in the Finder and create a folder on the drive called **Projects**. In the Project Window, click the folder icon next to the Location field and select `D:\Projects` (Windows) or `<Hard Drive Name>/Projects` (Mac) for the location. Maya will fill in all the other fields for you with defaults. Click Accept to create the necessary folders in your specified location. Figure 2.5 shows the completed Project Window in Mac OS X; except for the drive name, the values are the same on Windows.

After you create projects, you can switch between them by choosing File → Set Project and selecting the new project. Maya will then use that project's folders until you switch to or create another project. You may also select a recent project by choosing File → Recent

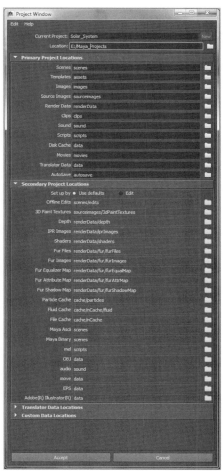

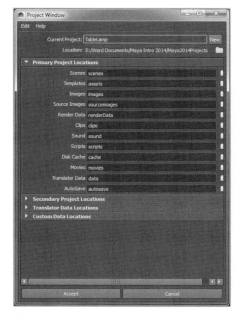

Figure 2.4

The Project Window

Figure 2.5

The completed Project Window

Projects. Maya by default will list four of your recent projects and scene files on the File menu for easy access.

DON'T FORGET TO ALWAYS SET YOUR PROJECT FIRST!

You should make sure to set your project before continuing with your work. The exercises in this book are based on projects, and you'll need to set your project whenever you start a new exercise—otherwise, the scene may not load properly, or your files may not save to the proper locations for that project.

The Production Process: Creating and Animating the Objects

As discussed in Chapter 1, "Introduction to Computer Graphics and 3D," production is typically divided into phases to make workflow easier to manage. In this project, you'll first create the sun, the planets, and their moons; then, you'll animate their respective orbits and rotations.

USE CUBES INSTEAD OF SPHERES

Feel free to create the planets and moons as cubes instead of spheres. That way, you can see each of their individual rotations much more easily so you can tell whether the animation is working properly for you.

Creating the Sun and the Planets

The first thing you'll do is create the sun and the planets. Follow these steps:

1. Choose File → New Scene (or press Ctrl+N). Maya asks if you want to save your current scene. Save the file if you need to, or click Don't Save to discard the scene.

2. By default, the screen should begin in an expanded perspective view. Press the spacebar to enable the four-panel view. When you're in the four-panel view, press the spacebar with the cursor inside the top view panel to select and maximize it.

3. To create the sun, you need a primitive sphere. A *primitive* is a basic 3D shape. Let's turn off a Maya feature called Interactive Creation that is on by default. Turning off Interactive Creation allows you to create the sphere at the center of the grid (the origin) without having to click and drag its size and then reposition it manually. Uncheck Create → NURBS Primitives → Interactive Creation to toggle it off, as shown

in Figure 2.6. For more on how to create primitives with interactive feedback, see the section "Work Panels and Navigation" in Chapter 3.

Figure 2.6

Turning off Interactive Creation

4. With Interactive Creation turned off, choose Create → NURBS Primitives → Sphere. Doing so places a NURBS sphere exactly at the origin—that is, at a position of 0,0,0 for *X,Y,Z*. This is good, because the origin of the workspace will be the center of the solar system, too.

5. Select the word *nurbsSphere1* in the Channel Box to the right of the Maya UI (shown in Figure 2.7), and enter **Sun** to rename it. If you don't see the Channel Box in your Maya window, please refer to the section "Maya's Layout" in Chapter 3.

Naming your objects right after creation is a good habit to develop. Doing so makes for a cleaner scene file and a more organized workspace. This is particularly important if anyone needs to alter your scene file; proper naming will keep them from getting frustrated when they work on your scene.

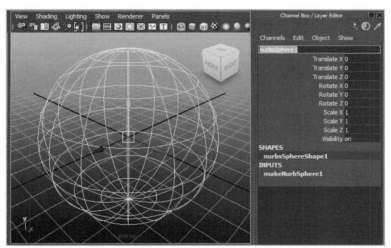

Figure 2.7

Renaming the sphere in the Channel Box

NURBS AND POLYGONS

NURBS and polygons are two types of geometry that you can create and edit in Maya. You'll explore the uses of each modeling type in Chapter 4, "Beginning Polygonal Modeling"; Chapter 5, "Modeling with NURBS, Surfaces, and Deformers"; and Chapter 6, "Practical Experience."

Always keep in mind that Maya is case sensitive. An object named "sun" is different from an object named "Sun."

Maya typically uses an object-naming structure called a *humpback style,* where words are slung together without spaces. The first letter of a new word in the humpback name is capitalized, such as the node name *nurbsSphere1.*

Figure 2.8

The Sun sphere's Scale values in the Channel Box (left) and in the Input box (right)

6. Choose the Scale tool in the Tool Box to activate the Scale Manipulator, and uniformly scale the Sun sphere up to about four times its creation scale of 1. (Make it a scale of about 4 in all three axes.) For more precision, you can do one of two things. You can select the sphere and enter a value of **4** in all three entry fields (the white window next to the attribute) for the Scale X, Scale Y, and Scale Z channels in the Channel Box shown on the left in Figure 2.8. Alternatively, you can enter a value of **4** in the Input box on the Status line along the top of the UI, as shown on the right of Figure 2.8. Don't worry; you'll take an in-depth look at both of these methods in the next chapter.

7. After you enter the final value through either method, press Enter, and the sphere will grow to be four times its original size (at a scale of 1). When you enter the values in either the Channel Box or the Input box, a scale of 4 appears in all three fields, as shown on the right in Figure 2.8, and your Sun sphere expands in size by a factor of 4. Entering exact values in the Channel Box or Input box is a way to scale the sphere precisely; using the Manipulator isn't as precise.

Creating the Planets

Next, you'll create the primitive spheres you'll be using for the planets. Leave Interactive Creation off, and follow these steps:

1. Create a NURBS sphere for Mercury just as you did before, by choosing Create → NURBS Primitives → Sphere. A new sphere appears at the origin. Click its name in the Channel Box, and change it to **Mercury**.

2. Choose the Move tool from the Tool Box to activate the Move Manipulator, and move Mercury a few grid units away from the Sun sphere in the positive *X* direction. (Click the red arrow and drag it to the right.) Leave about two grid units between Mercury and the Sun sphere.

3. Because Mercury is the second-smallest planet and is tiny compared to the sun, scale it down to 1/20 the size of the Sun sphere, or type **0.2** in all three axes of Scale if you choose to enter the values manually in the Channel Box.

4. Repeat steps 1 through 3 to create the rest of the planets and line them up, placing each one farther out along the *X*-axis. Be sure to keep about two grid units of space between them. Scale each one proportionally as follows:

These proportions aren't exactly the same as those found in the real solar system, but they will do nicely here. Figure 2.9 shows how your solar system should look now.

No, Pluto isn't actually a planet anymore, but for nostalgia's sake, we'll include it here in our solar system. Poor Pluto!

PLANET SPHERE SIZES	
Venus	0.5
Earth	0.5
Mars	0.4
Jupiter	1.0
Saturn	0.9
Uranus	0.7
Neptune	0.7
Pluto	0.15

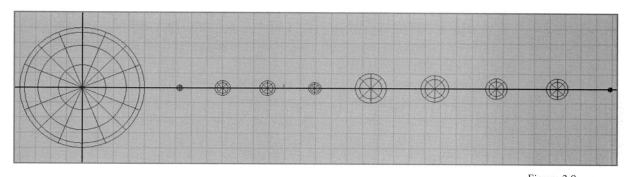

Figure 2.9

All the NURBS spheres are lined up in place (top view).

Using Snaps

Now is the perfect time to start using *snaps*. Some common snap icons are shown in Table 2.1. Snap icons are explained in greater depth in the next chapter. These icons run across the top of the UI just below the Main Menu bar, as shown here.

SNAP ICON	NAME	DESCRIPTION
	Snap To Grids	Snaps objects to intersections of the view's grid
	Snap To Curves	Snaps objects along a curve
	Snap To Points	Snaps objects to object points such as CVs or vertices
	Snap To Projected Center	Snaps an object to the center of another object
	Snap To View Planes	Snaps objects to view planes

Table 2.1

Snap icons

You use snaps to snap objects into place with precision, by placing them by their pivot points directly onto grid points, onto other object pivots, onto curve points, and so on.

Here you'll reposition all the planets slightly to center them on the nearest grid line intersection:

1. Select the first planet, Mercury. Choose the Move tool from the Tool Box, and toggle on *grid snaps* by clicking the Snap To Grids icon (▨).

2. The center of the Move Manipulator changes from a square to a circle, signaling that some form of snapping is active. Grab the Manipulator in the middle by this circle, and move it slightly to the left or right to snap it onto the closest grid intersection on the X-axis.

3. Select the remaining planets, and snap them all to the closest grid intersection on the X-axis, making sure to keep about two grid spaces between each of them. Because the Sun sphere was created at the origin and you haven't moved it, you don't need to snap it onto an intersection.

SAVING MULTIPLE VERSIONS OF YOUR WORK, INCREMENTAL SAVING, AND AUTOSAVE

As you're working on a project, you may want to save multiple versions of your files at various stages of completion. It's always good to keep as many versions of an animation as you can. Just keep your Scenes folder organized well—for example, by keeping older versions of scenes in separate subfolders—and you should have no problems.

Maya software's Incremental Save feature makes a backup of your scene file every time you save your scene with File → Save. To enable it, choose File → Save Scene ❑, and click the Incremental Save box. After you've done this, Maya will create a new folder within your Scenes folder with the name of your current scene file. It will then create a backup of your scene in that folder and append a number to the filename: for example, planets_001.mb. Every time you save your file, Maya will create a new backup until you disable the feature by choosing File → Save Scene ❑.

The scene files for the projects in this book are provided on the accompanying web page to give you a reference point for the major stages of each project. These files use a slightly different naming system than the names generated by Incremental Save (for example, the file on the web page is planets_v1.mb instead of planets_001.mb), so there is no risk of files overwriting each other.

Whether you save different versions of your scenes manually or use Incremental Save, it's a good idea to keep written notes about the differences in each version of a scene file so that whenever you make a significant change to a file, you have a record of your work.

If you prefer to name files manually, be sure to use an underscore (_) between the filename and version number instead of a space. Using spaces in your filenames may create problems with the software and some operating systems such as Linux.

Also handy is the AutoSave feature, which automatically saves your file to a specified folder at a set interval of time. To enable AutoSave, select Windows → Settings/Preferences → Preferences. In the Categories column on the left of the Preferences dialog box, select Settings → Files/Projects. You can enable AutoSave as well as set its time interval and save location under the AutoSave heading. This better ensures against data loss should your machine crash and is a pretty good idea to enable. AutoSave is off by default.

Making Saturn's Ring

Now, create the ring for Saturn. To do so, follow these steps:

1. Choose Create → NURBS Primitives → Torus to place a donut shape at the origin. Remember, Interactive Creation is turned off. You can also try creating the torus with the Interactive Creation option. In that case, click and drag the mouse to create the donut shape as you prefer. When you have a ring, use the Move tool to snap it to the same grid intersection as Saturn. This ensures that both the planet and its ring are on the same pivot point and share the same center.

2. Select the torus shape you've created, and name it **Ring** (if you haven't already done so) in the Channel Box.

3. While the torus shape is still selected in the top view, press the spacebar to display the four-panel layout. Place the mouse cursor in the persp view, and press the spacebar to maximize the Perspective window.

4. Press the F key to focus the perspective display on the ring and on Saturn. Pressing F centers and zooms in the panel on just the selected object(s).

5. Press 5 to get into Shaded mode, and with the torus selected, press 3 to increase the resolution display for the ring. Display resolutions are achieved by pressing the 1, 2, or 3 key and are further explained in the next chapter. Pressing 3 gives you the smoothest view of the torus in the view panels. That's a good thing.

6. From the Tool Box, select the Scale tool, and scale the torus down to 0 or close to 0 in the Y-axis (the torus's height, in this case) to flatten it.

   You'll notice that the ring is too fat and is cutting into the planet. You need to edit the attributes of the ring to increase the inside radius of the donut shape and create a gap between the planet and the ring.

7. Press Ctrl+A (Ctrl/Cmd+A will work on a Mac) to toggle the Attribute Editor if it's not on, and then click the makeNurbTorus1 tab to select its creation node (see Figure 2.10).

8. Increase the Radius attribute to about 1.5, and decrease the Height Ratio attribute to about 0.25 to get the desired effect.

   Now all your planets are complete, and you can move on to the moons.

Figure 2.10

Changing the creation attributes of the NURBS torus in the Attribute Editor

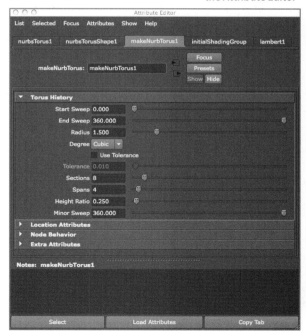

Changing the original attributes or parameters of an object, as you've just done with Saturn's ring, is often referred to as *parametric modeling*.

Saving Your Work

Save your work, unless you like to live on the edge. Saving frequently is a critical habit to develop. Power failures and other unforeseen circumstances (such as your pet jumping onto your keyboard) may not happen often, but they do happen—and usually at the wrong time. (As mentioned in the feature "Saving Multiple Versions of Your Work, Incremental Saving, and AutoSave," the Incremental Save and AutoSave features make it easy to maintain backups of your work.) Because you created this as a new project, the Save File window will direct you to the Scenes folder of that project. Save your scene as **planets** in the .mb (Maya Binary) format.

The file Planets_v1.mb in the Scenes folder of the Solar_System project on the web page shows what the scene should look like at this point.

Creating the Moons

For the planets with moons, create a new NURBS sphere for each moon. For simplicity's sake, create a maximum of only two moons for any planet. However, feel free to make all the moons for all the planets after you get a handle on this exercise.

The first moon will be Earth's. Use the top view to follow these steps:

1. Create a NURBS sphere, and scale it to about half the size of Earth using the Scale tool. Visually estimate the size of the moon.

2. Move the sphere to within half a unit of Earth, using the Move tool by the *X*-axis. There's no need to snap it to a grid point, so toggle off the Snap To Grids icon (⊞). Name the moon.

3. Repeat steps 1 and 2 for the remaining moons, placing them each within half a grid unit from their respective planets. When placing two moons, place them on opposite sides of the planet. Make sure to name your moons.

4. After you've finished with all the moons, their placements, and their sizes, select all the elements in the scene and press 3 to increase the display resolution on all the spheres. This gives you a smoother view of the NURBS spheres. When you're finished, you should have a scene similar to Figure 2.11 in perspective view. If you don't, it's clear Maya doesn't like you.

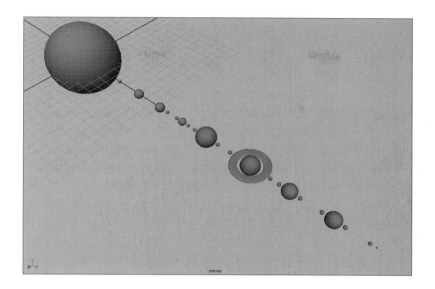

Figure 2.11

The planets and moons in position in perspective view

Applying a Simple Shader

To help distinguish one gray planet from another, attach simple shaders to each of the planets to give them color. Shaders, in short, are materials that give an object its particular look, whether it be color or a tactile texture. You can easily take care of this task using the Hypershade window. Follow these steps:

1. Choose Window → Rendering Editors → Hypershade to open the Hypershade window. This window lists, and allows you to edit, all the shaders and textures in the scene. With this window, you create the look of your objects by assigning colors, surface properties, and so on. You'll notice three default (or initial) shader icons already loaded (see Figure 2.12). For more on the Hypershade window, see Chapter 3.

Figure 2.12

The Hypershade window

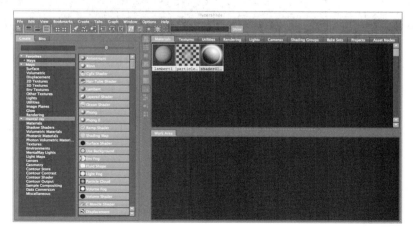

A BEGINNER'S TIP FOR SETTING KEYFRAMES

As with many other functions in Maya, you can set a keyframe in several ways. Switch to the Animation menu set by pressing F2. When you're first starting to learn Maya, the best way is to choose Animate → Set Key ▢ as shown here to display the Set Key Options box. Here, you're selecting the option box for that menu item by clicking the little empty box to the right of the menu item. The option box for any particular menu item allows you to set the options for that function. In this case, you're changing the options for the Set Key function.

If you choose Animate → Set Key without first changing those options, Maya sets a keyframe for all the keyable attributes for the selected object. Although this may seem convenient, it makes for a sloppy scene, especially if the scene must be heavily animated.

Having keyframes for attributes that may not actually be animated creates unnecessary clutter. In the Set Key Options box shown here, set the Set Keys On option to All Keyable Attributes instead of the default All Manipulator Handles And Keyable Attributes. Set Channels to From Channel Box instead of the default All Keyable. (These attributes will remain grayed out until you change to All Keyable Attributes.) Now, when you choose Animate → Set Key, you'll set a keyframe only for the channels that you specify explicitly through the Channel Box, giving you greater control and efficiency. All you have to do is highlight the channel you want to keyframe in the Channel Box and then choose Animate → Set Key. Save your settings by choosing Edit → Save Settings, and then click Close to close the dialog box.

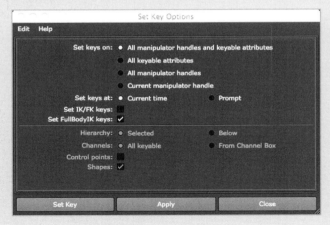

2. In the Create Maya Nodes panel on the left of the Hypershade window and under the Surface heading, click the Lambert icon (a gray sphere) to create a new Lambert shader node. It appears in the top and bottom of the Hypershade window. Click this icon eight more times to create a total of nine Lambert shading groups in the Hypershade window.

3. Click the first of the new Lambert nodes (lambert2) in the Hypershade window, and you should notice its attributes displayed in the Attribute Editor on the right of the UI. If you have the Channel Box displayed instead, double-click the shader's icon to open the Attribute Editor. At the top, replace lambert2 with **Mercury_Color** to identify this material as the one you'll use for Mercury.

4. Name each of the remaining planets in your animation (Venus, Earth, Mars, Jupiter, Saturn, Uranus, Neptune, and Pluto).

> To rename a node in the Hypershade window, you can also right-click the node's icon and choose Rename from the context menu that appears.

Again, keeping a well-named and organized scene is critical to a smooth animation experience. It's much more of a chore to root through dozens of unnamed nodes to find the one you want. When you've finished naming all the material nodes, save your work.

After you've created the shaders, you can assign the appropriate colors to each of them according to the planet they represent.

1. Double-click Mercury to open its Attribute Editor, if it's not currently open (see Figure 2.13).

2. To change the color of the shader, click the gray box next to the Color attribute. This opens the Color Chooser window, where you can choose a new color from the color wheel or by adjusting values with the HSV sliders. Because Mercury has a brownish red appearance, go with an orange color, such as in Figure 2.14 (take note of the HSV values).

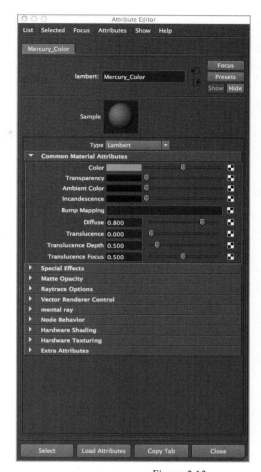

Figure 2.13

Mercury's shading group in the Attribute Editor

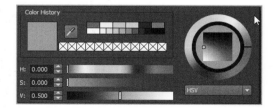

Figure 2.14

The Color Chooser window

3. Change the remainder of the shaders as follows:

Mercury	Orange-brown
Venus	Beige-yellow
Earth	Blue
Mars	Red-orange
Jupiter	Yellow-green
Saturn	Pale yellow
Uranus	Cyan
Neptune	Aqua blue
Pluto	Bright gray

Figure 2.15 shows the shading groups.

4. Next, apply shaders to the planets. Select a planet in the Perspective window, and right-click its corresponding material in the Hypershade window to open a marking menu. Drag up to highlight Assign Material To Selection, and release the button to select it. You can also use the middle mouse button to drag the material from the Hypershade window to its planet. Leave the moons set to the default gray color. When you're finished, you should have a scene similar to Figure 2.16.

Now that you're finished, you're ready to animate. Save this file; if you enabled Incremental Save as recommended earlier, your file won't be replaced with subsequent saves. This way, if you get lost in your animation and need to start fresh, you won't have to re-create everything from scratch.

Figure 2.15

The Hypershade window with all the colored planet shading groups

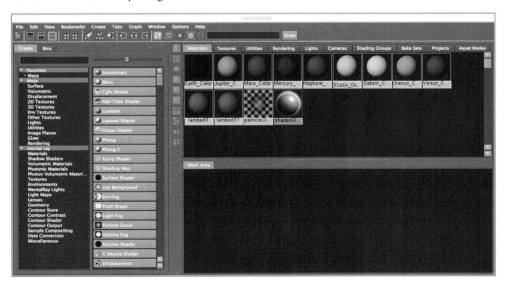

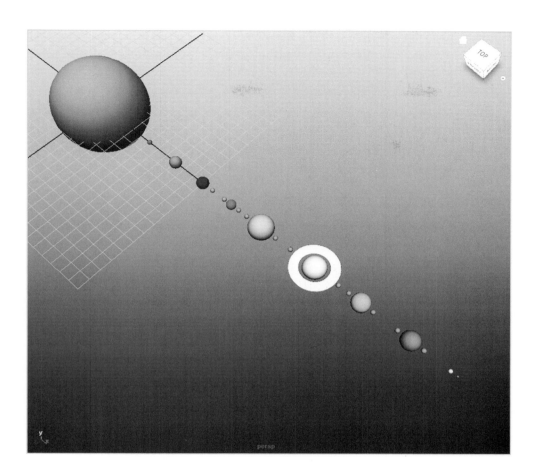

Figure 2.16

The shaded planets in perspective view

Creating the Animation

To begin this phase of the project, load the file Planets_v2.mb in the Scenes folder of the Solar_System project on the web page to your hard drive, or continue with your own scene file.

The animation you'll do for the orbits is straightforward. You'll rotate the planets around their own axes for their self-rotation, and then you'll animate the moons around the planets for their lunar orbits. Finally you'll make the planets and their moons orbit the Sun.

The premise of this exercise deals with hierarchy and pivot points. A *pivot point* is an object's center of balance of sorts. Every object or node that is created in Maya has a pivot point set at the origin. Because most objects, such as the spheres you created for the planets, appear at the origin upon creation, their pivot points are automatically centered.

When you move an object, as you've done to position the planets and moons, the pivot point moves with it. Therefore, the pivot points for all your planets and moons are already correctly positioned at the center of each planet and moon.

Now, you need to set up the animation settings for your scene file:

1. Press F2 to open the Animation menu set. *Menu sets* are groupings of menu headings in the Main Menu bar. They're organized according to the type of task at hand. You'll see the first several menu headings change when you switch from one menu set to another.

2. At the bottom of the UI, you'll notice a slider bar (the Range slider) directly below the strip of numbers counting off the frames (the Time slider) in the scene. Using the Range slider, you'll set the length of your animation to go from 1 to 240. Enter **1** in the Scene Start Frame and Range Start Frame boxes (Figure 2.17). Enter a value of **240** in the Scene End Frame and Range End Frame boxes, also as shown in Figure 2.17.

Figure 2.17

The Time and Range sliders

3. To the right of the Range slider, click the Animation Preferences icon () (shown here in the context of the lower-right corner of the Maya screen), click Settings, and set Time to NTSC (30fps), which is 30 frames per second, or NTSC video speed. Also see Figure 2.18.

4. Verify that Up Axis is set to *Y* and not *Z*, as shown in Figure 2.18. This ensures that you've designated the *Y*-axis to be pointing "up" in the Perspective window or pointing out at you from the monitor in the top view. *Y up*, as it's called, is the default, but it never hurts to make sure, especially if you're on a shared computer.

Choose Window → Settings/Preferences → Preferences to open the Preferences window. Under Settings → Undo, make sure Undo is on (if it isn't already), and set Queue to Infinite. Setting Queue to Infinite takes a little more system memory, but it's worth it. With this configuration, you can undo (press Crtl+Z [Command+Z on a Mac] or just Z), as many times as it takes to undo any blunders. To close the Preferences window, click Save.

Figure 2.18

Set Time to 30fps in the Settings tab of the Preferences window.

Mercury's Rotation

Now you're ready to animate Mercury's rotation. Follow these steps:

1. Select Mercury, and press E to activate the Rotate tool. The E key is the hotkey to invoke the Rotate tool in Maya; pressing it is the same as clicking the Rotate tool icon in the Tool Box, as you've been doing so far. Press F to focus on Mercury in the perspective view, or zoom in on it manually.

2. Make sure you're on frame 1 of your animation range by clicking and dragging the Scrub bar (refer back to Figure 2.17) to place it at the desired frame. You can also manually type the frame value of **1** in the Current Frame box.

3. For Mercury, you'll set your initial keyframe for the *Y*-axis rotation. Click the attribute name for Rotate Y in the Channel Box to select it (it's then highlighted in gray, as shown in Figure 2.19), and in the Main Menu bar, choose Animate → Set Key. This places a keyframe for a rotation of 0 in the *Y*-axis at frame 1 for the Mercury sphere. If you followed the advice in the sidebar "Setting Keyframes," earlier in this chapter, only the Value box in Rotate Y attributes turns from white to orange to indicate that a keyframe exists for that attribute. If you left the Set Key command at its defaults, choosing Animate → Set Key sets keys on all the attributes for the sphere, turning all their values orange in the Channel Box.

Figure 2.19

Setting the initial keyframe for Mercury's Y-axis rotation

4. Using the Scrub bar in the Time slider, go to frame 240. Grab the Rotation Manipulator handle by the *Y*-axis (the green circle), and turn it clockwise a few times to rotate the sphere clockwise. You'll notice that you can rotate the object only so far in one direction before it seems to reset to its original starting rotation. Rotate it as far as it will go, and release the mouse button. Then, click the Manipulator again, and drag to rotate the sphere as many times as necessary until you're satisfied.

5. Choose Animate → Set Key with the `Rotate Y` attribute still selected in the Channel Box. This sets a keyframe for the new *Y*-axis rotation at frame 240 for the Mercury sphere.

6. To play back your animation, you can scrub your Time slider. *Scrubbing* is using the mouse to move the Scrub bar back and forth so you can watch the animation play back in a window. Click in the Time slider on the Scrub bar, hold down the left mouse button, and move your cursor from side to side to scrub in real time. You'll see Mercury rotating in your active view panel, if you set your two keyframes as described.

Clicking so many things just to set two keyframes may seem like a lot of work, but you're doing this the long way right now; you're not yet using any shortcuts or hotkeys. You'll start using those for the next planet.

You have the self-rotation for Mercury worked out. Mercury has no moon, so let's get Mercury orbiting the Sun.

Grouping Mercury for a New Pivot Point

You've learned that every object in Maya is created with a pivot point around which it rotates, from which or to which it scales, and which acts as the placement point for its *X*-, *Y*-, and *Z*-coordinates. To orbit Mercury around the Sun sphere, the sphere must revolve around a pivot point that is placed in the middle of the Sun sphere. If the pivot point for Mercury is already at the center of itself, how can you revolve it around the Sun sphere?

One idea is to move its current pivot point from the center of itself to the center of the Sun sphere. That would, however, negate Mercury's own rotation, and it would no longer spin around its own center, so you can't do that. You need to create a new pivot point for this object. This way, you have the original pivot point at Mercury's center so it can self-rotate, and you have a second pivot point at the Sun sphere so that Mercury can revolve around that point around the Sun sphere. You'll accomplish this by creating a new *parent node* above Mercury in the hierarchy. What does that mean?

In order not to get too confusing, I'll take time in the following section to introduce the concept of Maya object structure: nodes and hierarchies. Save your progress so far, and open a new blank scene. After this explanation, you'll resume the solar system exercise.

Hierarchy and Maya Object Structure

Let's take a timeout from the solar system exercise and look at how objects and hierarchies work in Maya. On top of everything that you see in Maya—its interface—is a layer you don't see: the code. The layer of code keeps the objects in Maya organized through a network of nodes. How you relate these nodes defines how you've built your scene. In short, using Maya is essentially programming your computer directly to create 3D objects and animation.

So, having a solid understanding of how Maya defines objects and how they interact is essential to an efficient and successful animation process. This involves getting an intrinsic understanding of how nodes relate, whether it's a straightforward parent-child hierarchy in which one affects the other directly or a more complicated script-driven expression connecting 15 attributes of several objects to simplify a task.

Understanding Nodes

At its core, Maya relies on packets of information called *nodes*, and each node carries with it a group of attributes that in combination define an object. These attributes can be spatial coordinates, geometric descriptors, color values, and so on. Taken together, an object's attributes define it and how it animates. You can define, animate, and interconnect any or all of these attributes individually or in concert, which gives you amazing control over a scene.

Nodes that define the shape of a surface or a primitive are called *creation nodes* or *shape nodes*. These nodes carry the information that defines how that object is created. For example, a sphere's creation node has an attribute for its radius. Changing that attribute changes the radius of the sphere at its base level, making it a bigger or smaller sphere. This is *different* than scaling the sphere as you've done with the planets so far. Shape nodes are low on the hierarchy chain and are always child nodes of *transform nodes*. The sphere listens to its creation node attributes first and then moves down the chain to its other nodes' attributes (such as position, rotation, or scale).

Not all primitives are created with shape nodes, so changes at the creation level may not be possible on certain objects; some objects are created without a creation node. When you create a new primitive or an object, make sure the History button ( ) is turned on in the Status line (see Chapter 3 for more about the Status line and its icons). If it displays a small red *X* in the icon, History is off, and the primitive will be created without a shape node.

The most visible and used nodes are the transform nodes, also known as directed acyclic graph (DAG) nodes. These nodes contain all the transformation attributes for an object or a group of objects below it. *Transformations* are the values for translation (position), rotation, and scale. These nodes also hold hierarchy information about any other children or parent nodes to which they're attached. When you move or scale an object, you adjust attributes in this node.

Try This   As an example of working with transform nodes, you can create a sphere and see what happens in the Attribute Editor as you adjust its position and size. Follow these steps in a new Maya scene:

1. Press Ctrl+A to toggle the Attribute Editor on the right of the UI or to open it as its own window if you've set it up to do so in preferences. (Ctrl functions the same on a Mac as on a PC, so Mac users can also use their Ctrl key when called for in the text.)

   The tabs along the top of the window let you switch between the nodes that are attached to this object. The current tab should be on the sphere's shape node, called nurbsSphereShape1. This node contains specific information about the object, but it isn't typically a node that you edit.

2. Press W to select the Translate tool. With the sphere still selected, click the nurbsSphere1 tab in the Attribute Editor to access the sphere's transform node. Move the sphere a little in the *X* direction. Notice in the Attribute Editor that the Translate attribute for *X* has changed. You should also see the change in the Channel Box.

3. Press R to select the Scale tool. R is the hotkey by default in Maya for the Scale tool and is the same as clicking the Scale tool icon in the Tool Box ( ). Scale the sphere uniformly, meaning equally, in all directions by clicking and dragging the Center Manipulator handle (the cyan box). Notice that the Scale X, Scale Y, and Scale Z attributes of the sphere change in the Attribute Editor. In the Attribute Editor, enter **1.0** for the *X*, *Y*, and *Z* Scale values to reset the sphere to its original size.

4. In the creation node of makeNurbsSphere1, change the radius from 1.0 to **2.0**. The sphere doubles in size because its radius is doubled. Switch back to the transform node (nurbsSphere1), and note that the Scale X, Scale Y, and Scale Z attribute values are unchanged. This is because you affected the size of the sphere through its Radius attribute in the creation node at its root level, not through the Scale attributes in a higher node. Any changes you make to the Scale attributes take effect after changes in the lower node. This is a perfect example of how one node's output (here, the Radius attribute) changes another node.

Parents and Children

A *parent node* is simply a node that passes its transformations down the hierarchy chain to its children. A *child node* inherits the transforms of all the parents above it. So, by using hierarchies for the solar system exercise, you'll create a nested hierarchy of parents and children to animate the orbital rotation of the nine planets and some of their moons.

By creating parent-child relationships, you can easily animate the orbit of a moon around a planet while the planet orbits the sun. With the proper hierarchy, the animation of the planet orbiting the sun automatically translates to the moon. In effect, the planet takes the moon with it as it goes around the sun.

Child nodes have their own transformations that can be coupled with any inherited transforms from their parent, and these transformations affect them and any of their children down the line.

The revolution of one of the planets around the sun takes into account its moons, but those moons can have their own animation to spin themselves around their planets. You're about to experience this firsthand as you continue the solar system exercise. The more you hear about these concepts in different contexts, the easier they will be to master.

Figure 2.20 shows the Outliner and Hypergraph views with a simple hierarchy of objects for your reference. The Outliner and Hypergraph show you the objects in your scene in an outline and flowchart format, respectively. Both of these windows allow you to access the different levels of nodes (the hierarchy) in a scene and are discussed further in Chapter 3.

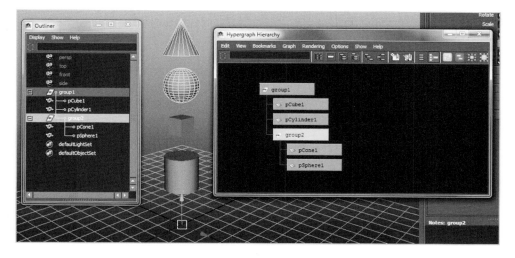

Figure 2.20

A simple hierarchy in both the Outliner and Hypergraph windows

A top parent node called group1 holds its children pCube1, pCylinder1, and the nested group node group2. The node group2 is the parent node of pCone1 and pSphere1.

The Solar System, Resumed

If you still feel a little unsure about nodes and hierarchies, take the time to reread the previous section and try the short exercise again. You'll practice these concepts as you resume the solar system exercise. By the time you've finished this exercise, you'll have a strong sense of how hierarchies work in Maya, although you should feel free to repeat the entire exercise if you think that will help you master hierarchies. Understanding nodes and hierarchies is important to animating in Maya.

If you're new to CG animation, take your time with the following section.

Animating Mercury's Orbit Around the Sun

Load your scene from where you last saved it. When you left off, you had created the self-rotation animation for Mercury and were about to create a second pivot point for the planet to orbit around the Sun sphere by creating a new parent node for the Mercury sphere.

To create a new pivot point by making a new parent node, follow these steps:

1. With `Mercury` selected, press E for the Rotate tool, and then choose Edit → Group from the Main Menu bar. The Channel Box displays attributes for a new node called `group1`. Notice that nothing about the Mercury sphere changed, except that the Rotation Manipulator handle jumped from where it was originally centered on Mercury all the way back to the origin, where the zero points of the *X*-, *Y*-, and *Z*-axes collide. Figure 2.21 shows the new `Mercury` group and its new pivot location.

Figure 2.21

Grouping Mercury to itself creates a new pivot point at the origin.

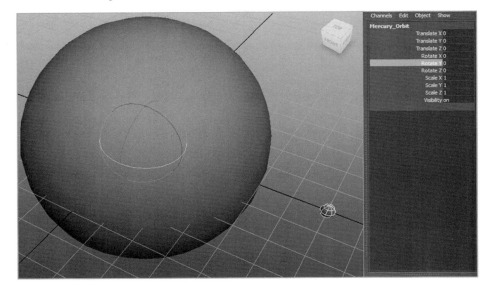

You just created a new Maya object by grouping Mercury to itself. In doing so, you also created a second pivot point for Mercury, which was placed by Maya at the origin by default. Because an object's Manipulator always centers on its pivot point when it's selected, Mercury's Rotate Manipulator jumped to the origin when the new parent node became selected upon its creation. That is fortunate for you, because that happens to be the center of the Sun sphere—exactly where you need it to be for Mercury to orbit the Sun sphere properly.

2. Without unselecting Mercury, click group1 in the Channel Box, and change the name of this new group to **Mercury_Orbit**. It's important to make the distinction between node names so you never get confused. Now you know that the Mercury node is the planet sphere itself, whereas Mercury_Orbit is the name of the new parent node, with which you'll orbit Mercury around the Sun sphere.

3. Click anywhere in an empty space in your view window to unselect Mercury_Orbit. Try selecting it again. Notice that when you click Mercury, you select only the planet and not the new parent node Mercury_Orbit, the group that has its pivot point at the center of the Sun sphere. This happens because you're in Object Selection mode (a.k.a. Object mode). To select the group Mercury_Orbit, you need to switch into Hierarchy mode by toggling its icon (![icon]) on the Status line at the top of the UI, as shown in Figure 2.22. Make sure you switch back to Object mode by clicking its icon (![icon]) in the Status line. For more on selection modes, see Chapter 3.

Figure 2.22

Toggling on the Hierarchy mode

4. Go back to frame 1 of your animation. Set a keyframe for Mercury_Orbit's Rotate Y attribute by selecting its name in the Channel Box and then choosing Animate → Set Key from the Main Menu bar.

5. Go to frame 240, grab Mercury_Orbit's Rotate Manipulator handle by the green *Y*-axis, and spin it around the Sun twice in either direction. (It doesn't matter if you go clockwise or counterclockwise.) You can also enter **720** (or **-720** in Object Selection mode to go in the other direction) in the Rotate Y attribute field in the Channel Box.

6. Choose Animate → Set Key to set a keyframe at frame 240 for Mercury_Orbit. Scrub your animation to play it back.

Does that make good sense? You'll have the chance to do this a few more times as you animate the other planets and their moons. However, if you still find yourself a little fuzzy on this concept (which is perfectly normal), repeat the steps to animate Mercury in a new scene file if need be. One down, eight to go.

Creating Venus

For your next planet, Venus, follow the same procedure as for Mercury's self-rotation, and animate it so that it rotates around itself. Then, create a new pivot point (placed by default at the origin) by grouping Venus to itself to create a new parent node for that sphere, and call the new parent node **Venus_Orbit**. Last, animate Venus_Orbit to revolve around the Sun sphere just as you did with Mercury_Orbit in the previous steps.

Earth and the Moon

Now you need to animate the third planet, Earth, in much the same way, except that this time there will be the added complication of a moon. In addition, instead of choosing Animate → Set Key to set your keyframes, you'll use the keyboard hotkey S. (Earth? Hey, I can see my house from here!)

Whenever you press S when an attribute is highlighted in the Channel Box, you're essentially choosing Animate → Set Key. In the Set Key Options box, be sure you've changed Set Keys On to All Keyable Attributes instead of the default All Manipulator Handles And Keyable Attributes. Also make sure you've set Channels to From Channel Box instead of the default All Keyable, as mentioned in the earlier sidebar.

To animate Earth and the moon, follow these steps:

1. Select Earth, and give it its self-rotation animation as you did for Mercury. But this time, select the rotation channel names in the Channel Box and press S, instead of choosing Animate → Set Key to set rotation keyframes. Again, if you left the Animate → Set Key ❐ at its defaults, pressing S sets keys for all attributes. But if you followed the advice given previously in the sidebar, only the selected channels are keyframed.

2. Select the moon, and give it its self-rotation animation by spinning it around itself and keyframing it as you've just done with Earth.

3. To spin the moon around Earth, do what you did earlier in this chapter to spin a planet around the Sun sphere: group the moon to itself by choosing Edit → Group, and name the new parent node **Moon_Orbit**.

This time, however, you need the pivot point to be at the center of Earth and not at the center of the Sun object, where it is currently. Follow these steps:

1. Turn on the grid snap, and then press the Insert key to activate the pivot point. If you're using a Macintosh, press the Home key. On either PC or Mac, you may also press and hold down the D key. The moon's Manipulator changes from a rotation handle to the *Pivot Point Manipulator*. This Manipulator acts just like the Move Manipulator, but instead of moving the object, it moves the object's pivot point.

Figure 2.23

Moving the moon's pivot point to the center of Earth

2. Grab the yellow circle in the middle of the Manipulator, and move the pivot point to snap it to the grid point located at the center of Earth (see Figure 2.23).

3. Press the Insert key again (or the Home key on a Macintosh; or release the D key) to return to the Rotation Manipulator for Moon_Orbit. At frame 1, set a keyframe for the moon's Y-axis rotation. Then, at frame 240, rotate the moon around the Y-axis and set a keyframe. Return to frame 1.

Grouping the Moon with Earth

To animate Earth's orbit of the Sun, you need to make sure the moon will also follow Earth around the Sun sphere. Instead of just selecting Earth and grouping it to itself as you've done for the other two planets, you need to include the Moon_Orbit node in that group. Follow these steps:

1. Select Earth. Shift+click the Moon_Orbit group while in Hierarchy mode ( ) to make sure you get the topmost node of the moon, and then choose Edit → Group. Name this new parent node **Earth_Orbit**. Remember, when you select just Earth or the moon in Object mode ( ), the Earth_Orbit node isn't selected. If you select Earth and then Shift+click the moon, you select both objects, but you still don't select the parent node Earth_Orbit, which is the group that contains both these objects and has its pivot point at the center of the Sun. Make sure you select the right group. Keep an eye on where the Manipulator is when you make your selection. If you have the Earth_Orbit node selected, its Manipulator should be in the middle of the Sun sphere. I'll deliberately illustrate this mistake and its consequences when you animate Pluto a little later.

> Make sure you use Hierarchy mode ( ) when you click the moon object to select Moon_Orbit and not just the moon sphere. Otherwise, you'll lose the animation of the moon orbiting Earth.

2. Set a keyframe for Earth_Orbit's Rotate Y attribute at frame 1 by highlighting Rotate Y in the Channel Box and pressing S for the Set Key command. This assumes you've changed the defaults in Animate → Set Key ❑ as discussed in the earlier sidebar.

3. Go to frame 240, spin Earth and the moon around the Sun sphere a few times in whichever direction and for however many revolutions you want, and set a keyframe at frame 240 as well.

Now the first three planets are going around themselves and around the sun, with a moon for Earth. If you haven't been saving your work, save it now. Just don't save over the unanimated version from earlier.

Creating the Other Planets' Moons

Repeat this animation procedure for the remaining planets and moons, but leave out Pluto for now. (Poor Pluto: first it loses out on being a planet, and now it has to wait for last.)

If you find that one of your moons is left behind by its planet or that it no longer revolves around the planet, you most likely made an error when grouping the moon and planet. Undo until you're at the point right before you grouped them, and try again. If that still doesn't work, start over from the earlier version of the file you saved just before you began animating it. You'll learn how to fix it in the section "Using the Outliner" later in this chapter.

Auto Keyframe

You can also use the Auto Keyframe feature when animating the planets and moons. Auto Keyframe automatically sets a keyframe for any attribute that changes from a previously set keyframe. For example, an initial keyframe for an attribute such as Y-Axis Rotation needs to be set at some point in the animation. The next time the Y-Axis Rotation is changed, Maya will set a keyframe at the current frame automatically.

To turn on Auto Keyframe, click the Auto Keyframe icon (▣), which is to the right of the Range slider. When the icon is red, Auto Keyframe is active.

To use Auto Keyframe to animate the moon orbiting Mars, follow these steps:

1. Turn on Auto Keyframe.

2. Start at frame 1. Select Mars's moon, and set a keyframe for its *Y*-axis orbit by highlighting Rotate Y in the Channel Box and pressing S.

3. Go to frame 240. Revolve the moon around Mars several times in a direction of your choosing. Maya automatically sets a frame for *Y* rotation at frame 240. Save your file.

Using the Outliner

The Outliner is an outline listing of all the objects and nodes in your scene. For an in-depth look at the Outliner, see Chapter 3. For now, let's look at how to use the Outliner to illustrate the hierarchies for the planets and moons. When all is good and proper, the Outliner should look like Figure 2.24. Choose Window → Outliner to open the Outliner window and take a peek at what you have. If you haven't yet properly named everything, including the moons, take this opportunity to do so by double-clicking a name in the Outliner and entering a new name.

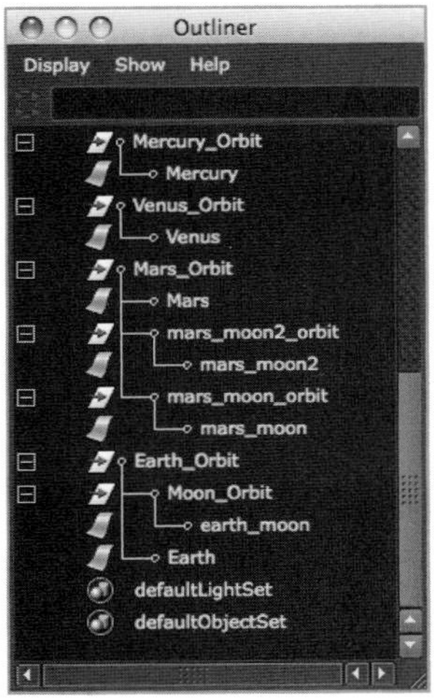

Figure 2.24

The Outliner view of the planet hierarchies

Let's look at the planet Mars and its layout in the Outliner to better understand the hierarchy for all the planets. All the other planets should be laid out exactly like Mars (except the planets that have just one or no moon).

At the bottom of the hierarchy are Mars's two moons, mars_moon and mars_moon2. Each of those moons is spinning on its own pivot point. You grouped each moon to itself, created the `mars_moon_orbit` and `mars_moon2_orbit` nodes, and placed their pivot points at the center of Mars to animate their orbits around Mars.

Mars is spinning on its own pivot point, but it needed another pivot point to be able to orbit the Sun. Because you had to make the moons go with it around the sun, you selected Mars, `mars_moon_orbit`, and `mars_moon2_orbit` (the top nodes of the moons that circle the planet Mars) and grouped them all together, placing that pivot point at the center of the sun. You called this node `Mars_Orbit`. This is the *parent node* because it's the topmost node for this group. Wherever this parent node goes, the child nodes that are under it will follow.

Hierarchies such as this are a cornerstone of Maya animation. It's imperative that you're comfortable with how they work and how to work with them. If you find yourself scratching your head even a little, try the exercise again. A proper foundation is critical. Remember, this learning 3D thing isn't easy, but patience and repetition help a lot.

Correcting Hierarchy Problems Using the Outliner

One of the most common problems you'll run into with this project is a planet revolving around the sun without its moon. To illustrate how to fix it using the Outliner, as opposed to undoing and redoing it as suggested earlier, the following steps will force you to make this error with Pluto. Usually, people learn more from mistakes than from doing things correctly.

Go to `Pluto`, start the same animation procedure as outlined earlier, and then follow these steps to force an error:

1. Create Pluto's own self-rotation by spinning it around itself and keyframing as before.

2. Do the same for Pluto's moon's rotation.

3. Group the moon to itself, and grid-snap the pivot point at the center of Pluto to create the moon's orbit of Pluto.

    When Pluto's moon (`pluto_moon`) is orbiting Pluto, you're ready to group the moon's orbit and Pluto together to create an orbit of the Sun sphere for both.

4. Here is where you make your mistake. In Object mode, select the sphere for Pluto's moon, and select the sphere for Pluto. Your error is that you're remaining in Object mode instead of switching to Hierarchy mode.

5. Choose Edit → Group to group them together, and call that new node **Pluto_Orbit** (following the naming convention you used for the others).

6. Animate `Pluto_Orbit` revolving around the Sun.

7. Play back the animation.

Figure 2.25

Pluto's incorrect hierarchy

Figure 2.26

Regrouping objects in the Outliner

Notice that the moon is no longer orbiting the planet. This is because you didn't include `pluto_moon_orbit` in your group `Pluto_Orbit`. The animation of the moon going around Pluto is stored in that node, and because it's no longer attached to `Pluto_Orbit`, there's no moon orbit of Pluto.

Figure 2.25 shows the hierarchy of Pluto and how it's different from that of the other planets: the moon's orbit node has been left out of the group. (Earth has been expanded as a contrasting example.)

Using the Outliner, you can easily fix this problem. Place the `pluto_moon_orbit` node under the `Pluto_Orbit` node. Go to frame 1 of the animation, grab the `pluto_moon_orbit` node in the Outliner, and use the middle mouse button to drag it to the `Pluto_Orbit` node so that it has a black horizontal line above and below it to show a connection, as in Figure 2.26.

You've just grouped `pluto_moon_orbit` under `Pluto_Orbit`, a practice known as *parenting*. Now you need to parent `pluto_moon` under `pluto_moon_orbit` as well. Use the middle mouse button to drag `pluto_moon` onto `pluto_moon_orbit`. When you play back the animation, you'll see that the moon is revolving around the planet, while at the same time Pluto and the moon are orbiting the Sun sphere. Now that you've corrected Pluto's layout in the Outliner, it's similar to the layouts for the other properly working planets.

The file `Planets_v3.mb` in the Scenes folder of the Solar_System project on the web page will give you an idea of how this project should look. The first five planet systems are grouped and animated as a reference, leaving the final four for you to finish.

> You can add objects to a group by MMB+dragging their listing onto the desired parent node in the Outliner. You can also remove objects from a group by MMB+dragging them out of the parent node to a different place in the Outliner.

GROUPING TERMINOLOGY

Grouping terminology can be confusing. Grouping Node A under Node B makes Node A a child of Node B. Node B is now the parent of Node A. Furthermore, any transformation or movement applied to the parent Node B will be inherited by the child Node A.

When you group Node A and Node B, both nodes become siblings under a newly created parent node, Node C. This new node is created just to be the parent of Nodes A and B and is otherwise known as a *null node*. To group objects, select them and choose Edit → Group. Parenting nodes together places the first selected node under the second selected node. For example, if you select Node A, Shift+select Node B, and then choose Edit → Parent, Node A will group under Node B and become its child. This is the same procedure as MMB+dragging Node B to Node A in the Outliner, as you did with Pluto's moon and Pluto itself.

Outputting Your Work: Playblasting

What's the use of animating all this work and not being able to show it? There are several ways of outputting your work in Maya, most of which involve rendering to images. One faster way of outputting your animation in a simple shaded view is called *playblasting*. Playblasting creates a sequence of images that play back on your computer at the proper frame rate. Only if your PC is slow or if you're playblasting a large sequence of frames will your playback degrade. In this case, playblasting 240 frames shouldn't be a problem.

A *playblast*, as it's called in Maya, outputs the view panel's view into an image sequence or AVI movie. You can also save the image sequence or AVI to disk if you like. Playblasting is done mainly to test the look and animation of a scene, especially when its playback is slow within Maya.

When you have your solar system animated, output a playblast by following these steps:

Figure 2.27

Selecting Playblast

1. With your animation completed, click in the Perspective panel to make it active in the four-panel layout (don't maximize the Perspective window). Press 5 to enter Shaded mode.

2. RMB+click in the Time slider, and select Playblast ❑ from the menu, as shown in Figure 2.27. The option box is shown for the Playblast options in Figure 2.28.

3. In the Playblast options, set Format to avi (displayed as qt for QuickTime when using a Macintosh) and Display Size to From Window. Check the Save To File option, and give your playblast a name. Set Scale to **1.0**.

Figure 2.28

The option box for creating a playblast preview

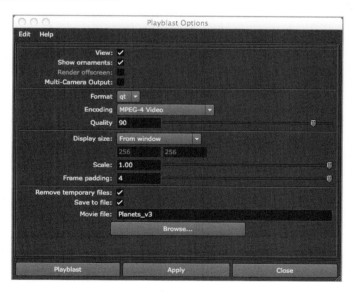

4. Because you checked the avi (or qt on a Mac) option, Maya runs through the animation and creates an AVI movie file on a PC or a QuickTime movie file on a Mac that is based on the Shaded-mode appearance of the currently active view panel (which should be the Perspective panel). Because you also checked the Save To File option, the movie file is saved to disk. By default, it's saved to the Images folder for the Solar_System project you created on your hard drive. You can also click the Browse button to store the playblast video file anywhere you like. For now, click Browse, and place the file on your desktop. Click the Playblast button.

5. When Maya runs through the animation, Windows Media Player on Windows or QuickTime on a Mac (or whatever your default movie player is set to in your OS) automatically opens and plays the move file of the animation at the proper speed of 30 fps, as shown in Figure 2.29. Now you can share your animation with others without having to open Maya and play it back in the scene.

When you're creating a playblast, make sure you don't cover the view panel with any other windows, such as an Internet browser, as you wait for the animation to complete. Doing so may create a display error in the playblast output. It's best to allow Maya to complete the playblast before you use the system again.

Figure 2.29

Creating a playblast movie file is easy.

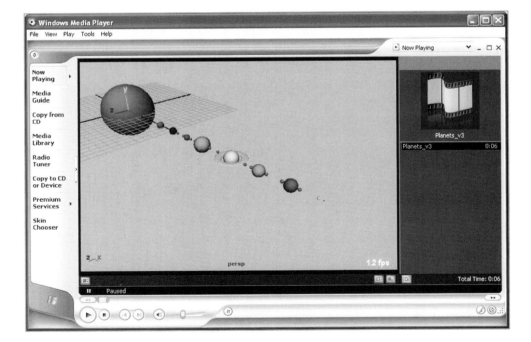

Summary

In this chapter, you learned how to start working in Maya by getting around the interface a bit and learning how to navigate the UI. Then, you began working by creating a new project, creating basic objects such as primitives, and placing objects in the scene. You learned how to place pivot points for objects and how to use snaps to place points precisely. You had some experience with the Channel Box and Attribute Editor to set an object's attributes. You then went on to create simple shaders for your objects and set keyframes to animate a solar system. You explored object hierarchy and grouping conventions to organize and set up your scene better, and finally you learned how to output a basic playblast video file of your completed animation.

The planet animation you created is based on a system of layering simple actions on top of each other to achieve a more elaborate result. If you work slowly and in segments, animation will be more straightforward to produce and generally of higher quality. Much of your time in actual animation, as opposed to setup or modeling, will be spent adjusting the small things. These small things give the scene life and character. You'll find that finishing 85 percent of a scene will take about 15 percent of the time. The remaining 85 percent of the time goes into perfecting the final 15 percent of the scene.

CHAPTER 3

The Autodesk Maya 2014 Interface

This chapter takes you on a guided tour of all the elements visible on the Autodesk® Maya® 2014 program's screen as you build a simple model of a decorative box. The chapter draws from the experience you had in Chapter 2, "Jumping in Headfirst, with Both Feet," with the solar system exercise. You'll visit the menus, icons, and shelves to become familiar with the interface basics as you build a model. For now, while you're first getting into this, knowing the name of everything and its purpose is a good idea. Don't get nervous; you won't need to retain a lot of information. Think of this more as a nickel tour.

This chapter also serves as a good reference when you're wondering about the purpose of a particular icon.

Learning Outcomes: In this chapter, you will be able to

- Recognize and use Maya UI elements
- Understand how Maya view panels and windows work
- Use Manipulators to transform objects in 3D space
- Create and use reference planes for modeling from pictures
- Use polygon modeling techniques
  - Extrude
  - Bevel
  - Edge loops
  - Interactive Split tool
  - Component editing—edges, faces, vertices
- Use the Layer Editor to organize your scene
- Render test frames to preview your work
- Gain confidence in using the Attribute Editor
- Better manage your scenes and object hierarchies with the Outliner

Navigating in Maya

The key to being a good digital artist or animator isn't knowing *where* to find all the tools and buttons, but knowing *how* to find the features you need. Maya is intricate, with layers of function sets and interface options separated into categories. The purpose of this chapter is to help you get to know Maya and how it operates, building on your experience so far. This chapter will also answer the questions you may have about the UI from the previous chapter.

Explore the interface. Using your mouse, check out the menus and the tools. Just be careful not to change any settings; the rest of this book and its projects assume your Maya settings are all at their defaults. If you do change some settings inadvertently, reverting to the defaults is easy. Choose Window → Settings/Preferences → Preferences. In the Preferences window, choose Edit → Restore Default Settings. Now all the settings and interface elements are restored to their default states.

Exploring the Maya Layout

Let's take another look at the initial Maya screen in Figure 3.1—this time with the Full Perspective window and not the four-panel layout you saw in the previous chapter.

Figure 3.1

The initial Maya screen

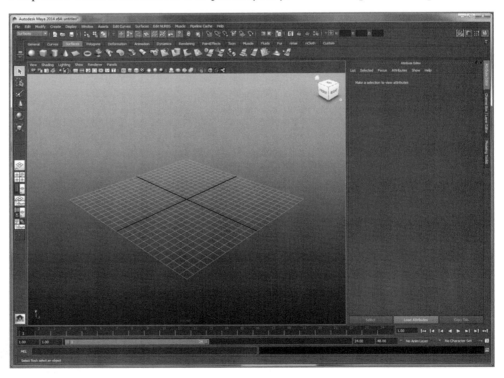

The *Main Menu bar*, *Status line*, and *Shelf* all run across the top of the screen. The Tool Box runs vertically on the left side of the screen. It contains icons for your Transform tools (such as Move, Rotate, and Scale) as well as quick-view selections to allow you to customize your panel layouts quickly. The Attribute Editor, Channel Box/Layer Editor, and Modeling Toolkit (the Attribute Editor is currently displayed in Figure 3.1) run down the right side of the screen. Finally, listed from the top down, the Time slider, the Range slider, the Character Set menu, the Auto Keyframe button, and the Animation Preferences button, some of which you've already used, run across the bottom of the screen.

REMINDER: MAYA MOUSE CONTROLS

In Maya, holding the Alt key on a PC or the Option key on a Mac along with the appropriate button allows you to move in the view panel. The left mouse button (LMB) acts as the primary selection button (as it does in many other programs) and lets you orbit around objects when used with the Alt key. The right mouse button (RMB) activates numerous context menus and lets you zoom with the Alt key. The middle mouse button (MMB) with the Alt key lets you move within the Maya interface, and the mouse's wheel can be used to zoom in and out as well.

The Main Menu Bar

In the Main Menu bar, shown in Figure 3.2, you'll find a few of the familiar menu choices you've come to expect in many applications, such as File, Edit, and Help.

Figure 3.2

The Main Menu bar is where the magic happens.

In Maya, menu choices are context sensitive; they depend on what you're doing. By switching menu sets, you change your menu choices and hence your available toolset. The menu sets in Maya are Animation, Polygons, Surfaces, Dynamics, Rendering, and nDynamics. You select a menu set using the drop-down menu in the Status line below the Main Menu bar, as shown in Figure 3.3.

When you're wondering where a particular toolset is, all you need to do is ask yourself, "What CG phase would that function fall under?" Because the menu sets are organized in phases of computer animation workflow—modeling (polygons and surfaces), animating, dynamics, and lighting/rendering—the task dictates which menu includes its toolset.

Figure 3.3

The Menu Set drop-down menu

No matter which menu set you're working in, the first six menu items are constant: File, Edit, Modify, Create, Display, and Window. The last menu, Help, is also constantly displayed no matter which menu set you choose.

Some plug-ins can also add menu items to the Main Menu bar. For example, Maya Muscle is a plug-in that comes with Maya and is on by default; it adds the Muscle menu to the Main Menu bar. If the plug-in is turned off, that menu item is removed. So, don't panic if you don't see the same Main Menu bar pictured throughout this book. Keep in mind that some menu headings are displayed when a feature or plug-in is enabled, so your Maya screen may show slightly different headings. The following menus typically stay no matter which menu set you are in (see the "Menu Sets" section for more):

File   Deals with file operations, from saving and opening to optimizing scene size and export/import.

Edit   Contains the commands you use to edit characteristics of the scene (for example, deleting and duplicating objects or undoing and redoing actions).

Modify   Lets you edit the characteristics of objects in the scene, such as moving or scaling them or changing their pivot points.

Create   Lets you make new objects, such as primitive geometries, curves, cameras, and so on.

Display   Contains commands for adjusting elements of the graphical user interface (GUI) in Maya as well as objects in the scene, allowing you to toggle, or switch on or off, the display of certain elements as well as components of objects, such as vertices, hulls, pivots, and so on.

Window   Gives you access to the many windows you'll come to rely on, such as the Attribute Editor, Outliner, Graph Editor, and Hypergraph. This menu is broken into submenus according to function, such as Rendering Editors and Animation Editors.

Assets   Used primarily in collaborative work and pipelines—where parts of an animation production are compartmentalized to different artists all working concurrently on the same thing. Assets allow you to control and streamline how scene objects are used within the scene.

Muscle   Another integrated plug-in that allows you to create more realistic skin deformation in animated characters by using underlying muscle objects in the rig of the character. I will not cover Muscle in this book because it is an advanced workflow.

Pipeline Cache   Needs to have a plug-in activated to appear on your UI, and should be on by default. Pipeline caching allows you to optimize large scenes by caching them to external files. This facilitates easier collaboration between artists working on the same project and reduces overhead in scenes. Since this is an advanced workflow, pipeline caches will not be covered in this book.

Help   Gives you access to the help files.

Submenus and the Option Box

You'll notice two different demarcations to the right of some menu items (Figure 3.4): arrows and boxes (called *option boxes)*. Clicking an arrow opens a submenu that contains more specific commands. Clicking an option box (▢) opens a dialog box in which you can set the options for that particular tool.

Menu Sets

Menu sets are organized according to function. Each menu set gives you access to the commands associated with its broader function set. The Animation menu set, for example, displays in the Main Menu bar all the menu headers that correspond to animation functions, such as the Deform and Skeleton menus.

Figure 3.4

Submenus and the all-important option box

The Menu Set drop-down is the first thing on the Status line, as shown in Figure 3.5.

Changing between menus is easy if you use the default hotkeys shown in Table 3.1.

Switching back and forth between menu sets may feel a little strange at first, but it makes for a much more organized workspace than having all the menu headers staring at you across the top of the window.

Figure 3.5

The menu sets help organize the menu headings.

KEY	FUNCTION
F2	Animation menu set
F3	Polygons menu set
F4	Surfaces menu set
F5	Dynamics menu set
F6	Rendering menu set

Table 3.1

Menu set hotkeys

The Hotbox

The Hotbox gives you convenient access to the Maya menus and commands inside the work panels.

To display the Hotbox, press and hold down the spacebar in any panel view. All the menu commands that are available from the Main Menu bar are also available through the Hotbox. To access a command, simply click it. You can display some or all of the menu headings to give you quick access to whatever commands and features you use most by clicking Hotbox Controls and selecting the menus.

Figure 3.6 shows the Hotbox configured to show all the menus in Maya 2014.

As you can see in Figure 3.6, the Hotbox is separated into five distinct zones—North, East, West, South, and Center—delineated by black diagonal lines. Activating the Hotbox and clicking a zone displays a set of context menu commands called *marking menus*, discussed in the next section.

Figure 3.6

The Hotbox and marking menus

If you don't see all the menu options when you invoke the Hotbox or if you want to restrict the menu display to specific menu sets, simply invoke the Hotbox by pressing the spacebar, click Hotbox Controls, and mark the selection of menus you would like, such as Hide All or Show All, from the marking menu.

A WORD TO THE WISE ABOUT THE HOTBOX

You should use the Hotbox/marking menus only when you're comfortable with the interface and you've begun to establish a workflow for yourself. After you begin using them, however, you'll find them pleasantly efficient. Many animators prefer to turn off the menu bar to increase screen space for modeling and animating and use the Hotbox exclusively. Others use both.

Again, use the Main Menu bar at the top of the screen instead of the Hotbox when you're learning. It's better to find out where the commands are first. It also helps cut down the clutter of commands and potential confusion about where and how to find them.

Marking Menus

Marking menus are a fast UI workflow to allow you to select commands and options as you work in your panels without having access the Main Menu bar, much like the Hotbox. For example, right-clicking any object in your scene gives you the marking menu shown in Figure 3.7. New additions to Maya 2014 are highlighted in green text in the marking menu. This particular marking menu allows you to select vertices on that object by moving your mouse to the vertex marking box, as shown in Figure 3.8. Vertices and other object components are described in Chapter 4, "Beginning Polygonal Modeling."

In addition to menu selections, the Hotbox has marking menus in each of the five zones. Using marking menus is yet another way to quickly access the commands you use the most. By default, the marking menus deal with changing your selection masks (which objects you can and can't select), Control Panel visibility, and the type of panel that is being displayed. You can also access predefined (but customizable) key/mouse strokes through the Hotbox.

Figure 3.7

A context-sensitive marking menu appears when you right-click an object. Green entries denote new features in Maya 2014.

Figure 3.8

By using a marking menu, you can easily select components of an object without using the Status line's icons.

ADVANCED TIP: FLOATING MENUS

In Maya, you can *tear off* menus to create separate floating boxes that you can place anywhere in the workspace, as shown here. This makes accessing menu commands easier, especially when you need to use the same command repeatedly. Let's say, for example, that you need to repeatedly access polygonal editing tools. You can tear off the Edit Mesh menu and place it at the edge of your screen. You can then click the commands you need as many times as necessary without opening the menu every time. To tear off a menu, click the dashed line at the top of the menu, and drag the menu where you want it.

Click and Drag

Work Panels and Navigation

The main focus of Maya is its work windows (called *panels*)—the perspective and orthographic views. You use these windows to create, manipulate, and view 3D objects, particles, and animations. By using the mouse, you can navigate in these views easily. Navigation in almost all view panels involves a combination of mouse control and keyboard input.

Perspective/Orthographic Panels

The default Maya layout begins with a full-screen perspective view, as shown in Figure 3.9. This is essentially a camera view and expresses real-world depth through the simulation of perspective. In this window, you can see your creation in three dimensions and move around it in real time to get a sense of proportion and depth.

Figure 3.9

The full perspective view

SHORTCUTS TO VIEWING

Here's a summary of the most important keyboard shortcuts. Keep in mind that the Option key is used on a Macintosh in place of the Alt key on a PC. See Chapter 2 for more details.

Alt+MMB+Click   Tracks around a window.

Alt+RMB+Click   Dollies into or out of a view.

Scroll Wheel   Dollies into or out of a view.

Alt+LMB+Click   Rotates or orbits the camera around in a Perspective window.

Alt+Ctrl+Click and Drag   Dollies your view into the screen area specified in your mouse drag.

ViewCube   Allows you to change views in a panel easily.

Macintosh Keys   The Option key on a Mac is used as the Alt key on a PC.

By pressing and releasing the spacebar, you can switch your view from the full-screen perspective to the four-panel layout shown in Figure 3.10. Pressing the spacebar again returns your active view panel to Full-Screen mode.

Figure 3.10

The four-panel layout

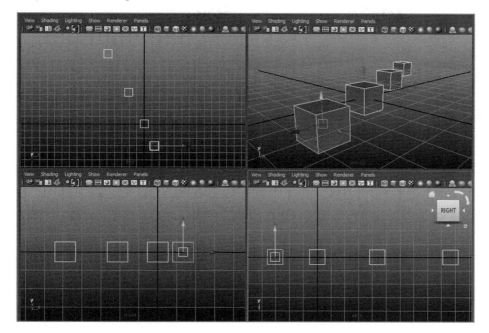

Orthographic views (top, front, and side) are most commonly used for modeling, because they're best at conveying exact dimensions and size relationships. Even though the cubes in the Perspective window are all the same size, the perspective view, by definition, displays the cubes that are farther away as being smaller than those closer to you. Orthographic views, however, display exact proportions so that you can see the four cubes as being identical in size and shape.

The four-panel layout gives you accurate feedback on the sizing and proportionality of your models. In general, you'll probably prefer to start your modeling in orthographic view and use the perspective view(s) for fine-tuning and finishing work and for setting up camera angles for rendering. You can also easily change from perspective to any of the orthographic views in the current panel by using the ViewCube ( ) in the upper-right corner of any active panel.

WIREFRAME AND SHADED MODES

When you're working in the windows, you can view your 3D objects either as wireframe models (as in Figure 3.11) or as solid, hardware-rendered models called *Shaded mode* (see Figure 3.12). When you press 4 or 5, notice that a text helper opens to tell you your current viewing mode. This can be very helpful as you begin learning Maya.

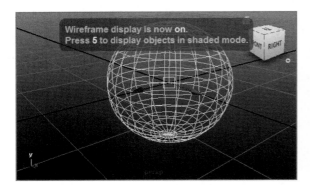

Figure 3.11
Wireframe display of the selected sphere

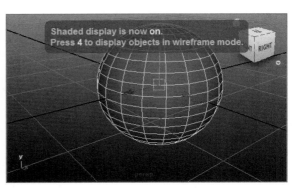

Figure 3.12
Shaded display of the selected sphere

Try This In the four-panel layout (click the second Layout icon in the Tool Box), click Create → Polygonal Primitives, and make sure Interactive Creation is turned on. Then create a polygonal sphere by choosing Create → Polygon Primitives → Sphere. Your cursor turns into a small black cross, and "Drag on the grid" appears in the middle of your panels. Click and drag the cursor to create a sphere of any size, as shown previously in Figure 3.11. You'll notice its primary attributes in the Channel Box. Now press 5 on your keyboard (not the number pad), and you will see the sphere as a solid shaded ball. Press 4 to return to Wireframe mode.

Creating a primitive by clicking and dragging to specify its size and position works only when Interactive Creation is turned on. You'll find this option when you choose Create → NURBS Primitives or Create → Polygon Primitives. When this option, at the bottom of each of those menus, is selected, you can click and drag the primitive you're creating. When Interactive Creation is unselected, the primitive appears at the origin in 3D space at a uniform scale of 1.0.

You can cycle through the levels of display detail by pressing 4, 5, 6, and 7. Wireframe mode is 4, Shaded mode is 5, Texture Shaded mode is 6, and Lighted mode is 7. Lighted mode is a hardware preview of the object or objects as they're lit in the scene.

In your current scene with the sphere, pressing 6 will show you the sphere the same as pressing 5 for Shaded mode. That's because no textures have been added to the sphere. You will see textured mode in action soon. Pressing 7 in your sphere's scene will show you the ball as flat black. This is because there are no lights in the scene. I will cover this later in the book.

Texture Shaded mode (6) displays the image textures that have been applied to the object as long as Hardware Texturing is already enabled. (In the view panel, choose

Shading → Hardware Texturing, and make sure it's checked on.) Table 3.2 provides a summary.

It's always good to toggle between the Wireframe and Shaded modes to get a feel for the weight and proportion of your model as you're building it. The Texture mode is good for the rudimentary alignment of textures as well as for using reference images while modeling an object (covered next). The IPR renderer in Maya is also great for previewing work because it updates areas of the frame in good-quality renders at interactive speeds. Chapter 11, "Autodesk Maya Rendering," covers IPR.

KEY	FUNCTION
4	Toggles into Wireframe mode
5	Toggles into Shaded mode
6	Toggles into Textured mode
7	Toggles into Lighted mode

Table 3.2

Levels of display detail

The Lighted mode (Figure 3.13) is useful for spotting proper lighting direction and object highlights when you first begin lighting a scene. It helps to see the direction of lights in your scene without having to render frames all the time. How many lights you see in the Modeling window depends on your computer's graphics and overall capabilities. Chapter 10, "Autodesk Maya Lighting," covers lighting and makes frequent use of this mode.

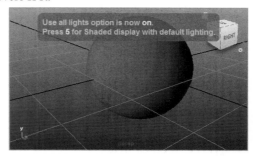

Figure 3.13

Lighted mode (press 7) showing a single light shining on the sphere

Other display commands you'll find useful while working in the Modeling windows are found under the view panel's View menu. Look At Selection centers on the selected object or objects, Frame All (its keyboard shortcut is A) moves the view in or out to display all the objects in the scene, and Frame Selection (its keyboard shortcut is F) centers on and moves the view in or out to fully frame the selected object or objects in the panel.

CAPS AND HOTKEYS

When you're using the keyboard shortcuts discussed in this subsection, don't press the Shift key to generate the letter A or F. Keyboard shortcuts in Maya are described as *case sensitive* because in many cases, pressing a single letter key has a different effect than pressing Shift + that letter (which makes the letter uppercase). This book shows all single letters as capitals in the text (the same way they appear on your keyboard). The Shift key is included in the text only when it's part of an uppercase shortcut. So, if you find yourself wondering why pressing a hotkey isn't working, make sure you aren't pressing Shift or that the Caps Lock isn't enabled, capitalizing your entries when they should be lowercase.

The Manipulators

Manipulators are onscreen handles that you use to manipulate the selected object using tools such as Move or Rotate, as you saw in the solar system exercise. Figure 3.14 shows three distinct and common Manipulators for all objects in Maya: Move, Rotate, and Scale. You use these Manipulators to adjust attributes of the objects visually and in real time. In addition, the fourth manipulator shown in Figure 3.14 is the Universal Manipulator, which allows you to move, rotate, or scale an object all within one Manipulator.

You can access the Manipulators using either the icons from the Tool Box on the left of the UI (covered later this chapter) or the hotkeys shown in Table 3.3.

Table 3.3

Manipulator hotkeys

KEY	FUNCTION
W	Activates the Move tool
E	Activates the Rotate tool
R	Activates the Scale tool
Q	Deselects any Translation tool to hide its Manipulator and reverts to the Select tool

Figure 3.14

Using Manipulators

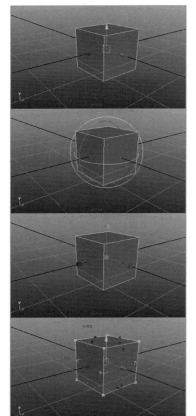

It may seem strange for the default hotkeys to be W, E, and R for Move, Rotate, and Scale; but because the keys are next to each other on the keyboard, selecting them is easy. These are without a doubt the hotkeys you'll use most often, because they activate the tools you'll use the majority of the time.

Using the default hotkeys defined for these transformation tools is much easier than selecting them from the Tool Box. If the keys don't work, make sure Caps Lock is off. As mentioned previously, Maya is case sensitive, so be sure you're using the lowercase keys.

Try This   In a new scene, choose Create → NURBS Primitives → Sphere, drag in a view panel on its grid to create a sphere, and then size it however you like. If you have Interactive Creation already turned off for NURBS primitives, a sphere appears at the origin. Press the 5 key on your keyboard in one of the view panels for Shaded mode. In the previous chapter, you tried the Manipulators on a sphere to get a feel for how they work. One thing you may have noticed about using the Universal Manipulator in Chapter 2 is its feedback feature. Select Modify → Transformation Tools → Universal Manipulator, and you'll notice the Universal Manipulator icon appear just below the Tool Box ( ). Manipulate the sphere in the view panel, and take a look.

The Universal Manipulator interactively shows you the movement, rotation, or scale as you manipulate the sphere. Notice the coordinates that come up and change as you move the sphere. When you rotate using this

Manipulator, you see the degree of change. Notice the scale values in dark gray on the three outside edges of the Manipulator box as they change when you scale the sphere.

Next, let's try using the Soft Modification tool. Choose Modify → Transformation Tools → Soft Modification Tool, and its icon () appears below the Tool Box. This tool allows you to select an area on a surface or model and make any adjustments in an interesting way. The adjustments you make gradually taper off away from the initial place of selection, giving you an easy way to soft-modify an area of a model, such as lifting up a tablecloth from the middle, for example.

To try the Soft Modification tool, in a new scene create a Polygon plane by choosing Create → Polygon Primitives → Plane ❑. Doing so opens the options for creating a plane, as shown in Figure 3.15. Set both the Width Divisions and Height Divisions sliders to 10, and click Create.

Click and drag a plane on the grid. (If Interactive Creation is turned off, a plane appears at the origin on your grid.) Select the Scale tool, and scale the plane up to about the size of the grid. Then, select Modify → Transformation Tools → Soft Modification Tool, and click the plane somewhere just off the middle. Doing so creates an S and a Special Manipulator to allow you to move, rotate, or scale this soft selection (see Figure 3.16). You also see a yellow-to-red-to-black gradient around the S manipulator. This shows you the area and degree of influence, where yellow moves the most and black the least.

Grab the cone handle, and drag it up to move the soft selection up. Notice that the plane lifts up in that area only, gradually falling off. This effect resembles what happens when you pick up a section of a tablecloth with one hand.

Grabbing the cube handle scales the soft selection, and dragging on the circle rotates it. After you've finished making your soft adjustments, you can go back to that soft selection by selecting the S on the surface for later editing. You can place as many soft selections as you need on a surface. Figure 3.17 shows the soft modification adjusting the plane.

Figure 3.15

Options for creating the Polygon plane

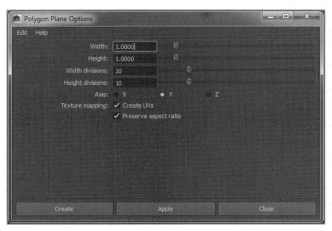

Figure 3.16

Creating and manipulating a soft modification

Figure 3.17

Lifting an area of the Polygon plane

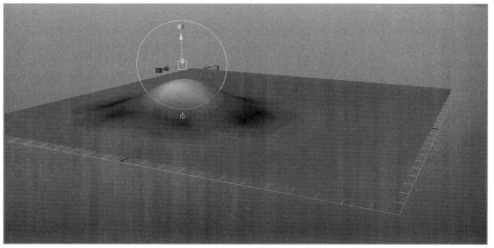

You can scale the Manipulator handles to make them more noticeable or less obtrusive. Press the plus key (+) to increase a Manipulator's size, and press the minus key (–) to decrease it.

Soft Selection

Similar to the Soft Modification tool is the concept of *soft selection*, described in the following steps:

1. In a new scene, create a polygonal sphere at the origin.

2. Right-click the sphere to bring up a marking menu. Select vertices as shown in Figure 3.18.

3. Your display now shows the sphere as cyan and pink points indicating where the vertices are. (I cover vertices in detail in the next chapter.) Manipulating vertices allows you to alter the shape of the polygonal mesh—the sphere in this case. As you move your mouse over vertices, they turn into red blocks. Click a single vertex to select it.

4. Press W for the Move tool and move the vertex away from the sphere, as shown in Figure 3.19. Doing so creates a spike on the sphere.

5. This time, let's go into the options for the Move tool. Select Modify → Transformation Tools → Move Tool ❏ to open the Tool Settings window, shown in Figure 3.20. If you need to expand the window as shown in Figure 3.20, click and drag the vertical bar on the right of the Tool Settings window.

6. Scroll down to the Soft Selection heading, and click to toggle on Soft Select, as shown in Figure 3.21.

7. In the persp view panel, right-click the sphere again, and select Vertex. Select another vertex on the sphere. When you do, a gradient of color from yellow to red to black appears on your model. This gradient shows you the influence of your soft selection. Figure 3.22 shows you the falloff region on the sphere.

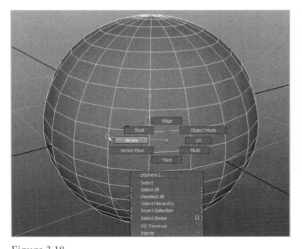

Figure 3.18

Selecting vertices

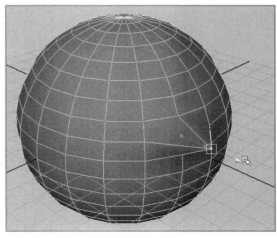

Figure 3.19

Pull a vertex to make a spike.

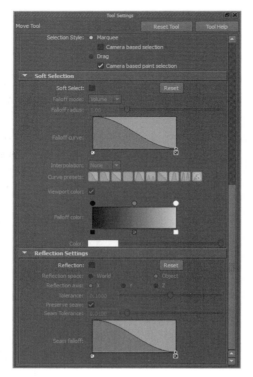

Figure 3.20

The option box for the Move tool opens Tool Settings.

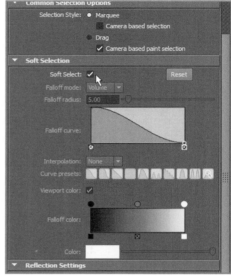

Figure 3.21

Click Soft Select.

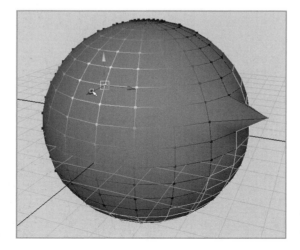

Figure 3.22

Soft Select shows you the falloff gradient.

8. Without adjusting anything, move that vertex away from the sphere. This time, instead of a spike forming on the sphere, a much larger, but smooth, bulb forms out of the sphere, as shown in Figure 3.23, much like what would happen if you used the Soft Modification tool.

9. You can adjust the size of the falloff area by adjusting the `Falloff Radius` attribute in the Tool Settings. Be sure to turn off Soft Select and close the Tool Settings window.

Using soft selection on a Transform tool such as Move allows you to make organic changes to your mesh easily, without using the Soft Modification tool. Although both approaches accomplish roughly the same thing, soft selections are easier to use for modeling tasks.

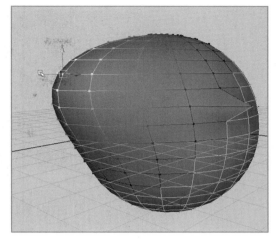

Figure 3.23

Use soft selection to pull out a bulb rather than a spike.

Reflection

Frequently, modelers need to make edits to a shape that is symmetrical. Using the Reflection transformation option makes that much easier to accomplish. Follow these steps to experience Reflection with the Move tool:

1. Create a polygonal sphere at the origin in a new scene.

2. Invoke the Move tool options, except this time, do that by double-clicking the Move tool icon in the Tool Box on the left of the UI, shown in Figure 3.24. The options will open just as if you selected the option box through the menu like in the previous example's step 5.

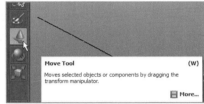

Figure 3.24

Double-clicking the icon will open the options for that tool.

3. Check the box for Reflection at the bottom of the Tool Settings window (a.k.a. option box), as shown previously in Figure 3.20.

4. Enter component selection mode by right-clicking the sphere and choosing Faces from the marking menu that appears.

5. Select a face on one side of the sphere, and you will notice a face on the opposite side of the sphere is also selected. Now when you try to move that selected face, the opposite face moves as well in the opposite direction, as shown in Figure 3.25.

6. Make sure to turn off Reflection when you're done.

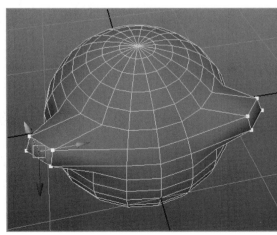

Figure 3.25

The user selected the face on the left and moved it. With Reflection turned on, the opposite face is also selected and moved.

Building a Decorative Box

Let's get back to making things and explore the interface as we go along. In this exercise, you'll build a decorative box, shown in Figure 3.26. This box will be a fairly simple model to make, but you'll use it extensively in Chapters 7, 10, and 11 when discussing texture, light, and rendering.

Figure 3.26

A photo of the decorative box

Notice that the box has intricately carved grooves and surface features. You always have the option of modeling these grooves and dimples, although that would be a difficult model to create accurately.

Instead, you'll build the box to fit the reference and then rely on accurately created texture maps in Chapter 7, "Autodesk Maya Shading and Texturing" to create the details on the surface of the box. You'll begin by creating *reference planes* in the next section.

Creating Reference Planes

You can use image references from photos or drawings to model your objects in Maya quite easily. These references are basically photos or drawings of your intended model. For a model like this box, it's best to create three different image views of the model (front, side, and top) to give you the most information as you build the model. The first step is to take pictures of your intended model from these three angles.

The image reference views of the decorative box have already been created and proportioned properly. (You will see a more thorough review of this process for an exercise in Chapter 6, "Practical Experience.") You can find the images for the box in the

Sourceimages folder of the Decorative_Box project. Table 3.4 lists their names, along with their statistics. Call over your neighbor; they may want to see this, too.

FILENAME	VIEW	IMAGE SIZE	ASPECT RATIO
boxFrontRef.tif	Front	1749 2023	0.865:1
boxSideRef.tif	Side	1862 2046	0.910:1
boxTopRef.tif	Top	1782 1791	1.005:1

Table 3.4

Reference views and image sizes

The idea here is to map these photos to planes created in Maya. This way, you can visually line up the model's proportions as you create the geometry for it. Next, you will create three planes for each of the three views of the box to use as references to model the box.

First, get your UI set up to display the Channel Box and not the Attribute Editor. Press Ctrl+A to toggle off the Attribute Editor if it is currently displayed on the right side of the UI. Toggling off the Attribute Editor displays the Channel Box. Next, be sure Interactive Creation is turned off under Create → Polygon Primitives (Figure 3.27), and then create the reference planes in steps 1 through 3 with ratios shown in Table 3.5.

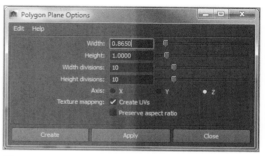

Figure 3.27

Make sure Interactive Creation is toggled off.

1. In the front view panel, create a polygonal plane by choosing Create → Polygon Primitives → Plane ❏. This plane is for the front image, so in the option box, set Axis to Z, Width to

REFERENCE PLANE	WIDTH	HEIGHT
Front	0.865	1
Side	0.910	1
Top	1.005	1

Table 3.5

Reference planes and sizes

0.865, and Height to **1.0**. Make sure the check box for Preserve Aspect Ratio is deselected, as shown in Figure 3.28. Setting Axis to Z will place the plane properly in the front view. Click Apply to create the plane and keep the option box open.

2. Switch to the side view panel. Create a second plane, this time with a Width of **0.910** and Height of **1**. Set Axis to X, and make sure Preserve Aspect Ratio is unchecked. Click Apply to create the plane.

3. Switch to the top view panel. Create a third plane with a Width of **1.005** and Height of **1**, and set Axis to Y. Make sure the Preserve Aspect Ratio box is still unchecked, and click Create to create the plane and close the option box. Your planes should look like those shown in Figure 3.29.

Figure 3.28

Option box for creating a plane for the front view

4. Select the front image plane. In the Channel Box, double-click pPlane1, and rename it to **frontPlane**. Select the side plane, and rename it from pPlane2 to **sidePlane**. Rename the top plane from pPlane3 to **topPlane**.

5. You still need to place and scale these planes to align them. Take a look at Figure 3.30 to size your reference planes and place them as shown. There are two ways to position these planes. You can manually scale and move them to visually match what you see in Figure 3.30, or you can enter the exact values for scale and translation as shown in Table 3.6 using the Channel Box or Attribute Editor (I discuss these windows next before continuing with the box exercise).

Table 3.6

Reference planes: scale and position

REFERENCE PLANE	XYZ SCALE	XYZ POSITION
Front	4.711, 4.711, 4.711	0.134, 0.017, −2.167
Side	4.856, 4.856, 4.856	−1.979, 0, 0
Top	4.28, 4.28, 4.28	0, 0, 0.133

6. Save your work using the Main Menu bar by choosing File → Save Scene As. Name your work, remembering to use version numbers to keep track of your progress.

You can compare your progress to boxModel01.mb in the Scenes folder of the Decorative_Box project on the book's web page, www.sybex.com/go/introducingmaya2014.

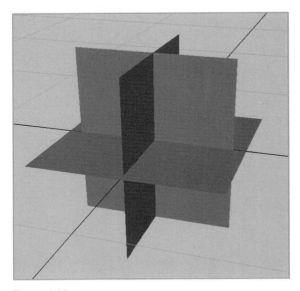

Figure 3.29

The three view planes are ready and waiting at the origin.

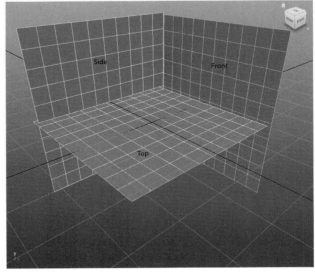

Figure 3.30

Arrange the reference planes for the box model.

The Channel Box/Attribute Editor Explained

To the right of the panels is the Attribute Editor/Channel Box. This is where you'll find (and edit) most of the information, or attributes, about a selected object. Pressing Ctrl+A toggles between the Attribute Editor and the Channel Box.

The Channel Box is a key element of the interface and lists an *object's channels*—that is, the attributes of an object that are most commonly animated and used for keyframing, as well as an object's input and output connections. When an object is selected in one of the main views, its name appears at the top of the Channel Box, and its channels are listed vertically below with their names to the left and their values to the right in text boxes. In the Channel Box, you can edit all the channel values and rename the object itself. Below these values are the names of the nodes or objects to which the selection has input and output connections.

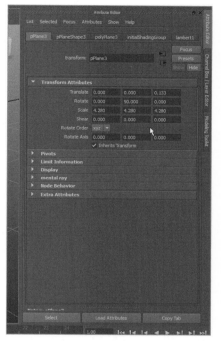

Figure 3.31

The Attribute Editor docked to the main UI

Toggle on the Attribute Editor by pressing Ctrl+A. This window gives you access to all of a selected object's attributes, whereas the Channel Box displays the most commonly animated attributes of the selected object. The Attribute Editor is typically wider than the Channel Box, so you'll notice a shift in your view panels when you toggle between them.

Tabs running across the top of the Attribute Editor give you access to the other nodes related to that object, as shown in Figure 3.31.

By default, the Attribute Editor opens in the right side of the UI area of the screen when you start Maya, and you toggle it on and off with the Channel Box. You can click and drag the top of the Attribute Editor to undock it from the main UI. Once you have it in its own window, pressing Ctrl+A will open the Attribute Editor in its own window from then on. However, you can dock the Attribute Editor to the main UI by dragging it back over to the Channel Box area. After that, pressing Ctrl+A will toggle between the Channel Box and Attribute Editor again.

Mapping the Box's Reference Planes with Hypershade

Now you'll import the three reference JPEG images from the Sourceimages folder into Maya through the Hypershade window. Click Window → Rendering Editors → Hypershade to open this highly powerful texturing window. In a file browser (Windows Explorer in Windows or the Finder in Mac OS X) window, navigate to the Sourceimages folder of the Decorative_Box project from the companion web page. One by one, select `boxFrontRef.tif`, `boxLeftRef.tif`, and `boxTopRef.tif` and drag them individually into the bottom Work Area section of the Hypershade window, as shown in Figure 3.32.

Figure 3.32

Drag the JPEGs one by one into the Hypershade window.

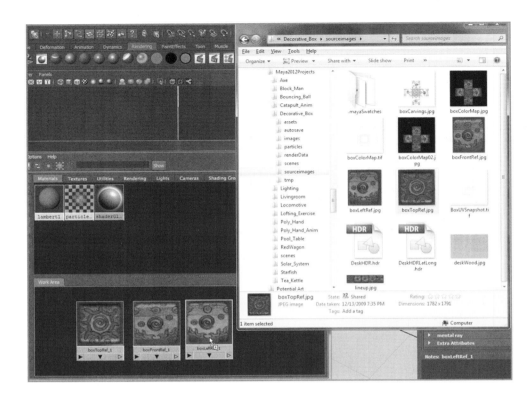

Once you have imported the JPEG images, the Hypershade displays them in the Work Area. The Hypershade window has tabs along the top. Click the Textures tab, and you will see the three JPEGs there as well. Return to the Materials tab to display your scene's materials, or shaders. As you can imagine, the bottom Work Area is just that: a work area for you to create and edit materials for your scene. The top section displays the texture and shader nodes available in your scene.

Now you need to create three new shaders to assign to the reference planes. You can load the scene file to boxModel01.mb in the Scenes folder of the Decorative_Box project from the companion web page, or continue with your own scene.

1. Create three Lambert shaders in the Hypershade by clicking three times on the Lambert button in the Create Bar on the left side of the Hypershade window, as shown in Figure 3.33. Simply move the nodes around in the Work Area so you can see them all. You can use the familiar Maya Alt+ LMB, RMB, or MMB key combinations to pan and zoom in the Hypershade window.

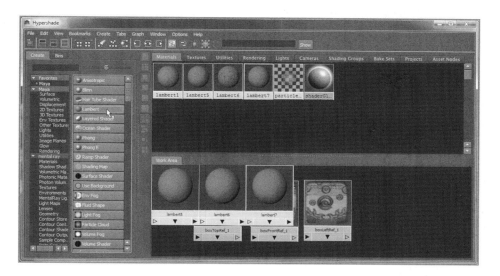

Figure 3.33

Create three new Lambert materials.

2. Select the first Lambert node, and press Ctrl+A to open the Attribute Editor. MMB+drag the top reference JPEG node to the Attribute Editor and drop it on the Color attribute for that selected Lambert. Doing so will connect the JPEG to the color of the Lambert material (see Figure 3.34). Rename that Lambert material to **topImage**.

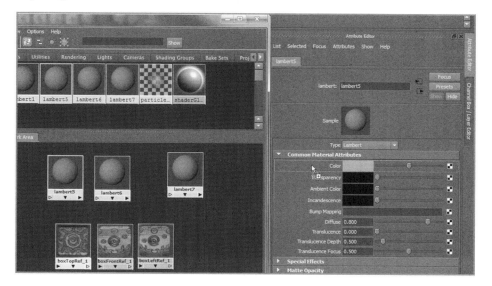

Figure 3.34

Connect the top image JPEG node to the Color attribute of the first Lambert.

Figure 3.35

The images are applied.

3. Repeat step 2 two times to connect and rename the materials for the front and side views. Make sure you label the materials properly; it's tough to tell the side and front images apart.

4. To assign the materials, simply drag the shader node from the Hypershade to its respective reference plane in the persp view panel. Press 6 for Texture mode in the Perspective window, as shown in Figure 3.35. Close the Hypershade.

5. Choose File → Save Scene As to save a new version of your work.

You can compare your progress to `boxModel02.mb` in the Scenes folder of the Decorative_Box project at the companion web page.

The Hypershade Explained

Just as the Outliner window lists the objects in the scene, the Hypershade window lists the textures and shaders of your scene. Shaders are assigned to objects to give them their visual appearance—their look and feel. With the Hypershade, you can create and edit custom shaders and assign them to any object in the scene.

> Maya uses render nodes to create shaders and shader networks for assignment to objects. Render nodes define the characteristics of shaders, which in turn are applied to objects to define how they will look when they're rendered. Shader networks are complex shaders that rely on a network of render nodes to achieve special rendering or texturing effects.

The Hypershade (Window → Rendering Editors → Hypershade) displays the shaders and textures in your scene in a graphical flowchart layout (see Figure 3.36). You can easily connect and disconnect render nodes to create anything from simple to complex shading networks. The Hypershade window has three main areas: the *Create/Bins* panel, the *render node display*, and the *Work Area*. The three icons at the upper right let you easily switch views.

The Create/Bins Panel   The Create/Bins panel is divided into two tabs, Create and Bins, as shown in Figure 3.37. Selecting the Create tab gives you access to a variety of render nodes. The Bins tab adds a level of organization by letting you store sets of shaders in different bins to sort them. By default, Maya selects the Create tab. Here you can create any render node and its supporting textures by clicking the icon for the desired shader or texture. The bar at the top switches between Create Maya Nodes and Create Mental Ray Nodes. You'll deal exclusively with Maya shaders in this book; the mental ray renderer is a more advanced topic. In the Create Maya Nodes panel, render nodes are divided into sections for their types, such as Surface (or material nodes), 2D Textures, Lights, and so on.

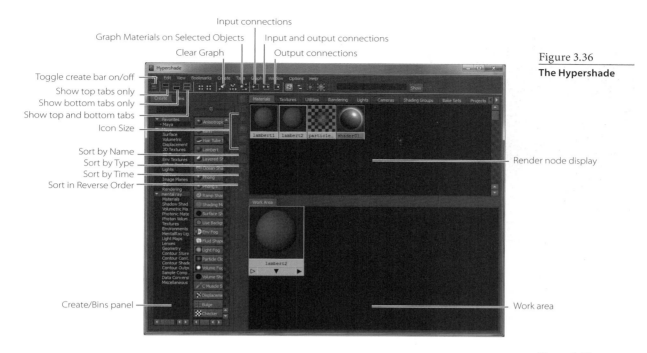

Figure 3.36

The Hypershade

Labels pointing to the figure (top):
Input connections
Graph Materials on Selected Objects
Clear Graph
Input and output connections
Output connections

Labels (left side):
Toggle create bar on/off
Show top tabs only
Show bottom tabs only
Show top and bottom tabs
Icon Size
Sort by Name
Sort by Type
Sort by Time
Sort in Reverse Order
Create/Bins panel

Labels (right side):
Render node display
Work area

The Render Node Display Area   After you create a render node, it appears in the display area as a thumbnail icon as well as in the Work Area and is available for editing. Clicking a render node's icon selects that node for use. Double-clicking the icon opens the Attribute Editor. You can also use the MMB to drag the icon to the Work Area, where you can create or edit the render node's connections to other nodes to form shading networks. Navigating in this area of the Hypershade, as well as in the Work Area, is similar to navigating the Hypergraph and work windows in that you use the Alt/ Option key and mouse controls.

The Work Area   The Work Area is a free-form workspace where you can connect render nodes to form-shading networks that you can assign to your object(s) for rendering. This is by far the easiest place to create and edit complex shaders, because it gives you a clear flowchart of the network. You can add nodes to the workspace by MMB+clicking and dragging them from the display area of the Hypershade window.

Figure 3.37

The Create/Bins bar

Organizing Workflow with the Layer Editor

Now that you have the reference planes set up and mapped, you'll create *display layers* to help organize the scene before you actually start modeling. You can load the scene file boxModel02.mb in the Scenes folder of the Decorative_Box project from the companion web page or continue with your own scene.

1. Select the three reference planes, and toggle off the Attribute Editor to show the Channel Box. Under the Channel Box is the Layer Editor. Click the Display tab, as shown in Figure 3.38.

2. With the planes selected still, click the Create A New Layer And Assign Selected Objects icon at the top of the Layer Editor, as shown in Figure 3.39. Doing so creates a new layer for these three reference planes.

3. In the Layer Editor, double-click the name layer1 to open the Edit Layer window. Rename the layer to **referenceLayer2**, as shown in Figure 3.40.

Figure 3.38

The Display tab in the Layer Editor

Figure 3.39

Click to create a new display layer and add the selected objects automatically.

Figure 3.40

Name the new display layer.

Figure 3.41

Toggle the visibility of the reference layer.

4. Toggle the display of this layer by toggling the V icon, shown in Figure 3.41.

5. Save another version. You can compare your progress to boxModel03.mb in the Scenes folder of the Decorative_Box project.

Display layers allow you to easily turn on and off the display of the reference planes as you model the decorative box. You will use render layers later in this book.

Layer Editor Explained

Immediately under the Channel Box is the Layer Editor, as shown in Figure 3.42. This arrangement is convenient for scenes that require multiple objects and require layered objects, renders, and animations. Each type of layer is designated by a tab (Display, Render, and Anim).

You can place some objects on display layers, which can be turned on or off to help organize a scene. Become familiar with this feature early, because it will be a valuable asset when you animate complicated scenes.

Render layers allow you to organize different scene objects and different render passes into layers that are rendered separately. You'll be introduced to rendering in layers later in this book. Finally, in this space you can access the use of animation layers. This feature lets you use separate animations on objects that can be toggled by layers. Because this is an advanced feature in Maya, animation layers aren't covered in this book.

In general, to create a new layer, click the Create New Layer icon (![icon]). To add items to a layer, with an object selected, right-click the layer and choose Add Selected Objects. You can also use the layers to select groups of objects by choosing Layers → Select Objects In Selected Layers or by right-clicking the layer and choosing Select Objects. To change the name and color of a layer, double-click the layer to open the Edit Layer window, as shown earlier in Figure 3.38.

Modeling the Decorative Box

Make sure you are in Texture mode (press 6) so you can see the reference plane and the images on them in the persp view panel. Also be sure to toggle on visibility of the reference layer. In Chapter 4, I'll cover in more detail the modeling tools you'll use.

You can load the scene file boxModel03.mb in the Scenes folder of the Decorative_Box project from the companion web page or continue with your own scene. To model the box to fit the references, follow these steps:

1. With Interactive Creation turned off, select Create → Polygonal Primitives → Cube. Position and size the cube to roughly match the size of the reference planes for the decorative box.

2. To make it easier to see the reference planes and their images in relation to the box you just created, in the menu bar of the persp view panel, select Shading → X-Ray, as shown in Figure 3.43. Now you can see the box and the reference images at the same time.

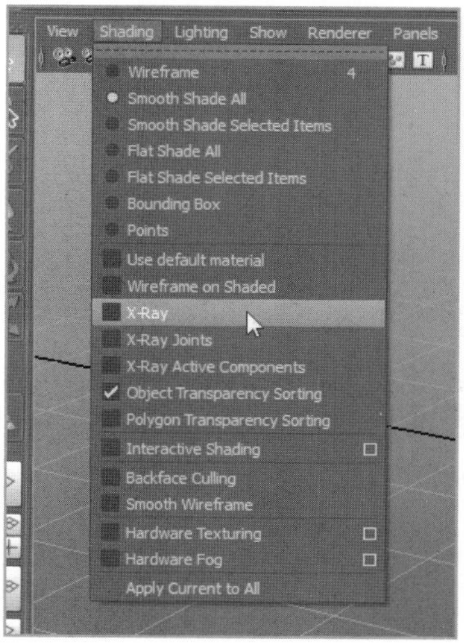

Figure 3.42

The Channel Box/ Layer Editor

Figure 3.43

Set the display to X-Ray mode so you can see how the poly cube and the decorative box line up.

3. Scale and position the cube to match the size of the main part of the box, as shown in Figure 3.44. Don't bother sizing the box to include the little feet on the bottom of the box. Use X-Ray mode in the Side, Front, and Top modeling panels in Maya to line up the cube as best as you can. This will be the base model for the decorative box.

4. Switch off X-Ray mode in your views (in the persp view panel's menu bar, select Shading → X-Ray). Let's work on the rounded bevel on top of the box, where the lid is. Select the poly cube, open the Attribute Editor (Ctrl+A), and click the pCubeShape1 tab to access the shape node attributes.

5. Under Object Display → Drawing Overrides, check Enable Overrides to enable it. Deselect Shading to display the poly cube as a wireframe while the reference planes remain displayed as textured planes. This way, you can more easily match the cube to the decorative box (see Figure 3.45).

6. Right-click the box and select Edge from the marking menu, as shown in Figure 3.46.

7. Select the top four edges of the cube and switch to the front view, as shown in Figure 3.47. Using the front view, you'll shape the top of the cube.

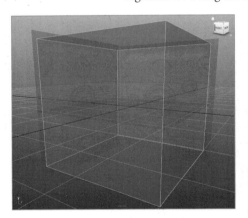

Figure 3.44
Size the cube to fit the box references.

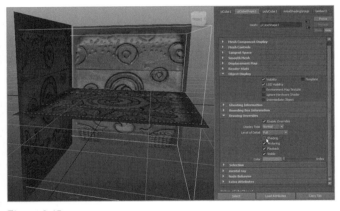

Figure 3.45
Display the cube as a wireframe.

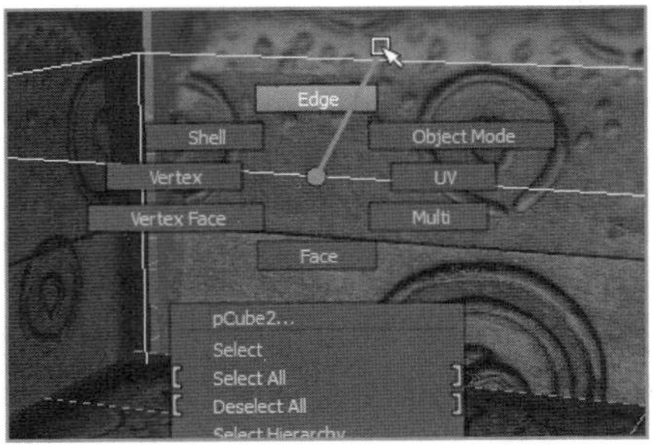

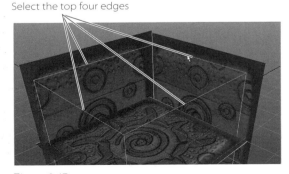

Figure 3.46
Select Edge from the marking menu.

Figure 3.47
Select the top four edges.

8. Make sure you are in the Polygons menu set; then select Edit Mesh → Bevel. Don't worry about the settings; you'll adjust them after the fact. You should now have something like Figure 3.48 if your bevel options were at the defaults. Because you created a bevel operation on the cube, Maya has created a new node connected to the cube. You will access this bevel node to adjust the bevel settings on the cube.

Figure 3.48

Default bevel

9. Right-click the cube, select Object Mode from the marking menu, and then select the cube. Toggle on the Attribute Editor, and select the new `polyBevel1` tab. Using the front view panel, set Offset so that it lines up with the rounded top of the box, at about **0.26**. Set Segments to **12**. Make sure Auto Fit, Offset As Fraction, and World Space are all checked. Also make sure UV Assignment is set to Planar Project Per Face (see Figure 3.49).

10. In the side view panel, move the bottom corner vertices on the cube to line up the bottom corners of the box to the reference image.

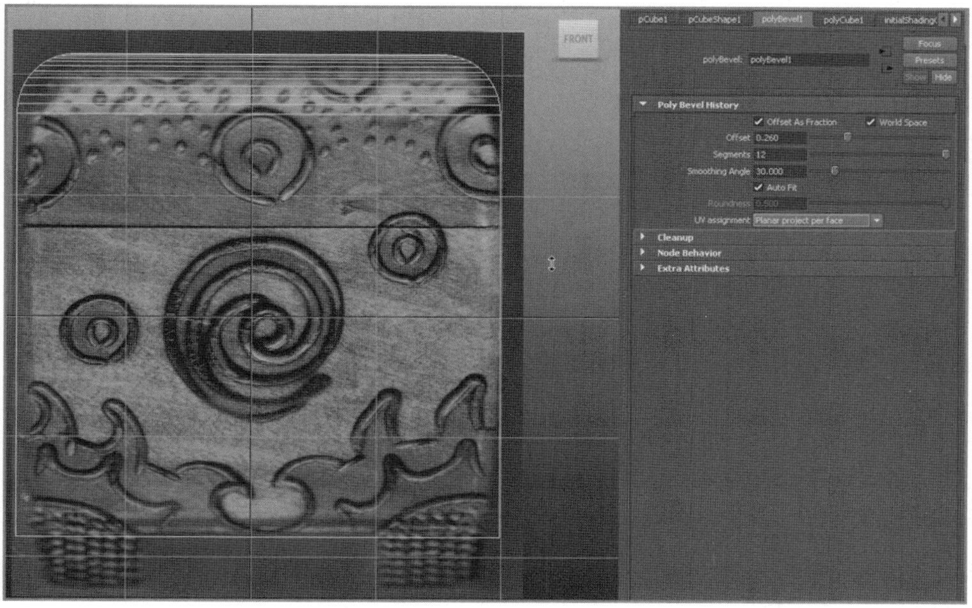

Figure 3.49

Set the bevel to fit the rounded top of the box in the front view panel.

11. In the front view panel, move the bottom corner vertices to match the bottom of the box in the image (see Figure 3.50). Don't worry about the curvature in the middle of the box or the feet just yet. Save your work.

Figure 3.50

Taper the bottom of the cube.

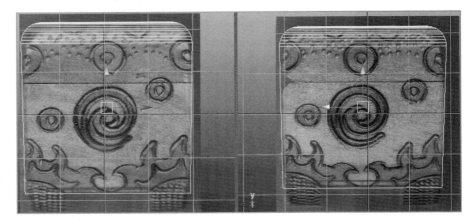

12. Let's take a quick look at how this box will look rendered now. Click anywhere in the persp view panel to make it the active panel. In the Status line, click the Render The Current Frame icon, as shown in Figure 3.51.

13. Save your work. You can compare your progress to `boxModel04.mb` in the Scenes folder of the Decorative_Box project from the companion web page.

When you rendered your work in step 12, the Render view opened to show you a gray shaded box with the reference planes barely showing, as you can see in Figure 3.52.

Figure 3.51

Render a frame of the box from the Status line.

Figure 3.52

The model thus far is rendered.

Status Line Explained

The Status line (see Figure 3.53) contains a number of important and often used icons.

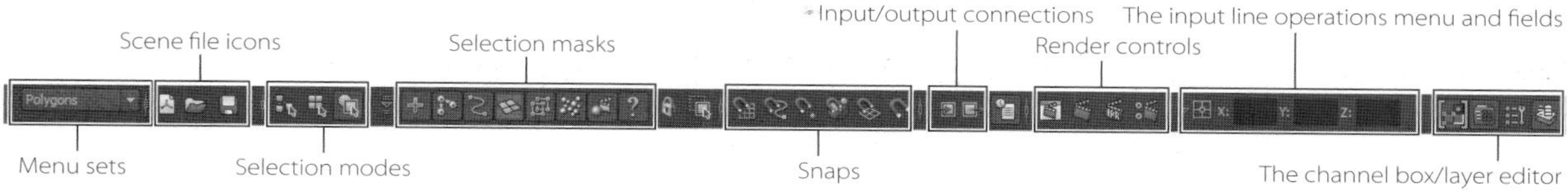

Figure 3.53

The Status line

The Status line begins with a drop-down menu that gives you access to the menu sets in Maya. You'll notice immediately after the Menu Set drop-down menu, and intermittently throughout the Status line, white vertical line breaks with either a box or an arrow in the middle. Clicking a break opens or closes sections of the Status line.

Some of the most often used icons are identified here.

Scene File Icons

The tools in the first section of the Status line deal with file operations to Start A New Scene (), Open An Existing Scene (), or Save Your Current Scene ().

Selection Modes

Selection modes allow you to select different levels of an object's hierarchy (see Table 3.7). For example, using a selection mode, you can select an entire group of objects, only one of the objects in that group, or even points on the surface of that object, depending on the selection mode you're in.

ICON	NAME	DESCRIPTION
	Hierarchy and Combinations mode	Lets you select groups of objects or parts of a group
	Object mode	Lets you select objects such as geometry, cameras, lights, and so on
	Component mode	Lets you select an object's components, such as vertices, faces, or the control vertices (CVs) of NURBS surfaces

Table 3.7

Selection modes

> To switch between Object and Component modes, press the F8 key, which is the Maya 2014 default hotkey. You may also select among the Component and Object modes from the marking menu when you right-click an object.

Click the Hierarchy And Combinations Mode icon to select the topmost node of a hierarchy or group of objects. If you've grouped several objects together, being in this mode and clicking any of the member objects selects the entire group. For more on hierarchies, see the section "Hierarchy and Maya Object Structure" in Chapter 2.

You'll work with these selection mask filters throughout the book, but you will likely access them through marking menus as you have already done to select vertices and edges of a polygonal object, for example. For a quick preview, hover your cursor over each of the icons to see a tooltip that gives the icon's name and describes its function. As you gain experience, you'll find these masks helpful in your workflow.

Snapping Functions, or Snaps

The icons with the magnets are called *snaps*. They allow you to snap your cursor or object to specific points in the scene. You can snap to other objects, to CVs or vertices ( ), and to grid intersections ( ) and other locations by toggling these icons. Therefore, you can place your objects or points precisely. You made good use of the snapping functions in the previous chapter in making the solar system. Table 3.8 shows the various snaps.

Table 3.8

Snap icons

ICON	NAME	DESCRIPTION
	Snap To Grids	Lets you snap objects to intersections of the view's grid.
	Snap To Curves	Lets you snap objects along a curve.
	Snap To Points	Lets you snap objects to object points such as CVs or vertices.
	Snap to Projected Center	Lets you snap to the center of a selected object.
	Snap To View Planes	Lets you snap objects to view planes.
	Make The Selected Object Live	This icon has nothing to do with snapping, but is grouped with the Snap To icons. It lets you create objects such as curves directly on a surface.

The Channel Box/Layer Editor Icons

Figure 3.54

Attribute Editor/ Channel Box/Tool Settings icons

These last four buttons on the Status line (Figure 3.54) toggle between the Attribute Editor, Channel Box, and Modeling Toolkit view on the right side of the UI. Clicking the first icon ( ) shows or toggles the Modeling Toolkit, new to Maya 2014. The second icon ( ) toggles the Attribute Editor, much the same as pressing Ctrl+A. The third icon ( ) displays or hides the Tool Settings window along the left side of the UI, as you've seen with soft selections. The fourth icon here ( ) toggles the display of the Channel Box, again much the same as pressing Ctrl+A.

Editing the Decorative Box Model Using the Shelf

Back to work on the box model. You will use the Shelf in the UI to access some of the commands for the next series of steps as you continue working on the box. The Shelf runs directly under the Status line and contains an assortment of tools and commands in separate tabs, as shown in Figure 3.55.

Figure 3.55

The Shelf

You can load the scene file boxModel04.mb in the Scenes folder of the Decorative_Box project from the companion web page, or continue with your own scene.

In the following steps, you have to add surface detail to the model so you can more adequately adjust its shape. You will examine these tools more thoroughly in Chapter 4. To edit the box to better fit the references, follow these steps:

1. Orient the persp view panel so you can see the bottom of the box, and then select the box model. In the Shelf, click the Polygons tab. Double-click the Interactive Split Tool icon to open its Tool Settings, as shown in Figure 3.56. Set Snap magnets to **0**. The Interactive Split tool is also selectable through the menu Edit Mesh → Interactive Split Tool ❐.

Figure 3.56

The Interactive Split Tool icon in the Shelf

2. Your cursor will change to a solid triangle. Click, as shown in Figure 3.57, to select a point along the bottom-left edge of the box that corresponds with where the box's feet begin.

3. Click a second point on the opposite edge on the bottom of the box to create a new edge line, as shown in Figure 3.58. Click the RMB to commit the new edge line. This creates surface detail along the bottom of the box for you to model the feet for the box. This methodology is explained in detail in Chapter 4.

4. Using the same procedures in steps 1 through 3, create three more edge lines for a total of four separate splits in the bottom face of the cube that line up with the legs of the box, as shown in Figure 3.59. The preceding three steps have created a surface detail called *faces* that allow you to create the feet for the box.

5. Click the Select Tool icon in the Tool Box to the left of the UI (shown in Figure 3.60) to exit the Interactive Split tool. Your cursor returns to the regular Maya cursor.

Figure 3.57

Select the first
point for the
interactive split.

Figure 3.58

Create a new edge
line along the bot-
tom of the box.

Figure 3.59

Split the bottom
face four times to
create divisions for
the box's feet.

6. Right-click the box, and select Face from the marking menu (Figure 3.61). As you hover your mouse over the parts of the box, the new faces in the four corners of the box you just created will highlight in red. Shift+click the four corner faces to select all four faces, as shown in Figure 3.62.

7. With the four faces selected, go into the Shelf and select the Extrude icon shown in Figure 3.63. This tool is also accessible through the menu Edit Mesh → Extrude.

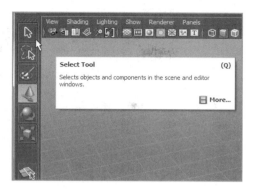

Figure 3.60

The Select Tool in the Tool Box

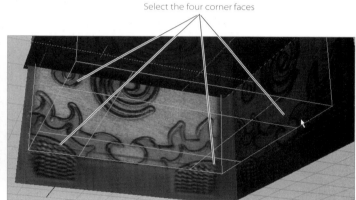

Select the four corner faces

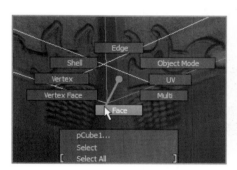

Figure 3.62

Select the four corner faces.

Figure 3.61

Select Face from the marking menu.

8. Your Manipulator will change, as shown in Figure 3.64. Grab the Z-axis move handle, and drag it down to "pull" the feet out of the bottom of the box as shown.

9. By moving vertices, taper the feet to match the reference images in the front and side view panels; see Figure 3.65.

10. Save your work. You can compare your progress to boxModel05.mb in the Scenes folder of the Decorative_Box project.

Figure 3.63

The Extrude icon in the Shelf

Figure 3.64

Extrude the feet.

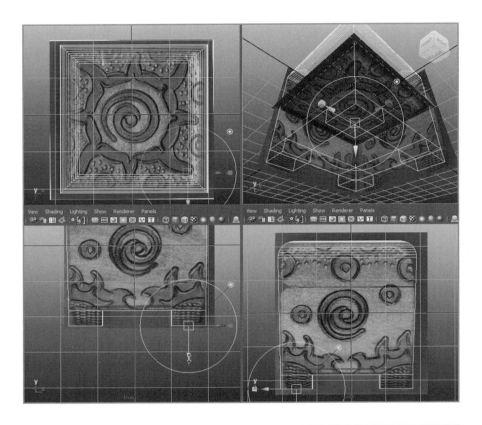

Figure 3.65

Move the vertices on the feet to line them up to the reference images.

The Shelf and Tool Box Explained

Here is a brief explanation of the tools and icons in the Shelf and Tool Box.

The Shelf

The *Shelf,* shown earlier in Figure 3.55, is an area where you keep icons for tools. It's divided into tabs that define functions for the tool icons in the Shelf. Whenever you start Maya, the tab you used in your previous session of Maya will be selected and displayed.

Each tab is broken out into different function sets, showing you icons that are useful for a particular set of functions such as creating surfaces or creating lights and textures. You can change the Shelf display to show the functions you'll be using by clicking the tabs. The Custom tab is empty so that you can create your own custom Shelf, populating it with the tools you find most useful.

Don't worry too much about the Shelf right now; it may be better to use the commands from the menus first before turning to icons and shelves. Doing so will build your proficiency at finding the tools you need, and it will also give you the chance to explore further every time you open a menu.

The Tool Box

The Tool Box, shown in Figure 3.66, displays the most commonly used tools. You have been accessing these tools, such as Move or Rotate, primarily through their hotkeys. Table 3.9 lists the icons and their functions.

In addition to the common commands, the Tool Box displays several choices for screen layouts that let you change the interface with a single click. This is convenient because different animations call for different view modes. Experiment with the layouts by clicking any of the six presets in the Tool Box.

Figure 3.66

The Tool Box

ICON	NAME	DESCRIPTION
	Select	Lets you select objects
	Lasso Select	Allows for a free-form selection using a lasso marquee
	Paint Selection Tool	Enables the Paint Selection tool
	Translate (Move)	Moves the selection
	Rotate	Rotates the selection
	Scale	Scales the selection
	Last Tool Used	Shows the currently selected tool (shown as Split Polygon Tool here)

Table 3.9

Tool Box icons

Continuing the Decorative Box Model

Back to work! You'll be spending more time getting the box in shape. You can load the scene file boxModel05.mb in the Scenes folder of the Decorative_Box project or continue with your own scene. In the following steps, you will add more faces and edges to the model surface (a.k.a. mesh) so you can add detail to the shape.

1. There is a little curve to the middle of the box. You will need to create a new edge line that runs across the middle of the box so you can bow out the sides in the middle. In the Layer Editor, toggle off visibility for the reference images by clicking the (⊡) icon for reference planes. Now you can see just the model of the box.

2. Select the box, and in the Polygons tab of the Shelf, double-click the Interactive Split Tool icon (⬛) for the options and set Snap Magnets to **1** and the Magnet Tolerance to **0.5**, as shown in Figure 3.67. (This tool is also selectable through the menu Edit Mesh → Interactive Split Tool ❏.) You will be using the Snap Magnets setting for this tool to help you place the new edge line you're about to create.

Figure 3.67
Interactive Split tool options

3. Move your triangle cursor along one of the box's edges. With Snap Magnets set to **1**, you will notice the cursor will snap at the corners and in the middle of the edge. Drag the mouse along the box's first edge to snap the placement in the middle of that edge, as shown in Figure 3.68.

4. Snap a new split point in the middle of the next edge of the box, creating an edge line along one side of the box. Continue to snap two more split points in the middle of each remaining edge to create a horizontal split line in the middle of the box, as shown in Figure 3.69. When you place your last point at the same point where you started, right-click to commit the action. You now have a horizontal split along the middle of the box.

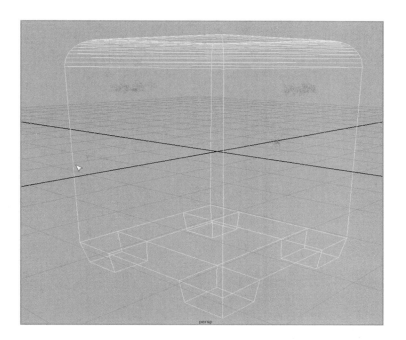

Figure 3.68
Click and drag the Interactive Split tool on this edge of the box, and snap the point at the middle.

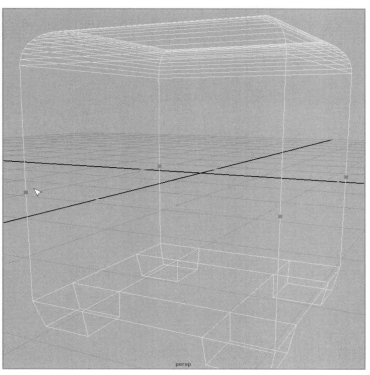

Figure 3.69
Create a horizontal edge line all the way around the box.

Figure 3.70

Adjust the cube to fit the reference images.

5. Click the Select Tool icon in the Tool Box to the left of the UI () to exit the Interactive Split tool, and close the Tools Settings panel to gain more screen space. Your cursor returns to the regular Maya cursor. Turn on the referencePlanes layer to show the image references.

6. Right-click the box, and choose Vertex from the marking menu. Move the new vertices in the middle of the box to bow out the box slightly. Move the rest of the vertices to match the model to the box images in the side and front view panels (see Figure 3.70).

7. Save your work. You can compare your progress to `boxModel06.mb` in the Scenes folder of the Decorative_Box project.

Time Slider and Help Line Explained

In this section, you will examine the bottom part of the UI where the Help line and Time slider live.

Time Slider/Range Slider

Running horizontally across the bottom of the screen are the Time slider and the Range slider, as shown in Figure 3.71. The Time slider displays the range of frames available in your animation and gives you a gray bar, known as the *Current Time indicator*. You can click it and then drag it back and forth in a scrubbing motion to move through time in your sequence. (When instructed in this book to *scrub* to a certain point in your animation, use this indicator to do so.)

The text box to the right of the Time slider gives you your current frame, but you can also use the text box to enter the frame you want to access. Immediately next to the current time readout is a set of DVD/DVR-type playback controls that you can use to play back your animation.

Below the Time slider is the Range slider, which you use to adjust the range of animation playback for your Time slider. The text boxes on either side of this slider give you readouts for the start and end frames of the scene and of the range selected.

Figure 3.71

The Time and Range sliders

You can adjust any of these settings by typing in these text boxes or by lengthening or shortening the slider with the handles on either end of the bar. When you change the range, you change only the viewable frame range of the scene; you don't adjust any of the animation.

Adjusting the Range Slider lets you zoom into sections of the timeline, which makes adjusting keyframes and timing much easier, especially in long animations. When you zoom into a particular section of your time frame, the Time slider displays only the frames and keyframes for that portion, making it easier to read.

Command Line/Help Line

Maya Embedded Language (MEL) is the user-accessible programming language of Maya. Every action you take invokes a MEL command or script that runs that particular function. You can write your own commands or scripts using either the Command line or the Script Editor. Use the Command line (see Figure 3.72) to enter single MEL commands directly from the keyboard in the white text box portion of the bar.

Figure 3.72

The Command line and the Help line

Below the Command line is the Help line. This bar provides a quick reference for almost everything on the screen. For the most part, it's a readout of functions when you point to icons. It also prompts you for the next step in a particular function or the next required input for a task's completion.

The Help line is very useful when you're not really sure about the next step in a command, such as which object to select next or which key to press to execute the command. You'll be surprised by how much you'll learn about tool functions by reading the prompts displayed here.

Finishing the Decorative Box Model

Now that you have the overall shape of the box finished, you need to add a few finishing details to the box. You will round out the edges of the box so they are not sharp, as well as add a line around the top of the box for the lid's seam and hinges. You can load the scene file boxModel06.mb in the Scenes folder of the Decorative_Box project or continue with your own scene.

When you build a model in CG, all the corners and edges will be sharp. To make a model more dynamic, you can round or *bevel* the edges to heighten the realism of the model when it is lit and rendered.

Figure 3.73

Hiding objects using the Outliner

1. Let's turn off the image reference planes again, but this time, let's do it a different way. Open the Outliner window by choosing Window → Outliner. You are already somewhat familiar with the Outliner from the solar system exercise in the previous chapter. Select frontPlane, sidePlane, and topPlane in the Outliner, and hide them by selecting Display → Hide → Hide Selection or by pressing Ctrl+H. This way, you can individually hide any object in your scene. Notice that when an object is hidden, its Outliner entry is grayed out (Figure 3.73).

2. Select the box, and open the Attribute Editor. Under the Object Display → Drawing Overrides headings, uncheck the Enable Overrides box, as shown in Figure 3.74, to display the box in Shaded mode again. This will help you see how the bevel works.

3. You will bevel the edges of the box throughout to soften the crisp corners of the cube that the real box doesn't have. Right-click the box and choose Edge from the marking menu. Shift+select all the outer edges of the cube, as shown in Figure 3.75.

4. With those edges selected, select Edit Mesh → Bevel □. Set everything to the defaults, but change Segments from 1 to **3**. Click Bevel, and your box should resemble the one shown in Figure 3.76.

5. Select the cube, and delete its history by selecting Edit → Delete By Type → History. This process essentially cleans up the model and the procedures it has undergone. You'll learn about History in the following chapters.

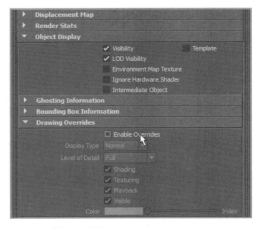

Figure 3.74

Turn off Drawing Overrides in the Attribute Editor to display the box in Shaded mode again.

6. You have one final detail to tend to on the lid. You need to add the hinge area you can see in the side view panel's reference image. Select the reference planes in the Outliner (pPlane1, pPlane2, and pPlane3), and press Shift+H to unhide them (you can also choose Display → Show → Show Selection). Make sure you're in Texture Shaded mode in your views (press 6) to see the box images.

7. Select the box. Turn its display back to wireframe by going into the Attribute Editor and, in the pCubeShape1 tab, turning on Enable Overrides under the Object Display → Drawing Overrides heading.

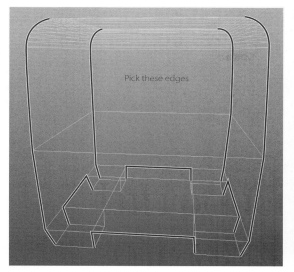

Figure 3.75
Select all of these edges for beveling.

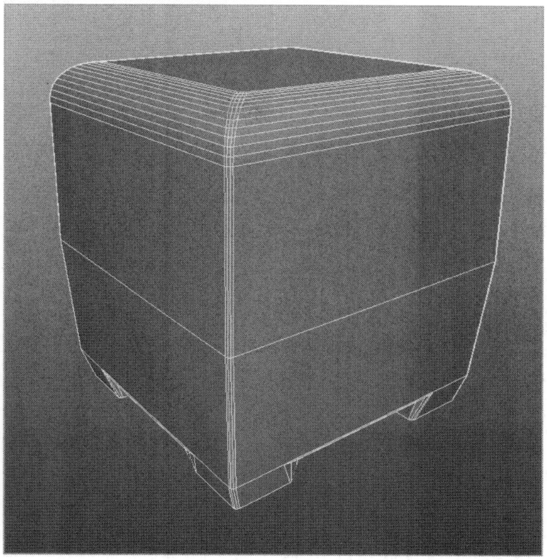

Figure 3.76
The beveled edges of the box

8. Select Edit Mesh → Insert Edge Loop Tool. This tool is like the Interactive Split tool in that it inserts new edges into a model. Your cursor will change to the solid triangle again. Click the upper edge of the box, and drag a dashed line to line up with the lid's seam in the box reference images, as shown in Figure 3.77. Once placed and you release the mouse button, the edge line will be completed, and the dashed line will turn solid.

Figure 3.77
Insert an edge loop to line up with the seam in the real box.

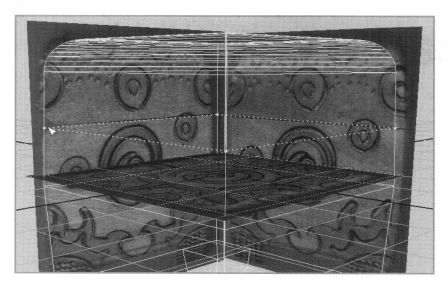

9. In the side view panel, insert four more horizontal edge loops for a total of five edge loops, as shown in Figure 3.78. This gives you edges with which to create the wedge cutout where the box is hinged, and that gives you a little indentation where the lid meets the box. You won't create a separate lid because you won't animate the box to open or close, and you don't need to see the inside.

Insert these five edges

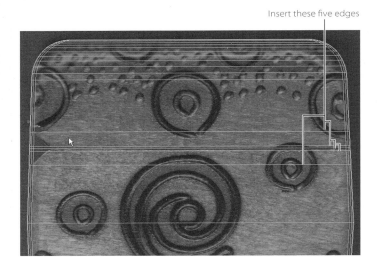

Figure 3.78

Insert these five edge loops for the lid of the box.

10. In the side view panel, select the appropriate vertices (see Figure 3.79), and move them to create the wedge-shaped indentation as shown.

Figure 3.79

Move the vertices to create the hinge area in the back of the box.

11. Choose Select → Select Edge Loop Tool. Select the middle edge loop you created earlier for the indent where the lid meets the box, as shown in Figure 3.80. Press R to scale the edge loop very slightly inward as shown.

Select this edge loop

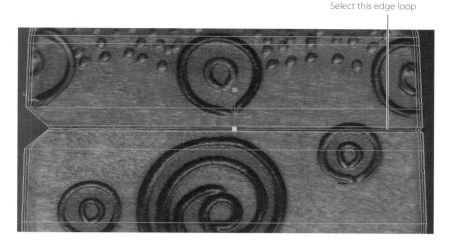

12. Hide the reference planes again through the Layer Editor, and turn Shading back on for the cube in the Attribute Editor. Figure 3.81 shows the completed box. But there's still a little snag. Notice the dark area where the lid meets the box, where you just created the slightly indented seam line. This is because of Normals. It makes the lid look as if it's angled inward.

13. Select the box, and choose Normals → Set Normal Angle. In the Set Normal Angle window that pops open, set Angle to the default of **30**, and click Apply And Close. Doing so fixes the darkening, as shown in Figure 3.82. For more on Normals, see the note in this section. Select the box, and delete its history by choosing Edit → Delete By Type → History.

14. Save your work, grab someone you love, and give them a hug.

Figure 3.81

The completed box needs one more adjustment.

Figure 3.82

The box now looks right.

You're finished with the modeling portion of this decorative box, and you've gotten to know the interface much better. In later chapters, you'll texture, light, and render the box with photo-realism in mind. You can load `boxModel07.mb` from the Scenes folder in the Decorative_Box project to compare your work.

NORMALS

Normals are imaginary lines that are perpendicular to a mesh's poly face and that define sides for that face. They also help determine how a renderer, such as mental ray, shades the surface. In some cases when you're modeling, you may notice an action that causes part of your model to display a darkened area as you saw in the decorative box in Figure 3.79. By manually setting a Normal angle for the box as you did in step 13 of the exercise, you override the seemingly display error. You'll learn more about Normals in Chapter 7.

The Attribute Editor and Outliner Explained

You have worked with the Attribute Editor and Outliner several times already. Here's a brief overview of these all-important windows the workflow in Maya.

The Attribute Editor Window

To use the Attribute Editor, select Window → Attribute Editor (Ctrl+A). The Attribute Editor window is arguably the most important window in Maya. Every object is defined by a series of attributes, and you edit these attributes using the Attribute Editor. This window displays every attribute of an object, and you can use it to change them, set keyframes, connect to other attributes, attach expressions, or simply view the attributes.

The Attribute Editor has tabs that correspond to the object's node structure. You learned a little about the Maya object structure in the previous chapter. As you can see, each tab displays different attributes of the object.

Try This   In a new scene, create a NURBS sphere with Interactive Creation turned off (Create → NURBS Primitives → Sphere). Select the sphere, press Ctrl+A to open the Attribute Editor, and click the `makeNurbSphere1` tab. Grab the top of the Attribute Editor if it is docked to the UI, and drag it off to the right to undock it. This will automatically display the Channel Box, as shown in Figure 3.83.

You'll notice that the Channel Box has the primary attributes (Translate X, Translate Y, Translate Z, Rotate X, and so on) of the sphere listed. Below them, you'll find the shapes node named nurbsSphereShape1 and the inputs node makeNurbSphere1 listed. If you click the makeNurbSphere1 entry in the Channel Box, it will expand to show you select attributes from the tab of the same name in the Attribute Editor. These attributes, despite being shown in two places, are the same. If you edit one in the Channel Box, it will be reflected in the Attribute Editor, and vice versa. The Channel Box is essentially a quick reference, giving you access to the most likely animated attributes of an object. The Attribute Editor goes into detail, giving you access to everything that makes up that object and the other nodes that influence it.

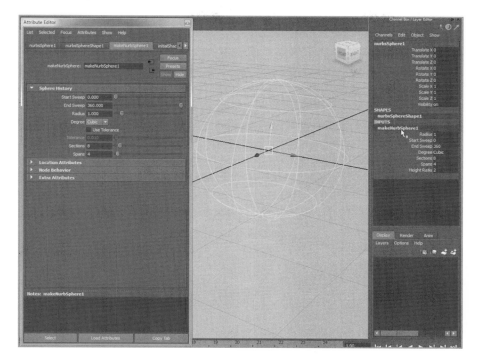

Figure 3.83

The Attribute Editor is undocked, and the Channel Box appears again.

Try changing some of the settings in this window and see how doing so affects the sphere in the view panels. For example, changing the Radius attribute under the nurbsSphereShape1 tab changes the size of the sphere. Click the nurbsSphere1 tab next, and you'll see the primary attributes listed. Try entering some different values for the Translate and Scale attributes to see what happens to the sphere in the view panels.

On the flip side, press W to activate the Move tool, and move the sphere around one of the view planes. Notice that the respective Translate attributes update in almost real time in both the Attribute Editor and the Channel Box. You'll see an area for writing notes at the bottom of the Attribute Editor. This is handy because you can put reminders here of important events, such as how you set up an object or even a birthday or an anniversary. If you drag the horizontal bar, you can adjust the size of the notes space, as shown in Figure 3.84.

Because you'll use the Attribute Editor constantly, you may want to keep the window open all the time and just move it around. You can also press the Ctrl+A hotkey to open the window more easily.

Figure 3.84

You can keep notes with an object's attributes in the Attribute Editor.

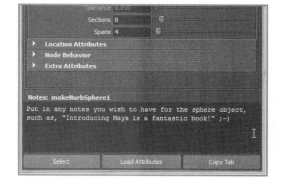

The Outliner

When you're well into an animation or a complex model, you'll invariably have several elements in your scene. Without a roadmap, finding the correct object to select or manipulate can be difficult. Using the Outliner, as you have already, greatly increases your efficiency. The Outliner is perfect for organizing, grouping objects, renaming nodes, and so forth, as you've already seen.

To use the Outliner, select Window → Outliner (see Figure 3.85). It displays all the objects in your scene as an outline. You can select any object in a scene by clicking its name.

The objects are listed by order of creation within the scene, but you can easily reorganize them by MMB+clicking and dragging an object to a new location in the window; doing so lets you group certain objects in the list. This is a fantastic way to keep your scene organized.

Additionally, you can easily rename an object by double-clicking its Outliner entry and typing a new name. It's crucial to an efficient animation process to keep things well named and properly organized. By doing so, you can quickly identify parts of your scene for later editing and troubleshooting.

A separator bar in the Outliner lets you split the display into two separate outline views. By clicking and dragging this bar up or down, you can see either end of a long list, with both ends having independent scrolling control.

Introducing the Modeling Toolkit

As you've seen in the interface, alongside the right of the UI where the Attribute Editor and Channel Box reside is a third tab called Modeling Toolkit shown in Figure 3.86. This suite of tools makes polygon modeling more efficient since most often used tools are centralized into one place. In addition, the Modeling Toolkit, when activated, allows for faster and easier component selection and editing.

In the Modeling Toolkit, the top half centers around making selections, while the bottom half lists important polygon workflow tools such as Bevel and Extrude. All of the Modeling Toolkit tools work slightly differently than the standard Maya tools of the same name; however, the results of the executed tool are identical.

Figure 3.85

The Outliner

Figure 3.86

Modeling Toolkit tab

Newly integrated into the Maya UI from a popular plug-in called NEX, the Modeling Toolkit is a powerful aid in working faster with polygons. This toolset is explored in depth and put to good use in Chapter 4.

Summary

In this chapter, you learned more about the user interface and the primary windows used in Maya as you worked on modeling the decorative box. The user interface combines mouse and keyboard input as well as plenty of menu and tool icons that you can select and use to accomplish your tasks. It also gives you a host of options to customize Maya to suit your needs.

You'll be quizzed in 10 minutes. Do you have it all memorized? Don't worry if you haven't absorbed all the information in this chapter. Now that you've had some exposure to the Maya user interface, you'll be familiar with the various windows when you really get to work.

You can always come back to this chapter to refresh your memory. Remember, you should learn the Maya program using its default settings. When in doubt, remember to access the Maya Help system, as shown in Figure 3.87.

To start, concentrate on using the menus to access most commands. After you're comfortable working in Maya, you can begin using hotkeys and shortcuts, and eventually you may even customize them. At this stage, though, focus on getting a clear understanding of the tools and what they do. You'll be introduced to various hotkeys and shortcuts as you work through the exercises in this book.

Figure 3.87

Maya Help—the best menu…ever!

CHAPTER 4

Beginning Polygonal Modeling

Simple objects call for simple models, and complicated objects call for a complex arrangement of simple models. Like a sculptor, you must analyze the object and deconstruct its design to learn how to create it.

The Autodesk® Maya® software primarily uses two types of modeling: polygons and NURBS. Both require a process that begins with deciding how best to achieve your design, although it's common to mix modeling methods in a scene.

To help you decide where to begin, this chapter starts with an overview of modeling, briefly describing the two popular methods and how they differ. You'll also learn about primitives. The second part of the chapter takes a detailed look at modeling with polygons. (The next two chapters cover the process of modeling with polygons and NURBS surfaces and how to bring them together in one model.)

Learning Outcomes: In this chapter, you will be able to

- Discern how to better plan your model
- Edit polygon geometry in traditional Maya as well as Modeling Toolkit workflows
- Navigate the Modeling Toolkit interface
- Work with the Modeling Toolkit selection workflow
- Extrude, bevel, and wedge polygons
- Use edge loops to create detail
- Create curves and then use the Revolve function to turn them into polygon meshes
- Adjust grouping and hierarchies in a complex model

Planning Your Model

Dissecting the components of an object into primitive shapes will help you translate and re-create it in 3D terms. You create the elements in Maya and then join them together to form the desired object.

Take reference pictures from many angles, get dimensions, and even write down a description of the object. The more perspectives from which you see your subject, the better you'll understand and be able to interpret your model.

Decide the purpose for your model. Then, determine the level of detail at which it will be seen in your CG scene. Consider the two scenes in Figure 4.1. If you need to create a park bench that is shown in a far shot (left), it will be a waste of time and effort to model all the details such as the grooves in the armrest. However, if your bench is shown in a close-up (right), you'll need those details.

Figure 4.1

The level of detail you need to include in a model depends on how it will be seen in the animation.

If you aren't certain how much detail you'll need, it's better to create a higher level of detail rather than skimping. You can more easily pare down detail than create it later.

Keep in mind that you can also add detail to the look of your model in the texturing phase of production, as you'll see with the decorative box later in the book. (Chapter 7, "Autodesk Maya Shading and Texturing," covers texturing.)

Choosing a Method

Polygon modeling involves tearing and extruding from larger pieces to form a desired shape. This method is typically preferred by most digital artists in the field.

NURBS modeling is great for organic shapes because the basis of all NURBS surfaces is smooth lines, or *curves*. However, NURBS tends to be more difficult in comparison since it's more difficult to create a complete model without several surfaces that must be perfectly stitched together, as you will see in the next chapter. Subdivision surfaces combine the best of both worlds but is not a popular workflow and is largely hidden in the interface now; therefore, it will not be covered in this book. But with subdivision surfaces, an artist can begin with a rough shape, chisel it out coarsely, and then switch to finely detailed sculpting by adding levels of detail to the sculpture only when and where needed. NURBS is covered in the next chapter.

In the end, when using NURBS, converting everything back to polygons is almost always preferable. Why? The available rendering applications all turn everything to polygons (a process called *tessellation*) when they render the scene. You can save yourself some memory and time and be the master of your own models by trying to go back to polygons as often as is reasonable.

An Overview of Polygons

Polygons consist of *faces*. A single polygon *face* is a flat surface made when three or more points called *vertices* are connected. The position of each *vertex* defines the shape and size of the face, usually a triangle. The line that connects one vertex to another is called an *edge*. Some polygonal faces have four vertices instead of three, creating a square face called a *quad* instead of a triangular one called a *triangle*.

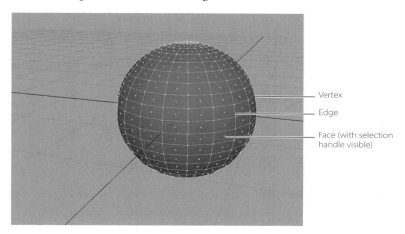

Figure 4.2

A polygonal sphere and its components

Vertex

Edge

Face (with selection handle visible)

Polygonal faces are attached along their polygonal edges to make up a more complex surface that constitutes your model (as shown with the polygonal sphere in Figure 4.2). A camping tent is a perfect example. The intersections of the poles are the faces' vertices. The poles are the edges of the faces, and the cloth draped over the tent's frame is the resultant surface.

Polygon models are the simplest for a computer to render. They're used for gaming applications, which need to render the models as the game is running. Gaming artists create models with a small number of polygons, called *low-count poly models*, which a PC or game console can render in real time. Higher-resolution polygon models are frequently used in television and film work. Because even complex polygon models can be made of a single object or mesh, they're useful for character animation work as well. Models in character animation bend and warp a good deal, so having a single surface that won't separate at the seams can be advantageous.

Using Primitives

Primitives are the simplest objects that you can generate in Maya (or in any 3D application). Primitives are simple geometric shapes—polygons or NURBS. Typically, they're used to sculpt models.

Because you can define the level of detail of the primitive's surface, primitives offer great sculpting versatility through vertex manipulation. You can create polygonal primitives using practically any level of subdivisions to define the number of vertices and faces.

You may find it helpful to analyze your modeling subjects into forms and shapes that fit in with Maya primitives to get a better sense of how to begin a modeling assignment. Figure 4.3 shows all of the primitives in Maya, including NURBS, polygons, and volume primitives. Quite different from geometry primitives, volume primitives are used for lighting and atmosphere effects, such as fog or haze, and don't play a part in modeling.

Figure 4.3

The Maya primitives

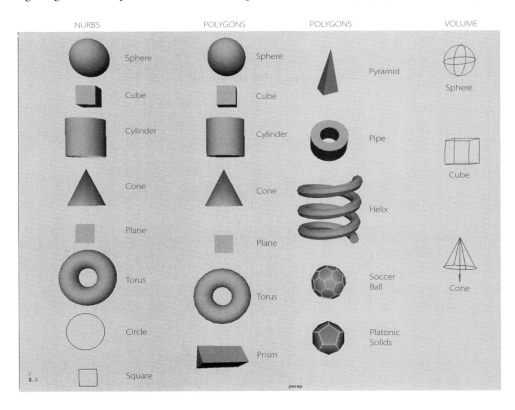

Polygon Basics

Polygon modeling is popular because its resulting models are usually one piece of geometry with many facets. You can, therefore, deform polygon models without fear of patches coming apart, as can happen with NURBS. Polygons, however, have a finite detail limitation and can look jagged up close or when scaled up. One solution to this problem in the Maya software is the Smooth tool.

A popular method of polygonal modeling, sometimes called *box modeling*, involves creating a base object, such as a simple cube, and then pulling and pushing faces to draw angles to create more faces. Whereas NURBS typically needs the creation of curves to start, complex polygons are usually created from basic-shaped polygons such as primitives.

A second method for creating poly surfaces uses the same curves that NURBS surfaces use or even converts a completed NURBS surface model to polygons. A third method is to create poly surfaces directly with the Polygon tool, which allows you to outline the shape of each face.

Creating Polygonal Primitives

The most notable difference between the options for a NURBS primitive and a poly primitive are the options for surface detail. With a NURBS surface, sections and spans define detail. With a poly mesh, detail is defined by *subdivisions*, which are the number of rows and columns of poly faces that run up, down, and across. The more subdivisions, the greater definition and detail the mesh is capable of.

Choosing Create → Polygon Primitives gives you access to the poly version of most of the NURBS primitives. Opening the option box for any of them gives you access to their creation options. To see an example, choose Create → Polygon Primitives → Sphere, and open the option box.

To get started, first make sure History is turned on, or there will be no creation node; then, click Create to make the poly sphere. Open the Attribute Editor, and switch to its creation node, called `polySphere1`. In the creation node `polySphere1` (in the option box, these are called Axis and Height Divisions), you'll find the Subdivisions Axis and Subdivisions Height sliders, which you can use to change the surface detail retroactively.

The Polygon Tool

You use the Polygon tool (switch to the Polygons menu set, and then choose Mesh → Create Polygon Tool) to create a single polygon face by laying down its vertices. When you select this tool, you can draw a polygon face in any shape by clicking to place each point or vertex. Aside from creating a polygon primitive by choosing Create → Polygon Primitives, this is the simplest way to create a polygon shape. Figure 4.4 shows some simple and complex single faces you can create with the Polygon tool.

Figure 4.4

Polygon faces created with the Polygon tool

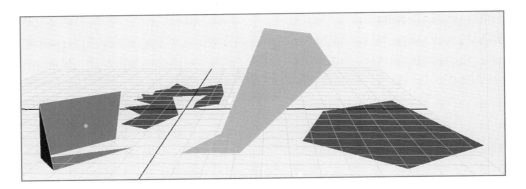

After you've laid down all your vertices, press Enter to create the poly face and exit the tool. For complex shapes, you may want to create more than just the single face so that you can manipulate the shape. For example, you may want to fold it.

Try This   The poly shown in Figure 4.5 was created with the Polygon tool and has only one face. Therefore, adjusting or deforming the surface is impossible. To fold this object, you need more faces and the edges between them. Make your own intricate poly shape with the Polygon tool by clicking vertices down in the different views to get vertices in all three axes.

With the surface selected, choose Mesh → Triangulate. The surface has more faces and edges and is easier to edit, but it's still simple to create because you start with a single face. If you need a uniquely shaped poly, start with this tool, and then triangulate your surface into several faces, as shown in Figure 4.6.

Faces that have too many edges (a.k.a. Ngons) may cause you troubles later in the work-flow, particularly in further manipulation of the mesh containing any Ngons and also when rendering.

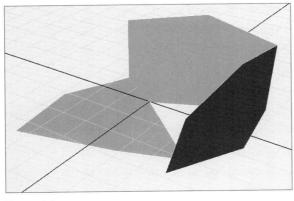

Figure 4.5

A single-faced polygon with a complex shape

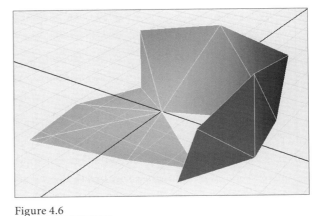

Figure 4.6

Complex shapes are better with more faces.

Poly Editing Tools

Here's a brief preview of what to expect in the world of poly editing. You should experiment with each tool on a primitive sphere as it's introduced, so saddle up to your Maya window and try each tool as you read along.

Later in this chapter, you'll deploy these new skills. In Chapter 6, "Practical Experience," you'll create a cute desk lamp to exercise your modeling skills. For most of the work in this chapter, you'll use the Polygons menu. Open the Edit Mesh menu, tear it off, and place it somewhere on your screen so you can get a good look at the tools and functions.

Modeling Toolkit

Modeling Toolkit used to be a plug-in called NEX that is now integrated with Maya 2014. It integrates component-level selection and editing tools (such as selecting vertices, edges, faces, etc., and extruding them, for example) together for a more streamlined modeling workflow. Modeling Toolkit can make tedious modeling chores much easier, especially for advanced modeling techniques. I will be covering some of the Modeling Toolkit workflow and how it's integrated into Maya 2014 alongside Maya traditional workflows, to give you a comparison and allow you to decide which workflow suits you. You'll take a look at the Modeling Toolkit and its interface later in the chapter.

The Poly Extrusion Tools

The most commonly used poly editing tool has to do with extrusion. You can use Extrude to pull out a face or an edge of a polygon surface to create additions to that surface. You access the tool at Edit Mesh → Extrude. Maya distinguishes between edge or face extrusion based on whether you've selected edges or faces. Follow these steps:

1. Select a face or multiple faces of a polygon, and choose Edit Mesh → Extrude. The regular Manipulator changes to a Special Manipulator, as shown in the left image in Figure 4.7.

2. Grab the Z-axis move handle (the blue arrow), and drag it away from the sphere, as shown in the center of Figure 4.7.

3. Using the scale handles (the boxes) scales the faces of the extrusion. The cyan circle rotates the face. The image at the right in Figure 4.7 shows the faces extruded, rotated, and scaled.

4. Choosing the Extrude command again without deselecting the faces lets you extrude even more, keeping the original extrusion shape and building on top of that.

5. Selecting the edges of the poly surface instead of the faces and choosing Edit Mesh → Extrude extrudes flat surfaces from the edges selected. The Special Manipulator works the same way as Extrude does for poly faces.

Figure 4.7

Extruding several faces at once on a sphere. The left image shows the selected faces, the middle image shows those faces extruded, and the right image shows those faces extruded with a rotation and smaller scale.

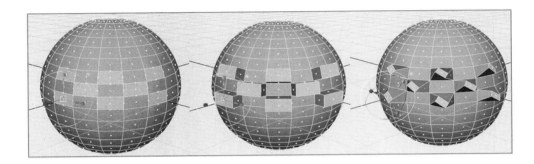

The face(s) you select pull out from the sphere, and new faces are created on the sides of the extrusion(s). The Extrude tool is an exceptionally powerful tool in that it allows you to easily create additions to any poly surface in any direction. It's particularly useful for modeling characters and creatures. Later in this chapter, you'll use it to make a simple human hand.

You can also use the direction and shape of a curve to extrude faces. Create a curve in the shape you want your extrusion to take, select the curve along with the face(s), and choose Extrude ▭. Taper decreases or increases the size of the face as it extrudes. Twist rotates the face as it extrudes, and Divisions increases the smoothness of the resulting extrusion. Choose Selected for the Curve setting. When you have your settings for those attributes, click the Extrude button (see Figure 4.8).

Figure 4.8

Extruding a face along a path curve

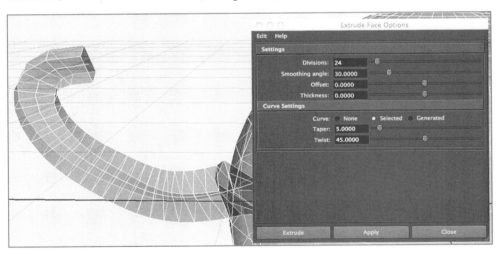

This seems to be strange behavior, but the Twist and Taper values are taken into account in the extrusion. You can edit these values when you uncheck, or you can reselect this option after you enter values for Twist and Taper. If your faces aren't extruding to the shape of the curve, increase the number of divisions.

Modeling Toolkit and Extrusions

Modeling Toolkit makes selecting and editing polygonal components more streamlined, making some workflows faster by incorporating tools into one place for ease of access as well as by reducing the amount of times you have to exit one tool or mode and enter another one. Since a lot of what Modeling Toolkit does centers around component selections, let's start there first.

Modeling Toolkit Interface

By default, the Modeling Toolkit plug-in should be enabled, which places the Modeling Toolkit menu on the Main Menu bar. If you don't see Modeling Toolkit, simply choose Window → Setting/Preferences → Plug-In Manager. About halfway down the list, you should see ModelingToolkit.dll. Check Loaded and Auto Load, as shown in Figure 4.9.

Modeling Toolkit also places an icon on your status bar, next to the XYZ input fields, shown next to the cursor and already turned on in Figure 4.10. When the Modeling Toolkit icon is turned on, Modeling Toolkit is automatically invoked whenever you enter into component selection mode. Go ahead and click the icon to turn Modeling Toolkit on if it isn't already.

In addition, Modeling Toolkit places a tab in the Channel Box, called Modeling Toolkit, to make displaying its tool set easier, as shown in Figure 4.11. You will notice toward the top of the Modeling Toolkit panel four icons for selecting, moving, rotating, and scaling. These operate in exactly the same way as transformation tools; however, they enable the Modeling Toolkit functionality. You'll see this in action throughout the book and introduced next.

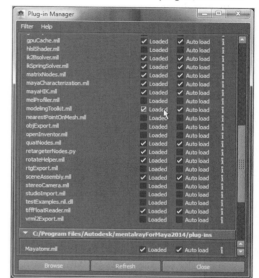

Figure 4.9

Loading the Modeling Toolkit plug-in, if needed

Figure 4.10

The Modeling Toolkit icon button

Modeling Toolkit Extrusion

Now that you have a little background on how Modeling Toolkit integrates with Maya 2014, let's use it in comparison to the Maya Extrude tool you just used on a sphere.

1. Make sure the Modeling Toolkit icon (🔲) in the status bar is active to see the Modeling Toolkit tab alongside the Attribute Editor and Channel Box/Layer Editor tabs. Then make sure the Modeling Toolkit button in the upper-right corner of the Modeling Toolkit is activated (🔵) so that it is lit blue.

2. Create a polygon sphere, and press 5 for Shaded mode.

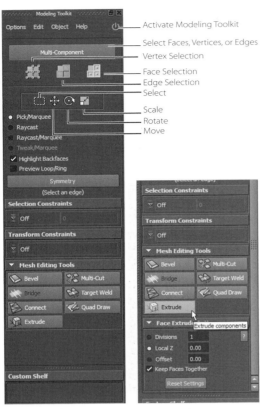

Figure 4.11
**The Modeling
Toolkit panel
and tab**

Figure 4.12
**Click Extrude in the
Modeling Toolkit panel.**

Figure 4.13
**Click and drag to
set the extrusion
amount.**

3. Right-click the sphere in your scene, and select Face from the marking menu for face selection mode. This is the easiest way to select components in Maya, which also works the same while using Modeling Toolkit.

4. Your faces are now highlighting differently than they do in Maya, as you saw when modeling the decorative box in Chapter 3, "The Autodesk Maya 2014 Interface." Now Modeling Toolkit selection turns the face dark red with a bold red highlight, instead of amber shading. Click a face to select it, or hold down Shift to select multiple faces. As soon as you click to select, the selected faces turn into the familiar Maya amber coloring while in Shaded mode. Select two faces side-by-side on the sphere.

5. In the Modeling Toolkit panel, click Extrude under the Mesh Editing Tools heading, as shown in Figure 4.12. The options appear below the button.

6. In the view panel, you'll see a yellow readout telling you the axis you will be extruding in, and your cursor will change to a double-headed horizontal arrow. Click and drag left or right to set the amount of extrusion (Figure 4.13).

7. In the Modeling Toolkit panel, click the Divisions button, and set the number to 3. This will give you multiple sections along your extrusion. You can also click and drag in the view panel to set the divisions number interactively.

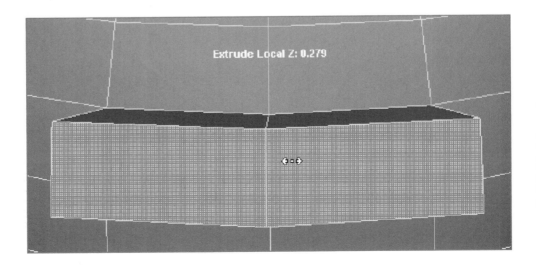

8. Click the Offset button, and click and drag in the viewport to make the extruded faces bigger or smaller. You may also enter a value in the Modeling Toolkit panel for Offset. Figure 4.14 shows an extrusion of 0.29 with a Divisions of 3 and an Offset of 0.04.

9. Finally, click the Keep Faces Together check box on and off in the Modeling Toolkit panel to see how the extrusion changes. Figure 4.15 shows the same extrusion as Figure 4.14, but with Keep Faces Together turned off. Whatever options you set will be used the next time you extrude in Modeling Toolkit. Simply turn off the Extrude button to exit the tool and commit the changes.

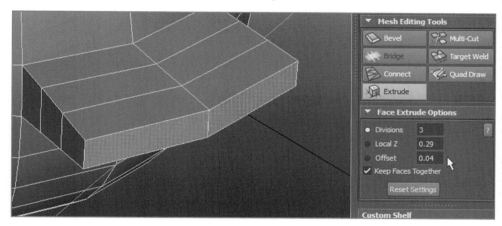

Figure 4.14

Modeling Toolkit extrusion in action

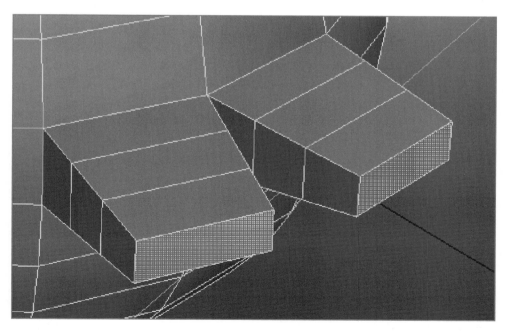

Figure 4.15

Keep Faces Together is turned off.

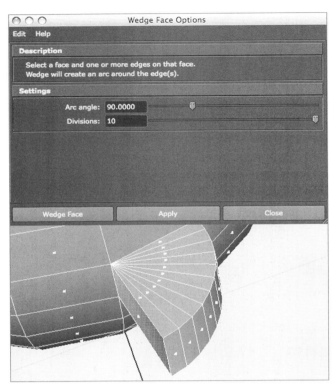

Figure 4.16

Executing a Wedge Face operation on a face of a sphere

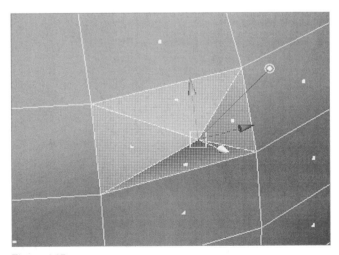

Figure 4.17

Poke Face helps create areas of detail in your model.

All of these extrusion options and settings are available in the Maya Extrude tool but are a little more streamlined and integrated in the Modeling Toolkit workflow. Experiment to see how you like to work. You will be using a combination of traditional Maya and Modeling Toolkit workflows throughout the chapter and other parts of the book.

The Wedge Face Tool

Similar to extruding faces, Wedge Face pulls out a poly face, but it does so in an arc instead of a straight line. For this tool, you need to select a face and an edge of the selected face for the pivot point of the corner. Here's how to do this. First deactivate Modeling Toolkit by clicking the icon ( ) to turn off the blue light.

Select a face, Shift+select one of its edges, and choose Edit Mesh → Wedge Face □. (To select a face and Shift+select an edge, right-click the sphere to display the marking menu. Choose Face, and select a face. Right-click again, and choose Edge on the marking menu. Then, Shift+select one of the face's edges.)

In the option box, you'll notice some help for the tool under the Description heading. Under the Settings heading, you can select the degree of turn in the Arc Angle (90 degrees is the default) as well as the number of faces used to create the wedge (by moving the Divisions slider), as shown in Figure 4.16.

To access selection filters more easily, you can right-click an object to display a marking menu. Drag the cursor in the direction of the selection type you want, and release the mouse button. Then, click or Shift+click your selection.

The Wedge Face tool is useful for items such as elbows, knees, archways, and tunnel curves.

The Poke Face Tool

Poke Face is great for creating detailed sections of a mesh (poly surface) and bumps or indentations. To use the Poke Face tool to add detail to a face, select a face and then choose Edit Mesh → Poke Face.

A vertex is added to the middle of the face, and the Move Manipulator appears on the screen, as shown in Figure 4.17. This lets you move the point to where you need it on the face. You can add bumps and depressions to your surface as well as create regions of extra detail. By selectively adding detail, you can subdivide specific areas of a polygon for extra detailed work, leaving lower poly counts in less-detailed areas for an efficient model.

The Bevel Tool

Use the Bevel tool to round sharp corners and edges. The Bevel tool requires that you select an edge or multiple edges and then use them to create multiple new faces to round that edge or corner.

Select an edge or edges, and choose Edit Mesh → Bevel ❑ to adjust your bevel. The Width slider sets the distance from the edge to the center of where the new face will be. This basically determines the size of the beveled corner. The Segments number defines how many segments are created for the bevel: the more segments, the smoother the beveled edge. Leaving Segments at 1 creates a sharp corner (see Figure 4.18).

The setting of the Roundness slider specifies the roundness of the corner. Setting the number too high will make the beveled edge stick out, as shown in Figure 4.19, although that can be a valid design choice. You can allow Maya to set the roundness automatically based on the size of the geometry being beveled. Select the Automatically Fit Bevel To Object check box to disable the Roundness slider. Move the Segments slider to set the number of new faces that are created on the bevel: the more segments, the smoother the bevel.

Use the Bevel tool to round polygonal edges. You can also use it to add extra surface detail, because Bevel creates more faces on the surface.

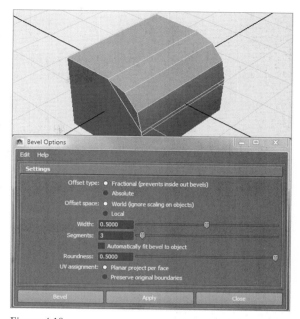

Figure 4.18

Increase Segments to create a rounder corner.

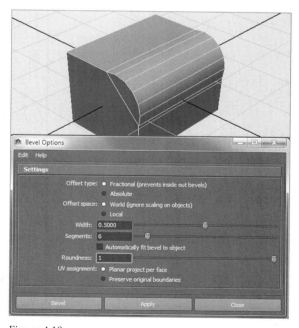

Figure 4.19

A poly bevel's roundness set too high

Modeling Toolkit Bevel

Just like the Maya Extrude and the Modeling Toolkit Extrude, there is a way to bevel inside Modeling Toolkit. Using the same example as earlier, a simple cube, you'll see how to bevel in the Modeling Toolkit here:

1. With the Modeling Toolkit Activate icon ( ) turned off for traditional Maya work-flow, enter edge selection mode by right-clicking a polygon cube in your scene and selecting Edge from the marking menu. When you move your mouse over an edge, it turns red, allowing you to select it. You don't need to select any edges right now. Now let's see how it works in Modeling Toolkit.

2. Turn on the Modeling Toolkit icon, and you'll remain in edge mode. Modeling Toolkit turns the edge red before you select it. However, this time, edges select when your cursor is near them and not directly on top of them as in traditional Maya selec-tion. This feature is one way where Modeling Toolkit improves the speed of modeling in Maya, allowing you to more easily and quickly select components without having to be right on top of them. This is true for vertices as well. You'll stay in Modeling Toolkit for this exercise.

3. Select an edge on the cube. Press W for the Move tool. You can also select Move from the Modeling Toolkit panel, but the traditional Maya hotkey of W works the same while in Modeling Toolkit. But because you have Modeling Toolkit enabled, your manipulator will have three circles added. Click and drag any of the circles to see that you can move that edge in any two-dimensional plane easily. Moving your mouse over any of the circles gives you the plane axes (Figure 4.20). Undo any moves you may have done, and you'll move on to the Modeling Toolkit Bevel command next.

Figure 4.20

Modeling Toolkit adds easy planar movement to components with its three circles in the manipulator.

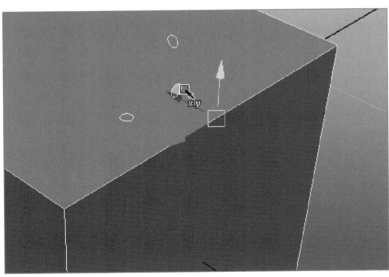

4. With an edge selected, click the Bevel button in the Modeling Toolkit panel. You can select either Divisions or Offset and click and drag in the view panel (as you did with the Modeling Toolkit Extrude tool in the extrusion example earlier in the chapter) to set their values. Offset is like Maya Bevel's Width attribute and makes the bevel large or smaller, while Divisions affects the rounding of the bevel. Figure 4.21 shows a Modeling Toolkit Bevel with an Offset of 0.5 and Segments of 3, which matches the Maya Bevel done earlier with a Width of 0.5 and Segments of 3. The result on the cube is the same if you compare it with the earlier Maya bevel shown in Figure 4.18.

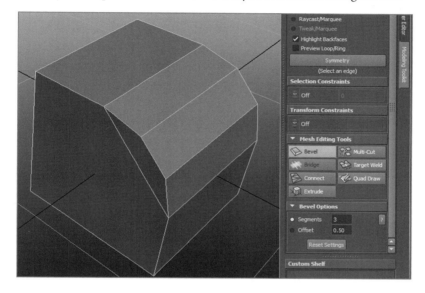

Figure 4.21

The Modeling Toolkit Bevel is the same as the Maya Bevel shown in Figure 4.18.

5. Click the Bevel button to exit the tool and commit your Bevel operation to the cube.

As you can see, using Modeling Toolkit makes the Bevel tool slightly easier and faster to accomplish with the same result as the Maya Bevel. As a matter of fact, Modeling Toolkit is only a workflow plug-in. It passes all of its changes and work into standard Maya attributes and nodes, making sharing files created using Modeling Toolkit workflow no different from ones created without Modeling Toolkit enabled. So, the cube you bevel in Modeling Toolkit is precisely the same as the one beveled in Maya software's traditional workflow. The attributes and history on that object are the same.

Having even a *slightly* rounded edge on a model—a box, for example—greatly enhances the look of that box when it's lighted and rendered, because the edges catch much more light, helping define the shape of the box. A perfectly flat corner with no bevel doesn't catch any light, making the model look weaker.

Putting the Tools to Use: Making a Simple Hand

Starting with a simple polygonal cube, you'll create a basic human hand using a mix of Maya and Modeling Toolkit workflows.

Either create a new project called Poly_Hand or download the entire project from the web page (www.sybex.com/go/introducingmaya2014) and use that. Follow these steps:

1. Create a polygonal cube. Open the Attribute Editor and, in the polyCube1 tab, set Subdivisions Width to **4**, Subdivisions Height to **1**, and Subdivisions Depth to **3**. If you don't have that tab in the Attribute Editor, click Undo, turn on History, and re-create the cube.

2. Scale the cube to $X = 1$, $Y = 0.25$, and $Z = 1.3$ so that it looks as shown in Figure 4.22.

3. Turn on the Modeling Toolkit icon (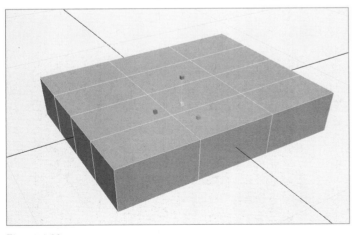) in the status bar. Click the Modeling Toolkit tab in the Channel Box to see the Modeling Toolkit tools if you need them. Right-click the cube and choose Face from the marking menu.

4. Select the front face that is in the corner closest to you. You'll extrude the face to make the first part of the index finger. Before you extrude, though, rotate the face a bit in the Y-axis, away from the rest of the hand, to angle the extrusion toward where the thumb would be.

5. In the Modeling Toolkit panel, click the Extrude button. Set Divisions to **3**. Click the Local Z radial button, and click and drag in the view panel until the Extrude Local Z readout in yellow reads about 1.1. Exit the Extrude tool. Figure 4.23 shows the full index finger with the slight rotation away from the hand.

   Save your work, and compare it to the scene file poly_hand_v1.mb in the Poly_Hand project on the web page.

6. Repeat steps 4 and 5 for the remaining three fingers. Remember, if you rotate the initial face of each finger slightly away from the previous finger, the extrusions will have small gaps between them, as shown in Figure 4.24. Otherwise, the fingers will extrude right up against each other, like a glove with the fingers glued together. Also remember to exit the Extrude tool in the Modeling Toolkit panel by clicking it off after each extrusion is complete to move on to the next finger.

Figure 4.22

The poly cube in position to make the hand

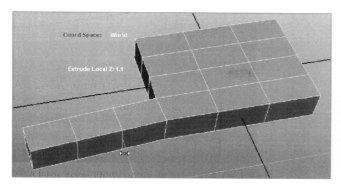

Figure 4.23

The index finger

Figure 4.24

Four fingers

Use Table 4.1 as a guide for the extrusion lengths for each finger.

When you're finished with the four fingers, select the hand; in the Perspective panel, press 2 to give you a smooth preview of the hand. With a polygonal object, pressing the 1, 2, and 3 keys previews the smoothness your model will likely have when it's smoothed (a polygonal modeling operation about to be discussed). When you press 2, your hand is previewed smoothed. Doing so also shows the original shape of the hand as a wireframe cage (see Figure 4.25).

FINGER	EXTRUDE LOCAL Z VALUE
Middle	1.2
Ring	1.16
Pinkie	0.95

Table 4.1

Extrusion length guide

With the hand still selected, press 3. The original wireframe cage disappears, as shown in Figure 4.26. This doesn't alter your model in any way; if you render, your hand will still be blocky, just as you modeled it. Press 1 to exit the smooth preview and return to the original model view. The scene file poly_hand_v2.mb shows the hand with the four fingers created.

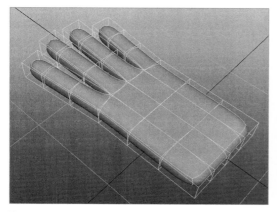

Figure 4.25

A smoothed preview of the hand, with the original shape shown as a cage

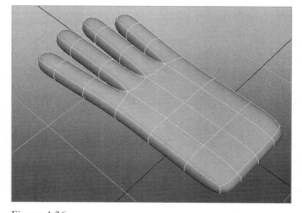

Figure 4.26

A full smooth preview of the hand

7. Let's work on the thumb. You need to move a couple of edges to make room for where the thumb attaches to the hand. Select the three edges on the index finger side of the hand, and move them up toward the tip of the hand, as shown in Figure 4.27. This creates an elongated face to start the thumb.

Figure 4.27

Creating an elongated face for the thumb

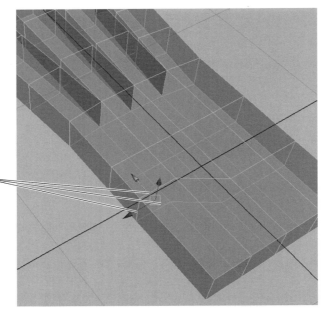

Select these three edges.

8. You'll use the Wedge Face tool to start the thumb. Select the elongated face. Right-click the object to display the marking menu, and choose Edge. Shift+select the edge on the left side of that face (see Figure 4.28). It's OK that you still have Modeling Toolkit active, even though the next command is not Modeling Toolkit related.

9. In the Main Menu bar, choose Edit Mesh → Wedge Face ❐. In the option box, set Arc Angle to **65** and set Divisions to **5**. Click Wedge Face. With that wedged face still selected, scale it down in the *X*-axis to just under half its width to make it less broad, and rotate it toward the hand a bit so it looks like the first image in Figure 4.29.

Figure 4.28

Select the face and edge for the Wedge Face function.

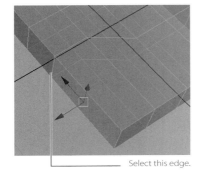

Select this edge.

10. To make the thumb itself, extrude that face in Modeling Toolkit first to **0.85** (by either clicking and dragging or typing **0.85** into the Modeling Toolkit panel's Local Z attribute) with a Divisions value of **2**. The hand looks awkward right now, especially the thumb area (see the second image in Figure 4.29).

11. Select the faces along the meaty part of the thumb, and move and rotate them to round out the hand. While you're at it, squeeze in the tips of the fingers to point them all by selecting and scaling the very top face of each finger.

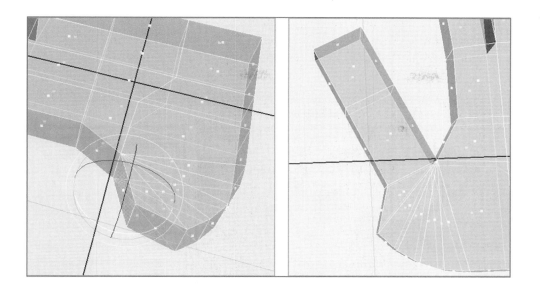

Figure 4.29

Rounding out the side for the thumb

12. Select the pinkie finger edges (not faces), and scale them in to narrow the pinkie.

13. Select the edges that make up the knuckle of each finger (one by one), and scale them out in the X-axis to fatten the knuckles a bit. Your results should be similar to Figure 4.30.

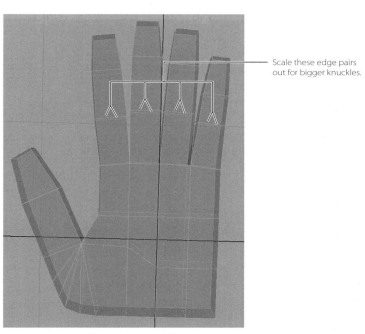

Scale these edge pairs out for bigger knuckles.

Figure 4.30

Better-proportioned fingers and knuckles

14. To add more detail to the hand, you'll raise the knuckles. You need to create new vertices for the knuckles where each finger meets the hand. Enter edge selection mode with Modeling Toolkit still active. In the Modeling Toolkit panel, click the Multi-Cut icon (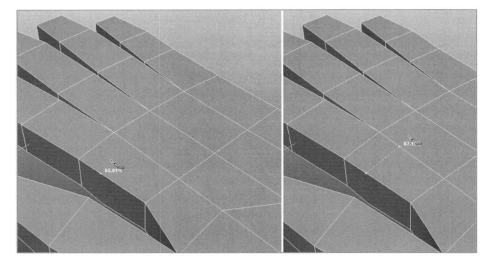 Multi-Cut). Click and drag along the edge between the thumb and the index finger, right below where the index finger attaches to the hand, until the yellow readout reads about 65%, as shown on the left of Figure 4.31. Release the mouse button to lay down the first point of the Multi-Cut operation.

15. Now click the opposite edge across at about 67 percent. You'll notice a green dashed line stretch across denoting where a new edge will be placed, as shown in Figure 4.31 (right).

Figure 4.31

Start a Multi-Cut operation on the hand for the knuckles (left). Continue the cut across the first face (right).

16. Click across the remaining knuckle faces to lay down a cut line across the top of the hand, as shown in Figure 4.32.

17. Exit the Multi-Cut tool in the Modeling Toolkit panel to commit the changes, and it will add four new edges (and hence four new faces) along the back of the hand for the knuckles. Select each of those new faces, and choose Edit Mesh → Poke Face to subdivide them into four triangles, with a vertex in the center. A Special Manipulator appears. Use the Z translate handle to pull those middle vertices up to make knuckles (see Figure 4.33).

18. Now that you have a simple hand, you can smooth out the mesh to make it less boxy. In Object mode, select the hand, and press 2 to see a preview of what the hand will look like after it's smoothed. Press 1 to exit the smooth preview. Choose Mesh → Smooth ❑; in the option box, set Division Levels to **2**, and leave the other options at their defaults (see Figure 4.34).

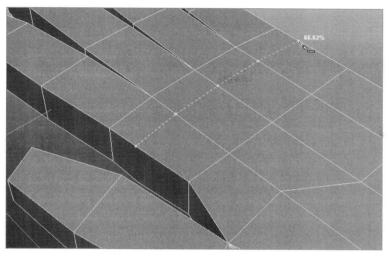

Figure 4.32

Adding a cut line across the hand for the knuckles with the Multi-Cut tool in Modeling Toolkit.

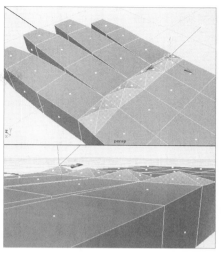

Figure 4.33

Use the Poke Face tool to raise the knuckles.

19. Click Smooth. Your hand should take on a smoother, rounder look—like a dish glove filled with air—and it should roughly resemble the preview mode when you press 3. This time, however, you've altered the geometry and actually made the mesh smoother and given it a higher density of polygons. Notice all the nodes listed under Inputs in the Channel Box in Figure 4.35. This is because History has been on for the entire duration of this exercise. At any time, you can select one of those nodes and edit something—the extrusion of the pinkie, for example. You don't need to do any of this now, so with the hand selected, choose Edit → Delete By Type → History to get rid of all those extra nodes. (Feel free to edit any of those nodes through the Attribute Editor if you like.)

Save your file again. To verify that you've been working correctly, you can load the finished hand file (with its history intact): poly_hand_v3.mb from the book's web page, www.sybex.com/go/introducingmaya2014.

Figure 4.34

Set the options for the Smooth operation.

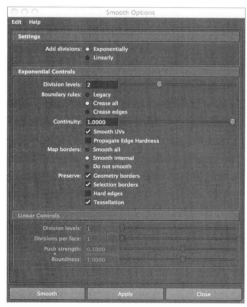

Figure 4.35

The smoothed hand with all its history nodes

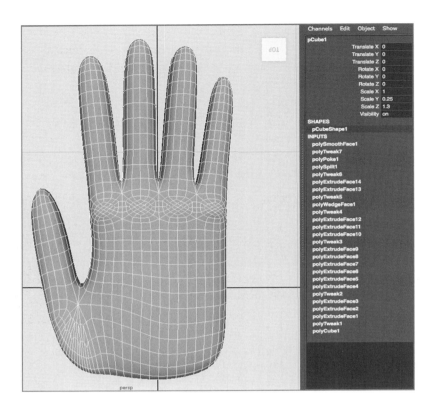

Creating Areas of Detail on a Poly Mesh

Figure 4.36

This detailed hand can be modeled in polygons, given a ton of time and love.

As you saw with the hand, it became necessary to add more faces to parts of the surface to create various details. The hand takes on better form when you devote time to detailing it. You began the hand shown in Figure 4.36 using the previous steps, but you detailed it by creating faces using the tools discussed in this section, moving vertices, and adding fin-

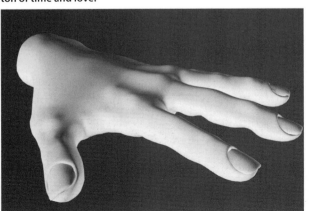

gernails. Don't expect to be able to model intricately right from the start unless you already have modeling experience. Start with simple objects, work your way up, and stay with it.

Maya provides several ways to add surface detail or increase a poly's subdivisions.

The Add Divisions Tool

You can use the Add Divisions tool to increase the number of faces of a poly surface by evenly dividing either all faces or just those selected. Select the poly surface face or faces, and choose Edit Mesh → Add

Divisions. In the option box, you can adjust the number of times the faces are divided by moving the Division Levels slider. The Mode drop-down menu gives you the choice to subdivide your faces into quads (four-sided faces, as on the left of Figure 4.37) or triangles (three-sided faces, as on the right in Figure 4.37).

You can also select a poly edge to divide. Running this tool on edges divides the edges into separate edges along the same face. It doesn't divide the face; rather, you use it to change the shape of the face by moving the divided edges, as shown in Figure 4.38.

You use the Add Divisions tool to create regions of detail on a poly surface. This is a broader approach than using the Poke Face tool, which adds detail for more pinpoint areas.

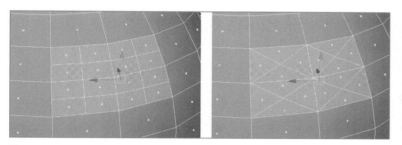

Figure 4.37

The Mode drop-down menu of the Add Divisions tool lets you subdivide faces into quads or triangles.

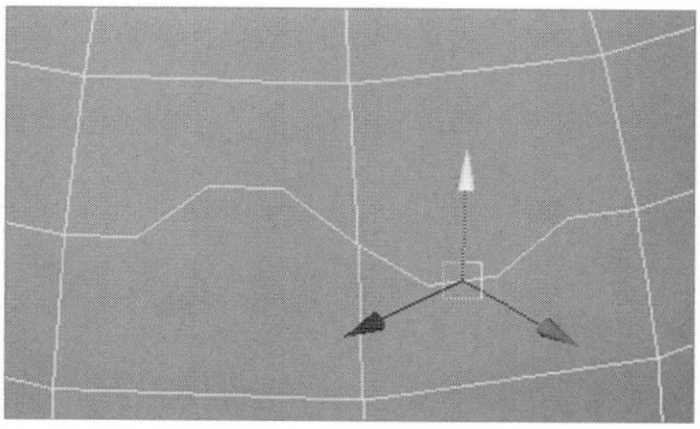

Figure 4.38

Dividing edges

Modeling Toolkit Multi-Cut Tool

As you saw when creating more faces and edges for the hand's knuckles in the previous exercise, Modeling Toolkit's Multi-Cut tool allows you to lay down edges along faces fairly easily. This tool (which turns your cursor into a knife shape) is essentially the same as the Interactive Split tool that you used on the decorative box exercise in Chapter 3 (and mentioned in the following section), but it's rolled into the Modeling Toolkit workflow for ease. It is accessed when Modeling Toolkit is enabled and through the Modeling Toolkit panel under the Mesh Editing Tools heading. You can also make multiple cuts on the same face, as shown in Figure 4.39.

Figure 4.39

The Modeling Toolkit Multi-Cut tool

The Interactive Split Tool

Another way to create detail is to use the Interactive Split tool, which does exactly what its name suggests. As you saw with the decorative box in Chapter 3, when you choose Edit Mesh → Interactive Split Tool ❑, your cursor changes to a triangle and the option box opens (Figure 4.40). Set Magnet Tolerance to **0** as shown. Use the triangle cursor to select two points along two edges

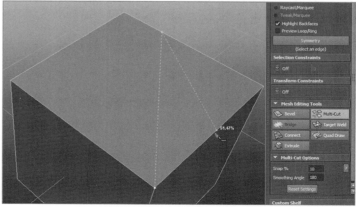

of a face. Doing so creates a line from the first to the second point, which serves as a new edge to divide that face into two halves. You can right-click to commit the new division or continue to create more splits on the same mesh, as shown in Figure 4.40. The Magnet Tolerance attribute allows you to snap the Interactive Split tool along the edge, for example, to the corners or middle of the edge. Again, simply right-click to commit the new division to the face(s). The tool remains active, so you can continue to split faces until you switch to another tool, such as by pressing W for the Move tool.

Using the Interactive Split tool is a flexible, accurate, and fast way to create surface subdivisions for your model.

The Insert Edge Loop Tool

This handy tool adds edges to a poly selection, much like the Interactive Split tool, but it does so more quickly by working along the entire poly surface, along common vertices. The Insert Edge Loop tool automatically runs a new edge along the poly surface perpendicular to the subdivision line you click, without requiring you to click multiple times as with the Interactive Split tool or Modeling Toolkit Multi-Cut. You used this tool in the decorative box in Chapter 3 and will continue using it throughout this book. You'll find it indispensable in creating polygonal models because it creates subdivisions quickly.

For instance, subdividing a polygonal cube is quicker than using the Interactive Split tool. With a poly cube selected, choose Edit Mesh → Insert Edge Loop Tool. Click an edge, and the tool places an edge running perpendicular from that point to the next edge across the surface and across to the next edge, as shown in Figure 4.41. If you click and drag along an edge, you can interactively position the new split edges.

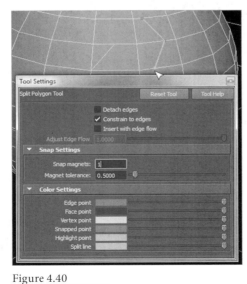

Figure 4.40
Splitting a polygon allows you to draw the new edge(s) to split the face.

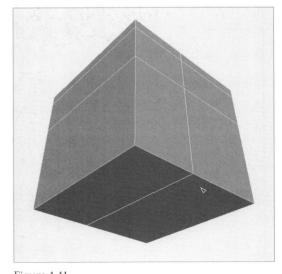

Figure 4.41
Using the Insert Edge Loop tool

The Offset Edge Loop Tool

Much like the Insert Edge Loop tool, the Offset Edge Loop tool inserts not one but two edge loop rings of edges across the surface of a poly. Edges are placed on either side of a selected edge, equally spaced on both sides. For example, create a polygon sphere and select one of the vertical edges, as shown in Figure 4.42. Maya displays two dashed lines on either side of the selected edge. Drag the mouse to place the offset edge loops, and release the mouse button to create the two new edge loops.

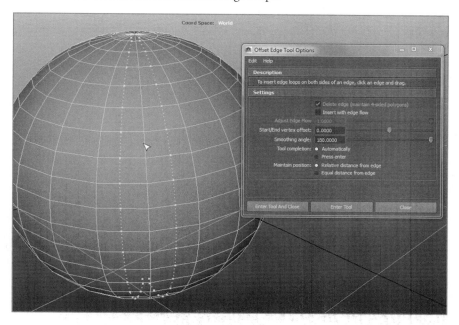

Figure 4.42

The Offset Edge Loop tool

The Offset Edge Loop tool is perfect for adding detail symmetrically on a surface quickly.

Modeling Toolkit Connect Tool

Very similar to the Insert Edge Loop tool is the Modeling Toolkit Connect function. While in Modeling Toolkit, simply select an edge, and click the Connect button in the Modeling Toolkit panel. This will create edges going around the object perpendicular to the selected edge. The Slide attribute places the perpendicular cut along the selected edge, which is slightly less interactive than Insert Edge Loop. However, the Segments attribute allows you to insert more than one ring of edges, while Pinch spaces those extra segments evenly (Figure 4.43).

Figure 4.43

Modeling Toolkit Connect tool creates edges much like Insert Edge Loop.

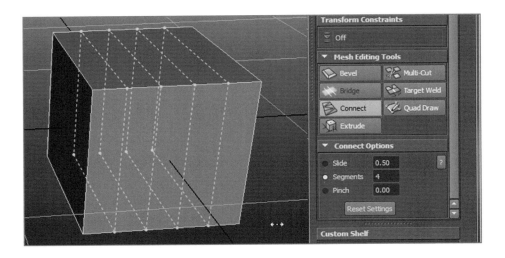

Modeling Toolkit Raycast Selection and Bridge Tool

One of Modeling Toolkit's nicest features is its Raycast selection mode. This allows you to essentially "paint" the components you want to select with your cursor instead of having to click every component.

Try This

1. Create a cube in an empty scene, and set Subdivisions Width to **1**, Subdivisions Height to **4**, and Subdivisions Depth to **5**, as shown in Figure 4.44. Figure 4.44 is shown in X-Ray mode, which is enabled in the Perspective panel's menu bar by choosing Shading → X-Ray.

Figure 4.44

Create a subdivided box.

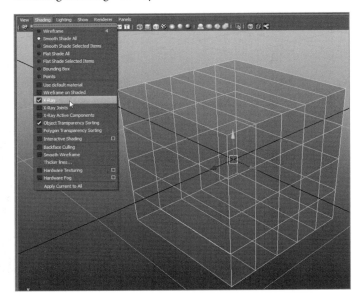

2. You are going to delete a square shape out of the front and back of the box. Exit X-Ray view mode (view panel menu: Shading → X-Ray).

3. Make sure the Modeling Toolkit icon in the status bar is enabled. Enter into face selection mode through the marking menu.

4. In the Modeling Toolkit panel, select the Raycast option under the transformation icons, as shown in Figure 4.45. Your selection cursor changes to a circle. Click one of the inside faces, and drag along a six-face square in the middle of the front of the cube, also in Figure 4.45.

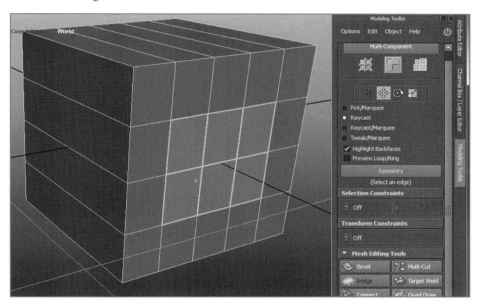

Figure 4.45

Raycast+select a six-face square on the front of the box.

5. Orbit your view to see the back of the box, hold down Shift, and Raycast+select the same six-face square on the back of the box.

6. Press Delete on your keyboard to delete the 12 selected faces, leaving you with a hollow box, as shown in Figure 4.46.

7. Now you're going to "fill in" the box to make a square-shaped tube. Switch to edge selection, and select the Pick/Marquee option in the Modeling Toolkit panel (it's right above the Raycast option). Click to select the two front and back edges shown in Figure 4.47 (left).

8. In the Modeling Toolkit panel, click Bridge, and two new faces will appear connecting the selected edges (Figure 4.47, right). Exit the Bridge tool.

Figure 4.46

Delete the square shapes out of the box.

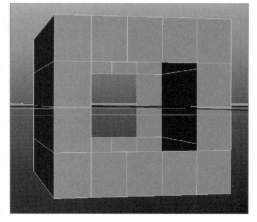

Figure 4.47

Select these edges (left), and bridge them (right).

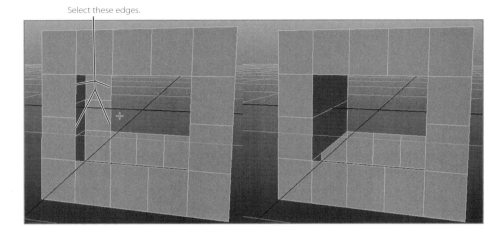

9. Repeat steps 7 and 8 on the bottom three edges to connect the bottom, as shown in Figure 4.48.

Figure 4.48

Bridge the bottom faces.

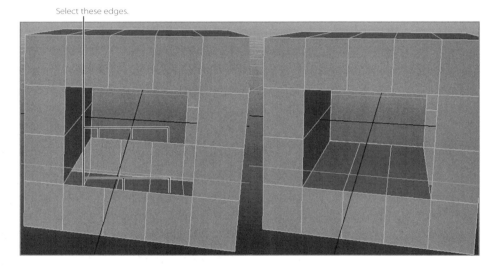

10. Repeat for the remaining edges to fill the holes making a square pipe that is now solid on the inside.

Experiment with the Divisions attribute for the Modeling Toolkit Bridge to get a curvature in the bridged faces.

Modeling Toolkit Symmetry Selections

One of the charms of Modeling Toolkit is its ability to select in symmetry, meaning the components you select on one side of a surface are automatically selected on the other side as well, making modeling appreciably faster. While Maya has its own Reflection feature in the transformation tools (Move, Rotate, Scale) covered in Chapter 3, it is limited to simple transforms. Tools such as Extrude or Bevel will not work in Reflection mode. Let's see how Modeling Toolkit Symmetry works.

Try This

1. Create a polygon sphere in a new scene. Enter **5** for Shaded view, and make sure Modeling Toolkit is enabled.

2. Select an edge on the sphere that you want to be the centerline for the symmetry.

3. In the Modeling Toolkit panel, check the Symmetry: Select Edge box. Once you do, the sphere's object name will display next to the check box, as shown in Figure 4.49.

4. Now enter face selection. As you move your mouse before you select, it is mirrored, and when you do select a face or faces, that selection will be mirrored on the other side of the mesh (Figure 4.50).

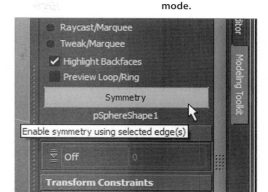

Figure 4.49

Turn on Symmetry mode.

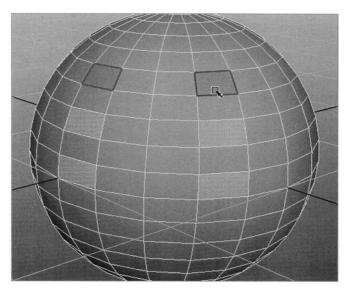

Figure 4.50

Selecting faces on one side selects them on the other.

Now if you engage any poly editing function, it will act on the symmetrically selected components.

Keep in mind that for Modeling Toolkit Symmetry to work, your mesh needs to be symmetrical itself. Uneven topology, where one side has a different number of faces than the other, will not work correctly.

The Combine and Merge Functions

The Combine function is important in cleaning up your model and creating a unified single mesh out of the many parts that form it. When modeling, you'll sometimes use several different polygon meshes and surfaces to generate your final shape. Using Combine, you can create a single polygonal object out of the pieces.

The Merge tool is important when you're creating a polygon model because it fuses multiple vertices at the same point into one vertex on the model. Frequently, when you're modeling a mesh, you'll need to fold over pieces and weld parts together. Doing so often leaves you with several vertices occupying the same space. Merging them simplifies the model and makes the mesh much nicer to work with, from rigging to rendering.

In the following simple example, you'll create two boxes that connect to each other along a common edge and then combine and merge them into one seamless polygonal mesh. To begin, follow these steps:

1. In a new scene, create two poly cubes, and place them apart from each other, more or less as shown in Figure 4.51.

2. Select the bottom edge of the cube on the right that faces the other cube, and choose Edit Mesh → Extrude. Pull the edge out a little to create a new face, as shown in Figure 4.52. This will be a flange connecting the two cubes. It isn't important how far you pull the edge out; you'll connect the two cubes by moving the vertices manually.

3. Select the first corner vertex on the newly extruded face, and snap it into place on the corner vertex of the other cube, as shown in Figure 4.53. Remember, you can click the Snap To Points icon (⬛) to snap the vertex onto the cube's corner.

4. Snap the other vertex to the opposite corner so that the cubes are connected with a flange along a common edge, as shown in Figure 4.54.

Figure 4.51

Place two polygonal cubes close to each other.

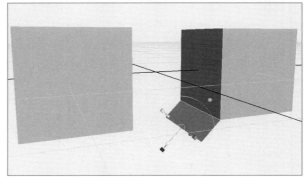

Figure 4.52

Extrude the bottom edge to create a flange.

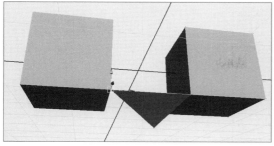

Figure 4.53

Snap the first corner vertex to the newly extruded face.

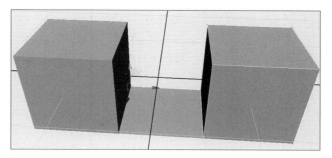

Figure 4.54

Snap the other corner vertex.

Even though the cubes seem to be connected at a common edge, they're still two separate polygonal meshes. You can easily select and move just one of the stacked vertices and disconnect the connective face of the two cubes. You need to merge the stacked vertices of the cubes into a single vertex. However, the Merge function won't work on vertices from two separate meshes; you must first combine the cubes into a single poly mesh. The following steps continue this task.

5. Select the two cubes (one has the extra flange on the bottom, of course), and choose Mesh → Combine. Doing so makes a single poly mesh out of the two cubes. You can now use the Merge function.

6. Even though the cubes are now one mesh, you still have two vertices at each of the connecting corners of the cube on the left. As you can see in Figure 4.55, you can disconnect the flange by selecting a single vertex at the corner and moving it. (Click the vertex to select just one. Don't use a marquee selection, because that will select both vertices at once.) If you move one of the corner vertices, press the Z key to undo and return the flange to its connected position.

7. To merge the vertices at the corners, select both the vertices at the near corner (you can use a marquee selection), and then choose Edit Mesh → Merge. The two vertices become one. Repeat the procedure for the far corner. Your connected cubes become a single mesh with no redundant vertices. As you can see in Figure 4.56, if you select a vertex at a corner and move it, the cube and the flange both move; there is no disconnect.

> To separate a combined mesh back into its component meshes, choose Mesh → Separate. But you can't use Separate if the mesh you've combined has merged vertices.

You'll notice fewer errors and issues with clean models when you animate, light, and render them. Combining meshes makes them easier to deal with, and Merge cuts down on unwanted vertices.

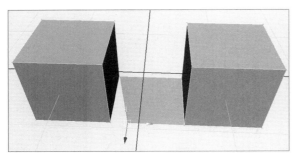

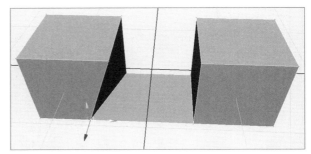

Figure 4.55

There are still two different vertices at the corner, and the boxes aren't really connected.

Figure 4.56

The cubes are now connected properly at the corners.

If the Merge function isn't working on vertices in your model, make sure the model is a single mesh.

The Cut Faces Tool

The Cut Faces tool lets you cut across a poly surface to create a series of edges for subdivisions, pull off a section of the poly, or delete a section (see Figure 4.57). Select the poly object, and choose Edit Mesh → Cut Faces Tool. Click the option box if you want to extract or delete the section.

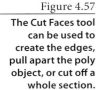

Figure 4.57

The Cut Faces tool can be used to create the edges, pull apart the poly object, or cut off a whole section.

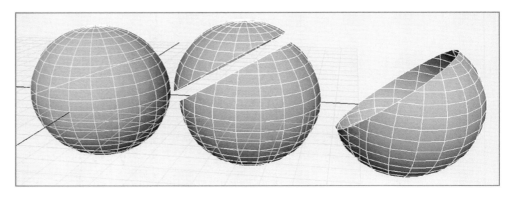

You can use the Cut Faces tool to create extra surface detail, to slice portions off the surface, or to create a straight edge on the model by trimming off the excess.

The Duplicate Face Tool

Select one or more faces, and choose Edit Mesh → Duplicate Face to create a copy of the selected face(s). You can use the Manipulator that appears to move, scale, or rotate your copied face(s).

The Extract Tool

The Extract tool is similar to the Extrude tool, but it doesn't create any extra faces. Select the face(s), and choose Mesh → Extract to pull the faces off the surface (see Figure 4.58). If the Separate Extracted Faces option is enabled, the extracted face will be a separate poly object; otherwise, it will remain part of the original.

This tool is useful for creating a new mesh from part of the original mesh you are extracting from. You can also use the Extract tool to create a hole in an object and still keep the original face(s). When you use this tool with the Interactive Split tool to make custom edges, you can create cutouts of almost any shape.

The Smooth Tool

The Smooth tool (choose Mesh → Smooth) evenly subdivides the poly surface or selected faces, creating several more faces to smooth and round out the original poly object.

The Sculpt Geometry Tool

You can use a Maya feature called *Artisan* to sculpt polygonal surfaces. Artisan is a painting system that allows you to paint attributes or influences directly onto an object. When you use Artisan through the Sculpt Geometry tool, you paint on a polygon surface to move the vertices in and out, essentially to mold the surface.

To access the tool in polygon modeling, select your poly object and choose Mesh → Sculpt Geometry Tool ❑.

For more on sculpting, see the section "Using Artisan to Sculpt NURBS" in Chapter 5, "Modeling with NURBS, Surfaces, and Deformers." The workflow is much the same as for sculpting with NURBS; the only difference when sculpting polygons is that the surface behaves in a slightly different manner when sculpted. If you create a poly with a large number of subdivisions, you'll have a smoother result when using the Sculpt Geometry tool (see Figure 4.59).

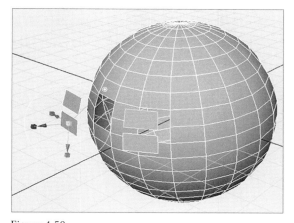

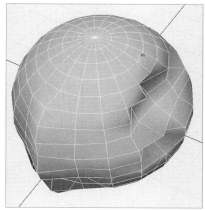

Figure 4.58
Pull off the faces.

Figure 4.59
The Sculpt Geometry tool deforms the surface.

Modeling a Catapult

This exercise will demonstrate the following polygonal modeling techniques:

- Extrusions and bevels
- Object duplication and mirror geometry
- Boolean operations
- Pivot placement
- The Insert Edge Loop tool
- CV curves and revolved surfaces
- Complex model hierarchy

You're going to create a catapult in this exercise using nothing but polygons. You'll use some sketches as a reference for the model. Since this is a more involved object than a hand, it's much better to start with good plans. This, of course, involves some research, web surfing, image gathering, or sketching to get a feel for what it truly is you're trying to make.

To begin, create a new project for all the files called Catapult, or copy the Catapult project from the companion website (www.sybex.com/go/introducingmaya2014) to your hard drive. If you do not create a new project, set your current project to the copied Catapult project on your drive. Choose File → Set Project, and select the Catapult project downloaded from the companion website. Remember that you can enable Incremental Save to make backups at any point in the exercise.

Now, on to modeling a design already sketched out for reference. To begin, study the design sketches included in the Sourceimages folder of the project. These sketches set up the intent rather easily.

In Chapter 8, "Introduction to Animation," you'll animate the catapult. When building any model, it's important to keep animation in mind, especially for grouping related objects in the scene hierarchy so that they will move as you intend. Creating a good scene hierarchy will be crucial to a smooth animation workflow, so throughout this exercise you'll use the Outliner to keep the catapult's component pieces organized as you create them.

The Production Process

The trick with a complex object model is to approach it part by part. Deconstruct the major elements of the original into distinct shapes that you can approach one by one. The catapult can be broken down to five distinct objects, each with its own subobjects:

- Base
- Wheels
- Fulcrum assembly
- Winch assembly
- Arm assembly

You will model each part separately based on the sketch in Figure 4.60 and the detailed schematic in Figure 4.61.

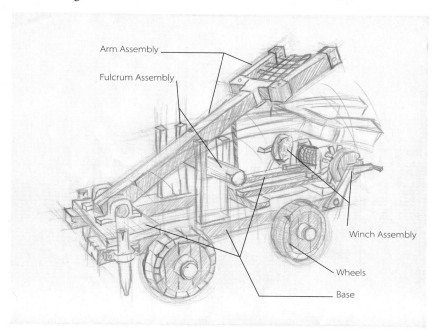

Arm Assembly

Fulcrum Assembly

Winch Assembly

Wheels

Base

Figure 4.60

A sketch of the catapult to model

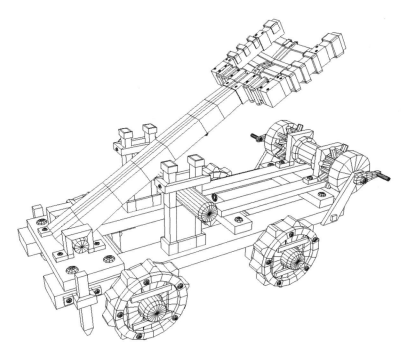

Figure 4.61

A schematic diagram of the finished model to show you your goal

The Base

The base consists of simple polygonal cubes representing timber and arranged to connect to each other. Keep in mind that in this exercise Interactive Creation for primitives is turned off (select Create → Polygon Primitives and make sure Interactive Creation is unchecked). Also, in the Perspective view, choose Shading → Wireframe On Shaded to turn on the wireframe lines while in Shaded mode to match the figures in this exercise.

Creating the Base Objects

To begin the catapult base, follow these steps:

1. Choose Create → Polygon Primitives → Cube to lay down your first cube. This will be for the two long, broad boards running alongside.

2. Scale the cube to 2.0 in *X*, 0.8 in *Y*, and 19.5 in *Z*. Move it off the center of the grid about two units to the right.

3. Now you'll add some detail to the simple cube by beveling the sides, using either Modeling Toolkit or traditional Bevel, as I will do here. Select the four edges running on top of the board. In the Main Menu bar, select Edit Mesh → Bevel ❑. Set Width to **0.1** and Segments to **2**, and click Apply. Figure 4.62 shows the resulting board.

4. Now select the remaining edges on the board, and bevel them to a Width of **0.5** and set Segments to **2**. See Figure 4.63. If you use Modeling Toolkit, enter an Offset value of **0.5** and a Segments value of **2**.

Figure 4.62

Create a bevel for the baseboard object.

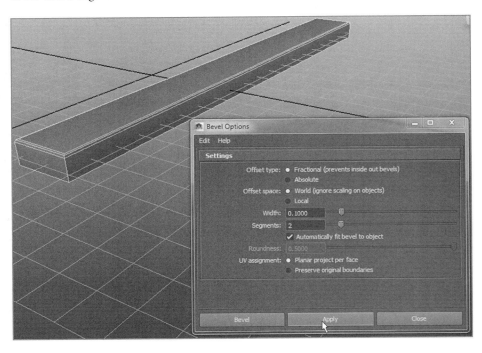

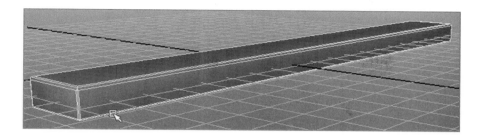

Figure 4.63

Beveling the bottom edges

Beveling the edges of your models can be an important detail. Light will pick up edges much better when they are beveled, even slightly. Perfect 90-degree corners can look too much like CG models and not real objects.

5. Select the board and choose Edit → Duplicate to place a copy of the board exactly where the original is in the scene. The new duplicated board is already selected for you, so just move the copy about 4 units to the left. You should now have something similar to Figure 4.64.

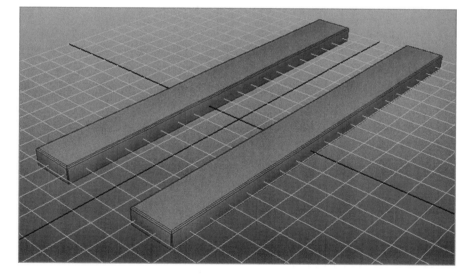

Figure 4.64

The long boards at the base

6. Now for the cross braces and platform. Create a poly cube and scale it 7.25 in *X*, 0.6 in *Y*, and 3.25 in *Z*. Place this platform on top of the two beams, at the end of the catapult's base.

7. With the first board that you beveled, you had a different bevel for the top edges than the bottom and sides. For this board, you'll have the same bevel width for all edges. Select the cube (not the edges as before), and choose Edit Mesh → Bevel ❑. Set Width to **0.2** and Segments to **2**, and click Bevel (or Apply). Figure 4.65 shows the platform board in place and beveled.

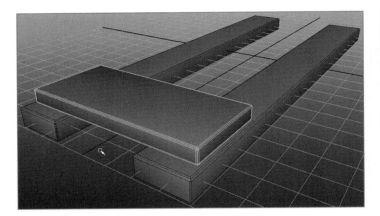

Figure 4.65

The platform board is in place.

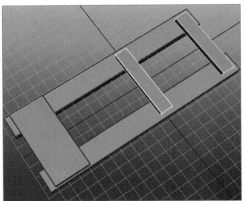

Figure 4.66

Cross bracing the base

8. Create a cube for the first of the top two cross braces, and scale it 6.5 in *X*, 0.6 in *Y*, and 1.2 in *Z*. Place it on top of the beams at the head of the base, and bevel this cube exactly as in the previous step.

9. Duplicate the cube, and move the copy about a third of the way down toward the end (Figure 4.66).

Using Booleans

You're going to add some detail as you go along, namely, the large screws that hold the timber together. The screws will basically be slotted screw heads placed at the intersection of the pieces. In this section, you will use Booleans to help create the screw heads.

Booleans are very impressive operations that allow you to, among other things, cut holes or shapes in a mesh fairly easily. Basically, a Boolean is a geometric operation that creates a shape from the addition of two shapes (Union), the subtraction of one shape from another (Difference), or the common intersection of two shapes (Intersection).

Be forewarned, however, that Boolean operations can be problematic. Sometimes you get a result that is wrong—or, even worse, the entire mesh disappears and you have to undo. Use Booleans sparingly and only on a mesh that is clean and prepared. You've cleaned and prepped your panel mesh, so there should be no problems. (Actually, there will be a problem—but that's half the fun of learning, so let's get on with it.)

First, you need to create the rounded screw head.

1. Create a polygonal sphere (Create → Polygon Primitives → Sphere) and move it from the origin off to the side in the *X*-axis of the base model. Scale the sphere down to 0.15 in *XYZ*.

2. With the sphere still selected, switch to the front view, and press F to frame. Right-click the sphere, and select Face from the marking menu (Figure 4.67). Select the bottom half of the sphere's faces, and press Delete on your keyboard to make a hemi-sphere (Figure 4.68).

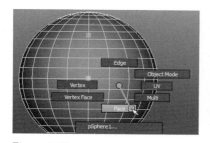

Figure 4.67

Use the marking menu to set the selection to Face.

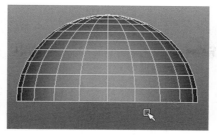

Figure 4.68

Delete the bottom half of the faces.

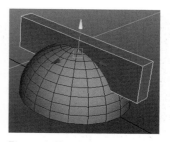

Figure 4.69

Place the scaled cube over the screw head.

3. Right-click the hemisphere, and select Object Mode from the marking menu; this exits face selection mode. Create a poly cube, and scale it to 0.4, 0.1, 0.04. Place it over the hemisphere as shown in Figure 4.69.

Now you have both objects that you need for a Boolean operation, and they are placed properly to create a slot in the top of the screw head.

4. Select the hemisphere and then the cube set into it. Select Mesh → Booleans → Difference (Figure 4.70). The cube disappears, and the screw head is left with a slot in the top, as shown in Figure 4.71.

Ngons!

Now if you take a good close look at the screw head, especially where the slot is, you will notice faces that have more than four sides, which makes them Ngons. As I noted earlier in the chapter, faces that have more than four edges may be problematic with further modeling or rendering. This simple screw head most likely will not pose any problems

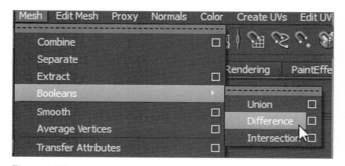

Figure 4.70

Selecting a Difference Boolean

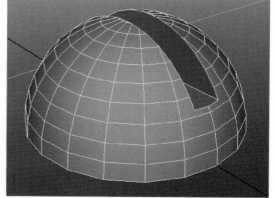

Figure 4.71

The screw head is slotted.

in the application here, but let's go over how to prevent any problems early on. You will select the potential problem faces (those around the slot) and triangulate them.

1. Select all the faces around the slot, as shown in Figure 4.72 (left). Choose Mesh → Triangulate. This is the easiest and fastest way to subdivide these faces from being Ngons without having to use Interactive Split to manually fix them. And although it may not look as clean as before (Figure 4.72, right), the geometry is clean and will not be a potential problem like Ngons would be.

Figure 4.72

Select the faces around the slot (left), and triangulate them (right).

2. Select the screw head, and choose Edit → Delete By Type → History. This cleans out any history on the object now that you're satisfied with it.

3. Notice that the screw head's pivot point is at the origin. With the object selected, choose Modify → Center Pivot.

4. Name the object **ScrewHead** and position it at one of the intersections of the boards you've built so far.

5. Duplicate that first screw head and place the copies one by one at all the other intersections on the base, as shown in Figure 4.73. These are pretty big screws, huh? For this simple catapult, they'll do fine. The workflow to make more realistic screws is the same if you want to make this again with more realism and scale.

6. Now take the objects in the scene and group them into a logical order, as shown in the Outliner in Figure 4.73.

Save your file, and compare it to `catapult_v1.mb` in the Catapult project from the companion website to see what the completed base should look like.

The time you spend keeping your scene objects organized now will pay off later when you animate the catapult in Chapter 8.

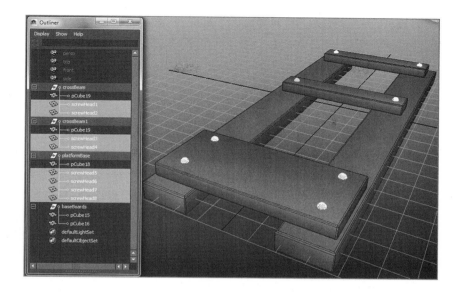

Figure 4.73

Place the screw heads on the base and organize your scene.

The Winch Baseboards

Next to model for the base are the bars that hold the winch assembly to the base. Refer to the sketch of the catapult (Figure 4.60) to refresh yourself on the layout of the catapult and its pieces. Follow these steps:

1. Create two long, narrow, beveled poly cubes for the baseboards of the winch, and position them across the top two side braces. Put a couple of screws on the middle crossbeam (see Figure 4.74).

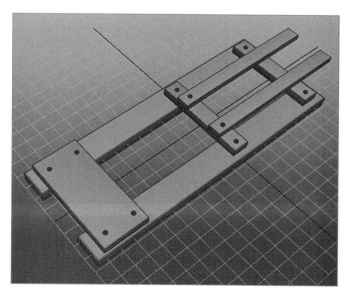

Figure 4.74

Adding the winch baseboards

2. For the brackets that hold down the winch, create a small poly cube, and move it off to the side of the base to get it out of the way. Scale the cube to 0.5, 0.3, 0.45. Enable Modeling Toolkit, select the side face, and click the Extrude button in the Modeling Toolkit panel. Type **0.8** for the Local Z attribute, and click the Extrude button off to commit the extrusion, as shown in Figure 4.75.

Figure 4.75

**Modeling Toolkit
Extrude the face.**

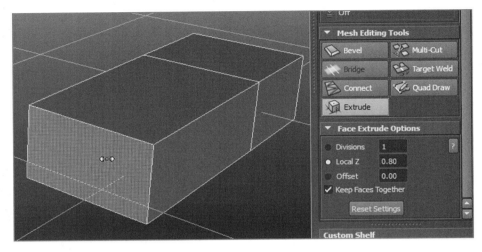

3. Select the top face of the original cube, and Modeling Toolkit Extrude it to a Local Z of **1.54** to take it up to an L shape. Select the two inside vertices on the top of the *L*, and move them up to create about a 45-degree angle at the tip, as shown in Figure 4.76.

4. Select that angled face, and select Edit Mesh → Extrude for a Maya extrusion. Click the cyan-colored switch icon above the Extrude Manipulator (shown next to the cursor in Figure 4.77, left). This will switch the extrusion axis (Figure 4.77, center) so you can pull the faces out straight and not angled up. Then grab the *Z* Move Manipulator and pull the extrusion out about 0.75 units.

5. Press W to exit the Extrude tool and enter Rotate. Select the end face and rotate it to make it flat vertically, and scale it down in *Y*-axis to prevent it from flaring upward (Figure 4.77 right).

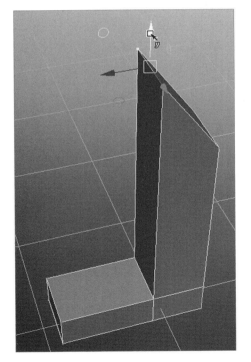

Figure 4.76

**Modeling Toolkit Extrude the top out to create an L shape;
then move the vertices up to angle the top of the *L*.**

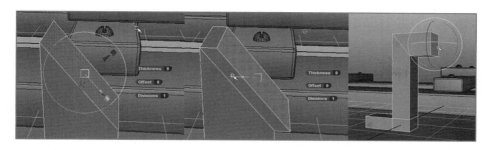

Figure 4.77

Click the switch icon (left) to switch the axis of extrusion (center). Rotate and scale the face to square it (right).

6. This shape forms half of the braces you need. To create the other half, select the face shown in Figure 4.78 (left) and delete it (press Delete). Enter Object mode, select the mesh, and choose Mesh → Mirror Geometry ❑. Set Mirror Direction to -Z, and leave the options as shown in Figure 4.78 (right). Click Mirror, and you will have a full bracket.

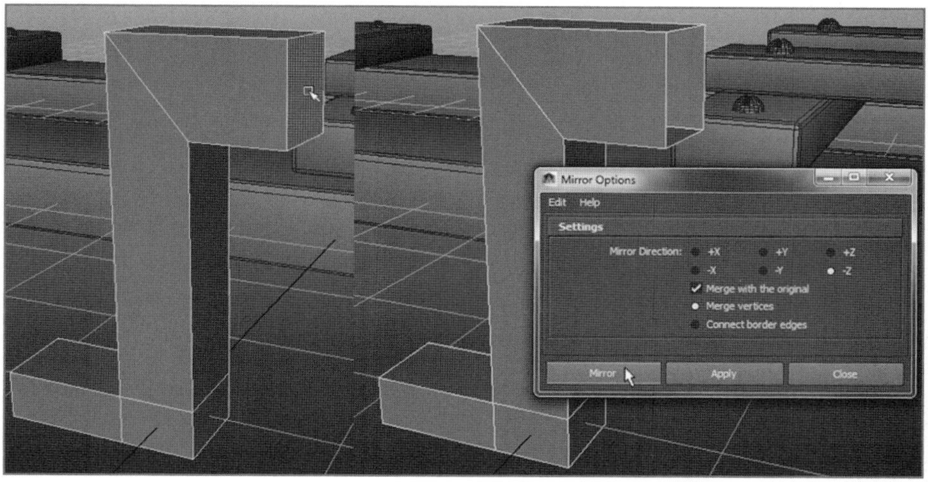

Figure 4.78

Delete the face (left), and set the Mirror Geometry options (right).

7. Name the object **bracket**, and move it on top of one of the baseboards for the winch; then place a duplicated screw head on the flanges of the bracket. Group the bracket and screw heads together by selecting them and choosing Edit → Group; call the group **bracketGroup**.

8. Duplicate bracketGroup, and move the copy to the other baseboard, as shown in Figure 4.79. Organize your scene as shown in the Outliner in Figure 4.79.

Figure 4.79

The winch's base completed

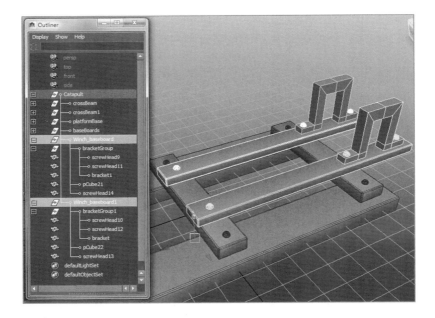

Figure 4.80

MMB dragging the duplicated bracketGroup to another location in the Outliner removes the group from the Winch_baseboard1 group.

The Ground Spikes

The last items you need for the base are the spikes that secure the base into the ground at the foot of the catapult. Follow these steps:

1. Duplicate a bracket group, and name it **bracketGroupCOPY**. Remove the group from its current hierarchy (the baseboard group) by MMB dragging it to another location in the Outliner. (See Figure 4.80.) Center its pivot (Modify → Center Pivot).

2. Move the bracket to the other side of the base. Rotate it on its side, scale it to about half its size in all three axes, and place it as shown in Figure 4.81 (left). Select the top vertices and move them closer to the base, as shown in Figure 4.81 (right).

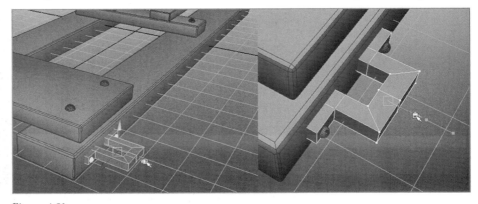

Figure 4.81

Position and scale the bracket assembly for the ground spikes (left). Move the vertices to reduce the depth (right).

3. Now for the spike itself. Create a poly cube, and position and scale it to fit through the bracket. Scale the spike cube to about 3.5 in the *Y*-axis. Select the bottom face of the spike cube, and choose Edit Mesh → Extrude. Click the Thickness helper, and type in a Thickness of **0.5** and an Offset of **0.15**, as shown in Figure 4.82. Click in an empty area to commit the extrusion. You can also use Modeling Toolkit to create the extruded spike.

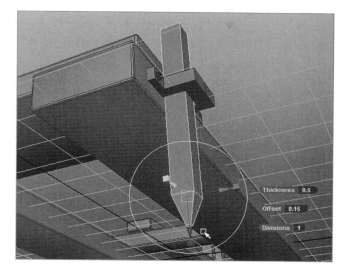

Figure 4.82

Creating the spike.

4. Bevel the spike if you'd like. Then select the `spike` and `bracketGroupCOPY` and group them together, calling the new group **stakeGroup**; center its pivot.

5. Duplicate the stake group, and move and rotate it 180 degrees in the *Y*-axis to fit to the other side of the base. Organize everything into a parent Catapult group (see Figure 4.83), and save your scene as a new version.

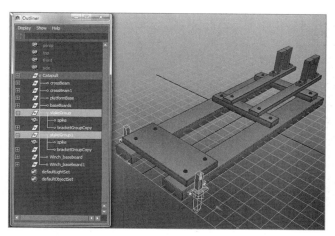

Figure 4.83

The completed base

The scene file `catapult_v2.mb` in the Catapult project from the companion website has the completed base for comparison.

The Wheels

What's a catapult if you can't move it around to vanquish your enemies? So now, you will create the wheels. Follow these steps:

1. First is the axle. Create a polygon cylinder (Create → Polygon Primitives → Cylinder), and then scale, rotate, and place it as shown in Figure 4.84 to be the rear axle.

2. Duplicate one of the stake assembly's bracket groups (`bracketGroupCOPY`) two times; then move and scale each of the two copies to hold the axle on either side. Move down the top vertices of the bracket to make the bracket fit snugly around the axle as needed, as in Figure 4.85. Remember to move the duplicated brackets out of their existing hierarchy in the `stakeGroups`. Group both the axle brackets together, and name the group **Axle_Brackets**. You are not grouping the brackets with the axle cylinder. Keep them separate. You'll organize the hierarchy better a little later.

3. To make the axle a little more interesting, let's add a taper at the ends. You will insert new edges around the ends by using Insert Edge Loop, which will be much faster than the Interactive Split tool in this case. Select the rear axle cylinder, and choose Edit Mesh → Insert Edge Loop Tool. Your cursor turns into a triangle. Select one of the horizontal edges on the cylinder toward one end, as shown in Figure 4.86. A dashed line will appear running vertically around the cylinder. Drag the cursor to place the dashed line as shown in Figure 4.86, and release the mouse button to commit the new edges to that location. Repeat the procedure for the other side.

4. Select the end cap faces and scale them down on each side of the axle cylinder, as shown in Figure 4.87, to create tapered ends. Name the cylinder **rearAxle**. Now you're ready for the rear wheels.

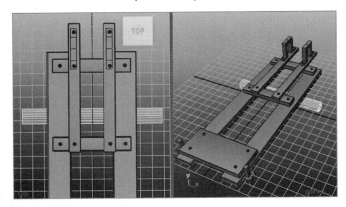

Figure 4.84

Place the rear axle.

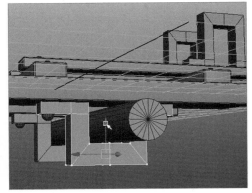

Figure 4.85

Place brackets to hold the rear axle, and adjust the vertices to make it fit.

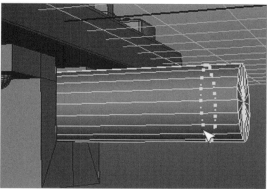

Figure 4.86

Insert an edge loop around the end of the cylinder.

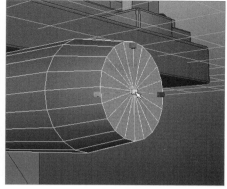

Figure 4.87

Taper the ends of the axle.

5. To model a wheel, first you'll use NURBS curves to lay out a profile to revolve. Go into the front view. Choose Create → CV Curve Tool ❐, and select 1 Linear for Curve Degree. Since the wheel's profile will have no smooth curves, you can create a linear CV curve like that in Figure 4.88. It's important for the design to create three spans for the top part of the curve. Place the pivot point (hold down the D key, or press Insert on a PC or Home on a Mac) about 3/4 of a unit below the curve as shown. This curve will be the profile of the front of the wheel.

6. Place the profile above the rear axle. To make sure the pivot point for the profile lines up with the center of the axle, turn on Snap To Points (a.k.a. Point Snap) (), and press and hold down D to move the pivot. Snap the pivot to the center of the axle, as shown in Figure 4.89. Turn off the Point Snap.

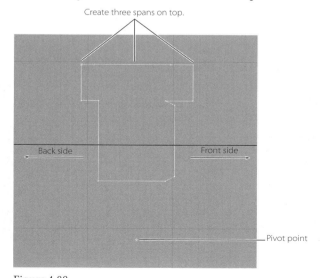

Figure 4.88

The profile curve for the wheel

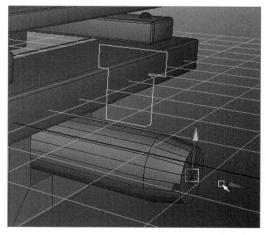

Figure 4.89

The profile curve is in place for the rear wheel.

Figure 4.90

**Switch to the
Surfaces menu set.**

7. Switch to the Surfaces menu set (Figure 4.90). Select the curve and revolve it by choosing Surfaces → Revolve ❑. In the option box, set Axis Preset to X to make it revolve correctly. Change Segments from the default 8 to **20** to give a smoother wheel. Set Output Geometry to Polygons, and set Tessellation Method to Control Points. This will create the edges of the faces along the CV points on the curve. Click Revolve, and there it is (Figure 4.91).

8. Select the wheel object and bevel it. With the wheel still selected, delete the history and the original NURBS curve since you won't need either again.

9. Next, add some detail to the wheel. Duplicate a screw head, and remove the copy from whatever group it was in by MMB dragging it out of the current group in the Outliner. Arrange a few of the screw heads around the front face of the wheel.

10. Add a couple of braces on the front of the wheel above and below the wheel's middle hole with two thin, stretched, and beveled poly cubes, with screws on either side. Again, make sure to remove the duplicated screw heads from whatever group you got them from, as shown in Figure 4.92.

11. Select all the objects of the wheel, group them together by pressing Ctrl+G, and call the group **wheel**. Center the wheel group's pivot point by choosing Modify → Center Pivot.

Figure 4.91

The wheel revolved

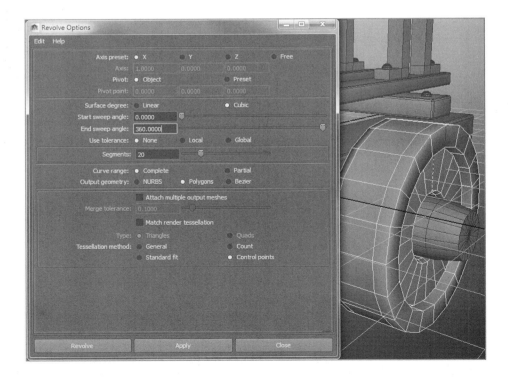

12. Adding studs to the wheel makes for better traction when moving the catapult through mud and also for a cooler-looking catapult. To create all the studs at once, grab every other middle face along the outside of the wheel and extrude them with a Thickness of -**0.3** and an Offset of **0.1**, as shown in Figure 4.93. You can use Modeling Toolkit Extrude instead to make the same extrusions if you prefer.

13. Copy the wheel group and rotate it 180 in the *Y*-axis to create the other rear wheel for the other side. Position it on the other side of the rear axle.

14. Group the two wheels with the rear axle, and call the new group node **Rear_Wheel**.

15. Select the Rear_Wheel node and the Axle_Brackets group node, and duplicate them by choosing Edit → Duplicate or by pressing the hot-key Ctrl+D. Move the objects to the foot of the catapult for the front wheels. Rename the wheel group node **Front_Wheel**.

16. Add the new axle bracket and wheel group nodes to the Catapult top node by MMB dragging them onto the Catapult node in the Outliner; save your scene. Figure 4.94 shows the positions and Outliner hierarchy of the wheels.

The file catapult_v3.mb in the Catapult project from the companion website reflects the finished wheels and base.

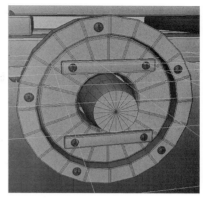

Figure 4.92
Adding detail to the wheel

Figure 4.93
Extrude out studs for the wheel.

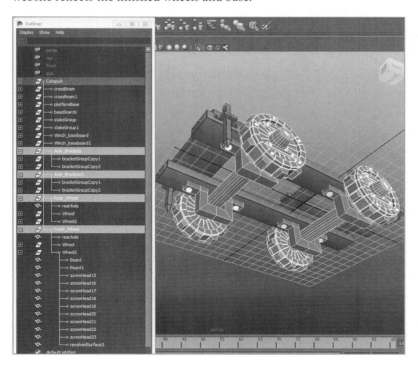

Figure 4.94
The wheels and brackets are positioned, and the hierarchy is organized.

The Winch Assembly

To be able to pull the catapult arm down to cock it to fire a projectile, you'll need the winch assembly to wind a rope that connects to the arm to wind it down into firing position. Since animating a rope can be a rather involved and advanced technique, the catapult will not actually be built with a rope. To build the winch assembly, follow these steps:

1. The first part of the winch is the pulley around which the rope winds. In the front view panel, create a profile curve for extrusion as you did with the wheel that looks more or less like the profile curve in Figure 4.95. In this figure, the first CV of the profile curve is on the left end of the curve. Place the pivot point of the curve at that first CV. Revolve the curve around the X-axis with only 12 segments (as opposed to the wheel's 20). Center its pivot, and you have the pulley.

2. Position the pulley at the rear of the catapult, placing the brackets in the grooves (see Figure 4.96).

3. Now you'll need some sort of geared wheel and handle to crank the pulley. Create a poly cylinder, and rotate it so it's on its side like one of the wheels. Scale it to a squat disk with scale values of **1.4** in the X- and Z-axes and **0.4** in the Y-axis. Select the disk and bevel it.

4. Off on the side of your scene, create another poly cylinder, and rotate it to its side as well. Scale it to be a long, thin stick. You'll use this as the first of eight gear teeth for the wheel. Position it at the top of the wheel as shown in Figure 4.97. Click the Snap To Points icon in the Status line (⬛), and snap the pivot point (press D to move the pivot) to the center of the wheel. Turn off Snap To Points.

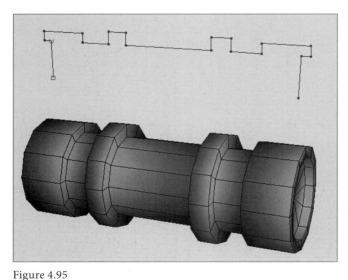

Figure 4.95

Create a profile curve and revolve it to create the object seen below the profile curve.

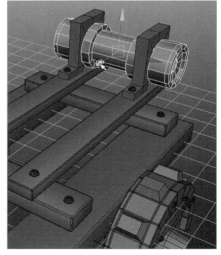

Figure 4.96

Place the pulley.

5. Instead of duplicating the gear tooth and positioning it seven more times, you'll use the array capabilities of the Duplicate Special tool. Select the tooth, and choose Edit → Duplicate Special ❏. In the option box, set Rotate to **45** in the *X*-axis, and set Number Of Copies to **7**. Since the pivot for the tooth is at the center of the wheel, as soon as you click the Duplicate Special button, Maya places seven copies around the wheel at 45-degree intervals (Figure 4.98).

6. Now for the handle, create a poly cube with enough segments for you to adjust vertices and faces to match the handle shown in Figure 4.99. Create cylinders for the crank axle and handle, and place them as shown. Group all the parts together, and snap the pivot point to the center of the gear wheel disk. Name the group **handle**. You can bevel the handle if you want.

7. Group the geometry together, call the object **Turn_Wheel**, and center its pivot. Place it at the end of the pulley. Place a copy (rotated 180 degrees) on the other side of the pulley. Figure 4.100 shows the placement.

8. Now you'll need gear teeth on the pulley cylinder shape. Create a poly cylinder to be a long, thin tube like the gear teeth, and position it at the end of the pulley. Place it so that it is in between two of the turning wheel gear teeth. Place the pivot at the center of the pulley using Snap To Points.

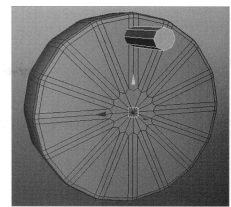

Figure 4.97

Making a gear wheel

Figure 4.98

Eight gear teeth in place

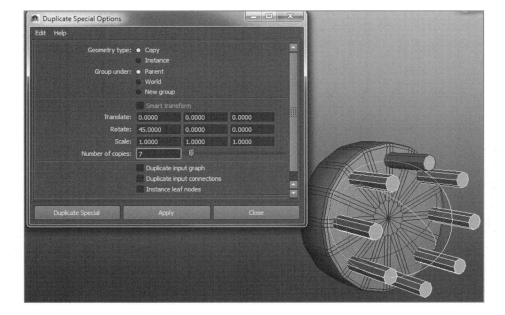

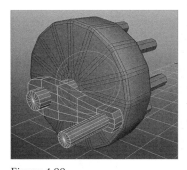

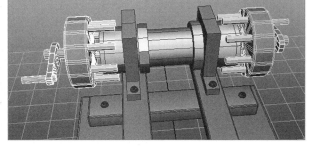

Figure 4.99

Use two cylinders and a poly cube to create the handle shapes.

Figure 4.100

Place the turn wheels.

9. Duplicate the new tooth seven times around the pulley at 45-degree intervals with Duplicate Special.

10. Make a copy of each of those eight teeth, and move the copies to the other side of the pulley for the other gear. Group the pulley and turning wheels together, and name the object **Winch**, as shown in Figure 4.101. Center the pivot.

11. Using a couple of poly cubes that you shape by moving vertices, make a winch arm on either side to brace the winch to the catapult. Bevel the shapes when you are happy with their shapes. Place the braces between the crank handle and the turning wheel on both sides, and bolt them to the catapult's base, as shown in Figure 4.102. Group them and add them to the hierarchy as shown. Save your scene file.

Figure 4.101

The winch gears and handles

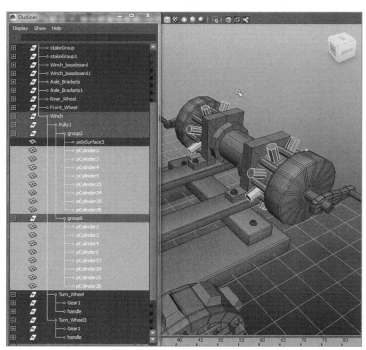

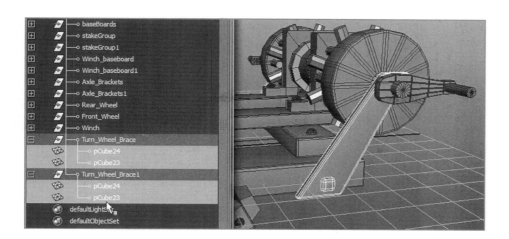

Figure 4.102
The assembled winch

To verify your work up to this point, compare it to `catapult_v4.mb` in the Catapult project from the companion website.

The Arm

OK, now I'm kicking you out of the nest to fly on your own! Try creating the arm (see Figure 4.103), without step-by-step instruction, using all the techniques you've learned and the following hints and diagrams:

- Create the intricate-looking arm with face extrusions. That's all you'll need for the arm geometry. Follow Figure 4.104 for subdivision positions to make the extrusions work correctly.

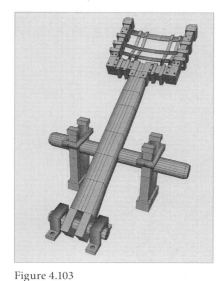

Figure 4.103

The catapult arm assembly

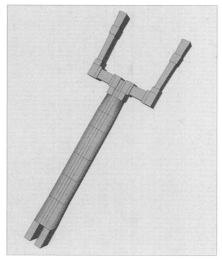

Figure 4.104

Follow the subdivisions on your model.

- Duplicate and place screw heads around the basket assembly, as shown in Figure 4.105.

Figure 4.105

Place screw heads around the basket arms.

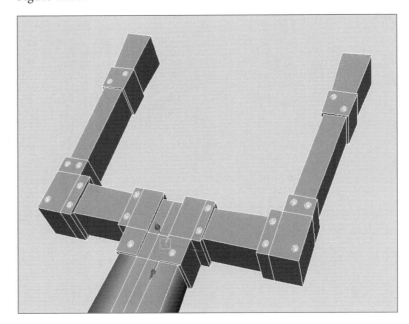

- Create the straps for the basket with poly cubes. It's easier than it looks. You'll just need to create and extrude the cubes with enough subdivisions to allow you to bend them to weave them together, as shown in Figure 4.106. The ends of the straps wrap around the arm's basket with extrusions.

Figure 4.106

Basket straps

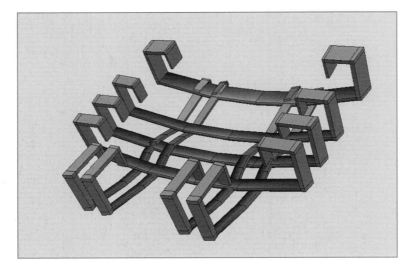

- Create the hinge for the arm with a couple of duplicated brackets and a cylinder.
- Create the arm's stand with multiple extrusions from a cube. Follow the subdivisions in Figure 4.107 for reference.

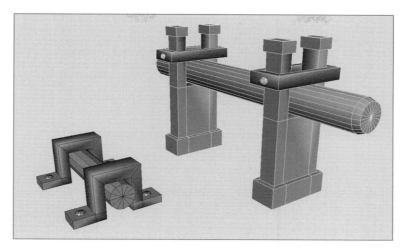

Figure 4.107

Follow the subdivisions on the arm stand.

- Bevel the parts you feel could use some nice edging, including the arm and stand pieces.
- Group the objects together and add their groups to the Catapult node.

When you've finished, save your scene file and compare it to catapult_v5.mb in the Catapult project from the companion website. Figure 4.108 shows the finished catapult.

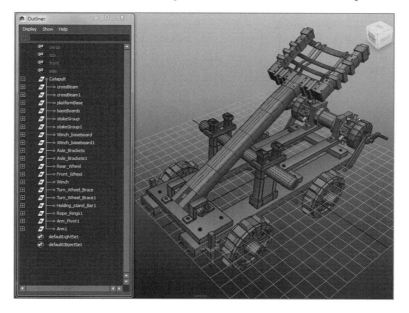

Figure 4.108

The completed catapult

Suggestions for Modeling Polygons

Poly modeling lends itself nicely to a wide range of objects—practically anything you can think of and some things you can't. Try modeling the following objects to fine-tune your skills and explore the tool set:

Dining Room Table and Chairs   This is an easy place to start. There is good amount of leeway in the design, which will give you as much of a challenge as you feel you can handle.

Computer Monitor   With all its angles and overall surface details, a monitor makes for a great extrusion and face-editing exercise.

Desk Lamp or Floor Lamp   This can be a quick exercise, so try to keep it highly detailed.

Car   This exercise can be a real challenge, so keep it simple at first and increase the amount of detail the next time. Try to keep your model to the overall shape of the car, and don't worry about making doors and windows that actually operate. Try to model the faces so that different parts of the car have different faces. Use NURBS surface tools to create poly patches to form the body of the car.

Summary

In this chapter, you learned about the basic modeling workflows with Maya and Modeling Toolkit and how best to approach a model. This chapter dealt with polygon modeling and covered several polygon creation and editing tools, as well as several polygon subdivision tools. You put those tools to good use by building a hand and smoothing it out, as well as making a model of an old-fashioned catapult using traditional Maya workflows as well as new Modeling Toolkit workflows. The latter exercise stressed the importance of putting a model together step-by-step and understanding how elements join together to form a whole in a proper hierarchy. You'll have a chance to make another model of that kind in Chapter 6, when you create a child's table lamp that is used to light and render later in the book.

Complex models become much easier to create when you recognize how to deconstruct them into their base components. You can divide even simple objects into more easily managed segments from which you can create a model.

The art of modeling with polygons is like anything else in Maya: your technique and workflow will improve with practice and time. It's less important to know all the tricks of the trade than it is to know how to approach a model and fit it into a wireframe mesh.

CHAPTER 5

Modeling with NURBS Surfaces and Deformers

As you read in the previous chapter, NURBS is based on organic mathematics, which means you can create smooth curves and surfaces. NURBS models can be made of a single surface molded to fit, or they can be a collection of patches connected like a quilt. In any event, NURBS provides ample power for creating smooth surfaces for your models.

Now that you've learned the basics of creating and editing poly meshes, getting into NURBS models and more advanced modeling techniques will more easily become part of your toolbox. This chapter explains how to use deformations to adjust a model, as opposed to editing the geometry directly as you did with the previous modeling methods.

Learning Outcomes: In this chapter, you will be able to

- Use the surfacing techniques to create surfaces: Loft, Set Planar, Revolve
- Convert NURBS geometry into polygons
- Create polygon meshes directly from NURBS techniques
- Model an organic shape using NURBS patches
- Create edits to existing models using lattices

NURBS! NURBS!

NURBS is an acronym for *Non-Uniform Rational B-Spline*. That's good to know for cocktail parties. NURBS models are typically used for applications in which the rendering is done in advance, such as animation for film or television. NURBS modeling excels at creating curved shapes and lines, so it's most often used for organic forms such as animals and people, as well as highly detailed cars. These organic shapes are typically created with a quilt of NURBS surfaces, called *patches*. Patch modeling can be powerful for creating complex shapes such as characters, but can also be tedious and sometimes difficult.

In essence, Bézier curves are created with a starting and an ending *control vertex* (CV) and usually two or more CVs in between that provide the curvature. As each CV is laid down, the curve or spline tries to go from the previous CV to the next one in the smoothest possible manner.

As shown in Figure 5.1, CVs control the curvature. The *hulls* connect the CVs and are useful for selecting multiple rows of CVs at a time. The starting CV appears in Autodesk® Maya® as a closed box. The second CV, which defines the curve's direction, is an open box, so you can easily see the direction in which a curve has been created. The curve ends, of course, on the endpoint CV. The start and end CVs are the only CVs that are always actually on the curve.

Figure 5.1

A Bézier curve and its components

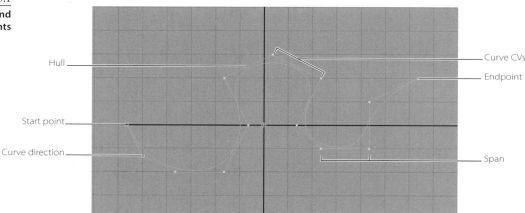

NURBS Modeling

NURBS surfaces are defined by curves called *isoparms*, which are created with CVs. The surface is created between these isoparms to form *spans* that follow the surface curvature defined by the isoparms, as in Figure 5.2. The more spans, the greater the detail and control over the surface—but this added detail makes greater demands on the computer, especially during rendering.

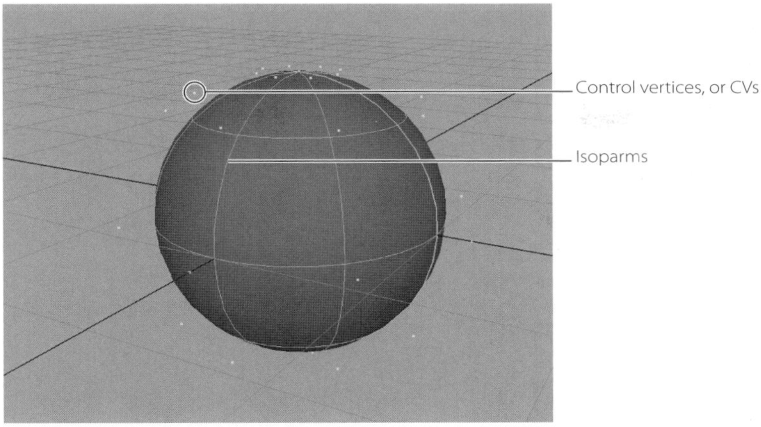

Figure 5.2

NURBS surfaces are created between isoparms. You can sculpt them by moving their CVs.

Control vertices, or CVs

Isoparms

It's easier to get a smooth deformation on a NURBS surface with few CVs. Achieving the same smooth look on a polygon would take much more surface detail. As you can see in Figure 5.3, NURBS modeling yields a smoother deformation, whereas polygons can become jagged at the edges.

Figure 5.3

A NURBS cylinder (left) and a polygonal cylinder (right) bent into a C shape. The NURBS cylinder remains smooth, and the polygon cylinder shows its edges.

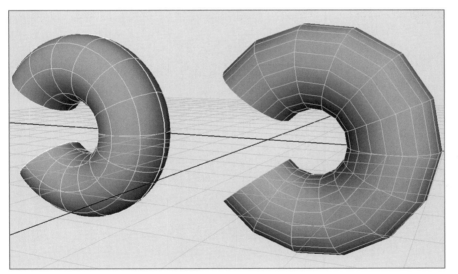

If your model requires smooth curves and organic shapes, use NURBS. You can convert NURBS to polygons at any time, but converting back to NURBS can be tricky.

Try This Open a new scene (choose File → New Scene). In the new scene, you'll create a few curves on the ground plane grid in the perspective (persp) panel. Maximize the perspective view by moving your cursor to it and pressing the spacebar. Choose Create → CV

Curve Tool. Your cursor turns into a cross. Lay down a series of points to define a curved line on the grid. Notice how the Bézier curve is created between the CVs as they're laid down.

> *Spans* are isoparms that run horizontally in a NURBS surface; *sections* are isoparms that run vertically in the object.

NURBS surfaces are created by connecting (or *spanning*) curves. Typical NURBS modeling pipelines first involve the creation of curves that define the edges, outline, paths, and/or boundaries of surfaces.

A surface's shape is defined by its isoparms. These surface curves, or curves that reside solely on a surface, show the outline of a surface's shape much as the chicken wire in a wire mesh sculpture does. CVs on the isoparms define and govern the shape of these isoparms just as they would regular curves. Adjusting a NURBS surface involves manipulating the CVs of the object.

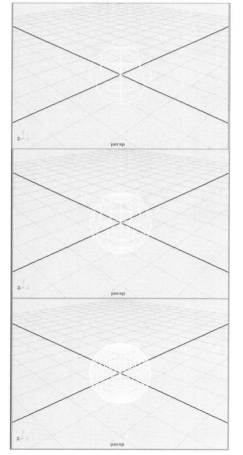

Figure 5.4

The degrees of NURBS display smoothness

Levels of Detail

NURBS is a type of surface in Maya that lets you adjust its detail level at any time to become more or less defined as needed. The display detail keys (1, 2, 3) adjust the level of NURBS detail shown in the panels only.

Press 2, and you'll see the wireframe mesh get denser. Press 3, and the mesh will get even denser. You can view all NURBS objects, such as this sphere, in three levels of display. Pressing 1, 2, or 3 toggles between detail levels for any selected NURBS object, as shown in Figure 5.4.

NURBS Surfacing Techniques

The easiest way to create a NURBS surface is to create a NURBS primitive. You can sculpt the primitive surface by moving its CVs, but you can also cut it apart to create different surface swatches or patches to use as needed, which you'll see in a steam pump model for an old-fashioned steam locomotive later in this chapter. Using the surfacing tools available under the Surfaces menu set, you can detach, cut, and attach pieces into and out of a primitive to get the exact shapes you need.

You can also make surfaces in several ways without using a primitive. All these methods involve first creating or using existing NURBS curves, or curves on another surface, to define a part or parts of the surface, and then using one of the methods described in the following sections to create the surfaces.

The newly integrated Modeling Toolkit suite and its workflow does not apply to NURBS modeling, because it is strictly a polygon toolset only.

Lofting

The most common surfacing method is *lofting*, which takes at least two curves and creates a surface span between each selected curve in the order in which they're selected. Figure 5.5 shows the result of lofting two curves together.

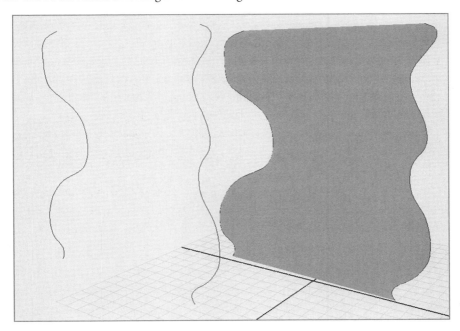

Figure 5.5

A simple loft created between two curves

To create a loft, follow these steps:

1. Switch to the Surfaces menu set (press F4).
2. Draw the two curves.
3. Select the curves in the order in which you want the surface to be generated.
4. Choose Surfaces → Loft, or click the Loft icon in the Surfaces shelf ( ).

When you define more curves for the loft, Maya can create more complex shapes. The more CVs for each curve, the more isoparms you have, and the more detail in the surface. Figure 5.6 shows how four curves can be lofted together to form a more complex surface. You can use almost any number of curves for a lofted surface.

Lofting works best when curves are drawn as cross-sectional slices of the object to be modeled. Lofting is used to make a variety of surfaces, which may be as simple as table-tops or as complex as human faces.

Revolved Surface

A *revolved surface* requires only one curve that is turned around a point in space to create a surface, like a woodworker shaping a table leg on a lathe. First you draw a *profile curve* to create a profile of the desired object, and then you revolve this curve (anywhere from 0 degrees to 360 degrees) around a single point in the scene to create the surface. The profile revolves around the object's pivot point, which is typically placed at the origin but can be moved (as seen in the solar system exercise in Chapter 2, "Jumping in Headfirst, with Both Feet"), and sweeps a new surface along its way. Figure 5.7 shows the profile curve for a wine glass.

The curve is then revolved around the *Y*-axis a full 360 degrees to create the wine glass. Figure 5.8 is the complete revolved surface with the profile revolved around the *Y*-axis.

To create a revolved surface, draw and select your profile curve, and then choose Surfaces → Revolve.

A revolved surface is useful for creating objects such as bottles, furniture legs, and baseball bats—anything that is symmetrical around an axis.

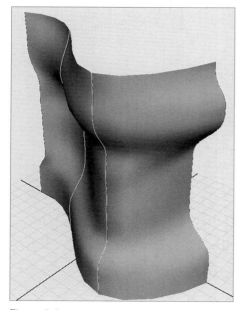

Figure 5.6

A loft created with four curves that are selected in order from left to right

Figure 5.7

A profile curve is drawn in the outline of a wine glass in the Y-axis.

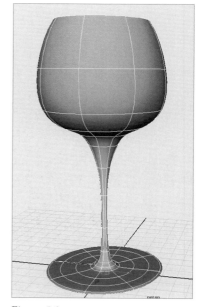

Figure 5.8

The revolved surface

Extruded Surface

An *extruded surface* uses two curves: a profile curve and a path curve. The profile curve is drawn to create the profile shape of the desired surface. It's then swept from one end of the path curve to its other end, creating spans of a surface along its travel. The higher the CV count on each curve, the more detail the surface will have. An extruded surface can also take the profile curve and simply stretch it to a specified distance straight along one direction or axis, doing away with the profile curve. Figure 5.9 shows the profile and path curves, and Figure 5.10 shows the resulting surface after the profile is extruded along the path.

Figure 5.9

The profile curve is drawn in the shape of an I, and the path curve comes up and bends toward the camera.

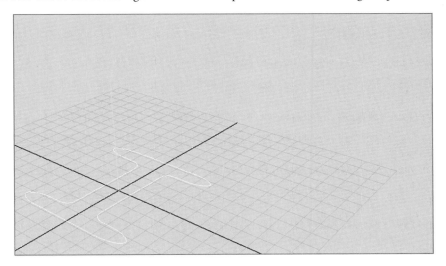

Figure 5.10

After extrusion, the surface becomes a bent I-beam.

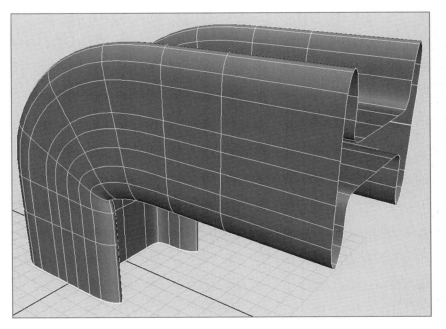

To create an extruded surface, follow these steps:

1. Draw both curves.

2. Select the profile curve.

3. Shift+click the path curve.

4. Choose Surfaces → Extrude.

An extruded surface is used to make items such as winding tunnels, coiled garden hoses, springs, and curtains.

Planar Surface

A *planar surface* uses one perfectly flat curve to make a two-dimensional cap in the shape of that curve. It does so by laying down a NURBS plane (a flat, square NURBS primitive) and carving out the shape of the curve like a cookie cutter. The resulting surface is a perfectly flat, cutout shape, also known as a *trimmed surface* because the "excess" outside the shape curve is trimmed away.

To create a planar surface, draw and select the curve, and then choose Surfaces → Planar.

You can also use multiple curves within each other to create a planar surface with holes in it. A simple planar surface is shown on the left side of Figure 5.11. When a second curve is added inside the original curve and both are selected, the planar surface is created with a hole. On the right side is the result when the outer curve is selected first and then the inner curve is selected before choosing Surfaces → Planar.

Figure 5.11

A planar surface based on a single curve (left); a planar surface based on a curve within a curve to create the cutout (right)

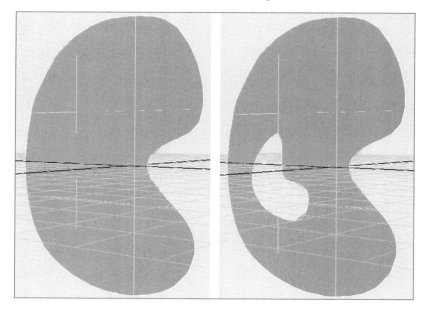

A planar surface is great for flat lettering, for pieces of a marionette doll or paper cut-out, or for capping the ends of a hollow extrusion. It's sometimes best to create the planar surface as a polygon. You'll see how to convert surfaces to polygons later in this chapter. The following quick exercise will give you an idea of what to look out for when creating polygons from surfacing techniques:

1. In the Surfaces menu set, select Create → NURBS Primitives → Circle twice to create two circles.

2. Scale the second circle to about three times its original size, as shown in Figure 5.12.

3. Select the larger circle first, then the smaller circle, and finally select Surfaces → Planar ❐. In the option box, select Polygons for Output Geometry, Quads for Type, and General for Tessellation Method, as shown in Figure 5.13.

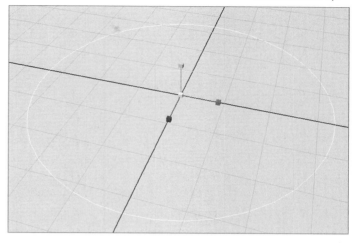

Figure 5.12

Scale the circle up.

4. Depending on how you create the geometry as poly-gons, you'll get different results, particularly around curves. Because Maya has to figure out where to put more faces to create a smoother outline, you have to set the Number U and Number V settings to best fit the curves of your resulting surface. At the current settings, your planar surface looks as shown in Figure 5.14. Notice the small gaps between the original outer NURBS circle and the surface outline.

5. Increase the Number U and Number V values, and you'll get tighter results at curves, although you'll have more faces on your model.

Keep this exercise in mind as you continue modeling. Whenever you need to create polygons from NURBS sur-faces—which should be quite often for some people—try the different creation methods for the best output. No one way works best all the time.

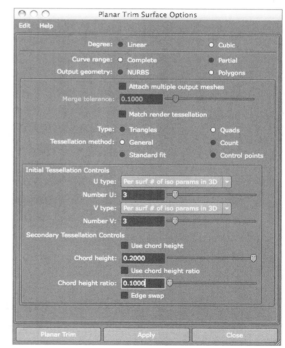

Figure 5.13

Choose these options.

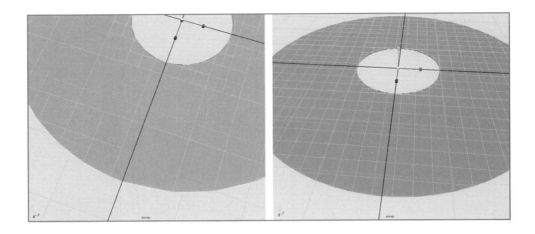

If you try creating a planar surface using a curve and notice that Maya doesn't allow it, verify that the curve(s) is perfectly flat. If any of the CVs aren't on the same plane as the others, the planar surface won't work.

Beveled Surface

Figure 5.15

A curve before and after it's beveled. The beveled surface has been given a planar cap.

The Bevel Surface function takes an open or closed curve and extrudes its outline to create a side surface. It creates a bevel on one or both corners of the resulting surface to create an edge that can be made smooth or sharp (see Figure 5.15). The many options in the Bevel tool allow you to control the size of the bevel and depth of extrusion, giving you great flexibility. When a bevel is created, you can easily cap the bevel with planar surfaces.

To create a bevel, draw and select your curve, and then choose Surfaces → Bevel.

Maya also offers a Bevel Plus surface, which has more creation options for advanced bevels. A beveled surface is great for creating 3D lettering, for creating items such as bottle caps or buttons, and for rounding out an object's edges.

Boundary Surface

A *boundary surface* is so named because it's created within the boundaries of three or four surrounding curves. For example, two vertical curves are drawn opposite each other to define the two side edges of the surface. Two horizontal curves are then drawn to define the upper and lower edges. These curves can have depth to them; they need not be flat for the boundary surface to work, unlike a planar surface. Although you can select the curves in any order, it's best to select them in opposing pairs. In Figure 5.16, four curves are created and arranged to form the edges of a surface to be created. First, select the vertical pair of curves, because they're opposing pairs; then, select the second two horizontal curves before choosing Surfaces → Boundary.

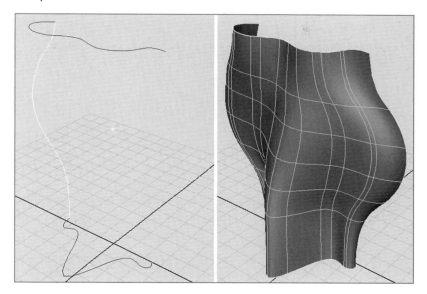

Figure 5.16

Four curves arranged to create the edges for a surface (left); the resulting boundary surface formed from the four curves (right)

A boundary surface is useful for creating shapes such as car hoods, fenders, and other formed panels.

Combining Techniques

You can use certain surfacing techniques in combination to create intricate models. For example, whenever a curve is required for a surface, you can use an isoparm instead to create a surface between two existing surfaces.

Try This   Take a couple of lofted surfaces, and connect them with a third surface. Figure 5.17 shows two surfaces with two intermediate curves between them. (Notice that the view panel's option Shading → X-ray is turned on so you can see through the shaded surfaces.) You'll select an isoparm from the first surface (on the left) and then the curve on the left, the curve on the right, and finally an isoparm on the second surface.

1. Either create two lofted surfaces and curves, as shown in Figure 5.17 , or load the Chap_5_Lofting_Exercise_1.ma file from the Lofting_Exercise project on the book's companion web page, www.sybex.com/go/introducingmaya2014.

Figure 5.17

Two lofted surfaces with two curves in between

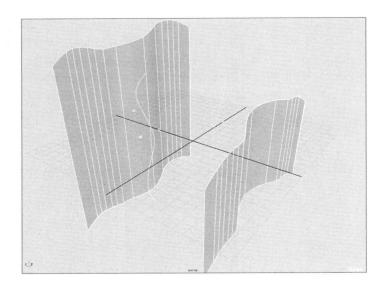

2. To select the first isoparm, press F8 for Component Selection mode, and click the Lines Selection Filter button ( ) in the Status line to allow you to select isoparms. You can also right-click the surface and choose Isoparm from the marking menu to enter Component Selection mode for isoparms.

3. Select an isoparm close to the left edge. Press F8 to return to Object Selection mode (or right-click the first curve and choose Object Mode from the marking menu), Shift+click the first curve, and then Shift+click the second curve. Press F8 again or use the marking menu again for Component Selection mode, and Shift+click an isoparm toward the left edge on the second surface, as in Figure 5.18.

Figure 5.18

Selecting the isoparm

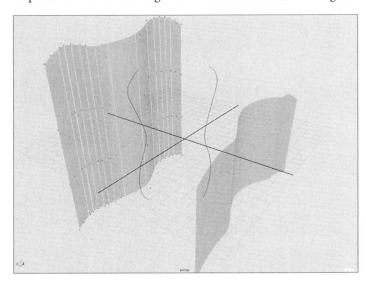

4. Choose Surfaces → Loft to create the intermediate surface between the existing lofts. Figure 5.19 shows how the new surface snakes from the first loft to the second loft by way of the two curves.

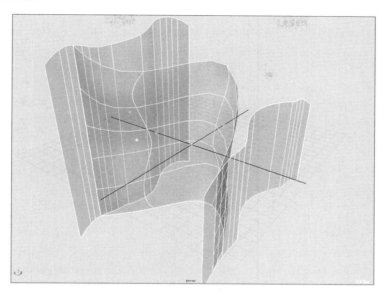

Figure 5.19

The spanning loft between the existing surfaces snakes from the first isoparm to the curves and then to the second isoparm

Surface History

In Chapter 3, "The Autodesk Maya 2014 Interface," you learned that clicking the History icon ( ) toggles History on and off. *History* has to do with how objects react to change. Leaving History on when creating primitives, as you did in Chapter 2, allows you to access an object's original parameters.

Leaving History on when creating NURBS surfaces allows the surface to update when any of its creation pieces change. For example, the loft you just created will update whenever the two original surfaces or curves you used to create the loft move or change shape. If you were to move the original loft on the left and rotate it back a bit, the new loft would adjust to keep its one side attached to the same isoparm. If one or more of the input curves were to change, the loft would bend to fit.

> You must toggle History on before you create the object(s) if you want History to be on for the object(s).

By lofting using isoparms and with History toggled on, you can keep the new surface permanently attached to the original loft, no matter how the isoparms move, as in Figure 5.20. This technique works with all surface techniques, not just with lofting, as long as History is turned on. History is useful for making adjustments and fine-tuning a surface, and it can be handy in animation if several surfaces need to deform but stay attached.

Figure 5.20

History updates the newly created loft to keep it attached to the isoparms and curves used to create it, even when they've been moved or altered.

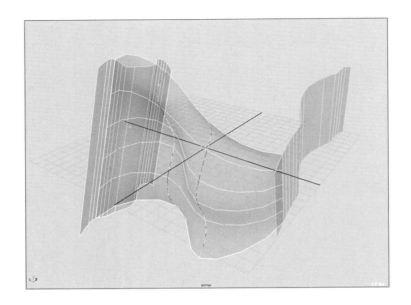

Figure 5.20

History updates the newly created loft to keep it attached to the isoparms and curves used to create it, even when they've been moved or altered.

Why wouldn't you want History turned on for everything? After a long day of modeling, having History on for every single object can slow down your scene file, adding unnecessary bloat to your workflow. But it isn't typically a problem on most surface types unless the scene is huge, so you should leave it on while you're still modeling.

If you no longer want a surface or an object to retain its History, you can selectively delete it from the surface. Select the surface, and choose Edit → Delete By Type → History. You can also rid the entire scene of History by choosing Edit → Delete All By Type → History. Just don't get them mixed up!

Using NURBS Surfacing to Create Polygons

You can create swatches of polygon surfaces by using NURBS surfacing tools, as you saw during the exercise on creating a planar surface.

To create a polygonal surface with any of the surfacing techniques in this chapter, open the option box for that particular NURBS tool. For example, create two simple curves. With both curves selected, choose Surfaces → Loft ❏. In the options for Output Geometry, click the Polygons button to display the options for creating the polygon surface and its detail level.

History for the surface will adjust the new polygonal surface. The detail of the surface will try to adjust as changes to the input curves are made. If you anticipate significant changes to the input curves, make sure you create the poly surface with a high poly count to accommodate major changes. This is probably the best way to create a single poly surface, especially if you prefer a NURBS workflow.

Try This Draw two CV curves as you did at the beginning of this chapter, both with the same number of CVs. Open the Loft option box, and click the Polygons option for Output Geometry.

The creation options that appear at the bottom of the window affect the tessellation of the resulting surface; that is, you use them to specify the level of detail and the number of faces with which the surface is created. Generally speaking, the more faces there are, the more detail you'll need. (That doesn't mean a detailed surface can't be efficient, with areas of high tessellation placed only where needed.)

The default Tessellation Method, Standard Fit, uses the fewest faces to create the surface without compromising overall integrity. The sliders adjust the resulting number of faces in order to fit the finer curvature of the input curves.

The lower the Fractional Tolerance setting, the smoother the surface and the greater the number of faces you need.

The Chord Height Ratio determines the amount of curve in a particular region, and calculates how many more faces to use to give an adequate representation of that curved area with polygons. This option is best used with surfaces that have multiple or very intense curves.

It isn't uncommon to create a surface, undo it, change the slider settings, re-create it, and repeat, to get just the right tessellation. That's why you should click the Apply button, which keeps the window open, rather than the Loft button, which closes the window after applying the settings.

The General Tessellation Method creates a specific number of lines, evenly dividing the horizontal (U) and vertical (V) into rows of polygon faces.

The Control Points method tessellates the surface according to the number of points on the input curves. As the number of CVs and spans on the curves increases, so does the number of divisions of polygons.

The Count method simply relies on how many faces you tell it to make—the higher the count, the higher the tessellation on the surface. Experiment with the options to get the best poly surface results.

TESSELLATION

In the rendering phase, all 3D objects are broken into polygonal triangles that form the surfaces that shape your objects. This process, called *tessellation*, happens on all rendered surfaces, whether polygonal or NURBS.

The computer calculates the position of each significant point on your surface and connects the points to form a skin representing your surface.

Converting a NURBS Model to Polygons

Some people prefer to model on NURBS curves and either create poly surfaces or convert to polygons after the entire model is done with NURBS surfaces. Ultimately, you'll find your own workflow preference, but it helps greatly if you're comfortable using all surfacing methods. Most modelers choose one way or another but are familiar with both methodologies. In the following section, you'll convert a NURBS model to polygons.

Try This Convert a NURBS-modeled axe into a poly model like one that might be needed in a game.

Open `axe_model_v1.mb` in the Scenes folder of the Axe project from the companion web page. The toughest part of this simple process is getting the poly model to follow all the curves in the axe with fidelity, so you'll have to convert parts of the axe differently. Follow these steps:

1. Grab the handle, and choose Modify → Convert → NURBS To Polygons ❐. Use the default presets. If need be, reestablish your settings by choosing Edit → Reset Settings; the handle converts well to polygons. Click Apply, and a poly version of the axe handle appears on top of the NURBS version. Move it 8 units to the right to get it out of the way. You'll move the other parts 8 units as well to assemble the poly axe properly.

2. Select the back part of the axe head. All those surfaces are grouped together to make selection easy. The default settings will work for this part as well, so click Apply and move the resulting model 8 units to the left.

3. The front of the axe head holds a lot of different arcs, so you'll have to create it with finer controls. Change Fractional Tolerance from 0.01 to 0.0005. This yields more polygons but finer-curved surfaces. Figure 5.21 shows the result.

If you were following this process for a conventional game engine, you'd normally be restricted to a low number of polygons, and your axe design would be different to better handle a low poly count.

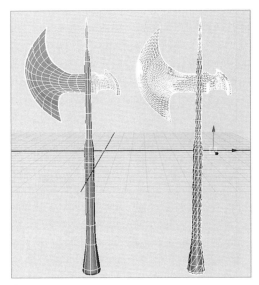

Figure 5.21
A faithful high-poly conversion (on the right) of a NURBS axe (on the left)

Editing NURBS Surfaces

As you've experienced, Maya provides numerous NURBS tools that you'll find useful when editing your surfaces. In addition to tools for moving CVs, some important functions and tools allow you to add realism to your model. This section gives you a quick overview of these tools—some you've already used, and others you'll need to try for yourself.

The following functions are all accessed through the Edit NURBS menu. Open and tear off the Edit NURBS menu so it remains open as you follow along.

Project Curve on Surface

The ability to project a curve onto a surface allows you to cut holes in the surface using the Trim tool (choose Edit NURBS → Trim Tool). It also lets you create, using History, another surface that is attached, following the outline of your projected curve, as you saw in the section "Combining Techniques" earlier in this chapter.

Similar to drawing a curve on a surface, projected curves project an existing curve onto the selected surface. That curve on the surface is now useful for patch modeling as well as tracing animation paths for objects to follow along a surface. For example, you can project a curve around a hilly landscape surface and assign a car to animate (drive) along that projected curve. The car will stick to the surface of the road with ease.

To use Project Curve On Surface, select the surface and the curve to project, and then choose Edit NURBS → Project Curve On Surface.

Trim and Untrim Surfaces

Trimming a surface (choose Edit NURBS → Trim Tool) creates holes in the surface using curves that are either drawn or projected onto the surface.

If you have a surface that has already been trimmed and it's too late to reverse the function with Undo, you can use Untrim Surfaces to remove either the last trim performed or all the surface trims. Choose Edit NURBS → Untrim Surfaces.

Attach Surfaces

Attach Surfaces does exactly that—it attaches two contiguous NURBS surfaces along two selected isoparms. Select an isoparm on the edge of the first surface, Shift+click an edge isoparm on a second surface, and choose Edit NURBS → Attach Surfaces to create a new surface from the two. As shown in Figure 5.22, the attach point is along the selected isoparms.

Figure 5.22

Attach Surfaces connects surfaces along their selected isoparms.

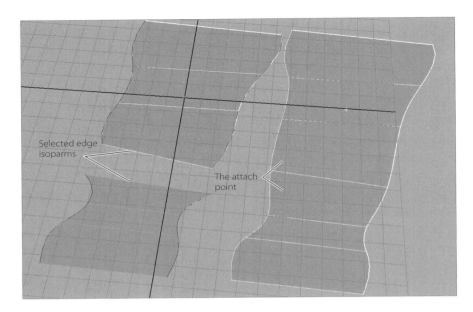

Detach Surfaces

Detach Surfaces is a highly useful tool for generating specific areas of a NURBS surface, or *patches*. Select an isoparm to define the line of detachment, and choose Edit NURBS → Detach Surfaces. The surface is cut along that isoparm to create two distinct surfaces (see Figure 5.23). You'll see plenty of Detach and Attach tools later in this chapter.

Figure 5.23

Detach Surfaces cuts a surface at the selected isoparms to create a new surface.

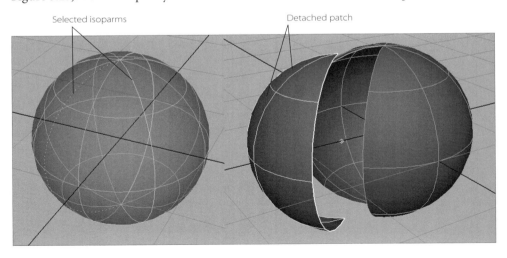

To select an isoparm that isn't displayed on the surface, click a viewable isoparm and drag the mouse to place the isoparm selection elsewhere on the surface. Release the button to make the selection; a dashed isoparm line is now selected. This is a valid surface isoparm, but it isn't one used to define the number of spans in the surface.

Insert Isoparms

Adding extra surface definition by adding spans is a matter of selecting an isoparm and choosing Edit NURBS → Insert Isoparms. This creates an isoparm and redefines the surface to add more spans to allow for smoother deformations—for example, adding an isoparm or two to the elbow joint of a model to make the arm bend with a cleaner crease (see Figure 5.24). You can either create a new isoparm between two existing ones or add isoparms to your own defined area.

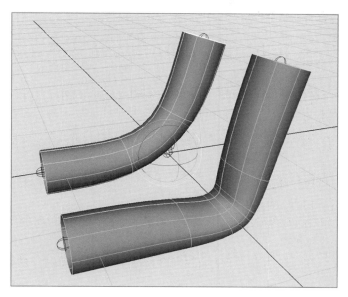

Figure 5.24

Inserting isoparms for a smoother deformation

Patch Modeling: A Locomotive Detail

With NURBS modeling, you frequently need to attach surfaces so that a model doesn't split at the seams. This process of aligning and attaching NURBS patches is called *stitching*, and this kind of modeling is called *patch modeling*.

You're jumping back in time to create a pump for a prebuilt polygonal locomotive. Since this part of the locomotive is perfect for smooth, organic modeling, you will use patches that you'll stitch together. This exercise gives you an idea of how patches work to pull together an organic shape using NURBS shapes. To show you what you're seeking to build, the finished model appears in Figure 5.25.

Keep in mind that patch modeling is a fairly involved process. If you don't feel comfortable with modeling quite yet, skip this exercise and move on to the "Using Artisan to Sculpt NURBS" section of this chapter. You can always return to this section to bone up on your patch modeling later.

Figure 5.25

The finished pump elements for a classic locomotive model are created in NURBS patches.

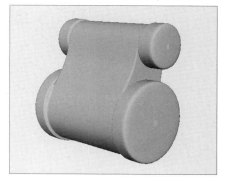

Starting the NURBS Pump

First, copy the Locomotive project from the companion web page to your hard drive and set it as your current project.

To start creating the locomotive pump, follow these steps:

1. In a new scene, create a NURBS cylinder with no caps by choosing Create → NURBS Primitives → Cylinder □. Under Caps in the option box, select None to create an open-ended cylinder. Set Axis to Z to create the cylinder on its side, and then click Create.

2. Size the cylinder down to **0.72** in *X* and *Y* and to 0.9 in *Z*.

3. Reset the cylinder so that its attributes are set back to normal. With the cylinder selected, choose Modify → Freeze Transformations □. In the option box, choose Edit → Reset Settings to reestablish the defaults, and then click Freeze Transform. Figure 5.26 shows the cylinder resized and after the application of Freeze Transformations.

4. You'll create slightly larger end pieces for the cylinder. Duplicate the cylinder once, move the copy, and scale it, as shown in Figure 5.27. Repeat to create the other end piece. The end pieces are roughly **1.075** in Scale X and Y and **0.18** in Scale Z and are moved slightly past the ends of the cylinder, leaving a slight gap, as shown. You should freeze transforms on the ends to reset their scale and positions back to the default.

5. Create a second copy of this assembly that is smaller in radius but is the same length (see Figure 5.28). Duplicate the three cylinders, and change their respective scales to **0.55** in *X* and *Y* but leave Scale Z set to 1. Remember, you froze their transforms, so their starting scales should have been at 1. Position the three cylinders as shown in Figure 5.28, slightly to the side and above the original larger cylinders. Freeze their transforms.

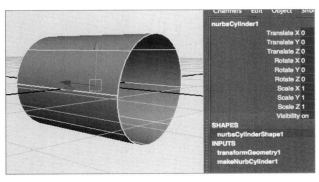

Figure 5.26

The first NURBS cylinder, after Freeze Transformations

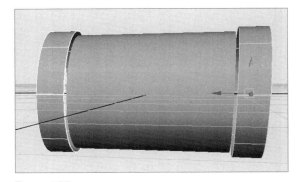

Figure 5.27

Create the end pieces.

6. Cut a couple of holes in the main cylinders. Cut at the top two isoparms on the sides of the larger cylinder first, as shown in Figure 5.29. To select the first isoparm, right-click the cylinder, choose Isoparm from the marking menu, and click the isoparm to select it. Next, Shift+click the isoparm on the other side so that both are selected.

7. In the Surfaces menu set, choose Edit NURBS → Detach Surfaces. The surface between the isoparms you just selected is now its own surface and can be deleted. This gives your first cut, as shown in Figure 5.30.

8. Use the same procedure to cut the smaller cylinder but at the sides so you can remove the bottom half. Select the isoparms on the sides of the smaller cylinder, and detach the surface by choosing Edit NURBS → Detach Surfaces again. Delete the bottom surface. Now your model should look like Figure 5.31.

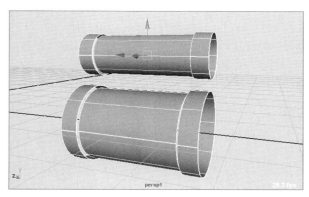

Figure 5.28
Create a smaller copy of the first cylinders, and place them higher for the top of the steam pump assembly.

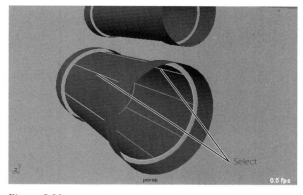

Figure 5.29
Select these isoparms to cut the top of the cylinder.

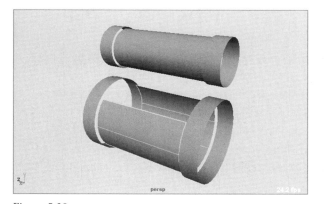

Figure 5.30
Cutting the cylinder's top

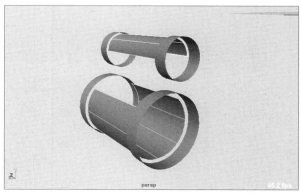

Figure 5.31
The cut cylinders

If detaching the surface doesn't work the first time, select the same isoparms again and detach surfaces again. This sometimes happens when you try to cut a NURBS surface at a side isoparm where the surface is beginning and ending.

Adding End Caps

At this point, you'll cap the ends of the cylinders to close them off. You can continue with your own file or load the file NURBS_pump_v01.mb from the Locomotive project from the companion web page and check your work so far. The trick will be to add four isoparms using the Insert Isoparms function you read about earlier in this chapter to create the caps.

To cap the ends, follow these steps:

1. Select the end cylinder, right-click the geometry, and select Isoparm from the marking menu. Select four isoparms (make sure you hold down Shift while selecting the isoparms so as not to deselect them), as shown in Figure 5.32, and choose Edit NURBS → Insert Isoparms ❐.

   Make sure your settings match those in Figure 5.33 (should be default settings: Insert Location set to At selection, Multiplicity set to Increase By, and the Multiplicity value set to **1**). This inserts four isoparms into the end cylinder that you can use to close the end to make the cap.

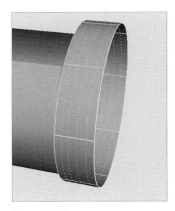

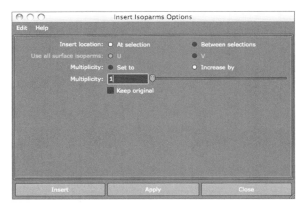

Figure 5.32

Select these four isoparms (shown as dashed lines).

Figure 5.33

The default Insert Isoparms Options settings

2. Select the end CVs to scale them down to close the cap. The easiest way to do this is to select the hull that controls all the edge CVs. Right-click the end cylinder and select Hull. Select the very outermost hull, and scale it down as shown in Figure 5.34. Doing so closes the end cap. Don't worry about leaving a small hole in the cap; you'll complete this pump when you finish the locomotive model.

3. Repeat the previous procedures to close off the other three end cylinders to create caps for both ends of both objects, as shown in Figure 5.35.

Figure 5.34

Scale down the outermost hull.

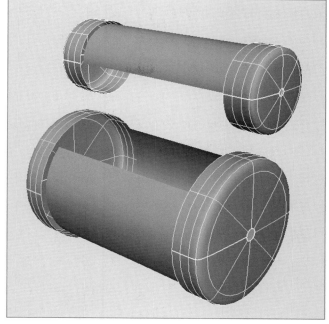

Figure 5.35

End caps for the pump pieces

4. Connect and patch the end caps to their cylinders. To do this, you need to line up a few new isoparms on the cylinders so you can stitch everything together properly. Using the previous workflow, add new isoparms to the bottom cylinder, as shown in Figure 5.36. (You may have to hide the end caps to create the isoparms on the cylinder. Select the end caps and use Display → Hide → Hide Selection. After you create the isoparms, select Display → Show → All.)

Figure 5.36

Add isoparms as shown here.

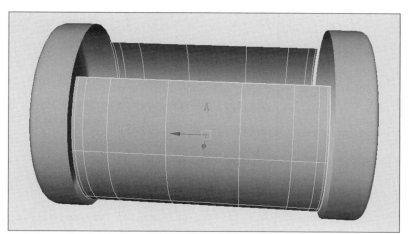

5. You need to prep the end cap to connect to the cylinder, by cutting a pie piece out of the cap, to line it up with the cut cylinder. On the end cap, select two isoparms to form a *V* that lines up with the cut edges of the main cylinder, as shown in Figure 5.37. Then, choose Edit NURBS → Detach Surfaces. Doing so cuts the *V* section out of the end cap. This aligns the end cap and the cylinder geometry at the edges so you can create a smooth connection between them in the next few steps.

Figure 5.37

Select two isoparms and detach the surfaces.

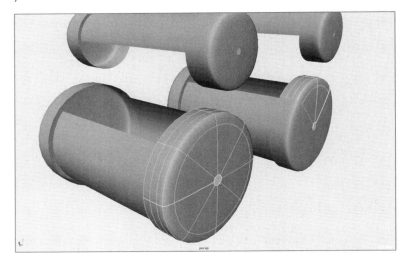

You can load the file NURBS_pump_v02.mb from the Locomotive project to compare your work with it. Or, if you skipped the previous steps, you can proceed from here to attach the end cap.

6. You need to pull the end of the cylinder to line it up with the edge of the end cap. Select the end four vertical hulls, as shown in Figure 5.38, and move them so that the edges of the cylinder and end cap align. Repeat this to line up the other end of the cylinder with the other cap.

7. Create the pieces to connect the caps to the cylinder using lofts. Right-click the cylinder, and choose Isoparm from the marking menu. Select the edge isoparm on the cylinder. Right-click the end cap, and choose Isoparm from the marking menu. Shift+click the edge isoparm of the end cap, as shown in Figure 5.39. Choose Surfaces → Loft ❑. Make sure you're using the default settings for the loft: in the option box, choose Edit → Reset Settings.

8. The previous step creates a surface to bridge the cylinder and the end cap. You'll notice that it's rather jagged—almost a diamond shape as opposed to a smooth ring. With the loft selected, press 3 on the keyboard to see it with a smooth display in the panel. Figure 5.40 shows the loft.

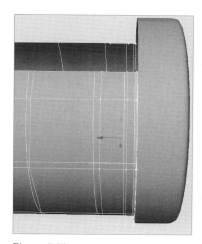

Figure 5.38

Select the four end hulls and move them to line up.

Figure 5.39

Shift+click the edge isoparm.

Figure 5.40

Lofting the end cap to the cylinder

Stitching and Tangency

Smooth seams are essential to organic modeling. The trick for creating a good patch model is to make sure all the patches line up; this is called *tangency*. In animation and texture setup, it's important that tangency be correct; otherwise, you may notice tearing at the seams during deformations or texture maps that don't line up quite right. It can be a tedious process, but here is a taste of it. To continue with the patch model of the loco-motive pump, follow these steps:

1. Create a smooth piece that connects the cylinder and the end caps using the lofts created in steps 7 and 8 in the previous section and shown in Figure 5.40. Select the cylinder and the connector loft, as shown in Figure 5.41, and attach them by choos-ing Edit NURBS → Attach Surfaces ❐. Make sure the tool is set to the default (choose Edit → Reset Settings). Turn off Keep Originals and click Attach. This blends the two surfaces into one, creates a smooth transition between them, and deletes the original surfaces.

2. Here's the funny part: you need to disconnect the surfaces. Select the isoparm at the location where the patches originally met, and choose Edit NURBS → Detach Surfaces. Again, make sure the tool is reset to the default so as not to keep the origi-nal patches. This gives you tangency across the two patches as well as a smooth tran-sition in the model.

3. Repeat steps 1 and 2 for the other end of the cylinder and its end cap and also for the upper cylinder and its two end caps. You should now have end caps with smooth attachments to the cylinders, as shown in Figure 5.42.

Figure 5.41

Attach the patches.

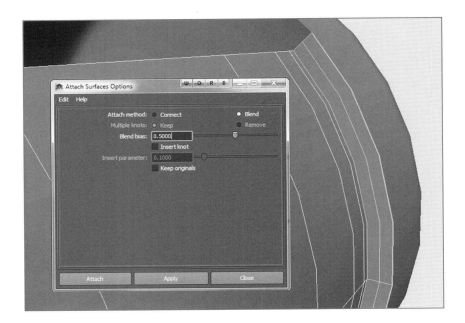

Figure 5.42

The end caps attach to the cylinders—smooth as low-cholesterol butter!

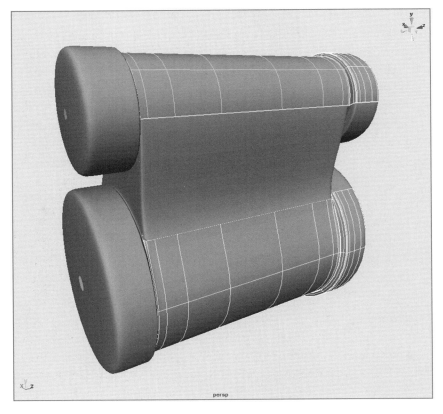

4. Connecting the upper and lower cylinders is next. Select the edge isoparms of both cylinders, and choose Surfaces → Loft ❑. Set Section Spans to **2** in the option box, and click Apply. Repeat to create a loft on the back side of the cylinders as well. Figure 5.43 shows the resulting surfaces.

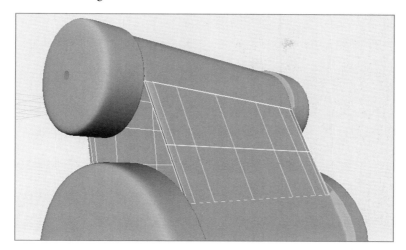

Figure 5.43

Lofting the two cylinders together

5. Individually select the middle hulls of both of the lofts, and move them back to create a bit of curvature to the surfaces, as shown in Figure 5.44. Remember, you can select hulls by right-clicking the surface and using the marking menu.

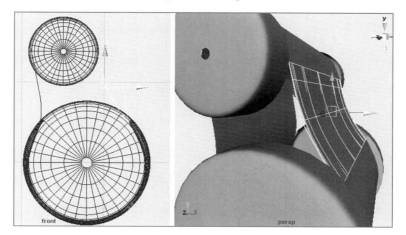

Figure 5.44

Move back the middle and lower-middle hulls.

6. Select the edge isoparms of the lofts you just created, and loft between them with two spans. Make sure you reset the loft settings by choosing Edit → Reset Settings in the option box, and then set Section Spans to **2** before you create the loft. Repeat for the other side. Figure 5.45 shows the closed ends.

Figure 5.45

Closing the sides

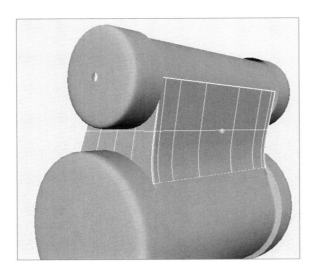

7. Go into CV mode, and move the CVs to line up the edges of the newly formed closed ends with the bottom and top cylinders. Repeat for the other side, as shown in Figure 5.46.

Figure 5.46

In CV mode, line up the ends and cylinders.

8. As you did in steps 1 and 2, attach and then detach the loft you just edited with CVs (I'll call it the *side panel*) and the front panel, as shown in Figure 5.47, to set up a smooth transition and a tangency. Repeat for the back panel and the other end of the cylinders to make the other side panel.

9. Shift your attention to one of the end caps on the lower cylinder. In step 5 in the previous section, and as shown in Figure 5.37, you detached a pizza-slice shape out of

the end caps. Select the detached slice, and insert two isoparms between the existing ones. Your model should resemble the one in Figure 5.48 with the added isoparms. This is set up for another attachment in a moment. Repeat for the other end cap on the lower cylinder.

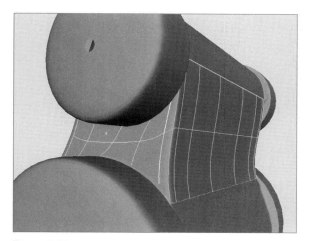

Figure 5.47
Create a smooth transition between the surfaces.

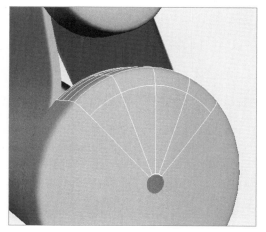

Figure 5.48
Insert isoparms into the end cap slice.

10. Select isoparms on the edges of the end cap and the side panel, and loft between them with two spans. Repeat for the other side. Doing so plugs the hole between the end cap and the side panels. You can, if you like, run another attach and detach to smooth out the groove between the end caps and the side panels. Figure 5.49 shows the end result of the groove.

11. You're getting kicked out into the cold now to run the same set of procedures on the upper cylinder and its end caps. These should be simpler, because there are fewer sections to deal with. Go ahead and finish the model from here to form the connections shown in Figure 5.50 (left) and to form the final model shown in Figure 5.50 (right). Save your NURBS pump scene file.

Figure 5.49
The groove connecting the end cap with the side panel

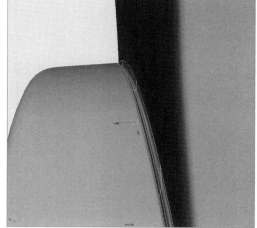

There is quite a bit of lofting, attaching, and detaching between surface patches in patch modeling. The key to becoming good at it is to be able to line up isoparms easily and cleverly and to be able to attach them again smoothly; it takes a lot of practice to get used to this technique. You'll make a lot of mistakes along the way, but that is how you'll learn the most! It's easy to see how this kind of modeling is useful for making organic shapes such as faces.

Figure 5.50

Finishing the top part of the NURBS pump (left) and the completed pump (right)

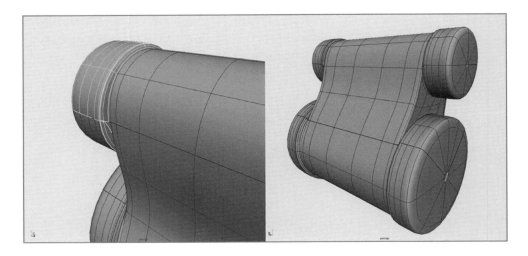

Integrating the Pump into the Locomotive Model: Importing a Scene

Now that you have the scene completed and saved, let's insert it into the locomotive model file by importing this saved file. This often happens in CG workflow, where you combine separate scene files into a single file to assemble a larger model. To import your NURBS pump, follow these steps:

1. Open the file `fancy_locomotive.mb` from the Scenes folder in the Locomotive project from the companion website. You will notice an area of the locomotive that is ready for the pump, as shown in Figure 5.51 (left).

2. Choose File → Import. A File dialog window opens much like the Open File dialog window you've seen many times. This time, however, you are importing a file into the existing open scene.

Figure 5.51

The locomotive is missing its steam pump (left); place the NURBS pump on to the locomotive (right).

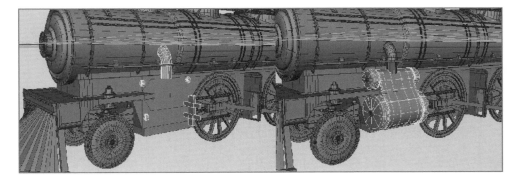

3. Navigate to your saved NURBS pump scene file and select it. Click Import, and the model will be brought into your locomotive scene. Group all its parts together, if you haven't already, and position the group as shown in Figure 5.51 (right). Make sure to group them into the existing hierarchy for the locomotive; there is a place for it all set aside for you to find and use. The group name is `steam_pump_LT_side`, and it's found in the Outliner.

4. The opposite side of the locomotive needs the pump as well. You can import the pump scene again, or simply copy the pump you already imported, and move the duplicate to the other side. Make sure to group that as well under the `steam_pump_RT_side` node.

Even though the pump you created is a NURBS model, it will work wonderfully with the polygonal locomotive. You may also opt to convert the surfaces into polygons.

Using Artisan to Sculpt NURBS

Imagine that you can create a NURBS surface and sculpt it using your cursor the way hands mold the surface of wet clay. You can do just that with a Maya module called Artisan—and without the mess!

Try This   Artisan is a basic 3D painting system that allows you to paint directly on a surface. By painting on the surface with the Sculpt Geometry tool, you move the CV points in and out, effectively molding the surface.

1. In Shaded mode (press 5), maximize the Perspective window (press the spacebar) for a nice big view. Create a NURBS sphere, and open the Attribute Editor. In the sphere's creation node (`makeNurbsSphere1`), set Sections to **24** and Spans to **12**. The greater the surface definition, the more detailed the sculpting.

2. Select the sphere, and choose Edit NURBS → Sculpt Geometry Tool ❑. Clicking the option box opens the tool settings. You'll need those almost every time you paint with Artisan to change brush sizes and so forth.

   Your cursor changes to the Artisan brush, as shown in Figure 5.52. The red circle around the brush cursor and the lettering display the type of brush you're currently using. When the red lines point outside the circle and the lettering reads *Ps*, you're using the *push* brush that pushes in the surface as you paint it. The black arrow pointing toward the sphere's center is a measurement of the Max Displacement slider in the tool settings. This sets how far each stroke pushes in the surface. The lower the number, the less the brush affects the surface.

Figure 5.52

The Sculpt Geometry tool lets you mold your surface by painting on it. Here, the brush is set to push in the surface of the sphere as you paint.

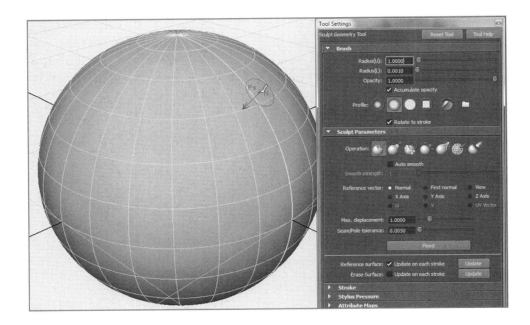

3. Click and drag the cursor across the surface of the sphere to get a feel for how the surface deforms under your tool. Use the Max Displacement slider to control the force of the brush, and use Radius (U) and Radius (L) to set the size of the brush.

4. Switch your brush type to *pull*. Your cursor changes to read *Pl*, and the red lines appear on the inside of the circle (see Figure 5.53). You can then pull out the surface.

The Opacity slider also controls the force of the brush, but it's subtler than Max Displacement to give you greater control. Because this is, after all, a 3D Painting tool, Opacity controls how much value you paint onto the surface. The value in this case isn't a color but how far the surface is deformed. You'll see how Artisan comes into play in other aspects of Maya later in the book.

Figure 5.53

With a pull brush, your cursor changes to read Pl.

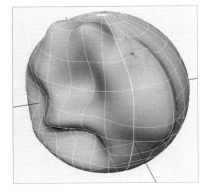

Additionally, *Smooth* blends the pushed-in and pulled-out areas of the surface to yield a smoother result. *Erase* simply erases the deformations on the surface, setting it back to the way it was before.

If you plan to sculpt a more detailed surface, be sure to create the surface with plenty of surface spans and sections. If you want to paint only a specific area of a NURBS surface, choose Edit NURBS → Insert Isoparms to add extra detail to that area before you begin painting, although you can add isoparms after you paint. When you begin to sculpt this way, going back into the surface's creation node to increase its sections and spans will ruin your results.

AUTODESK MUDBOX AND PIXOLOGIC ZBRUSH FOR SCULPTING

Although sculpting a surface in Maya with Artisan is convenient, the tool can take you only so far with your sculpture. For intricate sculpting and modeling, artists frequently use Autodesk Mudbox or Pixologic's ZBrush programs. Both interface with Maya easily and give you very intricate control while sculpting your model. The workflow can start with a basic model shaped out in Maya, transferred to the sculpting package, and then detailed. It's then exported from that package and reimported into Maya to be integrated back into the scene as needed.

Modeling with Simple Deformers

In many ways, deformers are the Swiss Army knives of Maya animation, except you can't open a bottle with them. *Deformers* are handy for creating and editing modeled shapes in Maya. These tools allow you to change the shape of an object easily. Rather than using CVs or vertices to distort or bend an object manually, you can use a deformer to affect the entire object. Popular deformers, such as Bend and Flare, can be powerful tools for adjusting your models quickly and evenly, as you're about to see.

Nonlinear deformers, such as Bend and Flare, create simple shape adjustments for the attached geometry, such as bending the object. You can also use deformers in animation to create effects or deformations in your objects. We'll explore this later in the book.

Modeling Using the Bend Deformer

Let's apply a deformer. In a new Maya scene, you'll create a polygonal cylinder and bend it to get a quick idea of how deformers work. Follow these steps:

1. Choose Create → Polygon Primitives, and turn on Interactive Creation. Then, choose Create → Polygon Primitives → Cylinder. Click and drag to create the base. Make it a few units in diameter; the exact sizing isn't important here. Click and drag to make the height of the cylinder 7 or 8 units, as shown in Figure 5.54. Make sure your create options are set to the defaults so that they're consistent with these directions.

   To make sure the settings are at their defaults, open the command's option box and click the Reset Settings button.

2. Let's jump right in and create the Bend deformer. With the cylinder selected, switch to the Animation menu set by pressing F2 and choosing Create Deformers → Nonlinear → Bend. Your cylinder turns magenta, and a thin line appears at the center of the cylinder, running lengthwise. Figure 5.55 shows the deformer and its Channel Box attributes. Depending on your settings, your deformer may be created in a different axis than the one pictured. You can reset the deformer's options as needed. Click bend1 in the Channel Box to expand the deformer's attributes shown in the figure.

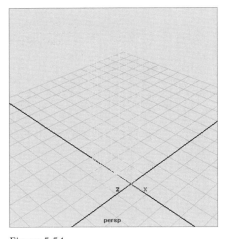

Figure 5.54
Create a cylinder to bend.

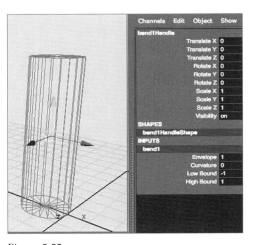

Figure 5.55
Creating the Bend deformer

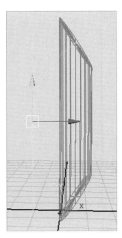

Figure 5.56
Notice the problem with this cylinder?

3. Click Curvature, and enter a value of **1**. Notice that the cylinder takes on an odd shape, as shown in Figure 5.56. The Bend deformer itself is bending nicely, but the geometry isn't. As a matter of fact, the geometry is now offset from its original location. It's offset because there aren't enough divisions in the geometry to allow for a smooth bend.

4. Select the cylinder, and click polyCylinder1 in the Channel Box to expand the shape node's attributes. Enter a value of **12** for the Subdivisions Height attribute (see Figure 5.57), and your cylinder will bend with the deformer properly, as shown in Figure 5.58.

Figure 5.57
Increase Subdivisions Height to 12.

5. Try adjusting the Bend deformer's Low and High Bound attributes. This allows you to bend one part of the cylinder without affecting the other. Figure 5.59 shows the cylinder with the Bend deformer's High Bound set to 0.25 instead of 1. This causes the top half of the cylinder to bend only one quarter of the way up and continue straight from there.

Experiment with moving the Bend deformer, and see how doing so affects the geometry of the cylinder. The deformer's position plays an important role in how it shapes an object's geometry.

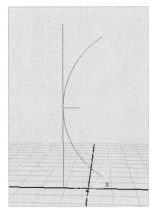

Figure 5.58
The cylinder bends properly now that it has the right number of divisions.

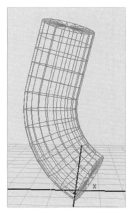

Figure 5.59
Using High Bound to change the effect of the Bend deformer

Adjusting an Existing Axe Model

In this exercise, you'll take an existing NURBS model of an axe and fine-tune the backend of the axe head. In the existing model, the backend of the axe head is blunt, as you can see in Figure 5.60. You'll need to sharpen the blunt end with a nonlinear deformer. Open the AxeHead_v01.ma file in the Scenes folder of the Axe project from the companion web page, and follow these steps:

Figure 5.60
The axe head is blunt.

1. Select the top group of the axe head's backend. To do so, open the Outliner, and select axeHead_Back (see Figure 5.61).

2. Press F2 to switch to the Animation menu set.

3. Create a Flare deformer by choosing Create Deformers → Nonlinear → Flare. The Flare deformer appears as a cylindrical object (see Figure 5.62).

4. Rotate the deformer 90 degrees in the Z-axis, as shown in Figure 5.63.

5. Open the Attribute Editor (Ctrl+A), click the flare1 tab to access the Flare controls, and enter the following values:

ATTRIBUTE	VALUE
Start Flare Z	0.020
High Bound	0.50

These values taper in the end of that part of the axe head, as shown in Figure 5.64. This is a much easier way of sharpening the blunt end than adjusting the individual CVs of the NURBS surfaces.

Deformers use History to distort the geometry to which they're attached. You can animate any of the attributes that control the deformer shapes, but in this case you're using the deformer as a means to adjust a model. When you get the desired shape, as shown in Figure 5.65, you can discard the deformer. However, simply selecting and deleting the deformer will reset the geometry to its original blunt shape. You need to pick the axeHead_Back geometry group (not the deformer) and delete its History by choosing Edit → Delete By Type → History.

Figure 5.61
Select the back of the axe head.

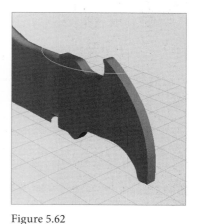

Figure 5.62
The Flare deformer appears as a cylinder.

Figure 5.63

**Rotate the deformer
90 degrees in the
Z-axis.**

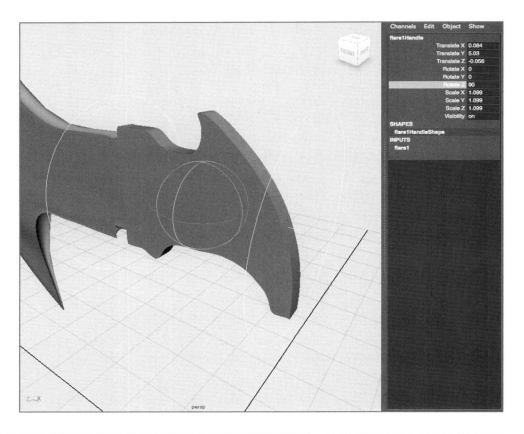

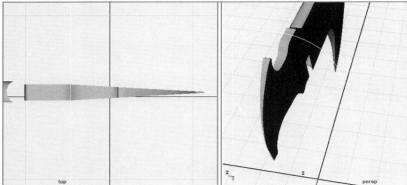

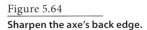

Figure 5.64

Sharpen the axe's back edge.

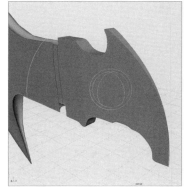

Figure 5.65

**Another view of the back of the axe
head with the Flare deformer**

The Lattice Deformer

A simple deformer, such as a Bend or Flare, will get you only so far; when a model requires more intricate editing with a deformer, you'll need to use a lattice.

A *lattice* is a scaffold that fits around your geometry. The lattice object controls the shape of the geometry. When a lattice point is moved, the lattice smoothly deforms the underlying geometry. The more lattice points, the greater control you have. The more divisions the geometry has, the more smoothly the geometry will deform.

Lattices are especially useful when you need to edit a relatively complex poly mesh or NURBS surface that is too dense to edit efficiently directly with CVs or vertices. With a lattice, you don't have to move the individual surface points.

Lattices can work on any surface type, and a single lattice can affect multiple surfaces simultaneously. You can also move an object through a lattice (or vice versa) to animate a deformation effect, such as a golf ball sliding through a garden hose.

Creating an Alien Hand

Make sure you're in the Animation menu set. To adjust an existing model or surface, select the model(s) or applicable groups to deform, and choose Create Deformers → Lattice. Figure 5.66 shows a polygonal hand model with a default lattice applied. The top node of the hand has been selected and the lattice applied.

Figure 5.66

A lattice is applied to the polygonal hand model.

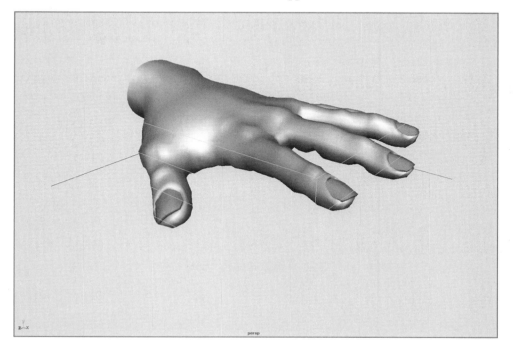

To experience how this works, you'll remodel the poly hand using a few different lattices. Your objective is to create an alien hand by thinning and elongating the hand and each of the fingers—we all know aliens have long, gawky fingers. Because it would take a lot of time and effort to achieve this by moving the vertices of the poly mesh itself, using lattices here is ideal.

To elongate and thin the entire hand, load the scene file detailed_poly_hand.ma from the Poly_Hand project from the companion web page, and follow these steps:

1. Select the top node of the hand (poly_hand) in the Outliner, and choose Create Deformers → Lattice. Doing so creates a default lattice that affects the entire hand, fingernails and all. Although you can change the lattice settings in the option box upon creation, you'll edit the lattice after it's applied to the hand.

2. The lattice is selected after it's created. Open the Attribute Editor, and click the ffd1LatticeShape tab. The three attributes of interest here are S Divisions, T Divisions, and U Divisions. These sliders control how many divisions the lattice uses to deform its geometry. Set S Divisions to **3**, T Divisions to **2**, and U Divisions to **3** for the result shown in Figure 5.67.

   A 3×2×3 lattice refers to the number of division lines in the lattice as opposed to the number of sections; otherwise, this would be a 2×1×2 lattice!

3. With the lattice selected, press F8 to switch to Component mode and display the lattice's points. These points act just like the vertices on a polygonal shape. You'll use them to change the overall shape of the hand without moving the vertices of the hand. Select the vertices on the thumb side of the hand, and move them to squeeze in that half of the hand. Notice how only that zone of the model is affected by that part of the lattice.

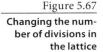

Figure 5.67

Changing the number of divisions in the lattice

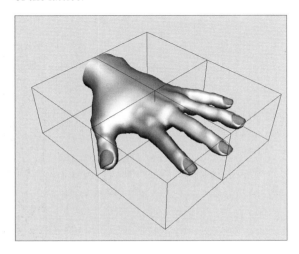

4. Toggle back to Object mode (press F8 again), and scale the entire lattice to be thinner in the *Z*-axis and longer in the *X*-axis. The entire hand is deformed in accordance with how the lattice is scaled (see Figure 5.68).

5. Now that you've altered the hand, you have no need for this lattice. If you delete the lattice, the hand will snap back to its original shape. You don't want this to happen. Instead, you need to delete the construction history on the hand to get rid of the lattice, as you did with the axe head exercise earlier in this chapter.

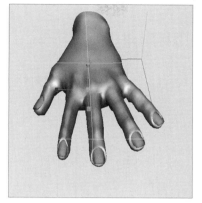

Figure 5.68

Lengthen the hand using the deformer.

   Select the top node of the hand, and choose Edit → Delete By Type → History.

Creating Alien Fingers

The next step is to elongate the individual fingers and widen the knuckles. Let's begin with the index finger. Follow these steps:

1. Select the top node of the hand, and create a new lattice as before. It forms around the entire hand.

   Although you can divide the lattice so that its divisions line up with the fingers, it's much easier and more interactive to scale and position the entire lattice so it fits around the index finger only.

2. Simply moving and scaling the selected lattice will deform the hand geometry. You don't want to do this. Instead, you need to select the lattice and its base node. This lets you change the lattice without affecting the hand. In the Outliner, select both the ffd1Lattice and ffd1Base nodes (see Figure 5.69).

3. Scale, rotate, and transform the lattice to fit around the index finger, as shown in Figure 5.70.

4. Deselect the base, and set the lattice S Divisions to **7**, T Divisions to **2**, and U Divisions to **3**.

5. Adjust the lattice to lengthen the finger by pulling the lattice points (see Figure 5.71). Pick the lattice points around each of the knuckles individually, and scale them sideways to widen them.

6. To delete the lattice and keep the changes to the finger, select the top node of the hand and delete its History. Repeat this entire procedure for the rest of the fingers to finish your alien hand. (Try to creep out your younger sister with it.)

Figure 5.69

Select the lattice and base nodes.

The alien hand in Figure 5.72 was created by adjusting the polygonal hand from this exercise using only lattices.

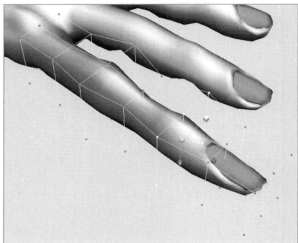

Figure 5.70
Position the lattice and its base to fit around the index finger.

Figure 5.71
Flare out the knuckles.

Figure 5.72
The human hand model is transformed into an alien hand by using lattices to deform the geometry.

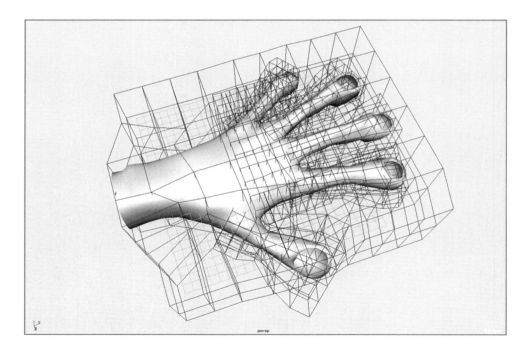

As you can see, lattices give you powerful editing capabilities without the complication of dealing with surface points directly. Lattices can help you reshape an entire complex model quickly or adjust minor details on parts of a larger whole.

In Chapter 8, "Introduction to Animation," you'll animate an object using another type of deformer. You'll also learn how to deform an object along a path.

Animating Through a Lattice

Lattices don't only work on polygons; they can be used on any geometry in Maya and at any stage in your workflow to create or adjust models. You can also use lattices to create animated effects. In the next exercise, you'll animate an object through a simple lattice.

In the previous example, if you moved the hand geometry through the lattice while it was still applied to one of the fingers, you would have seen an interesting effect before you deleted the last of your lattices. The parts of the geometry of the hand deformed as the hand traveled through the lattice. Think of ways you can use this warping effect in an animation. For example, you can create the effect of a balloon squeezing through a pipe by animating the balloon geometry through a lattice.

In the following exercise, you'll create a NURBS sphere with 8 sections and 16 spans and an open-ended NURBS cylinder that has no end caps:

1. Choose Create → NURBS Primitives → Sphere ❏, set Sections to **8** and Spans to **16**, and create the sphere.

2. Choose Create → NURBS Primitives → Cylinder ❏, and check None for the Caps option. Scale and arrange the sphere balloon and cylinder pipe as shown in Figure 5.73.

3. Select the balloon, and create a lattice for it (see Figure 5.74). (From the Animation menu set, choose Create Deformers → Lattice.) Set the S, T, and U Divisions to **4**, **19**, and **4**, respectively. You set this number of lattice divisions to create a smoother deformation when the sphere goes through the pipe.

Figure 5.73

Arrange the balloon and pipe.

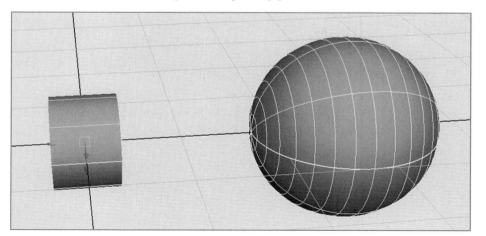

Figure 5.74

Create a lattice for the sphere.

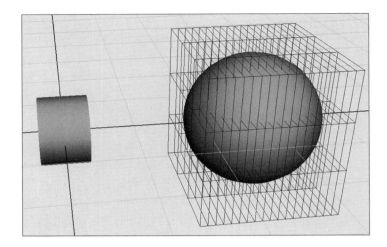

4. Select the lattice and its base in the Outliner (ffd1Lattice and ffd1Base nodes), and move the middle of the lattice so it fits over the length of the pipe (see Figure 5.75).

Figure 5.75

Relocate the lattice to the cylinder.

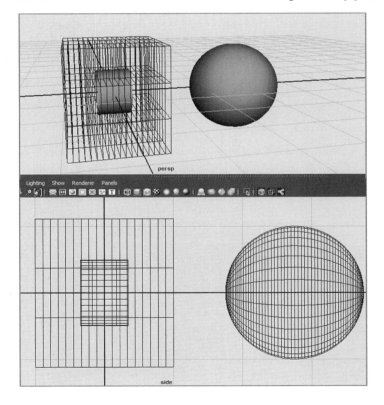

5. Deselect the lattice base, and choose Component mode for the lattice. Select the appropriate points, and shape the lattice so the middle of the lattice fits into the cylinder (see Figure 5.76).

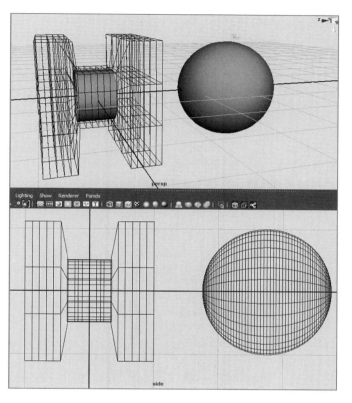

Figure 5.76

Squeeze in the lattice points to fit the cylinder.

6. Select the sphere, and move it back and forth through the pipe and lattice. Notice how it squeezes to fit through. If you look closely, you'll see that the sphere starts to squeeze a little before it enters the pipe. You'll also see parts of the sphere sticking out of the very ends of the pipe. This effect, in which geometry passes through itself or another surface, is called *interpenetration*. You can avoid this by using a more highly segmented sphere and lattice. If you try this exercise with a lower-segmented sphere and/or lattice, you'll notice the interpenetrations even more. Figure 5.77 shows the balloon squeezing through the pipe.

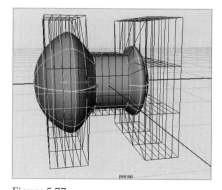

Figure 5.77

Squeezing the balloon through the pipe using a Lattice deformer

In a similar fashion, you can create a lattice along a curve path and have an object travel through it. You'll try this in Chapter 8.

Summary

In this chapter, you tackled NURBS modeling by going through the usual surfacing tools, from lofting and revolving to bevels and boundary surfaces. Then you explored the implications of surface History, and how surfaces adjust to changes when History is enabled. You learned about different editing methods for NURBS surfaces, such as inserting isoparms and attaching surfaces together as well as converting those surfaces to poly meshes. You then put those lessons to work on creating a NURBS patch model for a steam pump for a locomotive model, which you then imported into the locomotive scene file. Also in this chapter, I introduced you to the Artisan tool and how to use it to sculpt a NURBS surface.

This chapter covered various modeling techniques to help you break away from typical ways of thinking. You learned how to use a lattice to adjust a polygon hand model into an alien hand, as well as how to animate a balloon pushing through a pipe. As you saw in this and in the previous chapter and as you'll see in the next chapter, you can accomplish a modeling task in several ways. Different workflows give you the flexibility to choose your own modeling style. To make good choices, however, you'll need to practice. Good modelers have a strong eye for detail and a high tolerance for work that is repetitious. They also love assembling a complex object, and they're thrilled by the eventual outcome.

Keep at it; model everything you get your hands and eyes on. Try the same model a few different ways; switch between NURBS and polygons to become comfortable with the toolset in Maya. As you're doing that, stay on top of how you organize your nodes, and keep everything named and organized: the organization of your scenes is extremely important.

For further practice, use this chapter as a reference to create some of the following models using NURBS surfaces and lattices to aid in shaping polygons:

Bathroom Sink   Snap a few digital stills of your bathroom sink, or find some pictures on the Internet. A sink will give you a great chance to explore NURBS surfacing, making pristine curves and smooth surfaces. It may be a bit involved, but it's not overwhelming.

Cartoon Head   Use Maya Artisan and the Sculpt Geometry tool to turn an ordinary sphere into a cartoonish head. It's fun to use Sculpt Geometry to model. Try to make the head using only Artisan.

Computer Mouse   A PC or Mac mouse makes a great simple NURBS model.

CHAPTER 6

Practical Experience

It's time to put what you've learned so far into action. In this chapter, you'll build a child's table lamp. The lamp project uses poly and NURBS modeling techniques to give you some practical experience with a larger project in the Autodesk® Maya® software.

Learning Outcomes: In this chapter, you will be able to

- Use bevels and extrusions efficiently
- Manipulate curves to create poly meshes with Revolve → Surface
- Create a shape with a path extrusion
- See the differences between the Maya and Modeling Toolkit workflows
- Use reference images to shape your models
- See how to set up views with grid lines to align reference images for modeling
- See how images are lined up to make reference images for modeling
- Work in the Hypershade to assign image maps to objects in the scene
- Use a Boolean operation to cut holes in a mesh
- Use Maya referencing to easily share files between stages of workflow

Evaluating the Table Lamp

Download the entire TableLamp project folder structure from the book's companion web page (www.sybex.com/go/introducingmaya2014) to your computer's hard drive and set your project to that location.

Figure 6.1 shows the lamp you'll be modeling first in this chapter. There's certainly enough detail in this object to make it a good exercise, but it won't be difficult to complete. You can always return to this exercise to add more of your own detail or even redesign it for more challenge, which is something I highly recommend.

Figure 6.1

The table lamp is cute!

Study the photo carefully to get an understanding of the components that make up this object. You will model the parts individually instead of attacking the entire shape as a single object. This way of thinking helps complex objects become easier to understand and model. The lamp consists of the base, stem, lampshade, and toy airplane. In Chapter 3's decorative box exercise, you used reference planes to give you an accurate guide to build the box. With the lamp, since it's a relatively simple shape, you can use the profile photos in Figure 6.2 and Figure 6.3 as visual guides. You will not be importing them as reference planes into Maya since there's enough perspective in the photos that it will not allow for a clean side or front profile (like you had for the decorative box in Chapter 3). But that's OK for the lamp itself. When you set out to model the toy airplane later in this chapter, you'll use proper reference images.

Figure 6.2
The side photo of the lamp

Figure 6.3
The front photo of the lamp

Modeling the Base

You'll start by modeling the base. As you can see in Figure 6.4, the base is a simple cylinder with a rounded bevel at the top and a sharper bevel at the bottom. Create a TableLamp project on your hard drive, or set your project to the one copied from the companion website.

Figure 6.4
The base

For this exercise, you'll enable Modeling Toolkit, except where noted. Make sure to set your project to the TableLamp project you downloaded from the website. You'll begin the model in the following steps:

1. In a new Maya scene, make sure Interactive Creation is turned off in the Create → Polygon Primitives menu, and then create a cylinder and name it **base**. Scale it to (**3, 0.35, 3**), as shown in Figure 6.5.

Figure 6.5

**Scale the cylinder to
the proportions of
the base.**

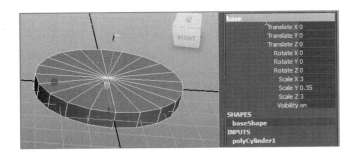

2. Select the base, and in the Channel Box, click the `polyCylinder1` entry to expand the attributes to adjust the subdivisions to make the base rounder. Set `Subdivisions Axis` to **60** and Subdivisions Caps to **4**.

3. To create the top round bevel, select the top loop of outer edges by right-clicking the cylinder and choosing Edge from the marking menu. Then double-click one of the top horizontal edges, as shown in Figure 6.6. Double-clicking will select the entire loop of edges automatically, whether you have Modeling Toolkit enabled or not. How convenient!

Figure 6.6

**Select the top loop
of edges.**

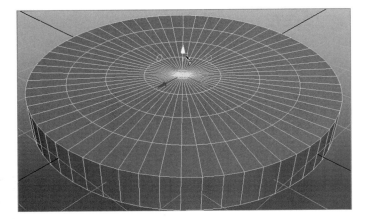

4. In the Modeling Toolkit under Mesh Editing Tools, choose Bevel. Your cursor turns into a double arrow, and a yellow readout appears in the top middle of your work panel. Click the Offset button under the Bevel Options heading in the Modeling Toolkit, and click and drag in your work window to set the Offset value to about **0.25**; then click the Segments button and click and drag to set Segments to **6**. Next, press the Bevel button again to turn it off, and then select the bottom loop of outer edges and repeat the bevel with an Offset value of **0.04** and a Segments value of **2**. Figure 6.7 shows the beveled base.

The scene file `lampModel_v01.mb` contains the finished base.

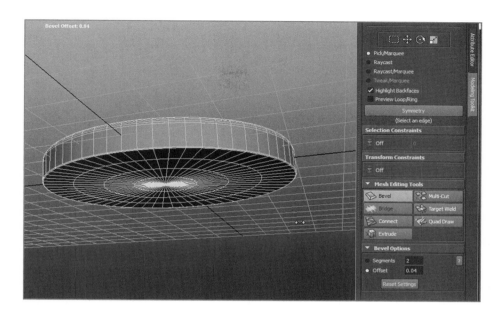

Figure 6.7
The beveled base

Creating the Lamp Stem

That's it; the base is completed. Continue with your own file to create the stem next, or load the file lampModel_v01.mb in the Scenes folder of the TableLamp project from the companion website.

In Figure 6.8, you can see the stem disassembled. It's a simple cylinder with a slight extrusion at the base and another one-third of the way up to the top, where the hooks for the lampshade and light bulb socket are. And since you don't see the light bulb behind the lampshade, you'll skip creating the bulb entirely.

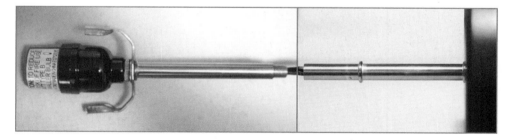

Figure 6.8
The stem of the lamp without the toy airplane

The Stem

To begin the stem, follow along here:

1. Create a poly cylinder, and scale it to (0.2, 4.8, 0.2); place it so its bottom touches the top of the base, as shown in Figure 6.9. Name it **stem**.

2. Choose Edit Mesh → Insert Edge Loop Tool, and insert an edge loop toward the bottom of the stem, as shown in Figure 6.10.

3. Select the bottom row of faces, and choose Extrude from the Mesh Editing tools section of the Modeling Toolkit panel. Set Local Z to **0.05** (Figure 6.11), and click off Extrude in the Modeling Toolkit panel to commit the extrusion.

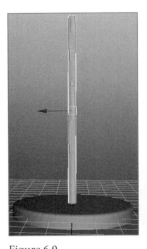

Figure 6.9

Place the cylinder on the base.

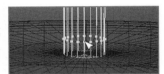

Figure 6.10

Insert an edge loop at the bottom of the stem.

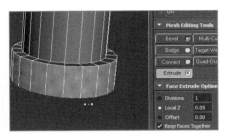

Figure 6.11

Create an extrusion at the bottom of the stem.

4. Select the top edge loop on the extruded bottom of the stem, and use either Modeling Toolkit's Bevel tool with an Offset of **0.35** and Segments of **2**, or a regular Maya Bevel with a Width of **0.35** and Segments of **2**. Figure 6.12 shows the beveled base.

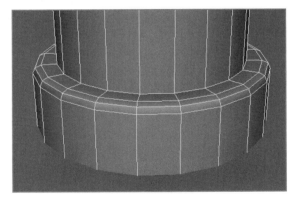

Figure 6.12

The extrusion is beveled.

5. About one-third of the way up the stem from the base, insert two new edge loops, as shown in Figure 6.13. These new faces will be used to create the second extrusion, as you did for the base.

6. Select the new faces between the new edge loops, and use Extrude in the Modeling Toolkit with a Local Z of **0.05**. Select the top and bottom outer row of edges and use the Modeling Toolkit's Bevel tool on them with an Offset of **0.5** (or Width if you use Maya Bevel) and Segments of **2**. Figure 6.14 shows the beveled extrusion. Save your scene!

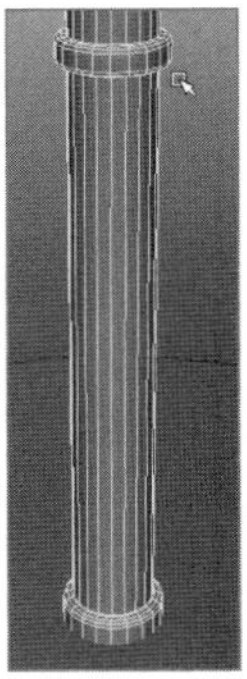

Figure 6.13

Insert two edge loops.

Figure 6.14

Creating the stem's middle extrusion

The Lampshade Bracket

Now that the stem is in place, on top of the lamp sits the light socket and the bracket that holds the lampshade (Figure 6.15 on the left), which you'll tackle here.

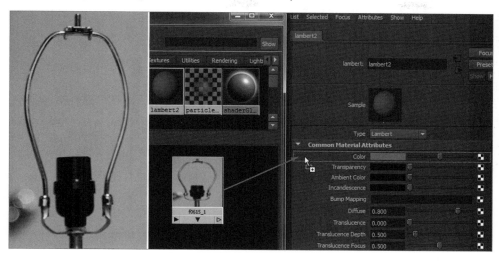

Figure 6.15

The lampshade bracket is shown on the left. Connecting the file node to the shader's Color attribute is shown on the right.

1. Create a poly plane, rotate it 90 degrees in the *X*-axis, and name it **reference**. In the front view panel, scale it to (4.6, 1, 9.75). You will put a reference image on this plane as you did in Chapter 3. This particular scale makes the photo image fit properly.

2. Choose Window → Rendering Editors → Hypershade. In the Hypershade, create a new Lambert shader. Navigate to the Sourceimages folder of the TableLamp project, and drag the image file stemTop.tif to the Hypershade. Click the Lambert shader, and open the Attribute Editor. MMB+drag the image file node in the Hypershade onto the Color attribute of the selected Lambert shader to map the image onto that shader, as shown in Figure 6.15 on the right.

3. Drag the new Lambert shader with the photo mapped to it onto the plane in the front view. Press 6 for Texture mode in the front view, and line up the plane with the top of the stem cylinder, as shown in Figure 6.16.

4. Choose Create → CV Curve Tool, and in the front view, trace the right-side outline of the light socket. Make sure to start laying CVs from the bottom up to the top; see Figure 6.17. This profile shape will create a hollow for the light bulb.

> If the curves you are tracing seem to disappear when you deselect them, they may be hiding behind the reference plane. Simply select the reference plane and move it back in the *Z*-axis a tiny bit, and the curves should show up again.

Figure 6.16

Placing the reference plane for the stem top

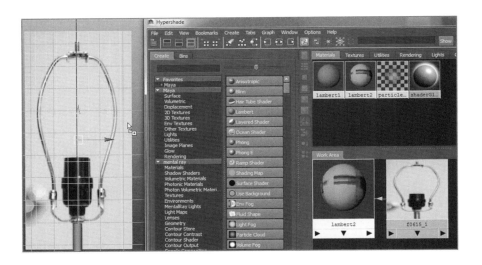

5. In the Surfaces menu set, select Surfaces → Revolve ❒. Set Axis Preset to Y and Output Geometry to Polygons. Then set Type to Quads and Tessellation Method to Standard Fit, as shown in Figure 6.18. Click Revolve.

6. In the front view, trace the left-side profile of one of the bell-shaped clasps on the lampshade bracket, as shown in Figure 6.19. With the new curve selected, choose Display → NURBS → CVs to display the CVs for the curve. Press D for Pivot Move mode, and click the Point Snaps icon (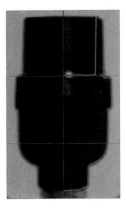) to snap the curve's pivot point to the top CV as shown.

Figure 6.17

Trace the right side of the socket.

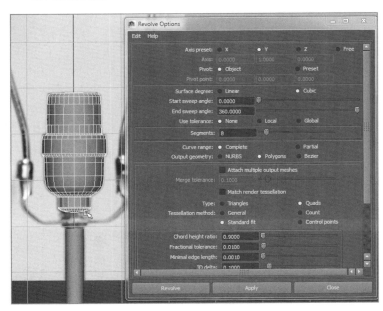

Figure 6.18

Revolve the socket shape.

7. Select Surfaces → Revolve ❑ again. Keep Axis Preset set to Y and Output Geometry to Polygons. Leave Type set to Quads and Tessellation Method to Standard Fit as well. Click Revolve, and you will see the bell-shaped clasp. Center the pivot point (Modify → Center Pivot), and then duplicate the bell shape (Ctrl+D) and move the copy to the other bell-shaped clasp, as shown in Figure 6.20.

8. Delete the profile curve shapes. Name the bell shapes **clasp** and **clasp1** and the socket geometry **socket**. Save your scene.

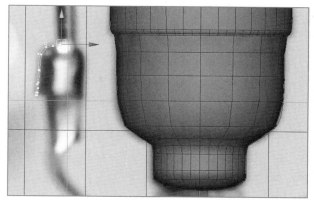

Figure 6.19

Trace the right half of the bell-shaped clasp.

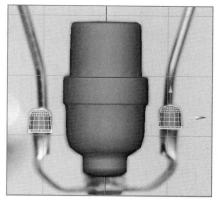

Figure 6.20

The bell-shaped clasps in place

The Bracket's Tube

To create the tubing for the top part of the bracket, follow these steps:

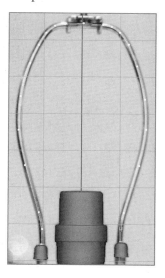

Figure 6.21

Trace a new CV curve.

1. In the front view, trace a new CV curve around the bracket shape, as shown in Figure 6.21. Use the CV placement shown as a reference to get the shape correct. This curve will be the path curve for a surface extrusion. With the new curve selected, turn on the CVs (Display → NURBS → CVs).

2. Select the right-side clasp (in this case, clasp1), and press Ctrl+H to hide it from view temporarily. Later you'll turn on visibility again through the Outliner.

3. Select Create → NURBS Primitives, and make sure the Interactive Creation check box is off. Then choose Create → NURBS Primitives → Circle to place a circle at the origin. Using Point Snaps (🔾), snap the circle

Figure 6.22

Snap the circle to the path's end CV.

to the right-side end of the bracket's path curve you created in step 1, as shown in Figure 6.22. This circle is the profile curve for the extrusion you will create in the next step.

4. Still in the Surfaces menu set, select Surfaces → Extrude ❑. In the options, set Result Position to At Path and Output Geometry to Polygons, leaving Type set to Quads and Tessellation Method set to Standard Fit, as shown in Figure 6.23. Click Extrude, and a tube will be created for the lampshade bracket. Name the tube **bracketTop**, and delete the circle and path curve.

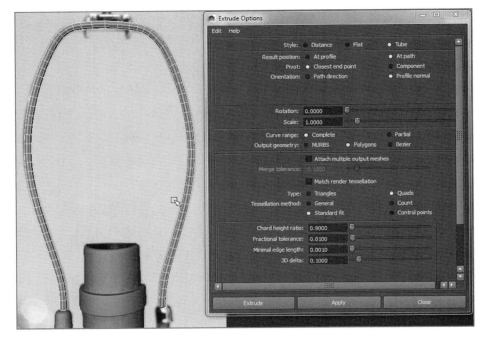

Figure 6.23

Create the tube for the bracket.

5. In the Outliner (Window → Outliner), select the hidden clasp (shown in Figure 6.24 as the grayed-out `clasp1` node). Select Display → Show → Show Selection.

6. Make sure to position the clasps if needed to fit over the ends of the `bracketTop` tube you just created. Now all that remains for the lampshade bracket is the bottom bracket and the nuts that hold it in place to the stem.

Figure 6.24

Select and show the hidden clasp object.

The Bracket's Bottom Part

Now for the rest of the bracket.

1. Open the Polygons menu set. Create a poly cube, and then scale and position it as shown in Figure 6.25.

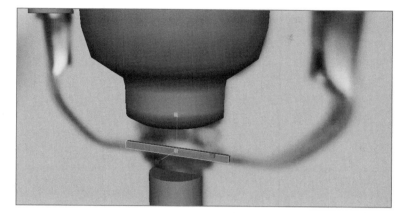

Figure 6.25

Place a cube.

2. Select both end faces of the new cube and use the Modeling Toolkit's Extrude tool to extrude them with a Local Z value of **0.25**, as shown in Figure 6.26. Turn off Extrude to commit the change.

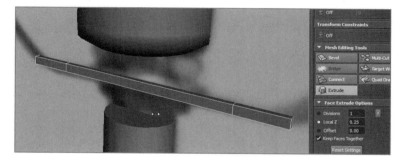

Figure 6.26

Extrude both end faces.

3. Move the two new end faces to create a bit of a downward arc, as shown in Figure 6.27.

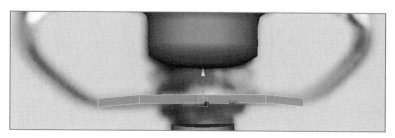

Figure 6.27

Create a slight downward curve.

4. With the two end faces selected, use Modeling Toolkit's Extrude to extrude them with a Local Z of **0.06** and turn off Extrude. Then click the Extrude button in the Modeling Toolkit panel to extrude again, this time with a Local Z value of **0.4**. Select the two new end faces and move them up to align with the bracket in the Front window. Then select each face individually in the perspective view, and rotate them to make the faces horizontal. Lastly, scale the faces in the X-axis to match the perspective view in Figure 6.28.

Figure 6.28

Adjust the extruded cube to fit the bracket shape.

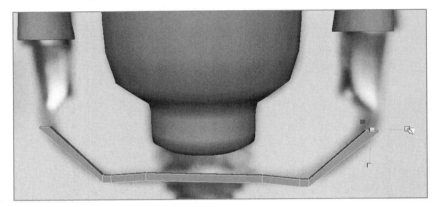

5. With the end faces selected, extrude them with a Local Z of **0.15**. With the faces still selected, turn Extrude off and on again to extrude once more, this time with a Local Z of **0.6** and an Offset of **-0.05** to flare them out a bit, as shown in Figure 6.29.

Figure 6.29

Extrude up the bracket.

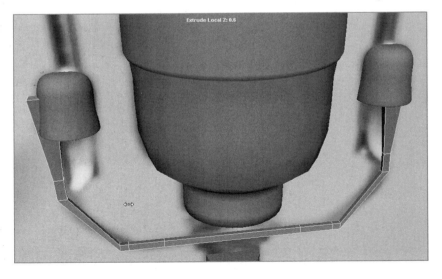

6. Press W for the Move tool. Select the top end faces individually and move them into the bell-shaped clasps. Figure 6.30 shows the bracket ends inside the clasps.

Figure 6.30

Place the ends of the brackets inside the clasps.

7. Select the reference plane, and press Ctrl+H to hide it. Insert an edge loop along the middle of the bottom bracket mesh, as shown in Figure 6.31. You'll use this extra detail to create a valley in the bracket.

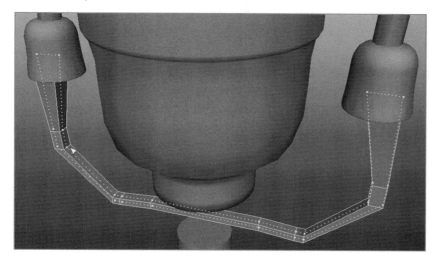

Figure 6.31

Create an edge loop.

8. Select only the inside edges of that new edge loop (the part that faces the light socket), and scale them out to create a ridge inside the bracket, as shown in Figure 6.32.

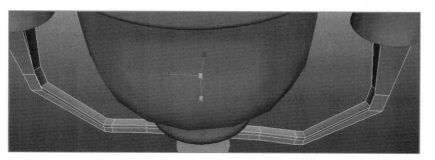

Figure 6.32

Create a ridge.

9. Use the Outliner to turn on the reference plane again. Move vertices on the bracket to shape the bracket to the reference image (Figure 6.33). Since this part of the lamp is barely visible when the lampshade is put on the lamp, you'll leave the detail level low. Feel free to study the pictures of the lamp bracket and create a more detailed version on your own as extra practice.

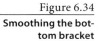

Figure 6.33

Shape the bracket to match.

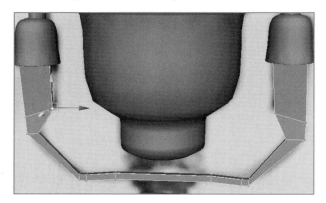

10. Select the bottom bracket piece and press 3 to see a smooth preview. It's just a little too round, which means the mesh needs a few more subdivisions to smooth better. Press 1 to get back to the mesh's normal view.

11. With the bracket geometry selected, choose Edit Mesh → Add Divisions □, set Division Levels to **1**, and click Add Divisions. This will tessellate the mesh a little better. Preview again by pressing 3, and you should get a much nicer smoothing result. Press 1 to exit smooth preview.

12. Let's smooth the mesh for real now. Select the bracket, and choose Mesh → Smooth □. Set Add Divisions to Exponentially and Division Levels to **1**. Name the mesh **bracketBottom**. Click Smooth, and check your result against Figure 6.34. Do the same to the base of the lamp to smooth that as well.

Figure 6.34

Smoothing the bottom bracket

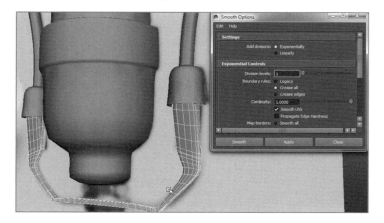

Ah, Nuts!

Now you'll add the nuts that hold the bracket to the stem.

1. In the top view, create a poly torus, name it **nut**, and move it to the side in the *X*-axis so you can work on it unimpeded. In the Channel Box, click polyTorus1, and change Subdivisions Axis to **6** and Subdivisions Height to **5**.

2. Scale the nut down in the *Y*-axis to flatten it out (you can see its thickness in the left side of Figure 6.35). Position the nut, and scale it uniformly to fit between the bracket and the stem, as shown in the right side of Figure 6.35.

3. Duplicate the nut, and place it above the bracket.

4. Duplicate the nut again, and place it between the first copied nut and the light socket.

5. Rotate them in the *Y*-axis to offset the three nuts from each other, as shown in Figure 6.36.

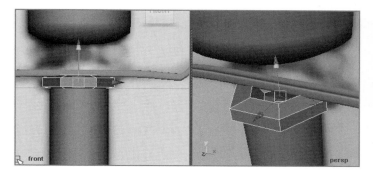

Figure 6.35

Create and place the first nut.

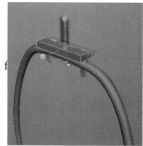

Figure 6.36

Place and orient the nuts to hold the bracket to the stem.

Lampshade Mount

Finally, for the lampshade bracket, you need the lampshade mount (Figure 6.37) at the top of the tubing you created.

1. Create a poly cube. Scale and position it to the top of the tube, as shown in Figure 6.38.

2. Place two edge loops on either end of the cube, as shown in Figure 6.39.

Figure 6.37

The lampshade mount

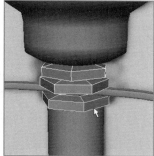

Figure 6.38

Place a cube to begin the mount's model.

3. Select the bottom faces on both ends and extrude them with a Thickness of **0.35** to create the flanges on the mount, as shown in Figure 6.40.

4. Select the mount as an object (not in component mode) and choose Edit Mesh → Bevel ❏ to bevel it using traditional Maya Beveling with a Width of **0.7** and Segments of **2**, as shown in Figure 6.41. Name the mesh **mount**.

Figure 6.39

Place edge loops on both sides.

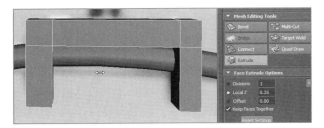

Figure 6.40

Extrude down the flanges.

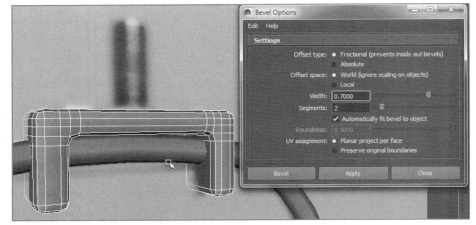

Figure 6.41

Bevel the mount to finish it off.

5. Place a properly sized poly cylinder on top for the screw, and name it **screw**. Select the top edge loop and put a bevel on it, and the lamp's lampshade bracket is complete. Select the reference plane and delete it; you don't need it anymore.

Figure 6.42 shows the lamp so far. Save your work.

Figure 6.42

The table lamp is ready for its lampshade.

Modeling the Lampshade

The lampshade will be fairly easy to create. You can continue with your own scene or load lampModel_v02.mb from the Scenes folder of the TableLamp project from the companion website. You will use another reference to create the lampshade here:

1. In the front view panel, create a poly plane and rotate it 90 degrees in the X-axis. Move it up to the lampshade bracket and name it **reference2**.

2. Open the Hypershade (Window → Rendering Editors → Hypershade) and create a new Lambert shader.

3. In the Sourceimages folder of the TableLamp project, drag the image file lampShade.tif into the Hypershade. Select the new Lambert shader, and open the Attribute Editor. MMB+drag the new lampShade.tif image file node onto the Color attribute of the new Lambert shader, and assign it to the new reference plane.

4. The photo is a perfect square, so you need only uniformly scale the reference plane and then position it, as shown in Figure 6.43.

5. You will create the blue stripes and the white lampshade as separate objects. First, trace a CV curve starting at the top and running down along the right edge of the lampshade. Before completing the curve, at the bottom of the shade, lay down CVs to loop back up along the edge a little to the left to make the line double wide, as shown in Figure 6.44.

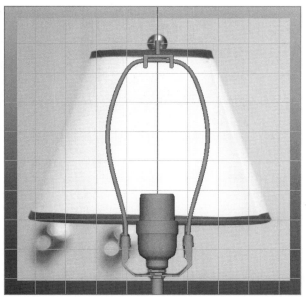

Figure 6.43

Place the new reference for the lampshade.

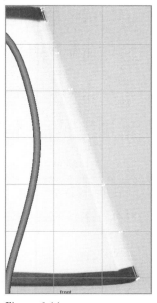

Figure 6.44

Create the curve for the profile of the lampshade.

6. This curve is open at the top (Figure 6.45, left), so you will have to close it. Select the profile curve, and in the Surfaces menu set, choose Edit Curves → Open/Close Curves. The curve closes but in a bizarre way (Figure 6.45, middle). Select the offending CVs, and move them to make the line more like Figure 6.45, right.

Figure 6.45

The profile curve (left) is closed (middle) and then adjusted to fit better (right).

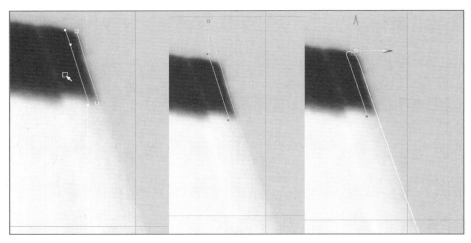

7. Select the closed profile curve, and in the Surfaces menu set, choose Surfaces → Revolve ❑. Keep the Axis preset at Y, Output Geometry at Polygons, and Tessellation Method as Standard Fit as before. This time, set 3D Delta to **0.04** for a cleaner resulting mesh. Click Revolve, and your lampshade is created. It seems to be offset, however, as you can see in Figure 6.46.

Figure 6.46

The lampshade looks offset.

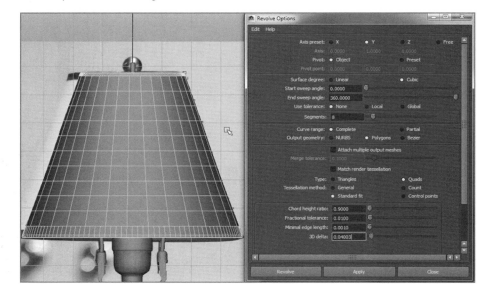

Nothing is perfect, including this little lampshade. It's OK if the reference image does not exactly line up with the geometry in this exercise. If you were building something to exact scale, you would start with exact photos. In this case, though, you can simply cheat.

8. Select the profile curve for the lampshade (use the Outliner if you need to). Simply move the profile curve to the right to make the lampshade wider. Construction History allows the lampshade mesh to adjust as you move the profile curve. When you have a satisfactory sizing of the lampshade (Figure 6.47), delete the profile curve. Name the lampshade geometry **lampshade**.

Figure 6.47

Cheating the size of the lampshade

9. Now for the blue trim. Create a NURBS circle, rotate it 90 degrees in the X-axis, and place and scale it in the front view panel at the upper edge of the lampshade, as shown in Figure 6.48. You should have an oval shape oriented as shown.

Figure 6.48

Place a circle for a profile curve for the blue trim.

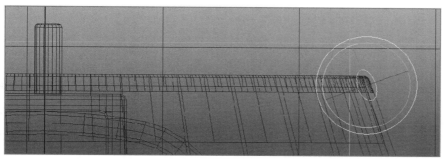

10. Press and hold D, and move the circle's pivot point to the middle of the lampshade, as shown in Figure 6.49.

11. Copy the oval shape, and place it at the bottom-right corner of the lampshade (Figure 6.50). Make sure to move its pivot point to the centerline of the lamp as well.

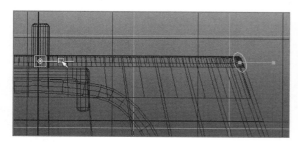

Figure 6.49

Move the circle's pivot to the center point of the lamp.

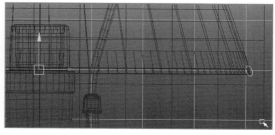

Figure 6.50

Place a copy of the oval at the bottom of the lampshade.

12. Now you are ready to revolve the ovals to make the upper and lower blue trim. Select both ovals, and in the Surfaces menu set, select Surfaces → Revolve ❑. Keeping the same settings as before in step 7, click Revolve, and compare your results to Figure 6.51.

Figure 6.51

The trim is in place.

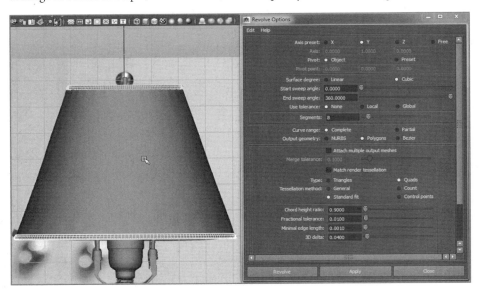

13. Name the trim objects **upperTrim** and **lowerTrim**, respectively, and delete the oval profile curves as well as the reference plane. You don't need them anymore.

As you can see in Figure 6.52, the lampshade has three metal tubes connecting it to the bracket with a metal ball over the screw. You'll create those in the following steps:

1. Create a polygon cylinder and flatten it to make a disc. Place the disc on top of the lampshade mount, around the screw. Bevel the top and bottom loop of edges, as shown in Figure 6.53. Name the object **disc**.

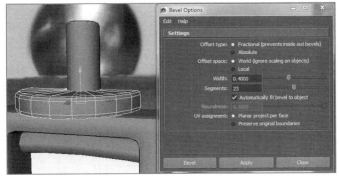

Figure 6.52

The lampshade is connected to the bracket by three metal tubes.

Figure 6.53

Place a beveled disc on the mount.

2. Create a poly cylinder, rotate it 90 degrees in the *Z*-axis to place it on its side in the front view panel, and name it **brace**. Scale it to be a long, thin tube at about the same thickness as the bracket top tube. Place it on top of the lampshade, as shown in Figure 6.54, and set its pivot point to the middle of the lampshade mount disc. This tube should go from the middle of the disc you just placed in the last step to the inside top of the lampshade trim.

3. Duplicate that brace tube twice, and orient and place the copies as shown in Figure 6.55.

4. You're almost finished with the main lamp model. Place a poly sphere at the top of the lampshade over the screw, and name it **button**.

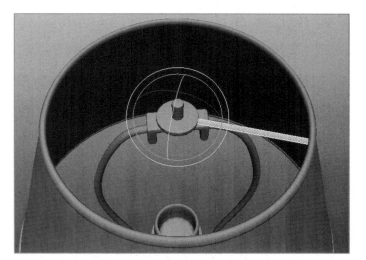

Figure 6.54

Place the first tube.

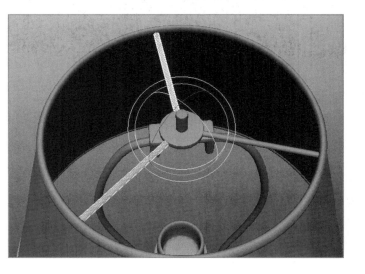

Figure 6.55

Place the duplicated bracing tubes as shown.

Voila! You're finished with the lamp itself and can move on to the toy airplane on its stem. Figure 6.56 shows the lamp so far and the Outliner view of its objects. You can check your work against the `lampModel_v03.mb` scene file in the Scenes folder of the TableLamp project from the companion website.

Figure 6.56

The main part of the lamp is complete.

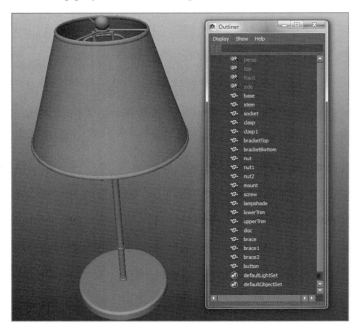

Making the Toy Airplane

Now all you need to add is the cute airplane to the middle of the lamp stem to complete this model. In this section, you will create the toy airplane in a new scene file, and then you'll learn how to *reference* the airplane model into the master lamp scene. *Referencing* in Maya is similar to importing a file into an open scene. However, with a referenced scene, any changes made to the original referenced scene will automatically be reflected into the object(s) referenced into the master scene. This is great for when you are continuously making adjustments to a model used in an animation or lighting scene. The model is updated as you make the changes. It also allows for an easier workflow when more than one person is working on a project. I'll explain referencing scenes in detail later in this chapter.

Since the toy airplane is a more complex shape than the lamp itself, you will use three image reference planes similar to those you used to create the decorative box in Chapter 3.

Reference Images

Reference images aren't just for fun! As you've seen, you can import images into Maya to work directly on the reference. For a model like this airplane, it's best to create three different image views of the model (front, side, and top) to give you the most information as you build the model. The first step, of course, is to take pictures of your intended model from these three angles. Figure 6.57, Figure 6.58, and Figure 6.59 show photos taken of the front, side, and top views of the toy airplane.

Figure 6.57

The airplane's front view

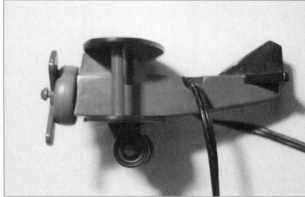

Figure 6.58

The airplane's side view

The trick here is to bring the photos into an image-editing program, such as Adobe Photoshop, and scale and edit the images to line them up as shown in Figure 6.60. The images have been copied and pasted into a larger frame, and grid lines are used to line up the major portions of the airplane, such as its wings and wheels.

Figure 6.59

The airplane's top view

Keep in mind that when you take a photo, in most cases there will be *perspective shift*, or *parallax*, in the image. Because of that shift, the different views of the same object will never exactly line up. As you can see in Figure 6.60, the bottom of the airplane wheels don't exactly line up between the front view and the side view, even though all the other major elements of the plane are in alignment. This is because of perspective differences in the photos.

Complete accuracy isn't what you're after in this situation. You just want to have a reasonable reference, and this will be more than adequate. Now, you'll import the images and create the model reference planes on which to work.

Figure 6.60

The views of the airplane roughly lined up in Photoshop

Creating Reference Planes for the Images

The reference views of the toy airplane have already been created for you. You can find them in the Sourceimages folder of the TableLamp project from the companion website. They're shown in Table 6.1.

Table 6.1

Reference views and sizes

FILENAME	VIEW	IMAGE SIZE	ASPECT RATIO
airplaneFront.jpg	Front	2000×1479	1:0.740
airplaneSide.jpg	Side	2400×1648	1:0.687
airplaneTop.jpg	Top	2400×2060	1:0.858

Why is the image resolution important? Well, it's not so much the resolution of the photos but rather the aspect ratio of each image. To properly map these images onto the planes you'll use in Maya, each plane has to be the same ratio in scale as its image. For example, an image that is 100×50 pixels has an aspect ratio of 2:1 and is, therefore, a wide horizontal rectangle. For it to map properly, the plane on which it's mapped in Maya must have a scale ratio of 2:1 as well so that it's also a wide horizontal rectangle. Otherwise, the image may distort. The more accurate your model needs to be, the more accurate your photos and their reference planes need to be.

You'll need to create three planes for each of the three views. First make sure Interactive Creation is turned off, and then follow these steps:

1. In a new scene, go to the front view panel, and create a polygonal plane by choosing Create → Polygon Primitives → Plane ▫. This plane is for the front image, so in the option box set Axis to **Z**, Width to **1**, and Height to **0.740**. Set Width Divisions and Height Divisions both to **1**. Make sure the check box for Preserve Aspect Ratio is deselected, as shown in Figure 6.61. Setting Axis to Z will place the plane properly in the front view.

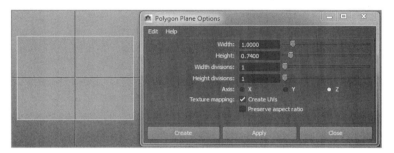

Figure 6.61

Creating a plane for the top view

2. Switch to the side view panel. Create a second plane, this time with a Width value of **1** and a Height value of **0.687**. Set Axis to X, and make sure the Preserve Aspect Ratio check box is not checked.

3. Switch to the top view panel. Create a third plane with Width set to **1**, Height set to **0.858**, and Axis set to **Y**. Make sure the Preserve Aspect Ratio box is still unchecked. Your Perspective panel should look like Figure 6.62.

Figure 6.62

The three view planes are ready.

Now that all three image planes have been created with the proper aspect ratios, you're ready to map the photos to them to create the reference for the model. You've already done this earlier in the chapter, but let's take a closer look at the process now.

Mapping the Reference Planes

The pesky wire has been painted out of these reference photos. To map the photos of the airplane to the reference planes, follow these steps:

1. Open the Hypershade (Window → Rendering Editors → Hypershade). Open a file browser in your OS, and navigate to the Sourceimages folder of the TableLamp project on your hard drive.

2. Click the `airplaneFront.jpg` file in your file browser, and drag it into the Work Area of the Hypershade window to import the file image. Drag the other two images (`airplaneSide.jpg` and `airplaneTop.jpg`) into the Hypershade as well, as shown in Figure 6.63.

If you don't see the image of the airplane in the icons in the Hypershade as you see in Figure 6.63, simply right-click the file node icon and select Refresh Swatch from the marking menu.

Figure 6.63

Importing the photos into the Hypershade window

3. Before you can assign the images to their respective planes, you must create shaders for each of the planes. In the left panel of the Hypershade window, click the Lambert icon three times to create three new Lambert shaders, as shown in Figure 6.64. For more information about shaders and texturing, see Chapter 7, "Autodesk Maya Shading and Texturing."

4. While still in the Hypershade Work Area, hold down the Ctrl key and MMB+drag the side-view photo swatch onto the first Lambert shader icon. Maya automatically maps the image to the color of the Lambert shader, as shown in Figure 6.65. You can also MMB+drag the image to the Lambert Shader's `Color` attribute in the Attribute Editor like you did earlier in the chapter.

5. Ctrl+MMB+drag the other two images onto their respective Lambert shaders to connect them. Name the shaders **lambertSide**, **lambertFront**, and **lambertTop**, respectively, by double-clicking them to open the Attribute Editor and changing their names; see Figure 6.65.

6. Assign the shaders to the reference planes. To do so, MMB+drag the Lambert shader that is connected to the side-view image to the side-view plane in the Perspective panel. Switch the perspective view into Texture mode by pressing 6 while in that panel. You should see the image of the airplane appear, as shown in Figure 6.66.

7. Drag the top-view Lambert shader to the top reference plane and the front Lambert shader to the front reference plane to assign the other two views. You should now have the three reference planes laid out as shown in Figure 6.67.

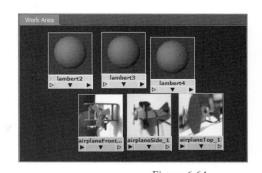

Figure 6.64

Create three new Lambert shaders.

Figure 6.65

Naming the Lambert shaders

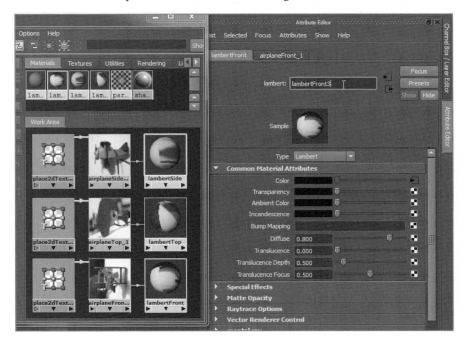

Figure 6.66

The side-view photo is mapped to the side view plane.

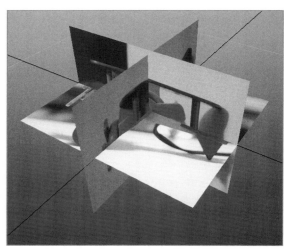

Figure 6.67

All three reference planes are mapped.

8. All isn't rosy yet! The front reference view and the side reference view seem to match up, but the top reference view is off. Select the top reference plane, and rotate it 90 degrees in the *Y*-axis. Although it's oriented properly now, the top view is larger than the side view plane, and the images still don't line up.

9. Uniformly scale and slightly move the top reference plane to match to the width of the airplane side view plane, as shown in Figure 6.68.

10. Uniformly scale and move the front reference plane as well to get the airplane images to line up better, as shown in Figure 6.69.

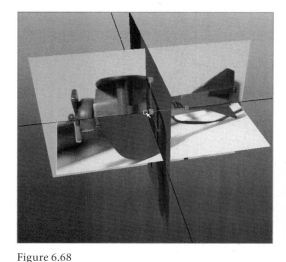

Figure 6.68

Scale and move the top reference airplane to match the side reference airplane.

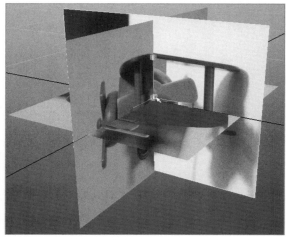

Figure 6.69

Line up the image reference planes.

11. Remember that the scale of these planes is small right now. You don't need to use real-world units for this project. However, you should scale the reference planes so that you have a larger scale with which to work. The base of the lamp you built was 6 units across, so the airplane should be about 6 units across. You will make the final adjustments later to fit the airplane into the lamp. For now, select all three reference planes and group them together by pressing Ctrl+G. Name the group node **referencePlaneGroup**.

12. Select the top group node and uniformly scale it so the reference planes are about 6 units large, as in Figure 6.70.

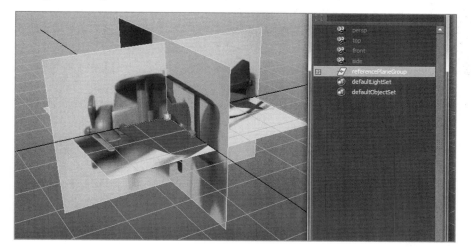

Figure 6.70

Group and then scale the planes up.

13. To give yourself more room to work, select the front view plane and move it back, as shown in Figure 6.71.

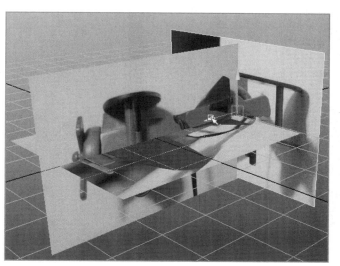

Figure 6.71

Move the front reference plane back.

14. Create a display layer for the planes to make it easy to manage them later. To do so, in Layer Editor below the Channel Box, click the Create A New Layer icon ().

    Double-click the new layer, and name it **referencePlanes** in the window that pops up (see Figure 6.72). Click Save. Your Layer Editor should resemble the one shown in Figure 6.73.

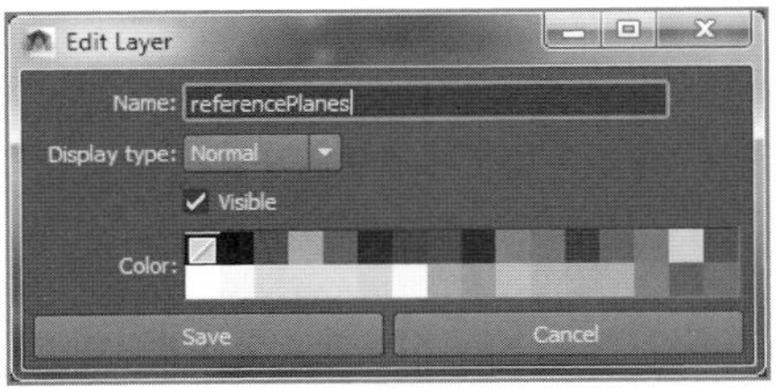

Figure 6.72

Name the new layer.

15. Select the top group node for the three reference planes (`referencePlaneGroup`), RMB+click the referencePlanes layer, and choose Add Selected Objects from the context menu. For more on Layer Editor, see the "Organizing Workflow with Layer Editor" section in Chapter 3, "The Autodesk Maya 2014 Interface." To toggle the display of the reference planes to get them out of the way, simply toggle the box to the extreme left of the layer name. It's currently checked with a V for Visible in Figure 6.73.

Save your work, and "version up" so you don't write over your previous scene files. You can download the scene file `airplaneModel_v01.ma` from the Scenes folder of the TableLamp project from the companion website to check your work or skip to this point. Just be sure to set your project to the TableLamp project on your hard drive after downloading the entire project from the website.

Figure 6.73

The new layer in Layer Editor

> To remain in step with this chapter, make sure Interactive Creation is turned off when you create any new primitives.

Creating the Fuselage

The main part of this airplane is its body, or *fuselage*. This will start with a cube in the following steps:

1. In the top view, press 6 to see Textured mode, if you haven't already. In the Layer Editor, click twice on the check box next to the Visibility toggle for the referencePlanes layer so you see an *R* appear, as shown in Figure 6.74. This sets that layer as a reference layer and makes the objects in the layer nonselectable.

Figure 6.74

Set the reference Planes layer to Reference.

2. Create a poly cube. You need to see the cube as a wireframe but still see the reference image as a textured object. In the top view panel's menu (not the main Maya menu bar), select Shading → X-Ray to allow you to see through the box but not lose your reference image display. Place and scale the cube over the fuselage of the plane, and then move the corner vertices to match the shape of the body, as shown in Figure 6.75.

3. Switch to the side view panel, and enable X-Ray mode (Shading → X-Ray). Move the corner vertices to get the general shape of the fuselage from the side, as shown in Figure 6.76.

4. Switch to Object mode to select the cube, and in the Polygon menu set, choose Edit Mesh → Insert Edge Loop Tool. Then insert two edge loops toward the back of the wing, where it meets the fuselage, as shown in Figure 6.77.

5. Use vertices to further shape the fuselage in the side and top views. Figure 6.78 shows the result.

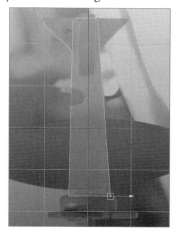

Figure 6.75

Shape a cube over the body of the plane.

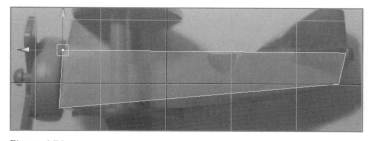

Figure 6.76

Shape the fuselage in the side view.

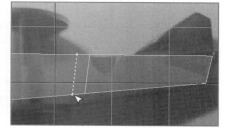

Figure 6.77

Insert two edge loops.

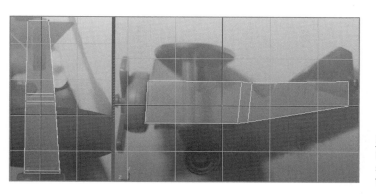

Figure 6.78

Further refine the outline shape of the fuselage using the top and side views.

6. Using the top view, insert an edge loop at the front of the tail wings. Switch to the side view, and choose Edit Mesh → Interactive Split Tool ⬚. In the option box, set Snap Magnets to **0**, and place a new edge split along the bottom of the tail wing, as shown in Figure 6.79. Do not click the right mouse button or hit Enter to commit the split yet.

7. Switch to the persp view, and continue the edge split around the back of the fuselage, as shown in Figure 6.80. Right-click to commit the new edges. Again, be careful not to click extra times when using the Interactive Split tool because you may inadvertently create vertices where you don't want or see them. This can cause issues later in the modeling pipeline without warning.

New edge split ——

New edge loop ——

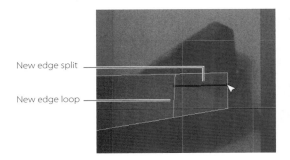

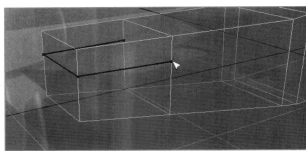

Figure 6.79
Starting the edges for the tail wings

Figure 6.80
Taking the split around the back

If you feel comfortable, you may also opt to use Modeling Toolkit's Multi-Cut tool in the Modeling Toolkit panel for steps 6 and 7 to make these edges instead of the Interactive Split tool. For more on how to use Multi-Cut, see Chapter 4.

8. Select both new faces on the sides of the fuselage and use the Modeling Toolkit's Extrude to extrude them with a Local Z of **0.7** or so. Use your top view to help you gauge how far to extrude the tail wings. Move the vertices in the top and side views to shape the tail wings, as shown in Figure 6.81.

Figure 6.81
Creating the tail wing shape

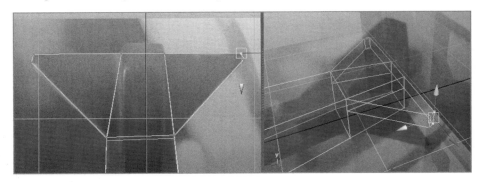

This is an inexpensive table lamp for a child's room. The airplane is not exactly uniform and even on both sides, so your model will also not be exactly uniform, either. You may certainly want to make your version more symmetrical.

9. For the vertical wing (the stabilizer) for the tail, insert an edge loop using the top view to line it up with the vertical stabilizer. Because of the splits you created earlier in this part of the geometry, the Insert Edge Loop tool creates an edge only across the top face, as shown in Figure 6.82. Luckily, that's exactly what you need.

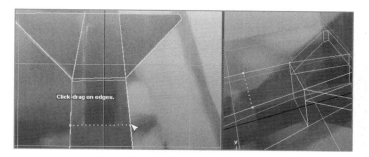

Figure 6.82

Create an edge loop for the vertical stabilizer wing.

10. Enter Object mode, and select the fuselage. Press W to exit the Insert Edge Loop tool; then choose Edit Mesh → Interactive Split Tool, and place a new split as shown in Figure 6.83. Make sure to right-click to commit the new split.

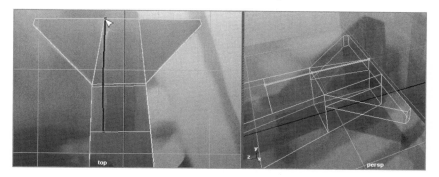

Figure 6.83

Insert a new edge split.

11. Create another split on the other side of the vertical wing (Figure 6.84).

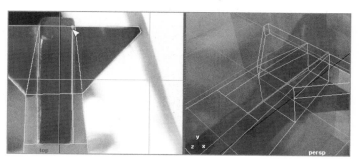

Figure 6.84

Create a split for the other side of the vertical stabilizer wing.

12. Select the top-center faces you just created with the Interactive Split tool, and extrude them with a Local Z of **0.7**, as shown in Figure 6.85.

13. Using the top view panel, move vertices to shape the vertical wing. Go through and move any vertices to shape the horizontal tail wings as well. Figure 6.86 shows the overall tail shape in all four view panels.

> Sometimes, things will not line up perfectly with photographed reference images like those of the lamp's toy airplane. It's up to you to shape the model to fit as best you can. For example, the tail section will differ slightly between the side and top views in Figure 6.86, but that's perfectly normal at this stage.

14. Now to concentrate on the front of the plane. There is a block that extends up from the fuselage to the top wing, as you can see in the earlier reference photo in Figure 6.3 and in your side view. Let's disable X-Ray view for the side view panel by unchecking Shading → X-Ray. This will make the reference image easier to see. However, the geometry of the fuselage blocks the reference, so let's set a display override for the mesh. Select the fuselage, and open the Attribute Editor. Under the Object Display → Drawing Overrides section, check Enable Overrides, and uncheck Shading. The fuselage is now displayed as a wireframe while the reference planes are still shaded and textured.

15. Insert an edge loop toward the front of the plane, as shown in Figure 6.87. Select the top face from the newly created section and extrude it up to just under the top wing as shown. Move the front edge vertices in the side view to shape the block to fit.

16. Select the top vertices of the block and taper the top using the front and side views as a guide for relative height. Keep in mind that perspective differences among the photos may mean the geometry may not line up exactly in all images, and that's OK; see Figure 6.88.

Save your work, and compare it to the scene file `airplaneModel_v02.ma` from the Scenes folder of the TableLamp project from the companion website to check your work, or skip to the next set of steps.

Figure 6.85

Extrude the vertical stabilizer wing shape.

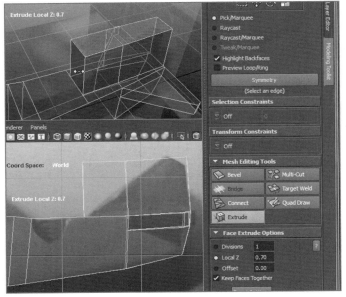

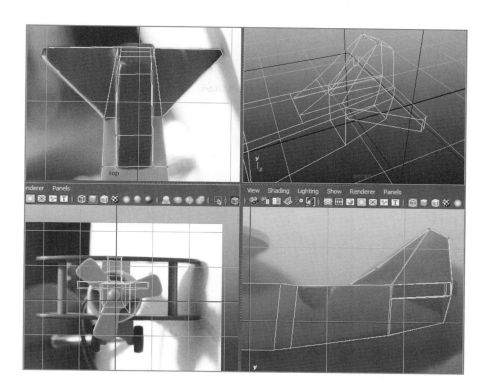

Figure 6.86

Shape the vertical and horizontal tail wings to fit.

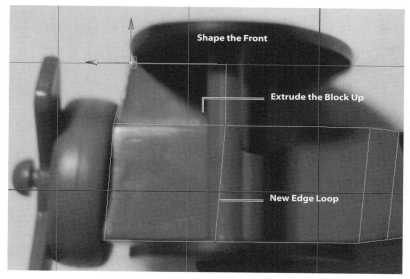

Figure 6.87

Create the block in the front of the airplane.

Figure 6.88

Fit the block.

Using Booleans to Finish the Fuselage

Before you're finished with the fuselage, you need to create the hole for the lamp's stem and the cockpit area using Booleans.

Booleans are very impressive operations that allow you to, among other things, cut holes in a mesh fairly easily. Basically, a Boolean is a geometric operation that creates a shape from the addition of two shapes together (Union), the subtraction of one shape from another (Difference), or the common intersection of two shapes (Intersection).

Be forewarned, however, that Boolean operations can be problematic. Sometimes you get a result that is wrong—or, even worse, the entire mesh disappears and you have to undo. Use Booleans sparingly and only on a mesh that is clean and prepared. You've cleaned and prepped your fuselage mesh, so there should be no problems.

To begin, let's create the hole for the lamp's stem. The plane (as shown earlier in Figures 6.2 and 6.3) sits on the stem at an angle. The hole in the fuselage needs to go between the biplane wings and the rear stabilizer wings and run from the left-top corner to the right-bottom corner. For a Boolean, you need two meshes. The fuselage is the first mesh to be affected, and the second mesh will be a polygonal cylinder to cut the hole into that fuselage.

1. Create a poly cylinder and use the reference planes as guides to move, rotate, and scale the cylinder to fit through the fuselage, as shown in Figure 6.89.

2. Turn off the drawing overrides for the fuselage in the Attribute Editor (in the Object Display section) so you can see the mesh as a shaded model now. With the fuselage selected, choose Edit → Delete By Type → History. This cleans out all the current history on the mesh, making the Boolean operation safer to run.

3. Select the fuselage first; then Shift+select the cylinder, and choose Mesh → Booleans → Difference. The cylinder disappears, and there is now a hole in the mesh, as shown in Figure 6.90.

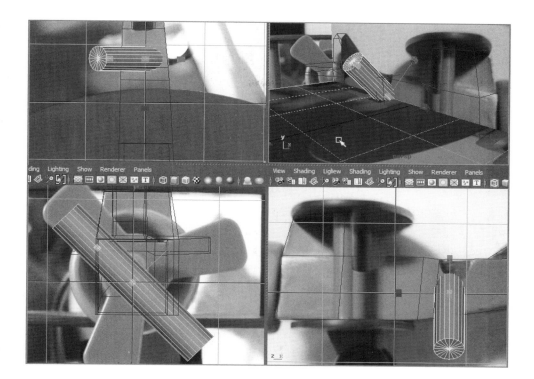

Figure 6.89

Place a cylinder that you'll use to cut the hole.

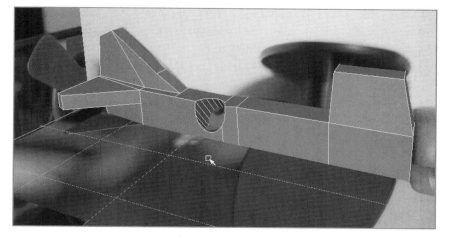

Figure 6.90

The Boolean made a hole!

4. Now for the cockpit. With the fuselage mesh selected, delete its history as in step 2.

5. With the fuselage selected, go into the Attribute Editor, and turn off shading in `Drawing Overrides` again to turn it into a wireframe. Using the reference planes, create and then position and scale another poly cylinder, as shown in Figure 6.91.

Figure 6.91

Place another cylinder to cut the shape of the cockpit.

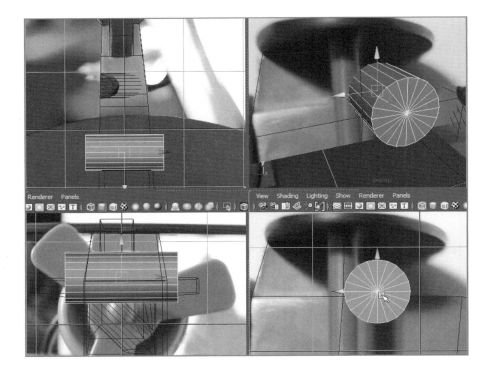

6. Select the fuselage first and then the new cylinder, and choose Mesh → Booleans → Difference. Bam! There's a cutout for the cockpit (Figure 6.92). Delete the history on the new fuselage and save your work.

Figure 6.92

Creating the cockpit shape

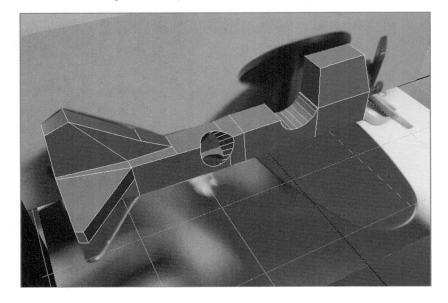

Cleaning Up the Fuselage

Now that you have the shape down for the fuselage, you'll clean it up and give the outer edges some bevels. Use your model scene or airplaneModel_v03.ma to follow along here:

1. Select all the outer edges around the mesh shown in Figure 6.93. You are not selecting two of the edges close to the hole and the edges around the stem's hole on purpose. You will do those edges separately to avoid problems. Choose Edit Mesh → Bevel ❑ for the traditional Maya Bevel tool. Set Offset Space to World (Ignore Scaling On Objects), Segments to **2**, and Width to **1.25**, as shown in Figure 6.94; then click Bevel.

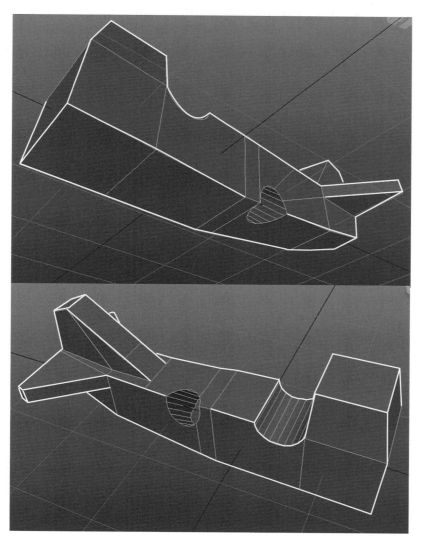

Figure 6.93

Select the outer edges of the fuselage.

2. Select the top edge you did not bevel in the previous step, as shown in Figure 6.95 (top). Maya Bevel that on its own (Figure 6.95, bottom).

3. Select the edge you didn't bevel on the bottom of the plane, as shown in Figure 6.96. You will need to bevel this with a lower Width to avoid a weird result, since this edge is so close to the stem's hole. Bevel the edge with a Width of **0.8** (you may have to go higher or lower if your model is slightly different).

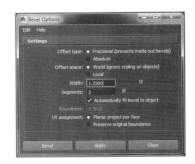

Figure 6.94

Set your bevel options.

Figure 6.95

Select this edge and bevel with the previous settings.

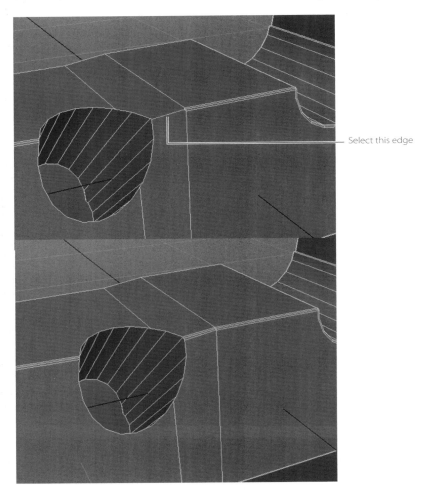

Select this edge

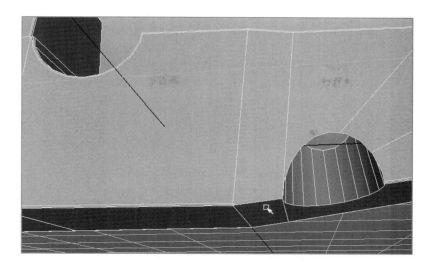

Figure 6.96

Select the edge close to the hole on the bottom of the plane.

4. This bevel isn't quite the same size as the other bevels. This is because some of the edges near the stem's hole are quite short and will not be able to bevel at a Width of 1.25. Your geometry may differ a little. You will manually move the vertices to make the bevel wider, as you can see in Figure 6.97.

Figure 6.97

Move the vertices at the new bevel to make it wider.

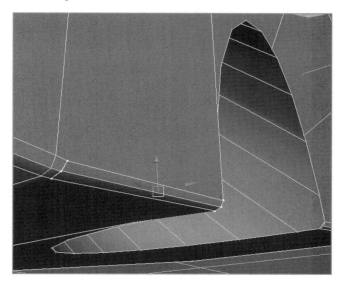

5. You may notice a small hole or tear where the stem hole meets the newly adjusted bevel (Figure 6.98). This is a normal part of modeling; check the mesh for any parts that may be torn or left open when you run operations like Booleans and bevels. Simply move the vertex shown in Figure 6.98 and snap it (by holding down V while you move the vertex) to the vertex at the bottom of the bevel, as shown in Figure 6.99.

This is a small tear and could be left alone if you choose to skip these steps. But it's always good to get into the habit of being very detail oriented when creating models, even if the issue may never be seen in renders.

Figure 6.98

Select this vertex on the hole.

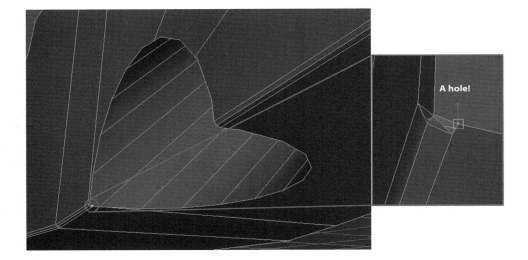

6. Select both the vertices that are now top of each other and choose Edit Mesh → Merge, and you've fixed the hole! Figure 6.100 shows the result.

Now that you've finished the base shape of the fuselage, it's time to clean it up to get rid of Ngons. If you recall, Ngons are polygons that have more than four sides. This may sometimes cause problems and inefficiencies with most renderers, like mental ray, so it's always a good idea to make sure your geometry is clean. For example, if you try beveling a mesh or some edges and you get a failed result, you can try cleaning up the mesh, as you're about to do next.

Figure 6.99

Snap the vertex down to close the hole.

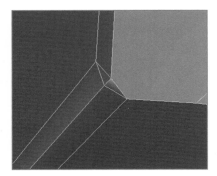

Figure 6.100

The hole is fixed.

Select the fuselage mesh, and choose Mesh → Cleanup. In the window that opens, select Faces With More Than 4 Sides and Edges With Zero Length, leaving the Length tolerance at the default, as shown in Figure 6.101. Click Cleanup, and the mesh should change ever so slightly. You will notice that some of the faces around the areas where you used a Boolean have been subdivided a bit in Figure 6.102. That is because those faces had more than four sides. Save your work and compare it to `airplaneModel_v04.ma`.

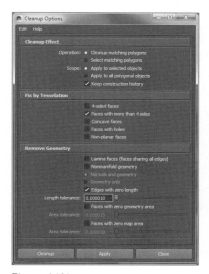

Figure 6.101
Set the Cleanup Options as shown for the fuselage mesh.

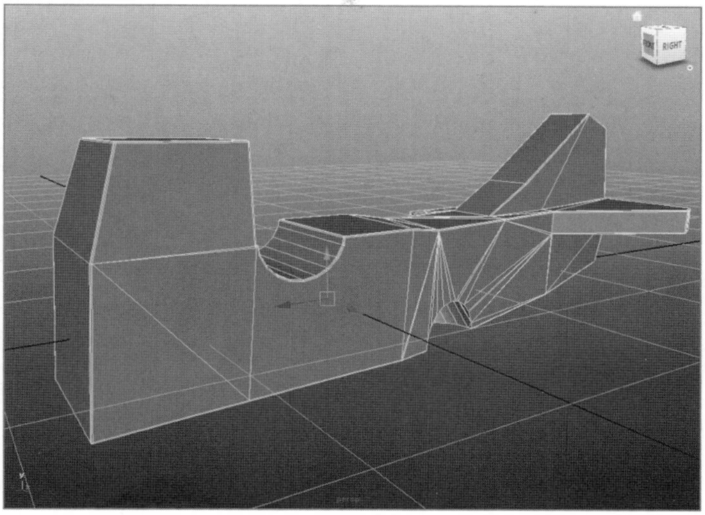

Figure 6.102
Cleaning up the Ngons

Creating the Propeller and Nose

Now that you've finished the main fuselage of the plane, you can move on to the other parts: wings, propeller, and wheels. Let's begin with the propeller, using your work so far or the file `airplaneModel_v04.ma`.

1. Create a poly cylinder with Height Divisions of **2** and Cap Divisions of **5**. Place, rotate, and scale the cylinder to match Figure 6.103. You will have to enable Drawing Overrides to turn off shading for the cylinder so you can place it while looking at the reference planes. The placement should be centered on the front of your fuselage geometry, even if it looks slightly off in the reference. Remember, perspective in the photos makes the reference less than perfect.

2. Select the loop of edges shown in Figure 6.104 (left), and scale the edges out as shown in Figure 6.104 (right).

Figure 6.103

Start with a cylinder in place.

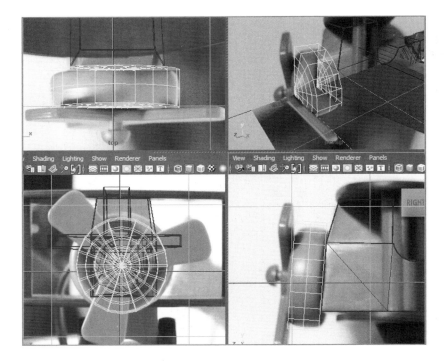

Figure 6.104

Select this edge loop (left), and scale the edges out (right).

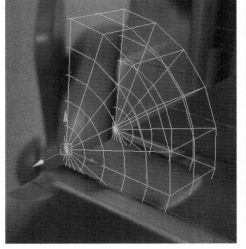
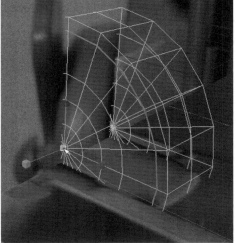

3. Disable Drawing Overrides for a moment. Select the two edge loops shown in Figure 6.105, and move them inward as shown.

4. Repeat steps 2 and 3 for the other side of the cylinder to create the same divot on the other side.

Move these edge loops

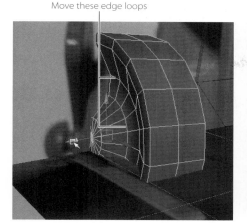

Figure 6.105
Create a divot by moving back the edge loops.

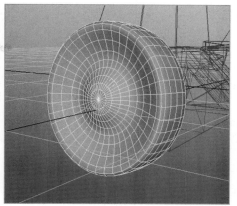

Figure 6.106
The propeller cap is done.

5. Select the cylinder, and name it **propCap**. Press 3 to see a smooth preview to verify how it will look smoothed. It looks exactly like you need it. Press 1 to exit Smooth Preview.

6. With the `propCap` selected, choose Mesh → Smooth □. In the option box, choose Edit → Reset Settings, and click Smooth. The `propCap` looks great in Figure 6.106 with the reference planes turned off. Reenable Drawing Overrides for the `propCap` to turn it into a wireframe.

7. Create a new cylinder with Axis Divisions of **12**, Height Divisions of **1**, and Cap Divisions of **1**. Orient and scale it to fit centered on top of the `propCap`, as shown in Figure 6.107. This will be the start of the propeller itself. Name the mesh **prop**.

8. Enter Face Selection mode, and select three faces around the rim of the prop disc, as shown in Figure 6.108. Extrude these three faces with a Local Z value of **0.8**, as shown in Figure 6.109.

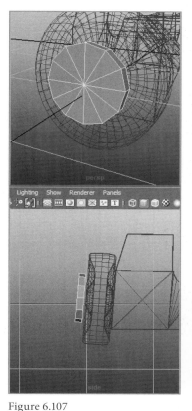

Figure 6.107
Starting the propeller mesh

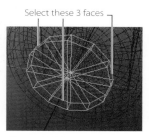

Select these 3 faces

Figure 6.108
Select these three faces.

Figure 6.109

Extrude the propeller blades out.

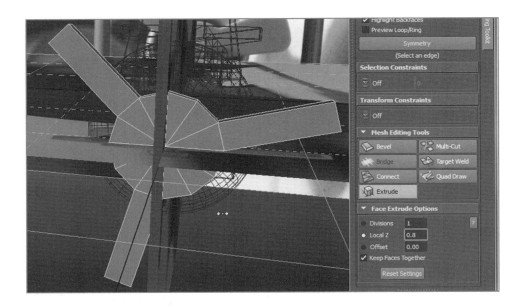

9. Select each of the blade's end faces individually, and one by one scale them to create a flare at each end of the blades, as shown in Figure 6.110.

10. If you press 3 for a smooth preview, the propeller doesn't look very good. You need to add some edge loops to prevent the prop from becoming too mushy and soft. Press 1 to exit the smooth preview, and use the Insert Edge Loop tool to place edge loops as shown in Figure 6.111.

11. Now if you press 3, you will have a nicer result in the smooth preview. Exit the preview, and with the prop selected, choose Mesh → Smooth. It's not an exact fit to the toy plane's propeller, so you may want to adjust your model accordingly; however, it will do great for your needs here.

12. For the button holding the prop to the propCap, you need a simple shape, and there's no need to make a hole in the prop for it either, since you won't see the hole behind the button. Create a poly cylinder, and place it in front of the center of the prop, as shown in Figure 6.112.

Figure 6.110

Flare out the ends of the blades individually.

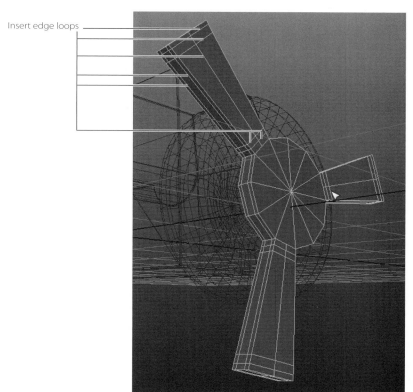

Figure 6.111

Insert these edge loops.

Insert edge loops

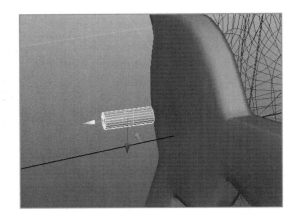

13. Select the vertex at the center of the end cap for the cylinder, and pull it out to form a point like a pencil. Then, as shown in Figure 6.113, insert two edge loops close to each other at the top.

Figure 6.113

Make a point and place two edge loops close to each other.

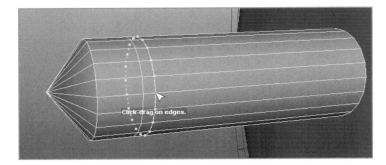

14. Select the faces of the pointed tip and scale them up as in Figure 6.114. Select the mesh, and choose Edit → Smooth to create a rounded button. Place the button into the prop, as shown in Figure 6.115.

Figure 6.114

Scale up the faces of the pointed cap.

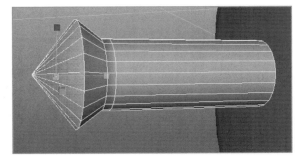

Figure 6.115

Smooth the mesh and place it into the prop. Scale it to fit.

Name the mesh **propButton**, and name the fuselage mesh **fuselage**. You can turn off Drawing Overrides for everything now. Group the airplane parts together, and call the group **biplane**. Save your work and compare it to `airplaneModel_v05.mb`.

Using Maya File References

The toy airplane is not finished yet, but you're going to place it onto the lamp now using the Maya Reference function. References work by importing (called *referencing*) a Maya file into another Maya scene. When the referenced file is updated, it is automatically also updated within the scene where it was referenced. You can also very easily swap out versions of the reference file and not lose any position or animation information in the main scene. Let's bring the airplane into the lamp now.

1. Open the last lamp model file you created, or open `lampModel_v03.mb` from the Scenes folder. It's the completed lamp.

2. Choose File → Create Reference, and navigate to your latest airplane file, or use `airplaneModel_v05.mb` from the Scenes folder. Click Reference, and the airplane is referenced into the lamp scene, reference planes and all, as shown in Figure 6.116.

Figure 6.116

The airplane model and its reference planes are referenced into the scene.

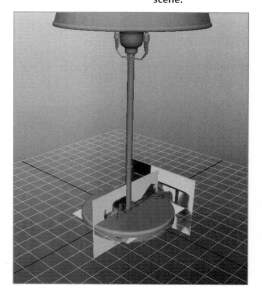

Figure 6.117

Turn off the reference plane layer.

Figure 6.118

Group the lamp properly.

3. Save this file. You can compare it to `lampScene_v01.mb` if you want.

4. If you select any part of the airplane model, you will notice that you cannot delete it. Referenced assets cannot be deleted in the master scene; you would need to go back into that Maya file itself to make such adjustments.

5. Notice in Figure 6.117 that the reference image planes' layer is also inserted into the scene. Until you delete these reference planes in the airplane model's file, you can just turn this layer off for now.

6. Open the Outliner, and at the bottom you'll notice two new nodes in your scene that have a blue diamond next to them. This signifies a reference. You'll also see that the lamp is in a mess. It's not grouped at all. Silly us! Follow along with the Outliner shown in Figure 6.118 to group your lamp's nodes. Then save your file (compare it to `lampScene_v02.mb`).

7. Now that the scene is cleaned up and saved, let's place the airplane on the stem. Select the top group node of the toy airplane, and position it so that the plane rests on the stem about one-third of the way up.

8. Now that the plane is in position, you will notice that the plane is smaller than it looks in the photos from the beginning of the chapter. Select the top node again, and press D to move the pivot. Move the pivot to where the stem and the airplane meet and then release the D key.

9. With the pivot placed at the stem, scale the top node of the biplane to **1.2** in all three axes. Again, make sure you are doing all these actions to the top node of the biplane. Figure 6.119 shows the placement and scaling.

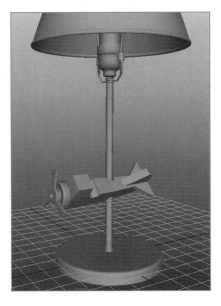

Figure 6.119

The plane is placed and scaled correctly.

Now your toy airplane is in position on the lamp (Figure 6.119), but it doesn't have any wings or wheels. Next, you'll go back into the airplane model file and finish the model properly. Version up and save your work. You can check against the file `lampScene_v03.mb` in the Scenes folder.

Finishing the Toy Airplane

You can continue with your own airplane model file or open the scene file `airplaneModel_v05.ma` to begin modeling the wings. Keep in mind that anytime you bevel in the rest of this exercise, you are using the Maya Bevel and not the Modeling Toolkit's Bevel tool. You may choose to use Modeling Toolkit's Bevel, in which case you should use the value given for Width in Maya Bevel for use as the Offset value in Modeling Toolkit's Bevel.

1. Create a poly cube with a Width Divisions value of **9** and a Depth Divisions value of **4**, and use the top and side reference planes to place, rotate, and scale it as the top wing, as shown in Figure 6.120. Move the vertices to shape the wing in the top view.

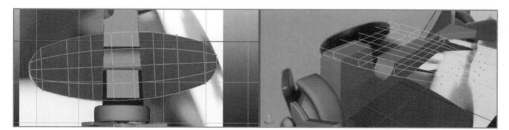

Figure 6.120

Place and shape the top wing cube.

2. Select the top and bottom edge loops around the outside edge of the wing, as shown in Figure 6.121, and bevel them with a Width value of **0.5** and a Segments value of **2**.

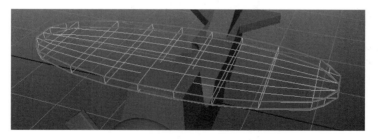

Figure 6.121

Bevel the wing.

3. Press 3 to preview the smooth version of the wing, and make any adjustments you want. When you are satisfied with the shape, select the wing, and choose Mesh → Smooth ❑. Make sure Add Divisions is set to Exponentially and Division Levels is at **1**. Click Smooth and compare the wing to the one shown later in Figure 6.122. The wing should have a much closer shape to the reference shape.

Figure 6.122

**Creating the bi-
wings and grouping
them properly**

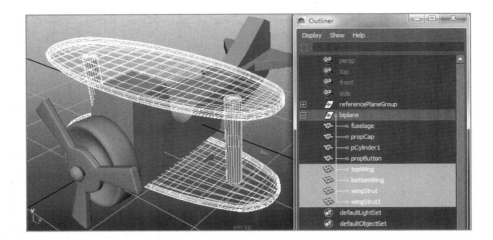

4. Duplicate the wing and move it down to where the bottom wing is to create the bi-wings. Name the top wing mesh **topWing** and the bottom one **bottomWing**.

5. Use the front view to create and place two poly cylinders as the wing supports, and call them **wingStrut** and **wingStrut1**. Place the four new meshes into the biPlane group as shown in the Outliner. Figure 6.122 shows both wings in place with the reference planes turned off. Go ahead and turn off Drawing Overrides for the wings.

Making the Wheels

Now for the wheel assembly below the bottom wing.

1. Create a poly cube with a Width Divisions value of **9** and a Depth Divisions value of **2**. Turn off Shading in Drawing Overrides in the Attribute Editor, and then place the cube using the reference images. Move vertices to shape the mesh, as shown in Figure 6.123.

Figure 6.123

**Place and shape the
wheel assembly.**

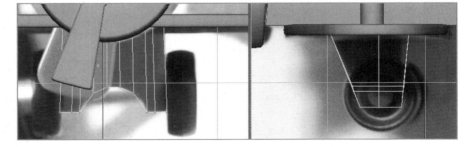

2. Select the outer edges (Figure 6.124), and bevel them with a Width value of **0.3** and a Segments value of **2**.

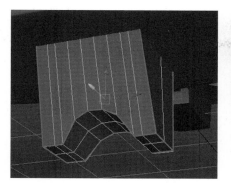

Figure 6.124

Select these edges and bevel them.

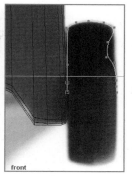

Figure 6.125

Shape a curve for the profile of the wheel.

3. In the front view, create a curve to match the outline of the wheel, as shown in Figure 6.125. Make sure the bottom two vertices are even with each other in the *Y*-axis. Call the mesh **wheelAssembly**.

4. Select the curve, and turn on CV display (Display → NURBS → CVs). Hold down the D key and use Point Snaps ( ) to snap the pivot point to the first CV of the profile curve.

5. Select the curve and switch to the Surfaces menu set. Select Surfaces → Revolve ❐. Set the attributes as shown in Figure 6.126, and click Revolve to make the wheel; name the mesh **wheel**. Center its pivot (Modify → Center Pivot).

Figure 6.126

The first wheel

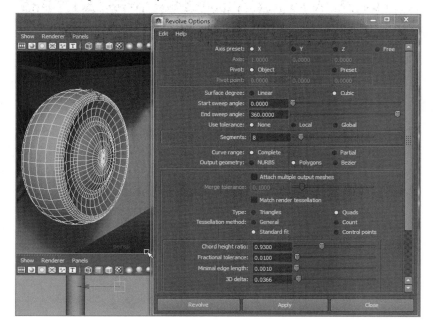

6. Delete the profile curve if you are happy with the shape. Turn off Drawing Overrides for the wheel assembly mesh. Duplicate the wheel, give the copy a scale of **–1.0** in the *X*-axis, and move it to the other side of the wheel assembly mesh.

7. Select both wheels, and choose Modify → Freeze Transformations. Place the wheel and wheel assembly nodes under the biplane node, as shown in Figure 6.127. Your biplane is finished!

Figure 6.127

The biplane is finished.

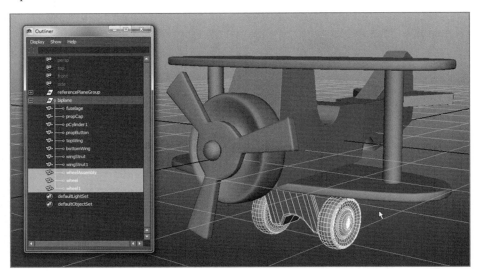

8. Select the reference planes' group (referencePlaneGroup) in the Outliner, and delete the reference planes. Right-click the referencePlanes layer in Layer Editor, and select Delete Layer to clean up the scene.

Save your work, and compare it to the scene file airplaneModel_v06.ma.

Updating the File Reference

Now that the biplane is finished, you need to go back into the scene file and update the biplane in that file. Open the scene file lampScene_v03.ma or open your own latest lamp scene file. Choose File → Reference Editor (Figure 6.128). In the Reference Editor window, click the airplaneModel_v04RN airplaneModel_v05.mb entry, and choose Reference → Replace Reference. Select the airplaneModel_v06.mb file, and click Reference. Save your new scene, and compare it to lampScene_v04.mb.

The biplane model will immediately update to reflect all the changes you made to add the wings and wheels. In addition, the reference planes and their display layer are gone from the scene since you deleted them from the original model file. Figure 6.129 shows the completed lamp scene.

References are a powerful way for collaboration where two people or more can work in tandem on different parts of a scene. References are also great for easily updating parts of a larger scene and in better managing these parts (a.k.a. assets). Be aware, however, that the more complicated models and hierarchies become, the more careful you have to be in keeping your scenes clean to avoid trouble with references.

Summary

In this chapter, you flexed your knowledge from the previous chapters and concentrated on creating a model of a child's table lamp. You used many of the tools discussed in the previous chapters, from extruding to adding edge loops to using bevels and even to sculpting by moving vertices and welding them together. You also used Booleans to create the notches and holes you needed in the airplane's fuselage, and then you fixed the problems that sometimes arise in modeling. And throughout, you used Maya references to easily update parts of a larger scene file.

Creating a model can be a lot of hard and sometimes tedious work, but when you start seeing it take shape, the excitement begins to build. From the basic shaping of the lamp's parts to the detail of adding the airplane, you rolled up your sleeves and worked hard in this chapter to create the table lamp.

In the following chapter, you'll tackle some simple texturing and see how to work with UVs. You'll then add detail to the decorative box from earlier in the book by creating maps for displacement as well as color. Later in the book, you'll light and render the table lamp and decorative box to make them look as photo-real as possible.

This doesn't mean your modeling experience is over! There's still plenty of detailing you can add to the table lamp and its toy airplane. For example, you can create a light bulb for behind the lampshade and even a power cord that comes out of the base.

You can also take the procedures you used in this chapter to build your own lamp or decorative box design. The important lesson to take away from this chapter is how in-depth you can get with a model and how a lengthy modeling process takes shape. Along the way, don't forget to name your pieces and group everything in a sensible fashion.

Figure 6.128

The Reference Editor

Figure 6.129

The lamp is updated and ready to go.

CHAPTER 7

Autodesk Maya Shading and Texturing

Shading *is the term* for applying colors and textures to create *materials*, also known in the Autodesk® Maya® software as *shaders*. A shader defines an object's look—its color, tactile texture, transparency, luminescence, glow, and so forth.

Learning Outcomes: In this chapter, you will be able to

- Differentiate between different shader types
- Create and edit shader networks in the Hypershade window
- Apply shaders and textures to a model
- Set up UVs on a model for the best texture placement
- Understand the steps to set up texture images to fit a model's UV layout
- Tweak UVs to align texture details

Maya Shading

When you create any objects, Maya assigns a default shader to them called Lambert1, which has a neutral gray color. The shader allows your objects to render and display properly. If no shader is attached to a surface, an object can't be seen when rendered. In the Maya view panels, it will appear wireframe all the time, even in Shaded view.

Shading is the proper term for applying a renderable color, surface bumps, transparency, reflection, shine, or similar attributes to an object in Maya. It's closely related to, but distinct from, *texturing*, which is what you do when you apply a map or other node to an *attribute of a shader* to create some sort of surface detail. For example, adding a scanned photo of a brick wall to the Color attribute of a shader is considered applying texture. Adding another scanned photo of the bumps and contours of the same brick wall to the Bump Mapping attribute is also considered applying a texture. Nevertheless, because textures are often applied to shaders, the entire process of shading is sometimes informally referred to as *texturing*. Applying textures to shaders is also called *texture mapping* or simply *mapping*. You map a texture to the color node of a shader that is assigned or applied to a Maya object.

Shaders are based on nodes. Each node holds the attributes that define the shader. You create shader networks of interconnected shading nodes, akin to the hierarchies and groups of models. These networks can be simple, or they can be intricate and involved, like when several render nodes are used to create complex shading effects.

Each shader, also known as a *shading group*, comprises a set of *material nodes*. Material nodes are the Maya nodes that hold all the pertinent rendering information about the object to which they're assigned, such as their color, opacity, or shininess. The shading groups are the nodes that allow the connection between the surface and the material you've created. When you edit the shader through the Attribute Editor, as you'll do later in this chapter, you edit its material node.

As you learn about shading in this chapter, you'll deal at length with the Hypershade window. See Chapter 2, "Jumping in Headfirst, with Both Feet," and Chapter 3, "The Autodesk Maya 2014 Interface," for the layout of this window and for a hands-on introduction. You can access the Hypershade window by choosing Window → Rendering Editors → Hypershade. Shading in Maya is almost always done hand in hand with lighting. At the very least, textures are tweaked and edited in the lighting stage of production.

Shader Types

Open the Hypershade window by choosing Window → Rendering Editors → Hypershade. In the left column of the Hypershade window, you'll see a listing of Maya shading nodes (Figure 7.1). The first section displays surface nodes, a.k.a. material nodes or shader types. Of these shader types, five are common to other animation packages as well. You'll use two of these later in this chapter.

Figure 7.1

The Maya shading nodes

To understand a bit more about shaders, consider what makes objects appear as they do in the real world. The short answer is light. The way light bounces off an object defines how you see that object. The surface of the object may have pigments that affect the wavelength of light that reflects off it, giving the surface color. Other features of that object's surface also dictate how light is reflected.

For the most part, shader types address the differences in how light bounces off surfaces. Most light, after it hits a surface, *diffuses* across an area of that surface. It may also reflect a hot spot called a *specular* highlight. The shaders in Maya differ in how they deal with specular and diffuse parameters according to the specific math that drives them. As you learn about the shader types, think of the things around you and what shader type would best fit them. Some Maya shaders are specific to creating special effects, such as the Hair Tube shader and the Use Background shader. It's important to learn the fundamentals first, so I'll cover the shading types you'll be using right off the bat.

The Lambert Shader Type

The most common shader type is *Lambert*, an evenly diffused shading type found in dull or matte surfaces. A sheet of paper, for example, is a Lambert surface.

A Lambert surface diffuses and scatters light evenly across its surface in all directions, as you can see in Figure 7.2.

The Phong Shader Type

Phong shading brings to a surface's rendering the notions of specular highlight and reflectivity. A Phong surface reflects light with a sharp hot spot, creating a specular highlight that drops off sharply, as shown in Figure 7.3. You'll find that glossy objects such as plastics, glass, and most metals take well to Phong shading.

Figure 7.2
A Lambert shader

Figure 7.3
A Phong shader

The Blinn Shader Type

The *Blinn* shading method brings to the surface a highly accurate specular lighting model that offers superior control over the specular's appearance (see Figure 7.4). A Blinn surface reflects light with a hot spot, creating a specular that diffuses somewhat more gradually than a Phong. The result is a shader that is good for use on shiny surfaces and metallic surfaces.

The Phong E Shader Type

The Phong E shader type expands the Phong shading model to include more control over the specular highlight. A Phong E surface reflects light much like a regular Phong does, but it has more detailed control over the specular settings to adjust the glossiness of the surface (see Figure 7.5). This creates a surface with a specular that drops off more gradually and yet remains sharper than a Blinn. Phong E also has greater color control over the specular than do Phong and Blinn, giving you more options for metallic reflections.

Figure 7.4
A Blinn shader

Figure 7.5
A Phong E shader

The Anisotropic Shader Type

The Anisotropic shader is good to use on surfaces that are deformed, such as a foil wrapper or warped plastic (see Figure 7.6).

Anisotropic refers to something whose properties differ according to direction. An anisotropic surface reflects light unevenly and creates an irregular-shaped specular highlight that is good for representing surfaces with directional grooves, like CDs. This creates a specular highlight that is uneven across the surface, changing according to the direction you specify on the surface. This is different than the Blinn and Phong shader types where the specular highlight is evenly distributed to make a circular highlight on the surface.

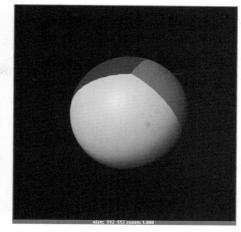

Figure 7.6

An Anisotropic shader

Figure 7.7

A Layered shader

The Layered Shader Type

A *Layered* shader allows the stacking of shaders to create complex shading effects, which is useful for creating objects composed of multiple materials (see Figure 7.7). By using the Layered shader to texture different materials on different parts of the object, you can avoid using excess geometry.

You control Layered shaders by using transparency maps to define which areas show which layers of the shader. You drag material nodes into the top area of the Attribute Editor and stack them from left to right, the left being the topmost layer assigned to the surface.

Layered shaders are valuable resources to control compound and complex shaders. They're perfect for putting labels on objects or adding dirt to aged surfaces.

The Ramp Shader Type

A *Ramp texture* is a gradient that can be attached to almost any attribute of a shader as a *texture node*. Ramps can create smooth transitions between colors and can even be used to control particles. (See Chapter 12, "Autodesk Maya Dynamics and Effects," to see how a ramp is used to control particles.) When used as a texture, a ramp can be connected to any attribute of a shader to create graduating color scales, transparency effects, increasing glow effects, and so on. You'll use Ramp textures later in this chapter.

The *Ramp shader* is a self-contained shader node that automatically has several Ramp texture nodes attached to its attributes. These ramps are attached within the shader itself, so there is no need to connect external Ramp texture nodes. This makes for a simplified editing environment for the shader because all the colors and handles are accessible through the Ramp shader's own Attribute Editor, as shown in Figure 7.8.

To create a new color in any of the horizontal ramps, click in the swatch to create a new ramp position. Edit its color through its Selected Color swatch. You can move the position by grabbing the circle right above the ramp and dragging left or right. To delete a color, click the box beneath it.

Ramp textures are automatically attached to the Color, Transparency, Incandescence, Specular Color, Reflectivity, and Environment attributes of a Ramp shader. In addition, a special curve ramp is attached to the Specular Roll Off attribute to allow for more precise control over how the specular highlight diminishes over the surface.

Shader Attributes

Shaders are composed of nodes just like other Maya objects. Within these nodes, attributes define what shaders do. Here is a brief rundown of the common shader attributes with which you'll be working:

Color An RGB or HSV value defines what color the shader is when it receives a neutral color light. For more on RGB and HSV, see Chapter 1, "Introduction to Computer Graphics and 3D."

Figure 7.8

A Ramp shader in its Attribute Editor

Transparency The higher the Transparency value, the less opaque and more see-through the object becomes.

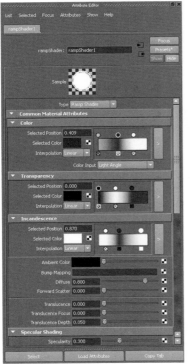

Although usually expressed in a black-to-white gradient, with black being opaque or solid and white being totally clear, transparency can have color. In a color transparency, the shader's color shifts because only some of its RGB values are transparent, as opposed to the whole.

Ambient Color This color affects the Color attribute of the shader as more ambient light is created in the scene. Ambient color tends to flatten an object because this attribute evenly colors the object. This attribute is primarily used to create flat areas and should be used with care. The default is black, which keeps the darker areas of a surface dark. The lighter the ambient color, the lighter those areas are. A bright Ambient Color setting flattens out an object, as shown in Figure 7.9.

Incandescence This attribute is the ability to self-illuminate. Objects that seem to give off or have their own light, such as an office's fluorescent light fixture, can be given an Incandescence value. Incandescence doesn't, however, light objects around it in regular renders, nor does it create a glow. It also serves to flatten the object into a pure color. As you'll see in Chapter 11, "Autodesk Maya Rendering," incandescence can also help light a scene in the mental ray® Final Gather rendering. The value of Incandescence (as well as the color) of an object is used to calculate the overall brightness in a Final Gather scene (see Figure 7.10).

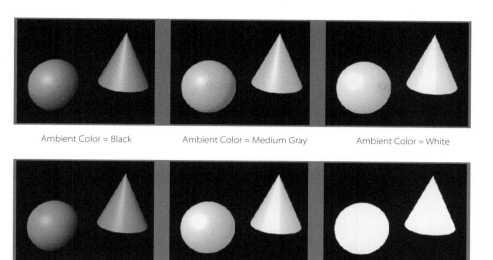

Ambient Color = Black   Ambient Color = Medium Gray   Ambient Color = White

Figure 7.9
**Ambient color
values**

Incandescence = 0   Incandescence = 0.5   Incandescence = 1

Figure 7.10
**Incandescence
values**

Bump Mapping   This attribute creates a textured feel for the surface by adding highlights and shadows to the render. It doesn't alter the surface of the geometry, although it makes the surface appear to have ridges, marks, scratches, and so forth. The bump map has to be a texture node such as a ramp, a fractal noise, or an image file. The more intense the variation in tones of that map, the greater the bump. Bump maps are frequently used to make surfaces look more real, because nothing in reality has a perfectly smooth surface. Using bumps very close up may create problems; bumps are generally good for adding inexpensive detail to a model that isn't in extreme close-up (see Figure 7.11).

Figure 7.11
**The effects of a
bump map**

No Bump Map   Fractal Texture Bump Map   Grid Texture Bump Map

Geometry when seen close up, where you have to change the topology of the model physically using texture maps, requires displacement maps. I'll cover displacement maps in Chapter 11.

Diffuse   This value governs how much light is reflected from the surface in all directions. When light strikes a surface, light disperses across the surface and helps illuminate it. The higher this value, the brighter its object is when lit, because more of the striking light is reflected from the surface. The lower the Diffuse value, the more light is "absorbed" into the surface, yielding a darker result, especially in areas that aren't well lit. Metals have very low Diffuse values because they rely on reflections and direct light (see Figure 7.12).

Figure 7.12

How a Diffuse value affects a shader's look

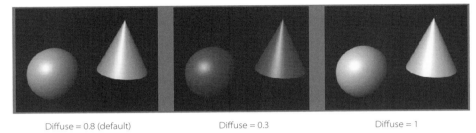

Diffuse = 0.8 (default)   Diffuse = 0.3   Diffuse = 1

Translucence and Translucence Focus   The Translucence and Translucence Focus attributes give the material the ability to transmit light through its surface, like a piece of canvas in front of a light. At a value of 1 for Translucence, all light shines through the object; at 0, none does. The Translucence Focus attribute specifies how much of that light is scattered. A light material such as paper should have a high translucence focus, and thicker surfaces should have low focus rates.

Glow Intensity   Found in the Special Effects section of the Attribute Editor, the Glow Intensity attribute adds a glow to the object, as if it were emitting light into a foggy area (see Figure 7.13). You'll add glow to an object in Chapter 10, "Autodesk Maya Lighting."

Figure 7.13

Adding a glow

Glow = 0   Glow = 0.5   Glow = 1

Matte Opacity   Objects rendered through Maya generate a solid *matte*. Where there is an object, the matte is white; where there is nothing, the matte is black. Mattes helps compositing programs, which bring together elements created independently into a single composite scene, to separate rendered CG from their backgrounds. Turning down the slider decreases the brightness of the object's matte, making it appear more transparent. This technique is usually used for compositing tricks or to make an object render in RGB but not appear in any composites. For more information about mattes, see the sidebar "Image Mattes" in this chapter, and see Chapter 11.

Raytrace Options   With raytracing, you can achieve true reflections and refractions in your scene. This subset of attributes allows you to set the shader's raytracing abilities. See Chapter 11 for more on raytracing.

Some attributes are available only with certain shader types. The following are the attributes for the Phong, Phong E, and Blinn shaders:

Specular Color   The color of the highlights on a shiny surface. Black produces no specular, and white creates a bright one.

Reflectivity   The amount of reflection visible in the surface. The higher the value, the more reflective the object will render. Increasing this value increases the visibility of the Reflected Color attribute or of true reflections in the scene when raytraced.

Reflected Color   Gives the surface a reflection. Texture maps are generally assigned to this attribute to give the object a reflection of whatever is in the image file or texture without having to generate time-consuming true reflections with a raytraced render. Using raytracing to get true reflections, however, is the only way to generate reflections of other objects in the scene.

Cosine Power   Available only with a Phong shader. This attribute changes the size of the shiny highlights (a.k.a. specular) on the surface. The higher the number, the smaller the highlight looks.

IMAGE MATTES

As you learned in Chapter 1 (and will explore further in Chapter 11), image files are stored with a red, a green, and a blue channel that keep the amount of each color in each pixel of the image. Some image formats, including TIFF and TARGA, also have an alpha channel, known as a *matte channel* or *image matte*. This is a grayscale channel that controls the opacity of an image. Completely white parts of the matte make those parts of the image opaque (solid), whereas black parts make those parts of the image fully transparent. Gray in the matte channel makes those parts of the image partly transparent. These mattes are used in *compositing*—bringing together elements created separately into a single composite scene. See Chapter 11 for an example of how an alpha channel works.

Roughness, Highlight Size, Whiteness   Control the specular highlight on a Phong E surface only. They control specular focus, amount of specular, and highlight color, respectively.

mental ray Attributes   Because Autodesk integrates features of the mental ray rendering engine into Maya, an object's Attribute Editor usually includes a set of mental ray options. Shaders are no different. If you open the Mental Ray heading in the Attribute Editor for a shader, you'll see attributes such as Reflection Blur and Irradiance, as well as a few ways to override the Maya shading attributes with those of mental ray.

An in-depth discussion of the mental ray attributes is beyond the scope of this introductory text. But it's a good idea to know that this brief section is available to you after you have more experience with rendering and you want to work with mental ray at its more advanced levels in Maya. You'll work with mental ray in Chapters 10 and 11.

The Autodesk website lists several premade shaders for your use. Maya also includes a shader library on its installation CD.

Shading and Texturing the Table Lamp

In the following section, you'll add shaders to the table lamp from Chapter 6, "Practical Experience." The lamp is fairly straightforward to shade. Use `lampScene_v04.mb` from the TableLamp project from the companion website. You have four different colors on the body of the biplane and lamp itself, a two-tone lampshade, and a metal stem. You'll start by making shaders in the Hypershade.

1. Open the Hypershade (Window → Rendering Editors → Hypershade). You'll notice that the shaders for the reference planes that have the pictures of the lamp are in the scene, and the names are in red (Figure 7.14). The red signifies that the shaders are part of a scene file that is referenced into the current scene. They cannot be deleted here; you will have to go into the original model scene to delete them. You'll do that in the next step. You'll also notice the Lambert shaders for the lamp shade reference planes used in the modeling phase.

2. Open `airplaneModel_v06.mb`, and then open the Hypershade window. Since you already deleted the geometry for the reference planes, it's easy to flush the now unused shaders for them. In the Hypershade, select Edit → Delete Unused Nodes, and they will disappear. Save the scene as `airplaneModel_v07.mb`.

Figure 7.14

The reference plane shaders are still here!

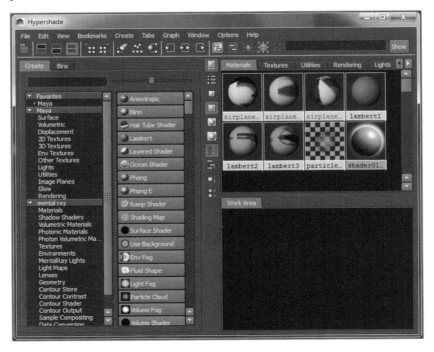

3. Open the `lampScene_v04.mb` file again, and then choose File → Reference Editor. Click the `airplaneModel_v06.mb` entry, and choose Reference → Replace Reference. Navigate to and select `airplaneModel_v07.mb` that you just saved in the Scenes folder. The biplane will disappear for a second and reappear back in place. The reference plan Lambert shaders are now gone. In the Hypershade, select Edit → Delete Unused Nodes to flush the lamp shade reference Lambert shaders as well. They were not referenced.

Figure 7.15

Create the blue shader.

4. Create four new Blinn shaders. Name them **blue**, **red**, **green**, and **black**. An organized Hypershade is a happy Hypershade.

5. Double-click the blue Blinn shader, and in the Attribute Editor, click the color swatch to open the Color Chooser. Set an HSV value of **234**, **0.91**, **.390**, as shown in Figure 7.15.

6. Go through the other three Blinn shaders and set their HSV colors according to Table 7.1. See also Figure 7.16.

WAGON COLOR	SHADER NAME	H VALUE	S VALUE	V VALUE
Red	red	4	0.81	0.64
Black	black	0	0	0.04
Green	green	105	0.56	0.35
Blue	blue	234	0.91	0.39

Table 7.1

HSV color values for the lamp's colors

7. Select the wings of the biplane and the base of the lamp, and assign the blue Blinn.

8. Select the propeller cap (named `propCap`) as shown in Figure 7.17, and assign the green Blinn.

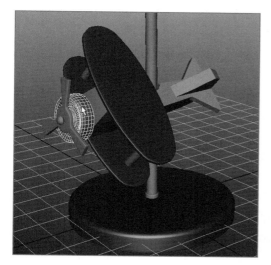

Figure 7.17

Assign the green Blinn to the propeller cap.

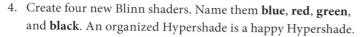

Figure 7.16

The four Blinn shaders

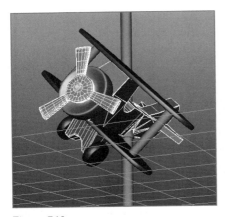

Figure 7.18

Assign the red Blinn to the biplane.

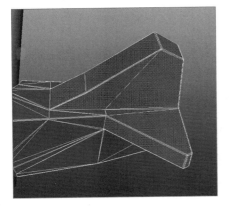

Figure 7.19

Assign blue to the faces of the back stabilizer wings.

Figure 7.20

Select the wing supports and make them red.

9. Select the wheels, and assign them to the black Blinn.

10. Select the body of the biplane, the wheel assembly (named `wheelAssembly`), and its propeller blades, and assign the red Blinn (Figure 7.18). Notice in the color photos in the Color Section of this book that the lamp's biplane body is red but has blue stabilizer wings.

11. Select the faces that make up the stabilizer wings (as shown in Figure 7.19), and assign them to the blue Blinn.

> Assigning shaders to the faces of a mesh and not the entire mesh itself works great in many cases; however, this is not a common practice in professional workflows, especially when using render layers expansively. Instead, UVs are laid out for the mesh, and different colors are assigned through maps. You will see this workflow later when you texture the wheels for a toy wagon. For your purposes just starting out, assigning to faces is a great way to explore multiple colors and materials on a single mesh.

12. Finally, select the wing support cylinders shown in Figure 7.20 and make them red as well.

The Socket, Stem, and Lampshade

Now let's get some shaders made for the rest of the lamp.

1. Create a new Phong shader, make it black in color like the wheel Blinn color, and call it **shinyBlack**. Select the light bulb socket, and assign the new black Phong to it. The Phong is just a bit shinier than the Blinn, perfect for the socket.

2. In the Hypershade, create a new Phong for the metal parts of the lamp. Give it a blue-gray color (HSV of **222**, **0.15**, **0.5**) and a low Diffuse value of **0.15**, as shown below the Color Chooser in Figure 7.21. Name the shader **metal**.

3. Select the stem and all the metal parts of the lamp shown in Figure 7.22, and assign the metal Phong shader to them. The metal parts will turn black in the view panel displays since metal is dependent on reflections for its look. You will not worry about that until a little later in this chapter and then again when you render the lamp in Chapter 11.

4. Finally, the lamp shade is a simple texture of an eggshell white color. Using a photo of the lampshade, you can create a texture swatch to use on the shade. Create a new Lambert shader, and call it **lampShade**.

5. Double-click the `lampShade` Lambert to open the Attribute Editor. Click the Map button next to the `Color` attribute. Select File to create a File Texture node attached to the `Color` attribute.

6. In the Attribute Editor, click the folder icon next to the Image Name text box, and navigate to the Sourceimages folder in the TableLamp project. Select the `lampShadePatch.jpg` file. Assign the Lambert to the lampshade as shown in Figure 7.22, but not the blue trim on the top and bottom. Press 6 in the persp view to enable Textured display mode.

Figure 7.21

Create the metal's Phong shader.

7. Set up your render parameters so that you can render your lamp using the default lighting already in the scene while you're tweaking shaders to get them right. Choose Window → Rendering Editors → Render Settings, or click the Render Settings icon (▓) in the menu bar to open the Render Settings window. Make sure Render Using is set to Maya Software.

Figure 7.22

Assigning the lamp-shade Lambert

8. In the Image Size section on the Common tab, set Presets to 640×480. In the Anti-Aliasing Quality section on the Maya Software tab, use the Intermediate Quality preset. This will give you a good look for the final render with a short render time.

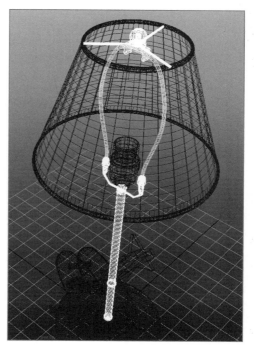

9. If you render a frame of the lamp, the lampshade's texture is a bit too stretched; it needs to tile a few times. In the Hypershade, select the `lampShade` Lambert node, and click the Input And Output Connections icon (▓). Click the `place2dTexture1` node, as shown in Figure 7.23, and open the Attribute Editor. Set the Repeat UV values to **4** and **4** as shown.

Figure 7.23

**Tile the lampshade
texture.**

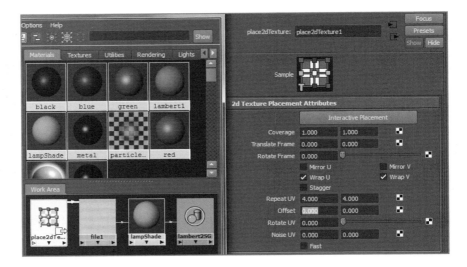

10. Render, and the lampshade should look nicer. Now for the blue trim. In the Hypershade, select the lampShade Lambert and choose Edit → Duplicate → Shading Network to create a copy of all the shading nodes. You will use this copy to make a blue version for the trim. Name the copy **lampShadeBlue**, as shown in Figure 7.24.

Figure 7.24

**Create a copy of
the lampShade
Lambert.**

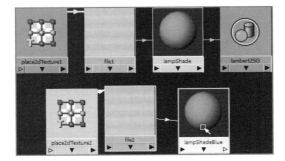

11. Click File2, and open the Attribute Editor. Under the Color Balance heading, click Color Gain, and give it a blue color with HSV of **234**, **0.91**, **0.39**. The eggshell white lamp shade now turns to blue in the copied shader network. Assign it to the top and bottom trim of the lamp shade, as shown in Figure 7.25.

Save your work. You can compare it to the lampScene_v05.mb file at this stage.

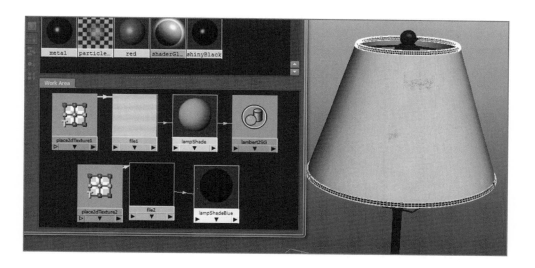

Figure 7.25

Assign the top and bottom trim to the blue-colored lampshade Lambert.

The Metal Parts

Now let's focus a little bit on the metal. Metal surfaces are all about reflections, as opposed to simple colors like the rest of the lamp.

1. Select the metal Phong shader. In the Attribute Editor, click the gray swatch for Specular Color. By changing this color, you control the hue and brightness of the highlights on this surface. Use a bright faded blue with HSV values of **208**, **0.20**, and **0.90**.

    Figure 7.26

    Assigning a Reflected Color texture.

2. In the Specular Shading heading, increase the spread of the specular highlights by changing Cosine Power from the default of 20 to **2.0**. Doing so creates a large area for the bright highlights, implying a polished reflective surface.

3. Rendering will still yield a black but shinier surface for the stem. You need reflections. You will explore this in detail in Chapter 11, but you will create a simple reflection "cheat" to use here by using an environment map. Select the metal Phong shader.

    Figure 7.27

    Select the Env Chrome texture.

4. In the Attribute Editor, click the Map button next to the Reflected Color attribute, as shown in Figure 7.26. Doing so attaches a new node to create a reflection and opens the Create Render Node window.

5. Click the Env Textures section, and select Env Chrome, as shown in Figure 7.27. An environment texture will provide an interesting reflection.

6. Move the Reflectivity slider from 0.50 to 0.85. The higher this number, the more prominent the reflected color in the surface. Figure 7.28 shows the lamp before (left) and after (right) mapping a reflection. The Env Chrome reflection texture makes the metal parts of the lamp look polished by reflecting a grid representing the ground and a bright blue sky.

The lamp is saved as lampScene_v06.mb to catch you up to this final point.

You can embellish a model a lot at the texturing level. The more you explore and experience shaders and modeling, the better you'll be at juggling modeling with texturing to get the most effective solution.

You'll begin UV layout and texturing a child's red wagon later in this chapter and then go into more detailed texturing with the decorative box, which you'll then light and render in mental ray. For even more practice, try loading the catapult model from Chapter 4, "Beginning Polygonal Modeling," and texturing it from top to bottom.

Figure 7.28

The lamp stem before (left) and after (right) a reflection is mapped onto the shader.

Textures and Surfaces

Texture nodes generate maps to connect to an attribute of a shader. There are two types of textures: procedural and bitmapped (sometimes called maps). *Procedural* textures use the Maya nodes attributes to generate an effect, such as ramp, checkerboard, or fractal noise textures. You can adjust each of these procedural textures by changing their attribute values.

A *map*, on the other hand, is a saved image file that is imported into the scene through a file texture node. These files are pregenerated through whatever imaging programs you have and include digital pictures and scanned photos. You need to place all texture nodes onto their surfaces through the shader. You can map them directly onto the surfaces' UV values or project them.

UV Mapping

UV mapping places the texture directly on the surface and uses the surface coordinates (called UVs) for its positioning. In this case, you must do a lot of work to line up the UVs on the surface to make sure the created images line up properly. What follows is a brief summary of how UV mapping works. You'll get hands-on experience with UV layout with the red wagon and decorative box exercises later in this chapter.

Just as 3D space is based on coordinates in *XYZ*, surfaces have coordinates denoted by *U* and *V* values along a 2D coordinate system for width and height. The UV value helps a texture position itself on the surface. The U and V values range from 0 to 1, with (0,0) UV being the origin point of the surface.

Maya creates UVs for primitive surfaces automatically, but frequently you need to edit UVs for proper texture placement, particularly on polygonal meshes after you've edited them. In some instances, placing textures on a poly mesh requires projecting the textures onto the mesh, because the poly UVs may not line up as expected after the mesh has been edited. See the next section, "Using Projections."

If the placement of your texture or image isn't quite right, simply use the 2D placement node of the texture node to position it properly. See the section "Texture Nodes" later in this chapter for more information.

Using Projections

You need to place textures on the surface. You can often do so using UV placement, but some textures need to be projected onto the surface. A *projection* is what it sounds like. The file image, ramp, or other texture being used can be *beamed* onto the object in several ways.

You can create any texture node as either a normal UV map or a projected texture. In the Create Render Node window, clicking a texture icon creates it as a normal mapped texture. To create the texture as a projection, you must right-click the icon and select Create As Projection (see Figure 7.29).

When you create a projected texture, a new node is attached to the texture node. This projection node controls the method of projection with an attached 3D placement node, which you saw in the axe exercise. Select the projection node to set the type of projection in the Attribute Editor (see Figure 7.30).

Setting the projection type will allow you to project an image or a texture without having it warp and distort, depending on the model you're mapping. For example, a planar projection on a sphere will warp the edges of the image as they stretch into infinity on the sides of the sphere.

Try This In a new scene, create a NURBS sphere and a NURBS cone, and place them side-by-side. Create a Blinn shader, and assign it to both objects. In the Blinn shader's Attribute Editor, set its Color attribute to a checkerboard pattern, as shown in Figure 7.31.

Try removing the color map from the Blinn shader. In the Blinn shader's Attribute Editor, right-click and hold the attribute's title word *Color*, and then choose Break Connection from the context menu. Doing so severs the connection to the checker texture map node and resets the color to gray. Now, re-create a new checker texture map for the color, but this time create it as a projection by right-clicking the icon in the Create Render Node window. In the illustration on the left in Figure 7.32, you see the perspective

Figure 7.29

Selecting the type of map layout

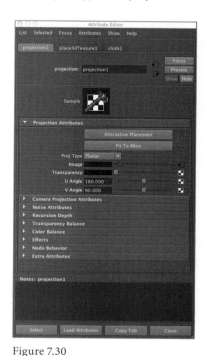

Figure 7.30

The projection node in the Attribute Editor

view in Texture mode (press the 6 key) with the two objects and the planar projection placement node.

Try moving the planar placement object around in the scene to see how the texture maps itself to the objects. The illustration on the right of Figure 7.32 shows the rendered objects.

Try the other projection types to see how they affect the texture being mapped.

Projection placement nodes control how the projection maps its image or texture onto the surface. Using a NURBS sphere with a spherical projected checker, with U and V wrap turned off on the checkerboard texture, you can see how manipulating the `place3dTexture` node affects the texture.

In addition to the Move, Rotate, and Scale tools, you can use the Special Manipulator tool (press T to activate or click the Show Manipulator Tool icon in the toolbar) to adjust the placement. Figure 7.33 shows this tool for a spherical projection.

Drag the handles on the Special Manipulator to change the coverage of the projection, orientation, size, and so forth. All projection types have Special Manipulators. Figure 7.34 shows the Manipulator wrapping the checkerboard pattern in a thin band all the way around the sphere.

To summarize, projection textures depend on a projector node to position the texture onto the geometry. If the object assigned to a projected texture is moving, consider grouping the projection placement node to the object itself in the Outliner.

Figure 7.31

Assign a checkerboard pattern to the sphere and cone with Normal checked.

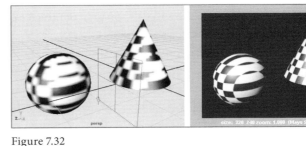

Figure 7.32

A planar projection checkerboard in the view panel (left) and rendered (right)

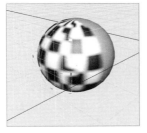

Figure 7.33

The spherical projection's Manipulator tool

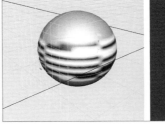

Figure 7.34

The Manipulator wrapping the checkerboard texture around the sphere (left, perspective view; right, rendered view).

Texture Nodes

You can create a number of texture nodes in Maya. This section covers the most important. All texture nodes, however, have common attributes that affect their final look. Open the Attribute Editor for any texture node (see Figure 7.35). The two top sections affect the color balance of the texture. The Color Balance and Effects sections are described here:

Color Balance   This set of attributes adjusts the overall brightness and color balance of your texture. Use these attributes to tint or brighten a texture (as you did with the blue trim of the lampshade) without having to change all the individual attributes of the shader.

Effects   You can invert the texture's color space by clicking the Invert check box. This changes black to white and white to black in addition to inverting the RGB values of colors.

You can map textures to almost any shader attribute for detail. Even the tiniest amount of texture on a surface's bump, specular, or color increases its realism.

Place2dTexture Nodes

The 2D texture nodes come with a 2D placement node that controls their repetition, rotation, size, offset, and so on. Adjust the setting in this node of your 2D texture in the Attribute Editor, as shown in Figure 7.36, to position it within the Shader network.

The Repeat UV setting controls how many times the texture is repeated on whatever shader attribute it's connected to, such as Color. The higher the wrap values, the smaller the texture appears, but the more times it appears on the surface.

The Wrap U and Wrap V check boxes allow the texture to wrap around the edges of their limits to repeat. When these check boxes are turned off, the texture appears only once, and the rest of the surface is the color of the Default Color attribute found in the texture node.

The Mirror U and Mirror V settings allow the texture to mirror itself when it repeats. The Coverage, Translate Frame, and Rotate Frame settings control where the image is mapped. They're useful for positioning a digital image or a scanned picture.

Ramp Texture

A *ramp* is a gradient in which one color transitions into the next color. You've already seen how useful a ramp can be in positioning materials in a Layered shader. It's also perfect for making color gradients, as shown in Figure 7.37.

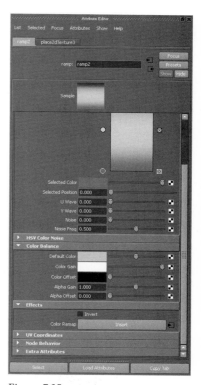

Figure 7.35

Some common attributes for all texture nodes

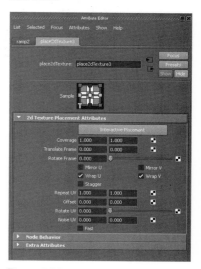

Figure 7.36

A 2D placement node in the Attribute Editor

Use the round handles to select the color and to move it up and down the ramp. The square handle to the right deletes the color. To create a new color, click inside the ramp.

The Ramp texture is different from the Ramp shader. The Ramp shader automatically has several Ramp textures mapped to some of its attributes.

The Type setting allows you to create a gradient running along the U or V direction of the surface, as well as to make circular, radial, diagonal, and other types of gradients. The Interpolation setting controls how the colors grade from one to the next.

The U Wave and V Wave attributes let you add a squiggle to the U or V coordinate of the ramp, and the Noise and Noise Freq (frequency) attributes specify randomness for the placement of the ramp colors throughout the surface.

Using the HSV Color Noise attributes, you can specify random noise patterns of Hue, Saturation, and Value to add some interest to your texture. The HSV Color Noise options are great for making your shader just a bit different to enhance its look.

Fractal, Noise, and Mountain Textures

These textures are used to create a random noise pattern to add to an object's Color, Transparency, or any other shader attribute. For example, when creating a surface, you'll almost always want to add a little dirt or a few surface blemishes to the shader to make the object look less CG. These textures are commonly used for creating bump maps.

Bulge, Cloth, Checker, Grid, and Water Textures

These textures help create surface features when used on a shader's Bump Mapping attribute. Each creates an interesting pattern to add to a surface to create tactile detail, but you can also use them to create color or specular irregularities.

When used as a texture for a bump, Grid is useful for creating the spacing between tiles, Cloth is perfect for clothing, and Checker is good for rubber grips. Placing a Water texture on a slight reflection makes for a nice poolside reflection in patio furniture.

The File Node

You use the file node to import image files into Maya for texturing. For instance, if you want to texture a CG face with a digital picture of your own face, you can use the file node to import a Maya-supported image file.

Figure 7.37

The Ramp texture

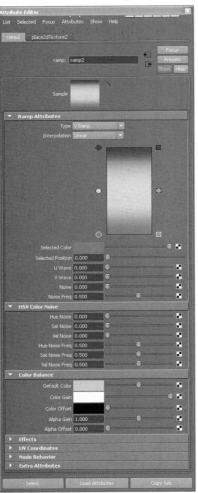

Importing an Image File as a Texture

To attach an image to the `Color` attribute of a Lambert shader, for example, follow these steps:

1. Create the Lambert shader. (Phong, Blinn, or any of the shaders will do.)

2. Click the Map button to map a texture on the `Color` attribute of the new Lambert shader. Select the file node as a normal texture. (You can also use a projected texture with an image file.) The Attribute Editor shows the attribute for the file node; see Figure 7.38.

3. Next to the `Image Name` attribute, click the Folder icon to open the file browser. Find the image file of choice on your computer. (It's best to put images to use as textures in the project's Sourceimages folder. As a matter of fact, the file browser defaults directly to the Sourceimages folder of your current project.) Double-click the file to load it.

4. After you import the image file, it connects to the `Color` attribute of that shader and also automatically connects the alpha to transparency if there is an alpha channel in the image. You can position it as you please by using its `place2dTexture` node or by manipulating the projection node if you created the file texture node as a projection.

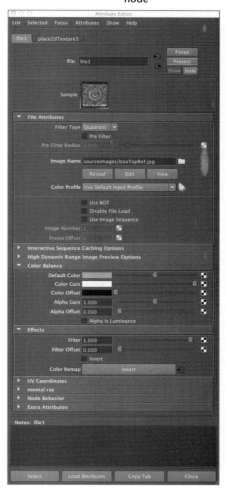

Figure 7.38

The file texture node

You can attach an image file to any attribute of a shader that is *mappable*, meaning it's able to accept a texture node. Frequently, image files are used for the color of a shader as well as for bump and transparency maps. You can replace the image file by double-clicking the file texture node in the Hypershade and choosing another image file with the file browser. Maya disconnects the current image file and connects the new file.

Using Photoshop Files: The PSD File Node

Maya can also use Adobe Photoshop PSD files as image files in creating shading networks. The advantage of using PSD files is that you can specify the layers within the Photoshop file for different attributes of the shader, as opposed to importing several image files to map onto each shader attribute separately. This, of course, requires a modest knowledge of Photoshop and some experience with Maya shading. As you learn how to shade with Maya, you'll come to appreciate the enhancements inherent in using Photoshop networks.

Try This You'll create a single Photoshop file that will shade this sphere with color as well as transparency and a bump. Again, you're doing this instead of creating three different image files (such as TIFFs) for each of those shading attributes.

1. Create a NURBS sphere in a new scene, and assign a new Lambert shader to it. You can do this through the Hypershade or by choosing Lighting/Shading → Assign New Material → Lambert in the Rendering menu set. This creates a new shader and assigns it to the selection, in this case your sphere.

2. Select the sphere, and choose Texturing → Create PSD Network. In the option box that opens, select Color, Transparency, and Bump from the list of attributes on the left side, and click the right arrow to move them to the Selected Attributes list on the right, as shown in Figure 7.39.

3. Select a location and filename for the image. By default, Maya places the PSD file it generates under the Sourceimages folder of your current project, named after the surface to which it applies. Click Create.

4. In Photoshop, open the newly created PSD file. You see three layers grouped under three folders named after the shader attributes you selected when creating the PSD file. There are folders for lambert2.bump, lambert2.transparency, and lambert2.color, as well as a layer called UVSnapShot.

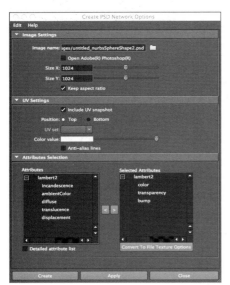

Figure 7.39

The Create PSD Network Options window

The UVSnapShot layer gives you a wireframe layout of the UVs on the sphere as a guideline to paint your textures. Because the sphere is an easy model, you don't need this layer, so turn it off. You'll use UV SnapShot later in this chapter when texturing a toy wagon.

You can now paint whatever image you want into each of the layers to create maps for each of the shader attributes, all in one convenient file. Save the PSD file. You can save over it or create a new filename for the painted file.

5. In Maya, open the Hypershade, and open the Attribute Editor for the Lambert shader assigned to the sphere (in this case, Lambert2). If you graph the connections to the Lambert shader in the Hypershade window's work panel, you see that the PSD file you generated is already connected to the Color, Bump, and Transparency attributes of the shader, with the proper layering set for you, as shown in Figure 7.40.

6. Open the file nodes for the shader, and replace the PSD file with your new painted PSD file. If you saved your PSD file with the same name, all you need to do is click the Reload button to update the psdFile node.

If you decide that you need to add another attribute to the PSD file's layering or if you need to remove an attribute, you can edit the PSD network. Select the shader in the Hypershade, and choose Edit → Edit PSD Network. In the option box, select new attributes to assign to the PSD file, or remove existing attributes and their corresponding Photoshop layer groups. When you click Apply or Edit, Maya saves over the PSD file with the new layout.

3D and Environment Textures

3D textures are projected within a 3D space. These textures are great for objects that need to reflect an environment, for example.

Instead of simply applying the texture to the plane of the surface as 2D textures do, 3D textures create an area in which the shader is affected. As an object moves through a scene with a 3D placement node, its shader looks as if it swims, unless that placement node is parented or constrained to that object. (For more on constraints, see Chapter 9, "More Animation!")

Disconnecting a Texture

Sometimes, the texture you've applied to an object isn't what you want, and you need to remove it from the shader. To do so, double-click the shader in the Hypershade to open its Attribute Editor.

You can then disconnect an image file or any other texture node from the shader's attribute by right-clicking the attribute's name in the Attribute Editor and choosing Break Connection from the context menu, as shown in Figure 7.41.

Figure 7.40

The PSD network for the Lambert shader in the Hypershade shows the connections to Color, Bump, and Transparency.

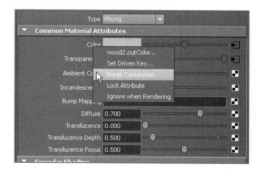

Figure 7.41

Right-clicking a shader's attribute allows you to disconnect a texture node from the shader.

Textures and UVs for the Red Wagon

Now you'll use a child's red wagon toy model, to which you will assign shaders. The real wagon is shown in Figure 7.42. Take a good look at the image of the toy wagon in the Color Section of this book to see how the red wagon is colored. The wagon is fairly simple; it will need a few colored shaders (Red, Black, Blue, and White) for the body, along with a few texture maps for the decals—which is where the real fun begins. The wagon will also require some more intricate work on the shaders and textures for the wood railings and silver metal screws, bolts, and handlebar; these will be a good foray into image maps and UVs.

Figure 7.42

The red wagon and its named parts

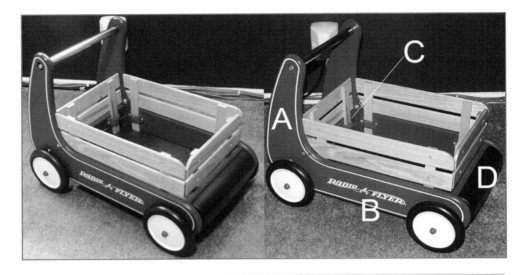

This exercise is a prime example of how lighting and shading go hand in hand.

Assigning Shaders

Load the file RedWagonModel.ma from the Scenes folder of the RedWagon project to begin shading the model of the wagon.

Shading is the common term for adding shaders to an object.

Study the color images of the wagon, and see how light reflects off its plastic, metal, and wood surfaces. Blinn shaders will be perfect for nearly all the parts of the wagon. Follow these steps:

1. Open the Hypershade window, and create four Blinn shaders.

2. Assign the following HSV values to the Color attribute of each Blinn shader, and name them as shown in Table 7.2 and in Figure 7.43. You'll create the Chrome Metal and Wood shaders later.

Figure 7.43

Create the four colored Blinn shaders.

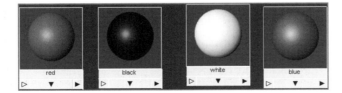

WAGON COLOR	SHADER NAME	H VALUE	S VALUE	V VALUE
Red	Red	355	0.910	0.650
Black	Black	0	0	0
White	White	0	0	1
Blue	Blue	220	0.775	0.560

Table 7.2

HSV color values for the wagon's colors

Initial Assignments

Look at the photo of the wagon in the Color Section in the middle of this book. The bull-nose and tires are black, the wheel rims are white, the floor is blue, the screws and bolts and handlebar are chrome metal, the railings are wood, and the main body is red. Assign shaders to the wagon according to the color photo and the following steps:

1. In the view panel, select the side panels (the A and B panels, without the screws and bolts) and the wheel rim caps, as shown in Figure 7.44, and assign the Red Blinn shader to them. Press 6 to enter Texture Display mode.

2. Select the `wheelMesh` objects for all four wheels, and assign them the White shader. The tires also turn white, but you'll fix that shortly; don't worry about it now. See Figure 7.45.

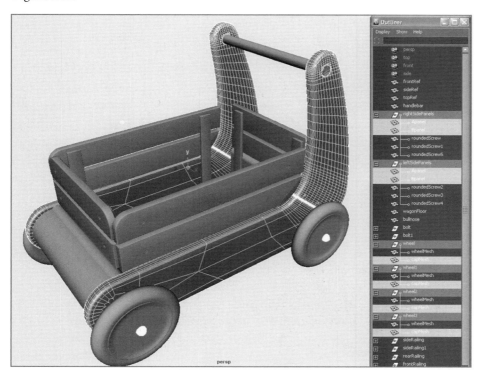

Figure 7.44

Assign the Red shader.

Figure 7.45

Assign the White shader.

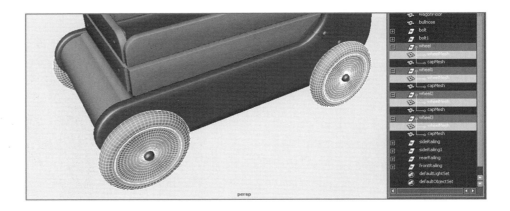

3. Select the bullnose (the rounded cylinder in front of the wagon), and assign it the Black Blinn.

4. Select the wagonFloor object, and assign it the Red shader, as shown in Figure 7.46. You'll notice that the front and back bodies of the wagon turn red as they're supposed to, but so does the floor of the wagon, which should be blue according to the photo in the Color Section. If you try to assign the Blue shader to the wagon floor mesh, the floor will be correct, but the front and back body of the wagon will be blue and not red. You'll fix this later.

Now you have initial assignments for the basic colors of the wagon's body. Let's tweak these shaders' colors next.

Figure 7.46

Assign the Red shader to the wagon floor just for now; you'll change it to blue later.

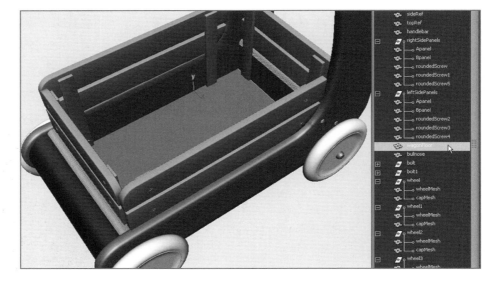

Creating a Shading Network for the Wheels

Refer to Figure 7.47 to observe how the materials are different for the rim and the tire of the wheel. The rim is glossier and has a tighter, sharper specular, whereas the tire has a very diffuse specular and is quite bumpy. You'll create a Layered shader for the wheels with white feeding into the rim portion and black into the tire portion, instead of assigning to faces like you did earlier with the lamp's biplane.

Figure 7.47

The tire on the wagon

Coloring the Wheel

First you need to determine where the white ends and the black starts on the surface of the wheel mesh.

1. Select the White shader in the Hypershade window. Click the Map icon (▣) next to the Color attribute. Right-click the Ramp texture icon, and select Create Texture. The wheel's color turns to a red, green, blue gradient, but in the wrong direction; you need the gradient to run from the center to the edge and not clockwise across the wheel. In the Ramp texture's Attribute Editor, set Type to U Ramp, as shown in Figure 7.48.

> If the ramp doesn't show up in your view panels, make sure you press 6 to enter Texture Display mode. If the colors and ramp texture still don't display, make sure Use Default Material isn't checked in the view panel's Shading menu.

2. Now the color gradient is running from the center (red) to the outside edge (green) to blue on the reverse side of the wheel. Move the blue ramp's handle in the ramp's Attribute Editor until its Selected Position value is about 0.6, as shown in Figure 7.49.

3. Delete the red handle in the ramp by clicking the checked box on the right of the handle. Change the blue color to black and the green color to white. Set the Interpolation attribute (found above the ramp color) to None so you get clean transitions from white to black, instead of a soft linear gradient where the black slowly grades to white. Name this ramp **wheelPositionRamp**.

Figure 7.48

Set the ramp to a U Ramp type.

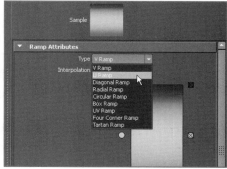

4. The backs of the wheels are solid black. In the wheelPositionRamp, click toward the top of the ramp to create a new color. Set that color to white, and set its position to about 0.920 to place white behind the wheels, keeping the black only where the tire is. See Figure 7.50.

Figure 7.49

Move the blue handle.

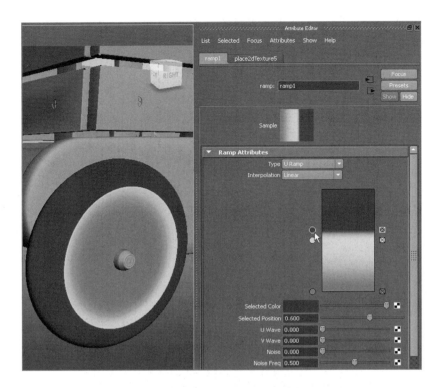

Figure 7.50

Setting the tire location using a ramp

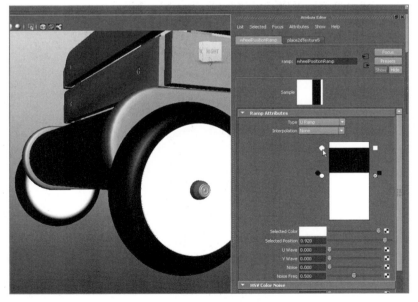

Now that you've pinpointed where the white rim ends and the black tire begins, you'll use this ramp as a transparency texture to place the Tire shader on top of the Rim shader in a Layered shader that you'll create later.

5. You don't need this Ramp shader on the color of the shader anymore—you did this so you could easily see the ramp color positions in the view panels. In the Hypershade, select the White shader, and click the Input And Output Connections icon (■) to graph the shader, as shown in Figure 7.51.

6. In the Attribute Editor, RMB+click the Color attribute, and select Break Connection from the context menu to disconnect the ramp from the color. Set the Color back to white. Notice that the link connecting the Ramp texture node to the White shader node disappears in the Hypershade window.

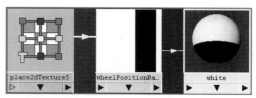

place2dTexture5   wheelPositionRa…   white

Figure 7.51

The White shader has the ramp attached as color.

7. Create a Layered shader. MMB+drag the White shader from the Hypershade to the top of the Layered Shader Attributes window, as shown in Figure 7.52. Delete the default Green shader in the Attribute Editor by clicking the checked box below its swatch.

8. Create a new Blinn shader, and set its color to black. Name the shader **tireShader**. Select the Layered shader, and then MMB+drag the new tireShader from the Hypershade to the Layered shader's Attribute Editor, placing it to the left of the White shader, as shown in Figure 7.53. Name the Layered shader **wheelShader**.

9. Select the wheels, and assign the wheelShader Layered shader to them. The wheels should appear all white. This is where the ramp you created earlier (wheelPositionRamp) comes into play.

10. Select the wheelShader, and click Input And Output Connections to graph the network in the Work Area of the Hypershade window. In the top panel of the Hypershade, click the Texture tab to display the texture nodes in the scene so you can see wheelPositionRamp's node.

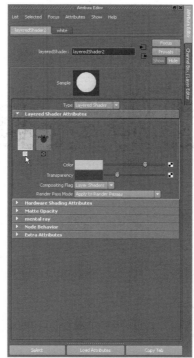

Figure 7.52

Drag the White shader to the Layered shader, and delete the default Green shader from it.

Figure 7.53

Add the black tireShader.

Figure 7.54

Attach the ramp to the Transparency attribute of the tireShader in the wheelShader.

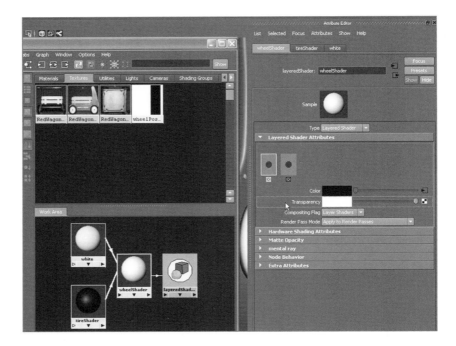

11. In the wheelShader's Attribute Editor, click the tireShader swatch on the left. MMB+drag the wheelPositionRamp node to the Transparency attribute, as shown in Figure 7.54.

12. When you attach the ramp, the wheelShader icon turns white on top and black on the bottom. Render a frame in the persp view panel to make sure the black tires line up properly, as shown in Figure 7.55. The wheel coloring is complete!

Figure 7.55

The tires are done!

Setting the Feel for the Materials and Adding a Bump Map

Because the material look and feel on the real wheels differs quite a bit between the rim and the tire, you'll further tweak the white rim and the black tire shaders. The rim is a smooth, glossy white, and the tire is a bumpy black with a broad specular. Follow these steps:

1. Let's set up a good angle of view for your test renders. Position your persp view panel to resemble the view in Figure 7.56. Render a frame.

2. Select the White shader, and set Eccentricity to **0.05** and Specular Roll Off to **0.5**. Doing so sharpens the specular highlight on the rim.

3. Select the black `tireShader`, and set Eccentricity to **0.375** and Specular Roll Off to **0.6** to make the highlight more diffuse across the tire. Set Reflectivity to **0.05**. Render a frame, and refer to Figure 7.57 to see how the specular highlight is broader and less glossy than in Figure 7.56.

4. Open the Attribute Editor for the tireShader, and click the Map icon (▣) next to the `Bump Mapping` attribute. In the Create Render Node window, click to create a Fractal texture map. Notice that the entire `wheelShader` icon becomes bumpy. Render a frame, and you'll see that the entire wheel is bumpy—not just the tire. (See Figure 7.58.) Argh!

Figure 7.56

Set your view to this angle, and render a frame.

Figure 7.57

Setting specular levels

Figure 7.58

The whole wheel becomes bumpy!

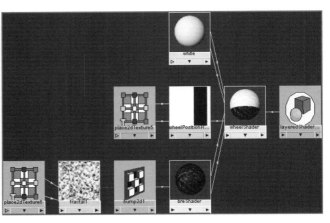

Figure 7.59

Graph the wheelShader network.

5. You have to use the `wheelPositionRamp` to prevent the bump from showing on the rim. Select the `wheelShader`, and click the Input And Output Connections icon () in the Hypershade to graph its network (Figure 7.59).

> Notice the single, blue connecting line between the fractal1 node and the bump2d1 node in the Hypershade. This means the alpha channel of the fractal feeds the amount of bump that is rendered on the `tireShader`. You have to alter the alpha coming out of the fractal node with the positioning ramp to block the rim from having any bump. The white areas of the ramp allow the bump map from the fractal to show on the tire, whereas the black area of the ramp keeps any bump from appearing. Because you already used this ramp to position the Rim shader and the Tire shader on the wheel, it will work perfectly for the bump position as well.

6. You have to use the `wheelPositionRamp` to prevent the bump from showing on the rim. Select the `wheelShader`, and click the Input And Output Connections icon () in the Hypershade to graph its network (Figure 7.59).

7. Select the fractal to display it in the Attribute Editor, and MMB+drag the `wheelPositionRamp` in the Hypershade to the `Alpha Gain` attribute for the fractal, as shown in Figure 7.60.

8. Render a frame, and you see that now the tire has no bump and the rim is bumpy (Figure 7.61).

9. This is easy enough to fix. All you need to do is reverse the ramp and then feed it into the `Alpha Gain` attribute of the fractal so that the tire is bumpy and the rim is smooth. In the Hypershade, in the Create pane on the left, click the Maya → Utilities heading, and then click the Reverse icon to create a reverse node in the Hypershade window. See Figure 7.62.

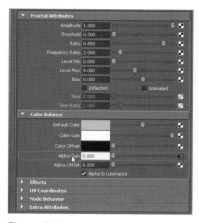

Figure 7.60

MMB+drag the ramp to the Alpha Gain attribute of the fractal.

Figure 7.61

The tire is smooth, and now the rim is bumpy.

Figure 7.62

Create a reverse node.

10. In the Hypershade, MMB+drag the `wheelPositionRamp` node onto the Reverse node, and select Input from the context menu when you release the mouse button. This connects the output of the ramp into the reverse node, which will then reverse the effect of the ramp on the fractal when you connect it in the next step.

11. MMB+drag the reverse node on top of the `fractal1` node, and select Other from the context menu. This opens the Connection Editor, which you first saw in Chapter 3. On the left the `reverse1` node is loaded, and on the right is the `fractal1` node. In the left pane, click the plus sign next to the `Output` attribute, and select outputX. In the right pane, select the `alphaGain` attribute, as shown in Figure 7.63.

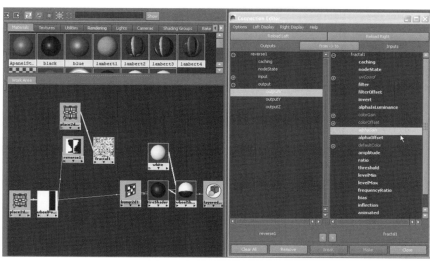

Figure 7.63

Connecting the reverse node to the fractal node

Figure 7.64

Set Quality to Production Quality.

Figure 7.65

Now you have the bump where you need it.

12. Open the Render Settings window by choosing Window → Rendering Editors → Render Settings. Click the Maya Software tab, and set Quality to Production Quality in the pull-down menu. (See Figure 7.64.) Render a frame: you finally have a bump on the tire and a smooth rim. See Figure 7.65.

13. It's not a very convincing bump yet, so select the fractal node, and set Ratio to **0.85**. Click the Placement tab for the fractal (it should be called something like *place2dTexture6*), and set the Repeat UV values to **18** and **48**, as shown in Figure 7.66. Doing so makes the fractal pattern finely speckled on the tire.

14. Render a frame; the fractal's scale on the bumpy tire looks too strong. Double-click the bump2d node in the Hypershade, and in the Attribute Editor, set `Bump Depth` to **0.04**. Render, and check your frame against Figure 7.67. The bump looks much better, if not a little strong from this angle; you can finesse it to taste from here.

Figure 7.66

Set the Repeat UV values for the fractal map.

Figure 7.67

The wheel looks pretty good.

Tire Summary

Congratulations! You've made your first somewhat complex shading network, as shown in Figure 7.68. By now, you should have a pretty good idea of how to get around the Hypershade and create shading networks. To recap, you're using a ramp to place the two Tire and Rim shaders on the wheel, as well as using it to place the bump map on just the tire by using a reverse node. The more you make these shading networks, the easier they will become to create.

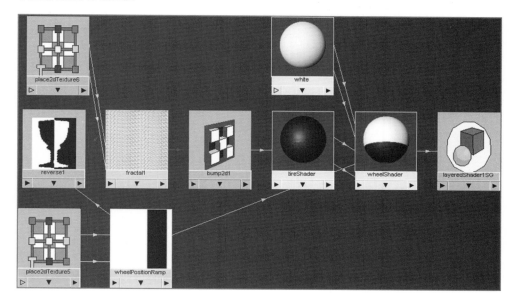

This type of shading is called *procedural shading*, because you used nothing but stock Maya texture nodes to accomplish what you needed for the wheels. In the following sections, you'll make good use of image mapping to create the decals for the wagon body as well as the wood for the railings.

You can load the file RedWagonTexture_v01.ma from the Scenes folder of the RedWagon project to check your work or skip to this point.

Putting Decals on the Body

Figure 7.69 shows you the decals that need to go onto the body of the wagon. They include the wagon's logo, which you'll replace with your own graphic design, and the white stripe that lines the side panels.

Figure 7.69

**You need to add the
body decals.**

Instead of trying to make a procedural texture as you did with the wheel, you'll create an image map that will texture the side panels' white stripe. The stripe is far too difficult to create otherwise. You'll create an image file using Photoshop (or another image editor) to make sure the white stripe (and later the red wagon logo) lines up correctly.

Working with UVs

Mapping polygons can involve the task of defining UV coordinates for them so that you can more easily paint an image map for the mesh. When you create a NURBS surface, UV coordinates are inherent to the surface. At the *origin* (or the beginning) of the surface, the UV coordinate is (0,0). When the surface extends all the way to the left and all the way up, the UV coordinate is (1,1). When you paint an 800×600–pixel image in Photoshop, for example, it's safe to assume that the first pixel of the image (at $X = 0$ and $Y = 0$ in Photoshop) will map directly to the UV coordinate (0,0) on the NURBS surface, whereas the top-right pixel in the image will map to the UV (1,1) of the surface. Toward that end, mapping an image to a NURBS surface is fairly straightforward. The bottom of the image will map to the bottom of the surface, the top to the top, and so on. Figure 7.70 shows how an image is mapped onto a NURBS plane and a NURBS sphere.

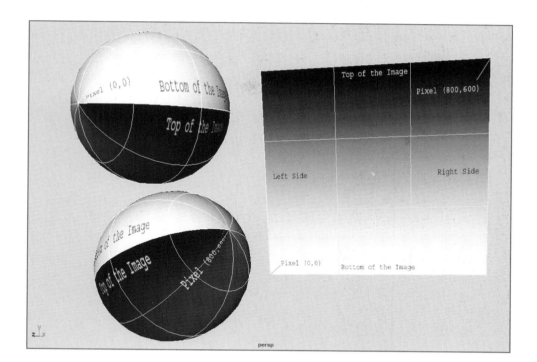

Figure 7.70

An image file is mapped to a NURBS plane and a NURBS sphere. Notice the locations marked in the image and how they map to the locations on the surface, with the pixel coordinates directly corresponding to the surface's UV coordinates.

The locations in the image, marked by text, correspond to the positions on the NURBS plane. The sphere, because it's a surface bent around spherically, shows that the origin of the UV coordinates is at the sphere's pole on the left and that the image wraps itself around it (bowing out in the middle) to meet at the seam along the front edge as shown.

When you're creating polygons, however, this isn't always the case. You must sometimes create your own UV coordinates on a polygonal surface to get a clean layout on which to paint in Photoshop. Although poly UV mapping becomes fairly involved and complicated, it's a concept that is important to grasp early. When poly models are created, they have UV coordinates; however, these coordinates may not be laid out in the best way for texture-image manipulation.

Working with the A Panels

Let's look at how the UVs are laid out for the A panel of the wagon model. Use Figure 7.42 earlier in the chapter to remind yourself where the A panel is.

1. Using the scene file RedWagonTexture_v01.ma from the Scenes folder of the RedWagon project, select the A panel on one side of the wagon, and choose Window → UV Texture Editor, as shown in Figure 7.71.

This section assumes you have some working knowledge of Adobe Photoshop. You can skip the creation of the maps and use the maps already on the companion web page, which are called out in the text later in the exercise.

The UV Texture window works almost like any other view panel. You may navigate the window and zoom in and out using the familiar Alt+mouse button combinations.

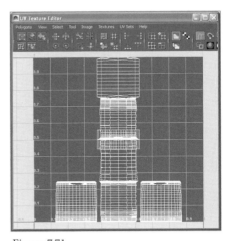

Figure 7.71

The A panel in the UV Texture Editor

2. RMB+click any part of the wireframe layout in the UV Texture Editor window, and select UV to enter the UV selection. Select the entire wireframe mesh at the lower right, as shown in Figure 7.72. Notice that green points are selected—almost as if they were vertices. These are UV points, and they're what define the UV coordinates on that part of the mesh. Look in the perspective view panel; the entire front face of the A panel is selected as well as the green UV points (also in Figure 7.72).

Feel free to select parts of the UV layout in the UV Texture Editor to see what corresponding points appear on the mesh in the persp view panel. This will help orient you as to how the UV layout works on this mesh.

3. You need to again lay out just this area of the mesh's UVs. Because you already have the entire front side of the panel selected in UVs, let's convert that selection to poly faces on the model. In the Polygons menu set and in the Maya Main Menu bar, choose Select → Convert Selection → To Faces. The front faces of the A panel mesh are selected, as shown in Figure 7.73. You can always manually select just the front faces of the mesh, but this conversion method is much faster. The UV Texture Editor shows just those faces now.

4. With those faces selected, make sure you're in the Polygons menu set. Choose Create UVs → Planar Mapping ❐ from the Main Menu bar. In the option box, set the Project From option to X Axis, check the Keep Image Width/Height Ratio option, and then click Project. (See Figure 7.74.) The UV Texture Editor shows the front A panel face.

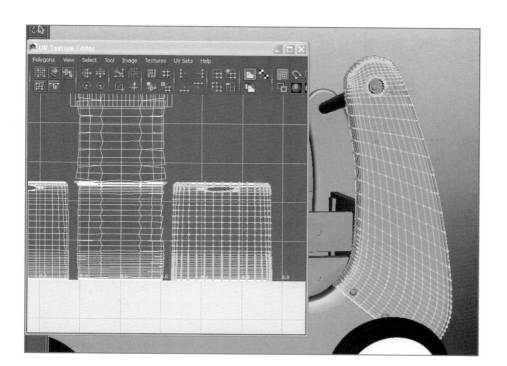

Figure 7.72

Select the UVs on this part of the A panel mesh.

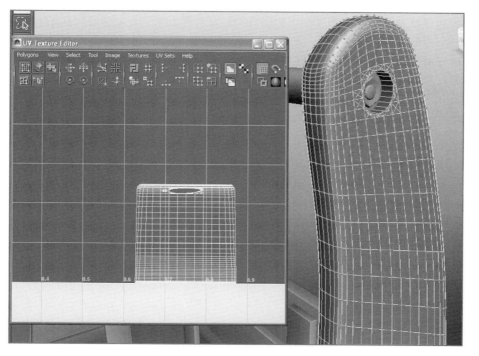

Figure 7.73

Convert the UVs you just selected to a face selection. This method easily isolates the front faces of the A panel for you to lay out their UVs again.

Figure 7.74

Create a planar projection for the UV layout.

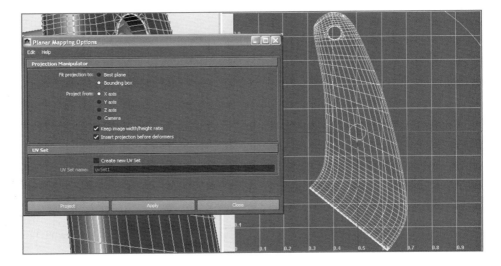

5. Now the front face has a much simpler UV layout from which to paint. However, it's centered in the UV Texture Editor and will overlap the other UVs of the same mesh. You should move and size it to fit into its original corner, more or less, to make sure no UVs double up on each other. In the UV Texture Editor, right-click the wireframe, and select UV to enter UV selection. Select all the UVs on those faces; all the UVs for the A panel mesh appear in the UV Texture Editor, and you can see the overlap. See Figure 7.75.

6. Press W for the Move tool, and move the selected UVs to the side of the UV Texture Editor. Press R for the Scale tool, and scale them down a bit to fit into the corner, as shown in Figure 7.76.

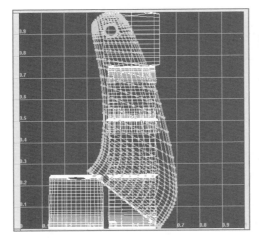

Figure 7.75

The UVs for the A panel, with the front side's UVs still selected

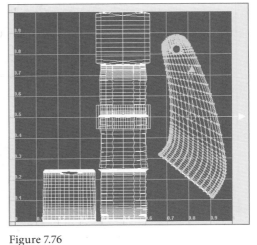

Figure 7.76

Position these UVs to make sure they don't overlap the rest of the A panel mesh's UVs.

7. Earlier in the chapter, you saw how to write out a PSD file with a UV snapshot as one of its layers. You'll use a similar technique to paint the decal for the panel. Click an empty area of the UV Texture Editor to deselect everything. Then, in Object Selection mode (press F8 if you need to exit Component Selection), select the A panel mesh in the persp view panel.

8. In the UV Texture Editor window, select Polygons → UV Snapshot to open the option box. Set both Size X and Size Y to **1024**. Change the image format to TIFF, click the Browse button at the top next to the File Name field, and navigate to the RedWagon project's Sourceimages folder on your hard drive. Name the file **ApanelUV.tif**, and click Save. Leave UV Range set to Normal (0 to 1), and click OK. See Figure 7.77.

Figure 7.77

Settings for the UV snapshot

WORKING IN PHOTOSHOP

Next, you'll go into Photoshop to paint your map according to the UV layout you just output.

1. In your OS file browser, navigate to the RedWagon project's Sourceimages folder, and open the file ApanelUV.tif in Photoshop. Figure 7.78 shows the layout of the UVs that you'll use to create the white stripe for the front of the A panel.

Figure 7.78

Using a UV snapshot makes working with the UV layout for the A panel easy.

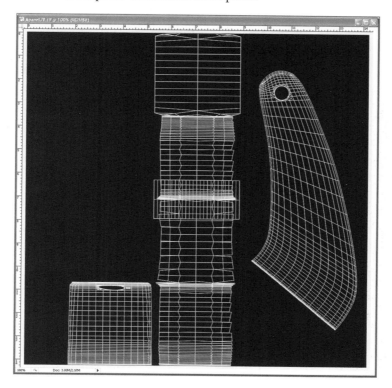

2. In Photoshop, create a new layer on top of the background layer that is the UV layout (white on black, as shown). Using the Bucket tool, fill that new layer with the same red you used on the shader in your scene. To do so, click the foreground color swatch in Photoshop, and set H to **355**, S to **91** percent, and B to **65** percent, as shown in Figure 7.79. Click OK.

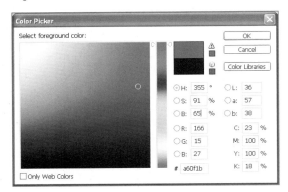

Figure 7.79

In Photoshop's Color Picker, create the same red you used for the wagon.

Figure 7.80

Set the opacity for the red layer in Photoshop so you can see the UV layout on the layer below.

3. Using the Bucket tool, click to fill the entire image with the red you just created. The trouble is that now you can't see the UV layout. Set the Opacity value of the red layer in Photoshop to **50** percent, as shown in Figure 7.80.

4. Set Photoshop's foreground color to white. Using the Line and Brush tools set to a width of about 6 pixels, draw a stripe following the UV layout lines, as shown in Figure 7.81. Doing so places that white stripe along the A panel's outer edge, because the UV lines you're following correspond to that area of the mesh. The rest will be left red.

5. You may have drawn directly on the red layer in Photoshop or created a new layer for the stripe. In either case, set the Opacity value of the red layer back to **100** percent so you can no longer see the UV layout. Your image file should look like the one in Figure 7.82. Save the image as **ApanelStripe.tif** in the Sourceimages folder of your RedWagon project. You may keep the layers in the TIFF file, or you may choose to flatten the image or merge the layers. It may be best to keep the stripe and red on separate layers so that you can go back into Photoshop and edit the stripe as needed.

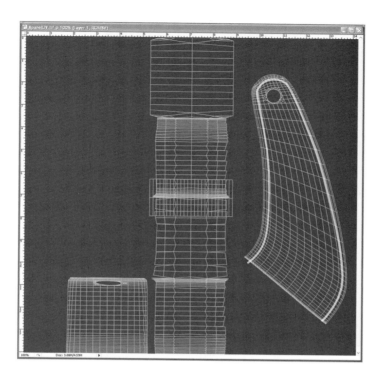

Figure 7.81

Follow the UV lines to draw the white stripe.

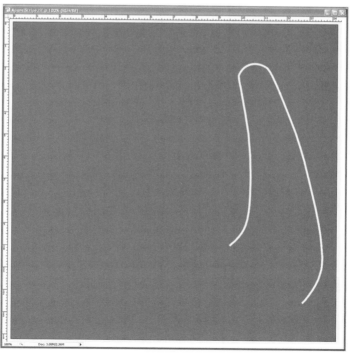

Figure 7.82

The striped image file

CREATING AND ASSIGNING THE SHADER

Now, let's create the shader and get it assigned to the geometry.

1. In Maya, open the Hypershade, and select the Red shader. Duplicate it by choosing Edit → Duplicate → Shading Network in the Hypershade window, as shown in Figure 7.83.

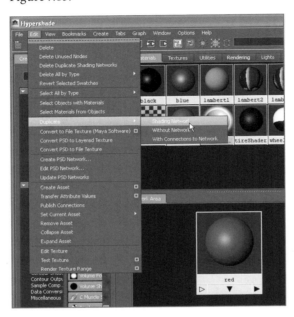

Figure 7.83

Duplicate the original Red shader.

2. Name the new shader (called `red1`) **ApanelStripe**. Open the Attribute Editor, click the Map icon (■) next to `Color`, and choose File. In the Attribute Editor, click the Folder icon next to the `Image Name` field. Navigate to your Sourceimages folder, and select `ApanelStripe.tif`, as shown in Figure 7.84.

3. In the Hypershade, you may see that the Shader icon has turned somewhat transparent. Maya is automatically mapping the Transparency attribute of the shader as well as the color. Double-click the shader to open its Attribute Editor, RMB+click `Transparency`, and select Break Connection from the context window. Doing so sets the shader to the same red you used earlier, but now it gives you a stripe along the side A panel.

4. Assign the `ApanelStripe` shader to the A panel mesh, and press 6 for Texture Display mode in the persp view panel. See Figure 7.85. The stripe lines up well.

You may skip the image creation using Photoshop and use the `ApanelStripe.tif` image file found in the Sourceimages folder of the RedWagon project on the companion web page instead.

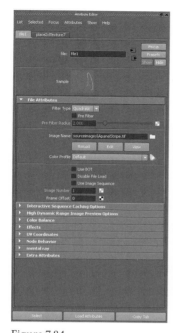

Figure 7.84

Select the ApanelStrip.tif file.

Figure 7.85

The stripe

COPYING UVS

You need to put the stripe on the other side's A panel. Select the other A panel, and assign the ApanelStripe shader to it. You'll notice that no stripe appears. (See Figure 7.86.) This is because the UV layout for this A panel hasn't been set up yet. Don't worry; you don't have to redo everything you did for the first A panel. You can essentially copy the UVs from the first A panel mesh to this one.

1. Select the first A panel (with the stripe) and the second panel (without the stripe). In the Polygons menu set, choose Mesh → Transfer Attributes ❒. In the option box, set Sample Space to Local, as shown in Figure 7.87, and click Transfer.

2. The stripe appears on the inside of the back A panel, not on the outside as you need. Select that A panel, and choose Modify → Center Pivot.

3. In the Channel Box, enter a value of –**1.0** for Scale X. The stripe flips to the correct side, as shown in Figure 7.88.

4. With that A panel still selected, choose Modify → Freeze Transformations.

You can load the file RedWagonTexture_v02.ma from the Scenes folder of the RedWagon project to check your work or skip to this point.

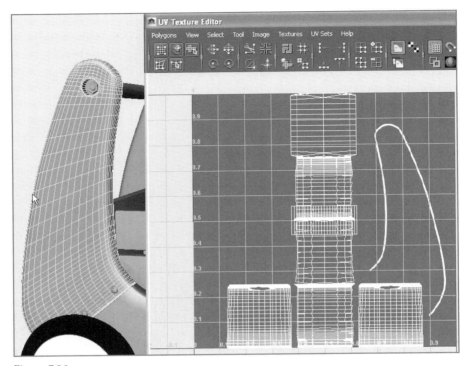

Figure 7.86
Assign the ApanelStripe shader to the other side's A panel.

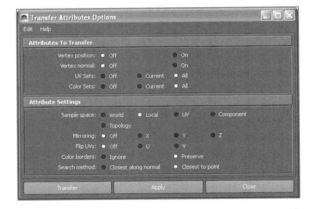

Figure 7.87
The Transfer Attributes settings

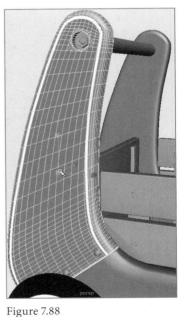

Figure 7.88
The stripe is on the correct side now.

The file texture you'll use for the panels was painted in Photoshop to place the stripes and logo properly on the wagon using their UV layouts. Study the image file, and see how it fits on the mesh of the wagon. Try adjusting the image file with your own artwork to see how your image map affects the placement on the mesh.

Working with the B Panels

With the A panels done, you'll move on to the B panels (Figure 7.42 earlier in the chapter), using much the same methodology you did with the A panels. To begin, follow these steps:

1. Select one of the B panels, shown in Figure 7.89, and open the UV Texture Editor window.

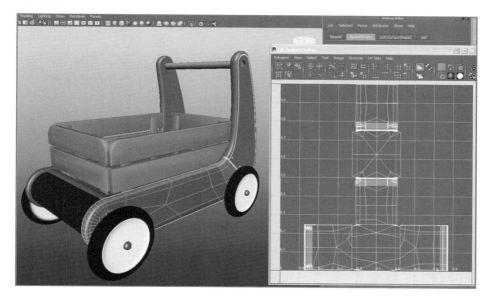

Figure 7.89

Starting on the B panels

2. As you did with the front face of the A panel, select the UVs on the lower-right side of the layout in the UV Texture Editor, as shown in Figure 7.90, to isolate the front face of the B panel.

3. Choose Select → Convert Selection → To Faces. You've isolated the front face of the B panel.

4. Choose Create UVs → Planar Mapping ❏. In the option box, set the Project From option to X Axis, and make sure the Keep Image Width/Height Ratio option is checked, just as before. Your B panel shows up nicely laid out in the UV Texture Editor. See Figure 7.91.

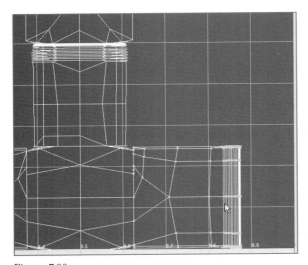

Figure 7.90

Select the front face UVs for the B panel.

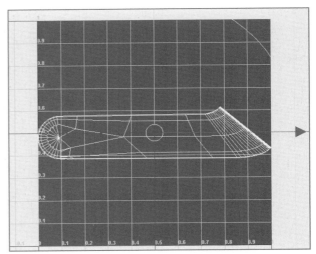

Figure 7.91

The planar projection creates a nice UV layout for the front faces of the B panel.

5. Convert the selection to UVs, and use Move (W), Scale (R), and Rotate (E) to position the UV layout for that front face, as shown in Figure 7.92.

6. Press F8, and select the B panel mesh. In the UV Texture Editor, save a UV snapshot called `BpanelUV.tif` to the Sourceimages folder of the RedWagon project.

7. Open the `BpanelUV.tif` image in Photoshop, and follow the same steps as you did for the A panel to lay down a red layer and paint a stripe along the layout, as shown in Figure 7.93. It's best to save the stripe on its own layer in Photoshop, because you'll probably need to edit and reposition the stripe to make sure it lines up with the A panel stripe after you assign the shader.

Figure 7.92

Put the front face UVs on the side.

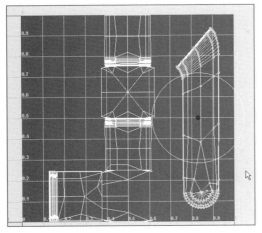

8. Create your own logo to place in the middle of panel B, and place it in the Photoshop image file, as shown in Figure 7.94. Save the image file as `BpanelStripe.tif` into the Sourceimages folder.

9. Duplicate another Red shader, and, as you did previously, assign the `BpanelStripe.tif` as its color map. If necessary, disconnect the transparency from the shader as you did with the A panel's shader. Name the shader **BpanelStripe**.

10. Assign the `BpanelStripe` shader to the B panel, as shown in Figure 7.95.

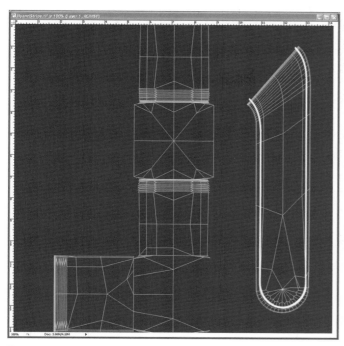

Figure 7.93

Create the B panel's stripe in Photoshop using the UV snapshot.

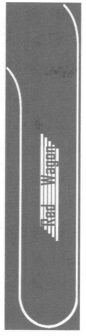

Figure 7.94

Create the logo in Photoshop.

Figure 7.95

The B panel has its decals.

You can skip the image creation in Photoshop and use the BpanelStripe.tif image file found in the Sourceimages folder of the RedWagon project on the companion web page.

CREATING THE OTHER B PANEL TEXTURE

Finally, you need to create the shader for the other side's B panel. Assign the BpanelStripe shader to the other B panel. Nothing happens, because the UVs for the second B panel aren't set up yet.

However, because there is a logo with text, setting up its UVs won't be as simple as copying the UVs from the first B panel and then mirroring the mesh, as you did with the A panel with a Scale X value of –1.0. Doing so will make the logo and text read backward. First you'll copy and flip the UVs to the other B panel.

1. Select the first B panel with the correct texture, and then select the other side's B panel and choose Mesh → Transfer Attributes ❑. Make sure Sample Space is still set to Local, and set Flip UVs to U. Click Transfer to copy the UVs, flipping them over, as you can see in Figure 7.96.

2. You have to go back to Photoshop and create a second BpanelStripe.tif image file with a mirrored logo. In Photoshop, create a marquee around the logo, and mirror or flip the canvas horizontally. See Figure 7.97.

3. Select the logo portion of the image and flip that vertically, as shown in Figure 7.98. Save the image as **BpanelStripe_2.tif**.

4. Duplicate the BpanelStripe shader in the Hypershade by selecting the shader and choosing Edit → Duplicate → Shading Network. The copy is called BpanelStripe1.

Figure 7.96

Copying and flipping the UVs to the other B panel

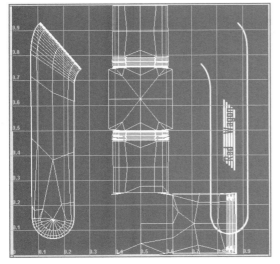

5. Select the newly copied BpanelStripe1 shader, and graph its input and output connections (▣) in the Hypershade. Select its file node, and open the Attribute Editor. Click the Folder icon to select a new image file, and then select the BpanelStripe_2.tif you just created in the Sourceimages folder. See Figure 7.99.

6. The stripe and logo display on the wrong side of the B panel. Select the mesh, and center its pivot.

7. Set the Scale X attribute for the B panel to **–1.0** to mirror it. The stripe and logo decals now show up on the correct side of the panel. Select the mesh and freeze its transforms. Figure 7.100 shows the wagon so far.

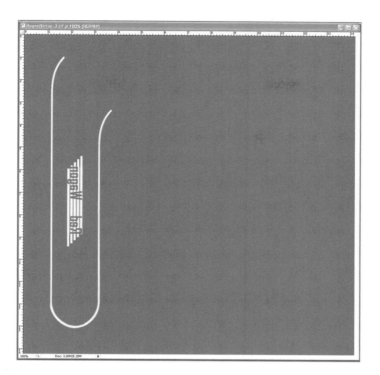

Figure 7.97

Flip the original image horizontally to fit the new UV layout of the second B panel.

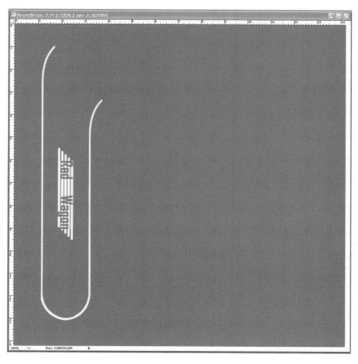

Figure 7.98

Flip the logo vertically, and save the image as its own file.

Figure 7.99

Assign the new image file to the new BpanelStripe1 shader.

Figure 7.100

The wagon has decals on both sides.

Texturing the Floor

Right now, the floor of the wagon is red, like the rest of its body. However, the real wagon has a blue floor, not red. If you select the mesh for the wagon's floor (named wagonFloor) and assign the Blue shader you created, the whole body of the wagon turns blue, and that isn't what you want. You need only the inside and bottom of the floor to be blue, not the front and back sides of the wagon's body.

You'll make a face assignment instead of dealing with UVs and image files. RMB+click the wagon floor mesh, and select Face from the marking menu. Select the two faces for the floor, as shown in Figure 7.101.

With the faces selected, assign the Blue shader from the Hypershade window, and you're finished! You have a blue floor. All that remains now are the screws, bolts, handle, and wood railings.

You can load the file RedWagonTexture_v03.ma from the Scenes folder of the RedWagon project to check your work or skip to this point.

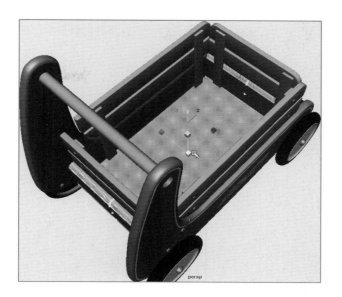

Figure 7.101

Select the floor faces.

Shading the Wood Railings

You'll use procedural shading to use the Wood texture available in Maya to create the wood railings. Begin here:

1. In the Hypershade, create a new Phong material.

2. Click the Color Map icon (▣), and choose the Wood texture from the 3D Textures heading in the Create pane in the Hypershade.

3. In the Attribute Editor for the Wood texture, set the Filler Color and Vein Color attributes according to Table 7.3.

ATTRIBUTE	H VALUE	S VALUE	V VALUE
Filler Color	43	0.25	1.0
Vein Color	10.7	0.315	0.9

Table 7.3

Filler Color and Vein Color attributes

4. Set Vein Spread to **0.5**, Layer Size to **0.5**, Randomness to **1.0**, Age to **10.0**, and Grain Contrast to **0.33**. In the Noise Attributes heading, set Amplitude X to **0.2** and Amplitude Y to **0.1**, as shown in Figure 7.102. Name the shader **Wood**.

5. Select all the wood railings and posts, and assign the Wood shader to them. Render a frame, and compare it to Figure 7.103. Notice the green cube place3dTexture node that is now in your scene. See Figure 7.104.

Figure 7.102

Setting the Wood texture

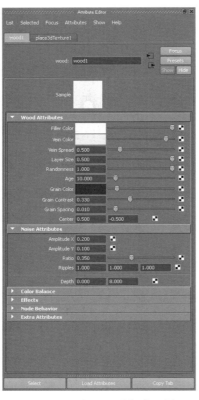

6. The side wood railings look fine; however, the wavy pattern on the front and back wood railings looks a bit odd. In the Hypershade, duplicate the shading network for the Wood shader, and call the new shader **woodFront**.

7. Assign that shader to the front and back railings and posts. Graph the network on the woodFront shader in the Hypershade window.

8. In the Hypershade, select the place3dTexture2 node (Figure 7.105) and the green cube in the view panels.

9. Rotate that placement node in the persp view panel 90 degrees to the right or left. Render a frame, and compare it to Figure 7.106. The wood should no longer have that awkward wavy pattern.

The wood railings are finished. Now, for some extra challenge, you can use pictures of real wood to map onto the railings for a more detailed look. The procedural Wood texture can give you only so much realism. If you create your own wood maps, use your experience with the side panels to create UV layouts for the railings so you can paint realistic wood textures using Photoshop. You'll use custom photos and texture image maps next to simulate the rich wood in the decorative box later in the chapter.

Figure 7.103

Assign the Wood shader.

Figure 7.104

The place3dTexture node for the wood texture

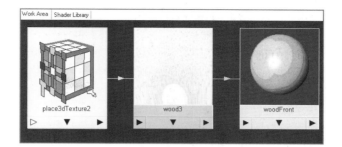

Figure 7.105

Select the place-ment node for the second Wood texture.

Figure 7.106

The wood on the front and back rail-ings looks better.

Finishing the Wagon

Now that the railings are done and you have test renders, there are only two parts left to texture: the bull-nose front of the wagon, and the metal handle and screws. From here, take your time and create a bump map based on a fractal, as you did for the tires, and apply it to the bullnose's black shader. Figure 7.107 shows a nice subtle bump map on the bullnose.

And last, you'll need a metal shader for the screws, bolts, and handlebar for the wagon. Use a Phong shader with a blue-gray color and a low dif-fuse value, and assign it to all the metal parts of the wagon, as shown in Figure 7.108. You can then add

Figure 7.107

A nice bump for the bullnose

an environment map to the reflection color like you did for the table lamp stem earlier in this chapter to give the metal a reflective look.

Because metal is a tricky material to render and a lot of a metal's look is derived from reflections, you'll finish setting the Metal shader's attributes in Chapter 11, when you render the wagon as well as the table lamp. You'll enable raytracing to get realistic reflections and gauge how to best set up the Metal shader for a great look.

Figure 7.109 shows the wagon with all its parts assigned to shaders. Figure 7.110 shows a quick render of the wagon as it is now.

You can load the file RedWagonTexture_v04.ma from the Scenes folder of the RedWagon project to check your work or skip to this point.

Figure 7.109

The wagon in the Perspective panel

Figure 7.110

A current render of the wagon

Photo-Real Mapping: The Decorative Box

With all the references you can find to any given object on the Internet, why not use real photos to create the textures for a model? That's exactly what you'll do here, with the decorative box you modeled in Chapter 3, using pictures of the real box.

You'll take this texturing exercise one important step further in Chapter 11 and experience how you can add detail to an object through displacement mapping, after you assign the colors in this chapter. This will allow you to add finer detail to a model without modeling those details.

Setting Up UVs (Blech!)

The UVs on the decorative box aren't too badly laid out by default, as you can see in Figure 7.111. The only parts of the box that are missing in the UV layout are the feet. That is a common issue when extruding polygons: their UVs are rarely laid out automatically as you extrude them. Frequently, they're bunched up together in a flat layout that is difficult, if not impossible, to see in the UV Texture Editor.

Open the file boxModel_v07.mb in the Scenes folder of the Decorative_Box project on the companion web page, or continue with your own model.

First you have to make room for the feet UVs.

1. Select all the UVs for the entire box in the UV Texture Editor. Press R for the Scale tool, and scale everything down uniformly to gain some space in the normalized UV space, shown in Figure 7.112.

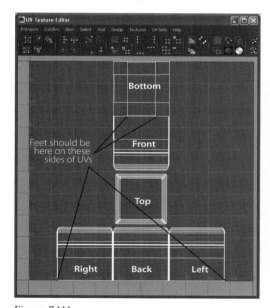

Figure 7.111
The feet UVs are missing from the box model.

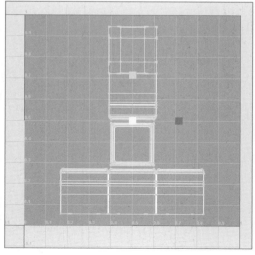

Figure 7.112
Scale all the UVs down a bit.

2. Now for the tedious part. You have to create new UVs for the four feet and then move them to where they should be in the full box's UV layout. Go into Component mode, and select the poly faces for the four feet, as shown in Figure 7.113.

Figure 7.113

Select the faces for the feet.

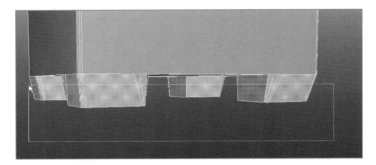

3. With the faces selected, go to the main Maya window. In the Polygons menu set, select Create UVs → Automatic Mapping. The feet now have UVs that you can see in Figure 7.114. However, they're all over the place. You have to individually select and move each face of each foot to its appropriate place on the box's overall UV layout.

4. Select all the feet UVs in the UV Texture Editor, scale them all down uniformly together. You want to scale them all so that one of the squares fits into the corner of the top shape, as shown in Figure 7.115 (left). Then move them all together off to the side, as shown in Figure 7.115 (right). You'll position and scale them to fit properly soon.

Laying out UVs can be a time-consuming affair, as you've seen with the wagon. Although it's recommended that you follow along with this exercise to lay out UVs for the box (because doing so will give you more practice and experience with UVs), you can skip straight to color-mapping the box in the next section by downloading the file boxTexture01.mb in the Scenes folder of the Decorative_Box project on the companion web page.

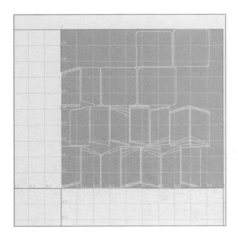

5. Now comes the task of figuring out which UV fits where. In the UV Texture Editor window, select the edges shown in Figure 7.116 by Shift+single-clicking them. Do not use a marquee selection to make sure you select only the single edges you need. Notice that as you select each edge, they become selected in the model as well as the feet UVs off on the side of the UV Texture Editor window. These are the edges where the outside sides of the feet meet the box. If you find it easier, you can select those edges from the model itself instead of the UV Texture Editor.

Figure 7.114

The automatic UV creation puts the UVs everywhere.

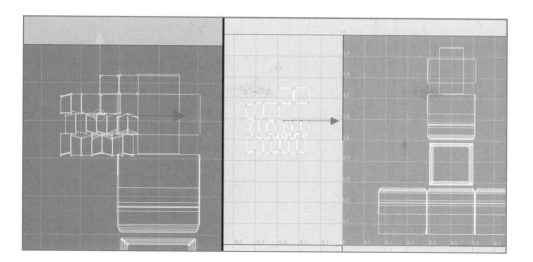

Figure 7.115

Scale the feet UVs to fit the size of the rest of the box's UVs (left).Then move the feet UVs to the side of the UV editor (right).

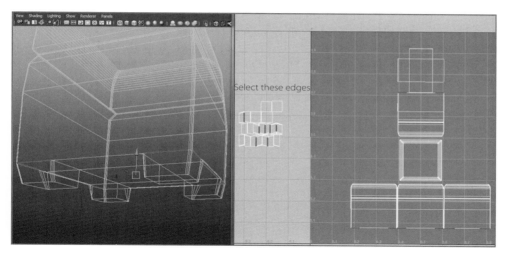

Figure 7.116

Select these individual edges either in the model view or in the UV Texture Editor.

6. With those edges selected, in the UV Texture Editor choose the Move And Sew The Selected Edges icon (Figure 7.117). This will snap the UVs for the outside sides of the feet to their respective sides on the box. If you did not scale the feet UVs in step 4 well enough, you will notice that the feet will stick out from the sides of the box's UVs, as shown in Figure 7.118 (left). If that is the case, it's easier to return to step 4 (press Z for undo until you reach step 4 again) and scale those feet UVs more accurately. This can have a little bit of back and forth. As long as you are within reasonable size, you will be fine. Figure 7.118 (right) shows a better matching scale of the feet after the UVs are sewn together.

Figure 7.117

The Move And Sew The Selected Edges icon in the UV Texture Editor

Figure 7.118

Sew the feet edges to the box. On the left, the feet UVs are scaled too big in step 4. On the right, the feet UVs are scaled properly.

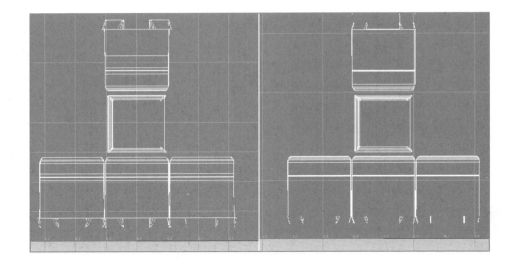

Figure 7.118

Sew the feet edges to the box. On the left, the feet UVs are scaled too big in step 4. On the right, the feet UVs are scaled properly.

7. Right-click in the UV Texture Editor, and select UV from the marking menu. Next, select just one corner UV from the bottom shape of the box, as shown in Figure 7.119 (left). In the UV Texture Editor, choose Select → Select Shell to select the entire bottom UV shape, and then press W to move the bottom UVs up in the UV Texture Editor a little bit, as shown in Figure 7.119 (right).

8. Figure 7.119 (right) also shows the remaining feet UVs off on the left side of the UV Texture Editor window. The four square shapes are the bottoms of the feet. Select just one corner UVs of the square shown in Figure 7.120 (left); then select the entire shell (Select → Select Shell) and move it to fit to the bottom UVs of the box as shown in Figure 7.120 (right).

Figure 7.119

Select one UV (left); then select the shell and move the bottom UVs up in the UV Texture Editor (right).

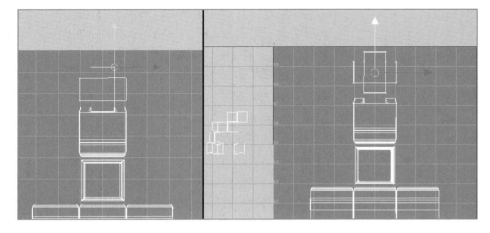

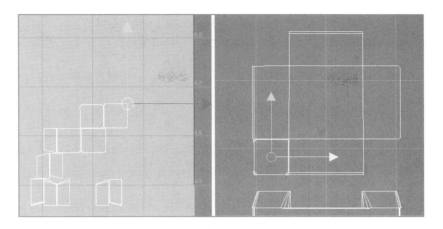

Figure 7.120
Select one UV in the corner (left); then select the shell and move it to fit the box bottom UV shape.

9. Repeat step 8 to place all the feet bottom shapes around the UVs of the bottom of the box, as shown in Figure 7.121.

10. Individually select the shells of the remaining feet UVs on the side of the UV Texture Editor, and line them up to the side of the box bottom as shown in Figure 7.121. Those remaining feet UVs are the inside faces of the feet and share the same generic wood texture as the bottom of the box, so aligning and sewing them together like you did for the outside faces of the feet in steps 5 and 6 is not necessary (Figure 7.122).

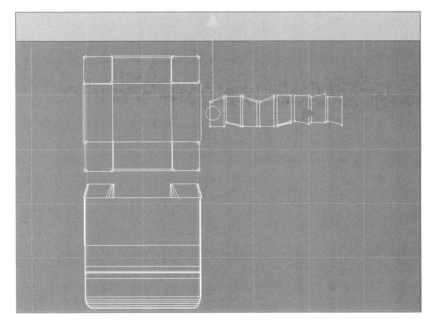

Figure 7.121
Place the feet bottoms to the box bottom and then line up the remaining feet UVs to the side.

Figure 7.122

These faces will have a generic wood texture like the bottom of the box and do not need to be carefully lined up.

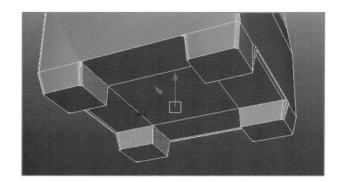

Figure 7.122

These faces will have a generic wood texture like the bottom of the box and do not need to be carefully lined up.

When you've finished, your UV Texture Editor should resemble the one shown in Figure 7.123. Because the box's decorations are seamless from the top of the box down to the four sides, let's lay out the UVs to make painting and editing in Photoshop easier.

Figure 7.123

Finally, you're finished with the feet UVs.

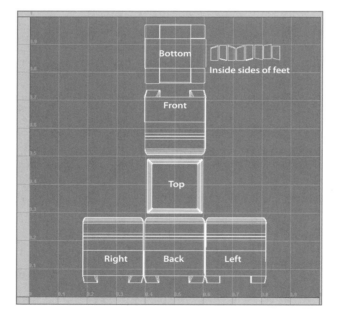

In the UV Texture Editor, select the box top's edges, as shown in Figure 7.124 (left). Then click the Move And Sew The Selected Edges icon (shown earlier in Figure 7.117) in the UV Texture Editor, and your UV layout should match Figure 7.124 (right). The top and sides of the box are all one UV shell now.

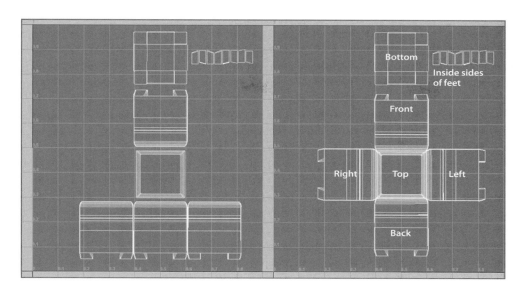

UV layout can be an exacting chore, but when it's completed, you're free to lay out your textures. You can check your work against the file boxTexture01.mb in the Scenes folder of the Decorative_Box project on the companion web page. You can also take a much needed breather. I sure hope you've been saving your work!

Color Mapping the Box

Now that you have a good UV layout, you can output a UV snapshot and get to work editing your photos of the box to make the color maps. Start with the following steps:

1. Select the box, and open the UV Texture Editor window. From the UV Texture Editor menu, select Polygons → UV Snapshot. In the UV Snapshot window, set Size X and Y to **2048**. Change Image Format to TIFF.

   Click the Browse button, and select a location for your UV snapshot image. Generally, the project's Sourceimages folder is the best place for it. Make sure you don't write over the UV snapshot already created for you. Type in a name for your UV snapshot, and click OK to create the image. Figure 7.125 shows the option box, and Figure 7.126 shows the UV snapshot image.

2. Open the UV snapshot image in Photoshop or your favorite image editor, and set it as its own layer. Rename the layer to **UV Snapshot**. I've done the heavy lifting for you and have prepared five photos of the decorative box that you can use to map the model. Figure 7.127 shows the photos of the box. This image file is included as lineup.jpg in the Sourceimages folder in the Decorative_Box project on the companion web page.

Figure 7.125

Setting the UV Snapshot options

Figure 7.126

The UV snapshot for the decorative box, shown as black lines on white. You may see white lines on black in Photoshop.

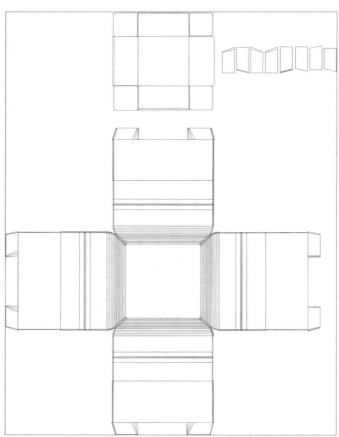

Figure 7.127

Photos of the box

Top	Right	Left	Front	Back

3. As you've probably guessed, you need to copy and paste the photos to their respective views over the UV Snapshot layer. Open the lineup.jpg file in Photoshop alongside the UV snapshot. Marquee+select a box around the top image (the one at the left in Figure 7.127), and copy it (Ctrl+C or Edit → Copy in Photoshop).

4. Go to the UV snapshot image in Photoshop, and paste the image on top. Rename the new layer to **Box Top**, and set the layer's Opacity to 50% so you can still see the UV layout, as shown in Figure 7.128.

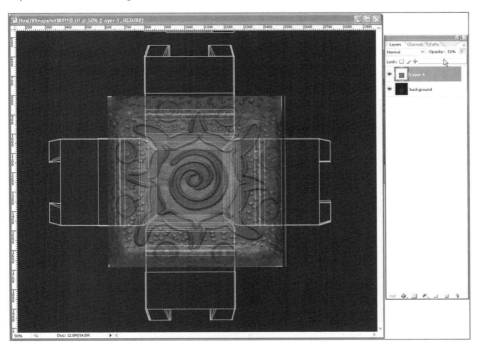

Figure 7.128

Paste the top image onto the UV snapshot image.

5. Use the Scale function in Photoshop (Edit → Transform → Scale) to move and scale the top image to fit over the top of the UV layout, as shown in Figure 7.129. Make sure you scale the box-top image uniformly to keep it from distorting. You can do this by holding the Shift key as you scale the image up or down.

These photo images of the box have been retouched and painted to create an overlap. This means that parts of the sides of the box show in the top image. As you can see in Figure 7.129, the top image extends slightly all around the four sides. This allows the different parts of the texture map (top and four sides) to overlap and blend with each other better when put on the model.

Save your work as **boxColorMap01.psd** in the project's Sourceimages folder. Saving as a Photoshop file will preserve the layers for easier editing.

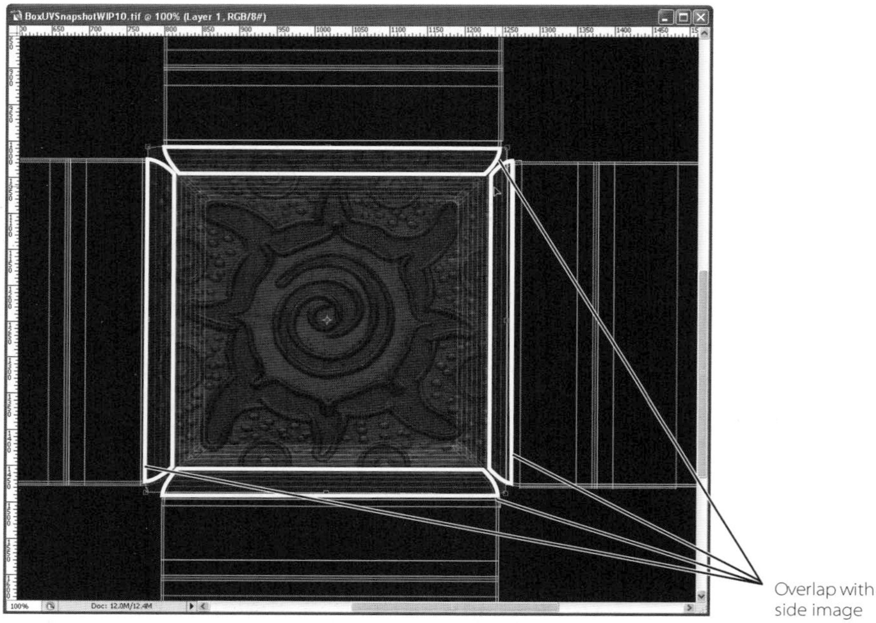

Figure 7.129

Position and scale the top image in Photoshop to line up with the UVs of the top of the model. Notice the overlap of the sides and the top.

Overlap with side image

6. Marquee+select the right-side image of the box (immediately to the right of the top image in lineup.jpg), and copy it. Paste it into boxColorMap01.psd in Photoshop. Do your best to align the right-side image with the top image, using the features of the box to line them up, as you can see in Figure 7.130. You can fix this later by adjusting both the map and the UVs on the box for a tighter fit. For now, be fairly accurate, and leave the finesse for later. Save the file.

7. Use the same procedures in Photoshop to line up the other sides of the box, as shown in Figure 7.131. Set the box-top image to be the topmost layer, make sure all the layers are at 100% opacity, and then turn off the UV Snapshot layer so it's not visible.

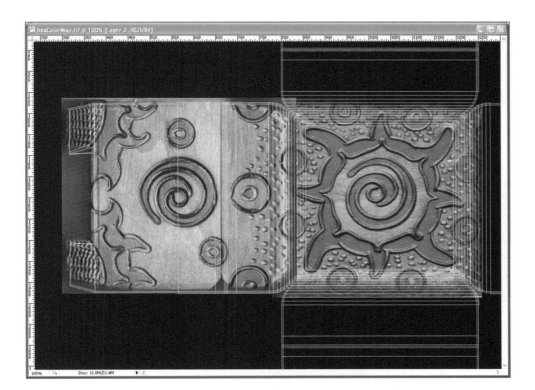

Figure 7.130
Align the right-side image with the right-side UVs.

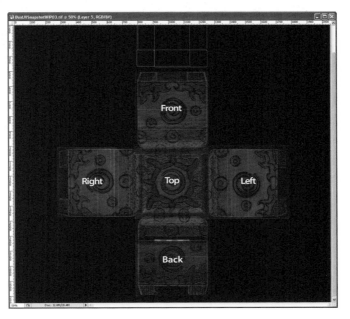

Figure 7.131
Copy, paste, and line up the box sides and the back to their respective UV areas.

8. And finally, open the file `boxBottomAndFeet.jpg` from the Sourceimages folder of the project. Select the entire image, and copy and paste into your `boxColorMap01.psd` file. Position and place the image to fit the bottom UVs of the box in your map in Photoshop. Just get close; you will fine-tune the placement of image to UV later.

9. Save the final Photoshop file. Then, resave the file as a JPEG called **`boxColorMap01.jpg`**. This is the file you'll map. (See Figure 7.132.)

Figure 7.132

The color map layout file boxColor-Map01.jpg

Mapping the Box

Let's map this color image to the box and see how it fits. Based on rendering the box, you can make adjustments to the UVs and the image map to get everything to line up. This, of course, requires more Photoshop and/or image-editing experience, which could be a series of books of its own. If you don't have enough image-editing experience, have no fear: the images have been created for you so you can get the experience of mapping them and learn about the underlying workflow that this sort of texturing requires. Follow these steps:

1. Back in Maya, open the Hypershade window, and create a new Phong shader. Open the Attribute Editor, click the Map icon (⬚) next to the `Color` attribute, and select File.

2. Double-click the `file1` node to open the Attribute Editor. Click the Folder icon next to the `Image Name` attribute, navigate to the Sourceimages folder for the project, and select the `boxColorMap01.jpg` file (not the PSD file). The icon in the Hypershade doesn't show the image because it's a large file. (See Figure 7.133.)

3. Double-click the `file1` node, and in the Attribute Editor, rename it to **boxColor-Map**. Right-click the newly named `boxColorMap` node in the Hypershade, and choose Refresh Swatch from the marking menu. The `boxColorMap` image is displayed as the boxColorMap icon. (See Figure 7.134.)

4. Select the box, and assign the Phong shader to it. Rename the Phong to **boxShader**. In the persp view panel, press 6 for texture view. The color map is fairly well aligned on the model. Not bad! (See Figure 7.135.)

5. Render a frame to see how the box looks (Figure 7.136). Notice that there are small alignment issues at the edges where the sides meet and where the top meets the sides. Save your Maya scene.

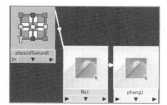

Figure 7.133

The color map's file node

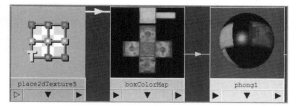

Figure 7.134

The icon is refreshed.

Figure 7.135

The color map fits pretty well already, but there are a few alignment issues at the edges.

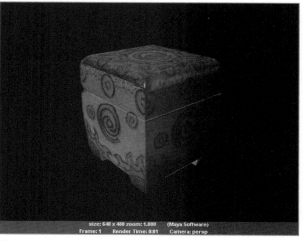

Figure 7.136

A render of the box so far

This gives you a pretty good place to work from. You need to adjust the color map image to be more seamless. The scene file boxTexture02.mb in the Scenes folder of the Decorative_Box project on the companion web page will catch you up to this point.

Photoshop Work

This is where image-editing experience is valuable. Here, it's all about working in Photoshop to further line up the sides to the top and the sides to each other to minimize alignment issues and yield a seamless texture map. Although I won't get into the minutia of photo editing here, I'll show the progression of the images and the general workflow used in Photoshop to make the color map's different sides and top line up or merge better. The images have already been created and are on the companion web page in the Sourceimages folder for this project.

For example, using masking in Photoshop, spend some time feathering the intersection of the box's sides in boxColorMap01.psd so there is no hard line between the different sides and the top. Figure 7.137 shows a smoother transition between the different parts. This image has been created for you; it's boxColorMap02.jpg in the Sourceimages folder. Make sure you don't overwrite that file if you're painting your own.

Figure 7.137

Use masks to feather the transitions between the different parts of the box.

In Maya, double-click the `boxColorMap` node in the Hypershade, and in the Attribute Editor, replace the original `boxColorMap01.jpg` with the `boxColorMap02.jpg` from the Sourceimages folder (or your own retouched image file). Render and compare the difference. The top and front should merge a little better. In the persp view panel, orbit

Figure 7.138

There are blank areas on the box as well as a little distortion.

around the box in Texture View mode (press 6) to identify any other lineup issues. In some cases, as you can see in Figure 7.138, gray or black is mapped onto the box on its right side, and there is a warped area. Also, the crease where the lid meets the box is lower than you've modeled.

The blank areas on the box are outside the bounds of the image in the Photoshop image and can be fixed by adjusting the UVs in Maya. The same goes for the distorted areas on the side of the box—you just need to adjust the UVs.

1. Select the box, and open the UV Texture Editor window. Figure 7.139 shows some primary areas for you to work on.

Figure 7.139

Here are the main problems to fix.

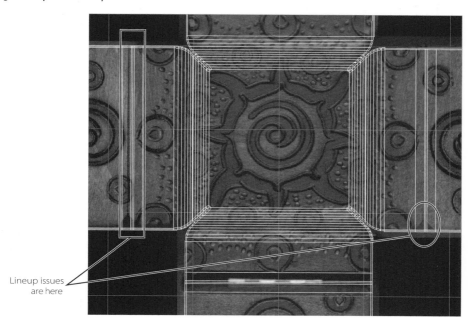

Lineup issues
are here

2. In the UV Texture Editor, select the UVs (right-click and choose UV) shown in Figure 7.140 on the left. Press W for the Move tool, and realign the UVs to the seam where the lid meets the box, as shown in Figure 7.140 on the right. As you make the changes in the UV Texture Editor, you should immediately notice them in the Perspective window (as long as you're in Texture View mode).

3. Look at the image on top in Figure 7.141. Move the appropriate UVs to align the edge of the UV layout to the image for the right side of the box, as shown on the bottom of Figure 7.141.

4. The distortion is getting better, and the texture fits nicer. But notice in the image on the left in Figure 7.142 that the right side of the box and the back of the box don't line up well. There are some other instances of the textures not lining up well all around the box. Using the Texture view mode (press 6) in the Perspective window and the UV Texture Editor, go around the box in its entirety and adjust the UVs, point by point as needed, so that they all line up to the image in the UV Texture Editor. Make sure that the sides line up at the edges of the box as well as you can. Figure 7.142's right image shows correctly aligned UVs for the right side/back side of the box. Don't forget to line up the bottom of the box and feet, too. That part should be much easier.

This part of tweaking the UVs takes time and patience. The key is to keep looking back and forth between the UV Texture Editor and the persp panel to see how the textures are lining up as you move the UVs. Figure 7.143 shows the UV Texture Editor and a persp

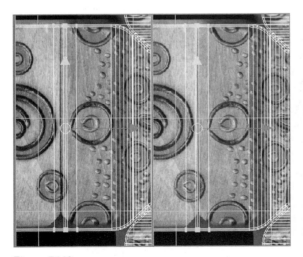

Figure 7.140
Move the UVs.

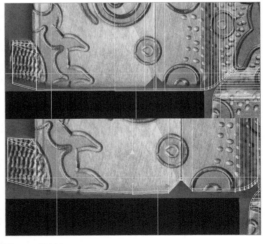

Figure 7.141
Line up the UVs to the image for the right side of the box.

view of the box with UVs lined up and reasonably ready to go. You can compare your work to the scene file `boxTexture03.mb` in the Scenes folder of the Decorative_Box project on the companion web page. Render a few different views to take in all the hard work. In Chapter 10, you'll light the box and prepare it for rendering, and in Chapter 11, you'll use displacement maps created from these photos to detail the indentations and carvings that are in the actual box. You've had enough excitement for one chapter.

Figure 7.142

Line up the UVs for the right-side/back-side edge of the box.

Figure 7.143

The UVs laid out for the decorative box

For Further Study

For a challenge and more experience, create new image maps for the wagon and try your own decal designs. You can even change the textures for the decorative box and make your own design. As previously suggested, you can try to create more realistic wood maps for the wagon's railings. In Chapter 10, you'll begin to see how shading and rendering go hand in hand; you'll adjust many of the shader attributes you created in this chapter to render the decorative box in Chapter 11.

You can also try to create textures to map onto the hand model you created in Chapter 4, using photos of your own hand with extensive UV manipulation.

Summary

In this chapter, you learned about the types of shaders and how they work. Each shader has a set of attributes that give material definition, and each attribute has a different effect on how a model looks.

To gain practice, you textured the table lamp scene using various shaders.

Next, you learned about the methods you can use to project textures onto a surface, and you learned about the Maya texture nodes, including PSD networks and the basics of UVs, and how to use them to place images onto your wagon and decorative box models in detailed exercises exposing you to manipulating UVs and using Photoshop to create maps.

Texturing a scene is never an isolated process. Making textures work involves render settings, lighting, and even geometry manipulation and creation. Your work in this chapter will be expanded in Chapters 10 and 11 with discussions of lighting and rendering.

Just like everything else in Maya, it's all about collaboration—the more experience you gain, the more you'll see how everything intertwines.

However, for Maya to be an effective tool for you, it's important to have a clear understanding of the look you want for your CG. This involves plenty of research into your project, downloading heaps of images to use as references, and a good measure of trial and error.

The single best weapon in your texturing arsenal, and indeed in all aspects of CG art, is your eye, specifically, your observations of the world around you and how they relate to the world you're creating in CG.

CHAPTER 8

Introduction to Animation

The best way to learn about animation is to start animating, so you'll begin this chapter with the classic exercise of bouncing a ball. You'll then take a closer look at the animation tools the Autodesk® Maya® software provides and how they work for your scene. You'll do that by throwing an axe. Finally, you'll tackle animating a more complex system of parts when you bring a locomotive to life.

Learning Outcomes: In this chapter, you will be able to

- Set keyframes to establish the movement scheme for an object
- Create the feeling of weight and mass for an animated object using scale animation
- Read animation curves in the Graph Editor
- Differentiate among different animation principles such as squash, stretch, anticipation, and follow-through
- Set up a hierarchy for better animation control
- Transfer animation between objects
- Create text
- Create motion trails and animate objects along a path
- Set up models for animation
- Use selection handles to speed up workflow
- Animate objects in time with each other

Keyframe Animation: Bouncing a Ball

No matter where you study animation, you'll always find the classic animation exercise of creating a bouncing ball. Although it's a straightforward exercise and you've probably seen it a hundred times on the Web and in other books, the bouncing ball is a perfect exercise with which to begin animating. You can imbue the ball with so much character that the possibilities are almost endless, so try to run this exercise as many times as you can handle. You'll improve with every attempt.

Animating a bouncing ball is a good exercise in real-world physical motion as well as in cartoon movement. First, you'll create a rubber ball and create a proper animation hierarchy for it. Then, you'll add cartoonish movement to accentuate some principles of the animation techniques discussed in the ultra-fabulous Chapter 1, "Introduction to Computer Graphics and 3D."

Creating a Cartoon Ball

First, you need to create the ball, as well as the project for this exercise. Follow these steps:

1. In a new scene, begin with a poly sphere, and then create a poly plane. Scale the plane up to be the ground plane.

2. Press 5 for Shaded mode.

3. Move the sphere 1.0 unit up in the *Y*-axis so that it's resting on the ground and not halfway through it, as shown in Figure 8.1.

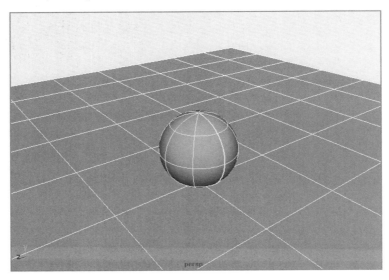

Figure 8.1

Place the ball on the ground.

4. Choose Modify → Freeze Transformations to set the ball's resting height to **0**, as opposed to 1. This action sets the ball's Translate attribute back to 0, effectively

resetting the object. This is called *freezing the transforms.* This is useful when you position, scale, and orient an object and need to set its new location, orientation, and size as the beginning state.

5. Choose File → Project Window to create a new project. Call the project **Bouncing_Ball**, and place it in the same parent folder as your Solar_System project folder. Choose Edit → Reset Settings to create the necessary folders in your project, and then click Accept. Save the scene file into that project.

Setting Up the Hierarchy

To make life easier, you'll set up the ball with three null nodes above it, listed here from the top parent node down: translate, scale, rotate. All the animation will be placed on these three nodes and not the sphere itself. This will allow you to easily animate the ball bouncing, squashing, stretching, and moving forward in space.

1. Select the sphere and press Ctrl+G to create the first group. In the Outliner, call this new group **rotate**.

2. With the rotate node selected, press Ctrl+G to create the **scale** group, and name it accordingly.

3. With the scale group selected, press Ctrl+G one last time to create the **translate** group and name it accordingly. Figure 8.2 shows the hierarchy.

   As you animate, you'll quickly see why you've set up a hierarchy for the ball, instead of just putting keys on the sphere.

Figure 8.2

The ball's hierarchy

Animating the Ball

Your next step is to keyframe the positions of the ball using the nodes above the sphere. You'll start with the *gross animation,* which is the overall movement scheme, a.k.a. *blocking.* First, you'll move the ball up and down to begin its choreography in these steps:

1. Press W to open the Translate tool, select the translate node, and move it up to the top of the frame, say about 10 units up in the Y-axis and 8 units back in the X-axis at (**–8,10,0**). Place the camera so that you'll have some room to work in the frame.

2. Instead of selecting the Translate attributes in the Channel Box and pressing S as you did in Chapter 2, "Jumping in Headfirst, with Both Feet," to set keyframes on the planets, you'll set keyframes for translation in an easier way.

   Press Shift+W to set keyframes on Translate X, Translate Y, and Translate Z at frame 1 for the top node of the ball (named translate). To make sure your scene is set up properly, set your animation speed to 30fps by choosing Window → Settings/Preferences → Preferences to open the Preferences window or by clicking the

Animation Preferences button (▦) next to the Auto-Key button. In the Settings category of the Preferences window, set Time to NTSC (30fps). A frame range of 1 to 120 is good for now. Figure 8.3 shows the ball's start position.

3. Click the Auto Keyframe button (▱) to turn it on; it turns red. Auto Keyframe automatically sets a keyframe at the current time for any attribute that has changed since its last keyframe for the selected object or node.

For the Auto Keyframe feature to work, you have to set an initial keyframe manually for each of the attributes you want to animate.

4. Disregarding any specific timing, go to frame 10, and move the ball down in the *Y*-axis until it's about one-quarter through the ground plane. Because you'll be creating squash and stretch for this cartoon ball (see Chapter 1 for a brief explanation), you need to send the ball through the ground a little bit. Then, move the ball about 3 units to the right, to about (**–5,–0.4,0**). The Auto Keyframe feature sets a keyframe in the *X* and *Y* axes at frame 10. Remember, this is all on the translate node.

5. Move to frame 20, and raise the ball back up to about half of its original height and to the right about 2.5 units (**–2.5,4,0**). Auto Keyframe sets X and Y Translation keyframes at frame 20 and will continue to set keyframes for the ball as you animate.

6. At frame 30, place the ball back down a little less than one-quarter of the way through the ground and about 2 units to the right, at about (**–0.5,–0.3,0**).

7. At frame 40, place the ball back up in the air in the *Y*-axis at a fraction of its original height and to the right about 1.5 units, at about (**1.1,1.85,0**).

Figure 8.3

Start the ball here and set a keyframe on the translate node.

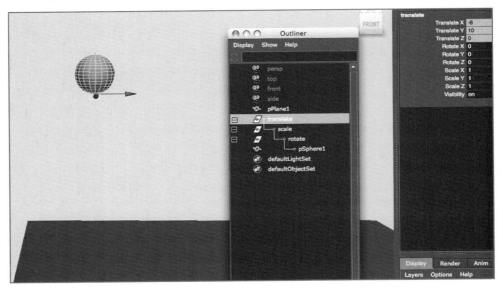

8. Repeat this procedure every 10 frames to about frame 110 so that you bounce the ball a few more times up and down and to the right (positive in the *X*-axis). Make sure you're decreasing the ball's height and traveling in *X* with each successive bounce and decreasing how much the ball passes through the ground with every landing until it rests on top of the ground plane. Open the Graph Editor for a peek into the ball's animation curves (see Figure 8.4). (Choose Window → Animation Editors → Graph Editor.)

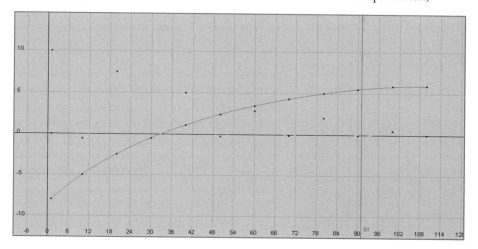

Figure 8.4

The Graph Editor curves for the ball's translate node

By holding down the Shift key as you pressed W in step 2, you set a keyframe for Translate. Likewise, you can keyframe Rotation and Scale. Here's a summary of the keystrokes for setting keyframes:

Shift+W   Sets a keyframe for the selection's position in all three axes at the current time

Shift+E   Sets a keyframe for the selection's rotation in all three axes at the current time

Shift+R   Sets a keyframe for the selection's scale in all three axes at the current time

You'll resume this exercise after a look at the Graph Editor.

The Graph Editor

To use the Maya Graph Editor, select Window → Animation Editors → Graph Editor. It's an unbelievably powerful tool for the animator (see Figure 8.5) to edit keyframes in animation.

Every movement that is set in Maya generates a graph of value versus time. The Graph Editor gives you direct access to the curves generated by your animation for fine-tuning your animation. The Graph Editor displays animation curves as value versus time, with value running vertically and time horizontally. Keyframes are represented on the curves as points that can be freely moved to adjust timing or value. The concept of the Graph Editor, and the process of editing animation using graph curves, may seem daunting at first, especially if you aren't mathematically inclined. However, this window is truly an animator's best friend. Using its graph view of where in space and time each keyframe lies, you can conveniently control your animation. Move a keyframe in time to the right (to be later in the timeline), for example, to slow the action. Move the same keyframe to the left (to be earlier in the timeline) to speed up the action.

The Graph Editor is divided into two sections. The left column, which is much like the Outliner, displays the selected objects and their hierarchy with a listing of their animated channels or attributes. By default, all of an object's keyframed channels are displayed as colored curves in the display to the right of the list. However, by selecting an object or an object's channel in the list, you can isolate only those curves that you want to see.

Figure 8.5

The Graph Editor

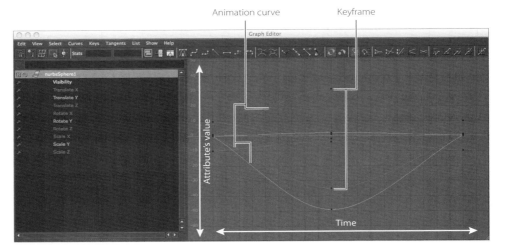

Reading the Curves in the Graph Editor

Using the Graph Editor to *read animation curves*, you can judge an object's direction, speed, acceleration, and timing.

You'll invariably come across problems and issues with your animation that require a careful review of their curves. The ability to see a curve and translate it into what your object is doing comes with time and practice. Here are a couple of key concepts to keep in mind.

First, the curves in the Graph Editor are like the NURBS curves you've modeled with so far. Instead of CVs on a NURBS curve controlling the curvature, points directly on an animation curve represent keyframes and control the curvature with their *tangency handles.* By grabbing one end of a key's handle and dragging it up or down, you adjust the curve.

Second, the graph is a representation of an object attribute's position (vertical) over time (horizontal). Every place on the curve represents where the object is in that axis;

there needn't be a keyframe on the curve. Not only does the placement of the keys on the curve make a big difference, so does the shape of the curve itself. Here is a quick primer on how to read a curve in the Graph Editor and, hence, how to edit it.

In Figure 8.6, the object's Translate Z attribute is being animated. At the beginning, the curve quickly begins to move positively (that is, to the right) in the Z-axis. The object shoots off to the right and comes to an *ease-out*, where it decelerates to a stop. The stop is signified by the flat part of the curve at the first keyframe at frame 41. The object then quickly accelerates in the negative *Z* direction (left) and maintains a fairly even speed until it hits frame 62, where it suddenly changes direction and goes back right for about 45 frames. It then slowly decelerates to a full stop in an ease-out.

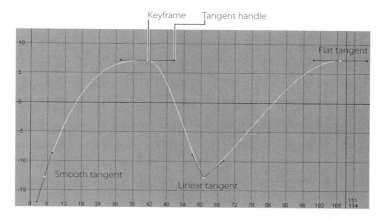

Figure 8.6

An animation curve

Consider a single object in motion. The shape of the curve in the Graph Editor defines how the object moves. The object shown in Figure 8.7 is moving in a steady manner in one direction.

Figure 8.7

Linear movement

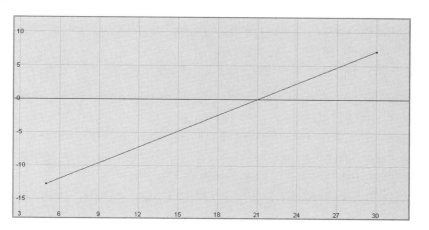

Figure 8.8 shows the object slowly accelerating toward frame 30, where it suddenly comes to a stop. If there is nothing beyond the end of the curve, there is no motion. The one exception deals with the *infinity* of curves, which is discussed shortly.

Figure 8.8

Acceleration (ease-in)

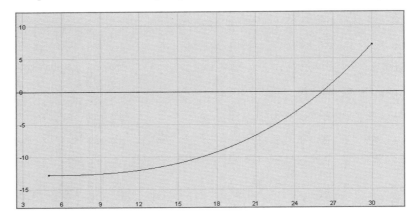

The object in Figure 8.9 begins moving immediately and comes to a slow stop by frame 27, where the curve first becomes flat.

Figure 8.9

Deceleration (ease-out)

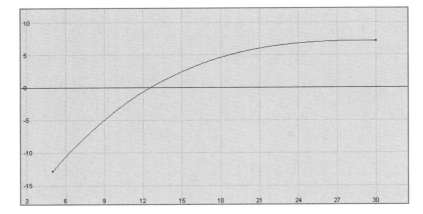

Cartoon Ball

Now, let's apply what you've learned about the Graph Editor to the bouncing ball. Follow these steps:

1. Open the Graph Editor, and look at the ball's animation curves. They should be similar to the curves shown in Figure 8.4.

2. Notice how only the *X*- and *Y*-axes' translates have curves, and yet Translate Z has a single keyframe but no curve. It's from the initial position keyframe you set at frame 1. Because you've moved the sphere only in the *X*- and *Y*-axes, Auto-Key hasn't set

any keys in the *Z*-axis. This is better than pressing S to set keys on everything, so if you don't have animation on something, it doesn't get keys. Keep your scene clean.

3. Play back the animation, and see how it feels. Be sure to open the Animation Preferences window. Click the Animation Preferences icon (🗊) to set the playback speed to Real-Time (30fps). You'll find this icon in the Playback section in the Time Slider category.

4. Timing is the main issue now, so you want to focus on how fast the ball bounces.

   - The ball is falling too fast initially, although the second and third bounces should look fine.

   - To fix the timing, move the keyframes in the Graph Editor. For the *X*- and *Y*-axes, select the keyframes at frame 10 and all the others beyond on both curves. Move them all back two frames. (See Figure 8.10.)

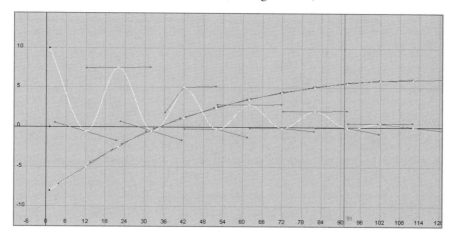

Figure 8.10

Move all the keyframes for both curves to the right to slow the initial fall by two frames, but leave the timing the same for the rest.

As the ball's bounce decays over time, it goes up less but still takes the same amount of time (10 frames) to go up the lesser distance. For better timing, adjust the last few bounces to occur faster. Select the keys on the last three bounces and move them, one by one, a frame or two to the left to decrease the time on the last short bounces. (See Figure 8.11.)

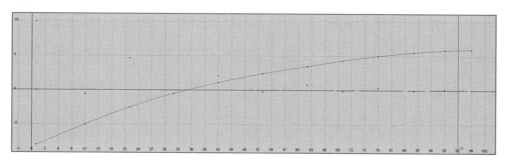

Figure 8.11

Move the keys to make the final short bounces quicker and the bounce height feel right.

To move a key in the Graph Editor, press W to open the Move tool, MMB+click, and drag the cursor in the Graph Editor window. Press the Shift key, and drag the cursor left and right or up and down to lock the movement to either horizontal or vertical to make it easier to control.

Understanding Timing

In animation, timing is all about getting the keyframes in the proper order. Judging the speed of an object in animation is critical to getting it to look right, and that comes down to timing. The more you animate, the better your timing will be, which is why the bouncing ball is such a popular exercise.

Download the file `ball_v01.mb` from the Bouncing_Ball project on the companion web page, `www.sybex.com/go/introducingmaya2014`, to get to this point.

When you play back the animation, it should look more natural. But it still looks fake, as if it's rising and falling on a wave as opposed to really impacting the ground and bouncing back. You need to edit the timing of the ball. The problem with the animation is that the ball eases in and out as it rises and falls. By default, setting a key in Maya sets the keyframes to have an ease-in and ease-out in their curves, meaning their curves are smooth like a NURBS curve.

Because of the smooth animation curve, the ball doesn't look natural in its timing. You need to accelerate the ball as it falls with a sharp valley in the curve, and you need to decelerate it as it rises with smooth peaks. Follow these steps:

1. In the Graph Editor, select the Translate Y entry in the left panel of the window to isolate your view to just that curve in the editor panel on the right. Select all the landing keyframes (the ones in the valleys of the curve), and change their interpolation from smooth to linear by clicking the Linear Tangents button (▧).

2. Likewise, select all the peak keyframes at the ball's rise, and change their tangents to flat by clicking the Flat Tangents icon (▭) to make the animation curve like the one shown in Figure 8.12.

Figure 8.12

The adjusted timing of the bounce

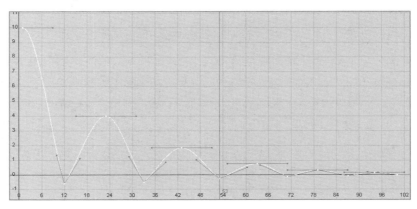

3. When you play back the animation, the ball seems to be moving more realistically. If you need to, adjust the keys a bit more to get the timing to feel right to you, before you move on to squash and stretch and rotation.

Squash and Stretch

The concept of *squash and stretch* has been an animation staple for as long as there has been animation. It's a way to convey the weight of an object by deforming it to react (usually in an exaggerated way) to gravity and motion.

In Maya, you use the Scale tool to squash and stretch your object—in this case, your ball, using only the scale node, not the sphere or translate node.

Download the file `ball_v02.mb` from the Bouncing_Ball project on the book's web page, and follow these steps:

1. Select the `scale` node, and select Modify → Center Pivot. This places the scale pivot point in the middle of the ball.

2. At frame 9, press R to set initial scale keyframes on the `scale` node of the ball, a couple of frames before the ball impacts the ground.

3. To initiate squash and stretch, go to frame 12, where the ball hits the floor the first time. With the `scale` node selected, press R to open the Scale tool; scale the ball down in the Y-axis until it no longer goes through the floor (about **0.6**), as shown in the image on the left in Figure 8.13. Set a keyframe for scale by pressing Shift+R.

4. Move ahead in the animation about three frames to frame 15. Scale the ball up in the Y-axis slightly past normal to stretch it up (about **1.15**) immediately after its bounce, as shown in the image on the right in Figure 8.13. Three frames later, at frame 18, set the Y-axis scale back to **1** to return the ball to its regular shape.

Figure 8.13

Squashing and stretching the ball to react to bouncing on the floor

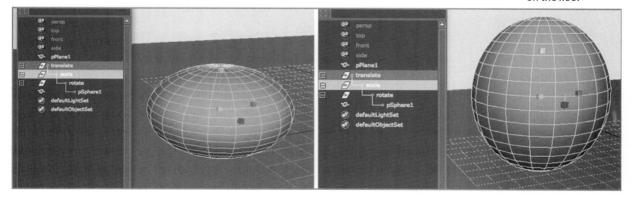

5. Scrub your animation, and you should see the ball begin stretching even before it hits the ground. That's a bit too much exaggeration, so open the Graph Editor and move the *Y*-axis scale key from 9 to 11. Now, the ball squashes when it hits the floor and stretches as it bounces up.

6. Repeat this procedure for the remaining bounces, squashing the ball as it hits the floor and stretching it as it bounces up. Remember to decay the scale factor as the ball's bouncing decays to a stop, like when you decayed the height of the ball's bounce earlier. The final bounce or two should have very little squash and stretch, if any.

Download the file `ball_v03.mb` from the Bouncing_Ball project on the book's web page to get to this point. And now, let's rotate the ball as it bounces.

Rotation

Let's add some roll to the ball in these steps:

1. Select the ball's `rotate` node, and select Modify → Center Pivot to set that node's pivot at the center of the ball.

2. At frame 1, press Shift+E to set keys for rotation at (**0,0,0**).

3. Scrub to the end of your animation (frame 100 in this example), and set a value of **−480** for Rotate Z in the Channel Box, as shown in Figure 8.14.

Figure 8.14

Setting a roll for the ball

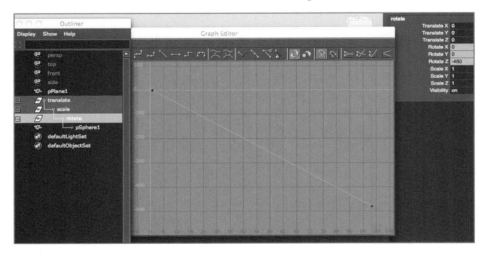

4. Open the Graph Editor to see the rotation curve on the ball's `rotate` node. It's a linear (straight) line angled down from 0 to −480. You need the rotation to slow to a stop at the end of the animation, so select the final keyframe and click (⬛) to make it a flat tangent.

Load the file `ball_v04.mb` from the Bouncing_Ball project from the companion web page to see an example of the finished bouncing ball. Although the bouncing of this ball looks okay, it could definitely use some finesse, a little timing change, and so on. Open the file, open the Graph Editor, and edit the file to get a feel for how the ball bounces and rolls. For example, it could continue rolling with no bouncing for another 20 frames or so.

Throwing an Axe

This next project will exercise your use of hierarchies and introduce you to creating and refining motion to achieve proper animation for a more complex scene than the bouncing ball. The workflow is simple but standard for properly setting up a scene for animation, also known as *rigging*. First, you'll model an axe and a target and then set up the grouping and pivots for how you want to animate. Then, you'll throw your axe!

Why won't you throw the NURBS axe you've already created and textured? Because later in this chapter, you'll need it for an exercise on importing and replacing an object in Maya while keeping the animation intact.

The Preproduction Process

To begin the animation right away, you'll create a basic axe, focusing on the animation and the technique. You'll also need to create a simple bull's-eye target at which to throw your axe, so look for some references for a target as well.

Create a new project; choose File → Project Window, and click the New button. Place this project in the same folder or drive as your other projects, call it **Axe**, and click Accept. Click the Animation Preferences button, and set the frames per second to 30fps. Later, you'll replace this simple axe with a finer axe model to learn how to replace objects and transfer animation.

Setting Up the Scene

To get started, model the axe and target from primitives, and set up their grouping and pivots. When your scene is set up properly, you'll animate. It's important to a healthy workflow that you make sure the scene is set up well before you begin animating.

Making the Axe

The axe will be made of two polygon primitives: a cylinder and a cube. Follow these steps:

1. Choose Create → Polygon Primitives → Cube ❏. Set Width Divisions to **4**, and click Create.

2. Call this cube **axe_head**.

3. Choose Create → Polygon Primitives → Cylinder to create a cylinder to be the handle for your axe, and call it **handle**.

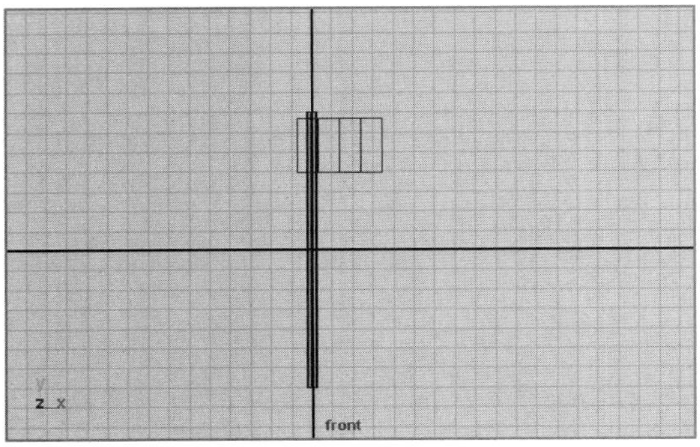

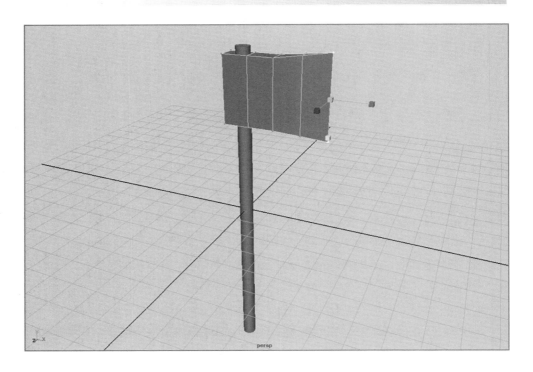

Figure 8.15

Placing the axe's head on the handle

4. Scale the cylinder so that it's about one-half unit across and about 14 units tall.

5. Move the cube to the top of the cylinder, leaving just a little of the tip showing, and scale it so that it's about 2.5 units high and 4 units wide in the front view. (See Figure 8.15.)

6. Scale the cube in the Z-axis so that it's just a little thicker than the handle.

7. To put a sharp edge on the axe, go into Component mode (F8). Select the four vertices on the very end of the cube, scale the vertices down in the Z-axis to a sharp edge, and scale them slightly up in the Y-axis. Select the next four vertices in from the edge, scale them down in the X-axis about halfway, and scale them up slightly in the Y-axis. (See Figure 8.16.)

> Most animation work of this kind doesn't depend on precise measurements. The key is using proportions and relative sizes. You can almost always use generic units in Maya (which are set to centimeters by default). The scope of your project will determine whether greater precision is necessary.

Figure 8.16

Creating a sharp edge for the axe

8. Press F8 to get back into Object mode, and select both pieces. Choose Edit → Group to group the pieces into one hierarchy, and call it **axe**.

Identifying the *center of balance* for this axe will give you the pivot point. Because the heaviest part of this axe is the head, the center of balance is toward the top and forward of the handle.

9. Press and hold down D (you can also press Insert on a PC or Home on a Mac) to activate the Pivot Manipulator, and move the pivot just under the axe head and about 1 unit from the handle, as in Figure 8.17.

Your scene should now look like the file axe_v1.mb in the Scenes folder of the Axe project from the companion web page.

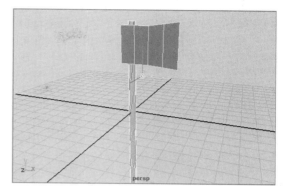

Figure 8.17

Find the axe's center of balance to determine the proper place for its pivot point.

Making the Target

Move the axe about 40 units in the negative *X*-axis away from the origin to make some room for the throw, and move it about 15 units up in the *Y*-axis. Now, you need to create a simple target for your axe to hit. Follow these steps:

1. Start with a polygonal cylinder.

2. Scale down the cylinder's height to make it squat, and rotate it just a bit past being perpendicular to the ground, facing somewhat toward the sky.

3. Scale the cylinder up about seven times its original size.

You also need to create a simple stand on which to rest the target. Follow these steps:

1. Choose Create → Polygon Primitives → Cube for the base.

2. Scale the cube so that the target fits on the base with some room to spare.

Figure 8.18

Positioning the cross braces for the target

3. Choose Create → Polygon Primitives → Cylinder to create two cylinders to make a cross brace for the back of the target.

4. Scale, rotate, and position the cylinders to fit behind the target and into the back of the base. Figure 8.18 shows the positions of the pieces to make up the target.

5. When you're happy with the target, group the four objects together, and name the group **Target**.

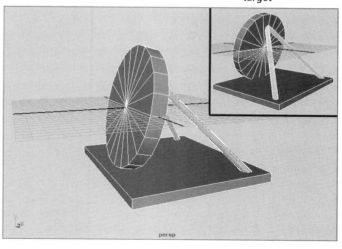

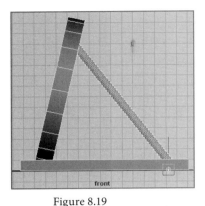

Figure 8.19

The proper placement of the target's pivot point

6. Move the target about 40 units in the positive *X*-axis away from the origin, and move it up in the *Y*-axis so its base is basically on the ground plane.

7. Hold the D key to move the target's pivot point to the bottom of the base, right where the cross beams connect to it. Figure 8.19 shows the proper pivot placement.

You place the pivot point at that location because the target will jerk up and back a little bit when the axe hits it. This is the best point for you to rotate around to lift the front of the base up a little to make it look like the axe is really hitting it. Save your file as your next version number. The scene is now ready for animation.

Preproduction: Keyframes and Motion Study

What separates good animation from bad animation is the feeling of weight that the audience infers from the animation. People instinctively understand how nature works in motion. You see an object in motion, how it moves, and how it affects its surroundings. From that, you can feel the essence of its motion, with its weight making a distinct, albeit subliminal, impression on you. As it pertains to animation, that essence is simply called *weight*, and its observation is called *motion study*.

Unfortunately, merely knowing how something should look while moving isn't all you need to animate it properly. Giving the axe believable weight is your primary job as an animator. Motion can make or break an animation.

A good feeling of weight in animation depends on timing and follow-through, which require practice.

It's a good idea first to try an action you want to animate. It may upset the cat if you grab a real axe and start throwing it around your house, but you can take a pen, remove its cap, and lob it across the room. Notice how it arcs through the air, how it spins around its center of balance, and how it hits its mark. Now put the cap on the pen, lob it again, and notice the subtle yet instrumental differences in motion caused by the cap's mass.

As an animator, this experimentation is part of your preproduction and motion study. It's important to have as thorough an understanding of your subject matter as possible. Just try not to take out anyone's eye with the pen.

According to some Internet research, the perfect axe throw should contain as few spins as possible. This is good information to know, because it will shape your animation and come in handy if you're ever cornered in a hatchet shop.

Animating the Axe: Keyframing Gross Animation

The next step is to keyframe the positions of the axe, starting with the *gross animation*— that is, the movement from one end of the axe's trajectory to the other.

Setting Initial Keyframes

You can start in your current scene or load the unanimated, premade axe and target from the companion web page (axe_v2.mb in the Scenes folder of the Axe project). Follow these steps:

1. Select the axe's top group node—not just the pieces. To make selecting groups such as this easier, display the object's selection handle. To do so, select the axe's top node, and choose Display → Transform Display → Selection Handles. Doing so displays a small cross, called a *selection handle* (⊕), at the axe's pivot point. You need only select this handle to select the top node of the axe.

> As you'll see later, in this chapter's catapult exercise, you can use selection handles to select the children of a group as well as the top node.

   Because this node is the parent node of the axe, the selection handle displays as a hollow cross at the node's current pivot point.

> You can turn on selection handles for practically any object in Maya—no matter where it is in a group's hierarchy—whether it's a child or a parent. If it isn't the top node, the selection handle appears as a regular cross (+).

2. With the axe selected, go to frame 1, and set a keyframe for the rotation and translation.

3. Hold down the Shift key, press W for the axe's translation keyframe, and then press E for the axe's rotation keyframe. You don't need to set a scale keyframe because you won't be changing its size. When you're finished, you'll have the initial keyframes for the axe at its start position.

Creating Anticipation

Instead of the axe just flying through the air toward the target, you'll animate the axe moving back first to create *anticipation*, as if an invisible arm were pulling the axe back before throwing it. Follow these steps:

1. Go to frame 15.

2. Move the axe back in the *X*-axis about 8 units, and rotate it counterclockwise about 45 degrees.

3. The Auto Keyframe feature sets keyframes for the position and new rotation at frame 15.

    Because you've moved the axe back only in the *X*-axis and made the rotation on the *Z*-axis, Auto Keyframe sets keyframes only for Translate X and Rotate Z. The other position and rotation axes aren't keyframed because their values didn't change.

4. Scrub through the animation, and notice how the axe moves back in anticipation.

> Auto Keyframe inserts a keyframe at the current time for the selected object's changed attributes only.

5. Go to frame 40, and move the axe so that its blade cuts into the center of the target.

    Notice that you have to move the axe in the *X*- and *Y*-axes, whereas before you had to move it back only in the *X*-axis to create anticipation. This is because the axis of motion for the axe rotates along with the axe. This is called the *Local axis*. The Local axis for any given object shifts according to the object's orientation. Because you angled the axe back about 45 degrees, its Local axis rotated back the same amount.

The file `axe_v3.mb` in the Scenes folder of the Axe project from the companion web page will catch you up to this point in the animation.

This last step reveals a problem with the animation. If you scrub your animation now, you'll notice that the axe's movement back is different from before, setting a keyframe at frame 40.

This is because of the Auto Keyframe feature. At frame 1, you set an initial keyframe for the *X*-, *Y*-, and *Z*-axes of translation and rotation. Then, at frame 15, you moved the axe back in the *X*-axis only (in addition to rotating it in the *Z*-axis only).

TROUBLESHOOTING AND AGGRAVATION

Why should you intentionally go through steps that create a problem, such as the axe's movement back? Understanding how to troubleshoot is the biggest challenge in learning a CG program. A good CG artist needs to know how to diagnose issues with a scene and be able to find a way to fix them. Your first forays into CG may be highly frustrating—riddled with simple troubles and issues that you just don't understand. When you can't figure out why things went wrong, you may turn red with aggravation and want to walk away. This is where you start molding yourself as a CG artist. Instead of giving up, ponder the steps you've taken, and see whether you can spot where your CG has taken a weird turn. You'll probably find yourself in such spots several times as you study this book. Instead of throwing the baby out with the bathwater, stay patient and try, try again. You'll learn more from your mistakes and missteps in the exercises in this book than you will if you follow everything to the letter.

Beginners' Gallery

On the following pages, you'll find some images from the book as well as images created by a few artists fairly new to the Autodesk® Maya® software. I hope these images will inspire your own creativity as you become more familiar with 3D in general and Maya specifically.

Some of these artists have been using Maya for only a short period of time, and already they've been able to use the tools and techniques they've learned to channel their artistic eye and creativity into some beautiful and interesting imagery. (All images are used with permission.)

This still life from Chapter 10, "Autodesk Maya Lighting" was modeled and textured by Maya students Juan Gutierrez and Robert Jauregui. The fruit still life was modeled by Juan using mostly polygons. The textures were created by Robert, who took this opportunity to learn all about UV texture space and mapping polygons because this was his first texturing experience with Maya. I laid out the scene, lit it, and rendered it to demonstrate some rendering concepts.

BELOW LEFT: This pool table was modeled by Victor J. Garza to demonstrate modeling techniques in an introductory Maya class and to show the students how to be creative when combining surfaces to form a complex object. After Victor modeled the table, he and I textured and lit the scene. **BELOW RIGHT:** A photo of the toy red wagon that was textured in Chapter 7, "Autodesk Maya Shading and Texturing." Take a look at not just the coloring but also the sense of surface and texture as you do the exercise in Chapter 7.

ABOVE: This living room scene was modeled by Huyen Dang of the Art Institute of California—Los Angeles for a lighting class; I lit it using global illumination in mental ray®. **MIDDLE:** The color render can be enhanced with the addition of an Ambient Occlusion pass to add detail and contact shadows. **BELOW:** The Ambient Occlusion render creates contact shadows and some further detail in the dark areas of the image to enhance the look of the color render. This pass is multiplied in a compositing package to add realism.

ABOVE: Yang Liu, my teaching assistant at the University of Southern California, created this fruit still life as a texturing exercise for his demo reel. Yang painted images for color, bump, and specular in Adobe Photoshop and applied them as maps with mental ray shaders, including Subsurface Scattering shading on the grapes to achieve their softly lit look. BELOW: Yang's thesis film creates a stylistic animation look. He created the scene entirely in Maya and rendered it with textures only. He used mental ray to render passes for the keylight, the Ambient Occlusion, and the vector outlines of the character to make it look 2D. He then painted on the passes in Photoshop, and composited everything in Adobe After Effects and The Foundry's Nuke.

ABOVE: Jordan Prieto, a student at the University of Southern California, created his look by using direct lighting techniques and raytrace shadows to light his interior space. He used point lights for the bulbs in the hallway and rendered using mental ray for Maya.
BELOW: Jordan created his character to fit into the style of his space, using mental ray shading for the subtle and stylized skin look for his character. The images for his project were rendered in passes, including Ambient Occlusion and Z-depth, and were composited together in postproduction.

ABOVE: Andre Champion created this still life render for my lighting and rendering course at Santa Monica College. The entire scene was modeled and rendered in Maya. The nontransparent objects were modeled out of simple geometric shapes, which were then unwrapped and brought into Photoshop to texture. Each of the glasses and the red wine objects were broken down into multiple pieces to create light refraction for a realistic feel. **BELOW:** Wen Huang of the University of Southern California's John C. Hench Division of Animation and Digital Arts created an illustrative style using clever texturing. His exterior scenes use mental ray Physical Sun And Sky in Maya for his lighting, with each shot of the short film fine-tuned based on the camera angle.

ABOVE: USC student Ryan Kravertz's goal for the lighting and rendering of his short film was to make the characters and the world feel like they existed in a real, tangible space. He used simple, direct lighting and rendered with mental ray with Final Gather for secondary light in his rich world. Ryan used a combination of Maya shaders and mental ray shaders for the characters, using custom-painted color, specular, and bump maps.

ABOVE: Christian Enriquez created this still life in my lighting and rendering class at Santa Monica College using an HDRI and some direct lights. The scene was rendered in mental ray and composited together in After Effects. **MIDDLE:** This still life was created by Natalya Sevastyanova, also from Santa Monica College, using a variety of models to create the composition. She rendered using mental ray for Maya after painting the color maps for her objects. **BELOW:** This is from University of Southern California student Louis Morton's mixed-media short film Shape Dance. The backgrounds were modeled, textured, and lit in Maya, and the characters were shot live action on green screen. The characters were then keyed in After Effects and imported onto an image plane in Maya to render within the CG environments. Final color correction and compositing work was done in After Effects.

Auto Keyframe set a keyframe for Translate X at frame 15. At frame 40, you moved the axe in *both* the X- and Y-axes to strike the target. Auto Keyframe set a keyframe at 40 for Translate X and Translate Y. Because the last keyframe for Translate Y was set at 1 and not at 15 as in the case of Translate X, there is now a bobble in the Y position of the axe between frames 1 and 15.

With the axe selected, open the Graph Editor (choose Window → Animation Editors → Graph Editor) to see what's happening. As you saw in the Bouncing_Ball project, using the Graph Editor is crucial, and the more practice you get with it, the better.

When you open the Graph Editor for this scene, you should see red, green, and blue line segments running up and down and left and right. You'll probably have to zoom your view to something more intelligible. By using the Alt key (or the Alt/Option key on a Mac) and mouse-button combinations, you can navigate the Graph Editor much as you can any of the modeling windows.

The hotkeys A and F also work in the Graph Editor. Click anywhere in the Graph Editor window to make sure it's the active window, and press A to zoom all your curves into view. Your window should look something like Figure 8.20.

The curves in the Graph Editor represent the values of the axe's position and rotation at any given time. The X-, Y-, Z-axes are in their representative red, green, or blue color, and the specific attributes are listed much as they are in the Outliner in the left column. Selecting an object or an attribute on the left displays its curves on the right.

You should also notice that the curves are all at different scales. The three rotate curves range in value from about –45 to 45, the Translate Y curve ranges from about 15 to 5, and Translate Z looks flat in the Graph Editor. It's tough to edit a curve with low values and still be able to see the timings of a larger value curve.

You can select the specific attribute and zoom in on its curve to see it better, or you can *normalize* the curves so that you can see them all in one view, with all their values in check. Click the Enable Normalized Curve Display icon in the top icon bar of the Graph Editor ( ). Doing so *normalizes* the view of all the curves within a scale of –1 to 1 to allow you to see the relative movement of all the curves at once.

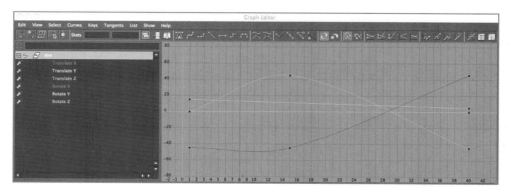

Figure 8.20

The Graph Editor displays the axe's animation curves.

Figure 8.21 shows the Graph Editor from Figure 8.19 after the curves have been normalized. Keep in mind that this doesn't change the animation in the slightest. All it does is allow you to see all the curves and their relative motion. You can denormalize the view by clicking the Disable Normalized Curve Display icon in the Graph Editor (⊠). Normalizing your view is particularly helpful in busy scenes when you want to adjust the smallest scale of values alongside the largest scale of values without having to zoom in and out of the Graph Editor constantly to see the appropriate curves.

Figure 8.21

The normalized view in the Graph Editor lets you see all the curves of an animation together in the same scale.

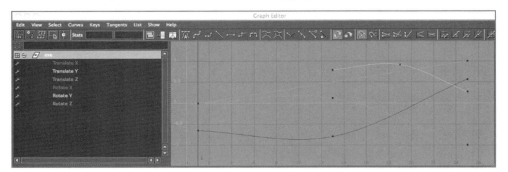

Notice that the Scale attributes on the axe aren't shown in this window; only animated attributes appear here.

Also notice that the curve for Translate Y has keyframes only at frames 1 and 40. The animation dips in the first 15 frames because there is no keyframe at frame 15 like there is for Translate Z. That dip wasn't there before you set the end keyframe at frame 40.

Continue the exercise by fixing this issue:

1. Move the first keyframe of Translate Y from frame 1 to frame 15 to fix the dip.

   - Press W to activate the Move tool in Maya, or click the Move Nearest Picked Key Tool icon (▦) in the Graph Editor.

   - Click the Time Snap On/Off icon (▩) to toggle it on.

   - Select the offending Translate Y keyframe at frame 1, and MMB+click and drag it to the right until it's at frame 15.

   Scrub your animation, and the backward movement looks like it did before. You might have prevented this problem by manually setting your keyframes for the axe instead of using Auto Keyframe. The more you work with Maya, the more valuable you'll find Auto Keyframe (although plenty of people get by without it just fine).

   The axe now needs an arc on its way to the target.

2. Go to the middle of the axe's flight, frame 27.

3. Move the axe up in the *Y*-axis a bit using the green handle of the Tool Manipulator.

If the axe is slightly rotated in frame, Auto Keyframe can set a key for both Translate Y and Translate X, although you were perhaps expecting only a key in Translate Y. Because the Move tool is on the axe's Local axis, and because the axe was slightly rotated at frame 27, there is a change in the *Y* and *X* positions in the World axis, which is the axis represented in the Graph Editor.

4. Select the Translate X key at frame 27, if one was created, and press Delete to delete it.

5. Now you'll add a full spin to the axe to give the animation more reality and life. You can spin it in one of two ways.

   - Go to frame 40, select the axe, and rotate it clockwise a full 360 degrees positive. Auto Keyframe enters a new rotation value at frame 40, overwriting the old value. You should see the Rotate Z curve angle down steeply as soon as you let go of the Rotate Manipulator.

   - In the Graph Editor, make sure you're at frame 40, grab the last keyframe on the Rotate Z curve, and MMB+click and drag it down, probably past the lower limit of the window. If you keep the middle mouse button pressed as you move the mouse, the keyframe keeps moving as you move the mouse, even if the keyframe has left the visible bounds of the Graph Editor.

If you hold down Shift as you MMB+click and drag the keyframe to move it in the Graph Editor, the keyframe will move in only one axis (up or down, left or right).

By moving the keyframe down, you change the Rotate Z value to a lower number, which spins the axe clockwise. Before you try that, though, move your Graph Editor window so you can see the axe in the Perspective window. As you move the Rotate Z keyframe down in the Graph Editor, you see the axe rotate interactively. Move the keyframe down until the axe does a full spin.

6. Play back the animation by clicking the Play button in the playback controls. If your animation looks blazingly fast, the Maya playback speed is probably set to Play Every Frame. Open the Animation Preferences window by clicking its icon (🖼), and set Playback Speed to Real-Time (30fps).

   Now, when you play back the animation, it should look slow. Maya is playing the scene back in real time, as long as the options in the Animation Preferences window are set to play back properly at 30fps. Even at 30fps, the scene should play back slowly, and this means the animation of the axe timing is too slow.

7. All you need to do is tinker in the Graph Editor a bit to get the right timing. For a good result in timing, move the first set of keyframes from 15 to 13. Then, grab the Translate Y keyframe at frame 27 and move it to 19. Finally, grab the keyframes at frame 40 and move them all back to frame 25. Play back the scene.

Changing the playback speed of an animation through the Animation Preferences window doesn't alter the timing of your animation. It only changes the speed at which Maya plays the animation back to you in its windows. To change the playback speed, choose Window → Setting/Preferences → Preferences to open the Preferences window, choose Settings → Working Units, and select the proper setting.

Adding Follow-Through

Load the axe_v4.mb file from the Axe project on the book's web page, or continue with your own file.

The axe is missing weight. You can add some finesse to the scene using follow-through and secondary motion to give more weight to the scene.

In the axe scene, follow-through motion is the axe blade driving farther into the target a little beyond its initial impact. Secondary motion is the recoil in the target as the momentum of the axe transfers into it. As you increase the amount of follow-through and secondary motion, you increase the axe's implied weight. You must, however, walk a fine line; you don't want to go too far with follow-through or secondary motion. Follow these steps:

1. Select the axe in the scene using its selection handle, and open the Graph Editor.

2. Because you'll add three frames to the end of this animation for follow-through, go to frame 28 (25 is the end of the current animation).

3. In the Perspective window, rotate the axe another 1.5 degrees in the Z-axis.

4. Rotating the axe in step 3 moves the axe's blade down a bit in the Y-axis. To bring the axe back up close to where it was before the extra rotation, move the axe up slightly using the Translate Y Manipulator handle. This also digs the axe into the target a little more. You'll see a keyframe for Translate Y and most probably for Translate X, as well as for Rotate Z.

   If you play back the animation, the follow-through doesn't look good. The axe hits the target and then digs into it as if the action were done in two separate moves by two different animators who never talked to each other. You need to smooth out the transition from the axe strike and its follow-through in the Graph Editor.

5. Highlight the Rotate Z attribute in the Graph Editor to get rid of the other curves in the window. Figure 8.22 shows the Rotate Z curve of the axe after the follow-through animation is added.

6. Focus on the last three frames of the curve and zoom into that range only. The curve, as it is now, dips down past where it should and recoils back up a small amount.

When you set keyframes, you create animation curves in the Graph Editor for the axe. These curves are Bézier splines, which stay as smooth as possible from beginning to end. When you set the new keyframe, rotating the axe about 1.5 more degrees for follow-through, the animation curve responds by creating a dip, as shown in Figure 8.22, to keep the whole curve as smooth as possible.

SECONDARY MOTION AND FOLLOW-THROUGH

Secondary motion in animation comprises all the little things in a scene that move because something else in the scene is moving. For example, when a superhero jumps from a tall building and his or her cape flutters in the wind, the cape's undulation is secondary motion.

Follow-through is the action in animation that immediately follows an object's or a character's main action. For example, after the superhero lands from their jump, his or her knees buckle a little, and the superhero bends at the waist, essentially squashing down a bit. That squashing motion is follow-through. The more follow-throughs, the more cartoon-like the animation appears.

The axe needs to hit the target with force and dig its way in, slowly coming to a stop. You need to adjust the curvature of the keyframes at frame 25 by using the keyframe's tangents. *Tangents* are handles that change the amount of curvature influence of a point on a b-spline (Bézier spline). Selecting the keyframe in question reveals its tangents, as shown in Figure 8.23.

7. Select the Out tangent for the `Rotate Z` attribute's key at frame 25, and MMB+click and drag it up to get rid of the dip. Notice that the tangency for the In tangent also changes.

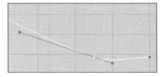

Figure 8.23

The tangent handles of a keyframe. The handle to the left of the keyframe is the In tangent, and the handle to the right is its Out tangent.

8. Press Z to undo your change. You need to break the tangent handles so that one doesn't disturb the other.

9. Select the Out handle, and click the Break Tangents icon (■) to break the tangent.

10. Move the handle up to get rid of the dip, so that the curve segment from frame 25 to frame 28 is a straight line, angled down. Figure 8.24 is zoomed into this segment of the curve after it's been fixed.

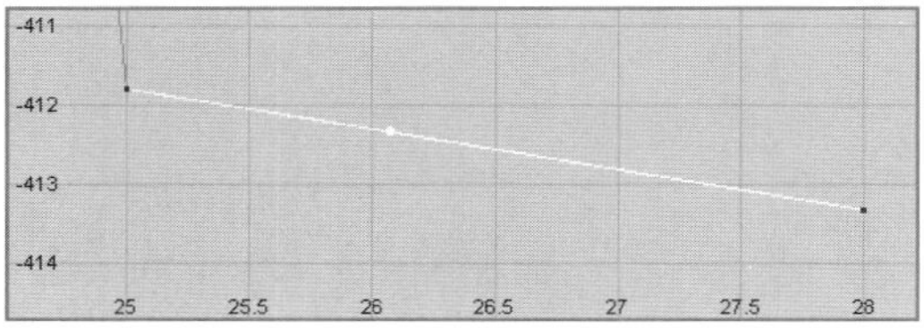

Figure 8.24

Zoomed into the end segment of the Rotate Z animation curve after the dip is fixed

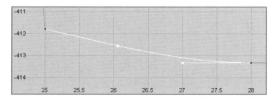

Now, to get the axe to stop slowly as it digs into the target, you need to curve that end segment of the Rotate Z curve to flatten it out.

11. Grab the last frame to reveal its handles. You can manually move the In handle to make it horizontal, or you can click the Flat Tangents icon (■) on the left side of the icon bar, under the menus in the Graph Editor.

The curve's final segment for Rotate Z should now look like Figure 8.25.

Figure 8.25

Zoomed into the end segment of the Rotate Z animation curve. Notice how the curve now smoothly comes to a stop by flattening out.

12. Adjust the keyframe tangents similarly for the axe's Translate Y and Translate X curves, as shown in Figure 8.26.

Figure 8.26

Smoothed translate curves to ease out the motion

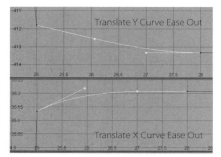

13. Play back the animation, and you should see the axe impact the target and sink into it a bit for its follow-through.

Now, you need to polish things up more.

Adding Secondary Motion

Load `axe_v5.mb` from the Axe project from the book's web page, or continue with your own scene file.

For secondary motion, you'll move the target in reaction to the impact from the axe's momentum.

An object in motion has momentum. Momentum is calculated by multiplying the mass of an object by its velocity. So, the heavier and faster an object is, the more momentum it has. When two objects collide, some or all momentum transfers from one object to the other.

In the axe scene's impact, the axe lodges in the target, and its momentum is almost fully transferred to the target. But because the target is much more massive than the axe, the target moves only slightly in reaction. The more you make the target recoil, the heavier the axe will seem.

First, group the axe's parent node under the target's parent node. The axe will be left behind to float in midair if you animate the target's parent node without grouping the axe under it. By grouping the axe under the target, you'll move the target to recoil while keeping the axe lodged in it. The animation on the axe won't change when you group the axe and target under a new node. We will use the Hypergraph instead of the Outliner, so let's take a quick look at its interface first.

The Hypergraph Explained

The Hypergraph: Hierarchy (referred to as just the Hypergraph in this book) displays all the objects in your scene in a graphical layout similar to a flowchart (see Figure 8.27). Select Window → Hypergraph: Hierarchy to see the relationships between objects in your scene more directly. This window will perhaps be somewhat more difficult for a novice

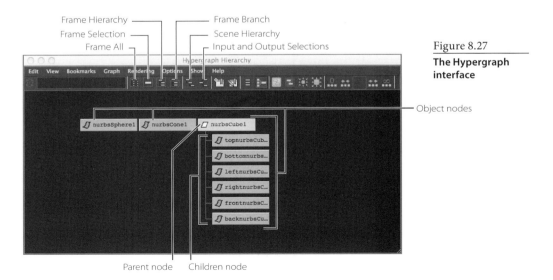

Figure 8.27
The Hypergraph interface

to decipher, but it affords you great control over object interconnectivity, hierarchy, and input and output connections. The Hypergraph: Connections window is technically called the Hypergraph window, but it shows you the interconnections of attributes among nodes as opposed to the node hierarchy in the scene.

Navigating the Hypergraph is the same as navigating any Modeling window, using the familiar Alt key and mouse combinations for tracking and zooming.

Continuing the Axe

First, you need to set the `target` node's `Translate` and `Rotate` attributes back to **0** and its `Scale` attributes back to **1**.

1. To freeze the transforms, select the parent target node, and then choose Modify → Freeze Transformations.

2. Select Window → Hypergraph: Hierarchy. MMB+click and drag the axe node to the target node in the Hypergraph to group the axe node under the target node. This can also be done in the Outliner.

3. Go to frame 25, the moment of impact, and set the position and rotation keyframes on Target.

4. Go to frame 28, rotate the target node in the Z-axis about 2.5 degrees, and move it up and back slightly in the Y- and X-axes, as shown in Figure 8.28.

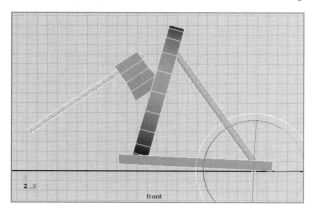

5. Go to frame 31. Rotate the target node back to 0 in the Z-axis, move it down to 0 in the Y-axis, and move it back a bit more in the X-axis.

6. Go to frame 35 and repeat step 4, but move it only half as much in Rotate Z, Translate X, and Translate Y.

7. Go to frame 40 and repeat step 5, but move Target back only slightly in the X-axis.

> If you don't freeze the transforms on the target's parent node before grouping the axe under it, the axe's animation will change and yield undesirable results.

The preceding steps should give you an animation similar to axe_v6.mb in the Axe project from the companion web page.

Motion Trails

You can see a moving object's trajectory, or *motion trail*—that is, its path of motion. Follow these steps:

1. Select the axe through its selection handle, and then, in the Animation menu set, choose Animate → Create Editable Motion Trail ❐ to open the window shown in Figure 8.29.

2. Make sure the Show Frame Numbers check box is selected.

3. Click Apply, and then click Close to close the window.

   The motion trail is useful for fine-tuning motion. Editing the animation curves in the Graph Editor and watching the motion trail adjust in the work panels shows you the precise trajectory of the axe throughout its movement. Play back your animation a few times to get a good sense of how the scene looks.

4. Select the axe, and open the Graph Editor.

5. Try adding more arc to the axe in the middle of its trajectory to the target.

6. In the Graph Editor, focus on the Translate Y curve, and select the keyframe at frame 19.

7. Move the keyframe up about 2 units, and watch the motion trail adjust to show you the higher arc.

8. Replay the animation with the higher arc in the middle.

Notice that the axe seems a little more solid than before. The extra height in the trajectory helps give the axe more substance. Figure 8.30 shows the axe and its motion trail after more height is added to its arc.

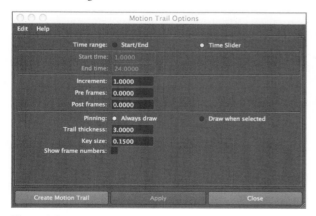

Figure 8.29

The Motion Trail Options box

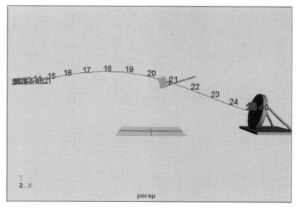

Figure 8.30

The axe and its motion trail

You can toggle the frame-number display on/off and change the display type of the motion trail from curve to points or locators through the motion trail's Attribute Editor. To get rid of the motion trail, select it and press Delete.

Path Animation

As an alternative to keyframing the position of the axe, you can animate it on a path. Path animation allows you to assign an object to move along the course of a curve, called a *path*.

Load axe_v7.mb from the Axe project from the companion web page. This is the finished axe animation. You'll delete most of your hard work by removing the translation animation on the axe, but you'll keep the rotation and everything else. You'll replace the translation keyframes you set up with a motion path instead. Follow these steps:

1. In the front window and with the motion trails turned on, trace the motion trail with a CV curve (choose Create → CV Curve Tool) from the beginning of the trail to the end, as shown in Figure 8.31. Make sure the CV Curve tool is set to make cubic (3) curves.

2. Take note of the frames on which you set important keyframes for the axe's position (for example, when it recoils and releases at frame 10 and when it hits the target at frame 25). Select the axe's top node (axe), and delete its translation animation. Select all three Translate attributes in the Channel Box, and right-click to display the context menu. Choose Break Connections to delete the animation from those channels. The axe now spins around, and it and the target recoil at the moment of impact, but the axe doesn't actually move.

3. Keep the motion trail in the scene for now to help with the timing you've already created.

4. Select the top axe node, and then Shift+select the path curve. In the Animation menu set, choose Animate → Motion Paths → Attach To Motion Path ❏.

5. In the option box, turn off the Follow check box.

    The Follow feature orients the object on the path so that its front always points in the direction of travel. Because the axe moves backward in anticipation before it's thrown forward, Follow would cause it to turn around twice, so turn this option off.

Figure 8.31

Trace the motion trail.

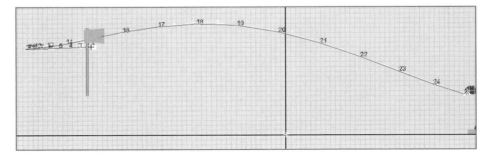

Now the axe will follow the curve end to end from frame 1 to frame 60. Of course, you have to adjust the timing to fit it, as before.

6. Select the motion trail, and move it down in the window to get it out of the way. But keep it lined up vertically with the path curve so you can figure out the timing again.

     The file `axe_path_v1.mb` in the Axe project will bring you up to this point.

7. Select the top `axe` node, and open the Graph Editor to see the axe's curves. The rotation curve is still intact, although the translation curves are missing. Click `motionPath1` in the Channel Box to highlight it; the `motionPath1.U Value` curve that took the place of the translation curves appears in the Graph Editor. On the left side of the Graph Editor, select the `motionPath1.U Value` curve to display only that. Zoom into it. (Press A to view all.)

8. The curve is an even, linear curve from 1 to 60. You need the axe to hit at frame 25, so move the end of the curve to frame 25 from frame 60.

9. Retime the backward movement. Scrub the animation until the axe moves all the way back (frame 4). Using the Insert Keys tool (🔲), insert a keyframe at frame 4. Select the animation curve, click the tool, and MMB+click the curve to create a key on it. You can MMB+click and drag the cursor to place the key precisely at frame 10 before releasing the mouse button.

10. Move this new keyframe to frame 10 (the frame where backward movement origi-nally ended).

11. Scrub the animation, and the timing is just about right. You'll have to adjust the tan-gents a bit to make the axe move more like before, but the movement is essentially there with path animation.

     The file `axe_path_v2.mb` in the Axe project will bring you up to this point.

Path animation is extremely useful for a number of tasks but especially for animating an object along a particular course. By adjusting the resulting animation curve in the Graph Editor, you can readjust the timing of the path animation easily.

A good path-animation exercise is to reanimate the Solar_System exercise with paths instead of the keyframes you set on the rotations.

GHOSTING

To see the position of an animated object a few frames before and after its current position, you can enable ghosting in Maya. For example, select the animated axe in your scene and, in the Animation menu set, choose Animate → Ghost Selected. Maya will display the axe's three frames before and after the current time. To turn off ghosting, choose Animate → Unghost Selected.

Axe Project Summation

In the Axe example, you furthered your use of layered animation by beginning with the gross animation to cover the basic movements of the axe. After those timings were set, you completed most of the remaining work in the Graph Editor by moving keyframes here and there to add detail to the motion. You added more keyframes to create follow-through and secondary movement to insinuate weight into the axe and target.

Without secondary movement in the target, the axe would seem to weigh nothing. With too much movement, however, the axe would seem too heavy, and the scene wouldn't look right. Subtle nuances can make stunning differences in the simplest of animations. You also went back into the animation and replaced the animation method entirely with path animation. This illustrates the multiple ways to accomplish a task in Maya; finding your own comfort zone with a workflow is one of the goals in learning Maya.

Replacing an Object

Aside from the need to model objects and texture them, there is the task of animation setup. Check your pivots, your geometry, and your grouping to make sure your scene will hold up when you animate it.

It's also common practice in setup to animate a *proxy* object—a simple stand-in model that you later replace. The next exercise will show you how to replace the axe you already animated with the fully textured NURBS axe from the previous chapter and how to copy an animation from one object to another.

Replacing the Axe

Load your completed, keyframed axe-animation scene (not the one using path animation), or switch to the Axe project and load the scene file axe_v7.mb from the book's web page. Now, follow these steps:

1. Choose File → Import.

2. Locate and import the Axe_Replace.ma scene file from the Scenes folder of the Axe project from the companion web page. The new axe appears at the origin in your scene.

Transferring Animation

Assuming all the properties and actions of the original axe requires some setup. Follow these steps:

1. Move the pivot on the new axe to the same relative position as the pivot on the original animated axe (up toward the top and a little out front of the handle, just under the blade). This ensures that the new axe has the same spin as the old axe. If you don't make sure the pivots line up, the animation won't look right when transferred to the new axe.

2. Rotate the new axe's top node 180 degrees in *Y* to get it to face the right direction.

3. Use grid snap to place the top node of the new axe at the origin.

4. Freeze transforms on the new axe group to reset all its attributes.

5. Choose Display → Transform Display → Selection Handles to turn on the selection handle of the new axe.

6. Go to frame 1. Select the original axe, open the Graph Editor, and choose Edit → Copy.

7. Select the new axe to display its curves in the Graph Editor. It has no curves to display yet. With the axe node selected in the Graph Editor, choose Edit → Paste. As shown in Figure 8.32, the new axe is slightly offset from the original axe.

> When you copy and paste curves in the Graph Editor, make sure you're on the first frame of the animation. Pasting curves places them at the current frame. Because the animation of the original axe started at frame 1, make sure you're at frame 1 when you paste the curves to the new axe.

8. Move the new axe to match the original. Because it's already animated, move it using the curves in the Graph Editor as opposed to moving it in the viewport. With the new axe selected, in the Graph Editor, select the Translate Y curve; move it up to match the height of the original axe.

9. Select the Translate X curve, and move it to match the axe's *X* position, as shown in Figure 8.33. Line up the axe handle as a guide.

   Scrub the animation, and notice that the new axe has the same animation except at the end when it hits the target. It doesn't have the same follow-through as the original axe. Remember that you grouped the original axe under the `target` node for follow-through animation. Place the new axe under this node as well.

   The file `axe_v8.mb` in the Axe project from the book's web page has the new axe imported and all the animation copied. It will get you caught up to this point.

10. After you scrub the animation and make sure the new axe animates properly, select the original axe's top node and delete it.

Animating Flying Text

It's inevitable. Sooner or later, someone will ask you to animate a flying logo or flying text for something or other. As late-1980s as that may sound, animating flying text—at least, the way you'll do it here—can teach you a thing or two about path animation and Lattice deformers. You can use the following steps to animate pretty much anything that has to twist, wind, and bend along a path; this technique isn't just for text.

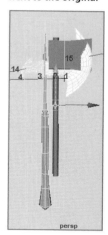

Figure 8.32

The new axe placed next to the original

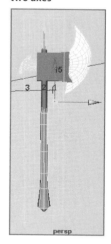

Figure 8.33

Lining up the two axes

You'll need to create the text, so follow these steps:

1. In a new scene, select Create → Text ❑. In the option box, enter your text, and select a font to use (see Figure 8.34). In this case, stick with Times New Roman. Set Type to Bevel.

Figure 8.34

The Text Curves Options box

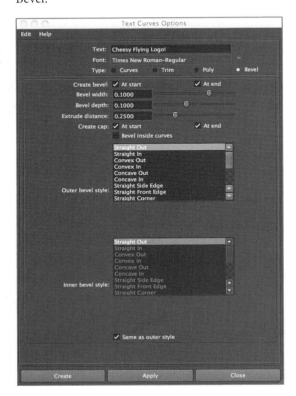

Setting the Type attribute to Poly for your text creates curve outlines for the text and planar faces for the letters, for a flat-text effect. Setting the Type Creation option to Curves gives you just the curve outlines. Finally, using Trim to create your text makes the letters out of flat planar NURBS surfaces. However, no surface history is created with text. To allow you to edit the text later, you must re-create the text and/or font type as needed.

2. Leave the rest of the creation methods at their defaults. Doing so creates the text as beveled faces to make the 3D text, as shown in Figure 8.35.

3. When you have the text, you need to create a curve for it to animate along. Using either the CV or EP Curve tool, create a winding curve like a roller coaster for the logo, as shown in Figure 8.36.

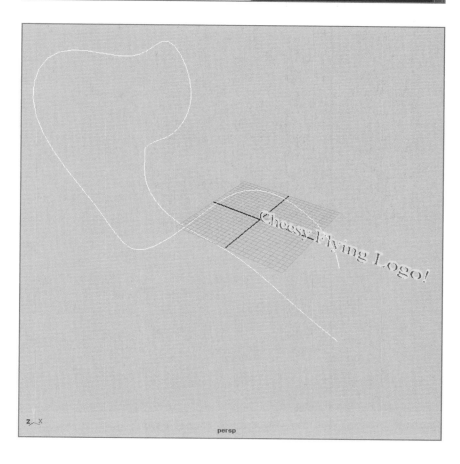

Figure 8.35

Creating the 3D text for the flying logo

Figure 8.36

Create a curve path for the text to follow.

4. Just as you did with the axe exercise, you'll assign the text object to this curve. Set your frame range to 1–100. Select the text, Shift+select the curve, and, in the Animation menu set, choose Animate → Motion Paths → Attach To Motion Path ❐. Set Front Axis to *X* and Up Axis to *Y*, and select the Bank check box, as shown in Figure 8.37.

   Depending on how you create your curve and text, you may need to experiment with the Front Axis and Up Axis attributes to get the text to fly the way you want. Notice that history is created with the path animation, so you can adjust the axes' attributes after the fact to see how they work on the curve you have.

5. Orbit the camera around to the other side, and you can see the text on the path, as shown in Figure 8.38. In the Attribute Editor for the motion path, notice the U Value attribute: this is the position of the text along the curve from 0 to 1. Scrub the animation, and the text should glide along the curve.

6. The text isn't bending along with the curve at all yet. To accomplish this, you need to add a lattice that bends the text to the curvature of the path. Select the text object, and choose Animate → Motion Paths → Flow Path Object ❐.

7. In the option box for the Flow Path Object, shown in Figure 8.39, set Divisions: Front to **120**, Up to **2**, and Side to **2**, and select Curve for Lattice Around. Make sure the Local Effect box is unchecked. Doing so creates a lattice that follows the curve, giving it 120 segments along the path. This lattice deforms the text as it travels along the path.

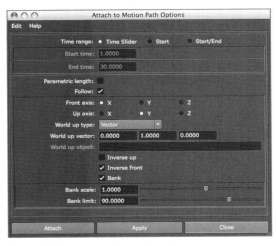

Figure 8.37

The Attach To Motion Path Options box

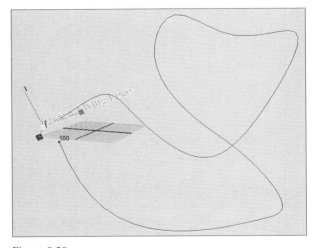

Figure 8.38

The text is on the path.

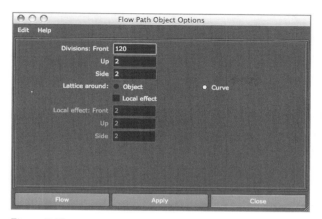

Figure 8.39
The Flow Path Object Options box

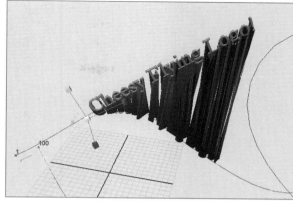

Figure 8.40
The geometry doesn't fit the lattice well.

8. Scrub your animation, and you see a fairly strange result: parts of the text explode out from the lattice, as shown in Figure 8.40.

9. The geometry is going outside the influence of the lattice, and this is causing the strange behavior. To fix the situation, select the lattice and base node, and scale up the lattice *and* its base node together to create a larger size of influence around the path (see Figure 8.41).

Scrub your animation to check the frame range and how well the text flies through the lattice. When the lattice and its base are large enough to handle the text along all of the path's corners and turns, voilà—Cheesy Flying Logo! (See Figure 8.42.)

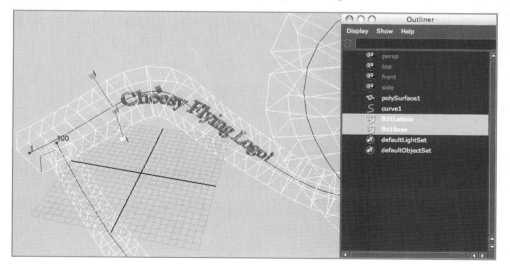

Figure 8.41
Scale the lattice and its base node to accommodate the flying text.

Figure 8.42

**Cheesy Flying Logo!
makes a nice turn.**

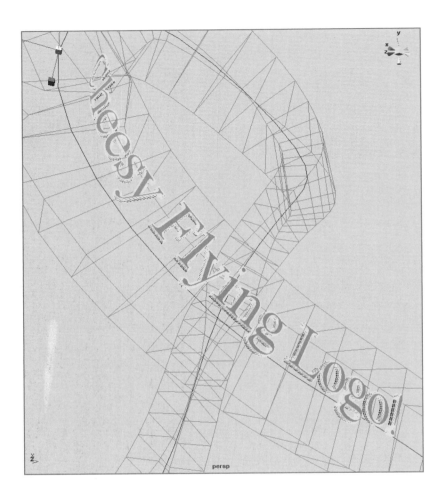

Rigging the Locomotive, Part 1

In this section, you'll return to a simple locomotive similar to the one for which you modeled a NURBS steam pump in Chapter 5, "Modeling with NURBS Surfaces and Deformers," and put your new animation skills to use.

Download the file locomotive_model.mb from the Scenes folder of the Locomotive project from the book's web page.

The Scene Setup

It's important to keep animation in mind as you build a model; hierarchy is crucial to getting a smooth animation workflow going. Now you're going into the locomotive scene to make sure you have good organization before beginning the task of rigging this thing for animation.

Figure 8.43 shows the organization of the locomotive as it stands in `locomotive_model.mb`. There already is a scene file with a locomotive that is grouped properly, using the intentions outlined here, but you'll go through the steps of rigging it here for the experience. First, you have to identify the parts of the locomotive that you need to rig, determine how they will move, and decide the best hierarchy for the model from there.

The major moving parts of the engine are the wheels and the steam pump drive mechanism. The wheels, of course, need to rotate, as wheels do, and the steam pump drives the wheel arms back and forth, which is what drives the main wheels to rotate. Aside from animating some steam pumping out of parts of the engine, which I'll cover in Chapter 12, "Autodesk Maya Dynamics and Effects," this is the basic rigging for the locomotive. First you need to make sure the hierarchies are settled well and the pivot points are in their proper places.

The `locomotive_model.mb` scene file has a well-organized hierarchy, but it needs some help to make rigging easier. Be sure all the individual wheel arms have their pivots at the base, as shown in Figure 8.44. Hold the D key (or Insert on a PC and Home key on a Mac) to move the pivots as needed. You'll rig these wheel arms using inverse kinematics (IK) bones in the next chapter.

Figure 8.43

The locomotive's Outliner view

Be sure all the elements that make up a wheel are grouped and that the group's pivot point is centered for all the wheel groups, as shown in Figure 8.45.

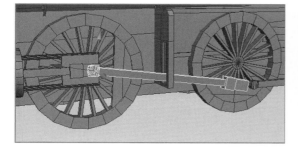

Figure 8.44

Check the pivot points.

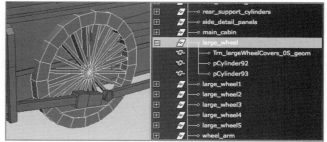

Figure 8.45

Check the hierarchy and pivot placement for the wheel.

Finally, for this simple rig, make sure the steam pump arm elements are properly grouped and that the pivot is placed as shown in Figure 8.46.

Figure 8.46

Place the pivot for the pump arm.

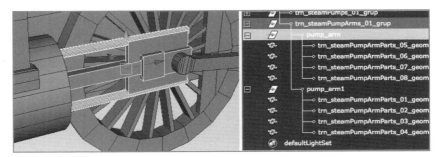

The scene file `locomotive_anim_v1.mb` in the Locomotive project from the companion web page has the locomotive scene file with the pivots and grouping already finished, as discussed earlier.

If the pivots and groupings are off, you'll notice as soon as you begin to animate; things just won't rotate on the correct axis, and pieces won't follow properly. The wheels, for example, may wobble around their axle.

For more practice in grouping and hierarchies, you can load `locomotive_anim_v1.mb` from the web page, ungroup everything in the scene, and piece it all back together. To ungroup everything, select the top node of the locomotive, and choose Edit → Ungroup. Doing so ungroups the major parts of the locomotive. With those groups selected, ungroup again to flush out individual geometry. You can also load `locomotive_anim_v1_B.mb` from the web page; it has all the major groupings removed. Then, regroup and repivot everything yourself for the shrill fun of it! This will definitely be great practice.

Figure 8.47

Selection handles make selecting a group of objects much easier.

Selection Handles

Using selection handles makes selection easier and workflow faster, so turn on selection handles for each of the groups you're animating. Select the wheel groups in the Outliner,

and then choose Display → Transform Display → Selection Handles. Select the wheel arm groups, and turn on their selection handles as well. Figure 8.47 shows the selection handles enabled for the wheel, pump arm, and wheel arm.

How selection handles work depends on the selection order in Maya. *Selection order*, which you can customize, sets the priority of one type of object over another when you try to select in a work window. After the selection handles for the locomotive's wheels and drive arms are turned on, only the handles will be selected (and not the whole locomotive) when you make a marquee selection that covers the entire locomotive. Handles have a high selection priority by default, so they're selected above anything else.

Animating the Locomotive

Animating most of the locomotive is straightforward. Simple rotations will make the wheels turn. Translating the locomotive's top node will move the entire object. This, however, leaves out the drive mechanism with the steam pump and the wheel and pump arms. You'll rig these to animate automatically in the next chapter, using IK handles and connections.

Animating the Catapult

As an exercise in animating a system of parts of a model, before you continue to animate the locomotive in the next chapter, you'll now animate the catapult from Chapter 4, "Beginning Polygonal Modeling." You'll turn its winch to bend back the catapult arm, which shoots the projectiles, and then you'll fire and watch the arm fly up.

Let's get acquainted with the scene file and make sure its pivots and hierarchies are set up properly. The scene file catapult_anim_v1.mb in the Catapult_Anim project from the companion web page has everything in order, although it's always good to make sure. Figure 8.48 shows the catapult with its winch selected and ready to animate.

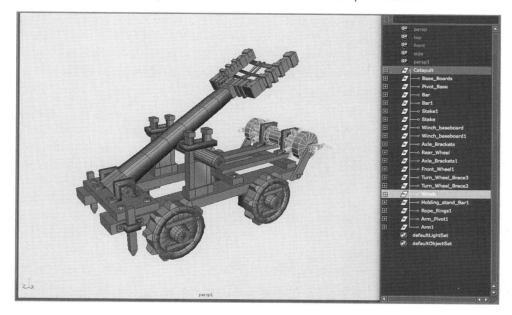

Figure 8.48

The catapult's winch is ready to animate.

Get a timing put down for the winch first, and use that to pull back the arm to fire. Follow these steps:

1. Select the Winch group with its selection handle. At frame 1, set a keyframe for rotation. If the selection handle isn't turned on, select Winch from the Outliner, and turn on the selection handle by choosing Display → Transform Display → Selection Handles. To keep it clean as you go along, instead of pressing Shift+E to set a key for all three axes of rotation, select only the Rotate X attribute in the Channel Box, right-click to open the context menu, and choose Key Selected. There only needs to be rotation in *X* for the winch.

2. Jump to frame 60.

3. Rotate the winch backward a few times, or enter **–400** or so for the Rotate X attribute.

4. Open the Graph Editor, ease in the curve a bit, and ease out the curve a lot so that the rotation starts casually but grinds to a stop as the arm becomes more difficult to pull back.

   Obviously, you're missing the rope between the winch and the arm. Because animating a rope is a fairly advanced task, the catapult is animated without its rope; but the principle of an imaginary rope pulling the arm down to create tension in the arm drives the animation.

5. To accentuate the more difficult winding at the end, add a key to the *X*-axis rotation through the Graph Editor. To do so, select the curve, and click the Insert Keys Tool icon (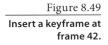) in the upper-left corner of the Graph Editor. Your cursor changes to a cross.

6. MMB+click frame 42 to add a keyframe already on the curve at frame 42. You can drag the key back and forth on the curve to place it directly at frame 42. It may help to turn on key snapping first. (See Figure 8.49.)

7. Move that keyframe down to create a stronger ease-out for the winch. Be careful not to let the curve dip down so that the winch switches directions. Adjust the handles to smooth the curve. You can also add a little recoil to the winch by inserting a new keyframe through the Graph Editor at frame 70. (See Figure 8.50.)

Figure 8.49

Insert a keyframe at frame 42.

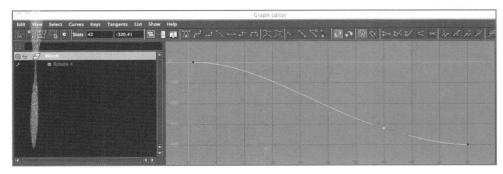

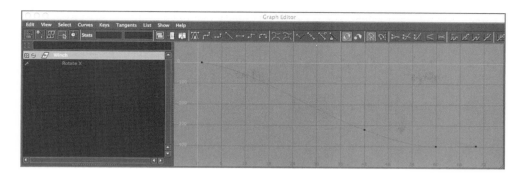

Figure 8.50

Creating a greater ease-out and adding a little recoil at the end

Animating with Deformers

It's time to animate the arm coiling back, using the winch's timing as it's driving the arm. Because the catapult's arm is supported by a brace and the whole idea of a catapult is based on tension, you have to bend the arm back as the winch pulls it.

You'll use a nonlinear deformer, just as you did in the axe head exercise in Chapter 5, but this time, you'll animate the deformer to create the bending of the catapult arm. Follow these steps:

1. Switch to the Animation menu set. Select the Arm1 group, and choose Create Deformers → Nonlinear → Bend to create a Bend deformer perpendicular to the arm. Select the deformer, and rotate it to line it up with the arm, as shown in Figure 8.51.

2. With the Bend deformer selected, look in the Channel Box for bend1 under the Inputs section, and click it to expand its attributes. Try entering **0.5** for Curvature. More than likely, the catapult arm will bend sideways. Rotate the deformer so that the arm is bending back and down instead, as shown in Figure 8.52.

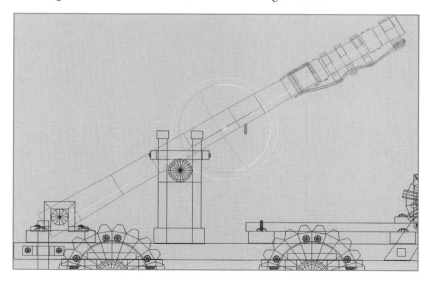

Figure 8.51

Align the Bend deformer with the catapult arm.

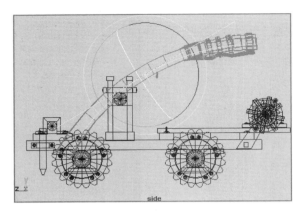

Figure 8.52

Orient the Bend deformer to bend the arm back and down.

3. You don't want the arm's base to bend back, just the basket side. You want it to bend at the brace point, not in the middle where it is now. Move the deformer down the length of the arm until the middle lines up with the arm's support brace.

4. To prevent the bottom of the arm from bending, change the Low Bound attribute to **0**. To keep the basket from bending, set the High Bound attribute to **0.9**.

5. Instead of trying to match the speed, ease in and out of the winch and set the gross keyframes for the arm pulling back first. Reset Curvature to **0**, and set a key for Curvature at frame 1. (Select bend1's Curvature in the Channel Box, right-click, and choose Key Selected from the context menu.)

> The Low Bound and High Bound attributes control how far up and down the deformer the object is affected. The Envelope attribute for a deformer governs how much the object is affected overall, with 0 not affecting the geometry at all.

6. Go to frame 60, and set Curvature to **0.8**. If Auto Key is turned on, this sets a keyframe; otherwise, set a key manually. (See Figure 8.53.)

7. If you play back the animation, notice that the way the winch winds back and the way the arm bends don't match. In the Graph Editor, you can adjust the animation curve on the Bend deformer to match the winch's curve.

Figure 8.53

Bend the arm back at frame 60 and set a keyframe.

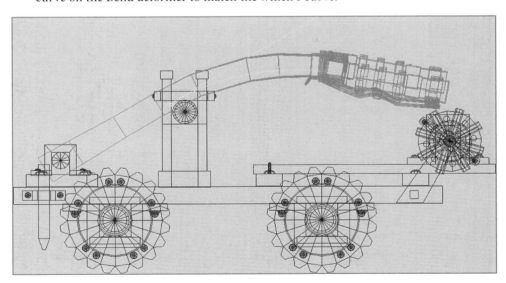

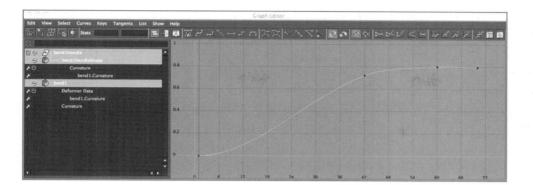

Figure 8.54

Try to match the relative curvature of the winch's animation curve with the Bend deformer's animation curve.

8. Insert a key on the Curvature curve at frame 42, and move it up to match the curvature you created for the winch.

9. Insert a new key at frame 70, and make the arm bend back up slightly as the winch recoils. Set Curvature to about **0.79** from 0.8. (See Figure 8.54.)

10. Go to frame 90, and set a key again at Curvature of **0**. Set a key at 0.82 for frame 97 to create anticipation, and then keyframe at frame 103 to release the arm and fire the imaginary payload with a Curvature of –**0.8**.

11. Add some rotation to the arm for dramatic effect. At about frame 100, during the release, the arm is almost straight. Select the Arm1 group, and set a rotation key on the X-axis. Go to frame 105, and rotate the arm 45 degrees to the left in the X-axis. If the starting rotation of the arm is at 30 (as it is in the sample file), set an X-axis rotation key of **75** at frame 105.

12. Notice that the arm is bending strangely now that it's being rotated. It's moving off the deformer, so its influence is changing for the worse. To fix this, go back to frame 100, and group the deformer node (called *bend1Handle*) under the Arm1 group, as shown in Figure 8.55. Now it rotates along with the arm, adding its own bending influence.

13. Work on setting keyframes on the deformer and the arm's rotation so that the arm falls back down onto the support brace and quivers until it becomes straight again. The animation curve for the Bend deformer should look like Figure 8.56. The rotation of the arm should look like Figure 8.57. Remember to make the tangents flat on the keys where the arm bounces off the brace linear and the peaks, like the ball's bounce from earlier in the chapter.

Figure 8.55

Group the deformer node under the Arm1 group node.

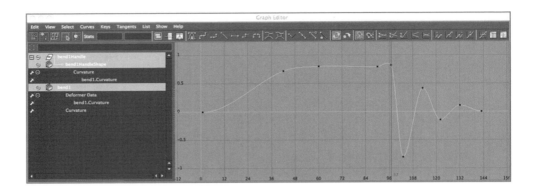

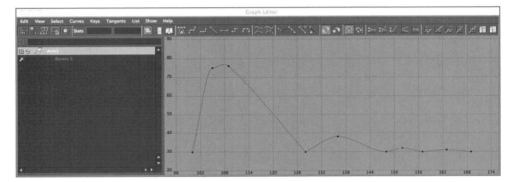

The file `catapult_anim_v2.mb` will give you a good reference to check out the timing of the arm bend and rotation.

Without getting into a lot more detail, try your hand at animating the catapult on your own. Here are some items you can animate to make this a complete animation:

- Spin the winch around as the arm releases, as if its rope is being yanked away from it.

- Animate the entire catapult rocking forward and backward as the arm releases, similar to the way a car rocks when you jump onto the hood.

- Move the catapult forward on a road, spinning its wheels as best you can to match the distance it travels.

- Design and build your own catapult, and animate it along the same lines.

Summary

In this chapter, you began to learn the fundamentals of animating a scene. Starting with a bouncing ball, you learned how to work in the Graph Editor to set up and adjust timing as well as how to add squash and stretch to the animation. The next exercise, throwing an axe, showed you how to set up a scene for animation, expanded on your experience of creating timing in the Graph Editor, and showed you how to add anticipation, follow-through, and secondary motion to your scene. You then learned how to adjust animation using motion trails and how to animate the axe throw using path animation. You went on to learn how to replace a proxy object that is already animated with a different finished model and how to transfer the animation. Using a simple version of the locomotive model you saw in Chapter 5, you began to set up the scene for further rigging in the next chapter by setting proper pivots and hierarchy. Finally, you used the catapult to animate with deformers and further your experience in the Graph Editor.

Animating a complex system, such as a catapult or a locomotive, involves creating layers of animation based on facets of the mechanics of the system's movement. With the catapult, you tackled the individual parts separately and then worked to unify the animations. You'll use rigging concepts in the next chapter to automate some of that process for the locomotive.

The same is true of the Bouncing_Ball and Axe_Throwing exercises. The different needs of the animation were addressed one by one, starting with the gross animation and ending with finishing touches to add weight. Finally, the art of timing brought the entire effort into a cohesive whole.

Even when animation is already applied, it's simple to change *how* the animation is accomplished, as you did with path animation, or even to replace the animated object entirely.

Animation is the art of observation, interpretation, and implementation. Learning to see how things move, deciphering why they move as they do, and then applying all that to your Maya scene is what animation is all about.

CHAPTER 9

More Animation!

Now that you have a little more animation experience, you can get into some more involved animation practices and toolsets, taking further the principles covered in this book and its examples. Animation is a growing exploration, and you should use this book as a stepping-off point. For everything you're being exposed to here, there are many more techniques to discover.

Learning Outcomes: In this chapter, you will be able to

- Use hierarchies to your advantage in animation tasks
- Create and manipulate a skeleton system for animation
- Group model pieces to a skeleton
- Create a walk cycle using forward kinematics for pose animation
- Copy and paste keyframes to extend animation
- Discern the three different ways—rigid, smooth, interactive—to bind a mesh to a skeleton in Maya
- Use inverse kinematics in a rig of a simple character
- Create a walk cycle using IK animation
- Use constraints to automate animation
- Create set-driven keys for animation rigging
- Rig a locomotive for automated animation
- Rig a simple character for basic character animation

Skeletons and Kinematics

If you don't have a skeleton, you probably aren't reading this book. In your body, your muscles move the bones of your skeleton, and as your bones move, parts of your body move.

In CG animation, a *skeleton* is an armature built into a 3D model that drives the geometry when the bones are moved. You insert a skeleton into a CG model and attach or bind it to the geometry. The skeleton's bones are animated, which in turn move the parts of the geometry to which they're attached. By using a skeleton, the Autodesk® Maya® software allows bending and deformation of the attached geometry at the skeleton's *joints*. A skeleton is useful for character work, but skeletons have many other uses. Any time you need to drive the geometry of a model with an internal system, such as a fly-fishing line or a tree bending in the wind, you can use skeletons. You'll use them to drive the locomotive wheels and a simple character later in this chapter.

Skeletons and Hierarchy

Skeletons rely on hierarchies (see Figure 9.1). Bones are created in a hierarchical manner, resulting in a *root joint* that is the parent of all the joints beneath it in the hierarchy. For example, a hip joint can be the root joint of a leg skeleton system in which the *knee joint* is the leg's child, the *ankle joint* belongs to the knee, and the five *toe joints* are the ankle's children.

Geometry need not deform to be attached to a bone system; objects can be grouped with or under joints. They move under their parent joint and rotate around that joint's pivot as opposed to their own pivot point.

A skeleton is really just a collection of grouped and properly positioned pivot points called *joints* that you use to move your geometry, whether it deforms or not. A *bone* is the length between each joint; bones only show you the skeletal system.

Inverse kinematics (IK) and *forward kinematics* (FK) are the methods you use to animate a skeletal system. FK rotates the bones directly at their top joint to assume poses. This method resembles *stop-motion animation*, in which a puppet, along with its underlying armature, is posed frame by frame. With FK, the animator moves the character into position by rotating the joints that run the geometry.

The rotation of a joint affects the position of the bones and joints beneath it in the hierarchy (see Figure 9.2). If you rotate the hip up, the knee and ankle swing up as if the character is kicking.

IK uses a more complex, but often easier, system of *IK handles* that are attached to the tip of a joint system. The corresponding base of the IK system is attached farther up the skeleton hierarchy to a joint determined to be the root of that IK segment. It need not be the root joint of the entire skeleton, though.

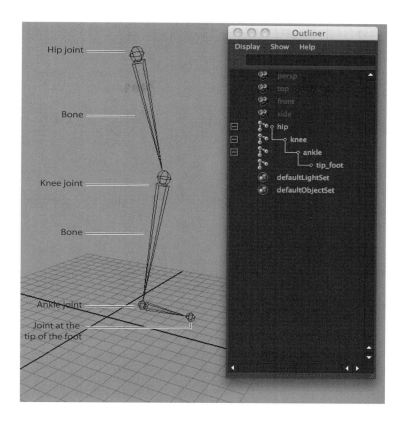

Figure 9.1

A leg skeleton and its hierarchy

The bones and joints in the IK chain are affected only by movement of the IK handle. When the handle moves, an *IK solver* figures out how to rotate all the joints to accommo-date the new position of the IK handle. Moving an IK handle causes the bones to rotate around their joints to accommodate a new position.

The effect is as if someone grabbed your hand and moved it. The person holding your hand is similar to an IK handle. Moving your hand causes the bones in your arm to rotate around the shoulder, elbow, and wrist. As you can see in Figure 9.3, the animation flows up the hierarchy and is therefore called inverse kinematics.

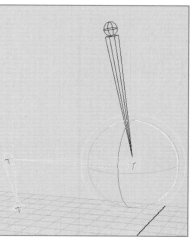

Figure 9.2

In forward kinematics, the joints are rotated directly.

Figure 9.3

In inverse kinematics, the joints rotate in response to the IK handle's position.

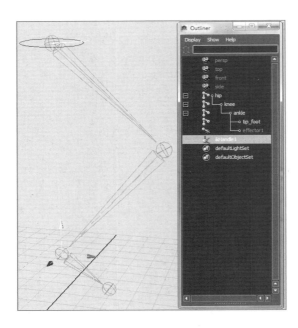

Forward Kinematics: The Block Man

To understand skeletal hierarchy, look at Figure 9.4, which shows a simple biped (two-legged) character made of primitive blocks. He's called the Block Man. (Surprise!) Each block represents part of the body, with gaps between the blocks representing points where the body pivots.

The pivot of each block is placed to represent the appropriate joint location. For example, the shin's pivot is located at the knee. Each block is grouped up the chain so that the foot moves with the shin, which moves with the thigh, which moves with the pelvis.

The hands are grouped under the arms, which are grouped under the shoulders, and so forth, down the spine to the pelvis. The head groups under the first neck block and so on down the spine to the pelvis. The pelvis is the center of the body, which is known as the *root* of the figure.

Figure 9.4

The Block Man's cubes arranged

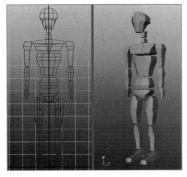

The way this figure is grouped (see Figure 9.5) represents how the hierarchy of a character works for the most part. Each body part is attached and becomes the child of the part above it in the chain.

Load the file `block_man_v02.mb` from the Block_Man project folder on the book's web page, `www.sybex.com/go/introducingmaya2014`, for a good reference of the grouping structure. This file shows you what a skeleton hierarchy does.

In the Hypergraph Hierarchy window, choose Options → Layout → Freeform Layout to position the nodes any way you want. To make selections easier, you can arrange the nodes as if they were on a body (see Figure 9.6). You can toggle between freeform and automatic, and your freeform layout will be retained.

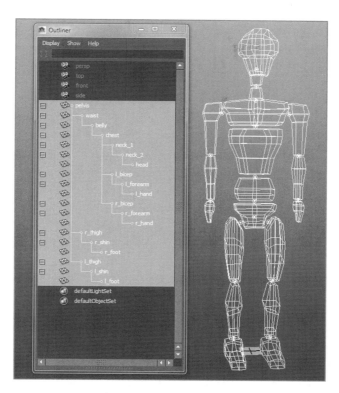

Figure 9.5

Pivot placements and grouping

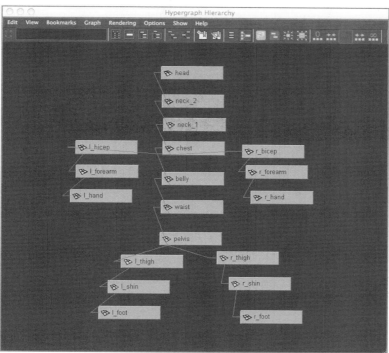

Figure 9.6

A freeform layout in the Hypergraph Hierarchy window

Creating the Skeleton

The basis of how the Block Man is laid out and grouped is what skeletons are all about. Skeletons make character animation easier by automating, at the very least, the hierarchy and pivot placement described earlier.

THE PELVIS AS ROOT

Traditionally, the pelvis is the basis of all biped setups. The root of any skeletal system (whether using bones or geometry as the example) is the character's pivot point—the center of balance. Because a biped character centers itself on two feet, its pelvis becomes the root of its skeletal system. In CG, the pelvis becomes the parent node of the whole system and is the node used to move or orient the entire character. In a skeleton system, this would be the root joint.

The root is then the top parent of the system below it and runs the entire chain. Therefore, selecting character parts straight from the Outliner or the Hypergraph is sometimes easier. You can see that a good naming convention is always important with character setups.

You'll use the Block Man to create a simple skeleton. Load `block_man_v01.mb` from the Block_Man project. This is the same as `block_man_v02.mb`, but this version isn't grouped.

1. Maximize the front view window. Switch to the Animation menu set by using the drop-down menu or by pressing F2.

2. Activate the Joint tool by choosing Skeleton → Joint Tool. Your cursor turns into a cross.

3. Click in the middle of the pelvis to place the first joint, which is the root joint of the skeleton.

4. Shift+click up to the space between the pelvis and the waist.

> The joint display sizes in your Maya window may not match those shown in the book. This isn't a problem; however, you can change the joint sizes by clicking Display → Animation → Joint Size.

By pressing Shift as you click, you create a joint in a straight line from the last joint placement. A bone is created between the two joints as a visual guide to the skeleton. The placement of the joints depends on the active view.

5. Click more joints up the spine at the gaps between the body parts, as shown in Figure 9.7. Place the second to last joint at the base of the skull, as shown in the side view in Figure 9.7. Place the last joint at the top of the head. Then press Enter to exit the Joint tool. Select the top joint at the head, and in a side view, move that joint toward the forehead as shown to make the angle in Figure 9.7.

6. Use Figure 9.7 as a guide to name all your joints. Now you need to start a new branch of joints leading into the legs and arms. Begin with the arms.

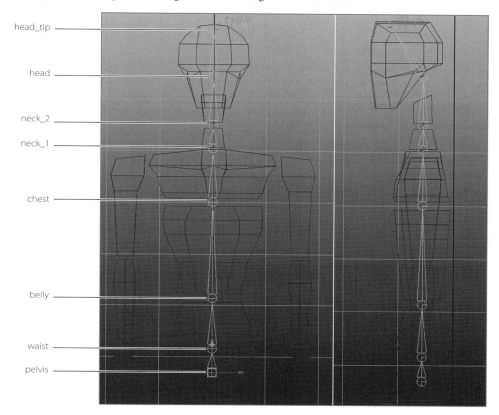

Figure 9.7

Place spine joints straight up the middle of the body, and offset the last joint in the head.

Pressing the Up arrow key takes you up one node in a hierarchy. Pressing the Down arrow key takes you down one node in a hierarchy. This approach also applies to skeletons, because they're hierarchies.

7. Enter the Joint tool (Skeleton → Joint Tool). In the front view, click to place a new joint at the top of the screen-left side of the upper chest just to the side of the joints you've already placed (Figure 9.8, left), and then click to place a second connected joint in the bicep at the shoulder. Click down to create joints at the elbow, the wrist, and the tip of the character's right hand (which is on the left side of your screen). Press Enter to complete that part of the skeleton.

8. Reenter the Joint tool, and repeat the previous step to create joints for the other arm, as shown in Figure 9.8 (right). Name your joints!

Figure 9.8

Place joints for the arm.

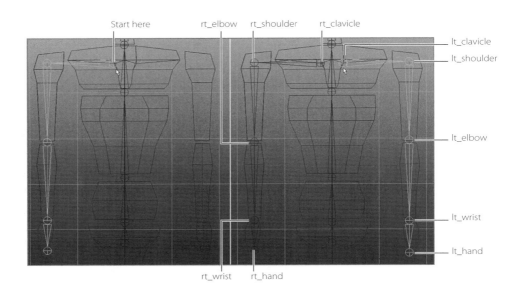

Pick-walking means you select one object or component in Maya and then use the Up or Down arrow key to pick the next object higher (or lower) in the hierarchy. You can use the Left or Right arrow key to pick-walk and select any siblings of the currently selected object in its hierarchy.

9. You'll notice that the arms are not part of the main skeleton yet. You need to connect them to the main skeleton. Open the Outliner, and select the lt_clavicle joint. MMB drag it to the chest node to group it to the chest (Figure 9.9). Notice that a new bone appears between these two joints. Group the rt_clavicle to the chest as well. Figure 9.10 shows the arms are now part of the main skeleton.

Figure 9.9

Group the lt_clavicle to the chest.

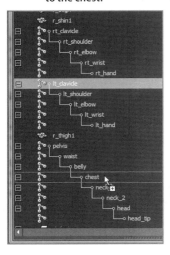

10. To start another string of joints in the first leg, enter the Joint tool. Then click the pelvis joint, selecting it. In the front view, place the first leg joint at the top of the screen-left thigh (the character's right thigh). Place the next joint between the thigh and knee and then another at the top of the foot where it meets the ankle. Do not exit the Joint tool yet!

11. Switch to the side view, and place another joint at the ankle, another in the middle bottom of the foot, and the last joint at the tip of the foot. Press Enter to exit the Joint tool, and you'll see that your leg is already attached to the pelvis; there's no need to group in the Outliner this time like with the clavicles.

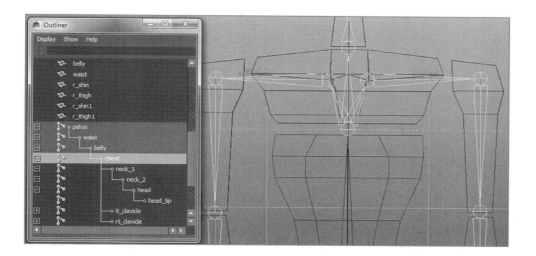

Figure 9.10

The arms are grouped to the chest, and the joints are connected with new bones.

12. In the side view, select the knee joint, and enter Pivot mode by pressing and holding the D key. Very slightly move the knee joint away from the front of the character, out toward the toe. This slight bend will be needed later when you continue the character rig. Using Pivot mode, make sure your joints are placed properly for the leg and foot using Figure 9.11 as a guide. Name your joints!

13. Select the rt_hip joint, and press Ctrl+D to duplicate the hip and the joints beneath it. In the front view, move the new rt_hip1 joint over to the other leg and place it as shown in Figure 9.12 (left). Rename those new joints as shown.

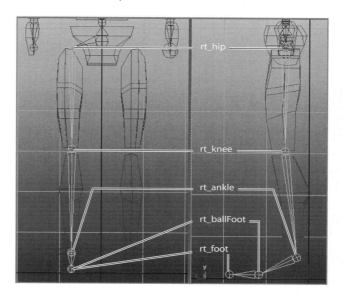

Figure 9.11

Place the leg joints and name them.

You're all done! You'll be adding to this later in the chapter as you create a more well-rounded rig for the character, but for now, check your work against Figure 9.12 (right) and the `block_man_skeleton_v01.mb` file from the Block_Man project.

Figure 9.12

Duplicate the leg joints, move them to the other leg, and name the new joints (left). The skeleton is complete (right).

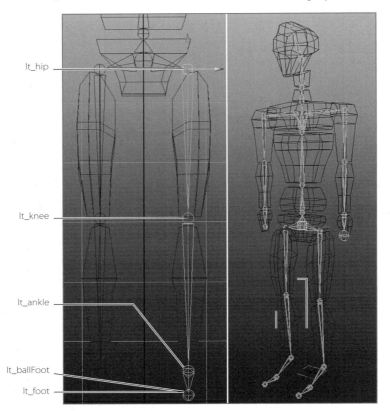

Attaching to the Skeleton

You now have a full skeleton for your character. To attach the geometry, all you need to do is parent the body parts under their appropriate joints. Before you get to that, take a few minutes and make sure all your joints are named in the Outliner to make the scene easier to manage. You can use Figure 9.13 as a naming reference.

You can also load the `block_man_skeleton_v01.mb` file from the Block_Man project to get to this point.

To parent the Block Man's geometry to the skeleton, follow these steps:

1. Starting with the pelvis, parent it under the `pelvis` joint by MMB+clicking and dragging it to the `pelvis` joint. Once it's in the group, MMB drag the `pelvis_geom` again, and place it between the `pelvis` and `waist` joints, as shown in Figure 9.13.

2. Continue the MMB dragging process in the Outliner to place all but the feet geometry in its proper place in the skeleton using the following list and Figure 9.14 as guides. You will deal with the feet a little differently. Figure 9.14 shows the finished hierarchy in the Outliner and Hypergraph.

- Shins under the knees and thighs under the hips
- Hands under the wrists and forearms under the elbows
- Biceps under the shoulder joints
- Head under the head joint (not the head_tip joint)
- Top neck geometry (neck_2) under neck_2 joint
- Bottom neck geometry (neck_1) under the neck_1 joint
- Chest under the chest joint
- Belly under the belly joint
- Waist under the waist joint

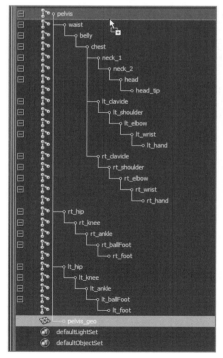

Figure 9.13

After you check your naming, you'll parent the pelvis geometry under the pelvis joint.

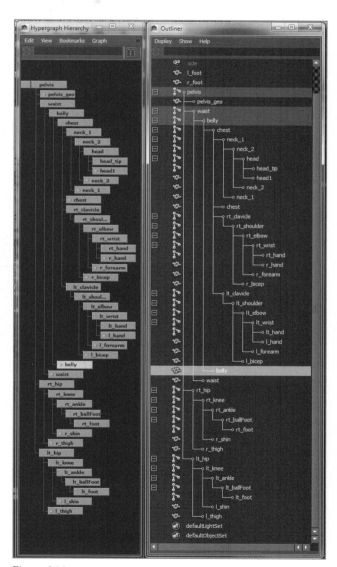

Figure 9.14

Parent all the geometry except the feet into its proper place in the skeleton. The finished hierarchy is shown in the Hypergraph and Outliner side-by-side.

3. Now you'll bind the feet to the foot joints, instead of grouping them. Since there is a joint in the middle of the foot, you'll want to bend the foot. You will explore binding in more detail later in the chapter, but for now, select the l_foot geometry in the Outliner; then press Ctrl, and select all three foot joints (lt_ankle, lt_ballFoot, and lt_foot) in the Outliner as well (Figure 9.15, left).

4. Select Skin → Bind Skin → Rigid Bind → Options, set Bind To to Selected Joints, and click the Bind Skin button. This will bind (a.k.a. skin) the foot geometry to the joints and allow for bending, or deformation, of the foot.

5. To test the bind, select the middle foot joint (lt_ballFoot) and rotate it; the tip of the foot should move. Select the ankle and rotate it, and the whole foot should move. Undo your rotations or set the rotations back to 0 so that the foot is at its rest pose (a.k.a. *bind pose*) again. Just don't undo the binding unless you need to redo steps 3 and 4. (See Figure 9.15, right.)

6. Repeat steps 3 and 4 for the other foot to bind the geometry and test its movement. Just remember to undo your rotations to return to the bind pose.

The Block Man is now set up with a skeleton that you'll use to make a simple walk cycle. This exercise will help get you more familiar and comfortable with animating a character. You will do more to this setup to make a better animation rig for the Block Man character later in the chapter.

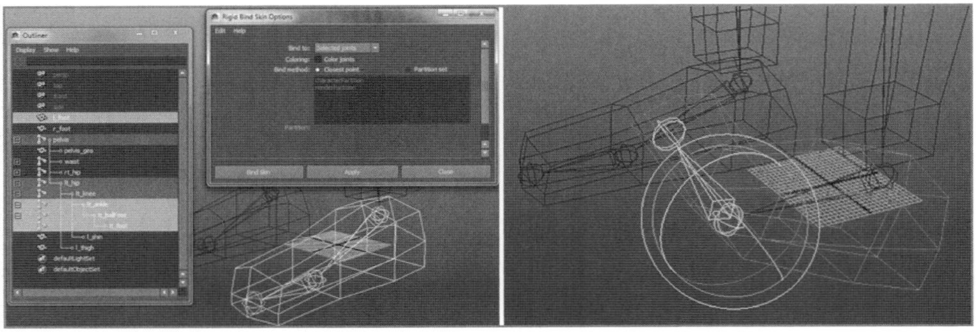

Figure 9.15

The Rigid Bind Skin Options: the left foot geometry and the left foot joints selected (left). Bind and test the left foot (right).

The Block Man: FK Walk Cycle

A *walk cycle* is an animation that takes the character through a few steps that can be repeated many times so that the character seems to be taking numerous steps. In a cycle, make sure the position of the first frame matches the position of the last frame so that when the animation sequence is cycled, no "pop" occurs in the motion at that point.

Now, try animating this character's walk cycle using FK on the skeleton. You'll find the workflow straightforward, as if you were adjusting positions on a doll.

Load the `block_man_skeleton_v02.mb` file from the Block_Man project from the companion web page for the properly grouped and bound model and skeleton. In addition, the right arm and leg have drawing overrides enabled in this file to make their wireframe display white to make it easier to distinguish between the right and left sides while working.

Use the key poses in the following figures to guide you in animating the body as it walks. You'll key at five-frame intervals to lay down the gross animation. You can go back and adjust the timing of the joint rotations in the Graph Editor to make the animation better later. The white leg and arm are behind the body, farther from the camera.

This animation is also called *pose animation* because you're posing the character from keyframe to keyframe.

Starting Out: Frames 1 and 5

Figure 9.16 shows the character's starting position. Here, you'll set a key for this position and then begin the walk cycle by moving the joints into their second position and key-framing that.

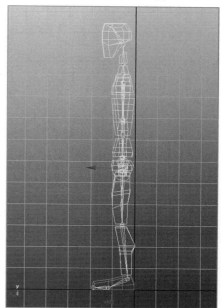

Figure 9.16

The character's starting position

1. At frame 1, set a key for the rotation of all the joints. The easiest way is to select all the joints (and only the joints) in the Outliner or the Hypergraph. With pose animation, you have to make sure that all the joints are keyframed at every step, even if Auto Keyframe is turned on. Also set a position keyframe for just the `pelvis` joint.

2. Go to frame 5. Rotate the back leg (the Block Man's right, white leg) back, rotate the `rt_ballFoot` joint to bend the foot, and bend the ankle to make the ball of the foot level again. Lower the body (select and move the `pelvis` joint) to line up the back heel with the ground. This will keep the man on the ground as he goes through the walk cycle, although he won't actually move forward yet.

3. Rotate the near leg (the man's left blue wireframe leg) forward, bend the knee, and pivot the foot up a bit.

SELECTING ONLY JOINTS IN THE OUTLINER

A quick way to select all the joints, and only the joints, is to filter the Outliner view to show only joints. In the Outliner, choose Show → Objects → Joints. To reset the Outliner, choose Show → Show All.

4. Rotate the back white wireframe arm forward, and rotate the near arm back (opposite from the legs). Bend the arms at the elbows.

5. Bend the man forward at the waist, bend neck_1 forward, and tilt the head back up to compensate a little. Figure 9.17 shows the pose at this point.

6. Select all the joints in the Outliner, and set a rotation key. You're setting a pose for all the joints, which will ensure that all the body parts are in synch.

If you don't key everything every step of the way, some parts of the body won't key with Auto Keyframe properly because the last time they moved may have been two steps previous. This may cause confusion, so it's best to key every joint at every step until you feel more comfortable editing character animation.

Frame 10

Figure 9.18 shows the position you'll keyframe at frame 10; it's approximately midstride for the first leg.

1. Go to frame 10. Rotate the back leg out further, and level the foot. Lower the body to place the man on the ground.

2. Rotate the front leg out, straighten the knee, and flatten the foot to place it on the ground. This is midstride. Swing the arms in their current direction a touch more. Bend the torso forward some more. Make sure you set a key for all the joints.

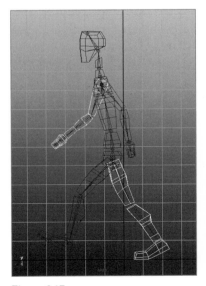

Figure 9.17

The second pose (frame 5)

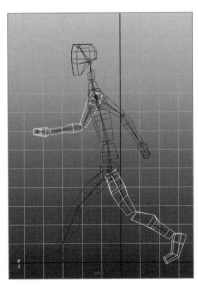

Figure 9.18

The third pose (frame 10)

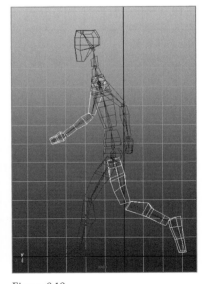

Figure 9.19

The fourth pose (frame 15)

Frame 15

Figure 9.19 shows the position you'll keyframe at frame 15. At this point, the character begins to shift his weight to the front leg as it plants on the ground, and the character also begins lifting the back leg.

1. Go to frame 15. Rotate the front leg back toward the body, and raise the body as the man steps to keep the front foot flat on the ground. Rotate the back knee up to lift the foot, and rotate the foot down to make him push off the toe.

2. Start swinging the arms in the opposite direction. Start straightening the torso back up, but bend the head forward a bit.

Frame 20

At frame 20, the man will shift all his weight onto the front leg and move his body over that leg, lifting his rear leg to begin its swing out front to finish the stride. Figure 9.20 shows the pose. Follow these steps:

1. Rotate the front leg almost straight under the man, and lift up the body to keep the front foot on the ground. Lift the rear leg, and swing it forward.

2. Straighten the torso, and keep the arms swinging in their new direction. Key all the joints.

Frame 25

Now, the man will swing his whole body forward, pivoting on the left leg (the dark one) to put himself off center and ready to fall forward into the next step. Figure 9.21 shows the pose. Here are the steps:

1. Go to frame 25.

2. Rotate the front (dark) leg back behind the man, and swing the white leg up and ready to take the next step. Lower the body to keep the now rear foot (the dark one) on the ground.

Frame 30

Use Figure 9.22 as a guide for creating the next pose. Notice that it's similar to the pose at frame 10. As a matter of fact, the only major differences are which leg and arm are in front. Everything else should be about the same. You'll want some variety in the exact positions to make the animation more interesting, but the poses are very similar.

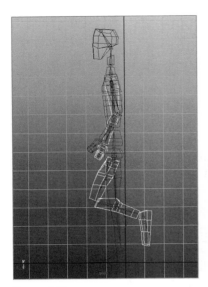

Figure 9.20

The fourth pose (frame 20)

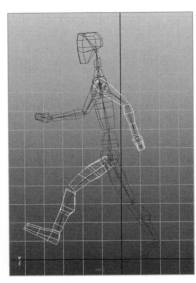

Figure 9.21

The sixth pose (frame 25)

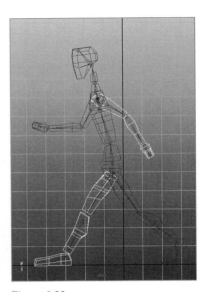

Figure 9.22

The seventh pose (frame 30)

Completing the First Steps

You've finished a set of poses for the character's first step. The next set of poses for your walk cycle corresponds to the first set, but now the other leg and arm correspond to these positions. For example, you animated the left leg taking a step forward in the first series of poses. The next series of poses has to do with the right leg. The pose at frame 35 corresponds to the pose at frame 15. Frame 40 matches frame 20. You will copy keyframes in the Graph Editor to make more steps, but first, let's retime these initial keys before continuing.

When a 30-frame section is complete, you need to return to the animation through the Graph Editor. Adjust all the keyframes that you initially set at these five-frame intervals to make the animation more realistic. Right now, you have only the gross keyframes in place, so the timing is off. Timing the frames properly is ultimately a matter of how the animation looks to you.

Logistically speaking, some poses take a little less time to achieve than the evenly spaced five frames you used. For example, achieving the second pose from the start position should take four frames. The third pose (see Figure 9.18, earlier in the chapter) from frame 5 to frame 10 should take four frames. The next frame section, originally from frame 10 to 15 (the fourth pose; see Figure 9.19, earlier in the chapter), should take only three frames. To accomplish this easily, follow these steps:

1. Select the top node of the skeleton (the pelvis), and open the Graph Editor. On the `pelvis` node in the left side of the Graph Editor, Shift+click the plus sign to open the

entire tree of nodes beneath the pelvis. All the animated channels show their curves, as shown in Figure 9.23 (top).

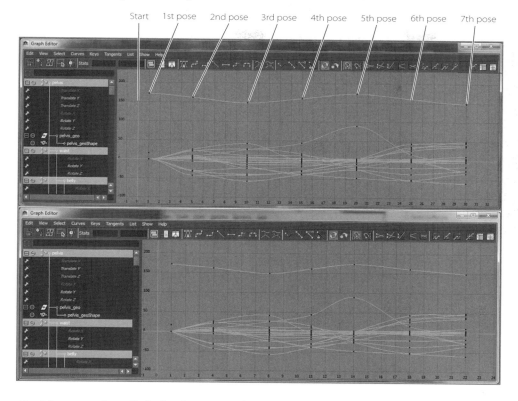

Figure 9.23

The Graph Editor shows the walk animation curves (top). The curves are retimed (bottom).

2. Marquee-select all the keyframes on the curves beyond frame 1, not including those at frame 1. Press the W key to activate the Translate tool. Shift+MMB+click in the Graph Editor (so you can move in only one axis), and drag the keys horizontally to move them all 1 unit (frame) to the left. All the keyframes move, and the second pose now goes from frame 5 to frame 4.

3. Deselect the keys now at frame 4 by holding down the Ctrl key (you also use the Ctrl key on a Mac) and marquee-deselecting all those keys at frame 4. Shift+MMB+click, and drag the remaining selected keys 1 unit to the left again. The third pose goes from being at frame 9 to frame 8.

4. Deselect the keys now at frame 8, and Shift+click and drag the other selected keys to the left two frames so that the fourth pose animates between frame 8 and frame 11. Deselect the frame 11 keys, and move the rest over two frames to the left again so that the next section runs from frame 11 to frame 14. The following section should

go from frame 14 to frame 18. The final section should go from frame 18 to frame 22. Figure 9.23 (bottom) shows the new layout for the curves.

5. Continue to set and adjust keys for another cycle or two of the walk. The majority of time spent in animating something like this involves using the Graph Editor to time out the keyframes to make the animation look believable. Also, try offsetting some of the arm rotations a frame to the left or right to break up the monotony that arises from having everything keyed on the same frame.

Load the file block_walk_v01.mov or block_walk_v01.avi of this walk cycle from the Images folder of the Block_Man project from the companion web page to see the animation in motion. It's a rough cycle, and you have to keep adjusting the character's height to keep the feet on the ground. This is where IK comes in handy, as you'll see later in this chapter. Also, the file block_man_skeleton_walk_v01.mb in the Block_Man project has the keyframed steps for you to play with and continue animating.

Copy and Paste Keyframes

Now that you have a base to work with, you'll copy and paste keyframes to extend the animation further. This can get a little tricky, so take this slow if you're not comfortable with the Graph Editor yet. Open the file block_man_skeleton_walk_v01.mb to follow along with these steps:

1. Extend the Time Range slider to 18 frames, and open the Graph Editor. Select the back (white) leg at the rt_hip joint.

2. In the Graph Editor, Shift+click the plus sign next to the rt_hip entry to see all the joints and all their curves beneath it in the hierarchy.

3. Marquee+select all the keys from frame 4 to frame 22. In the Graph Editor window, select Edit → Copy.

4. Move the Time slider to frame 30, and in the Graph Editor window, select Edit → Paste □. In the option box, set the Paste method to Merge. This setting is very important; otherwise, the curves will not paste properly for your use! Click Apply to paste the keys at frame 30. Figure 9.24 shows the pasted frames in the Graph Editor and the Paste options.

Figure 9.24

Copy and paste keys for the white colored leg.

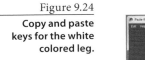
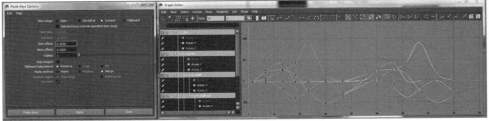

5. Select the other leg (lt_hip), and repeat steps 2 through 4 to copy all the keys from frames 4 through 22. Go to frame 30, and paste (with the Merge option as in step 3) the keys for this leg. Don't forget to Shift+click to expand all the joints beneath the hip joint in the Graph Editor to see, copy, and paste all the joints' keys as you did in step 1.

6. Repeat steps 2 through 4 for each of the two arms (rt_shoulder and lt_shoulder) to copy and paste their keys as well (copying keys from frame 4 through 22 and pasting at frame 30). Again, don't forget to Shift+click them in the Graph Editor (step 2)!

7. If you scrub your animation in the Timeline all the way to frame 48, you can verify that the animation copied properly for the arms and legs.

8. The body is not moving yet, so let's copy and paste those keys now. In the Outliner, Ctrl+select the waist, belly, chest, neck_1, neck_2, and head joints.

9. Repeat steps 3 and 4 to copy and paste keys from frames 4 through 22 to frame 30 as you did with the legs and arms. There is no need to Shift+click any of the joints in the Graph Editor (step 2) this time since you individually selected each of the joints you need. Figure 9.25 shows the pasted frames for the body movement.

10. Scrub your animation, and you'll see you need to copy and paste keys for the pelvis next. Select the pelvis joint.

11. In the Graph Editor, select all the keys from frame 1 to frame 22. This time, go to frame 27, and paste (with the Merge option as before!) the keys.

12. Scrub your animation, and everything should be working great! But around frame 25, you should see the character dip down too far. Simply raise him up and key the pelvis position at frame 25 to compensate, and you're done! The Block Man is walking for a full 48-frame clip now.

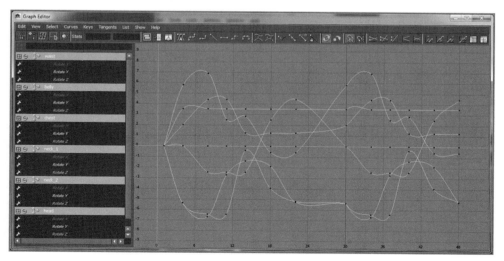

Figure 9.25

Copy and paste keys for the body movement.

Open the file `block_man_skeleton_walk_v02.mb` from the Block_Man project to check your work to this point.

Walk Cycle Wrap-Up

This walk cycle animation is more about getting comfortable with keyframing and skeletons than it is about creating great walk animation, so take some time to practice and get better. Character animation takes a lot of time and patience, and I encourage you to keep tweaking this animation and even create different walks of your own. Animating walk cycles is a good way to hone your skills. Several great books are devoted to character rigging and animation alone, and you can research the field for ways to become more proficient. But keep in mind that movement and timing are what make animation good, not the setup or the model.

Skeletons: The Hand

For another foray into a skeletal system, you can give yourself a hand—literally. You'll use a skeleton to deform the geometry and animate it as a hand would move.

Load the file `poly_hand_skeleton_v01.ma` from the Poly_Hand_Anim project from the companion web page. The hand is shown in Figure 9.26 (top).

You'll use it to create a bone structure to make the hand animate. This process is called *rigging*.

Rigging the Hand

To create the first bones of the hand, follow these steps:

1. Maximize the top view window. Switch to the Animation menu set by using the drop-down menu or by pressing F2.

2. Activate the Joint tool by choosing Skeleton → Joint Tool. Your cursor turns into a cross.

3. Click at the base of the wrist to place the first joint. This will be the root joint of the hand.

4. Shift+click the bottom part of the palm.

5. Place joints down through the thumb from this second joint, according to the corresponding bones in Figure 9.26 (bottom).

6. To start another string of joints into the palm, press the Up arrow key four times until you're at the second joint at the base of the palm.

7. The next joint you place will be a branch from this joint. Place that joint in the middle of the palm. Place another joint up further along the palm, and then branch it out

to the index finger. Press the Up arrow key to return to that upper palm joint, and start a new branch into the middle finger.

Repeat this procedure to place joints for the remaining fingers, as shown in Figure 9.27. With these joints placed, you have a simple skeleton rig for the hand. This rig allows you quite a bit of hand and finger movement.

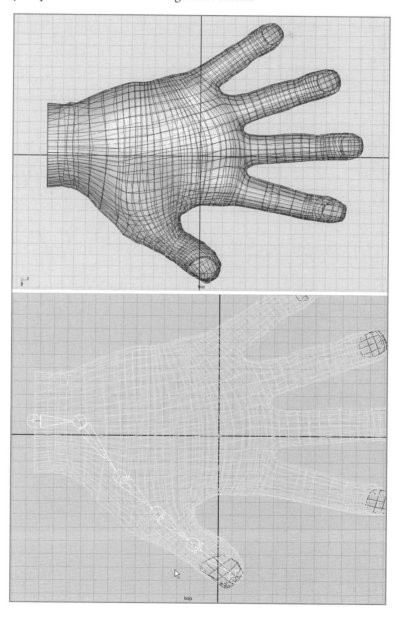

Figure 9.26

The hand mesh (top); placing joints in the hand (bottom)

Figure 9.27

**The joints in
the hand**

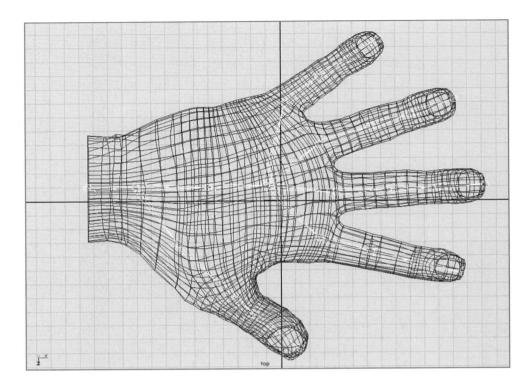

Check the other views (see Figure 9.28) to see where you need to tweak your joint positions to fit the hand. Ideally, you want the joints to be set inside your intended geometry in the same way that real bones are laid out.

To position the joints, you can use either of two Maya tools: Move or Move Pivot. First, you'll try the Move tool. Select the tip joint for the pinkie. It needs to be lowered into the pinkie itself. Select the Move tool (press W), and move it down into the tip of the pinkie. Now, move on to the top pinkie knuckle. Notice that if you move the knuckle, the tip moves as well. That's not such a great idea.

Instead, it's best to move joints as pivots. Because joints are nothing more than pivots, go into Move Pivot mode (hold down the D key to activate Move Pivot, or press the Ins key on Windows or the fn+Home key on a Mac) to move joints. Select the top pinkie-knuckle joint, and move it with Move Pivot instead. Only the joint moves, and the bones adjust to the new position. Set the positions on the remaining joints to be inside the hand properly, as shown in Figure 9.29 and Figure 9.30.

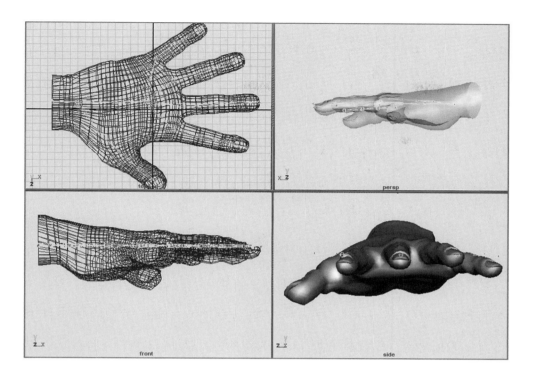

Figure 9.28

Four views of the hand with initial placement of the joints

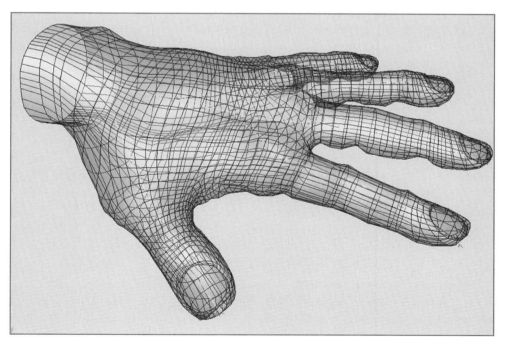

Figure 9.29

The joints of the hand placed properly in the geometry

Figure 9.30

Second view of the hand's skeleton

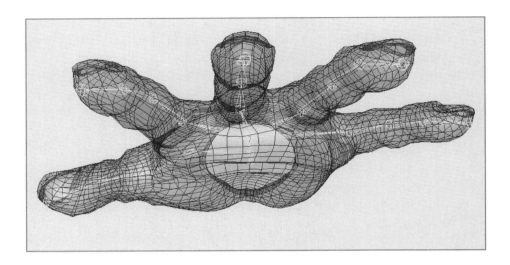

Binding to Geometry

An integral part of rigging a character or an object with a skeleton is *binding*, also known as *skinning*. Binding is another way to attach geometry to a skeletal system. With the Block Man, you directly attached the whole pieces of geometry to the bones through parenting, whereas binding involves attaching *clusters*, or groups of vertices or CVs, of the geometry to the skeleton to allow the skeleton to deform the model. This is typically how skeletons are used in character animation work. (For more on grouping and parenting, refer to the solar system exercise in Chapter 2, "Jumping in Headfirst, with Both Feet.")

The basic technique of binding a character is easy. However, Maya gives you tremendous control over how your geometry deforms.

Binding Overview

Binding is, in theory, identical to the Lattice deformer you saw in Chapter 5, "Modeling with NURBS Surfaces and Deformers." A lattice attached to an object exerts influence over parts of the model according to the sections of the lattice. Each section affects a NURBS surface's CVs or a polygon surface's vertices within its borders—and as a section of the lattice moves, it takes those points of the model with it.

Skeletal binding does much the same thing. It attaches the model's points to the bones, and as the bones pivot around their joints, the section of the model that is attached follows.

By attaching vertices or CVs (depending on your geometry) to a skeleton, you can bend or distort the geometry. When a bone moves or rotates about its joint, it pulls with it the points that are attached to it. The geometry then deforms to fit the new configuration of the bones bound to it.

You can directly bind geometry to a skeleton in three ways: using Smooth Bind, Interactive Skin Bind, and Rigid Bind. You can indirectly deform geometry using deformers and lattices attached to skeletons, but here you'll use the direct methods. Figure 9.31 shows a rigid bind, and Figure 9.32 shows a smooth bind. Note that an interactive skin bind will yield similar results to the smooth bind.

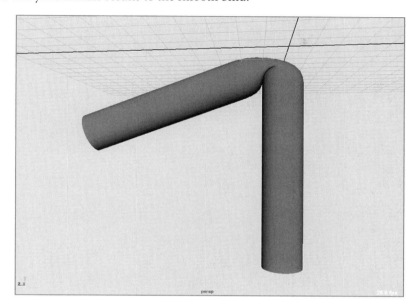

Figure 9.31

Rigid bind of a cylinder. The crease is pronounced.

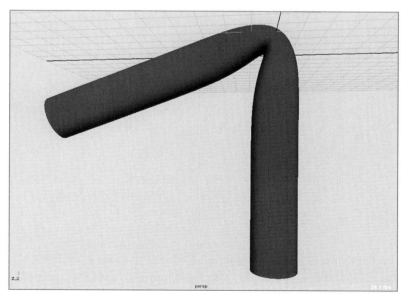

Figure 9.32

Smooth bind of the cylinder. The crease is smoother yet less defined. You may expect this result from the interactive skin bind as well.

Create a tall NURBS cylinder, with a span of 16 or more. The more spans you have in the deformable model, the better it will bend. Duplicate the cylinder, and move it over in your window. Now, in the front view, create a four-bone (five-joint) skeleton that starts at the bottom of the first cylinder and goes straight up the middle, ending at the tip. Duplicate the skeleton, and move it to the center of the second cylinder.

CREATING A RIGID BIND

A rigid bind is the simpler of the two because only one surface point (vertex or CV) is affected by a joint at a time. A *rigid* bind groups the CVs of a NURBS or the vertices of a polygon into *joint clusters* that are then attached to the bones. No one surface point is influenced by more than one joint. You created a rigid bind for the Block Man's feet earlier in the chapter.

Bending a model around a joint with a rigid bind yields a more articulate crease than a smooth bind. A smooth bind allows more than one joint to affect the CV or vertex, resulting in a more rounded and smooth bend.

To create a rigid bind, select the first skeleton and Shift+click its cylinder. In the Animation menu set, choose Skin → Bind Skin → Rigid Bind ❐.

In the option box, you'll find that almost everything you need is already set to the default. The Bind To parameter lets you rigid-bind the entire skeleton to the geometry or rigid-bind only the joints selected. Using Selected Joints gives you the option of using just part of a skeleton system to rigid-bind, which also gives you flexibility in how your rig affects the model. Leave that option set to Complete Skeleton to attach the whole thing.

Click the Color Joints check box to set a different color for each joint in the bind, which can make for an easier workflow. The Bind Method parameter deals with how the points in the model are attached. The default, Closest Point, organizes the points into skin point sets according to the joint to which they're closest. They're then assigned to be influenced by that joint only.

The Partition Set option lets you define your own points before you bind and select which points are set to which joints. If you define a partition set for each joint you have, Maya assigns each set to the nearest joint. For example, you can define some points at the top of the surface to be part of a set controlled by a joint in the bottom part. Closest Point is the best option for most work.

Use the defaults, turn on Color Joints, and click the Bind Skin button in the option box. The root of the skeleton is selected, and the cylinder turns magenta, signifying that it has input connections (such as history).

CREATING A SMOOTH BIND

A *smooth bind* allows a joint to influence more than one skin point on the model. This lets areas of the model farther from the joint bend when that joint rotates. Joints influence points to varying degrees between 0 and 1 across the surface, decreasing in influence the farther the point is from the joint. The multiple influences on a point need to add up to 1 across all the joints that influence it. Maya automatically generates the proper influence amounts upon binding, although the animator can change these values later.

To create a smooth bind, select the second skeleton and its cylinder, and choose Skin → Bind Skin → Smooth Bind ❏.

In the option box, you'll find the familiar Bind To parameter. You'll also find, under the Bind Method drop-down menu, the options Closest In Hierarchy, Heat Map, and Closest Distance. Choosing Closest In Hierarchy assigns the skin points to the nearest joint in the hierarchy. This option is most commonly used for character work, because it pays attention to the way the skeleton is laid out. For example, a surface point on the right leg wouldn't be affected by the thigh joint on the left leg simply because it's near it on the model. Closest Distance, on the other hand, disregards a joint's position in the hierarchy of the skeleton and assigns influences according to how far the point is from the joint. The Heat Map method uses a "heat diffusion" technique to create influence falloff radiating out from the joint.

Max Influences sets a limit on how many joints can affect a single point. Dropoff Rate determines how a joint's influence diminishes on points farther from it. For example, with Smooth Bind, one shoulder joint can influence, to varying degrees, points stretching down the arm and into the chest and belly. By limiting these two parameters, you can control how much of your model is pulled along by a particular joint.

Using all the defaults is typically best. So, click Bind Skin in the option box to smooth-bind your second cylinder to the bones.

Bend both cylinders to get a feel for how each creases at the bending joints. Figure 9.33 shows the difference.

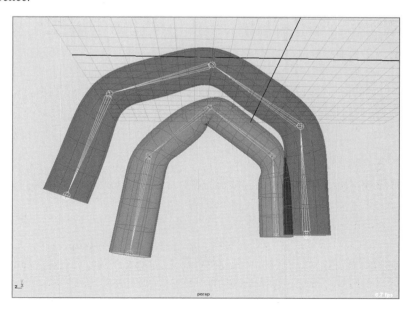

Figure 9.33

Rigid- and smooth-bound cylinders. The smaller cylinder is rigid bound, and the larger is smooth bound.

Interactive Skin Bind is practically the same as Smooth Bind and yields similar results to the smooth binding shown in Figure 9.33, but the editing of the influences is slightly different than for Smooth Bind. You will explore Interactive Skin Bind with the hand model later in this chapter.

DETACHING A SKELETON

If you want to do away with your binding, select the skeleton and its geometry, and choose Skin → Detach Skin. The model will snap to the shape it had before the bind was applied and the joints were rotated. It's common to bind and detach skeletons several times on the same model as you try to figure out the exact configuration that works best for you and your animation.

If you need to go back to the initial position of the skeleton at the point of binding it to the model, you can automatically set the skeleton back to the bind pose after any rotations have been applied to any of its joints. Simply select the skeleton and choose Skin → Go To Bind Pose to snap the skeleton and model into the position they were when you bound them together. It's also best to set your skeleton to the bind pose whenever you edit your binding weights.

A MODELING TRICK USING A SKELETON

An easy way to create bends and creases in a model is to create the surface without the bend and use a skeleton to deform it the way you want. You can then detach the skin and bake the history so that the surface retains its deformation but loses its connection to the skeleton. Bind your geometry to the skeleton chain using Smooth Bind or Rigid Bind. Bend the skeleton to deform the geometry, and then choose Skin → Detach Skin ❑. In the option box, set the History parameter to Bake History, and click Detach. The model will retain its deformed state but will lose all connections to the skeleton. This is just like using a Nonlinear or Lattice deformer on an object and then deleting the object's history to rid it of the deformer. With a detached skin, however, you won't lose any other history already applied to that object like you would if you deleted history through the Edit menu.

Binding the Hand: Rigid

Because you want definitive creases at the finger joints, you'll use Rigid Bind for the hand.

Load your hand and positioned skeleton, or use the file `poly_hand_skeleton_v02.ma` from the Poly_Hand_Anim project from the companion web page. Now, follow these steps to rigid-bind the hand:

1. Select the skeleton's root at the wrist, and Shift+click the top node of the hand. If you're using the file from the web page, select the hand's top node (`handTopNode`) to make sure you select the fingernails as well, as shown in Figure 9.34.

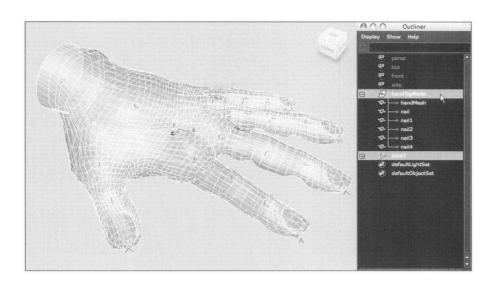

Figure 9.34

Figure 9.34

Select the root joint as well as the top node of the hand.

2. Choose Skin → Bind Skin → Rigid Bind ❐. Turn on Color Joints, and click the Bind Skin button in the option box. The skin is bound, and you're ready to animate the hand. The joints take on colors to help you identify them.

3. Select some of the finger joints and rotate them. Notice how the model creases at the knuckles, as shown with the index finger in Figure 9.35. If you rotate far enough, the model will fold in over itself.

Editing a Rigid Bind

Having a rigid bind doesn't mean your creases always have to be this hard. With *flexors* (basically lattices, as discussed in Chapter 5), you can smooth out specific areas of a joint for a better look. This is useful at shoulder joints or hip joints, where a crease such as on an elbow isn't desired. In this case, it will help smooth out the knuckles so the geometry doesn't fold over itself, as in Figure 9.35.

1. Choose Skin → Go To Bind Pose to reset your skeleton.

2. Select the middle knuckle of the index finger, and choose Skin → Edit Rigid Skin → Create Flexor to open the Create Flexor option box (Figure 9.36).

3. Notice that these options are similar to the lattice you created in Chapter 6, "Practical Experience," to edit the model. You can adjust the number of divisions later through the Attribute Editor, so you don't need to know exactly what you require before you create the flexor. Click Create to display a lattice at the joint position, as shown in Figure 9.37.

Figure 9.35

The crease at the knuckle is severe, and the geometry folds over into itself.

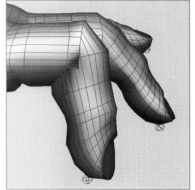

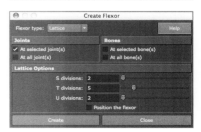

Figure 9.36

Creating a flexor

4. In the Outliner, drill down to the `jointFfd1LatticeGroup` node now attached under that knuckle joint in the hierarchy. Select the lattice as well as its base so you can adjust the size and, if need be, position of the flexor, just as you did on the lattice work earlier. Resize the flexor so that it better conforms to the knuckle, and elongate it so that it covers more of the finger, as shown in Figure 9.38.

5. Scaling and positioning the flexor (when both lattice and base nodes are selected) makes the joint bend more smoothly, without affecting it more than necessary. By elongating the flexor here, you smooth out the knuckle's bend, prevent the polygons from bending over each other, and still maintain a crisp crease, as shown in Figure 9.39.

6. Create flexors for the other knuckles that need them. Be sure to scale the flexors to make the most efficient use of them and fit them only where they need to be fitted. Figure 9.40 shows how the finger reacts when bending with flexors at each joint.

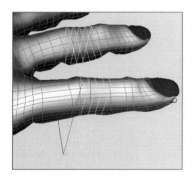

Figure 9.37

Creating a flexor at the middle knuckle

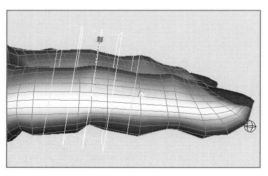

Figure 9.38

Scaling the flexor to fit better on the knuckle

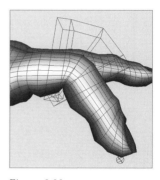

Figure 9.39

The knuckle's crease is now sharp, but the geometry doesn't fold over itself as before.

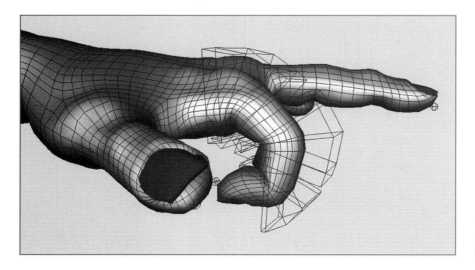

Figure 9.40

Flexors along the index finger

For reference, the scene `poly_hand_skeleton_v03.ma` from the Poly_Hand_Anim project on the companion web page has the hand rigid-bound with flexors on one finger. Start with it to create flexors for the rest of the fingers and animate the hand, making some sign language positions, grabbing a pencil, or pressing a button.

Binding the Hand: Smooth

Now, try skinning the hand with Smooth Bind.

Load your prebound hand or `poly_hand_skeleton_v02.ma` file from the Poly_Hand_ Anim project from the web page. Now, follow these steps to smooth-bind the hand:

1. Select the root at the wrist and the top node of the hand (if you're using the hand from the web page, make sure you have the nails as well). Choose Skin → Bind Skin → Smooth Bind.

2. Try rotating some of the knuckle joints to see how the fingers respond. Go back to the bind pose when you're finished.

3. Rotate the middle knuckle of the index finger down. Notice how the knuckle gets thinner the more you bend the finger there. Go to the top knuckle of the index finger and rotate that joint. Notice that part of the hand moves with the finger. This is again exaggerated because the hand is polygonal, so its deformations seem more severe than a NURBS model of the same hand. Figure 9.41 shows the result of bending at the index finger.

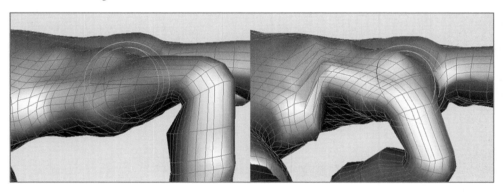

Figure 9.41

Bending at the index finger causes some unwanted deformation.

Editing a Smooth Bind

You usually edit a smooth bind by *painting skin weights*. Because points on the model are influenced by multiple joints in a smooth bind, you need to adjust just how much influence is exerted by these joints on the same points.

1. Make sure you're in Shaded mode (press 5). Select the hand, and then choose Skin → Edit Smooth Skin → Paint Skin Weights Tool ❐.

> You paint skin weights on the affected geometry and not on the joints themselves, so you need to select the model and not the skeleton before invoking this tool.

2. Your hand should turn black, with a bit of light gray at the wrist. The option box appears, listing the joints that are connected to the hand, as shown in Figure 9.42.

3. The color value (between white and black) determines how much binding influence the selected joint in the option box is exerting on that part of the geometry. It's best to name your joints properly so that selecting from this window is easier and more intuitive. If you loaded the file from the web page, you need to name the joints yourself to organize the scene and make working with it easier.

4. In the option box, make sure the Paint Operation button under the Influence section is set to Replace. Change the Value slider to 0. In the Stroke section, Radius(U) and Radius(L) govern the size of your brush. In the Influence section, make sure the Opacity slider is set to 1.

Figure 9.42

The option box for the Paint Skin Weights tool

> To change the size of your Artisan Brush while you're painting weights, you can hold down the B key and drag the mouse left or right to adjust the radius of the brush interactively.

5. Click and paint the black value around parts of the hand and palm that shouldn't be affected by the index finger bending at its top knuckle, as shown in Figure 9.43.

6. Smooth out the area where it goes from white to black. In the option box, in the Influence section, set Paint Operation to Smooth. Right-click to smooth the area around the knuckle for a cleaner deformation. Your index knuckle should now bend beautifully.

> Skin weights must always be normalized in a smooth bind, meaning the values have to add up to 1. When you reduce the influence of a joint on an area of the surface, the influence amount is automatically shifted to other joints in the hierarchy that have influence over that area; those joints are now more responsible for its movement.

You can exit the Paint Skin Weights tool by selecting another tool (press W for Translate, for example), and your view will return to regular Shaded mode. Try bending the rest of the fingers and painting their influences; then, animate the hand, making gestures or grabbing an object using FK animation to set keys on the rotations.

When you paint weights on polygons, keep in mind that you're painting using the UVs. You may need to re-create the UVs of a polygonal mesh with a UV projection map for the Paint Weights tool to function properly, especially when you're importing and exporting the weight maps from one mesh to another (a procedure you won't encounter until later in your Maya experience).

The scene `poly_hand_skeleton_v04.ma` from the Poly_Hand_Anim project from the companion web page has the hand smooth-bound with painted weights on the index finger for your reference. Try painting the other knuckles as needed for your animation.

Rigging work is essential for getting a good animation from your model. In a professional shop, it usually falls under the domain of a technical director (TD) who oversees the setup of characters and may also model their geometry. The more time I spent rigging scenes for the animators when I was a TD on the television show *South Park*, the easier and faster they were able to accomplish their animations.

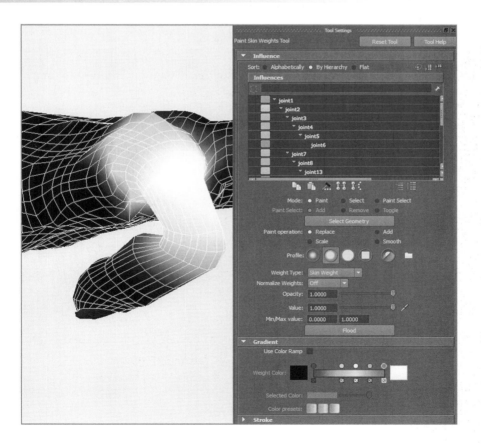

Figure 9.43

Paint the new weights to avoid unwanted deformations in the hand.

Binding the Hand: Interactive Skin Bind

Now, try skinning the hand with Interactive Skin Bind.

Load your own prebound hand or `poly_hand_skeleton_v02.ma` file from the Poly_Hand_Anim project from the web page.

The Interactive Skin Bind method is a bit easier to control when compared to the painting of the Smooth Bind weights. However, one limitation of Interactive Skin Bind compared to Smooth Bind is that it recognizes only a single mesh to be bound to the skeleton. In other words, you cannot bind the current hand as it is, since the fingernails are separate objects. But that is easy enough to fix.

1. Select the `handMesh` and all the nails in the Outliner, and in the Polygons menu set, choose Mesh → Combine. This turns all the different meshes into a single mesh.

2. The original nodes of the hand are still seen in the Outliner. With the new mesh still selected, choose Edit → Delete By Type → History to rid the mesh of any history. This will remove the original hand's nodes from the scene.

3. Rename the new mesh to **handMesh** in the Outliner.

4. Select the root joint at the wrist and the combined `handMesh` object, and choose Skin → Bind Skin → Interactive Skin Bind. Figure 9.44 shows the color scheme of a volume manipulator that allows you to set the initial skin weights of the hand easily.

5. In the Outliner, select the different joints of the hand to see how the interactive binding shows the volume influences. Then select the top knuckle of the index finger. Figure 9.45 shows the influence. Select the red circle at the end of the volume manipulator and size it down to reduce the influence on the middle finger, as shown in Figure 9.46.

Figure 9.44

The volume manipulator shows the influence of the selected joint.

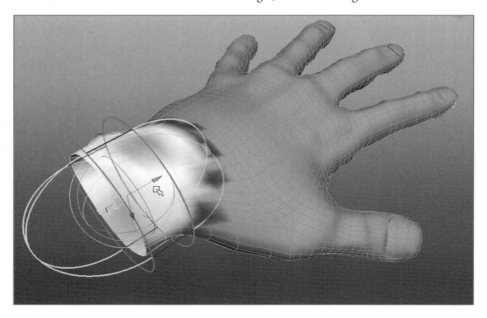

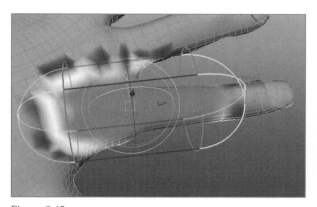

Figure 9.45

The index finger's first knuckle influences the middle finger, too.

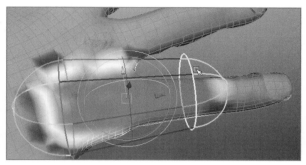

Figure 9.46

Use the volume manipulator to reduce the influence on the middle finger.

6. Grab the green, spherical end, and you can see that you can move that in or out to lengthen or shorten the volume manipulator. You can use the move or rotate handles to move the volume as well. Make adjustments to the finger to remove influences on the middle finger and other undesired areas of the hand, as shown in Figure 9.47. This is a bit similar to placing flexors as you did with the rigid binding earlier in this chapter.

Figure 9.47

Set the influences by adjusting the volume manipulator.

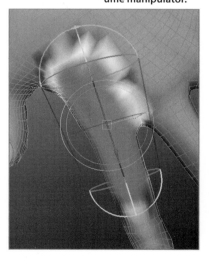

Editing the interactive skin bind, as you can see, is very easy using the volume manipulators. If you exited the tool when you first created the bind and no longer see the volume manipulators, you can access them by choosing Skin → Edit Smooth Skin → Interactive Skin Bind Tool. When you access this tool, the volume manipulators appear again, and you're able to adjust your skin's influences.

When you are happy with the proper level of influence, keep picking the other joints in the index finger to make sure your binding is proper. Then continue to the other fingers to set up the binding on the hand properly. This is definitely easier than painting weights as before, though not as controllable. Test the bind by bending the joints. You can compare your work to the prebound hand found in the `poly_hand_interactiveBind_v01.ma` scene file in the Poly_Hand_Anim project.

Inverse Kinematics

With IK, you have tools that let you plant a foot where it needs to be so you're not always moving the skeleton or model to compensate and keep the heel in place.

For legs, IK is nothing short of a blessing. There is no clearly preferable workflow to suggest when dealing with rigging arms and hands, however. Many people use IK on hands as well, but it can be better to animate the legs with IK and animate every other part of the body with FK. IK is best used when parts of the body (such as the feet) need to be planted at times. Planting the hands isn't necessary for a walk cycle, and having IK handles on the arms may create additional work while you are animating them. You will create a more well-rounded character rig that uses IK and easy-to-use character controls at the end of the chapter. First, let's get familiar with how IK works.

Rigging IK Legs

Back to the Block Man. Switch to that project, and load your version or the block_man_ skeleton_v02.mb file from the Block_Man project from the companion web page.

You'll create an IK chain from the hip to the ankle on each foot. Creating the IK from the hip to the toe won't work.

Because IK automatically bends the joints in its chain according to where its end effector, or IK handle, is located, it has to choose which way to bend at a particular joint. This is why you created the legs slightly bent in the Block Man rig earlier in the chapter.

If you did not do this or your setup has straight legs for whatever reason, select the two knee joints, and in Pivot mode (hold down the D key), move the knees forward a bit over the feet to create a slight crook in the legs. Don't go too far; a slight amount is enough. This lets the IK solver know which way those joints are supposed to go.

Now, on to creating the IK:

1. Open the IK Handle tool by choosing Skeleton ⇒ IK Handle Tool. Your cursor changes to a cross.

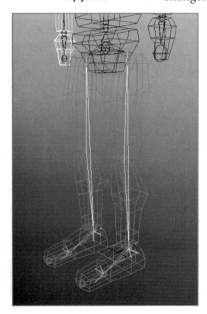

Figure 9.48

IK handles on both ankles with the roots at the hip joints

2. Select the start joint for the IK chain. This will be the root of this chain. Click the left thigh joint, and then pick your end effector at the ankle joint. The bones in the IK chain turn brown. Repeat this procedure for the other leg. Figure 9.48 shows handles on both ankles.

    If for some reason you can't manage to pick a joint for the IK tool, make sure Show ⇒ Pivots is turned on in your view panel. Also, if you have difficulty seeing the handles, you can increase their size by choosing Display ⇒ Animation ⇒ IK Handle Size.

3. Move the IK handles around, and see how the legs react. When you're finished, reset the IK handle positions.

4. Grab the top joint of the skeleton, which is the pelvis joint. Move the joint, and the entire body moves with it. Select both ankle IK handles, and set a translation key for them (press Shift+W). Grab the pelvis joint again and move it. The feet stick to their positions on the ground. Move the pelvis down, and the legs bend at the knees. Notice how the feet bend into the ground, though (see Figure 9.49, left).

5. Move the pelvis back to the origin. You can create an IK handle for the foot so that the foot stays flat on the ground. Open the IK Handle tool. For the start joint, select the first ankle; for the end effector, select the joint in the middle of that foot (lt_ballFoot or rt_ballFoot). Repeat for the other foot.

You can invoke the last tool you used by pressing Y.

7. Set a translate key for the foot IK handles. Move the pelvis down; the legs bend at the knees and the ankle, keeping the feet flush on the ground (see Figure 9.49, right).

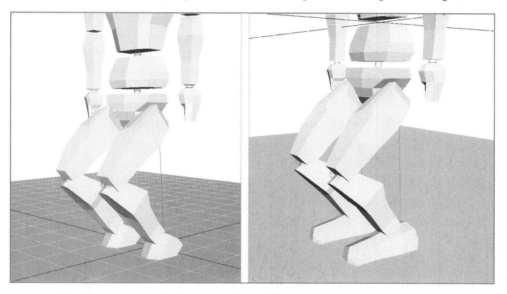

Figure 9.49

Creating another IK chain from the ankle to the tip of the foot and setting keyframes makes the feet stay on the ground (right) and not rotate into the ground (left).

Creating an IK Walk Animation

Because the Block Man's feet will stick to the ground, creating a walk cycle with IK animation is far easier than using FK (why didn't you tell us that before?). Making the animation look good is still a tough job that requires a lot of practice, though.

Load the scene file block_man_IK_v01.mb from the Block_Man project from the companion web page, or use your own IK-rigged Block Man with handles at the ankles and feet. The white leg and arm are, again, on the far side of the character. You'll set keys every five frames again for the gross animation. To keep this short, I'll just discuss setting poses with the feet. You can always return to the scene to add animation to the upper body with FK, as you did earlier in this chapter. Follow these steps:

1. On frame 1, set translate keys on the pelvis joint and all four IK handles for their start position.

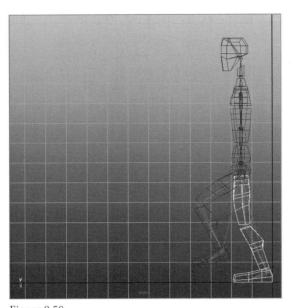

Figure 9.50
Step 3's pose (frame 5)

2. Go to frame 5, and move the pelvis forward about 1 unit. The legs and feet lift off the ground a bit and strain to keep their position, but they stay back. Lower the pelvis to get the feet flat on the ground again. Set a key for the pelvis. Because Auto Keyframe is turned on, all keys are set for this animation. (With the FK animation, you set keys for everything at every pose.)

3. Grab both near IK handles for the ankle and foot (blue leg), and move them forward and up to match the pose shown in Figure 9.50.

4. Go to frame 10. Move the front foot forward, and plant it on the ground. Move the pelvis another three-fourths of a unit. Set translation keys for the rear ankle and foot handles where they are. Be sure to place the pelvis so that the rear foot is almost flat on the ground. Match the pose shown in Figure 9.51.

5. Go to frame 15. Move the pelvis another 2 units to center the body over the front foot. Lift the rear ankle and foot IK handles up to bend the knee, and bring the knee up a bit. Match the pose shown in Figure 9.52.

6. Go to frame 20. Move the pelvis forward 1 unit, and swing the white leg forward as in the pose shown in Figure 9.53.

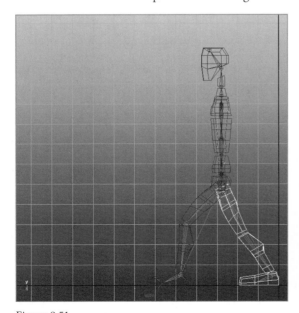

Figure 9.51
Step 4's pose (frame 10)

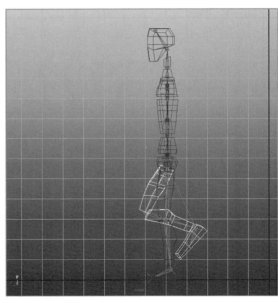

Figure 9.52
Step 5's pose (frame 15)

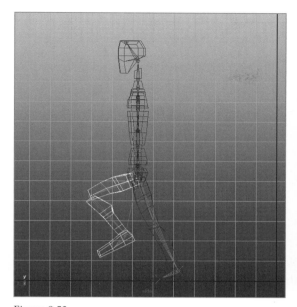

Figure 9.53

Step 6's pose (frame 20)

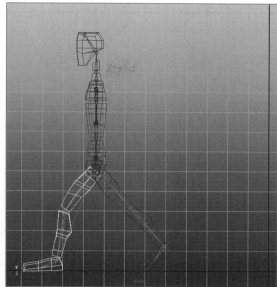

Figure 9.54

Step 7's pose (frame 25)

7. Move the pelvis three-fourths of a unit forward and plant the front leg down. Set keys for the rear leg and foot where they stand. Match the pose shown in Figure 9.54.

The next pose should match the pose in frame 10, although with the other leg. Continue the cycle, with each successive pose matching the one 15 frames before it on the opposite side.

At the end of this chapter, you'll take this one step further and create a simple character animation rig for the entire Block Man so you can have a nicely functioning character for animation.

Further Uses for IK Chains

Many animators use IK chains more often in effects animation than in character work. IK chains can drive whips and ropes, flutter flags, bounce ponytails, and pump pistons as well as move legs and arms. For example, you can use a different type of IK chain, the *spline* IK chain, to control the shape of your bone chain with a NURBS spline. This IK chain is great for snakes and other long, deforming objects.

To create a spline IK chain, choose Skeleton → IK Spline Handle Tool, and then select your top joint and end effector. Maya creates a spline running the length of the bone chain. Adjusting the curvature of the spline in turn drives the bones, which in turn drive the geometry bound to them. Figure 9.55 shows a spline curve affecting the curvature of the bones in its spline IK chain.

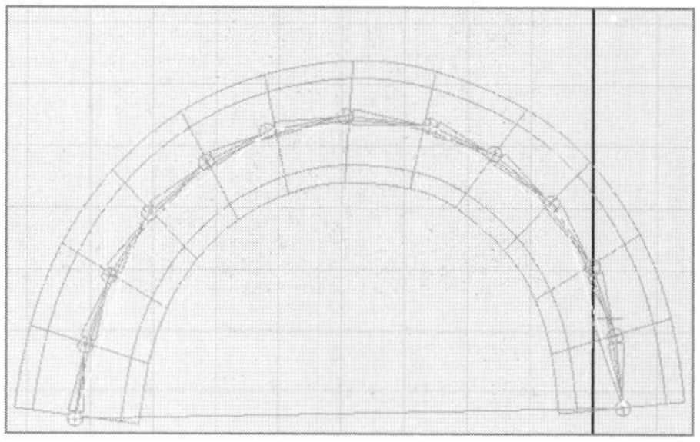

Figure 9.55

A spline IK chain is driven by the curvature of a NURBS spline. Adjusting the curve's CVs moves the joints.

Basic Relationships: Constraints

As you know, Maya is all about the relationships between object nodes. You can create animation on one object based on the animation of another object by setting up a relationship between the objects. The simplest way to do that (outside of grouping) is to create a *constraint*. For example, you can "glue" one object to another's position or rotation through a constraint.

A constraint creates a direct relationship between the source and the target object's Translate, Rotate, or Scale attributes. This section explores six types of constraints: point, orient, scale, aim, geometry, and normal.

The Point Constraint

To attach a source object to a target object but have the source follow only the position of the target, use a *point constraint*. A point constraint connects only the Translate attributes of the source to the target. To use this method, select the target object(s) and then Shift+click the source object. In the Animation menu set, choose Constrain → Point ❑.

Constraints are based on the pivots of the objects, so a point constraint snaps the source at its pivot point to the pivot point of the target and keeps it there, even in animation. But the options allow you to set an offset that creates a gap between the source and the target.

You can constrain the same source to more than one target object. The source then takes up the average position between the multiple targets. By setting the Weight slider in the option box, you can create more of an influence on the source by any of the targets.

In Figure 9.56, a cone has been point-constrained to a sphere. Wherever the sphere goes, the cone follows. This is different from parenting the cone to the sphere in that only its translations are affected by the sphere. If you rotate or scale the sphere, the cone won't rotate or scale with it.

Figure 9.56

A cone point that is constrained to a sphere follows that sphere's position.

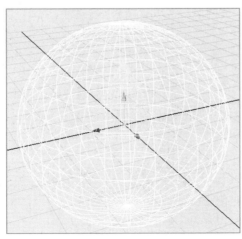

Although you can blend keyframe animation with constraint animation, as a beginner to Maya, consider that after you set a point constraint like that shown in Figure 9.56, you're unable to control the cone's Translate attributes because they're being driven by the sphere's translations.

Point constraints are perfect to animate a character carrying a cane or a sword, for example. The rotations on the sword are still free to animate, but the sword is attached to the character's belt and follows the character throughout the scene.

The Orient Constraint

An *orient constraint* attaches the source's Rotation attributes to the target's Rotation attributes. Select the target object(s) first, and then Shift+click the source object. In the Animation menu set, choose Constrain → Orient ☐.

The Offset parameter allows you to set an offset in any axis. Otherwise, the source assumes the exact orientation of the target. In the case of multiple targets, the source uses the average of their orientations. Figure 9.57 shows the cone's orientation following an elongated sphere (the target).

A rotation constraint saves a lot of hassle when you have to animate an object to keep rotating in the same direction as another object. For example, you can use the rotation of one wheel of a locomotive to drive the rotation of all the other wheels.

The Point on Poly Constraint

A *point on poly constraint* attaches a source object to a vertex of a mesh. Select the target object's vertex first, and then Shift+click the object you want to place at that point (Figure 9.58, left). In the Animation menu set, choose Constrain → Point On Poly ☐.

The object is snapped to the vertex of the target at its pivot point. Even if the target object is animated and deforming, like a character, the object will stay on that vertex. Figure 9.58 (right) shows the sphere pinned to the branch at the selected vertex location.

The point on poly constraint is good for pinning objects together, such as leaves on a branch.

Figure 9.57

The cone's rotations match the sphere's rotations.

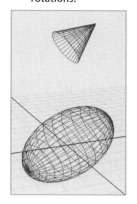

Figure 9.58

The red ball is placed on the tree branch like a fruit with a point on poly constraint.

Selected vertex

The Aim Constraint

The *aim constraint* adjusts the source's rotations so that the source always points to the target object. Select the target object(s) first, and then Shift+click the source object. In the Animation menu set, choose Constrain → Aim ❐.

The aim constraint has more options than the other constraints because you need to specify which axis of the source is to point to the target. You do so using the Aim Vector and Up Vector settings.

The Aim Vector setting specifies which axis of the source is the "front" and points to the target. In the cone and sphere examples, you set the Aim Vector of the cone to **(0,1,0)** to make the Y-axis the front so that the cone's point aims at the sphere. If Aim Vector is set to **(1,0,0)**, for example, the cone's side points to the sphere. Figure 9.59 shows the cone pointing to the sphere with an Aim Vector setting of (0,1,0).

Figure 9.59

The cone aiming at the sphere

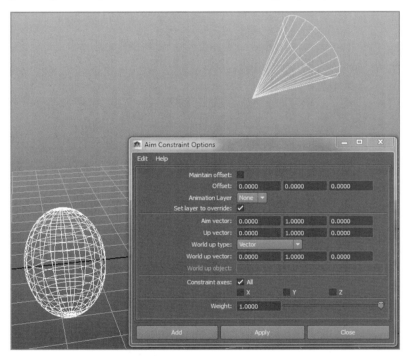

The Offset values create an offset on the source's Rotation attributes, tilting it one way or another. The Up Vector setting specifies which way the cone faces when it's pointing to the sphere.

Aim constraints are perfect for animating cameras to follow a subject, such as a car at a racetrack.

Geometry and Normal Constraints

The *geometry* and *normal constraints* constrain the source object to the surface of the target object (as long as it's a NURBS or poly mesh).

With a geometry constraint, the source object attaches, at its pivot point, to the surface of the target. It tries to keep its own position as best it can, shifting as its target surface changes beneath it. Again, select the target, select the source object, and choose Constrain → Geometry.

A geometry constraint is useful when you want to keep an object on a deforming surface, such as a floating boat on a lake. Figure 9.60 shows the cone after it has been geometry-constrained to a NURBS plane that is being deformed by a Wave deformer (choose Create Deformers → Nonlinear → Wave). The cone sits on the surface as the waves ripple through, but it doesn't rock back and forth to stay oriented with the surface.

Figure 9.60

With a geometry constraint, the cone sits on the deforming surface.

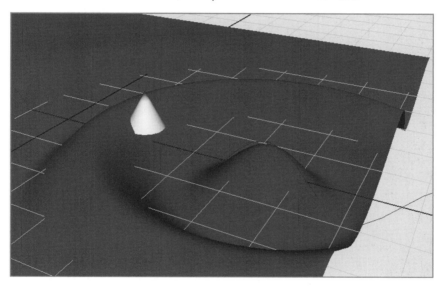

To get the cone to orient itself so that it truly floats on the surface, you need to use a normal constraint. Using a normal constraint rotates the cone to follow the surface's normals, keeping it perpendicular to the surface.

A *surface normal* is an imaginary perpendicular tangent line that emanates from all surfaces to give the surface direction.

The normal constraint is similar to the aim constraint, and its options are similar. Using the Aim Vector setting, you specify which way is up for the object to define the orientation that the source should maintain. However, this setting doesn't constrain the location of the source to the target. If you want a floating effect, use geometry and a normal constraint to get the cone to bob up and down and roll back and forth as the waves ripple along (see Figure 9.61).

Figure 9.61

The cone now animates to float on the water surface, using both geometry and normal constraints.

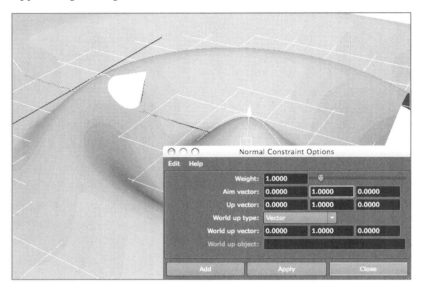

Scale, Parent, Tangent, and Pole Vector Constraints

Four more constraints are possible in Maya: the scale, parent, tangent, and pole vector constraints. Simply, a *scale constraint* attaches the source's Scale attributes to the target's Scale attributes. A *parent constraint* constrains an object's translation and rotation to another object by mimicking a parent-child relationship without actually parenting the objects. This keeps objects aligned without worrying about any grouping issues. You'll have a firsthand look at this in the exercise where you rig the locomotive later in this chapter. Lucky you!

A *tangent constraint* keeps an object's orientation so that the object always points along a curve's direction. This constraint is usually used with a geometry constraint or path animation to keep the object traveling along a curve pointed in the right direction, no matter the direction of the curve. A point on poly constraint allows you to select a vertex on a poly mesh and constrain an object to that vertex. *Pole vector constraints* are used extensively in character animation rigs to keep IK joints from flipping beyond 180 degrees of motion.

Basic Relationships: Set-Driven Keys

A favorite feature for animation riggers is the *set-driven key* (SDK). An SDK establishes a relationship for objects that lets you create controls that drive certain features of a character or an object in a scene.

Before you can use an SDK, you must create extra attributes and attach them to a character's top node. These new attributes drive part of the character's animation. The term *character* is used broadly here. For example, you can set up a vehicle so that an SDK turns its wheels.

Let's start with a simple SDK relationship between two objects. You'll create a relationship between a ball and a cone. As the ball moves up in the *Y*-axis, the cone spins in the *X*-axis. As the ball descends, the cone spins back. You'll then revisit the hand and set up an SDK on the skeleton that animates the model.

Creating a Set-Driven Key

To create a simple SDK to make a sphere control the animation of a cone's rotation, follow these steps:

1. Create a NURBS sphere and a cone in a new scene. Move the cone to the side of the sphere and lay it on its side, as shown in Figure 9.62.

2. Select the sphere, and in the Animation menu set, choose Animate → Set Driven Key → Set. The Set Driven Key window opens with the nurbsSphere1 object selected in the lower half of the window (the Driven section). Its attributes are listed on the right, as you can see in Figure 9.63.

3. You want the sphere to drive the animation of the cone, so you need to switch the sphere to be the driver and not what's driven. Click the Load Driver button to list the sphere in the top half of the window.

4. Select the cone, and click the Load Driven button to display the cone's attributes in the bottom half of the window.

5. In the Driver section, select the sphere's Translate Y attribute. In the Driven section, select the cone's Rotate X attribute. Click the Key button to set an SDK that essentially says that when the sphere is on the ground (*Y* = 0), the cone's *X* rotation is 0 because

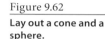

Figure 9.62

Lay out a cone and a sphere.

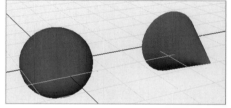

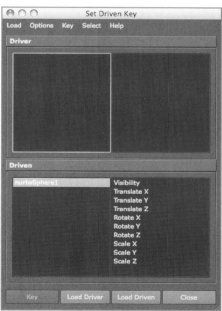

Figure 9.63

The Set Driven Key window

both attributes are currently 0. The cone's Rotate X attribute turns orange in the Channel Box, meaning a driven key has been set.

6. Select the sphere, and raise it in *Y* to a height of **5**. Select the cone, and rotate it in *X* to **1800** to make it spin properly. Click the Key button in the Set Driven Key window to specify that when the sphere is at a height of **5**, the cone's Rotate X attribute is **1800** degrees. As the sphere's height increases from 0 to 5, the cone spins from 0 to 1800 in *X*.

An Advanced Set-Driven Key: The Hand

Automating some animations on a character is indispensable to an animator. This can't be truer than when setting up an SDK for hand control. After you model and bind a hand to a skeleton, you're ready for an SDK.

Open the scene poly_hand_skeleton_v05.ma from the Poly_Hand_Anim project from the companion web page, or use your own file that has the hand and its skeleton and is bound (either smooth or rigid) to the skin. Your file shouldn't have animation, though. Set your hand to the bind pose before you begin.

Creating a New Attribute

First, you'll create a new attribute called index_pull to control a contracting finger.

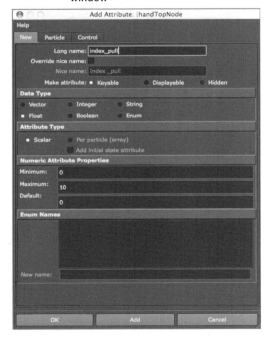

Figure 9.64

The Add Attribute window

1. Select the hand. (It's best to select the top node, handTopNode, instead of just the poly mesh of the hand.) In the handTopNode tab of the Attribute Editor, click the Extra Attributes section. For now, at least, this section is empty.

2. In the Attribute Editor menu, choose Attributes → Add Attributes to open the Add Attribute window, which is shown in Figure 9.64. In the Long Name field, enter **index_pull**. Maya will automatically display that attribute as Index Pull in the UI. Make sure the Make Attribute Keyable option is selected and that the Float option is selected in the Data Type section. In the Numeric Attribute Properties section, set Minimum to **0**, Maximum to **10**, and Default to **0**. Click OK.

After you click OK, the Index_Pull slider appears in the Attribute Editor and the Channel Box. This attribute alone will control the entire index finger.

Assigning the Set-Driven Key

To set up the relationships with the SDK, follow these steps:

1. With the top hand node selected, open the Set Driven Key window (choose Animate → Set Driven Key → Set). Click Load Driver to specify that the hand should drive the animation.

2. Because you're animating the index finger pulling back, you want to drive the rotations of the top three knuckles. Shift+click all three knuckles on the index finger. Click the Load Driven button. All three knuckles appear on the bottom.

3. Select the hand's Index Pull attribute and the three knuckles' Rotate Y attributes, as shown in Figure 9.65.

4. With the rotations of the knuckles at 0 and the index_pull attribute at 0 as well, click the Key button to set the first relationship. When index_pull is at 0, the finger is extended.

5. Select the top hand node, and set the index_pull attribute to 5.

6. Select the fingertip's knuckle (joint11 in the web page file), and rotate it in Y to 20. Select the next joint up the chain (the middle knuckle, joint10), and rotate it to 35 in the Y-axis. Select the final index knuckle (joint9), and rotate it in the Y-axis to 5. Click the Key button. When the index_pull attribute is at 5, the finger assumes this bent position.

7. Select the top hand node, and set index_pull to 10.

8. Select each of the three knuckles. Set the tip to rotate to 65 in Y. Set the middle knuckle to 60. Set the last knuckle to 50. Click the Key button to see the result shown in Figure 9.66.

Select the top hand node, and change the value of the index_pull attribute to animate your finger. All you need to do to pull the finger is to set keys on that attribute, without having to rotate the knuckles constantly. Furthermore, you can set up a single SDK to control the bending of all the fingers at once, or you can set up one SDK for each finger for more control.

Open the scene poly_hand_skeleton_v06.ma from the Poly_Hand_Anim project available on the companion web page to see the hand with the SDK set up on the index finger.

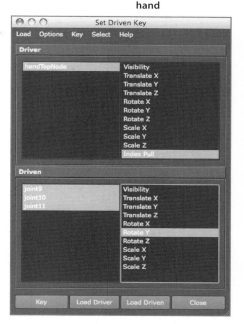

Figure 9.65

The Set Driven Key window for the hand

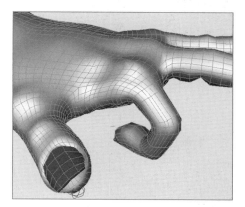

Figure 9.66

The bent index finger

Application: Rigging the Locomotive

Let's get back to our locomotive. In the previous chapter, you made sure the hierarchy and pivot placements were proper. In this exercise, you can use the `locomotive_anim_v1.mb` file from the previous chapter. You can also use a fancy version of the locomotive, called `fancy_locomotive_anim_v1.mb`; it's set up similarly to `locomotive_anim_v1.mb` for the exercise. This scene is shown in Figure 9.67.

Figure 9.67

The fancier locomotive model

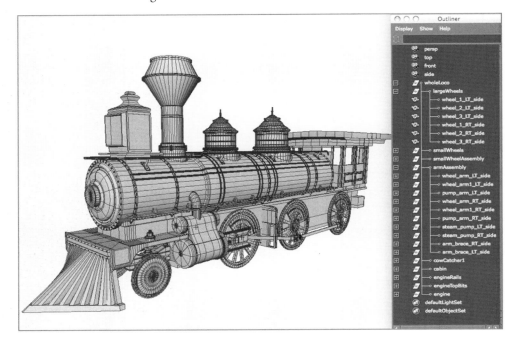

Setting Up Wheel Control

Your goal here is to rig the scene to animate all the secondary movements automatically based on some simple controls, such as you did for the hand earlier this chapter. In reality, the locomotive's steam pump drives the arms that then turn the wheels on the locomotive. You'll work backward, however, and use one wheel to drive the animation of everything else.

> As a challenge, you can also try this exercise of rigging the locomotive wheel's to rotate in unison by using rotation constraints instead of the Connection Editor.

Because all the large wheels have the same diameter, they rotate the same as the locomotive moves. In this case, you'll use the Connection Editor to attach the *X* Rotation on all the wheels to your main control wheel. You'll pick the middle wheel to be the control. To set up the locomotive, follow these steps:

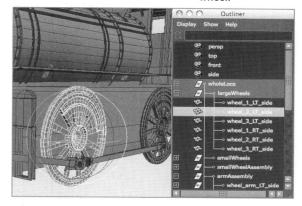

Figure 9.68

Select the middle wheel.

1. Select the middle wheel on the left side of the locomotive (node `wheel_2_LT_side`), as shown in Figure 9.68. Open the Connection Editor (choose Window → General Editors → Connection Editor). Click the Reload Left button to load the attributes of the selected middle wheel. Now, select the front wheel on the left side, and click the Reload Right button.

2. Scroll down in the Connection Editor until you find Rotate in both columns. Click to highlight Rotate in the left column, and then click to highlight Rotate in the right column. Doing so connects the two rotations so that they both rotate at the same time, effectively letting you drive the animation of both wheels from just the center wheel. Figure 9.69 shows the Connection Editor.

3. Select the back wheel on the left side (`wheel_3_LT_side`). Click the Reload Right button in the Connection Editor. Connect the Rotate attribute for the middle and back wheels. Close the Connection Editor, and select just the middle wheel. When you rotate the wheel, all three wheels rotate together.

4. Repeat this procedure to connect the rotations of the three wheels on the other side to this middle wheel as well. Now all six wheels rotate in sync with the one control wheel. When you select that left-side middle wheel (the control wheel), the other five wheels turn magenta, signifying a connection between these objects.

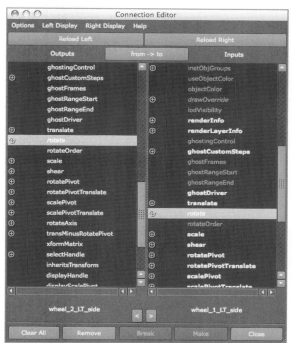

Figure 9.69

Connect the rotations of the two wheels.

If you get strange results when you connect the rotations of objects (for example, if the wheels flip over or rotate the opposite direction of the control wheel), try disconnecting all the connections, freezing transforms, and reconnecting the attributes.

Controlling the Wheel Arms

You've now automated the animation of the wheels. Next, you'll figure out how to connect the wheel arms to the wheels and drive their motion as well. To do so, follow these steps:

1. Create a single joint that lines up with the first wheel arm. The root joint is placed where the wheel arm meets the middle wheel (control wheel), and the end joint is placed where the wheel arm meets the pump arm, as shown in Figure 9.70. The pump arm has been templated in this graphic (displays in light gray wireframe) to show you the entire wheel arm and joint.

Figure 9.70

Create a joint from the middle wheel to the pump arm at the first wheel.

2. Group the joint under the control wheel's node, as shown in the Outliner in Figure 9.71. Then, group the wheel arm under the top joint. This way, the joint rotates with the control wheel, also shown in Figure 9.71, albeit incorrectly for the pump arm.

3. As you saw in Figure 9.71, the joint isn't rotating properly to make the pump arm work right. The other end of it needs to attach to the pump arm in front of the front wheel, not fly up in space. You can use an IK handle for this. Make sure the rotation of the control wheel and the joint/wheel arm are set back to **0** to place them in the original position. In the Animation menu set, choose Skeleton → IK Handle Tool. Make sure the settings are reset for the tool. Select the root joint as the start joint for the IK handle. Select the other tip of the bone as the end effector. You now have an IK handle at the tip where the wheel arm connects to the pump arm, as shown in Figure 9.72.

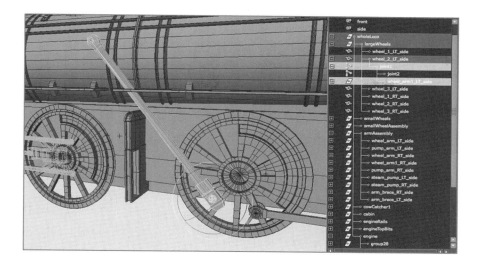

Figure 9.71

Group the top joint under the wheel, and then group the wheel arm under the top joint.

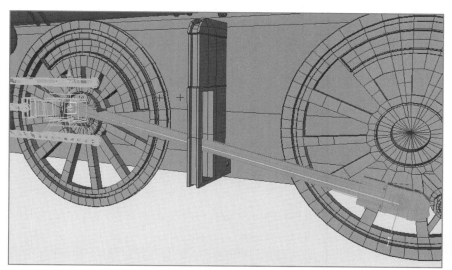

Figure 9.72

Place the end effector where the pump arm and the first wheel connect.

4. If you rotate the control wheel now, the wheel arm still separates from the pump arm. This is because the IK handle you just created needs a keyframe to keep it in position—that is, attached to the pump arm. Select the IK handle, and, at frame 1, set a position keyframe. Now, if you rotate the control wheel, the joint and wheel arm pump back and forth.

5. Group the IK handle (ikHandle1) under the top node of the locomotive (wholeLoco), as shown in Figure 9.73.

Figure 9.73

Group the IK handle under the locomotive's top node.

Controlling the Pump Arm

Next, you need to attach the pump arm to the wheel arm so that it pumps back and forth as the control wheel turns. If you simply group the pump arm with the end joint of the wheel arm's bone, the pump arm will float up and down as it pumps back and forth. You need to use a constraint to force the pump arm to move back and forth only in the Z-axis.

1. Make sure the control wheel is set back to 0 rotation. Select the pump arm, templated in Figure 9.74 so that you can see through to the wheel arm and joint, and line up its pivot with the end joint of the wheel arm bone.

2. Select the end joint (called `joint2`), Ctrl+click the pump arm group in the Outliner (called `pump_arm_LT_side`), and, in the Animation menu set, choose Constrain → Point ❑. In the option box, uncheck All under Constraint Axes, select only Z to constrain the pump arm only in the Z-axis, and click the Add button. Now if you rotate the control wheel, you see the pump arm and wheel arm connected. The pump arm pumps back and forth, although you'll immediately notice a need to adjust the model to make the piece fit when it animates. Figure 9.75 shows that the pump arm's geometry isn't yet quite right for animation. This is very normal for this process and luckily needs only a quick fix.

Figure 9.74

Line up the pivot of the pump arm with the end joint of the wheel arm joint.

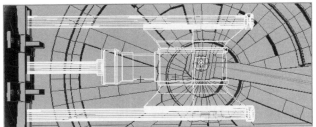

3. To fix the pump arm, select the vertices on the ends of the cylinders, and extend them to make them longer, as shown in Figure 9.76. Now the pump arm won't pull out of the steam pump assembly.

4. Adjust the pump arm so that the geometry fits when the pump pushes in as well.

The scene file `fancy_locomotive_anim_v2.mb` will catch you up to this point. Compare it to your work.

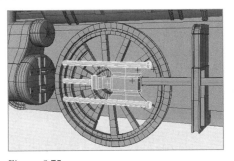

Figure 9.75

The pump arm is too short!

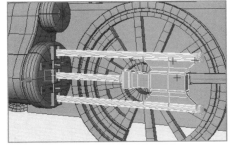

Figure 9.76

Use vertices to extend the pump arm.

Controlling the Back Wheel

All that remains is to control the animation of the back wheel and its wheel arm. To set up the wheel arm animation, follow these steps:

1. Using the methods described in the steps in the "Controlling the Wheel Arms" section, create a joint to follow along the wheel arm between the middle control wheel and the back wheel. The root of the joint is set at the control wheel, as shown in Figure 9.77.

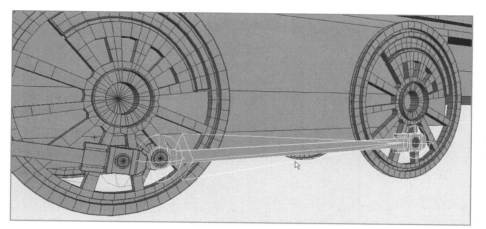

Figure 9.77

Create a joint to control the back wheel arm.

2. As before, create an IK handle for the end joint of this new bone, where it meets the back wheel, as shown in Figure 9.78. Make sure the handle is at the back wheel, not the middle control wheel.

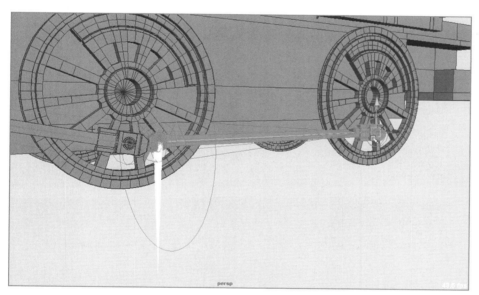

Figure 9.78

Create an IK handle to attach the wheel arm and the back wheel to the control wheel.

3. Group the new joint under the master wheel, and then group the wheel arm under this new joint. If you rotate the control wheel, the wheel arm rotates with the joint and wheel but doesn't connect to the back wheel yet. You need to attach the IK handle you just created for that joint to the back wheel.

If you group the IK handle, as shown in Figure 9.79, you'll run into a problem when you animate. Let's try it: group the IK handle (ikHandle2) under the end back wheel, as shown in Figure 9.79, and then rotate the control wheel. The wheel arm pumps back and forth along with the back wheel, but every now and then the wheel arm geometry flips over backward. This isn't good.

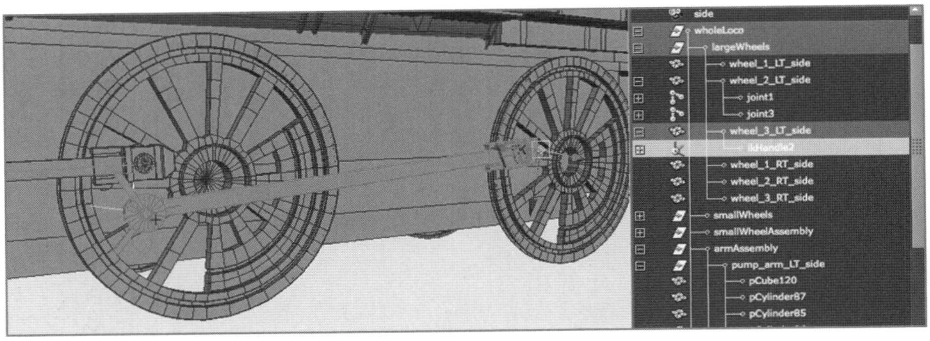

Figure 9.79

The wheel arm geometry flips over if you group the IK handle under the back wheel.

Fixing this is easy. The grouping of the IK handle to the back wheel is causing the issue. Although that is pretty much what you want to do, parenting the IK handle under the wheel is problematic. Here is where the parent constraint becomes extremely helpful. It gives you the desired result without the geometry flipping.

4. Make sure your control wheel is back to **0** rotation first. MMB+click in the Outliner, and place the IK handle outside the hierarchy of the locomotive to remove the IK handle from under the back wheel's node. You may also undo your past actions to the point before you grouped the IK handle (ikHandle2) under the back wheel. (You have to love Undo!)

5. Select the back wheel, Shift+click the IK handle (ikHandle2), and choose Constrain → Parent. Now, if you rotate the control wheel, everything works great.

6. Group the IK handle (ikHandle2) under the top node of the locomotive (wholeLoco). You can use fancy_locomotive_anim_v3.mb to compare your work.

Again, seeing procedures go slightly awry, like when the wheel arm flipped over, is important. Doing so gives you a taste of trouble and a chance to fix it. Troubleshooting is an integral skill for a good CG artist.

Finishing the Rig

You're almost home free with the locomotive wheel rigging. Everything works great when you rotate the control wheel. If you select the top node of the locomotive and translate the train back and forth, everything should work perfectly. Repeat the steps in the previous few sections to connect the wheel arms and wheels on the other side of the locomotive, and you're finished! Figure 9.80 shows the completed and rigged locomotive.

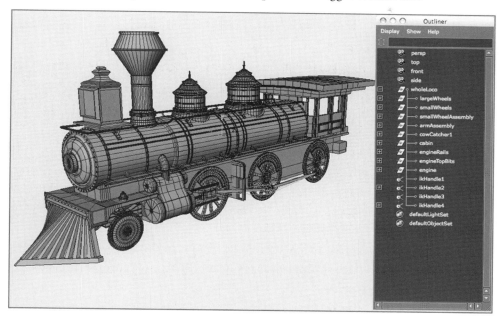

Figure 9.80

The rigged fancy locomotive

Creating a Simple Character Rig

In this section, you will revisit the Block Man setup to create a more well-rounded character rig with controls like professional animators use. This rig was created by Maks Naporowski, a fellow instructor at USC and CG animator/rigger as a fairly simple biped rig for animation. (You can see some of Maks' work in the Color Section of this book.) Bear in mind that character rigging is an involved process, and you are starting to scratch the surface here. When you are done with this rig, you will have a simple two-legged character that you can easily animate using the controls you will set up based on what you've already accomplished throughout this chapter.

Figure 9.81

Create IK handles for the arms and legs.

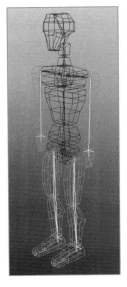

Creating Control Shapes

Animators hardly ever manipulate and keyframe IK handles or joints directly, when a good rig is available to them, and that's what you should keep in mind for the following rig:

1. Open the scene file block_man_skeleton_v02.mb from the Block_Man project.

2. In the Animation menu set, choose Skeleton → IK Handle Tool ❑. In the option box, set the Current solver attribute to ikRPsolver. Click one of the hip joints, and then click the ankle joint. This makes an IK chain for the leg. Repeat for the other leg. Name them **lt_ikHandle** and **rt_ikHandle**.

3. Create an IK chain for the arms, from the shoulder to the wrist, also making sure to use the ikRPsolver. Name them as well. Figure 9.81 shows all four IK handles created.

4. Create a circle (Create → NURBS Primitives → Circle). Scale it up and center it around the left wrist. Name this circle **lt_arm_CNTRL**. Duplicate the circle, move the copy to center on the right wrist, and name it **rt_arm_CNTRL**. Refer to Figure 9.82 for placement.

5. In the Channel Box/Layer Editor, click the Display tab in the Layer Editor and create two new layers: **lt_cntrls** (make it blue) and **rt_cntrls** (make it red). Assign the left wrist circle to lt_cntrls and the right wrist circle to rt_cntrls. This makes it easier to visualize and control. (See Figure 9.82.)

6. Select both circles, and select Modify → Freeze Transformations. This will zero out their positions. Name the left wrist circle **lt_arm_CNTRL** and the right wrist circle **rt_arm_CNTRL.**

7. Create two more circles, and adjust their CVs to make them oval to fit around the feet. Size and place them around the feet as shown in Figure 9.83. Assign each foot oval to the appropriate lt_cntrls or rt_cntrls display layers, and name the ovals **lt_foot_CNTRL** and **rt_foot_CNTRL**, respectively.

8. Create a large circle and center it around the pelvis joint (name it **body_CNTRL**). Make another large square shape, and place it on the floor around the feet (name it **main_CNTRL**). Assign these two shapes to a new display layer called **cn_cntrls** and make it green.

Figure 9.82

Create circles for the wrists, place them, and assign them to their own display layers.

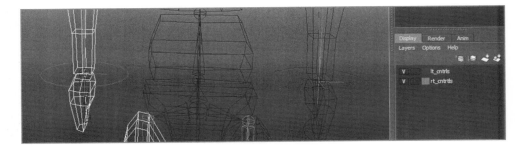

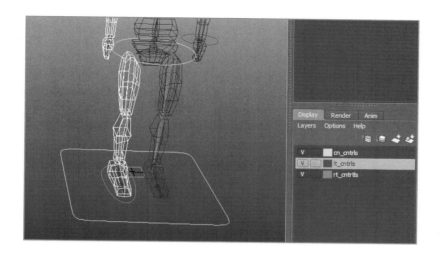

Figure 9.83

Create control shapes for the feet, pelvis, and body.

These shapes will be the primary controllers for the animation of the character. They are easy to select and manipulate and make animation much easier.

Setting up the Controls

Now comes the tough part of rigging it all to work! You'll group the shapes and create relationships to the skeleton here:

1. Parent the body_CNTRL under the main_CNTRL shape.

2. Parent the two arm controllers (rt_arm_CNTRL and lt_arm_CNTRL) under the main_CNTRL shape as well.

3. Parent each of the two wrist IK handles under each respective circle shape, as shown in Figure 9.84.

4. Select the left wrist circle and the lt_wrist joint, and choose Constraints → Orient ❑. In the option box, turn on Maintain Offset, and click Add. This allows you to control the hand's rotation with the circle, as well as the hand's position. Select the wrist circle and move and rotate it around to see how the arm reacts. The elbow can swing around a little much, so you'll add a control for the twist of the arm.

5. Select the left wrist circle, and open the Attribute Editor. Choose Attributes → Add Attribute. Enter the name **twist** to the wrist circle, and keep the options at their default (Data Type: Float).

6. Now you'll connect it to the IK handle. Select both the wrists' IK handle and the circle controller, and choose Window → Node Editor. The white circles on either side of the nodes are input and output sockets. (See Figure 9.85.)

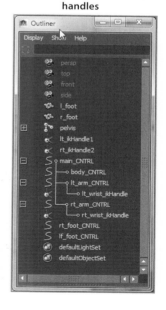

Figure 9.84

Grouping the controllers and IK handles

THE NODE EDITOR

The Node Editor is fairly new to Maya and gives you an easy way to create and manage connections between objects or nodes. You can navigate in it easily with Alt+mouse combinations like other Maya windows, and you can arrange the display of nodes however you want.

Figure 9.85

The Node Editor displays the IK handle and the circle control shape.

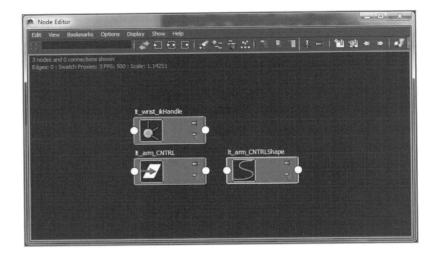

7. Click the output socket of the lt_arm_CNTRL node (the white circle on the right), and select Twist from the context menu. This connects a yellow rubber band to your cursor. Move the mouse to the input socket of the lt_wrist_ikHandle node (the white circle on the left), and click. Choose Twist from the menu. This automatically created an intermediate node but essentially connects these two attributes. (See Figure 9.86.)

Figure 9.86

You've connected the Twist attributes.

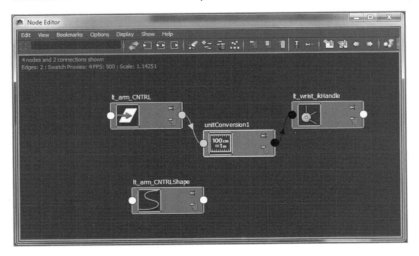

8. Now if you select the wrist circle and adjust the twist value, the arm will twist. If nothing happens, check your node connection and make sure you used the ikRPsolver when you created the IK handles in the previous section.

9. Repeat steps 4 through 8 for the right hand.

10. Now let's do the same for the feet for the Twist attribute. Select the left foot's control oval, and add a new attribute called **twist**. Select the oval and the ankle joint (lt_ikHandle1), and open the Node Editor and connect the Twist attributes as you did in step 7 for the arm. Repeat for the right leg.

11. Select the pelvis joint, and parent that under the body_CNTRL circle.

Setting Up Heel Controls

Now let's move on to creating some nice foot controls to allow the character to stand on his tiptoes or his heels easily. For that you will need to build a reverse joint chain to control the foot from the heel to supplement the existing leg joints.

1. In the side view, choose Skeleton → Joint Tool, and place a joint at the back of the left heel, as shown in Figure 9.87. Place the second joint exactly on the existing toe joint (lt_foot). Hold down V for point snaps when you create the joint so you can snap it exactly to that toe joint. Snap the third joint to the existing lt_ballFoot joint, and finally snap the fourth joint to the existing lt_ankle joint.

Figure 9.87

Create a reverse joint chain for the left foot.

2. Grab the top joint of this reverse chain, and parent it under the lt_foot_CNTRL oval. Name the joints as noted in Figure 9.88. Finally, parent the left ankle's IK handle (lt_ihHandle1) under the lt_rev_ankle joint as shown. Repeat for the other foot.

3. Next, parent both the foot control ovals under the main_CNTRL square. (See Figure 9.89.)

4. Select the main_CNTRL square, and move the rig around. The character moves along with it. Select the body_CNTRL circle. When you move the body control, the feet and hands stay because of IK (see Figure 9.90), and that's how you want it. Undo your moves.

5. Create a display layer called **rigging**. Select the lt_rev_heel and rt_rev_heel joints you just created and parented, and assign them to the new rigging display layer. This will make it easy to hide these extra reverse joints to keep them out of the way later.

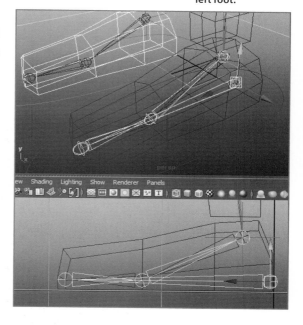

Figure 9.88

Parent the heel joints and ankle IK handles.

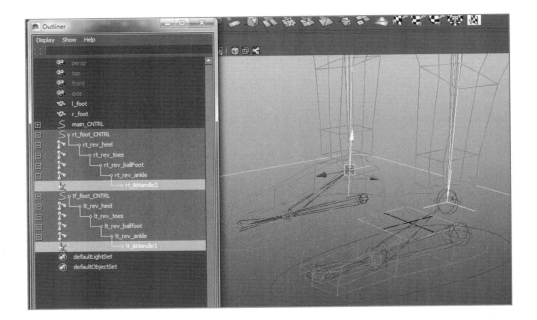

Figure 9.89

Parent the foot controls.

Figure 9.90

Moving the body control and the main control works perfectly.

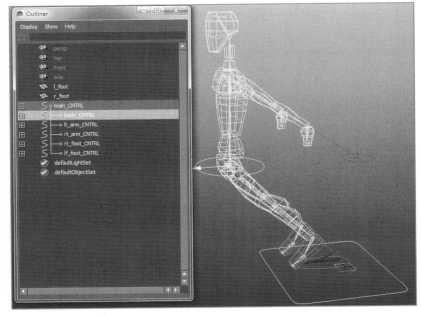

6. Select the `lt_rev_toes` joint first and then the `lt_ballfoot` joint (see Figure 9.91), and choose Constraints → Orient ❑. Make sure Maintain Offset is checked, and click Apply. The constraint node should appear under the `lt_ballFoot` node, as shown in the Outliner in Figure 9.91.

7. Select the `lt_rev_ballFoot` joint and then the `lt_ankle` joint, and create an Aim Constraint like in the previous step.

8. Repeat steps 6 and 7 for the right foot.

9. When you're done, your Outliner should be similar to the one shown in Figure 9.91. If your constraint nodes are not in the right places, check to make sure you selected the nodes in order in the steps 6 and 7 when you made the Aim Constraint.

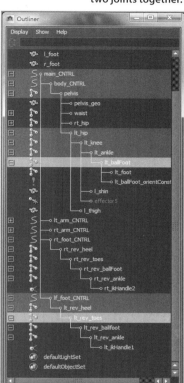

Figure 9.91

Aim constrain the two joints together.

Set-Driven Keys: Heel Controls

Now let's set up some fancy heel controls.

1. Select the left foot control oval, and add a new attribute to it called **heel**. In the options, change Data Type to Float, but give it a Minimum of **–5** and a Maximum of **10** (see Figure 9.92). Repeat for the right foot.

    You need to set up a set-driven key (SDK) to raise or lower the heel based on the value of the `Heel` attribute.

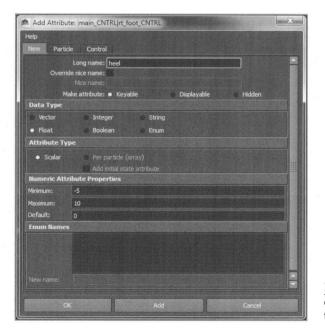

Figure 9.92

Create a new attribute for the foot control oval.

2. Select the left foot control oval, and choose Animate → Set Driven Key → Set. Click Load Driver to load the control oval as the driver of this SDK.

3. Select lt_rev_heel, and in the SDK window, click Load Driven.

4. In the SDK window, select Heel as the driver attribute on the oval and the RotateZ attribute on the driven joint (Figure 9.93).

5. Make sure the Heel attribute is set to **0** and the Rotate Z for the lt_rev_heel joint is also **0**. Click Key in the SDK window.

6. Set the Heel attribute to **–5**, and rotate the lt_rev_heel **45** degrees up in Z. Click Key in the SDK window. If you now select the foot control oval and change the Heel attribute to between **–5** and **0**, the heel will raise and lower. Make sure to set it back to **0** when you're done testing.

7. Select the lt_rev_ballFoot joint, and click Load Driven in the SDK window. Keep lf_foot_CNTRL's Heel as the driver. Select the RotateZ attribute for the driven joint (See Figure 9.94.)

8. Set Heel to **0**, and rotate in Z for the rev_ballFoot to **0**. Click Key in the SDK window.

9. Set Heel to **5**, and rotate in Z for the rev_ballFoot to **45** degrees. Click Key in the SDK window.

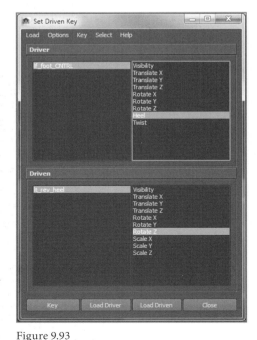

Figure 9.93

The first SDK relationship for the reverse heel joint

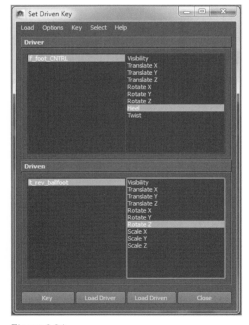

Figure 9.94

The next SDK relationship for the reverse ballFoot joint

10. Set Heel to **10**, and rotate in *Z* for the rev_ballFoot back to **0**. Click Key in the SDK window.

11. Test the Heel slider by sliding it to a value of 5, and you should see the back of the foot moving up, as shown in Figure 9.95. Set Heel to 10, and the heel comes back down.

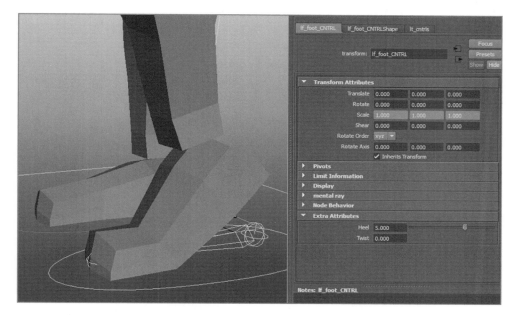

Figure 9.95

When the Heel attribute is at 5, the heel should raise up like shown.

12. Finally, select lt_rev_toes, and click Load Driven in the SDK window. Keep lf_foot_CNTRL's Heel as the driver. Select Rotate Z as the driven channel for the lt_rev_toes joint in the SDK window. Figure 9.96 shows the SDK relationship.

13. Set Heel to **5**, and make sure the lt_rev_toes joint's Rotate Z is **0**. Click Key in the SDK window.

14. Set Heel to 10, and rotate in Z the lt_rev_toes joint to **45** degrees. Click Key in the SDK window.

15. Test the Heel slider, and you'll see at a value of 10 that the foot is up and the toes are on the ground (see Figure 9.97).

16. Repeat steps 1 through 15 for the right foot. This time, you will use the rt_ nodes in place of the lt_ nodes you used earlier.

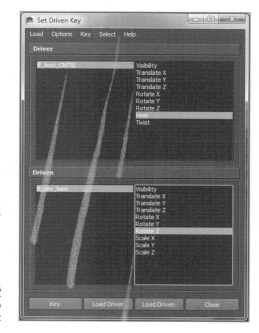

Figure 9.96

The final SDK relationship for the reverse toe joint

Figure 9.97

The foot position when Heel is set to 10

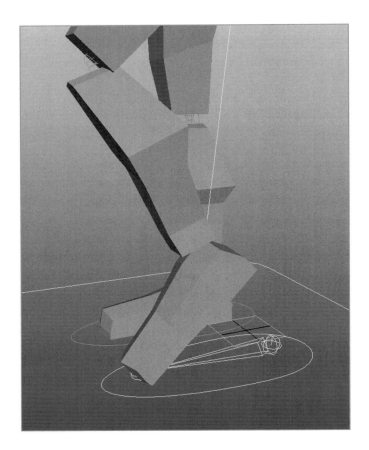

Make sure you're saving your progress as you go! When you're done, your rig should have some pretty handy controls. You will move the entire character using the main_CNTRL node. You can move the body itself while keeping sticky IK hands and feet by using the body_CNTRL node. And, of course, you control the arms/hands and legs/feet using the respective arm_CNTRL and foot_CNTRL nodes. All keyframes and animation should happen on these nodes only; you should not have to manipulate the joints or the IK handles directly at all. And that, in a somewhat confusing and long-winded nutshell, is the purpose of a character rig.

You can load the file character_rig_v01.mb from the Block_Man project to check your work or just to use as a rigged character for some animation fun!

For Further Study

Animation is as much a sport as it is an art, meaning practice makes you better. Use the rigged character from the end of this chapter to redo the walk animations from the beginning of the chapter. Also try different types and moods of walk. Can you animate a simple walk that looks happy and enthusiastic? Can you make that walk sad and lonely? Being able to convey emotion in your movement is key, and the more you try, the better you get.

Summary

In this chapter, you extended your experience with animation and learned about rigging techniques and automation. Starting with the simple Block Man, you learned how to set up a hierarchy for forward kinematics animation to create a walk cycle. Then, you used a skeleton to rig a hand for animation. Next, you learned how to bind the geometry of the hand to the skeleton using rigid, interactive, and smooth binds and how to edit the binding. You also learned how to create an IK system to drive the joints in the Block Man for an IK walk-cycle animation. After that, you learned how constraints can be used in rigging and how to set up set-driven keys to create easy controls to animate the hand. Then, you put all these rigging tricks together to rig the wheels of the locomotive to automate the animation of that complex system with a single control based on the middle wheel. And finally, you tackled a pretty tough rigging assignment in rigging the Block Man even further to have some nice options for movement using controllers.

The true work in animation comes from recognizing what to do in the face of certain challenges and how to approach their solutions. Maya offers a large animation toolset, and the more familiar you become with the tools, the better you'll be able to judge which tools to use in your work. Don't stop with this chapter; experiment with the features not covered here to see what happens.

Animation is about observation and interpretation. The animator's duty is to understand how and why something moves and to translate that into their medium without losing the movement's fidelity, tenacity, or honesty.

CHAPTER 10

Autodesk Maya Lighting

Light shapes the world by showing us what we see. It creates a sense of depth, it initiates the perception of color, and it allows us to distinguish shape and form. For a scene to be successful in CG, these realities of light need to be reproduced as faithfully as possible. The trick is learning to see light and its astonishing effects on the world around us.

Learning Outcomes: In this chapter, you will be able to

- Understand basic concepts for setting up CG lighting
- Choose the appropriate Autodesk® Maya® light for a scene based on light attributes
- Control which lights illuminate certain objects through light linking
- Create mood and realism with shadow maps and raytraced shadows
- Illuminate and render a scene with mental ray® Physical Sun and Sky
- Produce special lighting effects with volumetric lighting, lens flare, and shader glow
- Practice setting up a basic lighting solution for a lamp and decorative box
- Animate the attributes of a light and aim lights with the Special Manipulator

Basic Lighting Concepts

It's no surprise that lighting in Maya resembles actual direct-lighting techniques used in photography and filmmaking. Lights of various types are placed around a scene to illuminate the subjects as they would for a still life or a portrait. Your scene and what's in it dictate, to some degree at least, which lights you put where. The *type* of lights you use depends on the desired effect.

At the basic level, you want your lights to illuminate the scene. Without lights, your cameras have nothing to capture. Although it seems rather easy to throw your lights in, turn them all on, and render a scene, that couldn't be further from the truth.

Although it's easy to insert and configure lights, it's *how* you light that will make or break your scene. Knowing how to do that really comes only with a good deal of experience and experimentation, as well as a good eye and patience.

This chapter will familiarize you with the basic techniques of lighting a scene in Maya and start you on the road to finding out more.

Learning to See

There are many nuances to the real-world lighting around us that we take for granted; we infer a tremendous amount of visual information without much consideration. With CG lighting, you must re-create these nuances for your scene.

The most valuable thing you can do to improve your lighting technique is to relearn how you see your environment. Question why things look the way they do, and you'll find that the answers almost always come around to lighting. Take note of the distinction between light and dark in the room you're in now. Notice the difference in the brightness of highlights and how they dissipate into diffused light and then into shadow.

When you start understanding how real light affects objects, you'll be much better equipped to generate your own light. After all, the key to good lighting starts with the desire to create an interesting image.

What Your Scene Needs

Ideally, your scene needs areas of highlight and shadow. Overlighting a scene flattens everything and diminishes details. Figure 10.1 shows a still life with too many bright lights that only flatten the image and remove any sense of color and depth.

Similarly, underlighting your scene makes it muddy and lifeless, and it flattens the entire frame. Figure 10.2 shows the still life underlit. The bumps and curves of the mesh are hardly noticeable.

Like a photographer, you want your image to have the full range of exposure. You want the richest blacks to the brightest whites in your frame to create a deep sense of detail. As in Figure 10.3, light and shadow complement each other and work to show the features of your surface.

Figure 10.1

An overlit still life

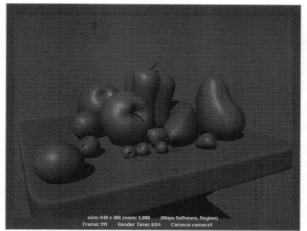

Figure 10.2

An underlit still life

Three-Point Lighting

Because your scene needs to be rendered and lighting can be a fairly heavy rendering process, your lighting needs to be efficient. That means not using dozens of lights for every part of the scene.

The traditional filmmaking and television approach to lighting is called *three-point lighting*. Three distinct roles are used to light the subject of a shot. More than one light can be used for each of the three roles, but the scene should seem to have only one primary (or *key*) light, a softer light to fill the scene, and a back light to pop the subject out from the background.

Three-point lighting ensures that the primary subject's features aren't just illuminated but featured with highlights and shadow. Using three directions and qualities of light creates the best level of depth. Figure 10.4 shows a schematic of a basic three-point setup.

Figure 10.3

Balanced lighting creates a more interesting picture.

Key Light

A *key light* is placed in front of the subject and off to the side to provide the principal light on the subject. Because it's usually off-center, the key light creates one side of brighter light, increasing the depth of the shot. This light also provides the primary shadows and gives the important sense of lighting direction in the shot.

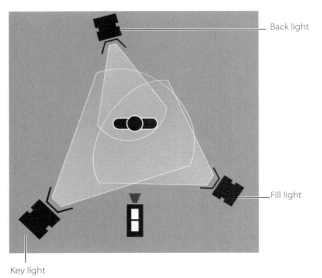

Back light

Fill light

Key light

Although it's possible for several lights to fulfill the role of key light in a scene—for example, three ceiling lights overhead—one light should dominate, creating a definitive direction. Figure 10.5 (left) shows the subject being lit by only a key light, although it's physically composed of two lights.

The direction of the two lights remains the same, and one takes intensity precedence over the other and casts shadows. The effect creates a single key light, which produces a moody still life.

Try This

1. Open the scene file still_life_v01.mb from the Lighting project downloaded from the book's web site.

Figure 10.4

A three-point lighting schematic

2. In the camera1 panel, press 7 for lighting mode. It should turn black; there are no lights.

3. Click Create → Lights → Point Light, and in the persp window, place it as your key light (Figure 10.5, right). Use the camera1 panel to gauge how the lighting composition is working for optimum placement of the Point light.

Fill Light

A more diffused light than the key light, the *fill light* seems directionless and evenly spread across the subject's dark side. This fills the rest of the subject with light and decreases the dark area caused by the key light.

Figure 10.5

Key light only

The fill light isn't meant to cast any shadows onto the subject or background itself and is actually used to help soften the shadows created by the key light. Figure 10.6 shows the still life with an added fill light. Notice how it softens the shadows and illuminates the dark areas the key light misses.

Typically, you place the fill light in front of the subject and aim it so that it comes from the opposite side of the key light to target the dark side of the subject. Even though the still life in Figure 10.6 is still a fairly moody composition, much more is visible than with only the key light in the previous figure.

Typically, you place the fill light in front of the subject and aim it so that it comes from the opposite side of the key light to target the dark side of the subject. Even though the still life in Figure 10.6 is still a fairly moody composition, much more is visible than with only the key light.

Figure 10.6

A fill light is now included.

Try This

1. In the existing scene that you started with a single Point light, choose Create → Lights → Directional Light. Where you place the light doesn't matter, but how you rotate it does.

2. Rotate the light so you get a lighting direction opposite to the direction of the key light from the Point light already in the scene.

3. With the Directional light selected, change its Intensity attribute in the Channel Box or the Attribute Editor from 1.0 to **0.5**. Use the camera1 panel to see how the fill light is working.

Back Light

The *back light*, or rim light, is placed behind the subject to create a bit of a halo, which helps pop the subject out in the shot. Therefore, the subject has more presence against its background. Figure 10.7 shows how helpful a back light can be.

The back light brings the fruit in this still life out from the background and adds some highlights to the edges, giving the composition more focus on the fruit.

Don't confuse the back light with the background light, which lights the environment behind the subject.

Try This

1. In your current scene with the two lights, create a third light to be a spotlight.

2. You can use Move and Rotate to position the light to shine from behind the fruit, or you can use the Special Manipulator. To use that, press T with the spotlight selected. You will see two move manipulators, one for the source of the light and one for the target.

3. Move the target to the front of the column stand, and move the target behind and slightly above the fruit (Figure 10.7, right). Use the camera1 panel to see how the back light should be placed.

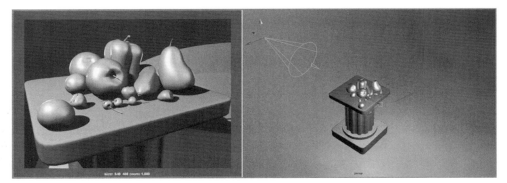

Figure 10.7

A back light makes the subject pop right out.

Using Three-Point Lighting

The three-point lighting system is used for the primary subject of the scene. Because it's based on position and angle of the subject to the camera, a new setup is needed when the camera is moved for a different shot in the same scene. Three-point lighting is, therefore, not scene specific but shot specific, as long as it does not break the overall continuity of the scene.

After the lighting is set up for the subject of a shot, the background must be lit. Use a directed primary light source that matches the direction of the key light for the main light, and use a softer fill light to illuminate the rest of the scene and soften the primary shadows.

Practical Lighting

Practical lighting is a theatrical term describing any lights in a scene that are cast from lighting objects within the scene. For example, a desk lamp on a table in the background of a scene would need practical lighting when it's on. You never want the practical lighting to interfere with the main lighting of the scene, unless the scene's lighting is explicitly coming from such a source.

Each light-emitting object in your CG scene doesn't necessarily need its own Maya light. Rendering tricks such as *glow* (for glow effects, see "Lighting Effects" later in this chapter) can simulate the effect that a light is turned on without actually having to use a Maya light. Of course, if you need the practical light to illuminate something in the scene, you need to create a light for it.

Maya Lights

Six types of light are available in Maya: Ambient, Directional, Point, Spot, Area, and Volume. These lights are also used when rendering in mental ray. How you use each dictates whether they become key, fill, or rim lights. Each light can fill any of those roles, although some are better for certain jobs than others. The most commonly used light types for most scenes are Spot, Directional, and Ambient. All of these Maya lights render in Maya Software as well as mental ray.

To create each light, choose Create → Lights, and click the light type.

Common Light Attributes

Lights in Maya are treated like any other object node. They can be transformed, rotated, scaled, duplicated, deleted, and so forth, and they are visible as nodes in the Hypergraph and Outliner alongside other objects in the scene. Like any other node, lights have attributes that govern how they function. Figure 10.8 shows the Attribute Editor for a typical light.

When you select any light type and then open the Attribute Editor, you'll see the following attributes and options:

Type This drop-down menu sets the type of light. You can change from one light type to another (for instance, from Spot to Point) at any time.

Color This attribute controls the color cast by the light. The darker the color, the dimmer the light will be. You can use Color in conjunction with Intensity to govern brightness, although it's best to leave that to Intensity only.

Figure 10.8

A typical light's Attribute Editor

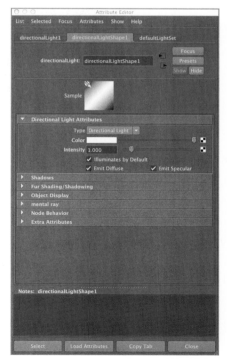

Intensity   This attribute specifies how much light is cast. The higher the intensity, the brighter the illumination will be.

Illuminates By Default   This check box deals with *light linking*, or the ability to illuminate specific objects with specific lights. Clearing this check box causes the light not to illuminate all objects by default, requiring you to link the light to objects you do want it to light. Keep this check box checked unless you're linking lights to specific objects. This chapter will briefly touch on light linking later.

Emit Diffuse and Emit Specular   These two check boxes aren't available with the Ambient light type. For all other light types, they toggle on or off the ability to cast diffuse lighting or specular highlights on an object (see Figure 10.9). This is useful for creating specific lighting effects. For example, if lighting an object makes it too shiny, you can disable the specular emission from one or more of the lights on that object to reduce the glare.

Figure 10.9

Lights can render diffuse or specular components if needed.

Full render   Diffuse only render   Specular only render

Light Types

Beyond the common light attributes, each light type carries its own attributes that govern its particular settings. In the following section, open the scene file still_life_v01.mb from the Lighting project, and create the light being described to see firsthand how that particular light affects the scene.

Ambient Lights

Ambient lights cast an even light across the entire scene. These lights are great for creating a quick, even illumination in a scene; but, as you can see in Figure 10.10, they run the risk of flattening the composition. They're perhaps best used sparingly and at low intensities as fill lights or background lights.

The Ambient Shade slider in the Attribute Editor governs how flat the lighting is. The lower the value, the flatter the lighting. Figure 10.11 shows the effect of two contrasting Ambient Shade settings.

Directional Lights

Directional lights cast a light in a general direction evenly across the scene (see Figure 10.12). These lights are perhaps second to Spot lights as the most commonly used light type. They're perfect for sunlight or general indoor lighting, for key lights, and for fill and back lights. They give an accurate sense of direction without having to emanate from a specific source.

Point Lights

A *Point light* casts light from a single specific point in space, similar to a bare light bulb. Its light is spread evenly from the emission point (see Figure 10.13).

Using the Decay Rate drop-down menu in the Attribute Editor, you can set how a Point light's intensity diminishes over distance. With No Decay, the Point light illuminates an object far away as evenly as it does up close. This is the most common setting for most applications.

Figure 10.10
Ambient light

Figure 10.11
A low Ambient Shade setting flattens the image.

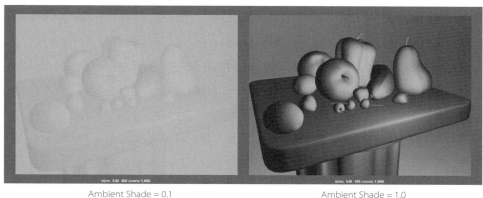

Ambient Shade = 0.1   Ambient Shade = 1.0

Figure 10.12
Directional light

Figure 10.13
A Point light placed in the front right of frame

Setting Decay Rate to Linear, Quadratic, or Cubic requires you to increase the intensity level exponentially to compensate for the decay. You can use Decay Rate settings to illuminate nearby objects and to leave distant ones unaffected. In reality, lights have decay rates. But in CG, they don't really need to decay unless the falloff effect is needed, as shown in Figure 10.14. Clever lighting can easily avoid this cumbersome calculation.

Point lights are good for effects such as candlelight or setting a mood.

Spot Lights

Spot lights are arguably the most used lights in Maya because they can be used for keys, fills, or rims; and they're highly efficient, casting light in specific areas, just like real spotlights.

Similar to Directional lights, Spot lights emphasize direction. But these lights emit from a specific point and radiate out in a cone shape, whereas Directional lights emit from an infinite source from a certain direction. As such, Spot lights can create a circular focus of light on the geometry much like a flashlight on a wall; Directionals spread the light evenly. Figure 10.15 shows a Spot light on the still life.

The following attributes govern the behavior of Spot lights:

Decay Rate Specifies the rate at which the light's intensity falls off with distance, as with the Point light. Again, the intensity needs to increase exponentially to account for any decay.

Cone Angle Sets the width of the cone of light emitted by the Spot light. The wider a cone, the more calculation intensive it becomes.

Penumbra Angle Specifies how much the intensity at the edges of the cone and hence the circular focus dissipate. (See Figure 10.16.) A negative value softens the light into the width of the cone, decreasing the size of the focus; a positive value softens away from the cone.

Figure 10.14
A Point light with a Decay Rate set

Figure 10.15
Using a Spot light

Figure 10.16

The Penumbra Angle attribute controls the softness of the edge of a Spot light.

Penumbra = 0   Penumbra = –10   Penumbra = 10

Dropoff   Specifies how much light is decayed along the distance of the cone. The higher the dropoff, the dimmer the light gets farther along the length of the cone. This effect is much better to use than a decay rate, and it gives similar results.

Most practical lights are created with Spot lights. For example, a desk lamp's light is best simulated with a Spot light. Spot lights are also the lights of choice to cast shadows. You'll find more on shadows later in the chapter. Remember, with a Spot light, you can press T for the Special Manipulator, allowing you to move the source and target of the spotlight easily to orient and place the light in your scene.

Area Lights

Area lights emit light from a flat rectangular shape only (see Figure 10.17). They behave similarly to Point lights, except they emit from an area and not from a single point. You can still set a decay rate, just as you can with Point lights. Area lights are the only lights whose scale affects their intensity. The larger an Area light, the brighter the light.

Because you can control the size of the area of light being emitted, these lights are good for creating effects such as a sliver of light falling onto an object from a crack in a door (as in Figure 10.18), overhead skylights, or the simulation of large, diffused lighting fixtures such as overhead office lights. Use Area lights when you need to light a specific area of an object.

Figure 10.17

An Area light and its placement

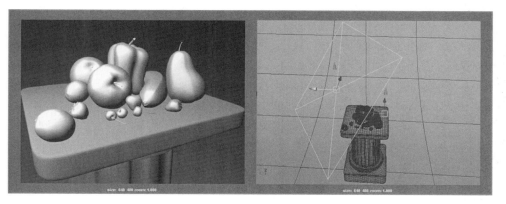

Figure 10.18

**An Area light as
a sliver and its
placement**

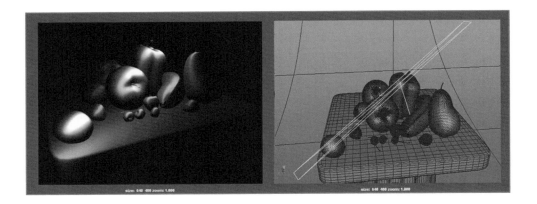

Volume Lights

Volume lights emit light from a specific 3D volumetric area as opposed to an Area light's flat rectangle (see Figure 10.19). Proximity is important for a Volume light, as is its scale.

A Volume light can have the following attributes:

Light Shape   A Volume light can be in the shape of a sphere, a box, a cylinder, or a cone. You select a shape from the Light Shape drop-down menu.

Color Range   This section of attributes sets the color of the light using a built-in ramp. The ramp (from right to left) specifies the color from inside to outside. For instance, a white-to-black ramp from right to left creates a white light at the center of the Volume light that grades down to black toward the outer edge.

Volume Light Dir   This attribute sets the direction for the light's color range: Outward lights from inside out, Inward lights from the volume's edge into the center, and Down Axis lights as a gradient in an axis of the light.

Arc And Cone End Radius   This attribute defines the shape for the volume.

Penumbra   For cylinder and cone shapes, this attribute adjusts how much the light dims along the edge of its length.

Figure 10.19

**A Volume light and
placement**

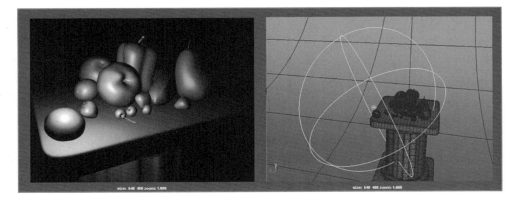

Use Volume lights when you need to control the specific area in which light is cast, or when you need an object to move into and out of a particular area of light. Volume lights are also great for creating volumetric lighting effects such as areas of lit fog. For volumetric effects, see the section "Volumetric Lighting" later in this chapter.

Lighting a Scene

It's best to start with just a couple types of light, such as Directional and Spot, before turning to the more sophisticated types, such as Area and Volume.

Getting the essence of lighting is far more important in the beginning than understanding the nuances of all the attributes of a light. At first, limit yourself to Spots and Directionals, and try to avoid any Ambient light use.

Light Linking

You can control which lights illuminate which objects by using Maya *light linking*. Inevitably, a time will come when you want to create a special light for part of your scene but not for all of it.

However, by default, lights created in your scene illuminate all objects in the scene. The easiest way to create an exclusive lighting relationship is first to create a light and then to turn off Illuminates By Default in the light's Attribute Editor. This ensures that this light won't cast light on any object unless specifically made to do so through light linking.

1. Open the scene file `still_life_linking_v01.mb` from the Lighting project, or use your own scene that already has at least three lights. Click the Render button (🖼) in the Status line to render a frame (Figure 10.20). There are no shadows; you'll deal with that in the next section.

2. Create a new Directional Light, and in the Attribute Editor, turn off the check box `Illuminates By Default` (it's right below the Intensity slider). Set Intensity to **1** or more. You can see the placement of the light in Figure 10.21.

3. Render a frame, and you won't see any change. Adding a new light with `Illuminates By Default` disabled won't increase the light level in the scene.

4. To assign your new light to the object(s) you want to illuminate exclusively, choose Window → Relationship Editors → Light Linking → Light-Centric. This opens the Relationship Editor and sets it for light linking. Light-Centric means the lights are featured in the left side of the panel, as shown in Figure 10.21, and the objects in your scene that will be lit are on the right.

Figure 10.20

All of the scene's lights illuminate the scene.

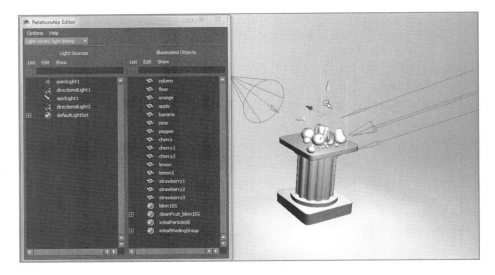

5. Now, select the light you want to link (in this case, the `directionalLight2` you just created) and the objects in the scene you'd like to link to (in this case, the apple and the pepper, as shown in Figure 10.22). Notice that no other objects on the right side of the Relationship Editor are selected; this means they will receive no illumination from this light source.

6. Render a frame, and you'll see that the objects you linked are lit by the new light. In this case, the apple and the pepper are brighter than the other fruit in the still life. (See Figure 10.23.)

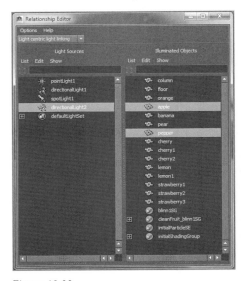

Figure 10.22

Select the scene objects to link to the
Directional light.

Figure 10.23

A linked light creates extra light for only the apple and the pepper behind it. The other objects aren't illuminated by that light.

When you're in Lighted mode (press 7 in the Shaded panel), however, keep in mind that linked lights aren't taken into account in the view panel displays. The linking comes through in the render. Light linking works with Maya Software and mental ray rendering.

Adding Shadows

Don't be too quick to create an abundance of light in your scene eager to show off your models and textures. Shrouding objects in darkness and shadow is just as important as revealing them in light. You can say a lot visually by not showing parts of a whole, leaving some interpretation to the audience.

A careful balance of light and dark is important for a composition. As Figure 10.24 shows, the realism of a scene is greatly increased with the simple addition of well-placed shadows. Don't be afraid of the dark. Use it liberally but in balance.

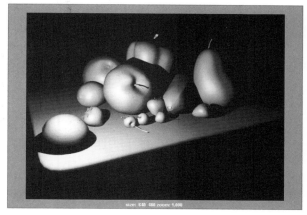

Figure 10.24

Darkness and shadow help add a sense of realism, depth, and mood to an otherwise simple still life.

Creating Shadows in Maya

Maya lights don't cast shadows by default; you need to enable this feature in the light's Attribute Editor. When you do that, however, lights can cast shadows in one of two ways, depending on how the scene is rendered: depth map shadows and raytraced shadows. Depth map shadows are faster and pretty accurate; however, with computing being as fast as it is now, it's usually just best to use raytraced shadows, which will be the predominate shadow type you'll use in this book.

When you enable *shadow maps* (by clicking the Use Depth Map Shadows check box in the Shadows area of a light's Attribute Editor), Maya generates shadow maps that locate where shadows fall by following the path of the light backward from the lighted object to the light itself. Shadow maps create fast, fairly accurate shadows through the Maya renderer.

The second method for casting shadows is achieved by raytracing with the Maya Software renderer or mental ray. *Raytracing* involves tracing a ray of light from every light source in all directions and tracing the reflection to the camera lens. Therefore, you can create more accurate shadows with raytracing. However, this render can take a little longer to calculate, particularly so when using soft shadows, which look more realistic.

You need to turn on raytraced shadows for each light when you want more accurate shadows—either soft and diffused or sharp and crisp edged—as well as enable raytracing in the Render Settings window. (See Figure 10.25 and Figure 10.26.)

Figure 10.25

A light with depth map shadows renders faster, though not as detailed as raytracing.

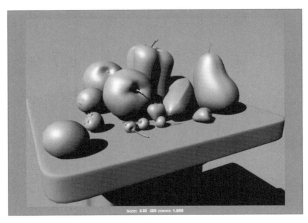

Figure 10.26

A light with raytraced shadows produces more detailed shadows.

Figure 10.27

Turning on shadow maps in the Attribute Editor for a Directional light

Shadow Map Shadows

For every light type except Ambient, you can turn on shadow maps through the light type's Attribute Editor, as shown in Figure 10.27.

The depth map resolution defaults at 512. The higher this resolution, the better defined the shadows. Most shadows are detailed enough with a depth map resolution of 1024 using a Spot light.

Spot lights create shadow maps with greater accuracy at lower depth map resolution settings and faster render times than other light types (especially over Directional lights), so if you must have shadow maps, use Spot lights. Figure 10.28 shows the same render with a Spot light and a depth map resolution setting of only 1024. Compare it to Figure 10.25, which is using a Directional light with a depth map shadow with four times the resolution.

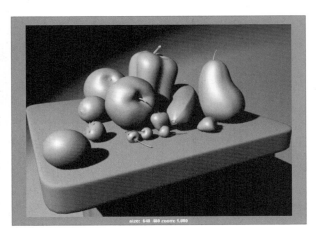

Figure 10.28

Spot lights cast faster and more detailed shadow map shadows.

Raytraced Shadows

To enable raytraced shadows, turn on the light's Use `Ray Trace Shadows` setting in the Attribute Editor (see Figure 10.29, toward the bottom of the Attribute Editor window). If you are rendering with Maya Software, open the Render Settings window by choosing Window → Rendering Editors → Render Settings or by clicking the Render Settings icon ( ) in the Status line; then enable the Raytracing check box under the Raytracing Quality heading. Let's add shadows to the scene.

1. In the file `still_life_linking_v01.mb` from the Lighting project, select the Point light. In the Attribute Editor, turn on Use Ray Trace Shadows under the Shadows → Raytrace Shadow Attributes heading (Figure 10.29, right).

2. Select the Directional light, and turn on Use Ray Trace Shadows as well.

3. Open the Render Settings window, and enable Raytracing (Figure 10.29, left).

4. Render a frame, and you'll see the scene looks more natural now with shadows (Figure 10.30). Turning on raytracing has also enabled reflections, which you'll look at later this chapter. Notice how the brighter key light (Point light) casts darker shadows than the darker fill light (Directional). As a general rule, you don't want too many lights in the scene all casting shadows; that may confuse the composition.

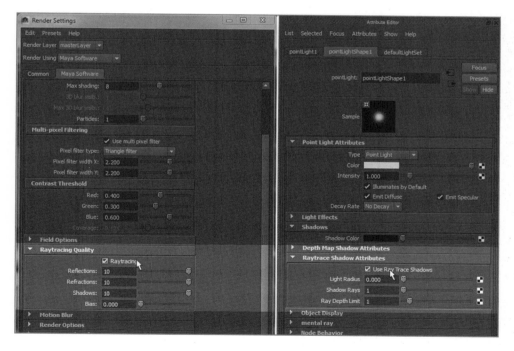

Figure 10.29

Enable raytraced shadows in the light (left), and enable raytracing for Maya Software in the Render Settings window (right).

Figure 10.30

Raytraced shadows add a lot to the scene.

For an object that has a transparency map applied to its shader, however, only raytraced shadows can cast proper shadows. On the left of Figure 10.31 is a plane with a mapped checkerboard transparency casting a raytraced shadow over the still life. On the right is the same light using shadow maps instead of raytraced shadows.

Figure 10.31

Only raytraced shadows work with transparencies.

Raytraced shadow   Shadow map shadow

Controlling Shadows per Object

To better control your lighting, you can specify whether an object can cast and receive shadows in Maya. For example, if you have geometry casting light in front of a shadow but you don't want it to cast a shadow, you can manually turn off that feature for that object only.

To turn off shadow casting for an object, follow these steps:

1. Select the foreground lemon in the `still_life_linking_v01.mb` scene, and open the Attribute Editor.

2. In the Render Stats section is a group of check boxes that control the render properties of the object, as shown in Figure 10.32 (left). Clear the Casts Shadows check box. If you don't want the object to receive shadows, clear the Receive Shadows check box.

3. Render a frame, and you'll see the lemon has no shadows on the column's tabletop; compare the render in Figure 10.32 (right) with Figure 10.30.

Figure 10.32

You easily can set whether an object casts or receives shadows in the Attribute Editor (left). The lemon does not cast a shadow anymore (compare with Figure 10.30).

Raytracing Soft Shadows

One interesting feature of shadows is that they can diffuse or soften as the shadow falls from its casting object. This small detail can greatly enhance the reality of any render. To use soft shadows, follow these steps:

Figure 10.33

Regular raytraced shadows

1. Open the still_life_shadows_v01.mb scene from the Lighting project. Check out the render settings. Raytracing is enabled. The key and fill lights have raytraced shadows enabled.

2. Render a frame, and notice that the shadows are sharp. Save that image into the render buffer by clicking the Keep Image () icon in the Render View settings. In Figure 10.33, you can see the still life rendered with sharp, raytraced shadows.

3. Select the Point light, and open the Attribute Editor. Under the Shadows → Raytrace Shadow Attributes heading, set Light Radius to **0.2**, as shown in Figure 10.34.

4. Select the `Directional light`, and set its Light Angle option to **4.0**. A Directional light's attribute is called Light Angle instead of Light Radius, but it does the same thing. Now render a frame, and compare it to the previous frame you rendered. The shadows are soft but very noisy, especially on the background (Figure 10.35). Save your image in the render buffer.

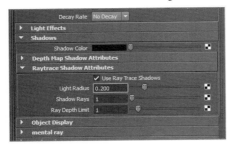

Figure 10.34

Setting the Light Radius value

The Directional light had a much higher light radius than the Point light because its shadows react differently. The Point light's distance from the subject plays a big part in how the light affects the shadows from the subject, so it is more sensitive to Light Radius values than is the non-position-dependent Directional light.

5. Now you'll mitigate the noise. Select the `Point light`, and in the Shadows → Raytrace Shadow Attributes heading, set `Shadow Rays` to **16**. Select the `Directional light`, and set its `Shadow Rays` value to **12**.

6. Render the frame, and your shadows should resemble the ones in Figure 10.36. The higher your Light Radius value, the higher you need to set your Shadow Rays setting to compensate for noise.

Notice how the shadows soften more toward the edge of the shadow; the shadow is still sharp at the point of contact. This gives a much nicer feeling of depth to the scene. There is an increase in render time—it's important to evaluate how much softening you need so you don't overdo the look or increase the render time too much.

Using soft shadows was easy! Make sure you enable raytracing in Render Settings, of course. These soft raytraced shadows work both in Maya Software rendering as well as mental ray rendering.

Figure 10.35

Soft but noisy shadows

Figure 10.36

A higher Shadow Rays setting makes for cleaner soft shadows.

mental ray Lighting

mental ray lighting and rendering opens up a large range of possibilities within Maya. As with all rendering, lighting plays the primary role. I'll cover mental ray rendering more in the next chapter; however, because rendering and lighting go hand in hand, it's tough to ignore it in this chapter. This section is a primer on mental ray light functionality.

> Open the Render Settings window by choosing Window → Rendering Editors → Render Settings. If you don't see the mental ray (or any other, such as the Maya Vector) option in the Render Using drop-down menu, you need to load the plug-in. Choose Window → Settings/ Preferences → Plug-in Manager to open the Plug-in Manager. Make sure `Mayatomr.mll` is checked for Loaded as well as for Auto Load to ensure that it loads by default.

Two important functions that mental ray brings to the Maya table are caustics and global illumination (GI). *Caustics* is the scattering of light reflections off and through semitransparent objects, such as the light that shines on the ceiling above an indoor pool or the sunshine at the bottom of an outdoor pool. *Global illumination* is the effect of light reflected from one object to another. For example, if you place colored spheres inside a gray box and shine a light into the box, the walls and floor of that box pick up the color of the spheres. The light from the spheres reflects onto the walls and tints them with the spheres' color. Furthermore, the light from the floor of the box bounces and helps illuminate the undersides of the balls.

For example, Figure 10.37 shows a scene file that has a dozen or so glass spheres inside an enclosed box. The box has four holes in the top, and two spotlights with shadows turned on are positioned outside the box, shining in through the holes. Figure 10.37 shows a typical software render. The spheres under the holes are visible, and the rest of the box is in shadow.

However, when rendering through mental ray for Maya (see Figure 10.38), the light that enters the box bounces around the scene and illuminates the other spheres. The color of the spheres also colors the area immediately around them because of GI. Additionally, the light shines through the semitransparent spheres and casts caustic highlights on the floor. (You can see the full effect in the Color Section of this book.)

Figure 10.37

The Maya Software render of the box of spheres scene

Figure 10.38

**The mental ray for
Maya render of the
scene**

Figure 10.38

**The mental ray for
Maya render of the
scene**

Global Illumination: A Downloadable PDF Exercise

Global illumination and caustics are both advanced lighting effects and won't be covered
in this book. However, a short GI exercise from a previous version of this book is available
for download from the book's web page, www.sybex.com/go/introducingmaya2014. The scene
files for this exercise are also available there. Once you download the exercise, you can
use Adobe Acrobat and the scene files to run through this livingroom exercise, where
you use simple GI techniques to explore this powerful rendering option in mental ray.

Image-Based Lighting

mental ray also brings image-based lighting (IBL) to Maya. This method of lighting uses
an image, typically a high dynamic range image (HDRI), to illuminate the scene using
Final Gather or GI. Final Gather is a form of global illumination that relies on direct as
well as indirect illumination. Direct illumination calculates the amount of light coming
directly from lights in the scene and renders the result. However, it misses an important
aspect of real-life lighting: diffuse reflections of light. Indirect illumination happens
when light bounces off objects in a scene in order to reach and therefore light the rest of
the scene—that is, diffuse reflections. Final Gather is typically a faster way than GI to get
indirect illumination in a scene.

I'll briefly touch on Final Gather here as we explore Physical Sun and Sky lighting in
the next section. However, I'll cover both IBL and Final Gather in depth in Chapter 11,
"Autodesk Maya Rendering" when you light the table lamp and decorative box model
(with displacement maps for box details as well).

mental ray Physical Sun and Sky

In Physical Sun and Sky lighting, mental ray for Maya creates nodes in your scene to simulate an open-air sunlight effect for your scene lighting. It's a quick way to create a nice-looking render. You'll place the textured red wagon into an open scene and apply a Physical Sun and Sky (PSAS) in the following exercise.

Use the scene file `WagonSunlight_v01.ma` from the Lighting project on the web page to follow along. Follow these steps:

1. The camera for this scene is already set up in the persp panel. Open the Render Settings window and switch to mental ray rendering in the Render Using pull-down menu at the top of the window, as shown in Figure 10.39.

2. In the Render Settings window, click the Indirect Lighting tab. Under the Environment heading, click the Create button next to Physical Sun And Sky. The Attribute Editor opens for the `mia_physicalsky1` node you just created, as shown in Figure 10.40.

3. Render a frame in the Perspective window, and compare it to Figure 10.41. It's a bit bright, but there's something very nice about this render. Notice that the metal handlebar takes on a good look right off the bat.

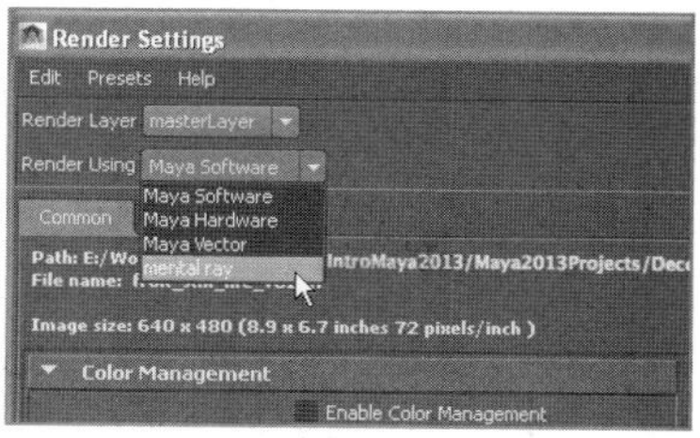

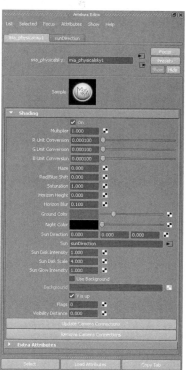

Figure 10.39
Enable mental ray rendering in Render Settings.

Figure 10.40
The mia_physicalsky1 node

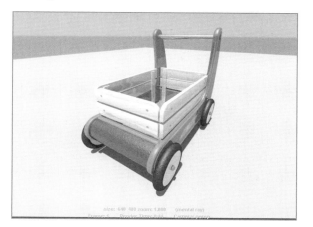

Figure 10.41
The first PSAS render doesn't look too shabby.

4. The render is too bright, and the wood slats for the railings shouldn't be reflective. Your render should also show that the fire-engine red of the wagon is a bit washed out.

    Let's first address the wood railings. Open the Hypershade, and double-click the first Wood shader. Change Reflectivity to 0.1 from **0.5**. Repeat for the second Wood shader.

5. In the Render View window, click and drag a box region around the wood railings, as shown in Figure 10.42. Click the Render Region button () to render that part of the frame only.

Figure 10.42

Render this region to check the reflection in the wood railings.

6. The wood looks much better now, so let's move on to the brightness of the scene. Open the Render Settings window, and go to the Indirect Lighting tab. Click the Input arrow next to the Physical Sun And Sky attribute's button (Figure 10.43). Doing so opens the Attribute Editor for the Physical Sun and Sky.

Figure 10.43

Click to open the attributes for the daylight system.

7. Change Multiplier to **0.5** from 1.0, and re-render the frame. The brightness comes down nicely, and the wagon is less blown out than in your previous renders. See Figure 10.44.

Figure 10.44

Bringing down the brightness of the sun

8. Let's play with the direction of the sun. Look in your persp panel, and you see a Directional light sitting smack in the middle of the scene. Maya uses this light to set the direction of the sunlight, and it doesn't contribute to the lighting of the scene in any other way. Only its rotation is important to PSAS. Its intensity, color, and other attributes are irrelevant. In this scene, the Directional light is called `sunDirection` and is in the wagon behind the third texture placement node, as you can see in Figure 10.45. The light is currently pointing sunlight almost straight down, as if the sun is high in the sky. It seems as if it's about noon. `RotateX` for the `sunDirection` light is –75.

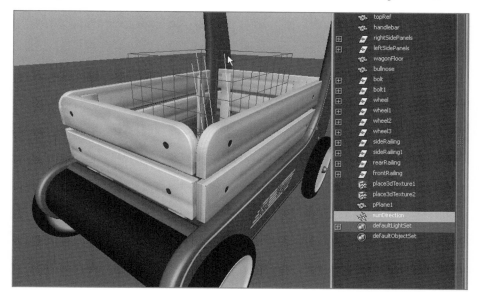

Figure 10.45

The sunDirection light adjusts only the direction of the sunlight in the scene.

9. That third texture placement node is getting in the way. To turn off its display easily, in the persp panel, click Show → Textures to uncheck it. The green box disappears in this view until you turn it back on through the Show menu. Now that you can see the Directional light better, you see that the sun is pointed slightly toward the back of the wagon. Rotate the light so that it's angled away from the camera even more, as shown in Figure 10.46. The sunDirection's RotateX should be about –**25**.

10. Render the frame, and you'll see quite a difference in the scene. Maya automatically adjusts PSAS settings to make the render appear as if the sun is about to set. This is because of the new angle. The scene (shown in Figure 10.47) not only shows a new lighting direction (the shadows fall toward the back and are longer) but also is a darker and warmer light, as if it were mid-to-late afternoon.

11. Angle the sunDirection light even more (so RotateX is at about –**2.5**), almost parallel with the ground plane, and render a frame. Now the sun has all but set, and it's dark dusk, just before night falls on the scene. See Figure 10.48.

12. Rotate the sunDirection even more so that it's at a RotateX of about **15**. It's now dark, and you can barely make out the wagon. (See Figure 10.49.) Time to go home before your mom gets mad. Remember, you can adjust the overall brightness of the scene by adjusting the mia_physicalsky1 node attributes, as you did in steps 6 and 7.

You can add lights to the scene as well; you aren't limited to the system's results. For example, Figure 10.50 shows a render of the wagon with the sun beginning to rise behind it, making the foreground a bit dark. Figure 10.51 shows the same render but with an added Directional light (with an Intensity of just **0.25**) pointing toward the front of the wagon. This helps define the front of the wagon, hinting that there is another light source, perhaps a porch light behind the camera.

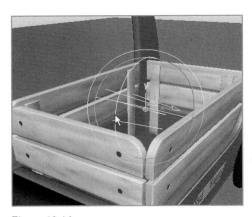

Figure 10.46
Angle the sun farther away from the camera.

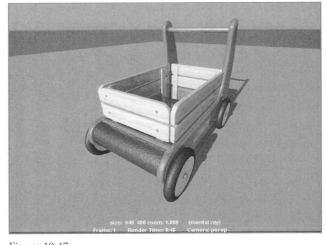

Figure 10.47
Now it's late afternoon.

Figure 10.48

It's getting late; you should get home before nightfall.

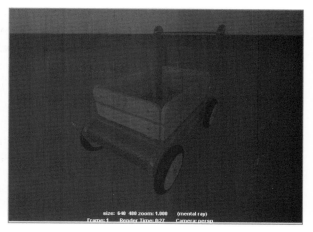

Figure 10.49

Ooh, it's dark—Mom is gonna be mad.

Figure 10.50

The sun also rises!

Figure 10.51

Adding a light to illuminate the front of the wagon in this sunrise scene from Figure 10.50

The PSAS system can get you some fairly nice results quickly. Keep experimenting with different sunDirection angles as well as the attributes for the system to see what results you can get for your scene. Add lights to create areas of detail in your model.

Unbeknownst to you, when you invoked the PSAS system, Maya turned on Final Gather in the mental ray settings. This enabled indirect lighting to work in the scene. You'll explore Final Gather in the next chapter. At the end of this chapter, though, I'll introduce HDRI and image-based lighting for a fairly photo-real rendering of the table lamp and decorative box.

This is the perfect time for a break, so save your work (as if I have to tell you that at this point!), go grab some iced tea, and rest your eyes for a bit. In the next section, I'll go over various special lighting effects before returning to the wagon.

Lighting Effects

In CG, you must fake certain traits of light in the real world. Using certain methods, you can create smoky light beams, glowing lights, and lens flares. Although some of these effects fall under the domain of rendering and shader tricks, they're best explored in the context of lighting, because they're created by light in the real world.

Volumetric Lighting

How do you create an effect such as a flashlight beam shining through fog? This lighting effect is called *volumetric lighting*, and you can use it to create some stunning results that can sometimes be time-consuming to render.

You can't apply volumetric effects to Ambient and Directional light types. To add a volumetric effect to any of the other types of lights, select the light and, in the Attribute Editor under the Light Effects section, click the checkered Map button to the right of the Light Fog attribute. This creates a new render node that appears in the Hypershade window. After you click the Map button, the Attribute Editor takes you to the lightFog node.

Maya handles volumetric lights by attaching a lightFog node to the light. The Color and Density attributes under this node control the brightness, thickness, and color of the fog attached to that light. Furthermore, in the light's Attribute Editor, you can control the fog with the Fog Spread and Fog Intensity settings. Fog Intensity increases the brightness of the fog, and Fog Spread controls how well the fog is defined within its confines. For example, a Spot light with fog shows the fog in its cone. Figure 10.52 shows how Fog Spread affects the conical fog shape.

> To remove a fog effect, right-click the Light Fog label in the light's Attribute Editor, and choose Break Connection from the context menu.

Figure 10.52

Fog Spread affects how the fog dissipates to the edges of the cone.

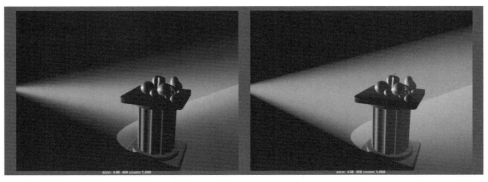

Fog Spread = 0.5   Fog Spread = 2.0

If you want the rays of light within the fog to cast shadows, check Use Depth Map Shadows for the light. You'll have to increase the depth map resolution for a higher-quality image.

Lens Flare

Lens flare and *light glow*, as illustrated in Figure 10.53, mimic the real-world effect created when light strikes a lens or when the light source is visible in the frame. The flare is created when the light hits the lens at a particular angle and causes a reflection of itself in the optics of the lens.

To enable a light glow, under the Light Effects section in the light's Attribute Editor, click the checkered Map button next to the Light Glow attribute to create an `OpticalFX` node that appears in the Hypershade. The Attribute Editor shifts focus to that new node, which controls the behavior of the light glow and lens flare. The `OpticalFX` node contains the following attributes and settings:

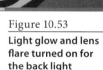

Glow Type   Setting this attribute specifies the kind of glow: Linear, Exponential, Ball, Lens Flare, and Rim Halo. These define the size and shape of the glow from the light.

Figure 10.53

Light glow and lens flare turned on for the back light

Halo Type   Specifying a halo creates a foggy halo around the light in addition to the glow. You can find controls for the halo in the Halo section in the Attribute Editor.

Star Points   Setting this attribute specifies the number of star points the glow generates.

Rotation   Setting this attribute rotates the orientation of the star points.

Radial Frequency   Used in conjunction with the Glow Radial Noise attribute (see the next item) in the Glow Attributes section, this attribute defines the smoothness of any added glow noise.

Glow Radial Noise   Setting this attribute adds noise to the glow effect, creating light and dark patches within the glow for a more random look, as shown in Figure 10.54.

Figure 10.54

Glow Radial Noise attribute

Glow Radial Noise = 0   Glow Radial Noise = 0.5

Glow Color   Setting this attribute specifies the color of the glow.

Glow Intensity and Spread   Setting these attributes specifies the brightness and thickness of the glow and how well it fades away.

To turn on a lens flare along with the light glow, click the Lens Flare check box at upper right in the Attribute Editor for OpticalFX. The attributes in the Lens Flare section control the look of the flare.

Light glows and flares can be highly effective in scenes, adding credibility to the lighting, but they're often misused or, worse, overused in CG. Used sparingly and with subtlety, lens flares can go a long way toward adding a nice touch to your scene.

Shader Glow Effects

To create a glowing effect, it's sometimes better to place a glow on a geometry's shader instead of the light itself. Because a light must be seen in the shot and pointed at the camera to see any light glow and flare, a shader glow is sometimes more desirable. This process will composite a glow on the object that is assigned the Glow shader to simulate a volumetric light, such as a street lamp on a foggy night. Shader glows have far less render cost than true volumetric lights.

Try This   To light a still-life scene, follow these steps:

1. Open the `still_life_v03.mb` file in the Lighting project on the web page. Create a Spot light, place it over the still life, and aim it directly down onto the fruit, as shown in Figure 10.55. Turn on Use Depth Map Shadows for the light, and set Resolution to **1024**. Set Penumbra Angle to **10** and Intensity to **1.5**. Press 7 for Lighted mode in the `Camera1` view panel to see how the light is being cast.

2. The Spot light provides the practical light in the scene. You'll place a bare bulb on a wire directly above the fruit. Create a NURBS sphere, and position it right over the fruit but in the frame for camera1 to see. In the `Render Stats` section of the Attribute Editor for the sphere, turn off Casts Shadows.

3. Create a long, thin cylinder for the light bulb's wire, and position it as if the bulb were hanging from it, as shown in Figure 10.56. Turn off Casts Shadows for the cylinder as well.

4. Create a black Phong E shader to assign to the cylinder.

5. Create a Phong shader for the bulb, and assign it to the NURBS sphere. Set its `Color` to a pale, light yellow, and make it about 50 percent transparent.

6. Select the Spot light, and set its `Color` to the same yellow. You can do this easily through the Color Chooser. With the shader for the bulb selected, open the Color Chooser by clicking the pale yellow color you just made. Click the right arrow to place the yellow color in the swatches to the right of the main color swatch, or right-click any of the swatches.

Figure 10.55

Aim a Spot light down toward the fruit.

Figure 10.56

Place a bulb on a wire over the fruit pedestal.

7. Pick the Spot light, and click its `Color` attribute to set the Color Chooser to that color. Click the yellow swatch you created to get the same color on the light. For detail's sake, make the light's color less saturated. Click Accept to close the Color Chooser window.

8. To make the shader glow for the bulb, open the Hypershade, and select the bulb's Phong material. In the Attribute Editor's `Special Effects` section, drag the Glow Intensity slider from 0 to **1.0**. If you render the frame, you'll see that the glow isn't quite enough to make a convincing light bulb. In the Hypershade, select the shader-Glow1 node; this node controls all the glows in the scene.

9. Set Quality to **0.1**. In the `Glow Attributes` section, set `Glow Intensity` to **6.0**, set `Glow Spread` to **0.5**, and set `Glow Radial Noise` to **0.2**.

The scene file `still_life_v04.mb` from the web page contains the full scene for your reference. See Figure 10.57 for the final result.

Figure 10.57

The bare light bulb over the still life is created with a shader glow.

size: 640 480 zoom: 1.000

Lighting the Table Lamp and Decorative Box

In this section, you'll set up the table lamp and decorative box together in a scene with lights so that you can render them. Furthermore, in the next chapter, you'll be using displacement maps for detail on the box and using HDRI, mental ray, and Final Gather to light the scene using the photo of the real lamp and box as a guide. Because most of your "lighting" look results from using an HDR image, the lighting you'll start with will be basic for now.

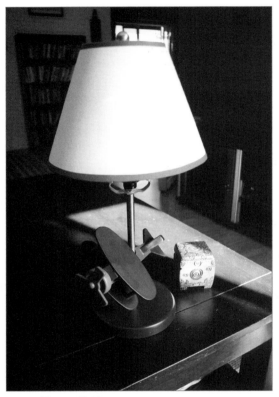

Figure 10.58

Lighting the lamp and decorative box using this practical lighting as general reference

The lighting conditions you'll use as a starting point are shown in Figure 10.58 as well as in the Color Section of this book. You can see that there is a primary key light coming from behind and to the right of the camera, with a fill from the left side and from the top back, which also gives a bit of a rim light. These lights will be easy to set up to get the general feel first. The finesse of this exercise will come from rendering through mental ray in the next chapter, using an HDR IBL, adding reflections to the box, adding displacement maps for the intricate carvings, and adjusting the shaders to taste for both the box and lamp. In the following exercise, you'll create a basic lighting setup for the lamp and decorative box and get a direct lighting solution first.

Set your current project to the TableLamp project, which you should have already downloaded from the book's web page. This is important to make sure Maya finds all the project files it needs, so it bears repeating: Set your project to TableLamp! Did you set your project yet?

How about now?

To begin lighting, open the lampScene_v07.mb scene file from the Scenes folder of the project. You'll bring in the decorative box first and place it in the scene with these steps:

1. Open the Outliner, and you'll be refreshed on how this scene was set up earlier in the book. There are a lampGroup node and a biplane node. The biplane is a referenced scene, if you recall, but it still needs to be grouped with the rest of the lamp. In the Outliner, MMB+drag the biplane reference node to the lampGroup node to parent the biplane to the rest of the lamp.

2. With the top node (lampGroup) selected, move the lamp up so that the bottom rests on the home grid. Create a poly plane for the ground plane, and scale to **25** in all *X*-, *Y*-, and *Z*-axes.

3. Choose File → Create Reference, and navigate to the Decorative_Box project. In the Scenes folder, select boxDetail01.mb to bring in the latest decorative box scene from Chapter 7, "Autodesk Maya Shading and Texturing" as a reference. This is actually the same scene file as boxTextures03.mb that you completed in Chapter 7 but cleaned up a bit to remove the image reference planes you used for modeling.

4. Scale the box to about three-fourths of its current size (**2.85** in X, Y, and Z); then position the box next to the lamp, using Figure 10.58 as a guide.

5. Create a new camera that you can use to render the scene. You'll keep using the persp camera to navigate through the scene. In one of the other view panels, click Panels → Perspective → New. persp1 is created. Then, choose View → Camera Attribute Editor. Maya shows you the persp1Shape tab. Your camera name may be slightly different (such as persp2Shape).

   In the Output Settings heading, make sure the Renderable box is checked. Click the persp1 tab in the Attribute Editor, and rename the camera from persp1 to **render-Cam** (persp1Shape is automatically renamed to renderCamShape).

   Select the original persp camera, and, in the Attribute Editor, make sure the Renderable box is unchecked. This ensures that only the correct camera (renderCam) will render.

6. Select the renderCam again, and set its Focal Length attribute to **24**. This places a 24mm lens on the renderCam to better match the camera taking the photo in Figure 10.58. Set up the renderCam to approximate the same angle of view in that photo for the lamp and box.

7. Press Ctrl+A to toggle off the Attribute Editor and show the Channel Box. In the Channel Box, select the renderCam's Translate and Rotate attributes, right-click, and select Lock Selected from the context menu shown in Figure 10.59. Doing so locks the camera in place, disallowing you from moving it. This way, you won't accidentally mess up the view. To be able to move that camera again, highlight those attributes, right-click them, and select Unlock Selected from the context menu.

8. In the renderCam panel, press 6 for textured display and then 7 for lighted and textured display. This way, you can more easily see how you orient the lights. Your objects should turn black since there are no lights yet.

9. Using the persp view, create a Directional light for the key light, and place it in front of the lamp and box and angled down at about 40 degrees, as shown in Figure 10.60. Set the Intensity to **1.2**, and turn on Use Ray Trace Shadows under the Shadows → Raytrace Shadow Attributes heading.

Figure 10.59

Match the camera angle and view; then lock the camera in place.

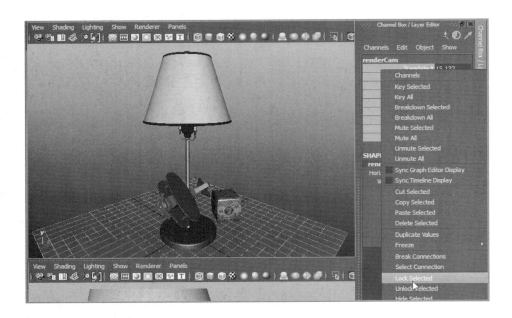

Figure 10.60

Create the key light, and place it as shown.

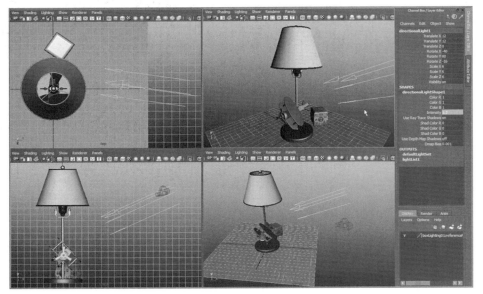

10. Create another Directional light, and place it as the fill light from the opposite angle from the left side and a bit higher and angled down more than the key light, as shown in Figure 10.61. Set `Intensity` to **0.25**, and turn on `Use Ray Trace Shadows`. Isn't this exciting?

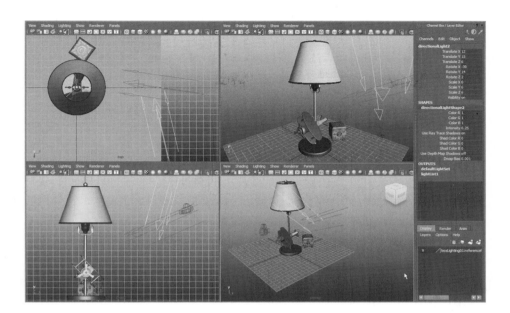

Figure 10.61
Create the fill light.

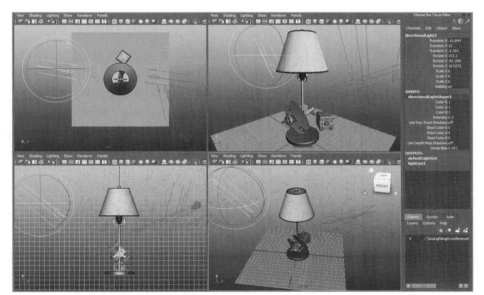

Figure 10.62
Create the back light.

11. Create a third Directional light. Place it behind the box on its left side, almost diametrically across from the camera and a bit higher than the box, as shown in Figure 10.62, so you get a nice light grazing across the top of the box. Set Intensity to **0.5**. Leave shadows off on this light.

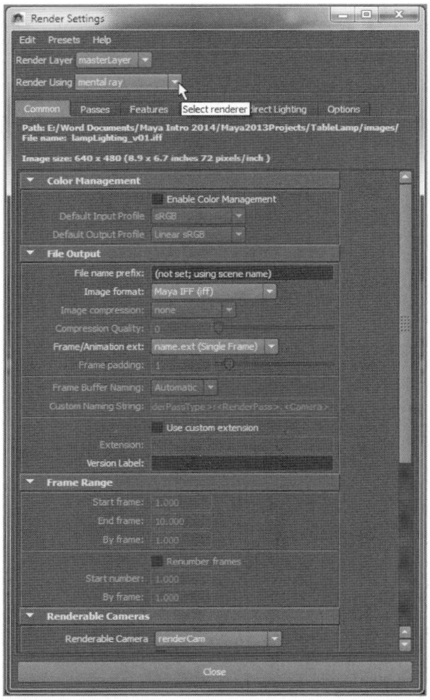

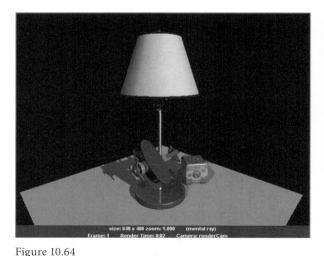

Figure 10.63

Change to mental ray in the Render Settings.

12. Open the Render Settings window, and select mental ray as the renderer. This also automatically turns on raytracing, which you need for the shadows from the key and fill lights. (See Figure 10.63.) Render a frame in the renderCam view.

Figure 10.64 shows the first render with these three lights. Notice that the gray floor is reflecting in the box because you have a Phong shader assigned to the box. You can use texture maps to adjust the reflective areas of the box and dial in the proper reflections in the next chapter as you render.

13. You can see the shadow behind the lamp falling off the edge of the ground plane. Scale it up to cover more of the floor. Select the key light (directionalLight1), and open the Attribute Editor. In the Raytrace Shadow Attributes heading, set a Light Angle setting of **3.5** and a Shadow Rays setting of **64**; then render the scene. The primary shadowing on the larger floor looks much nicer.

Select the fill light (directionalLight2), and set its Light Angle option to **7** with a Shadow Rays setting of **72** (see Figure 10.65). Play with the radii and number of rays to get the shadows to your liking. Notice how much longer the render takes with soft shadows enabled. You can temporarily use a smaller Shadow Rays setting on your lights until you're ready for final renders to save yourself some time. Just don't forget to turn those attributes back up to their full-quality looks!

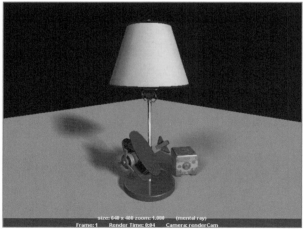

Figure 10.64

The render doesn't look too bad with just the three-point lighting.

Figure 10.65

Much nicer shadows on the floor

14. You may be bothered by the low-quality settings on the render and the slight fuzziness of the wood texture on the box. Open the Hypershade, and click the Textures tab in the top part of the window to show the texture nodes in the scene. Select the box's color texture node (boxDetail01:boxColorMap), and open the Attribute Editor. At the top, change Filter Type from the default Quadratic to Off. This prevents the renderer from slightly blurring the texture image to smooth it. (See Figure 10.66.) Do the same to turn off filtering for the lampshade's file textures (nodes file1 and file2).

Figure 10.66
Turn off filtering for the color texture image.

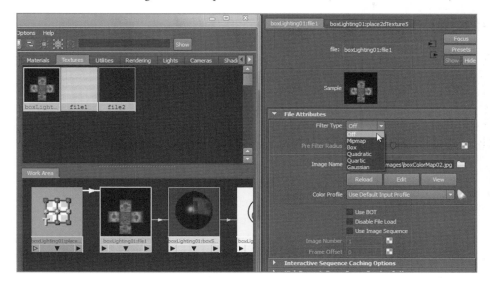

15. Open the Render Settings window (⊞), and click the Quality tab. Set Max Sample Level from 0 to **1**. (See Figure 10.67.)

16. Save your previous render in the buffer by clicking the Keep Image icon (⧉) in the Render View window. A scroll bar appears at the bottom of the Render View window. Render a frame of the persp panel now that you've turned off filtering for the texture file and increased a quality setting. Use the scroll bar in the Render View window to scrub back and forth between the older fuzzy render and the new unfiltered render. The box's decorative carvings and lines appear much stronger and crisper, as does the texture on the lampshade, as shown in Figure 10.68. It may be tough to compare the quality levels of the two renders in the book's black-and-white images, but you should notice them clearly in your Render View window.

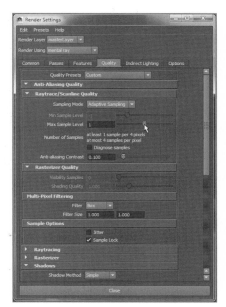

Figure 10.67
Select a slightly better render quality in the Render Settings window.

Figure 10.68

The render is much crisper and cleaner.

You've only just begun this process for the lamp and box scene. You'll pick up this exercise from this point in Chapter 11, where you'll add more texture maps to control reflections as well as add carving detail to the box, adjust shader settings for the lamp, and enable Final Gather to use an HDR image to light the scene to take it to a new level. Woo!

The scene file lampLighting_v01.mb in the Scenes folder of the TableLamp project gives you this lighting setup.

Further Lighting Practice

Lighting professionals in the CG field are called on to find the most efficient way to light a scene and bring it to the peak of its beauty. Again, this comes only from experience. The best way to become a crackerjack lighting artist is to spend months and years honing your eye and practicing the latest procedures, such as HDR lighting.

The file still_life_v01.mb in the Lighting project on the web page contains the scene of the still life with no lights, so you can play with lighting and shadow methods as well as light linking to create some extra focus on some parts of the frame. The file still_life_v02.mb contains the same scene but with three-point lighting already set up.

Notice in the still_life_v02.mb file that two lights make up the key light (spotLight1 and spotLight2). One light makes up the fill light (directionalLight1), and two lights (spotLight3 and spotLight4) make up the back light.

For practice, download some models from the Internet, and arrange them into your own still-life scenes to gain more lighting experience. Set up scenes, time the rendering process, and try to achieve the same lighting look using faster lighting setups that may not be as taxing on the renderer. Also, try taking pictures of situations and trying to match the lighting in the photo, like you're doing with the decorative box.

Try setting up simple scenes. Start with an indoor location that is lit by a single light bulb. Then, try the same scene in the following locations to expand your lighting repertoire:

- A photography studio
- Outside in the morning on a bright summer day
- Outside at dusk in the fall
- Outside at night under a street lamp
- Inside on a window ledge
- At the bottom of a closet lit by a nearby hallway light

Tips for Using and Animating Lights

When you're lighting a scene, invoking a lighting mode in your Perspective or Camera view panel will give you great feedback regarding the relative brightness and direction of your lights. Most computer systems' graphics cards can handle a maximum of eight lights in Lighted mode; some professional cards can handle more.

You invoke Lighted mode by pressing 7 on your keyboard (not through the number pad on the side). You must first be in Shaded mode (press 5) or Texture mode (press 6) to be able to press 7 for Lighted mode. Remember that Lighted mode displays linked lights as if they're lighting the entire scene. This can cause some confusion, so it's wise to take notes on any light linking in your scene.

The Maya IPR renderer is also useful when lighting a scene. This almost-real-time updating renderer will give you a high-quality render of your scene as you adjust your lights. Chapter 11 will explore the IPR renderer.

Animating a Light

Any attribute of a light can be animated in the same way that you animate any other object attribute. You can't, however, animate a light's type. To edit a light's animation, you need only select the light and open the Graph Editor to access its keyframes. You can set keyframes on Intensity, Penumbra Angle, Color, and so on, within the Channel Box or the Attribute Editor. Right-click the name of the attribute, and choose Key Selected from the context menu.

> By animating a light's intensity, you can simulate the real-world appearance of a light turning on or off. To turn on a light, create a quickly increasing curve so that its brightness arcs up slowly at first before climbing to full brightness. This animation mimics the way real lights turn on and off better than simply enabling or disabling them in your scene.

Animating the color of a light, as well as the color of a shader, sets keyframes for the color's RGB values as three separate keyframes. The Graph Editor shows a separate curve for the red, green, and blue channels of color when you animate a light's color. You can set all three keys at once by right-clicking the Color attribute in the Attribute Editor and choosing Set Key from the context menu, as shown in Figure 10.69.

Figure 10.69

Set a key for the light.

In addition, lights can be animated to be moved, scaled, and rotated like any other object. For further study, try animating the lighting for the simple scene(s) you set up to practice lighting from the previous section. Try creating animated lights to simulate a candle illuminating your scene, a campfire, or the flashing emergency lights you would find in your average space-station airlock.

Using the Show Manipulator Tool for Lights

As you saw earlier in the chapter, an easy way to manipulate lights is to use their Special Manipulator. For example, pressing T or choosing Modify → Transformation Tools → Show Manipulator tool with a Spot light selected gives you two Translate Manipulators in the view panel, as shown in Figure 10.70 and displays the icon ( ) below the Tool Box.

This allows you to move the source or target of the light to aim it better. By clicking the cyan circle that appears below the source's Translate Manipulator, you can toggle through a number of Manipulators to adjust the Spot light's settings, such as cone angle (two clicks clockwise) and penumbra angle (three clicks clockwise). Figure 10.71 shows the Manipulator for cone angle.

Source and Target Translate Manipulators are available for all light types through the Show Manipulator tool as well.

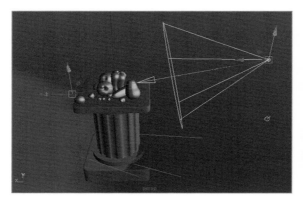

Figure 10.70

Using Special Manipulators to place and orient the Spot light

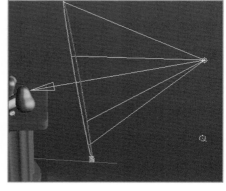

Figure 10.71

Adjusting the cone angle interactively with the Special Manipulator.

Summary

This chapter explored lighting in Maya, beginning with basic concepts that included the three-point lighting technique. You then learned about the different lights in Maya, how they work, and how you can use light linking to control your scene better. Shadows are an important part of lighting and were covered in this chapter, followed by a quick exploration of the Physical Sun and Sky system with mental ray and then lighting effects such as lens flare and light glows. You then created simple lighting for the table lamp and decorative box for a still rendering. Finally, you learned how to begin animating lights for use in your scenes.

Lighting is truly the linchpin of CG; it can make or break a scene. As you'll see in the next chapter, lighting goes hand in hand with rendering and shading, and the more you understand about all three functions, the better your scenes will look. Don't be afraid to experiment with lighting and shading schemes on all your projects.

CHAPTER 11

Autodesk Maya Rendering

Rendering is the last step in creating your CG work. It's the process by which the computer calculates the surface properties, lighting, shadows, movement, and shape of objects, and it saves a sequence of images. Although the computer does all the thinking at this point, you still need to set up your cameras and the render to get exactly what you want.

This chapter will show you how to render your scene using the Autodesk® Maya® Software renderer and mental ray® for Maya, and how to create reflections and refractions. In this chapter, you'll use a wine bottle and a still life from previous chapters, and you'll animate a camera to render a sequence.

Learning Outcomes: In this chapter, you will be able to

- Set up your scenes for output through rendering
- Choose resolutions, image formats, and other settings for rendering
- Create and edit cameras
- Render with motion blur and know how to differentiate between the types of motion blur
- Set up and use mental ray
- Render in layers and compose them back together
- Set render layer overrides settings for specific needs
- Use Final Gathering in mental ray renders for indirect lighting workflows
- Properly use Ambient Occlusion to create detail in crevices and for contact shadows
- Apply an HDRI map as a lighting source
- Apply a displacement map to create finer detail in a model

Rendering Setup

When your lighting scene from the previous chapter is complete, you've had a celebration smoothie for your hard work, and you're ready to start a render, you'll need to set up how you want it rendered. Although this is the last part of the CG process, from now on you should be thinking about rendering throughout your production. When you create models and textures with the final image in mind and you gear the lighting toward showing off the scene elegantly, the final touches are relatively easy to set up.

Decide which of the render engines included with Maya you'll use: Maya Software, Maya Hardware (or Hardware 2.0), mental ray for Maya (the most popular and what you started using in the previous chapter), or Maya Vector. Each engine has its own particular workflow and can yield entirely different results, although mental ray and Maya Software are close in appearance if you don't use the special features of mental ray. The choice of a rendering method depends on the final look you want and sometimes on the number of machines and licenses with which you can render. Maya Software rendering comes with an unlimited number of licenses, which means you can render on any machine you have (with Maya installed), although you can work with the Maya application only on as many machines for which you have licenses. There are also third-party developers in the CG field that have created other render engines that plug right into Maya, such as V-Ray® for Maya, Maxwell, and Pixar's RenderMan® for Maya.

No matter which renderer you use, the lighting and general setup are fairly common across the board. Even then, it's a good idea to choose your render engine as you begin creating your scene. It's best to begin with basic mental ray to pick up the fundamentals of lighting, texturing, and rendering before you venture into mental ray special features or try other renderers.

Regardless of the type of render, you need to specify a set of common attributes in the Render Settings window. Choose Window → Rendering Editors → Render Settings to open the Render Settings window. Figure 11.1 shows on the left the Render Settings window for the Maya Software renderer and its tabs: the Common tab and the Maya Software tab. You use the options in this window's Common tab to set up all your rendering preferences, including the resolution, file type, frame range, and so forth.

The Common tab contains the settings common to all the rendering methods, such as image size. The Maya Software tab gives you access to render-specific attributes, such as quality settings, raytracing settings, motion blur, and so on.

If you switch the Render Using pull-down menu from the default Maya Software setting to mental ray, you'll notice several tabs: Passes, Features, Quality, Indirect Lighting, and Options, as shown on the right in Figure 11.1. These tabs give you access to all the settings for the incredibly powerful mental ray renderer.

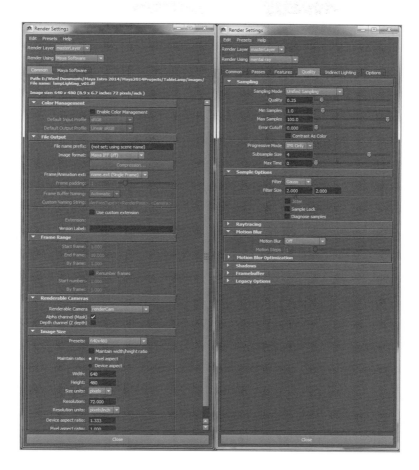

Figure 11.1

The Render Settings window

You may notice that some of the render engines like mental ray may not show up in the Render Settings window right away. In this case, the renderers' respective plug-ins must be loaded first. I'll discuss this further in the section "mental ray for Maya" later in this chapter.

Choosing a Filename

Rendered images are identified by a filename, a frame number, and an extension, in the form *name.#.ext*—for example, `stillife.0234.tif`.

In the File Name Prefix text box, enter the image sequence name. If you don't enter anything in this text box, Maya automatically names your rendered images after your scene file (`stillife` in the example). This is the preferred naming convention; using it, you can immediately identify the scene file from which a particular image file was rendered.

In the Frame/Animation Ext drop-down list box, select *name.#.ext* to render out a sequence of files. If you leave this setting at the default of *name.ext*, only a single frame will render, no matter what the animation range is in the Time slider.

> *Name.#.ext* is perhaps the most commonly used convention, as opposed to *name.ext.#* or *name.#*, because it allows you to identify the file type easily in Windows. Although Mac OS X isn't as picky about the order of the number and extension, most Mac compositing software applications (such as After Effects and Shake) want filenames that end in the three-letter extension. Therefore, it's best for both Mac and Windows users to employ the *name.#.ext* format.

The extension portion of the image name is a three-letter abbreviation for the type of file you're writing to disk to ensure that you can identify the file type.

Image Format

In the Image Format drop-down list box, select the type of image file you want to render. Maya will add the appropriate extension to the filename.

The image format you choose depends on your own preference and your output needs. For example, Joint Photographic Experts Group (JPEG) files may be great for the small file sizes preferred on the Internet, but their color compression and lack of alpha channel (a feature discussed later in this chapter) make them undesirable for most professional CG work beyond test renders.

It's best to render a sequence of images rather than a movie file for two reasons. First, you want your renders to be their best quality with little or no image compression. Second, if a render fails during a movie render, you must re-render the entire sequence. With an image sequence, however, you can pick up where the last frame left off.

The best file type format to render to is Tagged Image File Format (TIFF). This format enjoys universal support, has little to no compression, and supports an alpha channel. Almost all image-editing and compositing packages can read Targa- and TIFF-formatted files, so either is a safe choice most of the time. For more on image formats, see Chapter 1, "Introduction to Computer Graphics and 3D."

Frame Range

Maya defaults to the range 1–10, which you may need to change to render your entire sequence. You must choose a naming convention other than Name (Single Frame) to access the frame range. This is a common oversight when people first try to render their animations and see that only a single frame renders.

Enter the Start Frame and End Frame attributes for part of the sequence or the entire sequence. By specifying new start and end frames, you can render different portions of a sequence or pick up where a previous render left off.

The By Frame attribute specifies the intervals at which the sequence will render. For example, if you want to render only the odd-numbered frames, set the Start Frame attribute to 1, and set the By Frame attribute to 2. If you want to render only even-numbered frames, set Start Frame to 2, set By Frame to 2, and so on. Typically, you leave By Frame set to 1 so that Maya renders each frame.

The Frame Padding attribute and slider have to do with the way an operating system, such as Windows or Mac OS X, orders its files by inserting leading zeros in the frame number. For example, if Frame Padding is set to 4, the filename contains three leading zeros; therefore, frame 8 is `name.0008.tif` as opposed to `name.8.tif` (which is set to a padding of 1).

Large sequences of files are easier to organize if they all have a frame padding of at least 3. Figure 11.2 shows an image sequence without padding and with padding. The files without padding aren't shown in numeric order.

Figure 11.2

Images rendered without frame padding (left). Frame padding makes file sequences easier to organize (right).

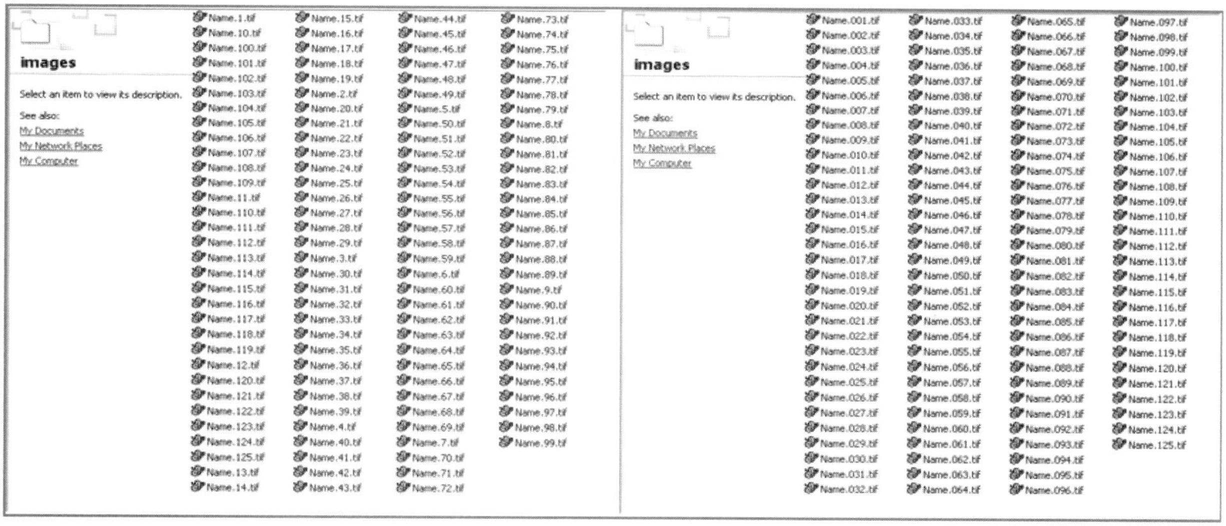

Camera and Channels

Under the Renderable Cameras heading, you choose the camera to render, and enable the Alpha and Depth channels.

Image files are composed of red, green, and blue channels. Each channel specifies the amount of the primary additive color (red, green, or blue, respectively) in the image. (See Chapter 1 for more on how computers define color.) Some file formats save a fourth channel, called the *alpha channel*. This channel defines the image's transparency level. Just as the red channel defines how much red is in an area of the image, the alpha channel defines how transparent the image is when layered or composited on another image. If the alpha channel is black, the image is perfectly see-through. If the alpha channel is white, the image is solid and opaque. The alpha channel is also known as the *matte*. An object with some transparency like tinted glass will render with a gray alpha channel, as shown in Figure 11.3.

The alpha channel can be displayed in the Render View window. As discussed later in this chapter, your test renders also display in this window.

To view an image's alpha channel in the Render View window, click the Display Alpha Channel icon (⬛). To reset the view to RGB (full-color view), click the Display RGB Channels icon (⬛).

Most renders have the alpha channels selected, so leave the Alpha Channel (Mask) check box selected at all times, as shown in Figure 11.4. Note, however, that JPEG,

Figure 11.4

Output an alpha channel.

Graphics Interchange Format (GIF), and Windows bitmap files don't support alpha channels, regardless of whether the Alpha Channel (Mask) check box is selected.

Only a few file formats, such as Maya IFF, support the depth channel. This grayscale channel resembles the alpha channel but conveys depth information—that is, the distance of an object from the camera. The Depth Channel (Z Depth) setting is typically used when compositing images.

Setting Resolution

The Width and Height attributes set the pixel size of the image to be rendered, a.k.a. the image *resolution*. In the Image Size section of the Render Settings window, you can select a resolution from the Presets drop-down list. The commonly used resolution for professional broadcast is 1920×1080 High Definition, which appears as HD 1080 in the Presets list. To composite Maya CG into a home-shot digital video (DV) movie, you use the standard DV resolution of 720×480 to render your scene, but you must enter that resolution manually in the Width and Height fields. (For more on resolutions, see Chapter 1.)

The Device Aspect Ratio and Pixel Aspect Ratio attributes adjust the width of the image to accommodate certain professional output needs; you do not need to adjust them here.

> Make sure your Pixel Aspect Ratio attribute is set to 1 before you render, especially HD resolutions, unless you need to render CCIR 601/Quantel NTSC or DV for television needs; otherwise, your image may look squeezed or widened compared to any live-action footage you use to composite.

The higher your resolution, the longer the scene will take to render. With large frame sequences, it's advisable to render tests at half the resolution of the final output or less to save time. In addition to turning down the resolution for a test, you can use a lower-quality render.

Selecting a Render Engine

Maya allows you to select a render engine in the Render Settings window. Although mental ray for Maya is most commonly used, the other rendering methods give you flexibility in choosing a final look for your project.

Maya Software

Maya Software, the default software rendering method, can capture just about everything you want in your scene, from reflections to motion blur and transparencies. You can use the software rendering method in a couple of ways.

USING RAYTRACING

Raytracing, a topic introduced in Chapter 10, "Autodesk Maya Lighting," is used to incorporate two optical effects into a rendering that the default software rendering method can't handle. *Raytracing* traces rays of light from each light source to every object in the shot and then traces the light's reflection from the object to the camera's lens. This allows true *reflections* and *refractions* to appear in the render as well as highly defined shadows (for more on shadows, see Chapter 10).

True Reflections   True reflections occur when every object in the scene is viewed in a reflective surface, as a reflection of course. You can also have objects with reflections explicitly turned off through the Render Stats section in the Attribute Editor in case you don't want a particular reflection, which is common. Although it's possible to simulate reflections in Maya Software using *reflection maps*, true reflections can be generated only through raytracing. (In Chapter 7, "Autodesk Maya Shading and Texturing," the TableLamp project shows how to apply reflection maps.)

Refractions   *Refractions* occur when light bends as it passes through one medium into another medium of different density. For example, a pencil in a glass of water appears to be broken. The light bouncing off the pencil refracts as it travels from the water into the air, bending a bit during the transition. That displaces the view of the pencil under the water, making it seem broken.

You saw in the previous chapter that raytracing is also a vital component of mental ray for Maya as well as the Maya Software renderer.

As with raytraced shadows, raytraced reflections need to be enabled. To do so, click Raytracing in the Raytracing Quality section of the Maya Software tab in the Render Settings window. Unlike raytraced shadows, however, raytraced reflections need not be explicitly turned on through the lights.

As soon as raytracing is enabled, any reflective surface receives a true reflection of the objects and environment in the scene. Even objects with reflection maps reflect other objects in addition to their reflection maps. For more on reflection maps, see the section "Reflections and Refractions" later in this chapter.

RENDER QUALITY

With software rendering, the render quality depends most noticeably on *anti-aliasing*. Anti-aliasing is the effect produced when pixels appear to blur together to soften a jagged edge on an angled line. Increasing the anti-aliasing level of a render produces an image that has smoother angles and curves. The Render Settings window contains presets that specify this level and a few others to set the quality of your render. Follow these steps:

1. In the Render Settings window, make sure Maya Software is selected in the Render Using drop-down list, and click the Maya Software tab.

2. In the Anti-aliasing Quality section, select either Preview Quality or Production Quality from the Quality preset drop-down list.

Figure 11.5 shows the fruit still life from Chapter 10 rendered with the Preview Quality preset and the same image with the Production Quality preset.

Figure 11.5

With Preview Quality (left), the edges of the fruit are jagged. With Production Quality (right), the jaggedness is gone.

Of course, the higher the quality, the longer the render will take. As you become more experienced, you'll be better able to balance uncompromised quality with efficient render times.

Maya Hardware and Hardware 2.0

The hardware rendering method uses your graphic card's processor to render the scene. Hardware renders are similar to what you may see when you play a 3D video game.

This method results in faster render times, but it lacks some of the features and quality you get from a software render. In Figure 11.6, the first image shows a wine bottle as rendered through hardware. The render time is blazingly fast, but the quality suffers. The second image shows the software render of the same frame. Hardware rendering becomes a good way to test-render a scene, although only some video cards fully support Maya Hardware rendering.

To use the Maya Hardware renderer, in the Render Settings window, make sure Maya Hardware is selected in the Render Using drop-down list. To specify hardware quality, select a level from the Number Of Samples drop-down list on the Maya Hardware tab.

Figure 11.6

The hardware-rendered wine bottle (left) lacks some subtleties. The software-rendered wine bottle shows better specularity and surface detail (right).

mental ray for Maya

mental ray for Maya has become a standard for rendering through Maya, supplanting the Maya Software renderer because of its stability and quality results. The mental ray for Maya rendering method can also let you emulate the behavior of light even more realistically than the other rendering methods, as you saw in the previous chapter's Physical Sun and Sky exercise. Based on raytracing, mental ray takes the concept further by adding photon maps to the light traces. That is, it projects photon particles from lights and records their behavior and trajectory. The end result allows the phenomena of light *caustics* and *bounce*, also known as *global illumination*.

The mental ray for Maya renderer can be an advanced and intricate rendering language with shaders and procedures all its own. This chapter briefly covers one of the popular mental ray methods called Final Gather using an HDR lighting dome. To use mental ray, you still need to be experienced with the basics of lighting and rendering. At its base, mental ray will give you results similar to those of Maya Software, without any of the bells and whistles enabled.

Maya Vector

Vector rendering lets you render your objects with an illustrated or cartoon look. You can render "ink" outlines of your characters to composite over flat-color passes. Figure 11.7 shows the fruit still life rendered with Maya Vector. This rendering method is different from the Maya toon-shading feature, which is briefly covered in Chapter 12, "Autodesk Maya Dynamics and Effects."

Figure 11.7

The fruit still life as a vector render

Maya Vector can output animated files in Adobe Flash format for direct use in web pages and animations, as well as Adobe Illustrator files and the usual list of image formats. To specify the attribute settings for Maya Vector, you use the Maya Vector tab in the Render Settings window (see Figure 11.8).

In the Fill Options section, click the Fill Objects check box, and select the number of colors for each object to set the look of the render. If you want the renderer to include an outline of the edges of your geometry, in the Edge Options section, click the Include Edges check box and set the line weights.

Previewing Your Render: The Render View Window

The Render View window automatically opens when you test-render a frame, as you've already seen in your work through this book. To open it manually, choose Window → Rendering Editors → Render View. Your current scene renders in the Render View window. Figure 11.9 shows the important icons in this window.

Redo Previous Render   Renders the last-rendered view panel.

Render Region   Renders only the selected portion of an image. To select a portion of an image, click within the image in the Render View window, and drag a red box around a region.

Snapshot   Grabs a snapshot of the currently selected modeling panel and inserts it as a background in the Render View. You can more easily do a render region this way.

Open Render Settings Window   Opens the Render Settings window (also known as the Render Globals window in previous versions of Maya).

Display RGB Channels   Displays the full color of the image.

Display Alpha Channel   Displays only the alpha matte of the render as a black-and-white image.

Display Real Size   Resets the image size to 100 percent to make sure the image displays properly. When the Render View window is resized or when you select a new render resolution, the image renders to fit the window, and the image is resized if needed. If your render looks blocky, make sure the Render View window is displaying at real size before adjusting the options in the Render Settings window.

Select Renderer   Lets you select the rendering method. This is the same as selecting it in the Render Settings window.

Information Readout   At the bottom of the Render View window is a readout of information about the frame rendered. This information tells you the resolution, renderer used, frame number, render time, and camera used to render. This readout is a huge help in comparing different render settings and different frames as you progress in your work, especially when you keep images in the buffer (as explained later).

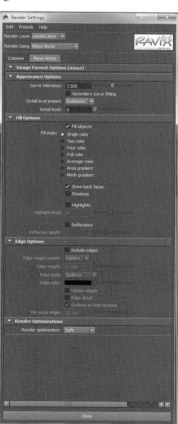

Figure 11.8

The Maya Vector rendering settings

Figure 11.9

The Render View window

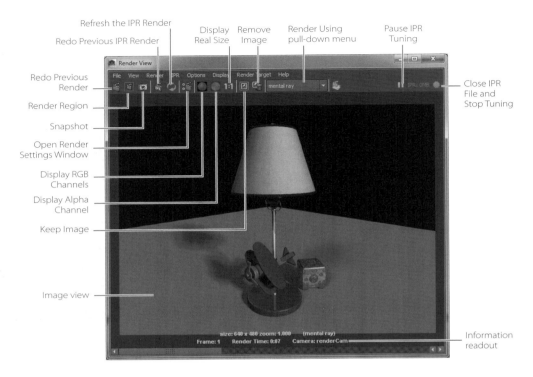

Saving/Loading an Image

Although you typically use the Render View window to test a scene, you can also use it to save single frames by choosing File → Save Image to save in any image formats supported in Maya. Likewise, choose File → Open Image to display any previously rendered image file in this window. If your task in Maya is to create a single frame, this is the best way to render and save it.

Keep/Remove Image

The Render View window is a prime place to see adjustments to various parts of your scene. You can store images in its buffer by clicking the Keep Image icon. When you do, a scroll bar appears at the bottom of the window, and you can scroll through any saved images. This is handy for making a change, rendering it, and scrolling back and forth between the old saved image and the new render to make sure the change is to your liking. You can store a number of images in the buffer. For a faster way to preview changes, use IPR rendering, as discussed next.

IPR Rendering

As you saw in Chapter 7, a fast way to preview changes to your scene is to use Maya Interactive Photorealistic Rendering (IPR). After you IPR-render a view panel, specify the region you want to tune by dragging a box around that area of the image in the Render View window. Maya updates that region every time you make a shader or lighting change to the scene. Figure 11.10 shows the decorative box as an IPR mental ray render as the color and specular levels are being fine-tuned against a wireframe snapshot of the model.

IPR is perfect for finding just the right lighting and specular levels. It will, however, register raytracing elements such as refractions and true reflections only if the scene is set to render through mental ray for Maya. Overall, IPR quality is fairly close to that of a full render while still allowing you to watch your tuning in near real time.

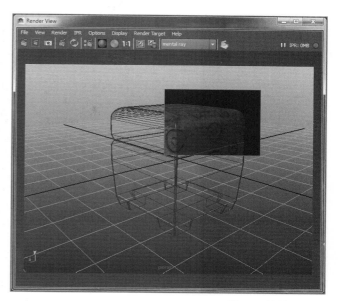

Figure 11.10

IPR rendering lets you fine-tune your textures and lighting with near-real-time feedback.

Reflections and Refractions

As you saw in Chapter 7, creating a "faked" reflection with a map for an object is pretty simple. To generate true reflections without the use of maps, however, you'll need to enable raytracing in either Maya Software or mental ray for Maya. With raytracing, Maya reflects any objects in the scene that fall in the proper line of sight.

> **RAYTRACING WITH MENTAL RAY**
>
> Enabling raytracing in mental ray is as simple as checking the Raytracing box in the Render Settings window on the Features tab.

Raytraced Reflections

To enable raytraced reflections, use a material with a Reflections attribute, such as a Phong, and open the Render Settings window. Choose Maya Software, and on the Maya Software tab, click the Raytracing check box in the Raytracing Quality section. (See Figure 11.11.)

Figure 11.11

Enabling raytracing in Maya Software rendering

Figure 11.12

Reflections set to 1 (left); Reflections set to 2 (right)

The sliders control the quality of the render by specifying how many times to reflect or refract for any given object. Setting Reflections to 2, for example, enables an object's reflection in a second object to appear as part of its reflection in a third object.

The first image in Figure 11.12 shows the still life reflecting onto the surface of its table. In this case, Reflections is set to 1. If you increase Reflections to 2, however, you'll see the reflections of the pieces of fruit in each other also reflecting in the surface of the table.

Notice the difference in the reflections of the fruit in the table between the two renders. Raytraced reflections can consume valuable render resources and time, so it's a good idea to make your scene efficient.

You can control the number of reflections on a per-object basis as opposed to setting limits on the entire scene through the Render Settings window. To access a shader's reflection limits, select the shader in the Hypershade, and open the Attribute Editor. In the Raytrace Options section, drag the Reflection Limit slider to set the maximum number of reflections for that shader. The lower value (either this value or the Reflections value in the Render Settings window) dictates how many reflections are rendered for every object attached to that shader. The default shader reflection limit is 1, so make sure you change the Reflections value as well as each shader's value if you want more than one level of reflection.

Furthermore, you may not want some objects to cast reflections in a scene with raytraced reflections. To specify that an object doesn't cast reflections, select the object in a Maya panel, and open the Attribute Editor. In the Render Stats section, clear the Visible In Reflections check box.

Rendering Refractions

Refractions are also a raytraced-only ability. Refractions require that an object be semi-transparent so that you can see through it to the object (or objects) behind it being refracted. To control refractions, use the shader.

To enable refractions, select the appropriate shader in the Hypershade, and open the Attribute Editor. In the Raytrace Options section, click the Refractions check box. Now you need to set a refractive index for the shader and a refraction limit, similar to the reflection limit.

The refractive index must be greater or less than 1 to cause a refraction. Typically, a number within 0.2 of 1 is perfect for most refraction effects. The first image in Figure 11.13 is raytraced with a refractive index of 1.2 on the wine bottle and glasses; the second image has a refractive index of 0.8 on both bottle and glasses.

You can specify whether an object is visible in a refracting object by clicking or clearing the Visible In Refractions check box in the Render Stats section of the object's Attribute Editor.

When rendering refractions, make sure the Refractions attribute under Raytracing Quality in the Maya Software tab of the Render Settings is set to at least 2 or higher; otherwise, your refraction may not appear properly. For mental ray, it is the Refractions attribute found under the Raytracing heading on the Quality tab, as shown in Figure 11.13 (right). You will also need to set the Refraction Limit found under the Raytrace Options heading in the Attribute Editor for the refractive shader in question.

Figure 11.13

Refractive index of 1.2 (left render); refractive index of 0.8 (middle render); setting the refraction quality in the Render Settings and the shader (right two windows)

Using Cameras

Cameras capture all the animation fun in the scene. The more you know about photography, the easier these concepts are to understand.

The term *camera*, in essence, refers to the perspective view. You can have as many cameras in the scene as you want, but it's wise to have a camera you're planning to render with placed to frame the shot and a different camera acting as the perspective work view so you can move around your scene as you work. The original persp view panel fits that latter role well, although it can be used as a render camera just as easily.

You can also render any of your work windows to test-render orthogonal views of your model the same way you render a perspective view.

Creating a Camera

The simplest way to create a new camera is to choose Panels → Perspective → New, as you've seen in a previous exercise. This creates a new camera node in Maya and sets that active panel to its view.

You can select a camera and transform it (move it, rotate it, scale it) just as you would select and transform any other object in Maya to be animated or positioned.

Furthermore, you can move a camera and rotate it using the Alt/Option key and mouse button combinations.

For example, click inside a new Maya Scene Perspective window to make it active. Select that view's camera by choosing View → Select Camera. The camera's attributes appear in the Channel Box. Try moving the view around using the Alt/Option key and mouse button combinations. Notice how the attributes change to reflect the new position and rotation of the camera. You can animate the camera—for example, zoom in or out or pan across the scene—by setting keyframes on any of these attributes.

Camera Types

You can create three types of nonstereo cameras for your scene: Camera; Camera And Aim; and Camera, Aim, And Up (also known as single-node, two-node, and three-node cameras, respectively). To create any of these cameras, choose Create → Cameras. You can also change the type of these cameras at any time through the Attribute Editor. The other two options for creating cameras are Stereo Camera and Multi Stereo Rig to allow for a stereoscopic effect, although they aren't covered in this book.

The single-node camera (Camera) is the most common (see Figure 11.14). This camera consists of a single camera node that you move and rotate as you would any other object for proper positioning. The persp view panel's camera is a single-node camera.

Figure 11.14

A single-node camera

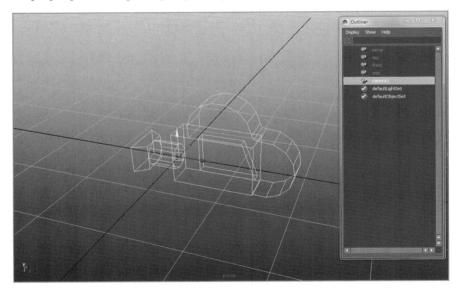

The two-node camera (Camera And Aim) consists of the camera node and an aim node. You use the aim node to point the camera as opposed to rotating it to orient it properly. This is useful for animating a camera following an object. You animate the movement of the aim node to follow your object much as you'd follow a car around a racetrack. The camera pivots to follow its aim point and, hence, the object. (See Figure 11.15.)

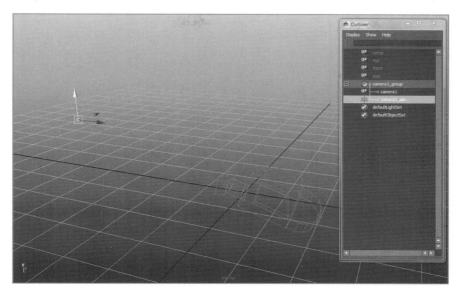

Figure 11.15

A two-node camera

The three-node camera (Camera, Aim, And Up) has a camera node, an aim node, and an up node. The additional up node is to orient the camera's up direction. This gives you the ability to animate the side-to-side rotation of the camera as well as its aim direction. (See Figure 11.16.)

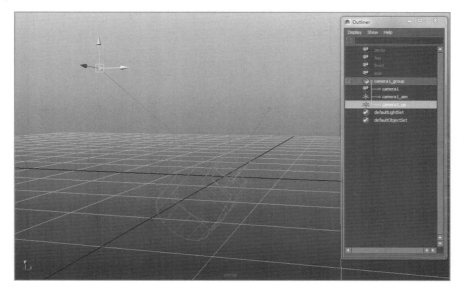

Figure 11.16

A three-node camera

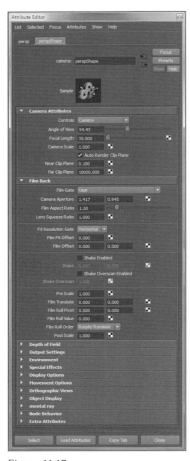

Figure 11.17

The Attribute Editor for the persp camera

Figure 11.18

Different focal lengths

Camera Attributes

As an example, set your project to Lighting, and download the
`still_life_render_v02.mb` scene from the Lighting project on the book's
web page, www.sybex.com/go/introducingmaya2014. You'll see a green box in
the persp view panel that displays the resolution (set to 640×480) and the
name of the camera (camera1).

Special attributes control the function of camera nodes. To set these attributes, follow these steps:

1. With `camera1` selected, open the Attribute Editor (press Ctrl+A or choose
   View → Camera Attribute Editor).

2. At the top of the window, select the type of camera controls you want.
   The Controls attribute sets the type of camera from single- to two- to
   three-control nodes. Figure 11.17 shows the Attribute Editor for the
   persp camera.

Focal Length

The Focal Length attribute specifies the length of the lens. The lower the
focal length (a.k.a. short lens), the wider the view. At very low numbers,
however, the image is distorted, as you can see in the comparison in
Figure 11.18. The higher the focal length, the closer the subject seems to
the camera.

Although adjusting the Focal Length attribute of a camera zooms in and
out, it isn't the same as moving the camera closer to your subject using the
Alt+right-click procedure to zoom in view panels (which is called *trucking*
the camera). Focal-length zooming can create optical distortions, such as can
be created with a fish-eye lens.

If you need to match some CG element in Maya to a photograph or video
that you've imported as an image plane, set your camera's focal length to
match that of the real camera used for the background photo.

Focal Length = 35   Focal Length = 8   Focal Length = 60

Clipping Planes

All cameras in Maya have clipping planes that restrict the amount of information that can be seen through them. The clipping plane is defined by the Near Clip Plane and Far Clip Plane attributes. These set the minimum and maximum distances, respectively, of the clipping plane. Any object or portion of an object that passes beyond these distances won't show in the window and should not render.

If you notice objects disappearing as you move your camera and create a scene, it may be because of the clipping plane. Increase the Far Clip Plane attribute, and the objects should reappear in the view.

Film Back

The Film Back attributes concern the type of output you'll be dealing with after your renders are finished and you're ready to put your animation on tape, DVD, film, or what have you.

Film Gate   Defines the aspect ratio of your camera's view. Images that are output to HD television have an aspect ratio of 1:1.78, which funnily enough does not have a preset in the Film Gate drop-down list. For an HD camera output, simply set Film Aspect Ratio to **1.78**. For standard-definition TV output, simply select 35mm TV Projection from the Film Gate drop-down list. (For more on aspect ratios, see Chapter 1.)

Fit Resolution Gate   Allows you to align footage you may have imported as an image plane to match up CG properly to live action.

Overscan

Found in the Display Options section for the camera's Attribute Editor, Overscan lets you resize the view without changing the film gate that will render. For example, the scene on the left in Figure 11.19 is set up with an Overscan setting of 1.3, allowing you to see more than what will render, which is defined by the outline box. The scene on the right in Figure 11.19 is set up with an Overscan setting of 2, which increases even more how much you see in the camera1 panel but doesn't change the view when rendered.

Figure 11.19

Overscan settings define how much you can see of your scene in the camera but not how much renders in the image.

You can turn the green box in the panel on and off through the camera's Attribute Editor. Also in the Display Options section are Display Film Gate and Display Resolution check boxes, shown in Figure 11.20. Ideally, these two green boxes should align perfectly

Figure 11.20

Camera display options

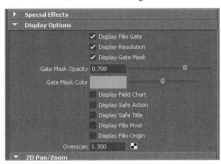

in the view pane. If the resolution box (the solid green line) doesn't line up with the film gate box (the dashed green line), change your film gate selection to match the resolution's aspect ratio in the Render Settings window. A resolution of 640×480, for example, has an aspect ratio of 1.33, the same as the 35mm TV Projection film gate currently selected for this scene.

Environment

In the Environment section, you'll find attributes to adjust the background color that renders and to create an image plane, as shown in Figure 11.21.

If you want to use a solid color as the camera's background when you render, click the color swatch next to Background Color to change the background color in your renders using the Color Chooser. The slider allows you to control the value, or brightness, of the current color. Neither changes the background color of your view panels, however.

CAMERA IMAGE PLANES

A camera image plane isn't like the reference planes you used for modeling the red wagon in Chapter 6, "Practical Experience." In this case, an image plane is created to be a background specific for that particular camera or view panel, but it's typically also used as a reference, much like the planes you created and mapped in Chapter 6. Camera image planes are useful

Figure 11.22

An image to import as a camera image plane

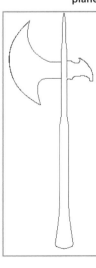

when you're matching your scene to existing footage or an image. For example, if you need to animate a flying saucer into a home video of a family gathering, you would import the video as an image sequence into Maya through a perspective camera to be able to line up your UFO properly to zap your cousins.

Figure 11.21

Adjusting the camera's environment and creating camera image planes

You can import an image plane by clicking the Create button in the Environment section of the Attribute Editor (see Figure 11.21) or directly through a view panel's menu, as you'll see in the next exercise.

In this exercise, you'll learn how to import a sketch of an axe into the Front view panel for a modeling assignment. (You won't actually model the axe, however.) The image, a sketch of a simple axe design, is to be used as a template for outlining the model. You can find the file Axe_outline_1.tif in the Sourceimages folder of the Axe project on the companion web page; it's shown in Figure 11.22.

Follow these steps:

1. Choose File → New Scene.

2. Import the sketch of the axe into Maya as a camera image plane for the Front view panel. In your Front window, choose View → Image Plane → Import Image.

3. Point to Axe_outline_1.tif in the Axe project's Sourceimages folder and load it. The sketch displays in your Front window and as a selected plane in the Perspective window (see Figure 11.23). You should see the image plane's attributes in the Attribute Editor. At first, the plane looks a little small in your view panels, but you can adjust the size of the image plane in the Attribute Editor under the Placement Extras heading using the Width and Height attributes. Just make sure that the Maintain Pic Aspect Ratio box is checked. In Figure 11.23, the Width and Height settings have been adjusted to 25.0×17.325.

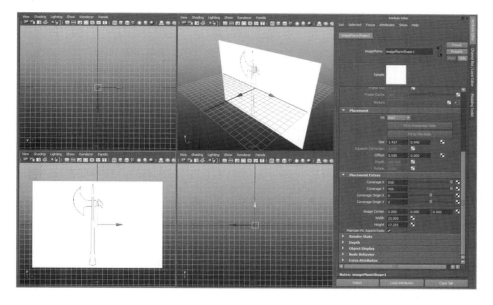

Figure 11.23

Importing a camera image plane into the Front view panel

Now you'd be ready to trace the outline of the axe easily in the Front view panel, if you were going to model the axe.

> If you can't see the image plane, click Show in the view panel, and make sure Cameras is checked.

IMAGE PLANE SEQUENCE

A movie file or a sequence of files can also be brought in to animate or to track motion (a.k.a. *matchmoving*) as a camera image plane. It's generally best to use a frame sequence, however. When you bring in an image for an image plane, check the Use Image Sequence box in the image plane's Attribute Editor window, as shown in Figure 11.24. Maya will automatically load the image to correspond to the frame number in the scene. For example, at frame 29 in your Maya animation, Maya loads frame 29 of your image sequence. But your image file sequence must be numbered correctly (such as `filename.###.tif`). You can import an image plane into any perspective view in exactly the same way.

> If the clutter of seeing a camera image plane in the other windows bothers you, under Image Plane Attributes in the Attribute Editor, change the radio button selection next to Display from In All Views to Looking Through Camera. This setting removes the image plane from the other windows.

Motion Blur

Motion blur is an optical phenomenon that occurs when an object moves quickly in front of a camera: the object looks blurred as it crosses the frame. Maya Software rendering renders motion blur in two ways—2D blur or 3D blur—although neither will render as reflections.

- In the 2D blur process, Maya calculates after the frame is rendered. Any objects moving in the frame are blurred with a 2D filter effect. The 2D blur is effective for most applications and faster than 3D blur.

- The 3D blur process is calculated while a frame of the sequence is rendering. Every motion blur–enabled object is blurred with typically better results than 2D blur but at a cost of a much longer render time.

I'll briefly cover motion blur in mental ray for Maya later in the chapter.

To enable motion blur for the Maya Software renderer, open the Render Settings window. In the Motion Blur section on the Maya Software tab, click the Motion Blur check box. Then, choose 2D or 3D blur.

Typically, you control the amount of blur rendered for 2D and 3D by setting the Blur By Frame attribute—the higher the number, the greater the blur. Using additional controls, however, you can increase or decrease the 2D blur effect in the render. The Blur Length attribute affects the streakiness of the blur to further increase or decrease the amount of motion blur set with the Blur By Frame attribute.

> Setting a camera's Shutter Angle attribute (in the camera's Attribute Editor in the Special Effects section) also affects the amount of blur rendered—the higher the number, the greater the blur.

Figure 11.24

Importing a sequence of image files as a camera image plane

Batch Rendering

So far, you've used single-frame rendering numerous times to see a scene in the Render View window. But how do you start rendering an animation sequence to disk? This is called *batch rendering* in Maya, whichever renderer you use. To batch-render an entire scene, follow these steps:

1. Open the Render Settings window.

2. Choose Maya Software to use to render, enter the start and end frames of your animation, and select your image format. Select your quality and resolution settings. Finally, set the camera you want to render in the `Renderable Camera` attribute.

> Be sure to select *name.#.ext* in the Frame/Animation Ext drop-down list to render a sequence of files. Remember, if you leave the default setting, which is *name.ext*, only a single frame renders.

Figure 11.25

The Batch Render Frame dialog box for Maya Software (top) and mental ray rendering (bottom)

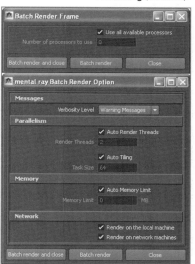

3. In the main Maya window under the Rendering menu set, choose Render → Batch Render ❏ to open the Batch Render Animation dialog box (or the Batch Render Frame box when rendering a single image). Figure 11.25 shows the Maya Software rendering batch options on top, and the bottom image shows the batch options for mental ray rendering.

4. If you have a multiprocessor, hyperthreading, or dual-core machine, select how many CPUs you would like to use to render your scene. A value of 0 will use all processors on the machine.

5. Click Batch Render to render the frame range you specified in the Render Settings window. The render occurs in the background, and you see progress updates in the Command line at the bottom of your Maya screen and in the Script Editor window if you open it.

To see a frame as the batch render progresses, choose Render → Show Batch Render. To cancel a batch render, choose Render → Cancel Batch Render.

When you batch render, your image files are written to the Images folder of the current project. Make sure your project is properly set; otherwise, your files will end up in an unexpected folder. You can always see the render path and the image name at the top of the Render Settings window, as shown in Figure 11.26.

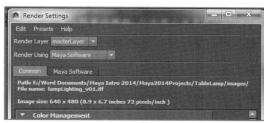

Figure 11.26

The Render Settings window shows you where the images will be rendered.

Rendering the Wine Bottle

In this section, you'll set up and render an animated camera to move over 25 frames of a wine bottle still life.

Set your current project to the Lighting project downloaded from the book's web page, and then load `still_life_render_v01.mb`. You'll adjust your render settings and some shader properties to make the wine bottle look more like glass.

Selecting Render Settings Options

Set your resolution and quality settings in the Render Settings window.

1. Open the Render Settings window, and select Maya Software. Click the Maya Software tab.

2. From the Quality drop-down list, select Production Quality. Doing so presets the appropriate settings to produce a high-quality render.

3. Click the Common tab. Set Frame/Animation Ext to *name.#.ext*, set Start Frame to **1**, set End Frame to **25**, and set Frame Padding to **2**.

4. From the Image Format drop-down list, select TIFF.

5. Make sure Renderable Camera is set to camera1. In the Image Size section, set Presets to 640×480.

Setting Up the Scene

Now, set up some of the objects in the scene. The wine bottle has been imported into the still life scene, and three wine glasses have been added. All the lights are in place, as is the camera.

Start by setting up this scene to raytrace to get true reflections and refractions.

1. Turn on refractions for the Glass shaders. In the Hypershade, select the Glasses material, and open the Attribute Editor. In the `Raytrace Options` section, click the Refractions check box, and set Refractive Index to **1.2**. Set Reflection Limit to **2**. Select the Wine_Bottle material, and repeat the previous steps.

2. You need to change your lights' shadows to raytraced shadows. Remember that semi-transparent objects cast solid shadows unless shadows are raytraced, so the glasses and wine bottle will cast shadows as if they were solid and not glass. In the Outliner, select `spotLight1`. In the Attribute Editor, in the `Shadows` section, enable Use Ray Trace Shadows. Repeat these steps for the remaining two shadow-casting lights: spotLight4 and spotLight3. Figure 11.27 shows the three shadow-casting lights in the scene in white.

3. Open the `Render Settings` window, and turn on raytracing in the Raytracing Quality section. Set Reflections to **2**.

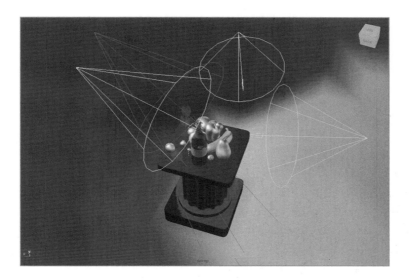

Figure 11.27

Shadow lights

You can't select all three lights at once to turn on raytraced shadows in the Attribute Editor. Any adjustments you make in the Attribute Editor affect only the most recently selected object, not multiple selections.

Setting Up the Camera

Next, you'll set up the camera to render the scene.

1. Open the camera's Attribute Editor through the `camera1` panel (choose View → Camera Attribute Editor).

2. Select the Display Film Gate option in the Display Options section to turn on a dashed green box in the `camera1` panel. Enable the Display Resolution option. Notice that the two boxes aren't aligned.

3. Because the resolution is 640×480, you'll use a 1.33 aspect ratio. Select 35mm TV Projection from the Film Gate drop-down list. The two green boxes now align. Although it's not absolutely necessary to match the resolution with the film gate, it's definitely good practice to do so, especially if you'll later insert CG in live-action videos.

4. As soon as you change the film gate, the framing of the scene changes. You must move the camera out to frame the entire still life. If you try to use the Alt key and mouse button combinations to zoom out, you'll notice that you can't move the camera in this scene: the movement attributes for the camera have been locked to prevent accidental movement that would disrupt the shot.

5. To unlock the camera, choose View → Select Camera. The camera's attributes appear in the Channel Box. Some are grayed out, signifying that they're locked and can't be changed. Highlight the locked attributes, and right-click Unlock Selected in the Channel Box.

6. Create an animated camera move to pull out and reveal the still life slowly over 25 frames. Set your Range slider to 1 to 25 frames. Go to frame 1. The `camera1` view should be similar to that shown in Figure 11.28. Select all three `Translate` and `Rotate` channels in the Channel Box, and right-click Key Selected to set keyframes for the first camera position.

7. Zoom (actually, truck) the camera out by pressing Alt+right-click to a wider framing to reveal the entire still life. Highlight the Translate and Rotate channels again in the Channel Box, and set keyframes for them. (See Figure 11.29.)

Scrub your animation, and you'll see a pullout revealing the full scene.

> You can lock the camera to prevent accidentally moving the view after you set your keyframes, especially if Auto Keyframe is on. Select the Translate and Rotate attributes in the Channel Box, and right-click Lock Selected.

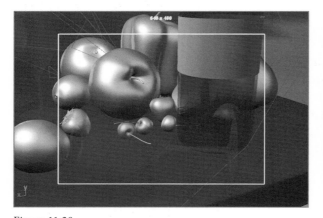

Figure 11.28

The camera view at the beginning of the animation

Figure 11.29

Pull out the camera.

Batch Rendering and Playing Back the Sequence

Now, you're ready to render out the 25-frame sequence. Choose Render → Batch Render.

Because you're raytracing this scene at full resolution, this render could take 20 minutes or longer. To chart the progress of the render, open the Script Editor by clicking its icon on the Help line or by choosing Window → General Editors → Script Editor.

To see the frames play back, you'll need a program that can load the images in sequence and play them back for you. You can also import the image sequence into a compositing or editing program, such as Adobe After Effects or Premiere, to play back as a clip and edit as you like.

You can also use FCheck, a frame viewer that is included with Maya. This small and surprisingly powerful program plays back your images in real time so that you can judge your finished animation. To use FCheck, follow these steps:

Figure 11.30

FCheck, shown here with a sample image, plays back your rendered sequence.

1. In Windows, choose Start → All Programs → Autodesk → Autodesk Maya 2014 → FCheck to open the FCheck window, as shown in Figure 11.30.

2. Choose File → Open Animation.

3. In the file browser, find your Images folder in your project, and click the first frame of the sequence you want to play back. FCheck loads the images frame by frame into RAM and then plays them back in real time. Just set your playback speed and use the DVD controls to play back your sequence.

mental ray for Maya

You had some experience with mental ray rendering in the previous chapter as you lighted using Physical Sun and Sky, which automatically used Final Gather to render. In this part of the chapter, I'll discuss mental ray options to begin to scratch the surface of this incredibly powerful renderer.

First, if you haven't done so already, be sure that mental ray is loaded. When you first start up, mental ray for Maya may not load because it's considered a plug-in. Choose Window → Settings/Preferences → Plug-in Manager to open the Plug-in Manager, shown in Figure 11.31. Make sure both the Loaded and Auto Load check boxes for `Mayatomr.mll` (or `Mayatomr.bundle` for Mac users) are checked so that mental ray for Maya loads by default.

Figure 11.31

Use the Plug-in Manager to load mental ray for Maya.

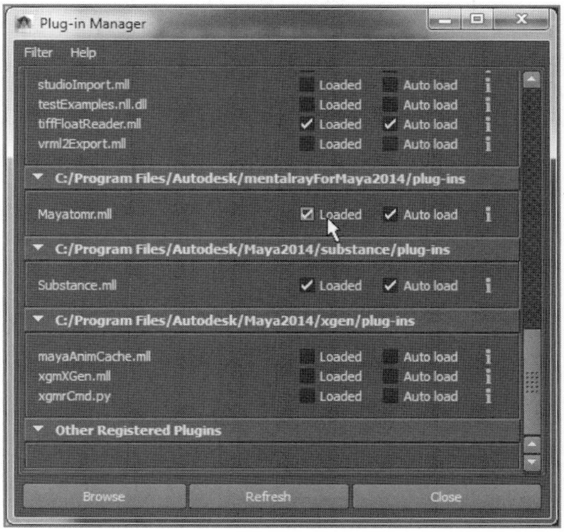

To render with mental ray, open the Render Settings window, and change the Render Using drop-down menu selection to mental ray, as shown in Figure 11.32 (shown with the Features tab selected). The Render Settings window now has the Common tab along with five other mental ray–specific tabs: Passes, Features, Quality, Indirect Lighting, and Options.

mental ray Quality Settings

As with the Maya Software renderer, the primary quality settings for the mental ray renderer center on anti-aliasing. However, mental ray for Maya offers you finer control over how you set the quality levels through the Render Settings window. Under the Anti-Aliasing Quality → Raytrace/Scanline Quality heading on the Quality tab, you'll find these attributes:

Sampling Mode (Under the Renderer Heading) This drop-down menu sets the type of sampling mental ray performs in the render. *Sampling* is the number of times mental ray reads and compares the color values of adjacent pixels in order to smooth the resulting render to avoid jagged lines. The choices are Unified Sampling (default), Legacy Rasterizer Mode, and Legacy Sampling Mode. Unified Sampling is generally the best choice because it sets the best range based on the Min and Max Samples you set along with a single Quality value. With the Min and Max Samples set to 1 and 100, respectively, the Quality value is key. A Quality setting at about 1.0 is considered good for production-quality renders, though you may need slightly higher than 1.0 in some cases. Quality of about 0.3 is a good fast render for previews. Experimenting with Min and Max Sample values will make more minor adjustments to the look of your render than would making changes to Quality.

For those who are already familiar with previous mental ray workflows, Legacy Sampling Mode will give you access to additional sampling modes available in previous versions of mental ray for Maya. Legacy Sampling is discussed in the "Legacy Sampling" sidebar. However, Unified Sampling mode attempts to greatly simplify the quality settings for mental ray for Maya and is preferred for use.

Figure 11.32

The Render Settings window for mental ray, showing the Features tab

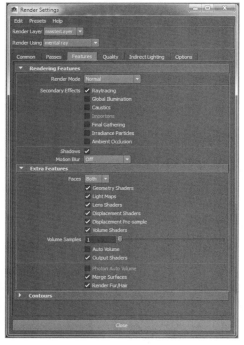

The Error Cutoff value (default at 0) and check boxes for Contrast as Color (default at off) are used for more advanced tweaking of quality settings and by and large should be left at their defaults.

Sample Options Heading Filtering is done on the results of the sampling of pixels to blend the pixels of a region together to form a coherent image. A high filter size tends to blur the image, whereas low filter values may look overly crisp. Box is the default filter and is the fastest to render, whereas Gaussian (Gauss) gives a slightly softer result with the slowest render times. Usually, render times don't vary much between different filter modes—it's not as if Gaussian takes four times longer to render the same frame over the Box filter type. But each gives a slightly different type of softness depending on its Filter Size setting.

LEGACY SAMPLING

When the Sampling Mode option is set to Legacy Sampling, you will have access to more controls over the quality of mental ray renders, which may be helpful if you are familiar with previous versions of mental ray. Under Legacy Sampling, you will see another Sampling Mode drop-down menu: Fixed Sampling, Adaptive Sampling (default), and Custom Sampling. Adaptive Sampling is generally the best choice because it sets the best range based on the Max Sample Level option you set. If you choose Custom, you can set your own sampling range with the Min and Max Sample Level options.

Number of Samples These Min and Max Sample Level values set the number of times mental ray samples a pixel to determine how best to anti-alias the result. The higher the number, the finer the detail and the smoother the appearance of your rendered lines will be. These settings are exponential, so a small increase yields a much greater quality and much longer render time. You won't need to set Max Sample Level above 2 for most uses. Both Max and Min Samples Level can be set into the negative numbers for fast renders, although you'll notice jagged edges. A good setting for most renders is 2 for Max Sample Level with the Adaptive Sampling mode.

What determines the exact sample level within the min and max range set by these attributes is dependent on the Anti-aliasing Contrast Threshold value.

Anti-aliasing Contrast The values here determine when mental ray turns up the number of samples in a particular region of the frame. If the contrast level from one pixel to its neighbor is below the threshold value, mental ray turns up the number of samples for that pixel to render a higher-quality result. Therefore, the lower the values set here, the higher the sample rate will be (within the Min and Max levels set).

Sample Lock is turned on to reduce noise and artifacts in rendered sequences that have lots of movement.

Rather than setting high sample rates with just the Min and Max Sample Level attributes, carefully increase the Quality value to force mental ray to use a sample rate closer to the Max Samples only where it needs to do so. You'll see this in action in the next section.

When you're ready to render your scene to disk, you still use batch rendering; however, the options in the Batch Render Option window are different (Figure 11.33) than they are for Maya Software.

Figure 11.33

mental ray batch render options

Render Settings in Action!

In this section, you'll look at how Quality values and how the number of Min and Max Samples work together to determine the quality of the render of a toy wagon. You can find the scene (`RedWagonRenderSettings.ma`) to render in the RedWagon project on the book's web page. Make sure to set your project to RedWagon. This scene is set up to use Final Gather with an IBL using an HDR image. I'll cover these methods later in this chapter.

Open the Render Settings window, making sure you are set to mental ray, and open the Quality tab. Set your Sampling Mode value to Unified Sampling. Occasionally you may see that Sampling Mode reverts to Legacy Sampling Mode when you open a file even though it was set to Unified Sampling. If that is the case, any settings you've created for Unified Sampling Mode do remain intact. Unified Sampling is mental ray's newest method to speed up rendering, replacing what is now called Legacy Sampling Mode. Quality should be set to **0.50**, Min Samples to **1.0**, and Max Samples to **1.0** in this file already.

These render quality settings are low at first and will yield the render shown in Figure 11.34, which took just less than two minutes. You can see jagged highlights on the wagon, especially the white lines on the side body, the reflections in the front black nose, and the edge of the white rims on the back wheel.

If you increase Max Samples Level to **100** and Min Samples Level to **1.0**, you'll see an immediate increase in quality (especially in the reflections of the wagon and the white decal lines) and a noticeable increase in render time (about 50 percent as long), as shown in Figure 11.35, which took just under three minutes to render.

You can get an even cleaner render. If you crank up the Quality value to the heavens, such as 2.0, you get a far cleaner render than before but with a much longer render time. Figure 11.36 shows the same frame with the Quality value set to 2.0 instead of the default of 0.5. The Min Sample Level option is still set to 1, and the Max Sample Level option is left

Figure 11.34

A toy wagon rendered with low sampling values. Notice the jagged highlights on the white decal lines and the back wheel.

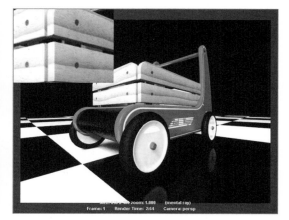

Figure 11.35

Better sampling improves the wagon's appearance.

at 100. The wood panels and the reflections of the wagon in the checkered floor are both noticeably nicer in this render. Your results as you render the scene on your own computer will be more noticeable than the images shown here. But this render took 4:35.

For very quick render to check composition and lighting, set your Quality, Min, and Max Samples all to **0.1**. You should get a super-fast render, though good luck discerning much detail. It's easy enough to crank the numbers to the sky, but render times will very quickly become unacceptable, especially when you have a supervisor or client breathing down your neck. Find just the right combination of numbers for acceptable results in a minimum of time. Each scene will be different.

Figure 11.36

The wagon has still better sampling with a higher Quality value. You'll see it better in your own renders.

Motion Blur with mental ray

Now that you have a primer on quality settings in mental ray for Maya, you'll learn how motion blur works.

1. Load the `Planets_motionBlur.ma` scene file from the Solar_System project on the web page. This is an animated scene of the solar system with just the first few planets and moons, as shown in Figure 11.37. A blast from the past!

2. Open the Render Settings window. The scene should already be set to render with mental ray. If your scene isn't, make sure the mental ray for Maya plug-in is loaded, and set the scene to render with mental ray.

Figure 11.37

The Solar_System project is back!

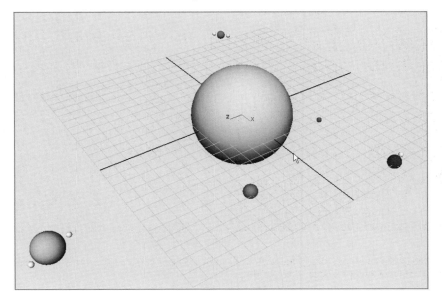

3. On the Common tab, set Frame/Animation Ext to *name.#.ext*, Frame Padding to **3**, Start Frame to **1**, and End Frame to **100**.

4. Set the Image Size to 640×480 for now, and leave the renderable camera to persp.

5. Go to frame 75, and render a frame from the persp view panel. Figure 11.38 shows the result.

6. In Render Settings, click to open the Features tab. In the Rendering Features heading, select No Deformation in the Motion Blur drop-down menu, as shown in Figure 11.39. This setting is the faster of two motion blur methods and works for objects that move in the scene without deformation. *Deformations* occur when the mesh or surface of an object changes, such as when you use a lattice or a skeleton rig like IK to drive a character. For deforming objects, you need to use Full as the Motion Blur setting.

7. Click to open the Quality tab in Render Settings. Set Sampling Mode to Unified Sampling, and set Quality to **0.5** and Min Samples and Max Samples each to **1.0**. In the Motion Blur → Motion Blur Optimization heading, set the Motion Blur By attribute from 1.0 to **3.0** for quite a bit of blur. Render a frame at frame 75. (See Figure 11.40.)

8. The render is very fast and shows quite a bit of blur; however, the quality is low. You see a lot of graininess in your render, especially with the yellow and red planets at the bottom of the screen. On the Quality tab of the Render Settings window, leave Sampling Mode at Unified Sampling, but change Max Samples to **50**. This render should be fast but cleaner, with a smoother but still-grainy motion blur for the planets. Notice, however, that the render time increases by about 50 percent! Now try Max Samples at **100** and Quality at **2.0** (Figure 11.41 shows this much cleaner render). You control the amount of motion blur in your scene with the Motion Blur By attribute (step 7) for your scene.

Figure 11.38

A render of frame 75 shows the planets in motion without any motion blur.

Figure 11.39

Turn on motion blur.

Figure 11.40

Render a frame with motion blur turned on.

Figure 11.41

Motion blur looks much better with higher sampling levels.

Render Layers

Most of the time, it's better to composite different elements together to form a final CG image. Professional CG workflow almost always requires multiple render passes that are composited together later for the maximum in efficiency and quality.

Maya does a great job of making rendering in layers much easier with render layers. As you saw earlier in this book, using display layers helps a lot in keeping your scene organized. Render layers operate in basically the same way, although they function by separating different elements of the scene into separate renders.

I'll address the most basic and commonly utilized render layer functionality here: separating objects into different renders. You'll select elements in a scene and assign them to different render layers. When you batch-render the scene, Maya will render each of the layers separately and save the files into their own subfolders in the Images folder of your current project. You'll then need to load all the different rendered layers into a compositing program, such as The Foundry's NUKE or Adobe After Effects, and composite the layers together.

Render Passes in mental ray

Two powerful features in mental ray rendering, Render Passes and Pass Contribution Maps, make rendering in passes and elements much more efficient. Passes allow you to separate shadows, reflections, diffuse color, and so on, from the render to give the most control in compositing over the image. This mental ray–specific workflow is fairly advanced and requires an existing knowledge of rendering and compositing render passes (such as you will do with render layers) to fully grasp. Thus, I won't cover these features in this book; however, you should be aware of this mental ray rendering pipeline as you move beyond this introduction and continue rendering with mental ray in your own work.

Rendering the Still Life in Layers

In this example, you'll separate a scene into different layers for rendering with mental ray, though the render layer workflow here applies to Maya Software rendering as well.

To separate a scene into different layers, follow these steps:

1. Set your project to the Lighting project downloaded from the book's web page, and open the still life scene (still_life_renderLayers_v01.mb from the Scenes folder to start there). The lights and a camera are already set up in this scene. Set your camera view to camera1. Open Render Settings, and make sure mental ray is the current renderer. Set Sampling Mode to Unified Sampling, set Quality to **2.0**, and set Min/Max Samples to **1.0** and **100**, respectively.

2. To separate the scene into different renders, in the Layer Editor, click the Render tab to switch to the render-layers view. Select the foreground lemon, and click the Create New Layer And Assign Selected Objects icon ( ). Doing so creates a new render layer called layer1 and assigns the lemon to it. (See Figure 11.42.)

3. Click layer1, and everything but the lemon disappears from the scene (see Figure 11.42). Double-click layer1 in the Layer Editor, and rename it **lemonPass**, as shown in Figure 11.43.

Figure 11.42

The newly created render layer with the foreground lemon assigned

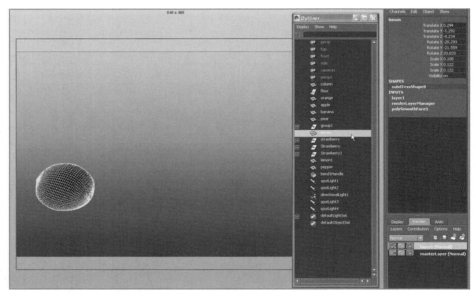

Figure 11.43

Rename the render layer to lemonPass.

4. If you test-render a frame, the frame should turn black. You need to assign your lights to the render layer as well. Select all the lights in the scene using the Outliner, as shown in Figure 11.44. Right-click the lemonPass layer in the Layer Editor, and select Add Selected Objects from the context menu. If you render a test frame now, the lemon renders as shown in Figure 11.45.

5. Create a render layer for the column and floor. Click the masterLayer render layer, and then select the column, the floor, and all the lights in the scene. As you did with the lemon, click the Create New Layer And Assign Selected Objects icon (), and then click the new layer to select and display it. Double-click the layer name to rename the render layer **columnPass** (see Figure 11.46).

6. Click back to the masterLayer; then select all the rest of the pieces of fruit, as shown in Figure 11.47, and create their render layer called **fruitPass**. You should now have three render layers and the default masterLayer. The masterLayer is always present to house all the elements of the scene. It switches to being not renderable as soon as you create a new render layer, as evidenced by the little red *X* in its Renderable icon ([icon]).

7. The first icon on each of the render layer entries in the Layer Editor toggles whether that layer will render or not. Make sure all your render layers are renderable, and leave the masterLayer off. Because all the elements of the scene are assigned to one render layer or another, the whole scene is covered. The masterLayer nonetheless is always present, because it represents all the objects in the scene, assigned to layers or not.

8. With the fruitPass render layer selected, test-render a frame, as shown in Figure 11.48. You should see just the fruit and not the background, column, or foreground lemon. Notice the reflections in the fruit.

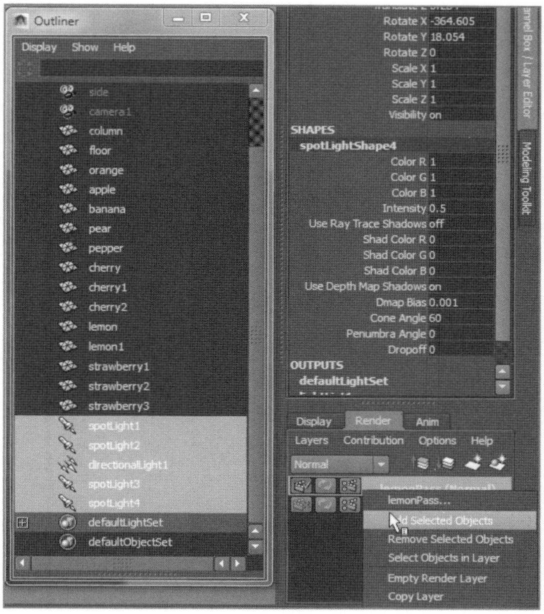

Figure 11.44

Add the lights to the lemonPass render layer.

Figure 11.45

The lemon rendered on its very own layer

Figure 11.46

The background is assigned to its own render layer.

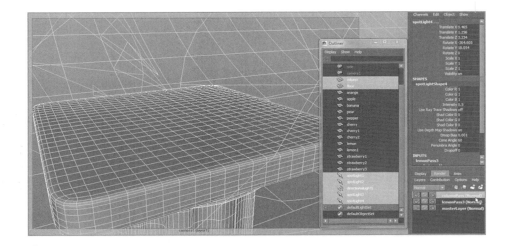

Figure 11.47

The newly created fruitPass render layer

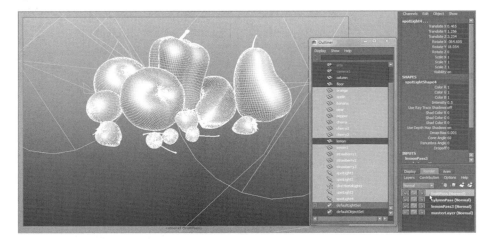

Figure 11.48

Rendering the rest of the fruit

Test-Rendering Everything Together

By default, Maya renders only the selected visible render layer. You can, however, tell Maya to test-render and show you all the layers composited together to give you a preview of what you'll end up with when you composite all the layers together after batch-rendering the scene.

Figure 11.49

Turn on Render All Layers.

To test-render all the layers together, click the Options menu in the Layer Editor, as shown in Figure 11.49, and toggle on Render All Layers by clicking the check box if it isn't already selected.

Now if you test-render a frame, Maya will render each layer separately and then composite them together. Test-render a frame with Render All Layers enabled, and you should notice that the foreground lemon is missing, as in Figure 11.50.

Figure 11.50

Rendering all the layers together

This is because the render layers in the Layer Editor need to be reordered so that columnPass is on the bottom, fruitPass is in the middle, and lemonPass is on top. This is the layer ordering for the composite. You can reorder the render layers by MMB+clicking a layer and dragging it up or down to its new location in the Layer Editor, as in Figure 11.51.

Now if you render the frame with Render All Layers enabled, you see the scene properly placed, as shown in Figure 11.52. Notice that shadows and reflections on the column's tabletop are missing, however. For that, you will need to create render layer overrides to allow reflections and shadows of an object to render, but without the object itself rendering.

Figure 11.51

Reorder the render layers.

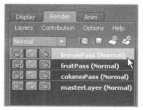

Figure 11.52

Now the lemon appears in the render.

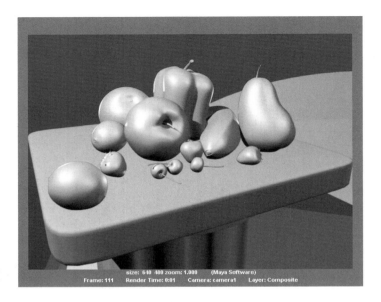

Render Layer Overrides

Where are the shadows and reflections? If you recall from earlier in this chapter, this scene renders with shadows, and this scene should have reflections as well. However, the reflections and shadow-casting objects are on different layers than the column. Shadows and reflections can't be cast from one layer onto another. In the following steps, you'll use render layer overrides to set up your `columnPass` layer to have shadows and reflections from the fruit but not render the fruit on top of the column:

> Render layers and overrides are very powerful workflow tools in Maya. Because there can be an obscene number of overrides in any given render layer, it's important to follow through this workflow carefully. Practice it to gain a comfort level before getting too fancy with render layers and overrides. Also, it helps to keep notes beside your keyboard to help you stay organized with render layers and overrides. And lastly, there are occasional problems when assigning shaders to the faces of a mesh (as opposed to the entire mesh) when using render layers. Try to always assign shaders to the entire mesh and not to faces in those cases.

1. Click to the `columnPass` render layer. In the Outliner, select all the fruit objects and add them to the layer (Figure 11.53).

2. If you render the layer now, it will render the fruit. To turn them off without removing them from the layer (and hence lose shadows and reflections), you'll set render layer overrides for each of the fruit objects. Select the orange, and open the Attribute Editor.

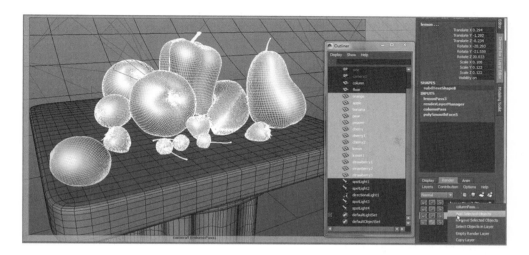

Figure 11.53
Add the fruit back into the layer.

3. On the orangeShape tab in the Attribute Editor, click to open the Render Stats heading. Here you see switches allowing for different ways to render the object. You want the orange to cast reflections and shadows in the scene, without rendering itself, so uncheck the Primary Visibility box. It will turn orange to signify that there is now a render layer override on that attribute for the current render layer (columnPass) only (Figure 11.54).

   As a matter of fact, if you click the other render layers with the orange still selected, you will notice that the Primary Visibility setting for the orange turns back on and loses its orange color in the Attribute Editor on the other render layers. Render layer overrides work only on the layers in which they were created.

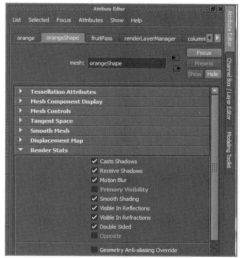

Figure 11.54
Turn off Primary Visibility to set a render layer override for the orange on the columnPass layer.

4. Now select each fruit model down the list in the Outliner individually, and turn off Primary Visibility one by one. You cannot select all the objects at once and turn off Primary Visibility in the Attribute Editor; it will register the action only for the last selected object and not them all.

> To change attribute values on multiple objects at once, such as Primary Visibility, you can use Window → General Editors → Attribute Spread Sheet. Be careful, though!

5. Turn off Render All Layers (in the Layer Editor, uncheck Options → Render All Layers). Render the columnPass layer, and you'll see the top of the column is rendering with shadows and reflections but not the fruit! (See Figure 11.55.)

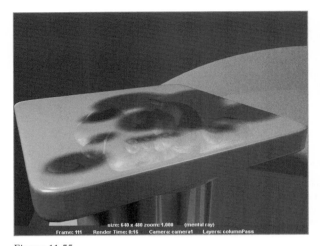

Figure 11.55

The column is rendering with shadows and reflections.

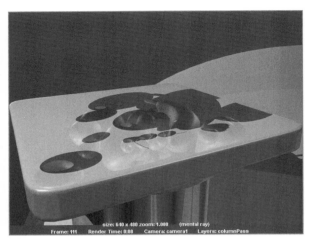

Figure 11.56

The shadows are crisp and clean but too sharp.

6. Finally, you make the shadows look nicer by using raytrace shadows. Select spotLight1, and in the Attribute Editor, under the Shadows → Depth Map Shadow Attributes heading, turn off Use Depth Map Shadows. Scroll down a bit until you see the Raytrace Shadow Attributes heading; open it, and turn on Use Ray Trace Shadows.

7. Repeat step 6 for spotLight3 and spotLight4. Render, and you'll see sharp shadows now on the column (Figure 11.56).

8. Let's enable soft shadows now for those three spotlights. Select spotLight1, and in the Raytrace Shadow Attributes, set Light Radius to **0.4** and Shadow Rays to **16**. Repeat the procedure for spotLight3 and spotLight4. The shadows will look much more believable now.

Figure 11.57

The layers all rendered together with soft shadows and reflections

9. Turn on Render All Layers, and render a frame to see the entire composition (Figure 11.57). Once you verify everything is working and looking good, you can now render your scene into separate layers for better control in compositing.

You can check your work against the file still_life_renderLayers_v02.mb from the Scenes folder of the Lighting project on the book's web page.

Batch Rendering with Render Layers

Now that you have everything separated into render layers, let's talk about batch-rendering the scene to composite later. Make the render layers you want to render renderable by making sure the Renderable icon next to each render layer is enabled, as shown in Figure 11.58.

In the Render Settings window, make sure Renderable Camera is set to camera1, as shown in Figure 11.59. Select your image file type and anything else you need to set in the Render Settings window. Then, in the main Maya window, choose Render → Batch Render to render the scene. Because render layers are enabled here, Maya renders the scene into different subfolders under the Images folder of your current project. Each render layer gets its own folder in the Images folder, as shown in Figure 11.60.

Figure 11.58

Check to make sure the layers you want to render are enabled.

I have only begun to scratch the surface here. When you get the hang of rendering and as your CG needs begin to grow, you'll find a plethora of options when rendering with layers and rendering with passes through mental ray. This section and the "Ambient Occlusion" section later in this chapter are here only to familiarize you with the basic workflow of render layers. You can find a wealth of information about rendering in layers and passes in the Maya online documentation under the Help menu.

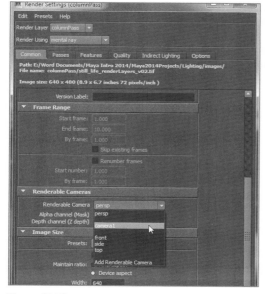

Figure 11.59

Select camera1 as your renderable camera in the Render Settings window.

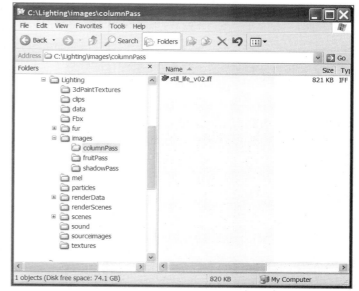

Figure 11.60

Render layers batch-render into subfolders in the Images folder of your project.

Final Gather

Final Gather (FG) is a type of rendering with mental ray that includes a simple light bounce within the scene. Final Gather traces light as it reflects off surfaces to illuminate the scene for a nicely realistic render that takes into account color bleed of light from one surface to another. For example, a red wall casts a red hue on the surface right next to it. FG is an intricate dance of settings and numbers that lets you get perfect renders. It's tough to cover in an introductory book such as this; however, this section will give you a primer to start using FG. In a follow-up section, you'll use a combination of lights and HDRI with Final Gather to render the decorative box.

The basic premise is that FG uses the illumination in the scene from lights as well as objects with color and incandescence set in their shaders to create a soft natural light. Its base settings will give you nice results right from the start.

To render the still life fruit scene with FG, begin by creating a dome light, which evenly illuminates a scene from a dome around the scene. (The term *dome light* is a bit of a misnomer, because a dome light isn't itself a light.) You'll construct a simple NURBS sphere, cut it in half to create a dome, and give it an Incandescent shader to provide the light for the scene. This type of quick FG setup is extremely useful for rendering out soft lighting and shadows to show off a model or a composition.

To light and render with FG, follow these steps:

1. Ensure that mental ray for Maya is loaded.

2. Load the still life scene file `still_life_mentalray_v01.mb` from the Lighting project from the book's web page. In the persp view panel (not the `camera1` panel), create a polygonal sphere, and scale it up to enclose the entire scene. Select the bottom half faces of the sphere, delete them to cut the sphere in half, and name the object **lightDome**. Place the dome to fit over the scene, as shown in Figure 11.61.

3. Add an Incandescent shader to the dome to give the scene some illumination through FG. To do so, in the Hypershade create a new Lambert shader. Turn up its incandescence to a medium light gray. Assign the new shader to the dome.

4. Maya automatically creates a general default light in a scene that has no lights when you try to render it. This is so you can test-render your scene quickly. However, because this incandescent dome light should be the only light source in the FG render, you have to turn off the default light feature before you render. Open the Render Settings window, and under the Common tab's Render Options heading (at the bottom of the Attribute Editor), turn off the Enable Default Light check box.

> Don't forget to turn Enable Default Light back on when you're finished with this FG exercise.

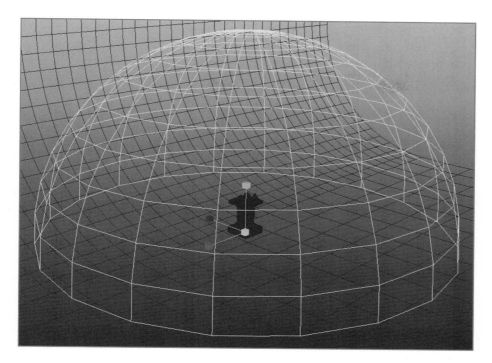

Figure 11.61

Create a sphere to act as a light dome.

5. At the top of the Render Settings window, switch the Render Using attribute to mental ray. You can keep the settings on the Common tab to render at 640×480. Choose the Quality tab to access its settings. Set Sampling Mode to Unified Sampling, and leave Min and Max Samples to 1.0 and 100, respectively, but set a Quality of **0.3**. Check to make sure that raytracing is enabled under the Raytracing heading. Figure 11.62 shows the Quality tab of the Render Settings window.

6. Click to open the Indirect Lighting tab, and click the Final Gathering heading to expand its attributes. Turn on Final Gathering by checking the box. You can leave the settings at their defaults for your first render. Figure 11.63 shows the Indirect Lighting tab for the Render Settings window with Final Gathering turned on.

7. You need to make sure the sphere you're using as a dome light doesn't render out in the scene. Select the sphere, and in its Attribute Editor under the Render Stats heading, turn off Primary Visibility. Since there are no render layers in the scene, it doesn't turn orange like with the previous section's exercise. Highlight the camera1 panel, and render the frame. Maya makes two passes at the scene and shows you something like Figure 11.64. You can control the brightness of the scene with the Incandescence attribute value of the dome's shader—the whiter the incandescence, the brighter the scene.

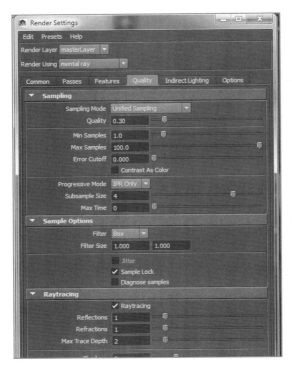

Figure 11.62

The Quality tab

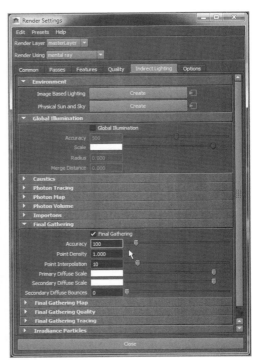

Figure 11.63

The Indirect Lighting tab accesses all the Final Gather settings.

Figure 11.64

The Final Gather render of the still life

Figure 11.65

Accuracy set at 500 increases the smoothness of the soft shadows. It's hard to see here, but you'll notice it in your own render.

You can adjust the level of lighting by increasing or decreasing the amount of incandescence on the light dome's shader. The proximity of the sphere also affects the light amount, so moving the sphere closer or farther away will change the lighting level as well. You can also insert lights into the scene as you see fit.

You can improve the quality of the render by adjusting any of the following three settings in the Indirect Lighting tab under the Final Gathering section of the Render Settings window:

Accuracy   Increase this number for a more accurate render. Don't increase it too much, however, because it will slow down your render. Earlier the still life was rendered with the default Accuracy setting of 100. In Figure 11.65, which uses a setting of 500, the soft shadows are noticeably smoother. Accuracy dictates the number of FG rays that are cast into the scene. The more rays, the better the quality of the render, although at a cost of rendering time.

Primary Diffuse Scale   Use this setting to adjust the overall lighting level globally in the scene. The higher the value of this color, the brighter the scene. You can type values greater than 1 in the Color Chooser.

Secondary Diffuse Bounces   Setting this attribute to 1 will add an additional bounce of light inside your scene, essentially brightening everything. Shadowed areas will pick up the biggest boost, and the scene lighting will be a bit more soft overall.

The Point Density and Point Interpolation attributes, along with several other attributes under the Final Gathering section, optimize and further control the FG settings for optimum efficiency and results, especially with animated scenes. Consider using the basic settings shown in this chapter to become familiar with mental ray for Maya, and then use FG to crank out fast and elegant renders to show off your models until you get more comfortable with mental ray.

Final Gather is a tough nut to crack; it will take you some time to become proficient at rendering with FG in scene files and especially with animated scenes. Later in this chapter, you'll try your hand at using FG, HDRI, and regular lights to render the decorative box from the previous chapters.

Ambient Occlusion

Ambient Occlusion is a special render pass that helps add depth and reality to a render. Ambient Occlusion goes by the premise that when two objects or surfaces are close to each other, they reduce the amount of light at the intersection. Ambient Occlusion passes make for great contact shadows and bring out the definition in surface creases and corners very nicely. Figure 11.66 shows an Ambient Occlusion pass for the living room scene from the PDF Global Illumination exercise included on the book's web page.

How the composite works is very simple. Ambient Occlusion gives you a black-and-white pass of the same geometry you've already rendered. This pass is then multiplied over the color render. That means a brightness value of white (a value of 1) in the Ambient Occlusion pass won't change the color of the original render (when the original color of the render is multiplied by 1, it stays the same color). The black parts of the frame (with a brightness value of 0) turn those parts of the original render black (when the original color of the render is multiplied by 0, it goes to black). The gray points of the multiplying image darken the original render. It sounds confusing, but when you see it, it makes much better sense.

The Living Room

You'll now take the living-room render made in the PDF file exercise on the web page and add an Ambient Occlusion pass using render layers. You don't have to read the PDF exercise to understand the concepts and practices for making an Ambient Occlusion pass here. However, if you'd like to understand how to light the living-room scene with Global Illumination, you may want to read that exercise on the web page now and then return to the following.

Set your current project to the Livingroom project you copied from the web page, open the livingRoom_v2.mb file from the Scenes folder, and follow these steps:

1. Make sure mental ray is loaded, of course, and that Render Settings is set to render with mental ray. As you did earlier, you need to create a new render layer for the Ambient Occlusion. This layer requires all the objects in the scene but the lights to be assigned to it. In this scene, the only light is a single Directional light. In the Outliner, select all the top nodes of the scene, but leave out the light, as shown in Figure 11.67.

2. Click the Render tab in the Layer Editor to switch to Render, and then click the Create New Layer And Assign Selected Objects icon ( ). Doing so creates a new layer (layer1) along with the preexisting master-Layer, as shown in Figure 11.68.

3. Click the new layer (layer1) to activate it. Everything in the scene should display as it did before, although the light disappears from view. Double-click layer1, and rename it **ambientOcclusion**.

4. You're going to use a preset to create a material override. This takes all the objects in the scene and assigns a single material to them: in this case, an Ambient Occlusion shader that generates the Ambient Occlusion pass for the entire scene. Right-click the ambientOcclusion layer, and select Attributes. In the Attribute Editor, click and hold down the Presets button. From the menu that appears, select Occlusion, as shown in Figure 11.69.

Figure 11.67

Select the scene objects for your Ambient Occlusion pass.

Figure 11.68

Create a new render layer.

If you're in Shaded mode, everything should turn black in the view panels. This is normal, because everything now has the Ambient Occlusion Surface Shader assigned, and that shader displays black in Maya panels. If you click the masterLayer, everything pops back into place.

5. When you select Occlusion from the Presets menu, your Attribute Editor window should display a new shader called surfaceShader1. Figure 11.70 shows the new Ambient Occlusion shader that is assigned throughout the scene. Rename that shader to **ambOccShader**. Don't worry if you don't see the surfaceShader1 in your Attribute Editor; you'll come back to it in later steps.

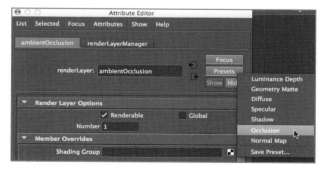

Figure 11.69

Setting an Occlusion preset for the layer

Figure 11.70

The Ambient Occlusion shader in the Hypershade

6. While still in the `ambientOcclusion` layer, render a frame. You should see something like Figure 11.71. You needn't worry about most of the settings in the Render Settings window; the layer preset takes care of it all. Well, almost all. It doesn't turn off the Global Illumination pass that you used for the original color render in the PDF exercise (which you can find on the web page); you need to turn that off manually in the next step.

Figure 11.71

The first render from the Ambient Occlusion pass doesn't look great— it's too dark.

7. In the Render Settings window, on the Indirect Lighting tab, you need to turn off Global Illumination, but just for the `ambientOcclusion` layer. With `ambientOcclusion` still selected in the Layer Editor, right-click the Global Illumination check box in Render Settings and choose Create Layer Override. The attribute lettering turns orange to signify that it's being overridden for that render layer, just like you saw before. Uncheck the box. It doesn't turn off GI for the masterLayer pass. You don't have to spend the time calculating any GI for this pass.

8. The render is mostly black, which darkens the original color render to black almost everywhere. You need the Ambient Occlusion shader to render mostly white with some darkening at the corners and where objects contact each other. You can adjust the Ambient Occlusion shader to fix this. Open the Hypershade window, and click `ambOccShader` (or `surfaceShader1`, if you didn't rename it earlier in step 5—rename it now).

9. Notice that the Out Color attribute has a texture connection to it (signified by the 🖼 icon). Click this button to display the `mib_amb_occlusion1` texture node in the Attribute Editor, as shown in Figure 11.72.

Figure 11.72

The Ambient Occlusion shader attributes

10. Set the Max Distance attribute to **4.0**, as shown in Figure 11.73, and render the frame again. Your Ambient Occlusion layer should look like Figure 11.74. It should have also taken less than half as long to render as the darker render from step 6.

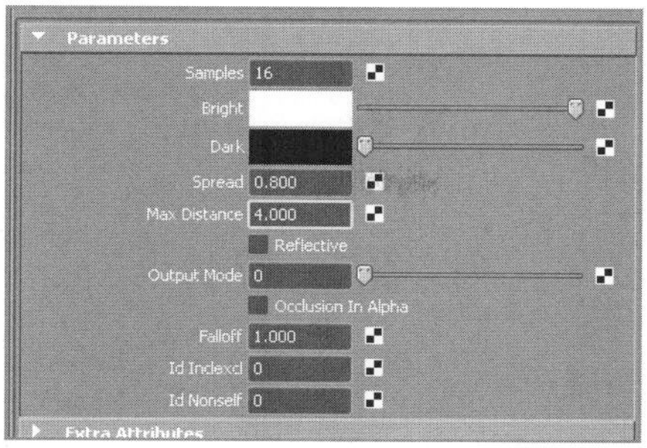

11. Notice that the glass in the window and the glass on the coffee table have shadows on them. Because glass is clear, they shouldn't have any Ambient Occlusion applied to them; it would look odd in the final composite. Select those pieces of geometry (Figure 11.75 shows the Outliner view for those pieces).

Figure 11.73
Set Max Distance to 4.

Figure 11.75
The Outliner view of the glass geometry in the scene

Figure 11.74
The Ambient Occlusion layer pass looks much better, but you aren't finished yet!

12. With the glass geometry selected, select Display → Hide → Hide Selection. Now the glass won't render in the Ambient Occlusion pass. But because you hid the objects only in this render layer, they still appear in the masterLayer; they will still render as glass in the color pass.

13. Render the frame, and you should have something similar to Figure 11.76. This is the Ambient Occlusion pass you need to composite.

Remember to check out the PDF exercise on the web page if you'd like to learn how this scene was lit with Global Illumination.

Figure 11.76

The Ambient Occlusion pass

Rendering the Results

You could save the image you just rendered in the Render View window to use in the composite and then render the masterLayer for the color pass in the Render View and save that frame as well. Instead, let's batch-render the scene to show how Maya handles rendering with layers enabled. To batch-render the scene, follow these steps:

1. Turn on the Renderable icon box (![icon]) for the masterLayer, and make sure it's on for the ambientOcclusion layer as well.

2. Click to activate the masterLayer. Open the Render Settings window, and on the Common tab, verify all the settings to render a single frame (*name.ext.#* in the Frame/Animation Ext field) at 639×360 (which is half 720p HD resolution). Also, select camera1 as the renderable camera.

3. If you batch-render (by choosing Render → Batch Render), Maya renders both render layers into the Images folder of your project in separate folders, as shown in Figure 11.77.

Figure 11.77

Maya renders the layers into their own folders by default.

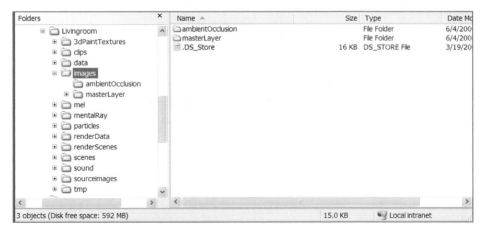

If for some reason your renders don't show up in your project's Images folder, open the Script Editor window and look at the batch-render report. The render feedback shows you where the rendered images were saved, as shown in Figure 11.78. You may also want to make sure you set your project to the Livingroom project from the web page.

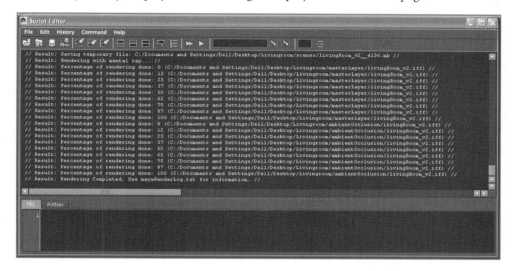

Figure 11.78

The Script Editor gives you feedback on the progress of the batch render.

Compositing the Results

Now that the two layers are rendered in their respective folders, load them into your favorite compositing package. You'll layer the Ambient Occlusion pass over the color render using a Multiply Transfer mode. This exercise uses Adobe After Effects CS4 to demonstrate how the Ambient Occlusion pass is composited over the original color render.

Figure 11.79 shows After Effects with the masterLayer color pass loaded. Figure 11.80 shows the ambientOcclusion pass layered on top of the color layer. Finally, Figure 11.81 shows the ambientOcclusion pass changed to a Multiply Transfer mode (as it's called in After Effects). Notice how the dark areas of the Ambient Occlusion pass help give contact shadows and depth to the color pass. *Voilà!*

This is a prime example of rendering different passes to achieve a more realistic result. Use different layers to put your final images together in composite.

You can see the difference Ambient Occlusion made to the living-room image in the Color Section of this book and on the web page.

Figure 11.79

The masterLayer
render pass is
loaded into After
Effects.

Figure 11.79

The masterLayer
render pass is
loaded into After
Effects.

Figure 11.80

The ambientOcclu-
sion render pass is
loaded into After
Effects.

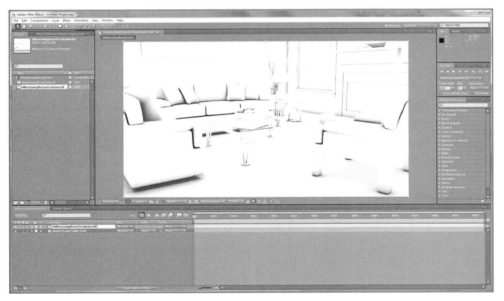

Figure 11.81
The ambientOc-
clusion pass is
multiplied over the
color pass and cre-
ates a more realistic
image.

HDRI

As you saw in the Final Gather section, FG rendering is based on the illumination in the scene from lights as well as the brightness of objects in the scene, such as a light dome. In a previous section, you used an incandescent dome to light the still-life scene. But what if you were to use an image instead of just white for the light dome?

Furthermore, what if the image you used was a high dynamic range image (HDRI)? In Chapter 1, I briefly discussed HDR images. Several photos at varying exposures are taken of the same subject, ranging from very dark (low exposure), to highlight only the brightest parts of the scene, and going all the way up to very bright (overexposure), to capture the absolute darkest parts of the scene. When these images (usually five or seven images) are compiled into an HDR image, you get a fantastic range of bright to dark for that one subject.

How does this help you light? With image-based lighting (IBL), mental ray creates an environment sphere in your scene to which you assign an image, usually an HDRI. That environment sphere, much like the white dome in the Final Gather exercise earlier in the chapter, uses the brightness of its image to cast light in your Maya scene.

The best type of image to capture for an IBL is sometimes called a *light probe*. This is a picture of an environment, such as the office reflected in a chrome ball shown on the left of Figure 11.82 or the stitched-together panoramic stills compiled into a map shown on the right of Figure 11.82. The stitched panoramic on the right of Figure 11.82 was photo-graphed at four 90-degree angles using a fish-eye camera lens capable of capturing a field of view of close to 180 degrees using a panoramic tripod attachment.

Figure 11.82

A light-probe photo of a desk is taken with a chrome ball (left) and a panoramic stitch (right).

Figure 11.82 shows the middle exposure of five exposures taken of the office and one of the four angles of the living room. Figure 11.83 shows five images in the range from underexposed (dark) to overexposed (bright) photos that were used to compile the HDRIs shown here. You will use an HDRI made from the living-room panoramic photos to light the decorative box in the next section.

The living-room photos are taken at 90-degree intervals inside the living room and then stitched and compiled in an HDRI file using a photographic software package (shown in Figure 11.84). The HDRI file is called livingRoomPanoramic.hdr and is in the Sourceimages folder of the TableLamp project on the web page for the next section's IBL lighting exercise. You won't be able to see the extensive range of the HDR, because the great majority of computer displays are limited to a display of 8-bit color.

The HDR will be mapped onto an IBL sphere. This is a large sphere that surrounds the environment in your Maya scene. The individual photos first need to be stitched together and converted to a rectangular image file, as shown in Figure 11.84. The full spherical panorama space captured in these photos and stitched together is laid out into a rectangular format that is suitable to project onto a sphere in Maya, just as if a geographic map on a school room globe was unwrapped into a rectangular sheet of paper.

Software such as HDRShop, available online for free, allows you to combine multiple images into an HDR. One useful program, PTGui from the Netherlands (available for a demo online at http://ptgui.com), allows you to stitch panoramas as well as merge HDR images, which makes it a fantastic tool for CG lighters and photographers. As long as the photos to be stitched were taken with enough overlap at the edges, PTGui is able to turn them into a large panoramic photo.

Figure 11.83

Five exposures make up the HDRI of a desk using a chrome ball (left); and a living room using a panoramic stitch (right), which is to be used in the next section

And if the proper exposure ranges were also taken, PTGui creates a solid HDR as well. I won't get into the details of creating the HDRI, because it's an advanced topic using Photoshop CS5, PTGui, and/or other software; however, it's good to know the origins of HDR images and how they come to be used in IBL.

Figure 11.84

Fish-eye photos are taken at four angles of the living room, each with several exposures from light to dark (above). The fish-eye photos are then warped and stitched together using the very handy software package PTGui and merged into an HDR image file (bottom).

Displacement Mapping the Decorative Box

Before continuing with the lighting and rendering for the lamp and decorative box, let's first address a need for detailing just the box by itself. Look at the photo of the box in Chapter 3, "The Autodesk Maya 2014 Interface." (Figure 3.24) and compare it to the close-up renders of the box in Chapter 10 (Figure 10.68); you'll see that the carved details in the CG box need more detail. Let's start by taking a closer look at the box by itself.

1. Make sure your project is set to the TableLamp project. Open the file lampLighting_v01.mb from the TableLamp project. An error may come up saying that the reference file cannot be found (if so, it will look like Figure 11.85). If that is the case, simply click Browse and navigate to where you have saved the Decorative_Box project's Scenes folder, where you will find the scene file boxDetail01.mb. Otherwise, the scene should open with no issues.

Figure 11.85

Oh no! Reference file not found!

Reference file not found: file:///E:/Word Documents/Maya Intro 2013/Maya2013Projects/Decorative_Box/scenes/boxLighting01.mb

| Abort File Read | Skip | Browse... | Retry |

Make path changes permanent

Remember these settings

2. Select the top node of the table lamp (lampGroup), and create a new display layer called **lampLayer**. Turn off visibility for the lampLayer.

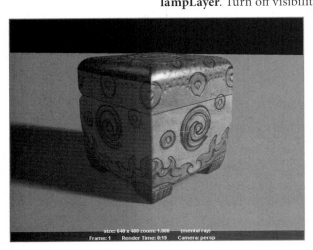

3. Use the persp camera (not the renderCam), and line up a view of the box to match the box render shown in Figure 11.86.

4. Render a frame, and you should notice more closely the lack of definition in the box when compared to the real photo of the box (Figure 3.24 in Chapter 3).

5. Save your work!

In the current render, the grooves are flat and shiny, whereas in the real box, they're carved into the wood and aren't glossy like the rest of the box. You will add definition to the model through textures next.

You can use the scene file lampLighting_v02 to catch up to this point or compare your camera angles.

Figure 11.86

The lamp and decorative box's current render when you finished the lighting in Chapter 10

Reflection Map

Just as you use a map to put color on the box, you can use similar maps to specify where and how much the box will reflect. Figure 11.87 shows the color map you used to texture the box in Chapter 7 side-by-side with a black-and-white map that shows only the carved regions of the box. This map was created with elbow grease and hard work to manually isolate just the carved areas of the box in Photoshop. See how much I do for you?

You'll first take the reflections out of the carved areas in the following steps:

1. Set your project to the Decorative_Box project from the companion website.

2. Open the boxDetail02.mb scene. This scene has the box set up with a few lights, a render camera and render settings preset, and a ground plane for you to focus on

Figure 11.87

The black-and-white map on the right shows only the carved areas of the box.

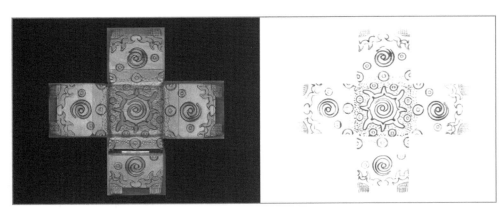

detailing just the box. Render a frame and study the outcome. Save it to the image buffer in the Render View window.

3. Open the Hypershade. In the Create bar on the left, click 2D Textures under the Maya heading, and choose File to open a new image file node (called `file2`). See Figure 11.88.

4. Double-click the file node, and navigate to find and choose the `boxCarvings.jpg` file in the Sourceimages folder of the Decorative_Box project. See Figure 11.89.

5. If the sample swatch at the top of the Attribute Editor for the file2 node doesn't show the image you just selected, it is because the image is too large for Maya to create a thumbnail swatch automatically. If this is the case, the file node in the Hypershade would also be blank. Right-click the file node, and choose Refresh Swatch from the marking menu. Figure 11.90 shows the swatch with the black-and-white image as a thumbnail. This isn't necessary, but it makes it easier for you to identify what file map is where.

Figure 11.88

Create a new file node.

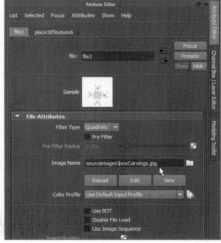

Figure 11.89

Select the proper image file.

6. MMB+drag the `phong1` node from the top of the Hypershade window down to the Work Area, alongside the `file2` node.

7. Double-click the `phong1` node to open the Attribute Editor. MMB+drag the `file2` node onto the `Reflectivity` attribute for the Phong2 shader, as shown in Figure 11.91.

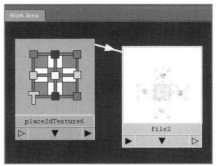

Figure 11.90

The swatch shows a thumbnail of the image you're using.

Figure 11.91

Map the new image file to the Reflectivity attribute.

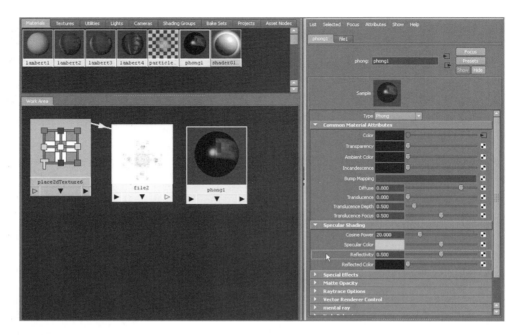

8. Notice the connection line in the Hypershade between the file2 and phong1 nodes. The white areas of the map tell the phong1 shader to have a reflectivity of 1, whereas the black areas have zero reflectivity. This effectively removes reflections from the box's carvings. Render a frame of the box in the renderCam view, and compare it to Figure 11.92.

9. In the Render View window, click the Keep Image icon (🖫) to store this render in the render buffer. Doing so allows you to easily compare renders to see the changes you make as you continue.

10. The box's reflections are now stronger all over, and the carvings still reflect. You need to turn on one switch. Select the file2 node, and open the Color Balance heading in the Attribute Editor. Check the box for the Alpha Is Luminance attribute. This instructs Maya to use the luminance values (basically the brightness) of the image to output to the reflectivity attribute of the phong1 shader. The box renders properly, and the carvings have no reflections, as shown in Figure 11.93. Save this render into the render buffer with the Keep Image icon (🖫).

11. You need to reduce the reflections on the rest of the box. Double-click the file2 node to open the Attribute Editor. In the Color Balance heading, set Alpha Gain to **0.4**, as shown in Figure 11.94. This sets the brightest part of the reflections to be capped at 0.4 and not the previous 1.0. Render, and you see a much better reflection in the box and no reflections in the carvings. (See Figure 11.95.) Save this to the render buffer.

12. Rename the file2 node to **reflectionMap** and the phong1 node to **boxShader,** and save your work to a new version.

Figure 11.92
The reflections are stronger; the entire box looks like a mirror.

Figure 11.93
The carvings don't reflect, but the rest of the box's reflections are still too strong.

You can open the scene file `boxDetail03.ma` from the Scenes folder in the Decorative_Box project to catch up to this point or to check your work so far.

Displacement Mapping

Now that the reflections are set up, you'll use the same image map to create displacements in the box to sink the carvings into the box. Isn't that convenient?

1. In the Hypershade, click to create a new file node, and select the `boxCarvings.jpg` file in the Sourceimages folder again. You don't want to reuse the same file node as you did for the reflections (`reflectionMap` node), because you need to change some of its attributes. Name the new file node **displacementMap**.

2. Double-click the `boxShader` node to open the Attribute Editor. MMB+drag the new `displacementMap` node onto the `boxShader` node in the Hypershade, and select Displacement Map from the context menu, as shown in Figure 11.96.

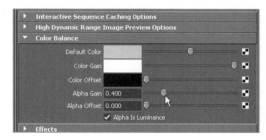

Figure 11.94
Set Alpha Gain to 0.4.

Figure 11.95
The reflections look much better now.

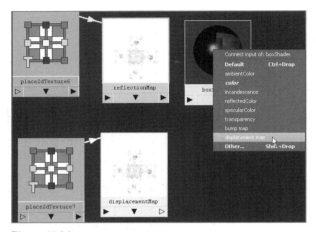

Figure 11.96

Add the new image map to the Displacement Map attribute.

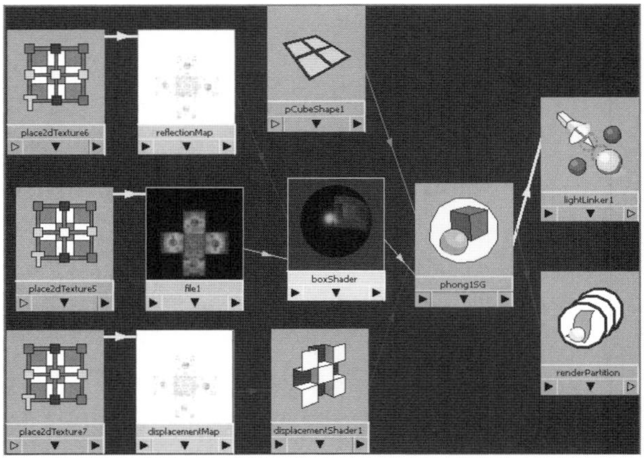

Figure 11.97

The shader network for the box

3. A new node appears called `displacementShader1`, but there is no connection apparent to the `boxShader`. Select the `boxShader`, and click the Input And Output Connections icon at the top of the Hypershade ( ). The Hypershade shows you the entire shader network, including the displacement map connection, as shown in Figure 11.97. Notice that the displacement connects to the `phong1SG` node and not directly to the `boxShader` node. This is normal and how it's always done.

4. Render the box, and see what happens now that you have a displacement map applied. Figure 11.98 shows how the box seems to have exploded!

> Occasionally when you click to view the input and output of a shader as you did in step 3, the Hypershade will put some nodes on top of others. If you don't see any of the nodes, try clicking and dragging some of the nodes around in the Hypershade to see whether there are any accidentally hidden nodes. These little touches make Maya extra fun!

Figure 11.98

The displacements seem to be wrong!

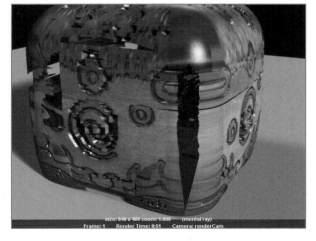

Not to worry—this is to be expected. The values coming from the black-and-white map dictate how much of the geometry is displaced (moved). Obviously, you don't have an image that works well for the amount of displacement, although it does look like the displacements are in the proper place to correspond to where the carvings are on the box.

5. Double-click the `displacementMap` node. In the Attribute Editor, open the `Effects` heading, and click the Invert check box. This turns the background to black and the carvings to white. Set Alpha Gain to **0.03** in the `Color Balance` heading, and make sure Alpha Is Luminance is also checked. (See Figure 11.99.) The Alpha Gain value reduces the amount of displacement, and inverting the image lets the rest of the box outside of the carvings not be displaced.

Figure 11.99

Set the attributes for the displacement image.

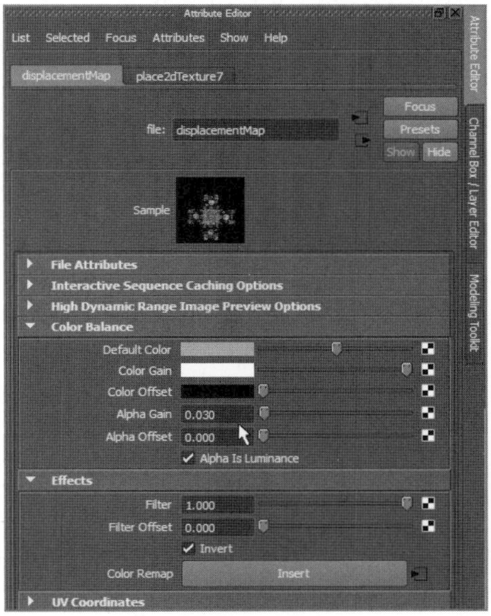

6. Render a frame, and compare it to Figure 11.100. It's not looking very good. The box isn't exploding anymore, and only the carvings are displacing, which is good. However, the carvings are sticking out, instead of in.

7. Set the Alpha Gain attribute to **–0.02** to push the carvings in a little instead of out. Render, and compare to Figure 11.101. The carvings are set into the wood as they should be, but the render looks bad. The displacements are very jagged and ill-defined.

8. The jagged look of the carvings has to do with the tessellation of the box—that is, the detail of the box's polygonal mesh. There are advanced ways to address how mental ray deals with displacements; however, the most basic method is to adjust the detail of the box's mesh. Figure 11.102 shows the current box's mesh. Notice that the sides of the box are very simply detailed. To increase the box's faces to add detail, select the box, and then, in the Polygons menu set, choose Edit Mesh → Add Divisions ❏. Set the options to Exponentially and Division Levels to **3**, as shown in Figure 11.103. Click Add Divisions to execute.

Figure 11.100

The carvings are displacing outward.

Figure 11.101

The carvings are inset into the wood, but they don't look good yet.

Figure 11.102

The current box's mesh isn't detailed enough.

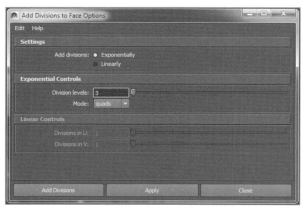

Figure 11.103

Set the Add Divisions values.

Figure 11.104

Added divisions

Figure 11.105

The displacements render much better now.

9. Figure 11.104 shows the newly tessellated box. It's far more detailed in the mesh. When you render, it gives a result similar to Figure 11.105. You can compare your work to the scene file boxDetail04.ma in the Scenes folder of the Decorative_Box project.

10. Now that you have the detail you want in the box, you need to prepare the box's scene file to be referenced back into your lamp lighting scene. Select the ground plane, the renderCam camera, and the three lights in the scene and delete them. Save your work to a new version.

Compare your work to the scene file `boxDetail05.ma` in the Scenes folder of the Decorative_Box project.

Notice that the render times increased because you increased the detail on the mesh in step 8. This increase is normal, but it can become a problem if the mesh is too divided and has more faces than you need. This box has fairly detailed carvings, so the level to which you set Add Divisions in step 8 gives a good result without being too detailed. As your experience increases in Maya and mental ray rendering, you'll learn how to use functions such as the mental ray Approximation Editor to keep the overall detail low on the mesh but with smooth displacement results when you render. This is an advanced technique, so I won't cover it in this book. You've taken in quite a lot by this point already.

The next time you select the box and open the Attribute Editor, you'll see a new tab called `polySubdFace1`. This is the node added with the Add Divisions function in step 8. Feel free to adjust the Subdivision Levels setting on that tab and render to see how the detail levels affect the final render. Also try better quality settings in Render Settings, as you did with the red wagon earlier in this chapter, to clean up the render to your satisfaction.

You'll next add an IBL sphere and use the HDR image you saw earlier in the chapter.

Rendering the Lamp and Decorative Box

You're all grown up and ready to light a full scene using Final Gather, IBL with HDRI, and regular lights to get the best bang for your buck out of mental ray rendering. In the previous chapter, you briefly lit the lamp and decorative box with key, fill, and rim lights (the three-point lighting system). In this exercise, you'll take this concept a few steps further, so take a deep breath, call your mother and tell her you love her, and let's get started!

Set your project to the TableLamp. Open the `lampLighting02.ma` file in the Scenes folder. This scene has the lights and soft shadows created in Chapter 10 and is set to render through mental ray with raytracing enabled already. Let's take a critical look at the render from the previous chapter in the earlier Figure 11.86.

Now that you have created a more detailed box, let's update the reference in this scene. Choose File → Reference Editor. You are currently reading in `boxDetail01.mb`. Click `boxDetail01.mb` to select the entry, and choose Reference → Replace Reference. Navigate to the Decorative_Box project's scene folder, and select `boxDetail05.mb`.

All your work detailing the box will now pop into the lamp lighting scene. Render a frame from the persp camera view. Figure 11.106 shows a comparison of the render from before the added detail (left) and the newly detailed box in the lamp lighting scene (right). The detailed box looks much nicer now, although you have to tweak the render quality settings in this scene later.

Figure 11.106

The render on the right shows all the added detail to the box missing from the render on the left.

Adding an IBL

Here's where things get fun. You'll add an IBL node to the scene and add the living-room HDR image to that IBL. First make sure you have mental ray selected as your renderer in the Render Settings window, and then follow along with these steps:

1. In your already open lampLighting02.ma scene, turn on the lampLayer visibility. Render a frame in the renderCam view, and save it to the buffer in the Render View window. You can also start moving around with your persp camera view again, since you're no longer focusing on the box.

2. In the Render Settings window, click the Indirect Lighting tab. At the top, in the Environment heading, click the Create button for Image Based Lighting, as shown in Figure 11.107.

3. The Attribute Editor opens to a view of the newly created IBL (named mentalrayIblShape1), as shown in Figure 11.108. Set Hardware Exposure to **3** to lighten up the view of the HDR image in the view panels.

4. Click the folder icon () next to the Image Name attribute. Navigate to the Sourceimages folder of the TableLamp project on your system, and select the file livingRoomPanoramic.hdr. You see in

Figure 11.107

Click to create an IBL.

your view panes that a large yellow sphere is created in your scene. The living-room panoramic HDR image is mapped. (See Figure 11.109.)

5. Use your persp camera to take a good look at the placement of the IBL sphere and the HDR image mapped to it. Select the IBL (you can click the IBL's yellow wireframe lines or select mentalrayIbl1 in the Outliner), and rotate the IBL sphere to 155 in the *Y*-axis so that the bright sun in the window is behind the renderCam and the window faces the top wing of the biplane on the lamp. Figure 11.110 shows the orientation of the IBL.

6. In the renderCam view, render a frame, and you'll see the HDR image in the background. However, the lighting is largely unchanged from before when you compare it to your earlier renders from step 1. You need to enable Final Gather to take advantage of the IBL and the HDRI mapped to it.

7. On the Render Settings window's Indirect Lighting tab, check the Final Gathering check box in the Final Gathering heading. Click the color swatch for Primary Diffuse, and enter a V (value) of **3.0**, as shown in Figure 11.111. This will boost the brightness of the HDRI and will therefore cast more light into the scene.

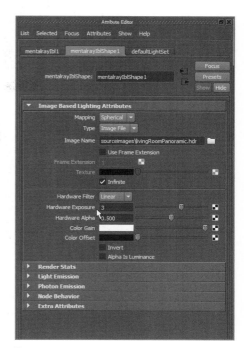

Figure 11.108

The Attribute Editor for the IBL node

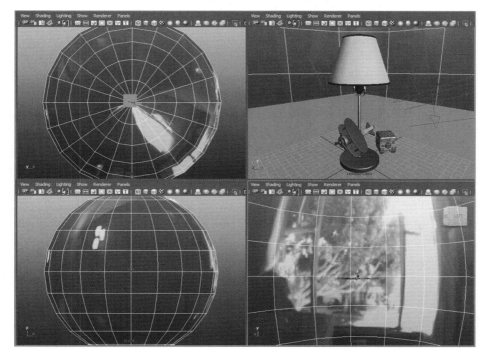

Figure 11.109

The IBL is in place and mapped to the office chrome ball HDRI.

Figure 11.110

Rotate the IBL sphere in the Y-axis to 155.

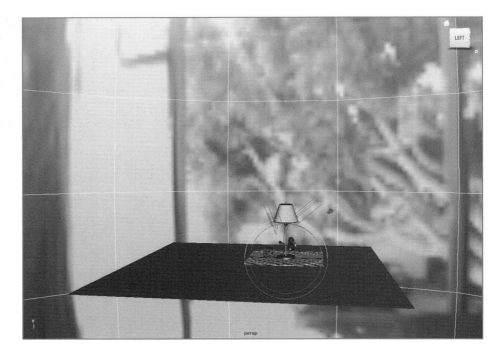

8. Render a frame, and compare it to the image in Figure 11.112. Save the image by clicking the Keep Image icon (🖻), and compare it to your earlier render before the IBL. Also notice the bounced light on the gray floor, which is a nice touch, albeit splotchy right now.

   The render is a little bright and quite noisy. You have three lights in the scene already and now an HDRI. Reduce the Intensity of the key light from 1.2 to **0.8**, the fill light from 0.25 to **0.15**, and the rim light from 0.5 to **0.4**.

9. Now, let's prevent the HDR image from showing up in the background. Select the IBL sphere, and in the Attribute Editor under the Render Stats heading, turn off Primary Visibility. The background renders black without the IBL. Feel free to select the IBL and change its rotation to a different orientation to see how it changes the look of the scene. Just don't forget to return it to its current orientation to stay consistent with the results shown in Figure 11.112 and the following section.

Figure 11.111

Enter a value of 3 to increase the brightness of the HDRI.

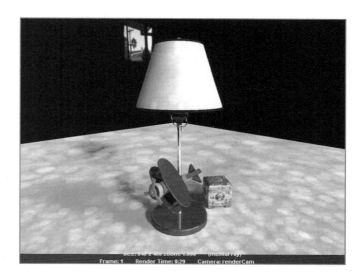

Figure 11.112
It's a noisy and bright render.

ORIENTING THE IBL

The image (HDRI or otherwise) used in an IBL and the IBL's orientation are huge factors in the lighting of a scene. Play around with the rotations of the IBL to see how the lighting differs until you settle on a look you like.

Fixing Final Gather Noise

The render from the previous section looks nice, except that it's noisy. Notice the blotches of light all over the floor. This is from having low-quality settings for FG. On the Render Settings' Indirect Lighting tab, increase Accuracy to **500** under the Final Gathering heading and Point Interpolation to **50**. Doing so dramatically increases the render time for the frame (almost doubling the previous time); however, it makes the scene look much better—practically eradicating the blotchy nature of the previous renders. The floor plane is still a bit blotchy, but you'll take care of it soon. The lamp and box have a nice glossy look to them thanks to the reflections and soft light from the HDRI. (See Figure 11.113.) Save the image to your Render View buffer.

Figure 11.113
Using higher-quality settings for FG makes a big difference.

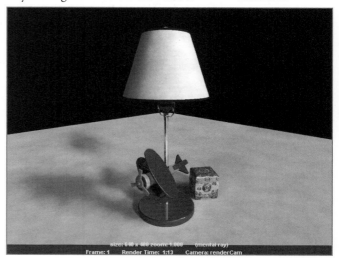

You can open the scene file lampLighting03.ma from the Scenes folder in the TableLamp project to catch up to this point or to check your work so far.

FG is a difficult beast to tame, especially with an IBL. It takes a lot of experience and practice to be able to use this powerful feature of mental ray successfully in scenes. Experiment with different HDR images that you can download from the Internet as well as adjusting the lights in the scene.

Blurring Reflections with the mia_material

Let's tweak the render a little more by making a new tabletop floor plane for the lamp and box to sit on to make the table look like a rich brown wood. You will use the mental ray mia_material shader:

1. Open the Hypershade, and in the Create panel, select Materials under the mental ray heading. Click mia_material to create the shader, as shown in Figure 11.114.

> The mia_material is quite different from the shaders I've covered. Although I will not cover this shader any further than this section, it is a powerful shader to use for glossy and reflective surfaces when using mental ray and especially so with Final Gather.

2. In the Attribute Editor for the mia_material, click the Map button next to the Color attribute under the Diffuse section, and apply a file node. Navigate to the Sourceimages folder of the TableLamp project, and select the tableWood.tif image file. This is a simple redwood texture.

3. In the Attribute Editor for the mia_material, set Reflectivity to **0.3** and Glossiness to **0.6**. The way the mia_material works allows you to have diffused or blurred reflections, which are set by the Glossiness attribute. The higher the number, the more mirror-like the sharpness of the reflection. Experiment with this powerful shader to see the results in changing the shading quality of the redwood table.

Figure 11.114

Create a mia_material shader.

4. Assign the `mia_material` to the floor plane. Name the shader **tableShader**.

5. Create two polygonal planes to make the corner of two walls behind the lamp and box, as shown in Figure 11.115, to have something in the background. Assign a light gray Lambert to the walls.

6. Render a frame, and you'll see that the lighting on the lamp and box has changed a bit, because the new walls and tabletop are bouncing more light than the earlier default gray plane. This is why indirect lighting can be more photo-realistic, though trickier to control. Figure 11.116 shows the render.

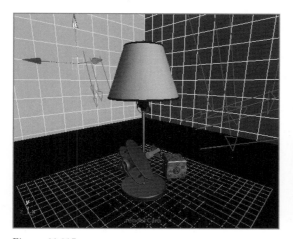

Figure 11.115
Create walls and a wood tabletop.

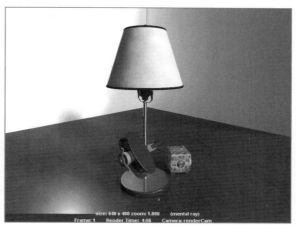

Figure 11.116
Not a bad render

Let's Get a Little Closer

Now that you have an overall look, let's create a new camera and get closer to the subjects.

1. Create a new camera, and call it **closeUpCam**.

2. In the Attribute Editor for the new camera, set Focal Length to **28** and frame the scene, as shown in Figure 11.117.

3. Render a frame, and compare it to Figure 11.118. If your render times are too long to wait for, you should reduce the FG values in the Render Settings window (Accuracy and Interpolation). Just remember to turn them back up for your final renders. Keep the image in your Render View buffer.

Figure 11.117

Create and frame the new camera for a close-up shot.

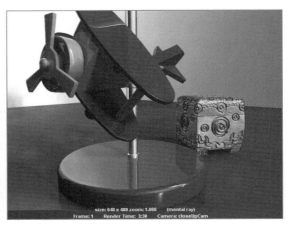

Figure 11.118

Render the close-up shot.

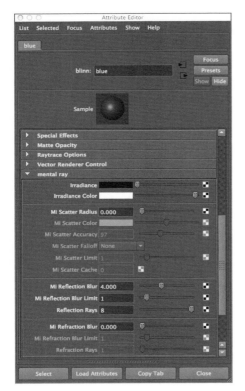

Figure 11.119

Create a blurred reflection for the blue shader.

4. In the render, the soft reflections in the tabletop look nice. The reflections in the lamp's base and biplane could benefit from softening as well. You don't have to make `mia_material` shaders for them to get blurred reflections, though. Open the Hypershade, and click the blue shader. In the Attribute Editor, click the mental ray heading to expand it. Set Mi Reflection Blur to **4.0** and Reflection Rays to **8**, as shown in Figure 11.119.

   The higher the Reflection Blur attribute, the blurrier the reflections. However, this comes at a slight cost in render time. The Reflection Rays attribute controls the detail and quality of the blurred reflections; the higher this attribute value, the better the reflections and the longer the render.

5. Repeat step 4 for the green and red shaders, and render a frame of the close-up view (Figure 11.120). Keep the image in the Render View window, and compare to the previous render with the nonblurred reflections in the biplane. It looks nicer, doesn't it? Experiment with the Reflection Rays attribute in the shaders to get a better reflection quality in the biplane and lamp base as desired.

Also try rendering the wider view in the other camera (`RenderCam`) and see how you can adjust lighting and shader settings for that angle.

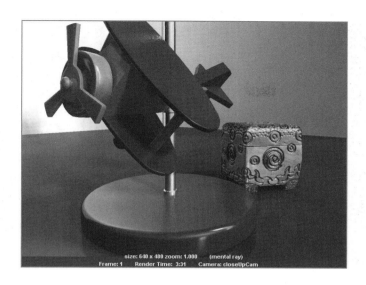

Save your work, and compare it to the `lampLighting_v04.mb` scene file found in the Scenes folder of the TableLamp project from the companion web page. And if you decide to batch-render this scene, make sure to select one of the two cameras you created for this scene in the Render Settings window.

> For a nice challenge, you could re-create the shaders for the objects using mia_materials to see the difference they can make in your renders. Many different materials could be simulated with the mia_materials shader.

Adding Depth of Field

One last item of interest is adding a depth of field (DOF) to the image. This effect adds blur to the render for the areas of the image that may be out of the lens's focal depth. It can greatly add to the photo-realism of a rendered image.

Select the `closeUpCam`, and open the Attribute Editor. In the Depth Of Field heading, check the `Depth Of Field` attribute. Set Focus Distance to **14,** and set F Stop to **11**. The F Stop setting, like a real lens, sets how much is in focus around the focal distance. With a higher F Stop value, the focus runs deeper than with a low F Stop value.

Figure 11.121 shows the final render of the lamp and box with DOF enabled. Your render times will be longer, and for a better render, you'll need to increase your Sample settings. Figure 11.121 was rendered with Min Samples of 0, Max Samples of 1, and Anti-Aliasing Contrast of 0.04 and took several minutes to complete.

Figure 11.121

The decorative box is in focus! We're finished!

The scene file `lampLighting_v04.ma` from the Scenes folder in the TableLamp project will take you to this point.

Notice from the render that the biplane is thrown out of focus, along with the back of the tabletop and the walls. Experiment with varying focus distance and F Stop values to try different looks for your scene. For example, keep the biplane in focus, but throw the box out of focus.

Depending on the need and the size of the render, you'll have to set the sampling levels to suit your needs—but be warned that your rendering times will dramatically increase, easily tripling depending on the quality settings. There are several ways to create DOF in a render that are faster or more controllable than what I've covered here. You can render out a depth pass to use with a lens filter in a compositing package such as Nuke to keep render times down. There are also more accurate DOF methods in mental ray and its lens shaders that you can experiment with when you've comfortably grasped the overall work-flow presented here.

Try also experimenting with the different sampling modes to see whether you can shave time off the render. The table lamp scenes are all set to legacy sampling settings, so setting it to a Unified Sampling Mode may get you faster results. Finally, adding an Ambient Occlusion pass isn't absolutely necessary for this render, although it may enhance the look of the contact shadows.

Wrapping Up the Lamp and Decorative Box

When you've learned a lot more about lighting and gained confidence with the processes of lighting, rendering, and compositing, you'll find a wealth of options when you render in several different layers. For example, if this lamp and decorative box scene were a professional job, its render would most likely be split into a flat color pass, a reflection pass, a specular highlight pass, a shadow pass, an Ambient Occlusion pass, a depth pass, and several different matte passes that separate parts of the scene to give the compositor the ultimate control in adjusting the image to taste.

You may not know what all those passes do right now, but understanding will come with time as long as you continue practicing your CG Kung Fu. Rendering your own color passes and Ambient Occlusions will give you some beautiful renders even without all the other passes. Keep in mind that small changes and additions can take you a long way toward a truly rich image.

> For an interesting challenge, take a photo in your house similar to the one on the cover of this book, render the lamp and box to match the lighting in the photo, and then composite the render against your photo.

Summary

In this chapter, you learned how to set up your scene for rendering. Starting with the Render Settings window and moving on to the different render engines available, you learned how to render your scene for a particular look. Then, I covered how to preview your render and how to use IPR for fast scene feedback. I moved on to how to render reflections and refractions, how to create and use cameras, and how to render motion blur. You tested your skill on a wine bottle scene, and to batch-render it out into a sequence of images, you checked it in a program like FCheck. You also used Maya render layers, overrides, and rendering an Ambient Occlusion pass to make your renders more realistic. Finally, you applied this knowledge to rendering the lamp and the decorative box using Final Gather and an HDR of a living room.

Getting to this point in a scene can take some work, but when you see the results playing back on your screen, all the work seems more than worth it. Always allow enough time to ensure that your animations render properly and at their best quality. Most beginners seriously underestimate the time needed to complete this step properly in CG production.

After you create numerous scenes and render them, you'll begin to understand how to construct your next scenes so that they render better and faster. Be sure to keep on top of your file management—rendering can produce an awful lot of files, and you don't want to have them scattered all over the place.

CHAPTER 12

Autodesk Maya Dynamics and Effects

Special effects animations simulate not only physical phenomena, such as smoke and fire, but also the natural movements of colliding bodies. Behind the latter type of animation is the Autodesk® Maya® dynamics engine, which is the sophisticated software that creates realistic-looking motion based on the principles of physics.

Another Maya animation tool, Paint Effects, can create dynamic fields of grass and flowers, a head full of hair, and other such systems in a matter of minutes. Maya also offers dynamic simulations for hair, fur, and cloth. In this chapter, I'll cover the basics of dynamics in Maya and let you practice working with particles by making steam.

Learning Outcomes: In this chapter, you will be able to

- Create rigid body dynamic objects and create forces to act upon them
- Keyframe animated passive rigid body objects to act on active rigid bodies
- Bake out simulations to keyframes and simplify animation curves
- Understand nParticle workflow
- Emit nParticles and have them move and render to simulate steam
- Draw Paint Effects strokes
- Render an object with a cartoon look easily
- Create an nCloth object (a.k.a. nMesh)
- Collide nMesh objects and add forces
- Cache your nDynamics to disk
- Customize the Maya interface

An Overview of Dynamics and Maya Nucleus

Dynamics is the simulation of motion through the application of the principles of physics. Rather than assigning keyframes to objects to animate them, with Maya dynamics you assign physical characteristics that define how an object behaves in a simulated world. You create the objects as usual in Maya, and then you convert them to *dynamic bodies*. Dynamic bodies are defined through dynamic attributes you add to them, which affect how the objects behave in a dynamic simulation.

Dynamic bodies are affected by external forces called *fields*, which exert a force on them to create motion. Fields can range from wind forces to gravity and can have their own specific effects on dynamic bodies.

In Maya, dynamic objects are categorized as bodies, particles, hair, and fluids. Dynamic bodies are created from geometric surfaces and are used for physical objects such as bouncing balls. *Particles* are points in space that have renderable properties and are used for numerous effects, such as fire and smoke. I'll cover particle basics in the latter half of this chapter. *Hair* consists of curves that behave dynamically, such as strings. *Fluids* are, in essence, volumetric particles that can exhibit surface properties. You can use fluid dynamics for natural effects such as billowing clouds or plumes of smoke.

Nucleus is a more stable and interactive way of calculating dynamic simulations in Maya than its traditional dynamics engine. Nucleus speeds up the creation and increases the stability of some dynamic effects in Maya, including particle effects and cloth simulation (through nCloth).

In the Maya 2009 release, Autodesk introduced nParticles. They're closely related to traditional particles in Maya but have been made easier to create and manage, requiring less-explicit expression controls than before.

I'll introduce nParticles (instead of traditional particles) later in this chapter; however, soft bodies, hair, nCloth, and fluid dynamics are advanced topics and won't be covered in this book.

Rigid and Soft Dynamic Bodies

The two types of dynamic bodies are rigid and soft. *Rigid bodies* are solid objects, such as a pair of dice or a baseball, that move and rotate according to the dynamics applied. Fields and collisions affect the entire object and move it accordingly. *Soft bodies* are malleable surfaces that deform dynamically, such as drapes in the wind or a bouncing rubber ball. In brief, this is accomplished by making the surface points (NURBS, CVs, or polygon vertices) of the soft body object dynamic instead of the whole object. The forces and collisions of the scene affect these surface points, making them move to deform their surface. In this section, you'll learn about rigid body dynamics.

Creating Active and Passive Rigid Body Objects

Any surface geometry in Maya can be converted to a rigid body. After it's converted, that surface can respond to the effects of fields and take part in collisions. Sounds like fun, eh?

The two types of rigid bodies are active and passive. An *active rigid body* is affected by collisions and fields. A *passive rigid body* isn't affected by fields and remains still when it collides with another object. A passive rigid body is used as a surface against which active rigid bodies collide.

The best way to see how the two types of rigid bodies behave is to create some and animate them. In this section, you'll do that in the classic animation exercise of a bouncing ball.

To create a bouncing ball using Maya rigid bodies, switch to the Dynamics menu and follow these steps:

1. Create a polygonal plane, and scale it to be a ground surface.

2. Create a poly sphere, and position it a number of units above the ground, as shown in Figure 12.1.

3. Make sure you're in the Dynamics menu set (choose Dynamics from the Status line's drop-down bar). Select the poly sphere, and choose Soft/Rigid Bodies → Create Active Rigid Body. The sphere's Translate and Rotate attributes turn yellow. There will be a dynamic input for those attributes, so you can't set keyframes on any of them.

4. Select the ground plane, and choose Soft/Rigid Bodies → Create Passive Rigid Body. Doing so sets the poly plane as the floor. For this exercise, stick with the default settings and ignore the various creation options and Rigid Body attributes.

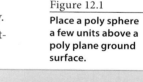

Figure 12.1

Place a poly sphere a few units above a poly plane ground surface.

5. To put the ball into motion, you need to create a field to affect it. Select the sphere, and choose Fields → Gravity. By selecting the active rigid object(s) while you create the field, you connect that field to the objects automatically. Fields affect only the active rigid bodies to which they're connected. If you hadn't established this connection initially, you could still do so later, through the Dynamic Relationships Editor. You'll find out more about this process later in this chapter.

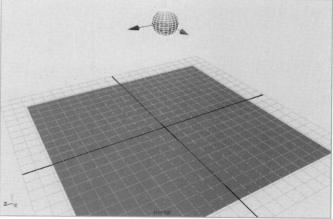

If you try to scrub the timeline, you'll notice that the animation doesn't run properly. Because dynamics simulates physics, no keyframes are set. You must play the scene from start to finish for the calculations to execute properly. You must also play the scene using the Play Every Frame option. Click the Animation Options button to the right of the Range slider, or choose Window → Settings/Preferences → Preferences. In the Preferences window, choose Time Slider under the Settings header. Choose Play Every Frame from the Playback Speed menu. You can also set the maximum frames per second that your scene will play back by setting the Max Playback Speed attribute.

To play back the simulation, set your frame range from 1 to at least 500. Go to frame 1, and click Play. Make sure you have the proper Playback Speed settings in your Preferences window; otherwise, the simulation won't play properly.

When the simulation plays, you'll notice that the sphere begins to fall after a few frames and collides with the ground plane, bouncing back up.

As an experiment, try turning the passive body plane into an active body using the following steps:

1. Select the plane, and open the Attribute Editor.

2. In the `rigidBody2` tab, select the Active check box. This switches the plane from a passive body to an active body.

3. Play the simulation. The ball falls to hit the plane and knock it away. Because the plane is now an active body, it's moved by collisions. But because it isn't connected to the gravity field, it doesn't fall with the ball.

To connect the now-active body plane to the gravity field, open the Dynamic Relationships Editor window, shown in Figure 12.2 (choose Window → Relationship Editors → Dynamic Relationships).

On the left is an Outliner list of the objects in your scene. On the right is a list from which you can choose a category of objects to list: Fields (default), Collisions, Emitters, or All. Select the geometry (`pPlane1`) on the left side, and then connect it to the gravity field by selecting the `gravityField1` node on the right.

Figure 12.2

The Dynamic Relationships Editor window

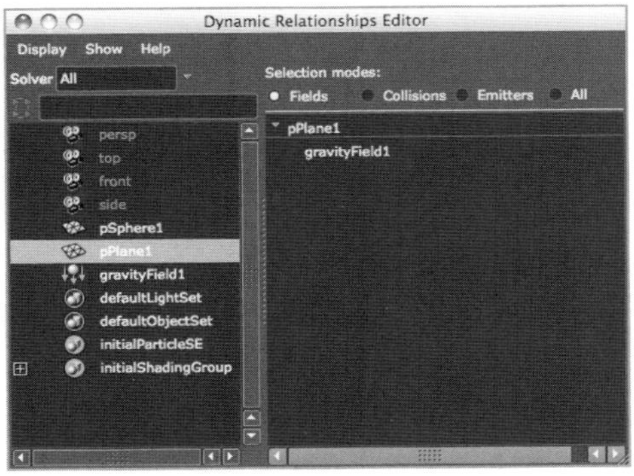

When you connect the gravity field to the plane and run the simulation, you'll see the plane fall away with the ball. Because the two fall at the same rate (the rate set by the single gravity field), they don't collide. To disconnect the plane from the gravity field, deselect the gravity field in the right panel.

You can also connect a dynamic object to a field by selecting the dynamic object or objects and then the desired field and choosing Fields → Affect Selected Object(s). This method is more useful for connecting multiple dynamic objects to a field.

Turning the active body plane back to a passive floor is as simple as returning to frame 1, the beginning of the simulation, and clearing the Active attribute in the Attribute Editor. By turning the active body back to a passive body, you regain an immovable floor upon which the ball can collide and bounce.

RELATIONSHIP EDITORS

The Relationship Editors, such as the Dynamic Relationships Editor window, are a means to connect two nodes to create a special relationship. The Dynamic Relationships Editor window specializes in connecting dynamic attributes so that fields, particles, and rigid bodies can interact in a simulation. Another example of a Relationship Editor is the Light Linking window mentioned in Chapter 10, "Autodesk Maya Lighting," which allows you to connect lights to geometry so that they light only a specific object or objects. These are fairly advanced topics; however, as you learn more about Maya, their use will become integral in your workflow.

Moving a Rigid Body

Because the Maya dynamics engine controls the movement of any active rigid bodies, you can't set keyframes on their translation or rotation. With a passive object, however, you can set keyframes on translation and rotation as you can with any other Maya object. You also can easily keyframe an object to turn either active or passive.

Any movement that the passive body has through regular keyframe animation is translated into momentum, which is passed on to any active rigid bodies with which the passive body collides. Think of a baseball bat that strikes a baseball. The bat is a passive rigid body that you have keyframed to swing. The baseball is an active rigid body that is hit by (collides with) the bat as it swings. The momentum of the bat is transferred to the ball, and the ball is sent flying into the stadium stands. You'll see an example of this in action in the next exercise.

Rigid Body Attributes

Here is a rundown of the more important attributes for both passive and active rigid bodies as they pertain to collisions:

Mass Sets the relative mass of the rigid body. Set on active or passive rigid bodies, *mass* is a factor in how much momentum is transferred from one object to another. A more massive object pushes a less massive one with less effort and is itself less prone to movement when hit. Mass is relative, so if all rigid bodies have the same mass value, there is no difference in the simulation.

Static and Dynamic Friction Sliders   Set how much friction the rigid body has while at rest (static) and while in motion (dynamic). *Friction* specifies how much the object resists moving or being moved. A friction of 0 makes the rigid body move freely, as if on ice.

Bounciness   Specifies how resilient the body is upon collision. The higher the *bounciness* value, the more bounce the object has upon collision.

Damping   Creates a drag on the object in dynamic motion so that it slows down over time. The higher the *damping*, the more the body's motion diminishes.

Animating with Dynamics: The Pool Table

This exercise will take you through the creation of a scene in which you'll use dynamics to animate a cue ball striking two balls on a pool table.

Creating the Pool Table and the Balls

You'll create a simple pool table as a collision surface for the pool balls. To create the table, follow these steps:

1. Create a polygonal plane for the surface of the table. Scale it to 10 along its height and length.

2. To create the pocket holes, make two holes in opposite corners. The easiest way is to duplicate the tabletop plane and offset it slightly in both directions, as shown in Figure 12.3. Doing so creates a pair of square holes in the corners for the ball to drop through. For this exercise, it will do perfectly well.

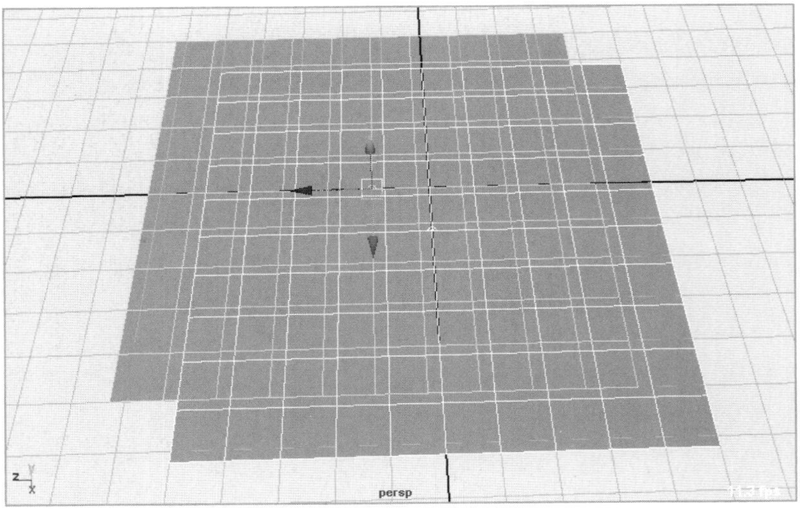

Figure 12.3

Duplicate the table-top plane, and offset it slightly in both directions.

3. Create a polygonal cube, and scale it to fit one edge of the plane to create a rail. Duplicate the cube three times, and then move and rotate the pieces to create the rails around the table, as shown in Figure 12.4.

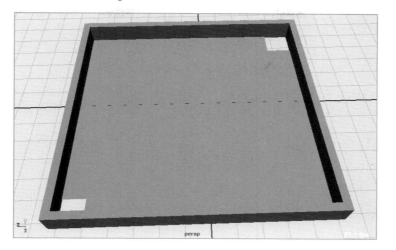

Figure 12.4

A simple pool table

4. Create three poly spheres, and then scale and place them as shown in Figure 12.5. It's important to place them slightly above the pool table surface. Although it's not imperative to have the exact location shown in the figure, it's a good idea to get close to the layout shown.

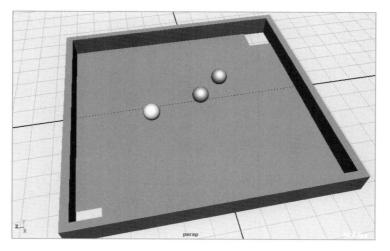

Figure 12.5

Scaling and placing the three spheres

5. Shade your pool balls to make each one different. The figures in this exercise show a solid white ball, a striped ball (it will be yellow on your screen), and a black eight ball, as shown in Figure 12.6.

Figure 12.6

The pool balls in texture view

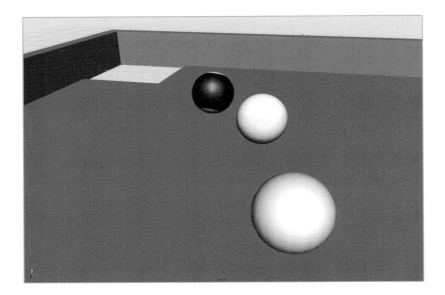

The spheres are placed a bit over the table surface so that their geometries' surfaces aren't accidentally crossing each other, an effect known as *interpenetrating*. When surfaces interpenetrate, the dynamics that result are usually as welcome as sand in your eyes. Starting all colliding rigid bodies slightly away from each other should guarantee that their surfaces don't interpenetrate. Using the simple pool table that you've set up will make the dynamics calculations quick and easy.

Use the file Table_v1.mb in the Scenes folder of the Pool_Table project on the book's companion web page, www.sybex.com/go/introducingmaya2014, as a reference or to catch up to this point.

Creating Rigid Bodies

Define the pool table as a passive rigid body, and define the pool balls as active rigid bodies. Follow these steps:

1. Select the two planes that make up the tabletop and the four cubes that are the side rails. Choose Soft/Rigid Bodies → Create Passive Rigid Body.

2. Select the three balls, and choose Soft/Rigid Bodies → Create Active Rigid Body to make them active rigid bodies.

3. With all three pool balls selected, create a gravity field by choosing Fields → Gravity. The gravity field automatically connects to all three balls.

4. Run the simulation. You should see the balls fall slightly onto the tabletop. Check to see that none of them interpenetrates the table surface. If any of them do, Maya will select the offending geometry and display an error message in the Command Feedback line, turning it red.

Animating Rigid Bodies

If you need to, enable texture view in your view panel by pressing 6.

The next step is to put the cue ball (the white sphere) into motion so that it hits the striped ball into the black eight ball to sink it into the corner pocket. Keyframe the cue ball's translation from its starting point to hit into the striped ball. However, because active rigid bodies can't be keyframed, you have to turn the cue ball into a passive rigid body. To do that, follow these steps:

1. Select the cue ball (the white ball). Notice the `Active` attribute in the Channel Box. (You may have to scroll down; it's at the bottom.) It's set to On.

2. Rewind your animation to the first frame. Choose Soft/Rigid Bodies → Set Passive Key. Notice that the `Active` attribute turns a dark yellow. You've set a keyframe for the active state of the cue ball, and it now says Off. You can toggle rigid bodies between passive and active. Maya has also set translation and rotation keyframes for the cue ball.

3. Go to frame 10. Move the cue ball with the Translate tool so that its outer surface slightly passes through the yellow-striped ball, as shown in Figure 12.7. Choose Soft/Rigid Bodies → Set Passive Key.

Figure 12.7

Move the cue ball with the Translate tool.

4. Go to frame 11, and choose Soft/Rigid Bodies → Set Active Key. This turns the cue ball back into an active rigid body in the frame after it strikes the striped ball.

By animating the ball as a passive rigid body, keyframing its translation, and then turning it back to active, you set the dynamic simulation in motion. The cue ball animates from its starting position and hits the striped ball. The Maya dynamics engine calculates the collisions on that ball and sets it into motion; the ball then strikes the black eight ball, which should roll into the corner pocket. The dynamics engine, at frame 11, also calculates the movement of the cue ball after it strikes the striped ball, so you don't have to animate its ricochet.

Go to the start frame, and play back the simulation. The cue ball knocks the striped ball into the eight ball. The eight ball rolls into the corner, and the striped ball bounces off to the right. If the eight ball doesn't go into the corner, you'll have to edit your cue ball's keyframes to hit the striped ball at the correct angle to hit the eight ball into the corner pocket.

At the current settings, however, the eight ball bounces out of the corner without falling through the hole. You need to control the bounciness of the collisions.

1. Go back to the first frame. Select all three balls. In the Channel Box, change the Bounciness attribute from 0.6 to **0.2**. After you set the attribute value in the Channel Box, Maya sets the value for all three spheres concurrently.

> Changing the Bounciness attribute through the Attribute Editor changes the value for only one sphere even when they're all selected. You have to change the value for each sphere individually in the Attribute Editor. This is true for all values changed on multiple objects through the Attribute Editor.

2. Play back the animation, and you'll see that the balls don't ricochet off each other and the sides of the pool table with as much spring. The eight ball should now fall through the hole. (See Figure 12.8.) You may need to increase your frame range if your ball doesn't quite make it by frame 120; try 200 frames instead.

You can download the scene file Table_v2.mb from the Pool_Table project on the web page to compare your work.

Figure 12.8

The eight ball falls through the hole.

Additional Rigid Body Attributes

In addition, while using the pool table setup without any animation, try playing with the rigid body attributes to see how they affect the rigid body in question. Some of these attributes are defined here:

Initial Velocity   Gives the rigid body an initial push to move it in the corresponding axis.

Initial Spin   Gives the rigid body object an initial twist to start the rotation of the object in that axis.

Impulse Position   Gives the object a constant push in that axis. The effect is cumulative; the object will accelerate if the impulse isn't turned off.

Spin Impulse   Rotates the object constantly in the desired axis. The spin will accelerate if the impulse isn't turned off.

Center of Mass (0,0,0)   Places the center of the object's mass at its pivot point, typically at its geometric center. This value offsets the center of mass, so the rigid body object behaves as if its center of balance is offset, like trick dice or a top-weighted ball.

Creating animation with rigid bodies is straightforward and can go a long way toward creating natural-looking motion for your scene. Integrating such animation into a final project can become fairly complicated, though, so it's prudent to become familiar with the workings of rigid body dynamics before relying on that sort of workflow for an animated project. You'll find that most professionals use rigid body dynamics as a springboard to create realistic motion for their projects. The dynamics are often converted to keyframes and further tweaked by the animator to fit into a larger scene.

Here are a few suggestions for scenes using rigid body dynamics:

Bowling Lane   The bowling ball is keyframed as a passive object until it hits the active rigid pins at the end of the lane. This scene is simple to create and manipulate.

Dice   Active rigid dice are thrown into a passive rigid craps table. This exercise challenges your dynamics abilities as well as your modeling skills if you create an accurate craps table.

Game of Marbles   This scene challenges your texturing and rendering abilities as well as your dynamics abilities as you animate marbles rolling into each other.

Baking Out a Simulation

Frequently, a dynamic simulation is created to fit into another scene, perhaps to interact with other objects. In instances such as this, you want to exchange the dynamic properties of the dynamic body you have set up in a simulation for regular, good old-fashioned animation curves that you can edit along with the rest of the animated scene, if need be.

You can easily take a simulation that you've created and bake it out to curves. As much fun as it is to think of cupcakes, *baking* is a somewhat catchall term used to describe converting one type of action or procedure into another; in this case, you're baking dynamics into keyframes.

You'll take the simulation you set up earlier with the pool balls and turn them into keyframes, to give you a quick idea of how it can be done and the curves you'll get. Dynamics is a deep layer of Maya, and there is a lot to learn about it. Keep in mind that you can use this introduction as a foundation for your own explorations.

To bake out the rigid body simulation of the pool balls, follow these steps:

1. Open the scene file Table_v2.mb from the Pool_Table project on the web page, or if you prefer, open your scene from the previous exercise.

2. Select all three pool balls, and choose Edit → Keys → Bake Simulation ❑. In the option box, shown in Figure 12.9, set Time Range to Time Slider (which should be set to 1 to 150). This, of course, sets the range you would like to bake into curves.

3. Set Hierarchy to Selected, and set Channels to From Channel Box. This ensures that you have control over which keys are created. Make sure Keep Unbaked Keys and Disable Implicit Control are checked and that Sparse Curve Bake is turned off. Before clicking the Bake or Apply button, select the Translate and Rotate channels in the Channel Box. Click Bake.

4. Maya runs through the simulation. Scrub the timeline back and forth. Notice how the pool balls move around normally as if the dynamic simulation were running—except that you can scrub in the timeline, which you can't do with a dynamics simulation. If you open the Graph Editor, you'll see something similar to Figure 12.10.

5. The curves are crowded; they have keyframes at every frame. A typical dynamics bake gives results like this. But you can set the Bake command to sparse the curves for you; that is, it can take out keyframes at frames that have values within a certain tolerance so that a minor change in the ball's position or rotation need not have a keyframe on the curve.

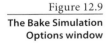

Figure 12.9

The Bake Simulation Options window

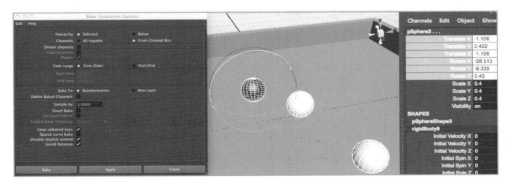

6. Let's go back in time and try this again. Press Z (Undo) until you back up to right before you baked out the simulation to curves. You can also close this scene and reopen it from the original project, if necessary. This time, select the balls, and choose Edit → Keys → Bake Simulation ❑. In the option box, turn on the Sparse Curve Bake setting, and set Sample By to **5**. Select the channels in the Channel Box, and click Bake. You're telling Maya to only look at every five frames of the simulation to set keyframes.

7. Maya runs through the simulation again and bakes everything out to curves. This time it makes a sparser animation curve for each channel because it's looking at five-frame intervals, as shown in Figure 12.11. If you open the Graph Editor, you'll notice that the curves are much friendlier to look at and edit.

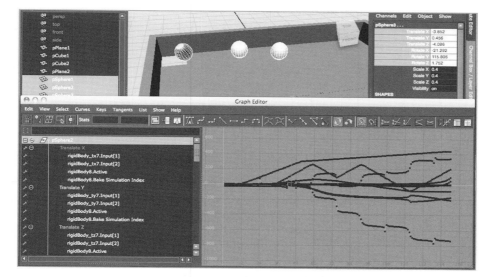

Figure 12.10

The pool balls have animation curves.

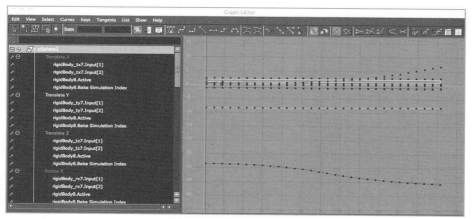

Figure 12.11

Sampling by fives makes a cleaner curve.

Sampling by fives may give you an easier curve to edit, but it can oversimplify the animation of your objects; make sure you use the best Sampling setting for your simulation when you need to convert it to curves for editing.

Simplifying Animation Curves

Despite a higher Sampling setting when you bake out the simulation, you can still be left with a lot of keyframes to deal with, especially if you have to modify the animation extensively from here. One last trick you can use is to simplify the curve further through the Graph Editor. You have to work with curves of the same relative size, so you'll start with the rotation curves, because they have larger values. To keep things simple, let's deal with one ball: the black eight ball. To simplify the curve in the Graph Editor, follow these steps:

1. Select the black eight ball, and open the Graph Editor. In the left Outliner side, select Rotate X, Rotate Y, and Rotate Z to display only these curves in the graph view. Figure 12.12 shows the curves.

2. In the left panel of the Graph Editor, select the rigidBody_rx8.Input(1) nodes displayed under the Rotate X, Y, and Z entries for all three curves, as shown in Figure 12.13. In the Graph Editor menu, choose Curves → Simplify Curve ❑. In the option box, set Time Range to All, set Simplify Method to Dense Data, set Time Tolerance to **0.2**, and set Value Tolerance to **0.5**. These are fairly high values, but because you're dealing with rotation of the ball, the degree values are high enough. For more intricate values such as Translation, you would use much lower tolerances when simplifying a curve.

Figure 12.12

The Graph Editor displays the rotation curves of the eight ball.

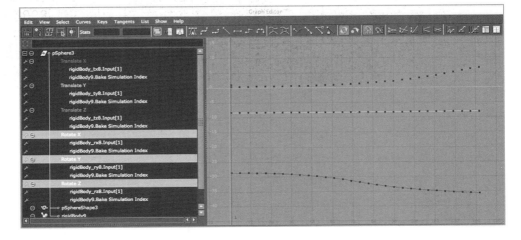

3. Click Simplify, and you see that the curve retains its basic shape but loses some of the unneeded keyframes. Figure 12.14 shows the simplified curve, which differs little from the original curve with keys at every five frames.

Simplifying curves is a handy way to convert a dynamic simulation to curves. Keep in mind that you may lose fidelity to the original animation after you simplify a curve, so use this technique with care. The curve simplification works with good old-fashioned keyframed curves as well; if you inherit a scene from another animator and need to simplify the curves, do it just as you did here.

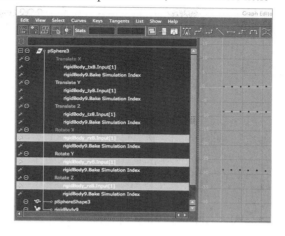

Figure 12.13

Select the curves to simplify them.

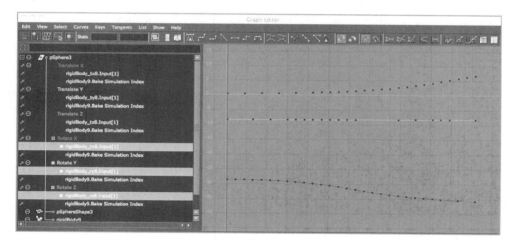

Figure 12.14

A simplified curve for the rotations of the eight ball

Fun Dynamics: Shoot the Catapult!

Now for a fun, quick exercise, you'll use Rigid Body Dynamics to shoot a projectile with the already animated catapult from Chapter 8. Open the scene file `catapult_anim_v2.mb` from the Catapult_Anim project downloaded from the companion website.

1. For the projectile, create a polygon sphere and place it above the basket, as shown in Figure 12.15.

2. Since dynamics takes a lot of calculations, to make things easier, you will create an invisible object to be the passive rigid body collider instead of the existing geometry of the basket itself. This is a frequent workflow in dynamics, where proxy geometry (often hidden) is used to alleviate calculations and speed up the scene. Create another poly sphere with Axis Divisions and Height Divisions both set to **40**.

3. Select the top half faces of the sphere and delete them, to create a bowl and place it over the catapult basket, as shown in Figure 12.16. Use the D key along with Point Snaps to place the bowl's pivot point on the top rim of the bowl, shown in Figure 12.16.

4. The animation of the catapult arm is driven by a Bend deformer, so simply placing and grouping the bowl to the basket will not work. You will use a point on poly constraint to rivet the bowl to a vertex on the arm. To do so, select the vertex shown in Figure 12.17; then Shift+select the bowl object. In the Animation menu set, choose Constrain → Point On Poly. The bowl will snap to the arm, as shown in Figure 12.18.

5. Select the bowl, and in the Channel Box, click the `pSphere2_pointOnPolyConstraint1` node. Set Offset Rotate Y to **-90** and Offset Rotate X to **8** to place the bowl in the basket better (Figure 12.19).

6. Go into the Dynamics menu set. Select the projectile sphere, and at frame 1 of the animation, choose Fields → Gravity. The ball will instantly become an active rigid body and will have a gravity attached. If you play back your scene, the ball will simply fall through the bowl and catapult.

7. Select the bowl object and choose Soft/Rigid Bodies → Create Passive Rigid Body to make the bowl a collision surface for the projectile ball. Play back your scene and *bam!* The projectile will bounce into the bowl as the catapult arm bends back, and the catapult will shoot the ball out.

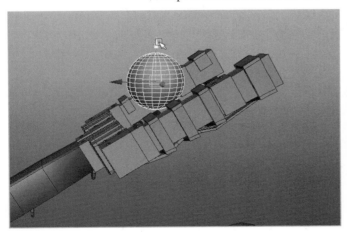

Figure 12.15

Place a sphere over the basket.

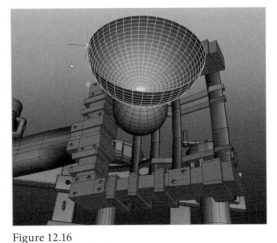

Figure 12.16

It puts the sphere in the basket, or else it gets the hose again.

8. Select the bowl object, and press Ctrl+H to hide it. Now when you play back your scene, the ball looks like it rests inside the catapult basket, as shown in Figure 12.20. The scene file `catapult_dynamics_v1.mb` will catch you up to this point.

If you play back the scene frame by frame, you'll notice that the arm and basket will briefly pass through the projectile ball for a few frames as the arm shoots back up around frames 102–104. Increasing the subdivisions of the ball and the bowl before making them rigid bodies will help the collisions, but for a fun exercise, this works great. Play with the placement of the ball at the start of the scene, as well as the gravity and any other fields you care to experiment with to try to land the projectile in different places in the scene.

Figure 12.17
Select the vertex.

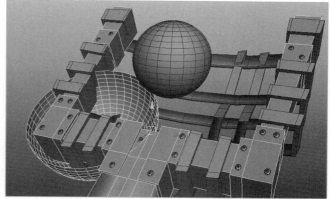

Figure 12.18
The bowl snaps to the arm at a weird angle.

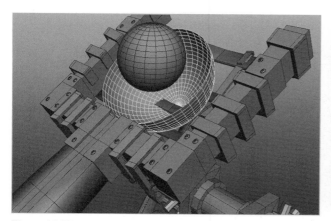

Figure 12.19
Set offsets to place the bowl properly inside the basket.

Figure 12.20
The ball shoots!

nParticle Dynamics

Like rigid body objects, particles are moved dynamically using collisions and fields. In short, a *particle* is a point in space that is given renderable properties—that is, it can render out. When particles are used en masse, they can create effects such as smoke, a swarm of insects, fireworks, and so on. nParticles are an implementation of particles through the Maya Nucleus solver, which provides better and easier simulations than traditional Maya particles.

Although particles (and nParticles) can be an advanced and involved aspect of Maya, it's important to have some exposure to them as you begin to learn Maya.

Much of what you learned about rigid body dynamics transfers to particles. However, it's important to think of particle animation as manipulating a larger system rather than as controlling every single particle in the simulation. Particles are most often used together in large numbers so that the entirety is rendered out to create an effect. You control fields and dynamic attributes to govern the motion of the system as a whole.

Emitting nParticles

A typical workflow for creating an nParticle effect in Maya breaks out into two parts: motion and rendering. First, you create and define the behavior of particles through emission. An *emitter* is a Maya object that creates the particles. After you create fields and adjust particle behavior within a dynamic simulation, much as you would do with rigid body motion, you give the particles renderable qualities to define how they look. This second aspect of the workflow defines how the particles come together to create the desired effect, such as steam. You'll make a locomotive pump steam later in this chapter.

To create an nParticle system, follow these steps:

Figure 12.21

Creation options for an nParticle emitter

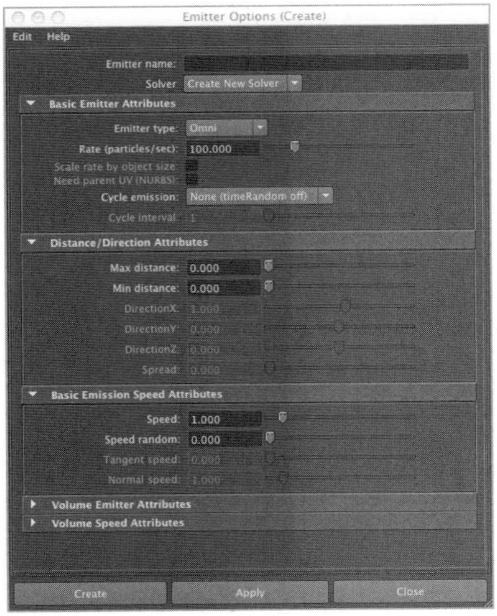

1. Make sure you're in the nDynamics menu set, choose nParticles → Create nParticles, and select Cloud. Choose nParticles → Create nParticles → Create Emitter ❏. The option box gives you various creation options for the nParticle emitter, as shown in Figure 12.21.

   The default settings create an Omni emitter with a rate of 100 particles per second and a speed of 1.0. Click Create. A small round object (the emitter) appears at the origin.

2. Click the Play button to play the scene. As with rigid body dynamics, you must also play back the scene using the Play Every Frame option. You can't scrub or reverse-play particles unless you create a cache file. You'll learn how to create a particle disk cache later in this chapter.

   You'll notice a mass of circles streaming out of the emitter in all directions (see Figure 12.22). These are the nParticles.

Emitter Attributes

You can control how particles are created and behave by changing the type of emitter and adjusting its attributes. Here are the most often used emitters:

Omni   Emits particles in all directions.

Directional   Emits a spray of particles in a specific direction, as shown in Figure 12.23.

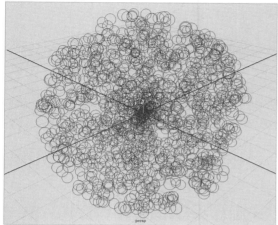

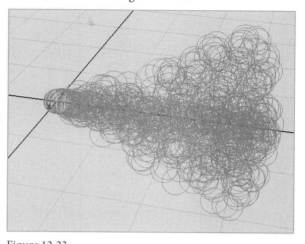

Figure 12.22

An Omni emitter emits a swarm of cloud particles in all directions.

Figure 12.23

Cloud nParticles are sprayed in a specific direction.

Volume   Emits particles from within a specified volume, as shown in Figure 12.24. The volume can be a cube, a sphere, a cylinder, a cone, or a torus. By default, the particles can leave the perimeter of the volume.

After you create an emitter, its attributes govern how the particles are released into the scene. Every emitter has the following attributes to control the emission:

Rate   Governs how many particles are emitted per second.

Speed   Specifies how fast the particles move out from the emitter.

Speed Random   Randomizes the speed of the particles as they're emitted, for a more natural look.

Min and Max Distance   Emits particles within an offset distance from the emitter. You enter values for the Min and Max Distance settings. Figure 12.25 shows a Directional emitter with Min and Max Distance settings of 3.

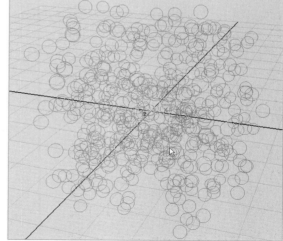

Figure 12.24

Cloud nParticles emit from anywhere inside the emitter's volume.

Figure 12.25

An emitter with Min and Max Distance settings of 3 emits cloud nParticles 3 units from itself.

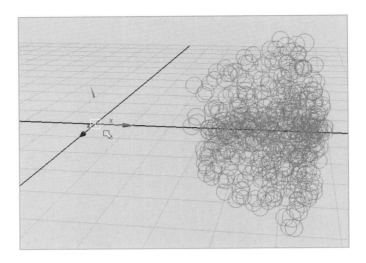

nParticle Attributes

After being created, or born, and set into motion by an emitter, nParticles rely on their own attributes and any fields or collisions in the scene to govern their motion, just like rigid body objects.

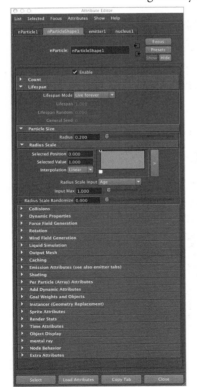

In Figure 12.26, the Attribute Editor shows a number of tabs for the selected particle object. nParticle1 is the particle object node. This has the familiar Translate, Rotate, and Scale attributes, like most other object nodes. But the shape node, nParticleShape1, is where all the important attributes are for a particle, and it's displayed by default when you select a particle object. The third tab in the Attribute Editor is the emitter1 node that belongs to the particle's emitter. This makes it easier to toggle back and forth to adjust emitter and particle settings.

The Lifespan Attributes

When any particle is born, you can give it a *lifespan*, which allows the particle to die when it reaches a certain point in time. As you'll see with the steam locomotive later in the chapter, a particle that has a lifespan can change over that lifespan. For example, a particle may start out as white and fade away at the end of its life. A lifespan also helps keep the total number of particles in a scene to a minimum, which helps the scene run more efficiently.

You use the Lifespan mode to select the type of lifespan for the nParticle.

Live Forever   The particles in the scene can exist indefinitely.

Figure 12.26

nParticle attributes

Constant   All particles die when their Lifespan value is reached. Lifespan is measured in seconds, so upon emission, a particle with a Lifespan of 1.0 will exist for 30 frames (in a scene set up at 30fps) before it disappears.

Random Range   This type sets a lifespan in Constant mode but assigns a range value via the Lifespan Random attribute to allow some particles to live longer than others for a more natural effect.

LifespanPP Only   This mode is used in conjunction with expressions that are programmed into the particle with Maya Embedded Language (MEL). Expressions are an advanced Maya concept and aren't used in this book.

The Shading Attributes

The Shading attributes determine how your particles look and how they will render. Two types of particle rendering are used in Maya: software and hardware. *Hardware particles* are typically rendered out separately from anything else in the scene and are then com-

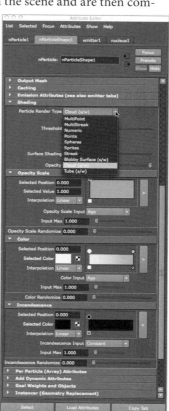

Figure 12.27

The Particle Render Type drop-down menu

posited with the rest of the scene. Because of this compound workflow for hardware particles, this book will introduce you to a software particle type called *Cloud*. Cloud, like other *software particles*, can be rendered with the rest of a scene through the software renderer.

With your particles selected, open the Attribute Editor. In the Shading section, you'll find the Particle Render Type drop-down menu (see Figure 12.27).

The three render types listed with the (s/w) suffix are software-rendered particles. All the other types can be rendered only through the Maya Hardware renderer. Select your render type, and Maya adds the proper attributes you'll need for the render type you selected.

For example, if you select the Points render type from the menu, your particles change from circles on the screen to dots, as shown in Figure 12.28.

Several new attributes that control the look of the particles appear when you switch the Particle Render Type setting. Each Particle Render Type setting has its own set of render attributes. Set your nParticles back to the Cloud type. The Cloud particle type attributes are Threshold, Surface Shading, and Opacity. (See Figure 12.29.)

Figure 12.28

Dots on the screen represent point particles.

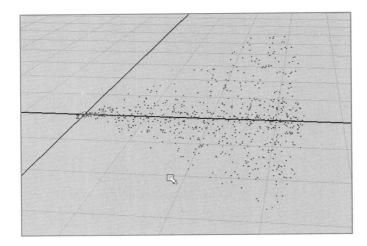

In the Shading heading, shown in Figure 12.30 for the cloud nParticles, are controls for the Opacity Scale, Color, and Incandescence attributes. They control how the particles look when simulated and rendered. Notice how each of these controls is based on ramps.

nParticles are already set up to allow you to control the color, opacity, and incandescence during the life of the particle. For example, by default, the Color attribute is set up with a white to cyan ramp. This means that each of the particles will begin life white in color and will gradually turn cyan toward the end of its lifespan, or Age setting.

Likewise, the Particle Size heading in the Attribute Editor contains a ramp for Radius Scale that works much the same way as the Color attribute just described. In this case, you use the Radius Scale ramp to increase or decrease the size of the particle along its Age setting.

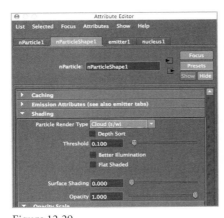

Figure 12.29

Each Particle Render Type setting displays its own set of attributes.

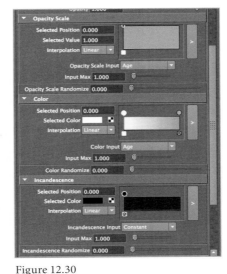

Figure 12.30

Controls for the Opacity Scale, Color, and Incandescence attributes

nCaching Particles

It would be nice to turn particles into cash, but I can only show you how to turn your particles into a cache. You can cache the motion of your particles to memory or to disk to make playback and editing of your particle animation easier. To cache particles to your system's fast RAM memory, select the nParticle object you want to cache, and open the Attribute Editor. In the Caching section, under Memory Caching, select the Cache Data check box. Play back your scene, and the particles cache into your memory for faster playback. You can also scrub your timeline to see your particle animation. If you make changes to your animation, the scene won't reflect the changes until you delete the cache from memory by selecting the particle object and unchecking the Memory Cache check box in the Attribute Editor. The amount of information the memory cache can hold depends on your machine's RAM.

Although memory caching is generally faster than disk caching, creating a disk cache lets you cache all the particles as they exist throughout their duration in your scene and ensures that the particles are rendered correctly, especially if you're rendering on multiple computers or across a network. You should create a particle disk cache before rendering.

If you make changes to your particle simulation but you don't see the changes reflected when you play back the scene, make sure you've turned off any memory or deleted any disk cache from previous versions of the simulation.

Creating an nCache on Disk

After you've created a particle scene and you want to be able to scrub the timeline back and forth to see your particle motion and how it acts in the scene, you can create a particle nCache to disk. This lets you play back the entire scene as you like, without running the simulation from the start and by every frame.

To create an nCache, switch to the nDynamics menu, select the nParticle object, and choose nCache → Create New Cache. Maya will run the simulation according to the timeline and save the position of all the particle systems in the scene to cache files in your current project's Data/Cache folder. You can then play or even scrub your animation back and forth, and the particles will run properly.

If you make any dynamics changes to the particles, such as emission rate or speed, you'll need to detach the cache file from the scene for the changes to take effect. Choose nCache → Delete Cache. You can open the option box to select whether you want to delete the cache files physically or merely detach them from the current nParticles.

Now that you understand the basics of particle dynamics, it's time to see for yourself how they work.

Animating a Particle Effect: Locomotive Steam

You'll create a spray of steam puffing out of the pump on the side of the locomotive that drives the wheels that you rigged previously. You'll use the scene fancy_locomotive_anim_v3.mb from Chapter 9, "More Animation!"

Emitting the nParticles

The first step is to create an emitter to spray from the steam pump and to set up the motion and behavior of the nParticles.

1. In the nDynamics menu, choose nParticles → Create nParticles. Cloud should still be checked in the Create nParticles menu. If it isn't, select Cloud, and then choose nParticles → Create nParticles → Create Emitter □. Set Emitter Type to Directional, and click Create. Place the emitter at the end of the pump, as shown in Figure 12.31.

Figure 12.31

Place the emitter at the end of the pump.

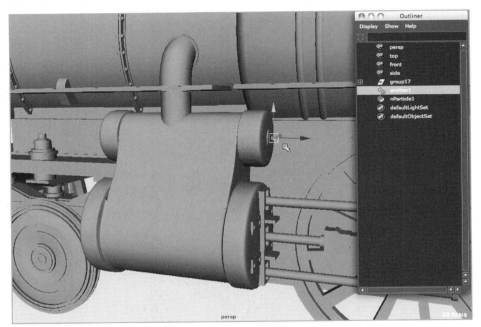

2. To set up the emission in the proper direction, adjust the attributes of the emitter. In the Distance/Direction Attributes section, set Direction Y to **0**, Direction X to **0**, and Direction Z to **1**. This emits the particles straight out of the pump over the first large wheel and toward the back of the engine.

The Direction attributes are relative. Entering a value of 1 for Direction X and a value of 2 for Direction Y makes the particles spray at twice the height (Y) of their lateral distance (X).

3. Play back your scene. The cloud nParticles emit in a straight line from the engine, as shown in Figure 12.32.

    You can load the file `Locomotive_Steam_v1.ma` from the Locomotive project on the web page to check your work.

4. To change the particle emission to more of a spray, adjust the Spread attribute for the emitter. Click the `emitter1` tab in the particle's Attribute Editor (or select the emitter to focus the Attribute Editor on it instead), and change Spread from 0 to **0.30**. Figure 12.33 shows the new cloud spray.

Figure 12.32
Cloud nParticles emit in a straight line from the pump.

The Spread attribute sets the cone angle for a directional emission. A value of 0 results in a thin line of particles. A value of 1 emits particles in a 180-degree arc.

5. The emission is rather slow for hot steam being pumped out as the locomotive drives the wheels, so change the Speed setting for the emitter from 1 to **2.0**, and change Speed Random from 0 to **1**. Doing so creates a random speed range between 1 and 3 for each particle. These two attributes are found in the emitter's Attribute Editor in the `Basic Emission Speed` Attributes section.

6. So that all the steam doesn't emit from the same point, keep the emitter's Min Distance at 0, but set its Max Distance to **0.3**. This creates a range of offset between 0 and 0.3 units for the particles to emit from, as shown in Figure 12.34.

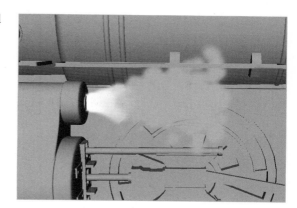

Figure 12.33
The emitter's Spread attribute widens the spray of particles.

Figure 12.34
A range of offset between 0 and 0.3 units creates a more believable emission.

Setting nParticle Attributes

It's always good to get the particles moving as closely to what you need as possible before you tend to their look. Now that you have the particles emitting properly from the steam pump, you'll adjust the nParticle attributes. Start by setting a lifespan for them, and then add rendering attributes.

Figure 12.35

The initial radius settings for the steam nParticles

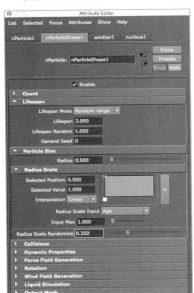

1. Select the nParticle object, and open the Attribute Editor. In the Lifespan section, set Lifespan Mode to Random Range. Set Lifespan to **2** and Lifespan Random to **1**. This creates a range of 1 to 3 for each particle's lifespan. (This is based on a lifespan of 2, plus or minus a random value from 0 to 1.)

2. You can control the radius of the particles as they're emitted from the pump. Under the Particle Size heading in the Attribute Editor, set a Radius attribute of **0.50**. Set the Radius Scale Randomize attribute to **0.25**. This allows you to have particles that emit with a radius range between 0.25 and 0.75. Figure 12.35 shows the attributes.

3. If you play back the simulation, you'll see the particles are quite large initially. Because steam expands as it travels, you need to adjust the size (radius) of your nParticles to make them smaller at birth; they will grow larger over their lifespan and produce a good look for your steam.

4. In the Radius Scale heading in the Attribute Editor, click the arrow to the right of the ramp to open a larger view of the ramp, as shown in Figure 12.36.

Figure 12.36

Open the Radius Scale ramp.

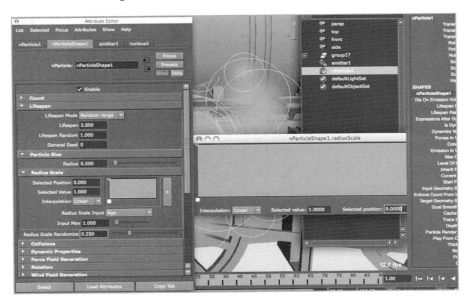

5. Click and drag the ramp's first and only handle (an open circle at the upper-left corner of the Ramp window) down to a value of about 0.25, as shown in Figure 12.37. The particles get smaller as you adjust the ramp value.

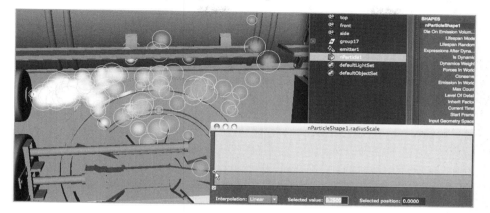

Figure 12.37

Decrease the radius of the nParticles using the Radius Scale ramp.

6. To allow the particles to grow in size, add a second handle to the scale curve by clicking anywhere on that line, and drag to a value of 1.0 and the position shown in Figure 12.38. The particles toward the end of the spray get larger.

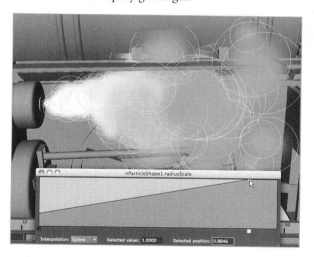

Figure 12.38

Adjust the Radius Scale ramp to grow the particles.

7. You can set up collisions so the nParticle steam doesn't travel right through the mesh of the locomotive. Select the meshes shown in Figure 12.39, and choose nMesh → Create Passive Collider.

8. In the Outliner, select the three nRigid nodes that were just created, and set the `Friction` attribute in the Channel Box to **0.0** from the default of 0.10. Play back your scene, and your particles now collide with the surface of the locomotive. (See Figure 12.40.)

Figure 12.39

Select the meshes with which the nParticles will collide.

Figure 12.40

The particles now react very nicely against the side of the locomotive.

If you want to check your work, download the file locomotive_steam_v2.ma from the Locomotive project on the web page.

Setting Rendering Attributes

After you define the nParticle movement to your liking, you can create the proper look for the nParticles. This means setting and adjusting their rendering parameters.

> **PARTICLE TYPE**
>
> Because Maya has several types of particles, the particles are set up according to their type; the workflow in this section applies only to the Cloud particle type.

1. Select the nParticle object, and open the Attribute Editor. Expand the Shading heading, and look at the Color ramp. By default, the particles go from white to light blue in color. Click the cyan color's circle handle on top of the ramp. The Selected Color attribute next to the ramp shows the cyan color. Click in the swatch to open the Color Chooser, and change the color to a very light gray.

2. Click the arrow bar to the right of the Opacity Scale ramp to open a larger ramp view. Grab the first handle in the upper-left corner, and drag it down to a value of **0.12**.

3. The steam needs to be less opaque at its birth, grow more opaque toward the middle of its life, and fade completely away at the end of the particle's life. Click to create new handles to create a curve for the ramp, as shown in Figure 12.41. The values for the five ramp handles shown from left to right are 0.12, 0.30, 0.20, 0.08, and 0.

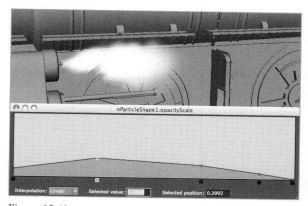

Figure 12.41

Creating an Opacity ramp for the steam

Figure 12.42

The steam seems too short and small.

4. In the Render Settings window, set Image Size to 640×480. On the Maya Software tab, set Quality to Intermediate Quality. Run the animation, and stop it when some steam has been emitted. Render a frame. It should look like Figure 12.42. The steam doesn't travel far enough along the engine; it disappears too soon.

   With the steam nParticles selected, open the Attribute Editor, and, in the Radius Scale, change the first handle's value from 0.25 to **0.35** to make the steam particles a bit larger. Below the Opacity Scale ramp is the Input Max slider; set that value to **1.6**.

5. Select the emitter1 tab, and change the Spread value for the emitter to **0.2**. Change Rate (Particles/Sec) to **200** and Speed to **3.0**. Play back the simulation, and render a frame to compare to Figure 12.43.

6. The Color ramp in the nParticle's Attribute Editor controls the color of the steam, and a shader is assigned to the particles. Select the steam nParticle object, and open the Hypershade window. In the Hypershade, click the Graph materials on the selected object's icon ( ), as shown in Figure 12.44.

Figure 12.43

A better emission, but a bit too solid

7. In the Hypershade, select the npCloudVolume shader, and open the Attribute Editor. Notice that the attributes in the Common Material Attributes section all have connections. The ramp controls in the nParticle Attribute Editor are controlling the attributes in this Particle Cloud shader.

8. Under the Transparency heading in the Attribute Editor for the shader, set Density to **0.35**. Try a render; the steam should look better. (See Figure 12.45.)

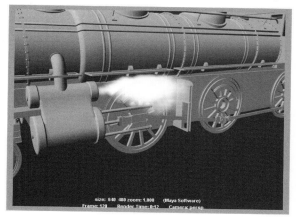

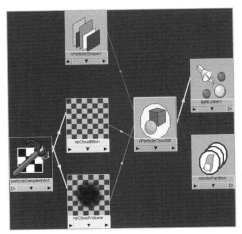

Figure 12.44

The shaders assigned to the cloud nParticle

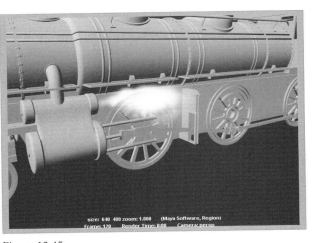

Figure 12.45

The steam is less flat and solid.

Batch-render a 200-frame sequence of the scene at a lower resolution, such as 320×240, to see how the particles look as they animate. (Check the frames with FCheck. Refer to Chapter 11, "Autodesk Maya Rendering," for more on FCheck.)

Download the file locomotive_steam_v3.ma from the Locomotive project on the web page to check your work.

Experiment with the steam by animating the Rate attribute of the emitter to make the steam pump out in time with the wheel arm. Also, try animating the Speed values and playing with different values in the Radius and Opacity ramps. The steam you'll get in this tutorial looks pretty good, but it isn't as lifelike as it could be. Particle animators are always learning new tricks and expanding their skills, and that comes from always trying new things and retrying the same effects with different methods.

When you feel comfortable with the steam exercise, try using the cloud nParticle to create steam for a mug of coffee. That steam moves much more slowly and is less defined than the blowing steam of the locomotive, and it should pose a new challenge. Also try your hand at creating a smoke trail for a rocket ship or a wafting stream of cigarette smoke, or even the billowing smoke coming from the engine's chimney.

Cloud nParticles are the perfect particle type with which to begin. As you feel more comfortable animating with clouds, experiment with the other render types. The more you experiment with all the types of nParticles, the easier they will be to harness.

Introduction to Paint Effects

One of the tools in the effects arsenal of Maya is called Paint Effects. Using Paint Effects, you can create a field of grass rippling in the wind, a head of hair or feathers, or even a colorful aurora in the sky. Paint Effects is a rendering effect found in the Rendering menu. It has incredible dynamic properties that can make leaves rustle or trees sway in a storm. Paint Effects uses its own dynamics calculations to create natural motion. It's one of the most powerful tools in Maya, with features that go far beyond the scope of this introductory book. Here you'll learn how to create a Paint Effects scene and how to access all the preset brushes to create your own effects.

Paint Effects uses brushes to paint effects into your 3D scene. The brushes create strokes on a surface or in the Maya modeling views that produce tubes, which render out through the Maya Software renderer. These Paint Effects tubes have dynamic properties, which means they can move according to their own forces. Therefore, you can easily create a field of blowing grass.

Try This   Create a field of blowing grass and flowers; it will take you all of five minutes.

1. Start with a new scene file. Maximize the perspective view. (Press the spacebar with the Perspective window active.)

2. Switch to the Rendering menu set (press F6). Choose Paint Effects → Get Brush to open the Visor window. The Visor window displays all the preset Paint Effects brushes that automatically create certain effects. Select the Grasses folder in the Visor's left panel to display the grass brushes available (see Figure 12.46). You can navigate the Visor window as you would navigate any other Maya window, using the Alt key and the mouse buttons.

3. Click the `grassWindWide.mel` brush to activate the Paint Effects tool and set it to this grass brush. Your cursor changes to a Pencil icon.

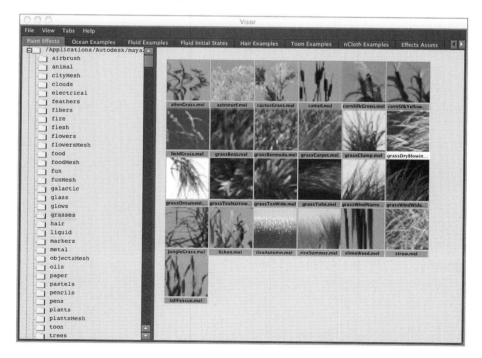

Figure 12.46

The preset grass brushes in the Visor window

4. In the Perspective window, click and drag two lines across the grid, as shown in Figure 12.47, to create two Paint Effects strokes of blowing grass. If you can't see the grass in your view panel, increase `Global Scale` in the Paint Effects Brush Settings in either the Attribute Editor or the Channel Box to see the grass being drawn onto the screen.

Figure 12.47

Click and drag two lines across the grid.

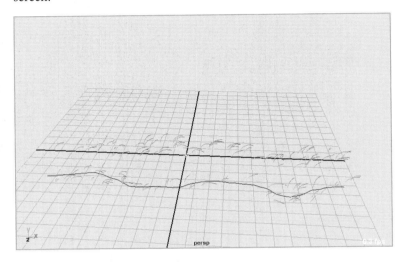

5. To change your brush so you can add some flowers between the grass, choose Paint Effects → Get Brush, and select the Flowers folder. Select the `dandelion_Yellow.mel` brush. Your Paint Effects tool is now set to paint yellow flowers.

6. Click and drag a new stroke between the strokes of grass, as shown in Figure 12.48.

Figure 12.48

Add new strokes to add flowers to the grass.

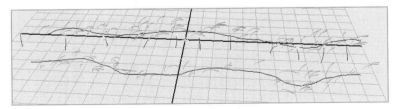

7. Position your camera, and render a frame. Make sure you're using Maya Software and not mental ray® to render through the Render Settings window and that you use a large enough resolution, such as 640×480, so that you can see the details. Render out a 120-frame sequence to see how the grass animates in the wind. Figure 12.49 shows a scene filled with grass strokes as well as a number of different flowers.

After you create a Paint Effects stroke, you can edit the look and movement of the effect through the Attribute Editor. You'll notice, however, that there are a large number of attributes to edit with Paint Effects. The next section introduces the attributes that are most useful to the beginning Maya user.

Figure 12.49
Paint Effects can add realistic flowers and grass to any scene.

Paint Effects Attributes

It's best to create a single stroke of Paint Effects in a blank scene and experiment with adjusting the various attributes to see how they affect the strokes. Select the stroke, and open the Attribute Editor. Switch to the stroke's tab to access the attributes. For example, for an African Lily Paint Effects stroke, the Attribute Editor tab is called africanLily1.

Each Paint Effects stroke produces tubes that render to create the desired effect. Each tube (you can think of a tube as a stalk) can grow to have branches, twigs, leaves, flowers, and buds. Each section of a tube has its own controls to give you the greatest flexibility in creating your effect. As you experiment with Paint Effects, you'll begin to understand how each attribute contributes to the final look of the effect.

Here is a summary of some Paint Effects attributes:

Brush Profile   Gives you control over how the tubes are generated from the stroke; this is done with the Brush Width attribute. This attribute makes tubes emit from a wider breadth from the stroke to cover more of an area.

Shading and Tube Shading   Gives you access to the color controls for the tubes on a stroke.

   Color1 and Color2   From bottom to top, graduates from Color1 to Color 2 along the stalk only. The leaves and branches have their own color attributes, which you can display by choosing Tubes → Growth.

   Incandescence1 and 2   Adds a gradient self-illumination to the tubes.

   Transparency1 and 2   Adds a gradient transparency to each tube.

   Hue/Sat/Value Rand   Add some randomness to the color of the tubes.

In the Tubes section, you'll find all the attributes to control the growth of the Paint Effects effect. In the Creation subsection, you can access the following:

Tubes Per Step   Controls the number of tubes along the stroke. For example, this setting increases or decreases the number of flowers for the africanLily1 stroke.

Length Min/Max   Controls how tall the tubes are grown to make taller flowers or grass (or other effects).

Tube Width1 and Width2   Controls the width of the tubes (the stalks of the flowers).

In the Growth subsection, you can access controls for branches, twigs, leaves, flowers, and buds for the Paint Effects strokes. Each attribute in these sections controls the number, size, and shape of those elements. Although not all Paint Effects strokes create flowers, all strokes contain these headings.

The Behavior subsection contains the controls for the dynamic forces affecting the tubes in a Paint Effects stroke. Adjust these attributes if you want your flowers to blow more in the wind.

Paint Effects are rendered as a *postprocess*, which means they won't render in reflections or refractions as is and they will not render in mental ray without conversion to polygons. They're processed and rendered after every other object in the scene is rendered out in Maya Software rendering only.

To render Paint Effects in mental ray, you can convert Paint Effects to polygonal surfaces. They will then render in the scene along with any other objects so that they may take part in reflections and refractions. To convert a Paint Effects stroke to polygons, select the stroke and choose Modify → Convert → Paint Effects To Polygons. The polygon Paint Effects tubes can still be edited by most of the Paint Effects attributes mentioned so far; however, some, such as color, don't affect the poly tubes. Instead, the color information is converted into a shader that is assigned to the polygons. It's best to finalize your Paint Effects strokes before converting to polygons, to avoid any confusion.

Paint Effects is a strong Maya tool, and you can use it to create complex effects such as a field of blowing flowers. A large number of controls to create a variety of effects come with that complexity. Fortunately, Maya comes with a generous sampling of preset brushes. Experiment with a few brushes and their attributes to see what kinds of effects and strange plants you can create.

Toon Shading

Paint Effects has been developed into a toon-shading system to make your animations render more like traditional cartoons. Using Paint Effects, Maya renders outlines for the objects in your scene, and using a Toon shader, Maya renders the objects in the scene with a flat cartoon-color look. Next, you'll take a quick look at how to apply toon shading to the wagon you textured in Chapter 7, "Autodesk Maya Shading and Texturing," to make it render like a cartoon.

Try This   Set your project to the RedWagon project, and open the `RedWagonModel.ma` scene file from the Scenes folder.

1. You'll see the wagon in a 3/4 view in the persp view panel. Select all the parts of the body of the wagon without the railings, as shown in Figure 12.50.

Figure 12.50

Select the main body of the wagon, without the wheels or the rails.

2. Switch to the Rendering menu set, and select Toon → Assign Fill Shader → Shaded Brightness Two Tone. The Attribute Editor opens, focused on a `Ramp` shader, as shown in Figure 12.51.

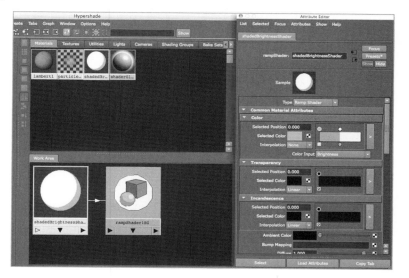

Figure 12.51

A Ramp shader is added to the scene and applied to the wagon's body.

3. Under the Color heading, set the color of the gray part of the ramp to a dark red, and set the white part of the ramp to a bright red. Your wagon should turn red in the persp view panel if you're in shaded or texture view. Render a frame, and you should see the wagon in only two tones of red but with gray railings and wheels (shown in grayscale in Figure 12.52).

4. Select the rail objects, and select Toon → Assign Fill Shader → Shaded Brightness Two Tone to create another Toon shader. Set the colors to a dark tan and a bright tan color in the Color ramp.

5. Select the handlebar and all four wheels and create another two-tone fill shader with a gray and white Color ramp (which is the default).

6. The frame, railings, and wheels now have a Toon shader as well. Notice the wheels in Figure 12.53 and how cool they look when toon shaded. Of course, adjust any of the colors to your liking.

7. Now for the toon outlines. Select all the parts of the wagon, and select Toon → Assign Outline → Add New Toon Outline. A black outline appears around the outside of the wagon's parts, and a new node called pfxToon1 appears in the Outliner or Hypergraph. The outlining is accomplished with Paint Effects.

8. Before you render a frame, set the background to white to make the black toon outlines pop. To do so, select the persp camera and open the Attribute Editor. Under the Environment heading, set Background Color to white.

9. Open the Render Settings window, and set the renderer to Maya Software. Render a frame, and compare to Figure 12.54. The outlines are too thick!

Figure 12.52
The wagon now has a toon-shaded body. The front side of the wagon is a darker red than the front because of the lighting in the scene.

Figure 12.53
The wagon has Toon shaders for the fill color applied.

The mental ray renderer doesn't render Paint Effects by default. You have to render with Maya Software rendering to be able to see Paint Effects strokes. To see Paint Effects with mental ray, you must convert the paint effects to polygons, a procedure briefly only mentioned in this chapter.

10. Select the `pfxToon1` node in the Outliner, and open the Attribute Editor window. Click the `pfxToonShape1` tab to open the attributes for the outlines. Set the `Line Width` attribute to **0.03**, and render a frame. Compare to Figure 12.55.

You can adjust the colors and the ramps of the fill shader to suit your tastes, and you can try the other Fill shader types, such as a three-tone shader to get a bit more detail in the coloring of the wagon. Adjust the toon outline thickness like you like, and have some fun playing with the toon outline's attributes to see how they affect the toon rendering of the wagon. This should be a quick primer to get you into toon shading. The rest, as always, is up to you. With some playing and experimenting, you'll be rendering some pretty nifty cartoon scenes in no time.

Figure 12.54
The black outlines are applied, but they're too thick.

Figure 12.55
The cartoon wagon

Getting Started with nCloth

nCloth, part of the nucleus dynamics in Autodesk Maya, is a simple yet very powerful way to create cloth simulations in your scene. From complex clothing on a moving character, to a simple flag, nCloth dynamics can create stunning movement, albeit with some serious setup. I will very briefly touch on the nCloth workflow here to give you a taste for it and familiarize you with the basics of getting started.

Making a Tablecloth

Switch to the nDynamics menu set. The nMesh menu is where you need to start to drape a simple tablecloth on a round table in the following steps:

1. Create a flat disc with a poly cylinder to make the basic table. Set the *Y* scale to **.175** and the *X* and *Z* scales to **5.25**. Set Subdivisions Axis to **36** for more segments to make the cylinder smoother.

2. Create a poly plane with a scale of **20**, to be larger than the cylinder. Set the Subdivisions Width and Height both to **40** for extra detail in the mesh. Place the square a few units above the cylinder, as shown in Figure 12.56.

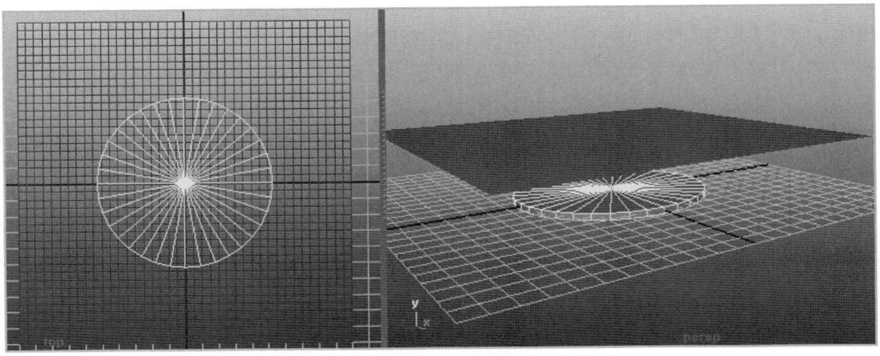

Figure 12.56

Place a square plane above a flat cylinder.

3. Now you'll set the plane to be a cloth object. Select the plane, and choose nMesh → Create nCloth. The plane will turn purple, and a pair of new nodes is added to the scene: nucleus1 and nCloth1.

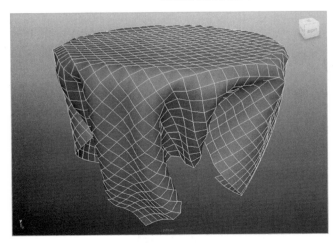

Figure 12.57

The cloth is working already!

4. Set your frame range to **1-240**, and click Play. The plane falls down and through the cylinder object. The nucleus engine has already set up the nCloth plane to have gravity.

5. Now let's define the cylinder as a collision object to make it the tabletop for our tablecloth. Select the cylinder, and choose nMesh → Create Passive Collider. That's it! Click Play, and watch the cloth fall onto the table and take shape around it. Figure 12.57.

Well, as easy as that was, there's a lot more to it to achieve the specific effect you may need. But you're on the road already. The first thing to understand is that the higher the resolution of the poly mesh, the better the look and movement of the cloth, at the cost of speed. At 40 subdivisions on the plane, the simulation runs pretty well, but you can see jagged areas of the tablecloth, so you would need to start with a much higher mesh for a smoother result.

Select the tablecloth, and open the Attribute Editor. There is a wide range of attributes to adjust for different cloth settings; however, you can choose from a number of built-in presets to make life easier. In the Attribute Editor, choose Presets*, as shown in Figure 12.58. Select Silk → Replace. As you can see, there are several Blend options in the submenu as well, allowing you to blend your current settings with the preset settings.

In this case, you've chosen Replace to set the tablecloth object to simulate like Silk. It will be lighter and airier than before. Figure 12.59 (left) shows the tablecloth at frame 200 with the silk preset. Now, in the Attribute Editor, choose Preset → thickLeather → Replace for a heavier cloth simulation (Figure 12.59, right). Notice the playback for the heavy leather was slower as well.

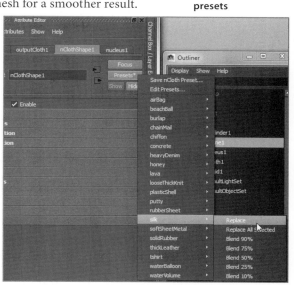

Figure 12.58

The built-in nCloth presets

As a beginner to Maya, it may be most helpful for you to go through the range of presets and see how the attributes for the nCloth changes. Here is a preliminary rundown of some of the nCloth attributes found under the Dynamic Properties heading in the Attribute Editor. Try changing some of these values to see how your tablecloth reacts, and you'll gain a finer appreciation for the mechanics of nCloth.

Stretch Resistance Controls how easily the nCloth will stretch. The lower this value, the more rubbery and elastic the cloth will behave.

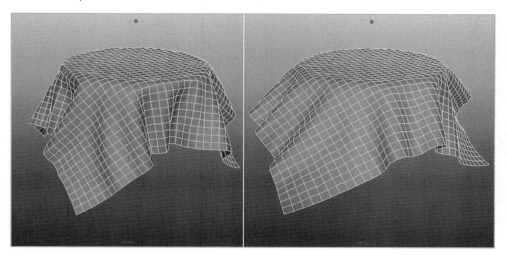

Figure 12.59

The silk cloth simulation is lighter (left); leather simulation is heavier and runs slower.

Bend Resistance   Controls how well the mesh will bend in reaction to external dynamic forces and collisions. The higher this value, the stiffer the cloth.

Rigidity   Sets the stiffness of the cloth object. Even a small value will have a stiffening impact on the simulation.

Input Mesh Attract   Compels the cloth mesh to reassume its original shape before the cloth simulation, which in our case is a flat square plane. At a value of 1, the cloth may not move at all. Using some Input Mesh Attract will also give the cloth object a more stiff and resilient/rubbery appearance.

Making a Flag

Now let's make a very quick flag simulation to get familiar with nConstraints.

1. Make a rectangular polygon plane that is scaled to (20, 14, 14) and with a subdivisions of **40** in width and height. Orient and place it above the home grid, as shown in Figure 12.60.

2. With the flag selected, choose nMesh → Create nCloth. Set your frame range to **1-240**, and click Play. The flag falls straight down. You need to keep one end from falling to simulate the flag being attached to a pole.

3. Select the edge vertices on the left side of the flag, as shown in Figure 12.61, and choose nConstraint → Transform. The vertices you selected turn green. Now click Play, and the flag falls, while one end is tethered as if on a pole (Figure 12.62).

4. Now you'll add wind to make the flag wave. Select the flag and open the Attribute Editor. Click the `nucleus1` tab, and under the Gravity and Wind heading, set the `Wind Speed` attribute to **16**. Figure 12.63 shows the flag flapping in the wind.

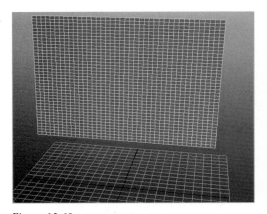

Figure 12.60
Create the mesh for the flag.

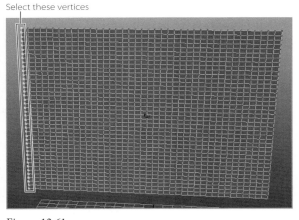

Select these vertices

Figure 12.61
Select the vertices for the nConstraint.

Adjust the `Air Density`, `Wind Speed`, `Wind Direction`, and `Wind Noise` attributes to adjust how the flag waves. You can use a similar workflow to create drapes blowing in an open window, for instance.

Caching an nCloth

Making a disk cache for a cloth simulation is important for better playback in your scene. Also, if you are rendering, it's always a good idea to cache your simulation to avoid any issues. Caching an nCloth is very simple. Select the cloth object, such as the flag from the previous example, and in the Main Menu bar, choose nCache → Create New Cache ❑. Figure 12.64

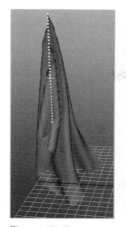

Figure 12.62

The flag is tethered to an imaginary pole now.

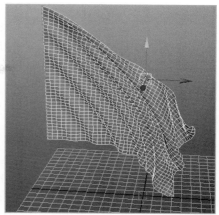

Figure 12.63

Wave the flag.

shows the options for the nCache. Here you can specify where the cache files are saved as well as the frame range for the cache. Once you create the cache, you will be able to scrub your playback back and forth.

In case you need to change your simulation, you will need to remove the cache first before changing nCloth or nucleus attributes. To do so, select the cloth object, and choose nCache → Delete Cache ❑. In the option box, you can select whether you want to delete the cache files or just disconnect them from the nCloth object.

You can reattach an existing cache file by selecting the nCloth object and choosing nCache → Attach Existing Cache File. That existing cache must be from that object or one with the same topology.

Figure 12.64

Create nCache Options dialog box

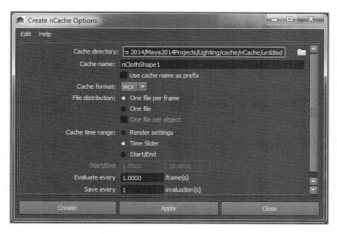

Customizing Maya

One of the most endearing features of Maya is its almost infinite customizability. Everyone has different tastes, and everyone works in their own way. Simply put, for everything there is to do in Maya, you have several ways of doing it; there are at least a couple of ways to access the Maya tools, features, and functions as well.

This flexibility may be confusing at first, but you'll discover that in the long run it's very advantageous. The ability to customize enables the greatest flexibility in individual workflow.

It's best to use Maya at its defaults as you first learn. However, when you feel comfortable enough with your progress, you can use this section to change some of the interface elements in Maya to better suit how you like to work.

Figure 12.65

The Settings/ Preferences menu

User Preferences

All the customization features are found under Window → Settings/Preferences, which displays the window shown in Figure 12.65.

The Preferences window (see Figure 12.66) lets you make changes to the look of the program as well as to toolset defaults by selecting from the categories listed in the left pane of the window.

The Preferences window is separated into categories that define different aspects of the program. Interface and Display deal with options to change the look of the program. Interface affects the main user interface, whereas Display affects how objects are displayed in the workspace.

Figure 12.66

The Preferences window

The Settings category lets you change the default values of several tools and their general operation. An essential aspect of this category is Working Units: these options set the working parameters of your scene (in particular, the Time setting).

By adjusting the Time setting, you tell Maya your frame rate of animation. If you're working in film, you use a frame rate of 24 frames per second (fps). If you're working in NTSC video (the standard video/television format in the Americas), you use the frame rate of 30fps.

The Applications category lets you specify which applications you want Maya to start automatically when a function is called. For example, while looking at the Attribute Editor for a texture image, you can click a single button to open that image in your favorite image editor, which you specify here.

> In the Settings section, click the Undo header, and set the Undo Queue to Infinite. Doing so allows you to undo as many actions as have occurred since you loaded the file. This feature is unbelievably handy, especially when you're first learning Maya.

Shelves

Under the Shelf Editor command (Window → Settings/Preferences → Shelf Editor) lurks a window that manages your shelves (see Figure 12.67). You can create or delete shelves or manage the items on the Shelf with this function. This is handy when you create your own workflow for a project. Simply click the Shelves tab to display the icons on that Shelf in the Shelf Editor window. Click in the Shelf Contents section to edit the icons and where they reside on that selected Shelf. Clicking the Command tab gives you access to the MEL command for that icon when it is single-clicked in the Shelf. Click the Double Click Command tab for the MEL command for the icon when it is double-clicked in the Shelf.

You can also edit Shelf icons from within the UI without the Shelf Editor window. To add a menu command to the current Shelf, hold down Ctrl+Alt+Shift, and click the function or command directly from its menu. Items from the Tool Box, pull-down menus, or the Script Editor can be added to any Shelf.

- To add an item from the Tool Box, MMB+drag its icon from the Tool Box into the appropriate Shelf.

- To add an item from a menu to the current Shelf, hold down the Ctrl+Alt+Shift keys while selecting the item from the menu.

Figure 12.67

The Shelf Editor

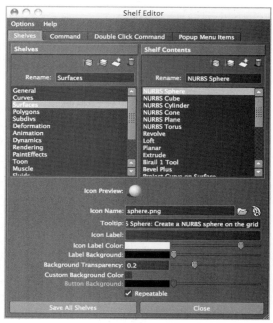

- To add an item (a MEL command) from the Script Editor, highlight the text of the MEL command in the Script Editor, and MMB+drag it onto the Shelf. A MEL icon will be created that will run the command when you click it.

- To remove an item from a Shelf, MMB+drag its icon to the Garbage Can icon at the end of the Shelf, or use Window → Settings/Preferences → Shelf Editor.

Hotkeys

Hotkeys are keyboard shortcuts that can access almost any Maya tool or command. You've already encountered a few in your exploration of the interface and in the solar system exercise in Chapter 2, "Jumping in Headfirst, with Both Feet." What fun! You can create even more hotkeys, as well as reassign existing hotkeys, through the Hotkey Editor, shown in Figure 12.68 (Window → Settings/Preferences → Hotkey Editor).

Through this monolith of a window, you can set a key combination to be used as a shortcut to virtually any command in Maya. This is the last customization you want to touch. Because so many tools have hotkeys assigned by default, it's important to get to know them first before you start changing things to suit how you work.

Every menu command is represented by menu categories on the left; the right side allows you to view the current hotkey or assign a new hotkey to the selected command. Ctrl and Alt key combinations may be used with any letter keys on the keyboard. Keep in mind that Maya is *case sensitive*, meaning that it differentiates between uppercase and lowercase letters. For example, one of my personal hotkeys is Ctrl+H to hide the selected object from view; Shift+Ctrl+H unhides it. (I'm sharing.)

Figure 12.68

The Hotkey Editor

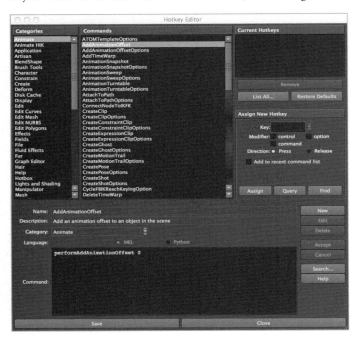

The lower section of this window displays the MEL command that the menu command invokes. It also allows you to type in your own MEL commands, name them as new commands, categorize them with the other commands, and assign hotkeys to them.

> The important thing to focus on right now is *discovering how to use the tools* to accomplish the tasks you need to perform and *establishing a basic workflow*. Toward that end, I strongly suggest learning Maya in its default configuration and *only* using the menu structure and default shelves to access all your commands at first, with the exception of the most basic hotkeys.

Color Settings

You can set the colors for almost any part of the interface to your liking through the Colors window shown in Figure 12.69 (Window → Settings/Preferences → Color Settings).

The window is separated into different aspects of the Maya interface by headings. The 3D Views heading lets you change the color of all the panels' backgrounds. For example, color settings give you a chance to set the interface to complement your office's décor as well as make certain items easier to read.

Customizing Maya is important. However—and this can't be stressed enough—it's important to get your bearings with default Maya settings before you venture out and change hotkeys and such. When you're ready, this section of this chapter will still be here for your reference.

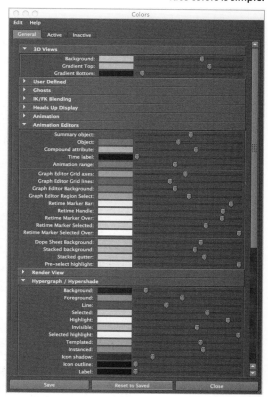

Figure 12.69

Changing the interface colors is simple.

Summary

In this chapter, you learned how to create dynamic objects and create simulations. Beginning with rigid body dynamics, you created a set of pool balls that you animated in the simulation to knock into each other. Then, you learned how to bake that simulation into animation curves for fine-tuning. A quick fun exercise had you shooting the catapult, after which you learned about particle effects by creating a steam effect for the locomotive animation using nParticles. Next, you learned a little about the Maya Paint Effects tool and how you can easily use it to create various effects such as grass and flowers. Then you used toon shading on a wagon and finally glossed over some of the customization options available in the Maya UI. Then you learned how to create cloth effects using nCloth to make a tablecloth and a flag, and finally, you learned how to customize Maya to suit your own preferences.

To further your learning, try creating a scene on a grassy hillside with train tracks running through. Animate the locomotive, steam and all, driving through the scene and blowing the grass as it passes. You can also create a train whistle and a steam effect when the whistle blows, and you can create various other trails of smoke and steam as the locomotive drives through.

The best way to be exposed to Maya dynamics is simply to experiment once you're familiar with the general workflow in Maya. You'll find that the workflow in dynamics is more iterative than other Maya workflows, because you're required to experiment frequently with different values to see how they affect the final simulation. With time, you'll develop a strong intuition, and you'll accomplish more complex simulations faster and with greater effect.

Where Do You Go from Here?

It's so hard to say goodbye! But this is really a "hello" to learning more about animation and 3D!

Please explore other resources and tutorials to expand your working knowledge of Maya. Several websites contain numerous tips, tricks, and tutorials for all aspects of Maya, and my own resources and instructional videos and links are online at http://koosh3d.com/ and on Facebook at facebook.com/IntroMaya.

Of course, www.autodesk.com/maya has a wide range of learning tools. Be sure to check out the sidebar "Suggested Reading" in the absolutely fabulous Chapter 1, "Introduction to Computer Graphics and 3D." Now that you've gained your all-important first exposure, you'll be better equipped to forge ahead confidently.

The most important thing you should have learned from this book is that proficiency and competence with Maya come with practice, but even more so from your own artistic exploration. Treat this text and your experience with its information as a formal introduction to a new language and way of working for yourself; doing so is imperative. The rest of it—the gorgeous still frames and eloquent animations—come with furthering your study of your own art, working diligently to achieve your vision, and having fun along the way. Enjoy, and good luck.

Index

Note to the reader: Throughout this index **boldfaced** page numbers indicate primary discussions of a topic. *Italicized* page numbers indicate illustrations.

N

T